THE
BALFOUR
DECLARATION

THE
BALFOUR
DECLARATION

THE ORIGINS OF THE
ARAB-ISRAELI CONFLICT

JONATHAN SCHNEER

BOND
STREET
BOOKS
DOUBLEDAY
CANADA

The Bond Street Books colophon is a trademark of
Random House of Canada Limited.

Library and Archives Canada Cataloguing in Publication

Schneer, Jonathan
The Balfour Declaration : the origins of the Arab-Israeli conflict / Jonathan Schneer.

Includes bibliographical references and index.

ISBN 978-0-385-66258-1

1. Balfour Declaration. 2. Zionism—Great Britain—History—20th century.
3. Zionism—History—20th century. 4. Arab-Israeli conflict. 5. Palestine—History—
1917-1948. I. Title.

DS125.5.S37 2010   956.04   C2010-902486-9

Book design by Christopher M. Zucker
Printed and bound in the USA

Published in Canada by Bond Street Books,
a division of Random House of Canada Limited

Visit Random House of Canada Limited's website: www.randomhouse.ca

10 9 8 7 6 5 4 3 2 1

This book is dedicated in loving memory to my parents.

In his indignation Cadmus killed the dragon, and by the advice
of Athena sowed its teeth. When they were sown there rose
from the ground armed men. . . .

APOLLODORUS 3.4.1
(Transl. J. G. Frazer)

Contents

CHAPTER 15   *Sokolow in France and Italy*   208
CHAPTER 16   *Revelation of the Sykes-Picot Agreement*   220

PART IV ***The Road Not Taken***

CHAPTER 17   *British Muslims, the Anglo-Ottoman Society,*
              and the Disillusioning of Marmaduke Pickthall   239
CHAPTER 18   *The Curious Venture of J. R. Pilling*   253
CHAPTER 19   *Henry Morgenthau and the Deceiving of*
              Chaim Weizmann   263
CHAPTER 20   *"The Man Who Was Greenmantle"*   275
CHAPTER 21   *The Zaharoff Gambit*   289

PART V ***Climax and Anticlimax***

CHAPTER 22   *The Ascendancy of Chaim Weizmann*   303
CHAPTER 23   *Lawrence and the Arabs on the Verge*   319
CHAPTER 24   *The Declaration at Last*   333
CHAPTER 25   *The Declaration Endangered*   347

Conclusion

CHAPTER 26   *A Drawing Together of Threads*   365

              Acknowledgments   377
              Notes   379
              Bibliography   409
              Index   417

Glossary of Names

(These brief notes are meant to provide only the most basic relevant information for those reading this book.)

AARONSOHN, AARON 1876–1919
He gained fame as the foremost agronomist in Palestine before World War I, but is best known for putting his knowledge of the land to use for Britain during the war and for his Zionist activities. He perished in an airplane crash.

ABDULLAH IBN HUSSEIN 1882–1951
Second son of Sharif Hussein, a member of the prewar Ottoman parliament, he helped to instigate and then took a leading role in the Arab Revolt. After the war he became emir of Transjordan, and when the British mandate ended in 1946, he became king of Transjordan and then in 1949 king of the Hashemite Kingdom of Jordan. He died by assassination.

ALI IBN HUSSEIN 1879–1935
First son of Sharif Hussein, he did not play a leading role in the Arab Revolt but nevertheless succeeded his father as king of the Hejaz in 1924, when the Wahhabi rebellion occurred. He abdicated one year later and spent the rest of his life in Baghdad in Iraq, where his brother Feisal ruled as king.

ALLENBY, SIR EDMUND 1861–1936

Promoted to general for his services on the Western Front, he took command of the British-led Egyptian Expeditionary Force in June 1917. His forces captured Gaza in October, Jerusalem in December, and Damascus in October 1918. He served as high commissioner for Egypt from 1919 to 1925.

ASQUITH, HERBERT HENRY
(FIRST EARL OF OXFORD AND ASQUITH) 1852–1928

The Liberal politician who served as prime minister from 1908 to 1916, he led Britain into the war and in May 1915 formed a coalition government with the Conservatives. Lloyd George replaced him as prime minister in December 1916.

AUDA ABU TAYI 1885–1924

The leader of a section of the Howeitat tribe of Bedouin Arabs, he threw his support behind the Arab Revolt and with Lawrence engineered the capture of Aqaba. Lawrence called him "the greatest fighting man in northern Arabia."

BALFOUR, ARTHUR JAMES (FIRST EARL OF BALFOUR) 1848–1930

The Conservative prime minister from 1902 to 1905, he served on Asquith's war council from the outbreak of hostilities until formation of the coalition government, upon which Asquith appointed him first lord of the Admiralty. When Lloyd George formed the second coalition government, he appointed Balfour to be his foreign secretary. After the war Balfour served in the Lloyd George government as lord president of the council.

CAILLARD, SIR VINCENT 1856–1930

A businessman with wide interests and direct experience of Turkey and the Ottoman Middle East, he served as financial director of Vickers armaments manufacturers from 1906 until after the war. In the attempt to arrange a separate peace with the Ottomans, he played the role of intermediary between Basil Zaharoff and David Lloyd George.

CECIL, ROBERT (FIRST VISCOUNT CECIL OF CHELWOOD) 1864–1958

Son of Prime Minister Lord Salisbury, cousin of Arthur Balfour, and himself a Conservative member of Parliament (although a free trader), he joined Asquith's coalition government in 1915 as parliamentary under secretary of state for foreign affairs, a post he held for four years. After the war he devoted himself to work for the League of Nations and international peace.

CHEETHAM, SIR MILNE 1869–1938
A career diplomat, after numerous postings he arrived in Cairo as first secretary to the British high commissioner. During the interval between Kitchener's departure in June 1914 and McMahon's arrival in January 1915, he served as acting high commissioner and helped compose an early letter to Grand Sharif Hussein.

CLAYTON, SIR GILBERT 1875–1929
Before the war he served Sir Reginald Wingate, governor general of Sudan, as director of intelligence in Sudan and agent in Cairo. With the outbreak of war he became director of military intelligence at British headquarters in Cairo, head of the Arab Bureau, and eventually chief political officer of the Egyptian Expeditionary Force and military governor of Palestine. After the war he continued to play an active role in Middle Eastern affairs, but his career was cut short by a fatal heart attack.

CURZON, NATHANIEL
(FIRST MARQUESS CURZON OF KEDLESTON) 1859–1925
A Conservative politician who had served as viceroy of India from 1898 to 1905, he joined Asquith's coalition government as lord privy seal in 1915. Lloyd George tapped him for his own coalition government a year and a half later, and for membership of the select War Cabinet, in which he served as lord president of the council. After the war Curzon replaced Balfour as foreign secretary and served until the Labour victory in the general election of 1923.

DJEMAL PASHA 1872–1922
An Ottoman military officer and early supporter of the CUP, he and Enver and Talaat effectively ruled the empire from 1913 until the end of the war. During 1915 and again in 1916 he led the Ottoman Fourth Army in unsuccessful attacks against British forces at Suez. Throughout the war he exercised dictatorial powers in Syria, earning widespread hatred. Afterward he fled to Germany, then to Switzerland, and finally to Central Asia. He was assassinated by an Armenian revolutionary.

ENVER PASHA 1881–1922

An Ottoman military officer and early supporter of the CUP, he was the architect of the triumvirate of three pashas who ruled the empire during 1913–18 and of the government's pro-German policy. During the war he occupied the position of war minister, although he was generally an unsuccessful military leader. With the Ottoman defeat in 1918, he fled first to Germany and eventually to the Soviet Union. An advocate of pan-Turanianism, he died fighting the Russians in Central Asia.

FARUKI, SHARIF MUHAMMAD AL- 1891–1920

A young Arab staff officer and member of the secret society al-Ahd, he crossed over to the British lines at Gallipoli, hoping to convince them to support Sharif Hussein's revolt and the Arabian kingdom adumbrated in the Damascus Protocol. He did so, although he did not formally represent al-Ahd. Later he became Sharif Hussein's agent in Cairo.

FEISAL IBN HUSSEIN 1885–1933

Third son of Sharif Hussein, leader and architect of the Arab Revolt, he became king of Syria for about four months in 1920, until the French kicked him out. The British made him king of Iraq in 1921, but they held a mandate to rule from the League of Nations so that Feisal's kingship was qualified. The British granted Iraq nominal independence in 1932.

FITZMAURICE, SIR GERALD 1865–1939

Senior dragoman, or Turkish-speaking consular officer, at the British embassy from 1907 to 1914, an inveterate intriguer with reactionary views, he hated the CUP government and longed unavailingly for restoration of the sultan. During the war he served in naval intelligence, mainly in London.

GASTER, MOSES 1856–1939

The chief rabbi, or *haham,* of Spanish and Portuguese Jews in England, Gaster was a renowned scholar and linguist who played a leading role among British Zionists, but he was an abrasive personality. Eventually Chaim Weizmann elbowed him aside.

GRAHAM, SIR RONALD 1870–1949

A career diplomat, at the beginning of the war he accepted the post of chief staff officer to Sir John Maxwell, the general officer commanding troops in Egypt. He returned to London in 1916 to become assistant under secretary of state at the Foreign Office.

GREENBERG, LEOPOLD 1861–1931

An early recruit to Zionism, a prominent figure among British Zionists during the prewar era, Greenberg was the principal shareholder and editor of the London *Jewish Chronicle*. During the war he indirectly introduced Weizmann to Sir Mark Sykes.

GREY, SIR EDWARD (FIRST VISCOUNT GREY OF FALLADON) 1862–1933

A Liberal politician who served as Asquith's foreign secretary, he opposed adding territory to the British Empire. Failing eyesight drove him from his post when Asquith's coalition government fell in December 1916.

HA'AM, AHAD 1856–1927

Asher Ginzberg's pen name means "One of the People" in Hebrew. A leading prewar Zionist essayist and thinker, he was famous for warning that Jews and Arabs in Palestine must learn to cooperate, and for emphasizing the spiritual but not the religious aspect of Judaism. Insofar as Weizmann acknowledged any mentor, Ahad Ha'am was it.

HARDINGE, CHARLES
(FIRST BARON HARDINGE OF PENSHURST) 1858–1944

A career diplomat and prewar viceroy of India, Hardinge favored aggressive military action in Mesopotamia once war began. This led to disaster at Ctesiphon in November 1915 and at Kut-al-Amara in April 1916. He returned to London shortly thereafter, where he served as permanent under secretary of the Foreign Office.

HERBERT, AUBREY 1880–1923

"The man who was Greenmantle," he knew well the Ottoman Empire and its CUP leaders. Despite being nearly blind, he joined the army upon the outbreak of war and was wounded and captured during the retreat from Mons. After his rescue and subsequent recovery, he accepted a posting to Egypt as an intelligence officer, where he came to favor the Arab Revolt. But always he hoped for peace between Britain and the Ottomans, and in 1917 he tried to arrange it.

HOGARTH, DAVID 1862–1927

A renowned archaeologist who served as keeper of the Ashmolean Museum at Oxford, during the early stages of the war he shuttled back and forth between London and the Middle East for the department of naval intelligence. From March 1916 Cairo was his permanent base, where he served as unofficial leader of the Arab Bureau. After the war he returned to Oxford.

HUSSEIN IBN ALI 1853–1931

Appointed emir or grand sharif of Mecca by Sultan Abdul Hamid II in 1908, he led the Arab Revolt against the Ottomans beginning in June 1916. Despite his ambition to rule an Arab empire, the Allies recognized him only as king of the Hejaz. This position he abdicated in favor of his son Ali in 1924. A year later they both fled the Wahhabi warriors of Abdul Azziz ibn Saud. He spent the rest of his life in exile.

KITCHENER, FIELD MARSHAL HORATIO (FIRST EARL KITCHENER) 1850–1916

A British soldier statesman, Kitchener served as Asquith's secretary of state for war starting in August 1914. He was the one who initiated wartime contact with Emir Hussein, dangling the possibility of the caliphate before him if he would side with the Allies in the war against the Central Powers. In early June 1916, while en route to Russia, he died when his ship struck a mine.

LAWRENCE, THOMAS EDWARD 1888–1935

Attached to the military intelligence department of the Egyptian Expeditionary Force in 1914, Lawrence eventually made contact with Feisal and soon proved to be a malevolent genius at guerrilla warfare. He left the Middle East thinking that Britain had betrayed the Arab struggle for independence.

LLOYD, GEORGE (FIRST BARON LLOYD) 1879–1941

He traveled the Middle East before the war, overlapping in Constantinople with Aubrey Herbert and Mark Sykes in 1905. In the House of Commons, to which he was elected in 1910, he specialized in imperial matters. Upon the outbreak of war he joined the military intelligence department of the Egyptian Expeditionary Force and wound up working for the Arab Bureau. After the war he would serve as high commissioner in Egypt.

LLOYD GEORGE, DAVID (FIRST EARL OF DWYFOR) 1863–1945

The great Liberal statesman who replaced Asquith as prime minister in December 1916, he was an "easterner" who sought a way around the Western Front and an entrance into Germany and Austria-Hungary through the Ottoman Empire.

MALCOLM, JAMES 1865–1952
An Armenian in London who represented his country's interests to the British government, he introduced Weizmann to Mark Sykes and continued during the war years to play a role as intermediary between Zionists and British officials.

MCMAHON, SIR HENRY 1862–1949
A British political officer in India, he replaced Kitchener as high commissioner of Egypt. He carried on the delicate and much-debated correspondence with Emir Hussein that led to the Arab Revolt. At the end of 1916 London replaced him in Cairo with Sir Reginald Wingate.

MILNER, ALFRED (FIRST VISCOUNT MILNER) 1854–1925
A leading British imperialist, he joined the War Cabinet of Lloyd George. He supported the Zionists but also supported a separate peace with the Ottoman Empire that might have left the Turkish flag flying over Jerusalem.

MONTAGU, EDWIN 1879–1924
A Jewish anti-Zionist and Liberal politician with close ties to Asquith, he earned the latter's enmity by joining the Lloyd George coalition government. He led the opposition in the cabinet to the Balfour Declaration, but just before the cabinet came to a final decision, he had to leave to take up a new post as secretary of state for India.

MONTEFIORE, CLAUDE 1858–1938
President of the Anglo-Jewish Association from 1896 to 1921 and an advocate of liberal (denationalized and deritualized) Judaism, he and Lucien Wolf fought hard against the Zionists and to maintain the long-standing connection between the British Foreign Office and advocates of Jewish assimilation.

MORGENTHAU, HENRY 1856–1946
The American ambassador to Turkey from 1913 to 1916, he developed ties to the Ottoman leaders. Early in 1917 he convinced President Wilson to send him to Palestine, where he could speak with responsible Ottomans about a separate peace between Turkey and the Allies. Weizmann headed him off at Gibraltar and convinced him to drop the plan.

MURRAY, GENERAL SIR ARCHIBALD 1860–1945
He took up command of British forces in Egypt in January 1916, defeated an Ottoman attack upon the Suez Canal in August, and advanced into and occupied the Sinai Peninsula. But he twice failed to take Gaza, and the government replaced him in June 1917 with General Allenby.

ORMSBY-GORE, WILLIAM (FOURTH BARON HARLECH) 1885–1964
A Conservative politician, in 1916 he joined the Arab Bureau in Cairo, where Aaron Aaronsohn converted him to Zionism. Recalled to London in 1917, he served as Milner's parliamentary private secretary and later as an assistant secretary to the cabinet, working with Mark Sykes. He knew Weizmann well. After the war he remained active in Conservative politics, eventually rising to colonial secretary in 1936.

PICKTHALL, MARMADUKE 1875–1936
An author of popular novels, many with Middle Eastern themes, he traveled and lived in the Middle East before the war and loved it. He opposed the British declaration of war against the Ottomans in 1914 and never relinquished hope of bringing the two countries into peaceful relations. In 1917 he converted to Islam. Later he wrote the first English translation of the Quran.

PICOT, FRANÇOIS GEORGES- 1870–1951
A French diplomat who, with Mark Sykes, redrew the map of the Middle East early in 1916, carving up the Ottoman Empire and basically allocating Syria, including Lebanon, to France and Mesopotamia to Great Britain. When they learned about this agreement, neither the Zionists nor the Arabs were pleased.

ROBERTSON, FIELD MARSHAL SIR WILLIAM 1860–1933
He served during most of the war as chief of the Imperial General Staff. A confirmed "westerner" who thought victory depended upon smashing through the German lines, he opposed those, including Prime Minister Lloyd George, who wanted to strengthen Britain's campaign in the East.

ROTHSCHILD, EDMOND DE 1845–1934
A member of the French branch of the famous banking family, he believed in Zionism and supported Chaim Weizmann.

ROTHSCHILD, WALTER (SECOND BARON ROTHSCHILD) 1868–1937
The oldest son of Baron Nathan Mayer Rothschild, Walter inherited the position of unofficial leader of the British Jewish community upon his father's death. Although most interested, probably, in zoology, Walter Rothschild lent his support to Zionism after falling under Weizmann's spell. Balfour addressed the famous letter promising British support for a Jewish homeland in Palestine to him.

RUMBOLD, SIR HORACE (NINTH BARONET) 1869–1941
A career diplomat, Rumbold served his country from 1916 to 1919 as envoy extraordinary and minister plenipotentiary to the Swiss Republic. There he kept tabs on agents of foreign powers and ran his own network of agents, including the inestimable Humbert Parodi. He had knowledge of most but not all British attempts to lure Turks into discussions of peace.

SACHER, HARRY 1881–1971
A journalist and Zionist based in Manchester, Sacher provided his friend Chaim Weizmann with the invaluable introduction to his editor at *The Manchester Guardian,* C. P. Scott. He helped to found the iconoclastic British Palestine Committee, which Weizmann sometimes considered to be a thorn in his side. Nevertheless he played a key role in helping Zionists frame the document that later became the Balfour Declaration.

SAMUEL, HERBERT (FIRST VISCOUNT SAMUEL) 1870–1963
A Liberal politician who rose to become president of the Board of Trade and then home secretary in Asquith's cabinet, he came from the "Cousinhood" of wealthy assimilated Jewish Britons, yet secretly nurtured Zionist beliefs. These he revealed to Asquith's cabinet and to Weizmann early in the war; later he helped bring Weizmann into contact with other important British officials. After the war he served for five years as Britain's first high commissioner in Palestine.

SCOTT, C. P. 1846–1932
He was the proprietor and editor of Britain's greatest Liberal and radical newspaper, *The Manchester Guardian.* Deeply impressed by Chaim Weizmann, whom he met in November 1914, he introduced the Zionist leader to David Lloyd George and other important Britons.

SOKOLOW, NAHUM 1861–1936

A leading official and representative of the World Zionist Organization, the Polish-born Sokolow spent the war years in London, where he was Weizmann's chief collaborator. At the suggestion of Mark Sykes, with whom he also worked closely, Sokolow traveled to France and Italy during the spring of 1917 and gained support from the governments of those countries for Zionist objectives. He was intimately involved from the Zionist side in the discussions that produced the Balfour Declaration.

STORRS, SIR RONALD 1881–1955

At the outbreak of the war he was serving in Cairo as the British high commissioner's oriental secretary. He already knew Sharif Abdullah and was involved in the drafting of the McMahon-Hussein correspondence. Later he joined the Arab Bureau and served as assistant political officer to the Anglo-French mission of the Egyptian Expeditionary Force and as military governor of Jerusalem.

SYKES, SIR MARK (SIXTH BARONET) 1879–1919

Having traveled and written about the Ottoman Empire and the Middle East before the war, he was assigned to the de Bunsen Committee by Kitchener and then sent by him to survey the Middle Eastern scene in person. Sykes negotiated the Sykes-Picot and Tripartite Agreements, dividing up the Ottoman Empire. He converted to Zionism and played a crucial role in promoting its leaders. He envisioned a remade Middle East based upon the autonomy of the small nationalities, most particularly Jews, Arabs, and Armenians.

TALAAT PASHA 1874–1921

A military officer, an early supporter of the CUP, the third member of the triumvirate that ruled the Ottoman Empire during World War I, he became grand vizier (prime minister) in 1917. He kept the door open for talks with Britain about a separate peace and, without informing Enver or Djemal, made more than one overture to the British during 1916–17. He died in Berlin at the hands of an assassin.

WEIZMANN, CHAIM 1874–1952

During the war he became the leading Zionist in Britain and played the crucial role from the Zionist side in fashioning the Zionist-British alliance and the Balfour Declaration.

WILSON, CYRIL 1873–1938

He headed the British mission at Jeddah as "pilgrimage officer" but really supervised the landing of supplies there. More important, he served as British liaison with King Hussein.

WINGATE, SIR FRANCIS REGINALD (FIRST BARONET) 1861–1953

An army officer and colonial governor, during the war he served first as sirdar of the Egyptian army and governor general of Sudan. He favored British support of the Arab Revolt and at the end of 1916 replaced McMahon as high commissioner for Egypt.

WOLF, LUCIEN 1857–1930

A journalist and expert commentator on British foreign affairs, he came to dominate the Conjoint Committee of the Anglo-Jewish Association and Board of Deputies of British Jews. One aim of these bodies, and of Wolf, was to persuade British policy makers to defend and to support Jewish interests outside Great Britain. He believed in Jewish assimilation and took a leading role among Jews in Britain who opposed Zionism.

ZAHAROFF, SIR BASIL 1849–1936

Of humble origin, Zaharoff attained great wealth as an arms dealer and rose to membership on the board of directors of the Vickers armaments manufacturer. He played a key role in engineering Greek entry into World War I on the side of the Allies and served as David Lloyd George's emissary to the Ottomans in search of a separate peace.

List of Maps

Postlude as Prelude

LONDON ON DECEMBER 2, 1917: a cold, rainy, windy day: gloomy weather to match British prospects in the stalemated Great War. The Italians had just met a disaster at Caporetto so complete that it seemed likely to take them out of combat altogether. The Russian Bolsheviks, who had seized power in Petrograd the month before, were preparing to negotiate their country's surrender to Germany. On the Western Front the Entente and German forces continued to wreak havoc upon each other with neither end nor breakthrough in sight. But the Germans were gathering for another tremendous offensive, intending to win the war before American troops arrived in sufficient number to tip the balance against them. Somehow Britain and France must summon the resolve and the resources to hang on.

On Kingsway, near the Strand, despite the rain and wind and generally awful war news, a steady stream of beaming men and women poured into the London Opera House. They filled the tiers of boxes, the auditorium, the saloons, lounges, and foyers, even the corridors. The handsome structure, designed to hold 2,700, was filled to capacity and more. People waited outside in the street under their umbrellas. They would not leave.

Inside about a dozen men gathered near the stage. Among them were a former Liberal cabinet minister, Herbert Samuel; the assistant foreign secretary, Robert Cecil; an assistant secretary to the War Cabinet, Sir Mark Sykes; the unofficial head of the British Jewish community, Lord Rothschild; and the two most important leaders of wartime British Zionism, Chaim Weizmann and Nahum Sokolow. They, and all the rest, beamed with pleasure. When finally the doors closed and the crowd settled, Lord Rothschild, hands in his pockets, spoke first to the breathless, happy audience. "We are met on the most momentous occasion in the history of Judaism for the last eighteen hundred years," he began. "We are here to return thanks to His Majesty's government for a declaration which marked an epoch . . . For the first time since the dispersion, the Jewish people have received their proper status by the declaration of one of the great Powers."

He referred, of course, to the Balfour Declaration, which the War Cabinet had agreed to one month earlier and published on November 9. By this document the British government pledged "to use their best endeavors to . . . [establish] in Palestine . . . a national home for the Jewish people."

One by one the men on the stage advanced to speak. One by one they offered thanks or congratulations and rosy predictions for the land to be freed, at long last, from the onerous Turkish yoke. Even an Arab spokesman, Sheikh Ismail Abdul al-Akki, foresaw the day when Palestine would again flow with milk and honey. Everyone said that the Declaration represented a historic gesture on the part of Britain and a historic achievement on the part of Zionism, the culmination of a joint effort that must lead to "Judea for the Jews," as Robert Cecil put it. And because the Declaration also promised that "nothing shall be done which may prejudice the civil and religious rights of existing non-Jewish communities in Palestine," they predicted that Jews and Arabs would share the land in harmony.

That last prophecy proved wishful thinking, but events have largely borne out the rest. Today we consider the Balfour Declaration a great marker in Jewish history, not merely a Zionist victory but a foundation stone of modern Israel. Some of us may know a bit about it: We may have read about the enormous effort, planning, and vision, as well as the unlikely alliances, prejudices, intrigues, and double-dealing, that went into its making. Few if any, however, can know that on the very day that the joyful throng gathered to celebrate at the London Opera House, Britain's prime minister and his agents were engaged in secret maneuverings to detach the Ottoman Empire from the Central Powers. They were offering, among other inducements, that the Turkish flag could continue to fly over Palestine. But the Zionists had long deemed Ottoman rule in Palestine to be one of their chief obstacles. Most of them viewed Turkish suzerainty, no matter how attenuated, as intolerable. Had the Turks accepted Lloyd George's offer, most Zionists, and certainly their most important leaders, would have felt that the British government had compromised, perhaps fatally, its recent pledge. In which case, no one today would pay much attention to the Balfour Declaration at all.

Of those secret dealings, two (or possibly three) men standing on the Opera House stage were well aware. They disapproved because they knew what the Zionist reaction would be, but they did not tell. Everyone else at the celebration remained in ignorance. That disparity of knowledge between government officials and the human objects of policy, and its potential for betrayal, encapsulates in a single moment the tortuous process that had led to the Balfour Declaration—and nearly to its swift negation. The meeting at the London Opera House on December 2 crystallized a convoluted history that too often has been conceived as an irresistible forward march. This book will show that the lead-up to the Balfour Declaration was anything but a simple triumphal progress. And since intrigue and double-dealing as much as bravery and vision were of its essence, the Balfour Declaration resulted not merely in celebration and congratulation but soon enough in disillusionment, distrust, and resentment. Nearly a century later these bitter emotions remain; compounded over the years, they continue tragically, bloodily, to unwind.

PART I

Sirocco

CHAPTER 1

Palestine Before World War I

THE LAND CALLED PALESTINE gave no indication, early in the twentieth century, that it would become the world's cockpit. Rather, if anything, the reverse. A century ago it was merely a strip of territory running along the east coast of the Mediterranean Sea. The remote, sleepy, backward, sparsely populated southwestern bit of Syria was still home to foxes, jackals, hyenas, wildcats, wolves, even cheetahs and leopards in its most unsettled parts. Loosely governed from Jerusalem in the south and from Beirut in the north by agents of the Ottoman Empire, Palestine's borders were vague. To the east it merged with the Jordanian plateau, to the south with the Arabian deserts, and to the north with the gray mountain masses of Lebanon. And it was small: Fewer than two hundred miles long and fifty miles wide, it was not much bigger than present-day Massachusetts (to put it in an American context) and about the size of Wales (to put it in the British).

The strip of land, resting mainly upon limestone, was devoid of coal, iron, copper, silver, or gold deposits and lacked oil, but it was happily porous ("calcareous," the geologists said), meaning that it was capable of absorbing moisture whenever the heavens should open, which they might do, especially when the wind came from the north. When it came from the east, however, as it frequently did in May and October, the wind was a malign enervating force. It was a furnace-blast sirocco in hot weather and a numbing chill in cold. The two mountain ranges that ran in rough parallel the length of the country from north to south could not block it. The western range, which includes "the Mount of the Amorites" of the Book of Deuteronomy, runs between the Jordan Valley (to its east) and the maritime plain (to its west). The eastern edge of this range is an escarpment that drops (precipitously in places) to the fabled Jordan River below. The second or eastern range of hills, which includes the mountains of Moab, Judea, and Galilee, is a continuation of a chain that begins in Lebanon and reaches southward into Jordan. To its west lies the river valley; to its east is a desert plateau. In the north of the country the mountains are quite tall: Mount Hermon rises more than 9,200 feet above sea level. (People ski there in winter now.) To the south the mountains are typically half as high, and the surrounding landscape is bleak, empty, and inhospitable.

For such a tiny land, Palestine contains extraordinary topographical contrasts. The Jordan River runs southward along a descending valley floor, passing some seventy miles from the clear waters of the Sea of Galilee, where the surrounding hills and fields are relatively green, welcoming, and fruitful. It empties into the brackish bitter Dead Sea, thirteen hundred feet below sea level, where the landscape is barren, freezing during winter, broiling in summer. In the Dead Sea area the Jordan Valley has never been cultivated, although at the turn of the twentieth century the wandering Bedouins might camp there. Even they, however, would move on during the hottest months, when temperatures scale 120 degrees Fahrenheit or higher and the land opens in cracks and fissures.

Elsewhere in Palestine, however, life flourished. "It drinketh of the rain of heaven," Moses is supposed to have said of his "Promised Land," and although it did not drink deep (rainfall averaged 28 to 32 inches annually, except in the south, where 6 inches marked a good year), and it rarely drank at all from March until November, nevertheless it drank sufficiently. Parts of the country were nearly luxuriant. In 1869 even that American innocent abroad, Samuel Clemens, whose wonderfully dyspeptic view of Palestine is legendary, could refer without irony to groves of lemon trees, "cool, shady, hung with fruit," by the village of Shunem near "Little Hermon," and to "breezy glades of thorn and oak," south of the Sea of Galilee near Mount Tabor. A horseman riding the Hauran plateau, east of the eastern mountain range, could view unbroken wheat fields extending to the horizon on every side. A British visitor to the Circassian village of Gerasa was reminded "of a Scotch glen, though the hills are not so high nor the land so barren." Local markets sold a diverse range of fruits and vegetables, some of remarkable size. "We have cauliflowers that measure at least a foot across, and water-

melons hardly to be spanned by a grown person's arms . . . grapes in clusters
from three to four feet in length . . . We have in their season [also] . . . apri-
cots, nectarines, plums, damsons, quince, mulberries, figs, lemons, oranges,
prickly pear, pomegranates and many kinds of nuts." In spring the countryside (some of it) ran riot with wildflowers: "anemones . . . hyacinths, ra-
nunculus, narcissus, honeysuckle, daisies, buttercups, cistus." The writer
lists a dozen additional varieties and claims to have seen "many more whose
names elude me now." Such reports may have been exaggerated—other
European visitors insisted the land was no cornucopia. But one hundred
years ago the countryside was far from being wasteland.

As many as 700,000 people lived there then, although figures vary and
are imprecise. Many were descended from the Canaanites or Philistines
(who gave the land its name) or from the Arabs, even from the ancient He-
brews. They spoke Arabic, and most of them may be termed Arabs, although commonly only nomadic Bedouins were referred to as "pure"
Arabs. The majority were Sunni Muslims, who accepted the caliphs as
Muhammad's legitimate successors, but some were Shiite Muslims, who
believed that Ali, son-in-law of Muhammad, originated the true line of succession. There were as well Druze and other Christians, some of them European or of European descent, and Jews, some of whom were also
European transplants or of European origin. Flocks of Christian tourists,
thousands every year, came to visit the holy land, and even greater numbers
of Muslim pilgrims passed through on their annual trek to Mecca.

Of the total permanent population, only a tiny fraction were rich. This
fortunate minority derived their wealth in one way or another from ownership of land, but they resided in the largest towns; their well-appointed
large brick houses were whitewashed with lime and built around court-
yards. The middle class, composed of well-to-do bankers, merchants, and
clerics, as well as a handful of professionals and local traders, lived more
modestly in the towns and villages, in stone houses well adapted for keeping out the heat of the sun. The vast majority of the inhabitants, however,
were poor. Many lived in tiny isolated villages, set on hilltops within high
walls, a reminder of the times, not long past, when safety demanded such
protection from Bedouin marauders. In northern and central Palestine the
typical village home was a square mud-plastered, whitewashed hut one
story high with a straw roof. In the south it was a rough straw shelter or, for
the semi-nomads based there part of the year, merely a tent. Inside these
dwellings one might see only a few mats, baskets, a sheepskin, and some
earthenware and wooden vessels.

Most villagers were fellahin, peasants. Within the village walls they sometimes worked in gardens or orchards or vineyards, for themselves or for their more wealthy neighbors; more commonly, they worked in the surrounding fields and pastures as sharecroppers for one of the great landowning families; or for the imperial Turkish state, which owned or controlled much Palestinian land; or for the villages themselves, since some villages owned land and periodically allocated it to residents for cultivation under a system called *musha*. Outsiders were impressed by the fellah's industry. "He abominates absence from his fields," observed one. And the fellah had a reputation for generosity, "such as his poverty allows."

Outside the towns and villages Bedouin nomads roamed ceaselessly, oblivious to boundaries and borders that, anyway, were vague to all. These "dwellers in the open land," or "people of the tent" as they called themselves, were the "pure Arabs" romanticized by certain Europeans for their swashbuckling behavior, independence, and egalitarianism. Divided among clans and tribes who occasionally made ritualistic and not very bloody war upon one another, the Bedouins might prey upon caravans and travelers, whom they viewed as fair game unless protected by previous agreement with a local sheikh, in which case the traveler's safety was inviolate. But robbery was only an interlude; mainly the Bedouin tribes wandered the countryside with their camels, sheep, goats, and donkeys in more or less regular patterns and rhythms according to the weather and needs of their livestock. Their material possessions were few. Their tents were little more than a few coverings of coarse goat or camel hair dyed black and spread over two or more small poles; on striking camp, they could quickly load their few possessions onto their beasts. When on the move, Bedouin tribes tended to skirt villages and to give towns an even wider berth. But this was a recent development: Within living memory Bedouins had raided them periodically.

Among the large towns of Palestine, Jerusalem was biggest and most important, containing sites holy to Jews, Muslims, and Christians alike. In 1911 its 60,000 inhabitants included 7,000 Muslims, 9,000 Christians, and 40,000 Jews. The city stood on a rocky plateau, 2,500 feet above sea level, overlooking hills and valleys except to the east, where the Mount of Olives looms 200 feet higher still. Peering down from that perch to the city below, one would have seen timber and red tiles among the vaulted white stone roofs of the more ancient structures: These hotels, hospices, hospitals, and schools were mainly the work of Christian missions embarked upon building programs. A pharmacy and a café opened at the Jaffa Gate, and in 1901 a clock tower and fountain were added. According to one visitor, the new structures displayed a "striking want of beauty, grandeur and harmony with their environment." Meanwhile Jerusalem had begun to overspill its ancient and massive walls. Now perhaps half the total population lived outside, in suburbs, of which Karl Baedeker, author of the famous guidebooks, deemed the Jaffa quarter most salubrious.

Overall, however, it was "a dirty town," as T. E. Lawrence observed. "The streets are ill-paved and crooked, many of them being blind alleys, and are excessively dirty after rain," sniffed Baedeker. Just before World War I the regime in Constantinople began to make improvements, but rubbish heaps continued to choke the alleyways, many cisterns were polluted, and dust thickened the air. As a result, typhoid, smallpox, diphtheria, and other epidemics remained common. But at least Jerusalem's provincialism was diminishing: After 1892 it connected with its port, Jaffa, by a paved road and a French-worked railway. Carriage roads extended to Bethlehem, Hebron, and Jericho. Christian tourists and, in season, as many as fifteen thousand Mecca-bound Muslim pilgrims clogged its streets. Residents did brisk business selling supplies, services, and trinkets typically of olive wood and mother-of-pearl. Local artisans were known for their work in tin and copper; skilled stonemasons were essential to the burgeoning building trade.

To the south of Jerusalem, the most significant towns were Gaza and Hebron; Beersheba, with only about eight hundred residents, was practically deserted by 1914. To the north and west, Nablus was a significant trading center: The fastidious Baedeker deemed its inhabitants "fanatical and quarrelsome." To the north and east stood Jericho, of whose residents Baedeker wrote, "They usually crowd round travelers with offers to execute a *'Fantasia,'* or dance, accompanied by singing, both of which are tiresome. The performers clap their own or each other's hands, and improvise verses in a monotonous tone." Farther up the coast lay Haifa, at the foot of Mount Carmel, at the southern end of the Bay of Acre. The best natural harbor on the Palestine coast, it increasingly overshadowed the older port, Acre, located at the northern end of the bay. A commercial hub, it connected by rail to Damascus.

Since 1517 Palestine had been governed more or less despotically by the sultans of the Ottoman Empire, which had been named for a Turkish Muslim warrior, Osman, whose followers were known as *Osmanliler* or Ottomans; the sultans made Constantinople their capital. When they conquered Arabia, they wrested the caliphate from the last survivor of the Abbasid line and made Constantinople its seat too. The two positions merged, and the sway of the caliph (or Prince of the Faithful) extended ostensibly to wherever Sunni Muslims might live, while the sway of the sultan extended, at its height, west and north through the Balkans all the way to Hungary; east into southern Ukraine, Georgia, and Armenia; south along the eastern and southern coasts of the Mediterranean Sea all the way to Algeria; and southeast all the way to Iraq and the Persian Gulf. Then the empire began to contract: The tsars of Russia nibbled from one direction, the Habsburgs of Austria from another. During the nineteenth century more or less successful independence movements developed in the Balkans.

For centuries the sultans paid little attention to Palestine, but during the nineteenth century conditions there slowly improved. Ottoman leaders realized they must modernize or perish at the hands of Russia or one of the great European powers. They instituted a program called Tanzimat (literally "reorganization"), which meant modernization in administration and in land tenure, among other things. The classic period of Tanzimat was 1839–76, but the last sultan of the nineteenth century, Abdul Hamid II (reigned 1876–1909), continued parts of it for longer. Abdul Hamid II was infamous for autocracy and brutality, employing many thousands of agents to spy upon his subjects; nevertheless, he favored the construction of roads, railways, schools, and hospitals throughout his dominions, and in Palestine, they led to increased domestic and external trade and to rising living standards for a fortunate few. The so-called Young Turks of the Committee of Union and Progress (CUP) who brought his reign to a generally unlamented end during 1908–09 continued the modernizing policies.

Wealthy and middle-class Palestinians benefited most from these improvements. Increasingly cosmopolitan, they commonly adopted European dress and were more aware of general European developments and European thinking than their parents and grandparents had been. They maintained closer contact with their Arab cousins than had previous generations, linked as they were by rail and telegraph lines and by journals of opinion and newspapers, seven of which were circulating in Jerusalem alone in 1914. These fortunate Palestinians knew not only their country's main towns but the greatest cities of the empire as well: They traveled regularly to Baghdad, Beirut, Damascus, and Constantinople, and to other Middle Eastern and North African cities, such as Cairo and Khartoum. For all that their land was backward by European standards, a new world was opening to them.

It was not opening yet to the Bedouins, who lived much as they always had. As for the fellahin, the backbone of the country, some left the land for the towns, where few prospered, but the vast majority remained where they had always been, to wrest such living as they could from the soil. For them, the forty years before 1914 were not so good. Land ownership was increasingly concentrated in the hands of a very few, and the fellah must work for whom he could, not for whom he would, for lower rates and longer hours than had been customary. To make ends meet, he often did double duty, laboring for more than one master at a time. His young children worked too, girls as well as boys, picking weeds and stones.

A main reason for the increasing pressure on the land and on the fellahin was the arrival in Palestine of a new and foreign element, although one that claimed an organic and ineradicable connection. They were European and Russian Jews, burning with the desire to live free, which they could not do in the countries of their birth. They were not themselves wealthy, but often they had wealthy patrons, and when land in the vicinity of Jaffa rose ten times in price over two decades, the patrons could afford to buy it while the typical fellah could not. In Palestine there had been occasional trouble, or anyway tension, between different elements of the population, Sunni and Shiite, Muslim and Christian and Jew. Relations among the various nomadic tribes had not always been peaceful; nor had been relations between Bedouin tribesmen and villagers. Now a new source of trouble had appeared, but what that would lead to was not yet apparent.

The Jews came because life at home had grown insupportable. Anti-Semitism in late-nineteenth-century Europe and Russia was increasingly pervasive. In western Europe it was usually more restrained, sometimes even genteel; but even there the conviction and harsh sentencing on fabricated evidence of the Jewish army captain Alfred Dreyfus in France, and the vehemence with which half the country supported this verdict, coupled with the electoral success of anti-Semitic political parties in Vienna, persuaded many western and central European Jews that true assimilation could never take place. But by and large they were not the ones who emigrated. In eastern Europe anti-Semitism was virulent, often dangerous. Discriminatory legislation against Jews made their daily existence a misery; violent pogroms threatened their lives and occasionally ended them. Western Europe and the new world beckoned, and many eastern European and Russian Jews moved to England, France, the United States, and Canada. But the Old Testament said that God had promised them Palestine. During the half century before 1914 the most sorely afflicted Jews, for whom religion or cultural identity was a decisive matter, increasingly turned their eyes in that direction.

Earlier in the nineteenth century it had been mainly elderly Jews who immigrated to Palestine. Predating the Zionists, they traveled alone, not part of any organized movement. They were seeking not to make a new start but rather to end their lives in the holy land. At midcentury these pathetic figures could be seen, ill clad and malnourished, begging for alms in the streets of Jerusalem, Hebron, Tiberias, and Safed, sacred cities for them. In 1845 perhaps twelve thousand Jews resided in Palestine, almost all in those four towns, and many of the immigrants among them depended upon charity; they were waiting, perhaps longing, for death.

But well-established and active Jewish communities already existed in Palestine, including "aboriginal Palestinian Jews," farmers near Acre. English observers, such as T. E. Lawrence, admired them: "They speak Arabic and good Hebrew; they have developed a standard and style of living suitable to the country and yet much better than the manner of the Arabs." In Jerusalem, where the Jews tended to congregate, Sephardim, whose forebears had arrived three centuries earlier from Iberia, still spoke old Spanish and Arabic; Persian Jews, originally from Bokhara, included a relatively prosperous group who still dressed in old-fashioned Persian costumes, boys in crimson garments, ladies "in the most beautiful sky-blue, green, scarlet, cherry, or lemon-colored silks." Outside Jerusalem's walls lived Jews from south Arabia and Yemen, who worked the land. They were not Zionists, but as successful cultivators of the soil, they were harbingers of what would prove to be a world-shaping movement.

That movement, Zionism, began to take shape in 1881, when Russian revolutionaries assassinated Tsar Alexander II. His son, Alexander III, blamed the Jews. Immediately he reimposed the anti-Semitic policies his father had relaxed, most notoriously the law confining Jews to settlements of ten thousand inhabitants or more. The tsar's adviser, his former tutor Constantin Pobiedonostsev, now chief procurator of the Holy Synod, vowed that one-third of Russian Jews would convert to the Orthodox Church, one-third would emigrate, and one-third would starve to death. Here was the stimulus for the great late-nineteenth-century Jewish exodus from Russia.

Russian and Russian-Polish Jews headed mainly west but secondarily for various regions in the Ottoman Empire, of which Palestine was the favorite. Seven thousand reached this last destination in 1882, the largest number in a single year since the Romans had destroyed the Second Temple. The seven thousand sought a peaceful life, not a place to die in peace; and the most energetic and idealistic among them were determined to practice the trade that was barred to them in Russia, namely agriculture. Jewish refugees from Romania, whose government gloried in making bloodcurdling pronouncements and issuing policies as harsh as the Russian, were of a like mind. Together Russians and Romanians composed the larger part of the "First Aliyah" (or "ascent" to the promised land). In a little more than twenty years, some thirty thousand Jewish immigrants made permanent pilgrimage to their ancient homeland as they deemed it.

They were not farmers, but in many of them burned fiercely the will to show the world that Jews could till land, could root themselves in their own soil and live upon it. They would demonstrate that they were not natural ghetto-dwellers. Within a few years they had established four agricultural colonies near Jaffa, plus one in the northern part of the Plain of Sharon and three in Galilee. At first the results were unsurprising: No colony prospered or even seemed likely to survive. Determination, no matter how strong, was no substitute for knowledge and expertise. But then the great Jewish philanthropists stepped in, Baron Edmond de Rothschild of Paris, members of the London branch of his family, and other wealthy coreligionists. Their subventions provided the necessary cushion when crops did not grow or, having grown, did not sell. They provided much else besides: funds for equipment, tools, seeds, teachers, schools, doctors, and administrators. And of course they gave funds to purchase land in the first place.

The Zionist movement, whose initial congress took place in Basel, Switzerland, in 1897, also aided the immigrants. Where the philanthropists helped the newcomers establish agricultural colonies in which they could live and work free from the scourge of anti-Semitism, Zionists sought to help them establish a national home. They may or may not have meant an independent state, purposively leaving it ambiguous, perhaps to avoid exciting antagonism, or perhaps because that goal seemed too ambitious even to them. Certainly they aimed for a national revival. They would reestablish Hebrew as the national tongue and found a great Jewish university in Jerusalem. Not that the Zionists ignored immediate practicalities: They discovered, for example, that the Jews from Yemen, if attracted to the land colonies, were much less likely than Europeans to desert for the towns. During this early crucial period the Yemeni Jews may have spelled the difference between survival and failure.

By 1914 Jews had purchased 130,000 acres, of which 90,000 were under cultivation in twenty-six separate colonies. These agricultural communities dotted the map of Palestine. Most struggled; a few flourished. It was a precarious foothold, a tenuous grip on a difficult life, but better than what the Jews had left behind.

Meanwhile the "Second Aliyah" had commenced in 1904: 33,000 settlers arrived, many preferring to live in towns from the outset. Some of them, believing in socialism, workers' rights, and cooperatives, produced the *kibbutz* and *moshav* settlements. Their leader, David Ben-Gurion, was to become Israel's first prime minister. During this Second Aliyah the Jewish population of Haifa tripled; in Jaffa it doubled, and next to Jaffa the Jews founded a new city, Tel Aviv. On the eve of World War I, when the Second Aliyah came to an end, about 85,000 Jews lived in Palestine. Of them perhaps half were self-consciously Jewish nationalists or Zionists; perhaps 12,000 lived in the agricultural settlements.

In 1914 Jews represented perhaps one-ninth of the Palestinian population. Friction arose between them and those who regarded them as interlopers, newcomers, strangers, regardless of the Old Testament. An immediate source of friction was Jewish purchase of land. Funded by their patrons and by the Zionist organization, Jews bought only large tracts, almost never small farms from an occupier-owner. The fellahin who had worked on a large estate, and perhaps lived on it, invariably were displaced, for the Jews were determined to be self-sufficient. Even if the fellah stayed nearby and continued to labor in adjoining fields, how could he not resent his changed situation? Moreover the Jews did not recognize the fellah's traditional right to pasture his flock on any field just harvested, which caused much hard feeling. "There was scarcely a Jewish colony which did not come into conflict at some time with its Arab neighbors," writes one authority, "and more often than not a land dispute of one form or another lay behind the graver collisions."

Other friction points emerged as well, including the religious one. The Prophet Muhammad had held that Jews had broken their covenant with God, had falsified their scriptures, and consequently were due for terrible chastisement on the day of reckoning. In a land whose people were accustomed to take the Quran as a guide to daily life, such teachings cannot have aided peaceful relations; still, Muslim law deemed Jews to be *ahl al-kitab,* possessors of a divine book, and therefore permitted to reside (albeit as second-class citizens) and to practice their religion wherever Islam held sway. That anti-Semitism existed in pre-1914 Palestine is indisputable; that it was as widespread, vicious, and dangerous as the eastern European and Russian is impossible, or else the Jews would not have continued to come.

In any event some Jews were equally hostile toward, equally contemptuous of, the Arabs. "Had we permitted the squalid, superstitious, ignorant fellahin . . . to live in close contact with the Jewish pioneers," wrote one, "the slender chances of success . . . would have been impaired, since we had no power . . . to enforce progressive methods or even to ensure respect for private property." This jarring tone was not uncommon. Palestinian farming, as practiced by the fellahin, suffered from "typical oriental lack of foresight," sniffed Samuel Tolkowsky, a Zionist leader who advocated the application of scientific methods to agriculture. "Ignorant and stupid as the Fellahin are," began one lecturer to the English Chovevi Zion Association, who then went on to damn with faint praise the fellah's "rude virtues." But again the disdain did not flow in one direction only: Some Arabs treated Jewish settlers as they treated the Christian tourists whom they hoped to fleece: their property and their money were fair game.

On the land and in the towns Jews and Arabs often competed. In the countryside, where the Jews employed the latest farming techniques, they were likely to win. "In the Arab orange groves 350 boxes of oranges per acre is considered a very good average yield," wrote a correspondent for the Zionist journal *Palestine*. "The Jewish planters obtain far higher returns and the writer himself had in 1912–13 an average crop of 638 boxes and in 1913–14 an average crop of 757 boxes per acre." In the towns Arab artisans and merchants likewise feared Jewish competitors. In 1891 authorities in Jerusalem sent a telegram to the Ottoman grand vizier begging him to prohibit Russian Jews from immigrating to their country. The quarter century before 1914 saw a stream of such communications and the formation of organizations designed to keep the Jews out, or at least to keep them from buying property, as well as anti-Zionist newspaper editorials and pamphlets. None of it had any effect—the Jews continued to arrive. In a typical piece a journalist in the Arab newspaper *al-Asmai* complained, "Their labor competes with the local population and creates their own means of sustenance. The local population cannot stand up to their competition."

Over time Arab protests grew more sophisticated and merged with a developing nationalist movement, of which anti-Zionism was merely a component. Suffice to say here that some politically conscious Arabs regarded Jews not merely as an economic threat to local merchants and farmers but rather as a geopolitical menace to a larger Arab cause. Five months before the outbreak of world war, one young Arab confided to his diary: "Palestine is the connecting link which binds the Arabian Peninsula with Egypt and Africa. If the Jews conquer [Palestine] they will prevent the linking of the Arab nation; indeed they will split it into two unconnected parts. This will weaken the cause of Arabism and will prevent its solidarity and unity as a nation." In another entry he put his finger on the crux of the matter, in words that continue to vex us even today: "If this country is the cradle of the Jews' spirituality and the birthplace of their history, then the Arabs have another undeniable right [to Palestine] which is that they propagated their language and culture in it. [The Jews'] right had died with the passage of time; our right is alive and unshakeable."

It may be correctly deduced that the Ottoman government held ambivalent feelings about Jews. On the one hand, it had no wish to see them established within the empire as an autonomous assembly cherishing national aspirations—the various ethnic groups already under its rule gave it enough to contend with. Both the sultan and the revolutionary Young Turks who deposed him were therefore resolutely anti-Zionist. On the other hand, the sultan and the Young Turks welcomed Jewish immigrants on an individual basis, deeming them potentially useful and industrious citizens. They tried to steer them into the Anatolian region of the empire, away from Palestine. But it was Palestine that beckoned to the Zionists, and they continued to find a way in, sometimes bribing Turkish officials who had been instructed by Constantinople to exclude them, sometimes simply relying on the inefficiency of imperial officials who could not be bothered to take action against them after they purchased land.

Such ambivalence and inefficiency offended many Arabs. Under Abdul Hamid II they had little scope for opposition; under the Young Turks they had more (although not much); but whether on the eve of World War I the Ottoman regime was generally unpopular in Palestine is a matter that divides historians. That the Jews were unpopular seems undeniable, although how deep and widespread their unpopularity was and what the antagonism might have led to under other circumstances remains uncertain. Every significant historical development has roots that may be traced back indefinitely. The Balfour Declaration was not, in and of itself, the source of trouble in a land that previously had been more or less at peace, but nor was it a mere signpost on a road heading undivertibly toward a cliff. No one can say what the course of events in Palestine might have been without it. What did come was the product of forces and factors entirely unforeseen.

CHAPTER 2

Ottomanism, Arabism, and Sharif Hussein

WHAT CAME WAS the most destructive and widespread war that humankind had yet experienced. One by one the great powers joined in. Few understood that Europe would be recast, the entire world irrevocably altered.

For twenty years the great powers had been aligning themselves. When war began, the alignments crystallized, with Germany, Austria-Hungary, and (belatedly) the Ottomans on one side, and Russia, France, and Great Britain on the other. During the blood-drenched years that followed, smaller countries chose sides according to their interests and calculations: Italy, Romania, and Greece sided with Britain and her allies; Bulgaria with the Germans. The opposing forces were very nearly evenly matched, and only when another great power, the United States, entered the fray in April 1917 on the side of the Allies could the German-led coalition finally be defeated.

The Turkish decision to side with Germany had been probable but not inevitable. Germany was the enemy of Turkey's greatest enemy, Russia. Russia was Turkey's enemy because she coveted free access to the Sea of Marmara and thence, through the Dardanelles, to the Aegean and Mediterranean Seas; Turkey controlled access to the Sea of Marmara and would not let the Russians through. Twice Russia tried to force the issue, and twice she had been thwarted. In 1856 Britain and France, who did not want the Russian navy in the Mediterranean, helped Turkey to defeat her in the Crimean War; in 1878 a concert of European powers, meeting at the Congress of Berlin, made her back off after she defeated the Ottomans in the Russo-Turkish War. (The Congress did permit weakening the Ottoman Empire in other ways, allowing Romania, Serbia, and Montenegro to declare independence and granting limited autonomy to Bulgaria.) In August 1914 Russia seemed ready to try again—and this time both Britain and France were her allies. Naturally Turkey turned to Germany for support.

It has been argued that this need not have happened, that Allied diplomacy with regard to the Ottomans was inept. Some Britons thought their country's alliance with Russia ill conceived, especially after the Young Turks and their Committee of Union and Progress led a successful revolution in 1908: better to ally with these advocates of modernization and representative government (however far they were from realizing those ideals), they felt, than with the tsar of Russia, the world's most autocratic major head of state. Others pointed out that it ill behooved Britain, with nearly a hundred million Muslim subjects in South Asia, Egypt, Sudan, and elsewhere, to make an enemy of the world's other great Muslim power, the Ottoman Empire, seat of the caliphate. When the war began, but before Turkey chose sides, some believed that Britain should make Russia declare she had no interest in taking Constantinople—that would have allayed Turkish fears. Others held that Winston Churchill, secretary of the British navy, was needlessly, if characteristically, provocative when, shortly after the German declaration of war but before the Ottomans chose sides, he commandeered two Turkish battleships (paid for by popular subscription in Turkey) that were under construction in British shipyards.

In fact, the Ottoman government was divided over which alliance to favor or whether simply to stay out of the conflict altogether. Enver Pasha, the minister of war and leader of the Young Turk movement, forced the issue. To make up for the two warships that the British had taken, Germany had given Turkey two more, the *Goeben* and the *Breslau*. Enver Pasha gave orders for Germans disguised as Turkish sailors aboard the two warships to bombard Russian ports on the other side of the Black Sea—without the knowledge of a majority in his cabinet. Some of its members never forgave him. Still, with Russia seemingly ready to advance, and with Britain and France both committed to Russia, it is hard to imagine Turkey doing anything significantly different. And with Turkey in the war and therefore in the crucible, so too were all her dominions, including Palestine.

In November 1914 the armies of Russia, a reactionary empire, and the

Ottoman, a decrepit one, lurched into gory battle near the Turkish fortress city of Erzurum. Long before then, however, the British had been considering how to weaken the Turkish foe and help their Russian ally. They recalled certain prewar talks with dissident Arabs. They recalled reports from their Middle Eastern agents and diplomats on the aspirations and activities of these people. Perhaps, mused the British, Arab discontent with Turkish rule could be turned to advantage.

In 1914 the Arab nationalist movement was not a major factor inside the Ottoman Empire; nor was it a negligible one. Its immediate progenitors were an assortment of mid- to late-nineteenth-century clerics and intellectuals from Persia, Egypt, Syria, and Mesopotamia. Virtually all of them longed for the empire to modernize and regain its former status as a great world power, able to protect the East, including Arabs, from the West. How this recovery would be accomplished remained a matter of contention. Some Arabs emphasized that Islam would confront the European threat; they became pan-Islamists. Others stressed that Arabs within pan-Islamism would not merely participate in the Ottoman revival but repossess the caliphate from Turkey. A few preached the unity of all Arabs within the empire regardless of religion. Historians group this bundle of approaches under a single term, *Ottomanism,* because they all envisioned revival of the Ottoman Empire.

Pan-Islamism and Ottomanism predate a third Middle Eastern ideology, Arabism, which emerged as a significant factor only during the six years before the outbreak of World War I. Advocates of Arabism looked forward to the revival of the empire and held views on religious and political questions as disparate as those of the champions of Ottomanism. But they went further than the Ottomanists in that they also wanted autonomy (home rule, as the British called it) for the various Arab groups inside the empire. They did not advocate complete separation and independence; full-fledged Arab nationalism envisioning separate sovereign Arab states did not appear as a noteworthy force until after 1914.

Sultan Abdul Hamid II probably helped delay the emergence of Arabism. A despot who reigned from 1876 to 1909, he was convinced of his divine right to rule but fearful of his people. At the outset he promised them liberal reforms and accepted a liberal constitution, but it was a pose designed to attract Western support. When the Western powers meddled and interfered with his modernizing projects instead of facilitating them, the sultan dropped it. He disavowed the constitution, imprisoned its author (a former grand vizier, or prime minister), and instituted personal rule that he never willingly relinquished. Paranoid, he employed ten thousand spies or more. They came to constitute a powerful and dangerous oligarchy within his realm, crisscrossing the empire and seeking out—or intentionally fabricating—accounts of disaffected subjects whose only defense against such charges was bribery. The spies' reports poured into the offices in Constantinople, stoking the sultan's fears. He had a harem of nine hundred women; one would check under his bed every night before he went to sleep. His tasters tried every morsel of food before he would touch it. His vigilant censors attempted to allay his terrors by cutting paragraphs, or entire stories, out of newspapers and journals and books, or by shutting down the presses altogether; but judges invariably confirmed his apprehensions with guilty verdicts in his corrupted courts. The sultan was subject to melancholia and fainting spells as well as murderous fits of rage: He ordered that his brother-in-law be strangled; also the grand vizier who had written the constitution and been imprisoned for his pains; also a slave girl who flirted with one of his sons.

But the sultan understood the necessity of maintaining good relations with Arab notables. During his reign they received scholarships to his military academies, commissions in the army, sinecures at the court, imperial postings, and relatively generous treatment. Whether by policy or merely by chance, the sultan surrounded himself with Arab advisers; the point is that he did not discriminate against them. He also understood the importance of religion to his Arab subjects. In order to facilitate the hajj, the annual pilgrimage of the devout to Mecca, he ordered that a railway be constructed to connect Damascus with that city. By 1908 it reached as far as Medina. Nothing could disguise the brutality of his rule, but then the brutality helped postpone the emergence of Arabism; moreover his generosity with the Arab notables, coupled with his religious policies, tempered criticism from that quarter.

Policies aimed at soothing Arabs did not necessarily appeal to Turks, however. The Turkish elite, army officers especially, increasingly despaired for their country and its empire, for the sultan was not merely cruel and brutal to his own people but ineffective in dealing with strangers. Where once Turkey had been a great power, now it was "the sick man of Europe." Ravenous wolves—which is to say the powers that were not sick, and those that were less sick (Austria-Hungary), and the smaller, newer nations that felt themselves in the springtime of youth (Serbia and Romania)—gathered around the sickbed and licked their chops or considered snatching a morsel then and there. Two years into Abdul Hamid's reign Russian soldiers marched to within ten miles of Constantinople; he gave in, but the Congress of Berlin saved him from the worst consequences of defeat, stripping him of much territory but not allowing the Russians access to the Mediterranean. In 1881, however, Abdul Hamid had to accept Greek occupation of Thessaly and, much worse, foreign control over the Ottoman national debt. In 1882 he had to accept British occupation and financial control of Egypt. In 1903 he had to accept the German plan to construct a railway through his territories from Berlin to Baghdad. He was unable to pacify his increasingly restive subjects in those Balkan territories that remained to him; Bulgaria finally achieved independence in 1908. He pacified his subjects in Armenia, or rather terrorized those who survived the twentieth century's first attempt at something approaching ethnic cleansing. (The entire world was outraged, or claimed to be.)

Organized resistance, when it came, originated in the army, which was warrened through and through by dissident Young Turk officers, members of secret societies, the most important of which was the Committee of Union and Progress. On July 3, 1908, a CUP major in the Third Army Corps stationed in Resna, Macedonia, raised the standard of revolt. His soldiers enthusiastically supported him. Troops sent to suppress the rebellion went over to the rebels. The uprising continued—indeed, it spread like wildfire. Within weeks the sultan surrendered. He restored the constitution of 1876 and reconvened the very parliament he had dissolved thirty-two years before. It decreed new elections, from which the CUP emerged victorious. The CUP proclaimed the equality of all Ottoman citizens regardless of ethnicity or religion. It pledged to uphold the reinstated constitution and parliamentary institutions. It promised to intensify Abdul Hamid II's modernizing efforts. Enthusiasm reigned among most Turks and non-Turks alike throughout the Ottoman Empire.

None of this pleased the sultan or his conservative supporters. Within months they were dabbling in counterrevolution, launching an attempt in April 1909. The army suppressed it; the CUP retained power. This meant the end for Abdul Hamid II and almost for the sultanate itself. The CUP deposed him and placed upon the throne an unappealing but relatively tractable figure, his younger brother. This gentleman served as a CUP puppet until his death in 1918, whereupon a third member of the family, Turkey's last sultan, took his place and served until 1923.

The empire's position among the great and smaller European powers continued to be perilous; the grasp on her remaining European possessions grew ever more tenuous. During the hectic six-year period before 1914 she lost nearly all of them: Bosnia and Herzegovina, Albania—in fact, everything except a slice of eastern Thrace. Meanwhile Italy had seized Libya and Rhodes in 1912 and Greece had annexed Crete. A hurricane raged outside the new regime's main gates.

Inside too the CUP was sorely tried. A Liberal Union Party, envisioning an empire composed of federated districts, won some key by-elections. More important, some CUP members were incompetent, unable to stem the loss of Balkan and other territory. In January 1913 army officers burst into a cabinet meeting. One of them shot and killed the minister of war then and there. The army officers authorized a new CUP government and outlawed the Liberals, but that hardly calmed things down. On June 11, 1913, the new grand vizier was murdered too.

For readers familiar with European history, the CUP may be usefully compared to the Jacobin Society led by Robespierre during the French Revolutionary era. It tamed a monarchy, as the Jacobins had done (or thought they had done). Like the Jacobin, the CUP held militantly secular views that sparked a conservative reaction. When the CUP replaced Islamic law with civil courts, when it opened schools for girls as well as boys, it offended devout Muslims. Like the Jacobins, the CUP was professedly democratic but, again like the Jacobins, it turned away from democratic practices in order to deal effectively with a national emergency. Finally, as the Jacobins had centralized power in eighteenth-century France, so did the CUP a little more than a hundred years later centralize the Ottoman Empire. This last policy caused the gravest difficulties of all.

Sultan Abdul Hamid II had conceived of Islam as the glue to which the vast majority of his subjects adhered; under his rule Muslims, whatever their ethnic background and wherever in the empire they might reside, had parity and deserved equal treatment by the state. But the Young Turks of the CUP exalted the Turkish element. They sought to strengthen its hold throughout the empire, among other things by making Turkish the official Ottoman language. They wished to extend Turkish rule wherever ethnic Turks lived, even outside the empire, even inside Russia. This Turkish nationalism, or pan-Turanianism, contradicted the CUP's 1908 statements about the equality of all Ottoman citizens. Inevitably it provoked a reaction.

Now Arabs began to organize against the CUP. Some held to Ottomanist goals; they tended to support the opposition Liberal Union Party, which they hoped still might revive the empire. Many more championed Arabism, aiming at a revived empire that would provide autonomy for Arabs. Others lodged somewhere between the Ottomanist and Arabist positions.

A variety of organizations spoke for these diverse discontents. A short-lived Ottoman-Arab Brotherhood hoped to strengthen ties between the two peoples; a Literary Club in Constantinople soon had branches in the major towns of Syria and Mesopotamia and thousands of members. Its quarters served as meeting grounds for the advocates of Ottomanism, Arabism, and dissident views in general. A Young Arab Society, founded in 1909 by Arabs in Paris, aimed "to awaken the Arab nation and raise it to the level of energetic nations." Reform societies appeared in Beirut, Damascus, Aleppo, Jerusalem, Baghdad, and Basra. They called for strengthening Syria and Mesopotamia (Iraq) in order to strengthen the empire and to facilitate resistance to the West. Most important was the Ottoman Decentralization Society, with headquarters in Egypt and branches throughout Syria. Its objectives with regard to the empire were apparent from its name. Meanwhile newspapers, journals, and Arab delegates to the CUP-dominated parliament in Constantinople maintained a steady stream of argument in favor of Ottomanist and Arabist ideals.

Secret societies emerged as well. Al-Qahtaniya preached the creation of a dual monarchy for Arabs and Turks, on the model of Austria-Hungary. Betrayed by one of its members, al-Qahtaniya ceased to meet within a year. But the dissatisfaction with Ottoman rule that had prompted its establishment remained unassuaged. Soon enough it reappeared in a new guise, as al-Ahd (the Covenant). This group's membership was limited largely to army officers. It advocated not only a dual monarchy but the establishment of autonomous entities for all ethnic groups within the empire; each group was to be permitted to use its native language, although Turkish would remain as a lingua franca. Al-Ahd maintained a central office in Damascus and its members paid a monthly subscription. By 1915 its treasury contained 100,000 Turkish lira. The members, who communicated by cipher, swore an oath on the Quran never to divulge the secrets of the society, "even if they are cut to pieces."

A second secret organization, al-Fatat, grew from the Young Arab Society, which maintained an above-ground presence. Seven Arab students in Paris founded the subterranean counterpart. The security issue loomed as large for them as for the members of al-Ahd; like them, they swore an oath of secrecy and admitted newcomers only after a careful vetting process and long period of probation. When the students returned to the Middle East, they changed al-Fatat's headquarters to Beirut in 1913 and to Damascus shortly thereafter. Al-Fatat was the civilian equivalent of the military-dominated al-Ahd. After the outbreak of war the two movements would merge and play an important role in the lead-up to the Arab Revolt of 1916.

The climax of prewar Arab nationalism occurred in Paris during June

1913, at a conference whose primary organizer was the Young Arab Society. This was the world's first Arab congress. Elected delegates from the secret societies attended. Telegrams of support arrived with 387 signatories: 79 Syrians, 101 Lebanese, 37 Iraqis, 139 Palestinians, 4 Egyptians, 16 Arabs resident in Europe, and 11 who were unidentifiable as to residence. On June 21 the congress made public its resolutions: One called for decentralization and another for recognition of Arabic in the Ottoman Parliament and as the official language throughout the Arab lands under Ottoman rule.

The growth of Arab nationalism, limited though its aims may have been before the outbreak of war, did not go unnoticed by the Turks. Turkish spies kept the regime in Constantinople well informed of Arab nationalist plans and actions.

Meanwhile the French, who had long-standing economic interests in Syria and Lebanon, were also keeping track of advocates of Arabism. They encouraged them, not without effect, to expand their horizons and look to France for support. A manifesto of Syrian nationalists, for example, read: "The heart's desire of the Christians in Syria is the occupation of Syria by France." We know about it because the French consul general in Beirut, François Georges-Picot, failed to burn this and other incriminating documents when he had to leave the city on the outbreak of World War I. Instead he hid them in a consulate safe, and then made the mistake (a deadly one for their authors) of telling the consulate's dragoman what he had done. The dragoman, whose duties were to act as interpreter and guide between the French, Arabs, and Ottomans, informed the latter of Picot's action. Not surprisingly, they immediately opened the safe. Since the Syrian document had been signed by "Christian members of the Executive Committee of the General Assembly elected by all the communal councils of the province of Beirut," the Turks could pick off one by one not only the principals but, if they chose to, even the men who had voted for them.

The British were paying close attention to Ottoman possessions in the Middle East as well. Southern Syria, a land bordering Egypt, through part of which ran the Suez Canal, overlooked England's economic jugular vein; moreover, the land route between Egypt and India, jewel in the crown of the British Empire, ran through Ottoman territory. For all that the British and French were allies against the Germans, and for all that they had settled many of their imperialist differences, French aspirations in Syria were unwelcome to the British. In fact, the British probably preferred a weak Ottoman regime there to a strong French one When, late in 1913, the Turks dispatched a new governor or *vali* to rule Lebanon, the twenty-fourth in five years, British observers permitted themselves some optimism. Competent Turkish rule would keep out the French, and the new *vali* was "a man of character, decision and enlightenment." Wrote one Foreign Office expert, "It is to be hoped he will remain long."

Even minor events in Ottoman territory attracted British attention. In May 1913, when Arabs protested corruption among the police of Basra, a detailed report found its way to the Foreign Office in London. When a few days later the protesters rioted because Turkish officials had taken no action, a Foreign Office official noted, possibly with alarm: "There is every sign of the approaching disintegration of Turkish rule in these regions." In December 1913 the Ottomans agreed to sponsor a new Islamic university in Medina, and a well-known Egyptian pan-Islamist laid the foundation stone; a report soon was circulating at the Foreign Office. So closely did the British watch the development of the Arab nationalist movement, in fact, that after the 1913 Paris Congress, a detailed report on individual participants soon made the rounds of the Foreign Office. "With one or two exceptions," the report concluded, after describing in detail nearly a dozen participants, "they are all young men of whom much is expected."

Only fourteen months later the European powers declared war upon one another, and in November 1914 Enver Pasha brought his country in on Germany's side. Few Arab nationalists supported this move enthusiastically, but even fewer opposed it openly. Still, at least one conservative Ottomanist recognized the war as an opportunity. If Turkey lost it, then her grip on Arab lands would be weakened, perhaps fatally, in which case he might realize his (vast) ambitions for himself and his family. He would do nothing rash, but it might not hurt just to reestablish relations with the British. (He distrusted the French.) After all, he had had some contact with them, direct and indirect, prior to the war, and he had conceived a great admiration for them.

The cautious individual who had decided to sound out the British was the emir, or grand sharif, Hussein of Mecca. A leader among Arabs, he was at this stage not an Arabist but a conservative Ottomanist deeply alienated by CUP rule. In 1914 he was a little more than sixty years old, of medium height and fair complexion, with fine and regular features. He possessed "large and expressive brown eyes . . . strongly marked eyebrows under an ample forehead . . . a short and delicately curved nose." His mouth was "full . . . [his] teeth well formed and well preserved. The beard thick and not long, grey almost to whiteness." "He is such an old dear," T. E.

Lawrence once wrote of him dismissively. But a second Briton judged him "outwardly so gentle and considerate as almost to seem weak, but this appearance hides a deep and subtle policy, wide ambitions and an un-Arabian foresight, strength of character and persistence."

Grand Sharif Hussein belonged to the Abadila clan, which claimed direct descent from the Prophet Muhammad. Only one other clan, the Dwahi Zeid, claimed a like lineage. Male members of the two clans possessed the aristocratic title *sharif;* only they could become emirs, or grand sharifs, of Mecca. Mecca was the capital city of the Hejaz, which is present-day Saudi Arabia.

Until the eighteenth century the grand sharifate was a prize worth having. Its holder was overlord of the Hejaz, although the Bedouin tribes who wandered the country were loath to acknowledge any temporal master. But the title conferred enormous religious authority too, because the Hejaz included not merely Mecca, where the prophet had been born, but also Medina, where he had been buried. Indeed, to Muslim eyes the grand sharif of Mecca probably ranked second only to the caliph as a holy and revered figure. The grand sharif oversaw arrangements for the annual pilgrimage, or hajj, to the two cities, an extremely lucrative business. In addition he received other monies, titles to land, and emoluments.

The position itself dated from the tenth century. In the sixteenth century, when the Ottomans took over the Hejaz, they chose to retain it as always, choosing the grand sharif from the two clans but making him govern in concert with a *vali,* whom they appointed in Constantinople. The Ottomans did not significantly reduce the grand sharifs' power because they feared alienating Muslim Arabs. Instead, they went the other way, exempting Hejazis from taxation and conscription and pouring money into the two holy cities, both of which prospered as a result.

In 1803 Muslim fundamentalists, Wahhabis who wished to purge Islam of innovations, swept like a cutting desert wind into Mecca in order to "purify" it. In 1819 the Ottomans restored their own rule but gripped tighter than before. Sultans now sought to control the grand sharifs partly through the *vali*s and partly by exercising stricter oversight from Constantinople; they encouraged rivalries within and between the two sharifian clans on the principle of divide and conquer. For the next ninety-five years the grand sharifs strove always to weaken the Ottoman hold, to regain the freedom of action they once had enjoyed. They engaged in sometimes deadly rivalry with the *vali*s. The Dwahi Zeid and the Abadila clans maneuvered against each other too, jockeying incessantly for favor and position at the Ottoman court. After 1819 the history of the grand sharifate was one long tale of intrigue. But of that intrigue Hussein, grand sharif of Mecca in 1914, was a master.

He was born in Constantinople in 1853, the son, grandson, and nephew of former emirs. Part of his childhood he spent in Mecca, part in the Ottoman capital. According to an early, sycophantic biographer, he displayed extraordinary qualities even as a youth: "integrity, energy and truth . . . unselfishness . . . gracious manners . . . love of virtue." One imagines this young paragon listening intently as his uncles, older cousins, father, and grandfather discussed how to best their Dwahi Zeid rivals, and how to manipulate the politicians of Constantinople and the *vali*s in Mecca. In secret his closest relatives may have discussed how to defeat their own cousins and uncles, since all longed to be appointed grand sharif. The youngster took it all in. During a second stint in Mecca, as an adult, Hussein supported the attempts of his uncle, Grand Sharif Aoun el-Hafik, to loosen the Ottoman reins. For this the sultan recalled him to Constantinople in 1891. There Hussein stayed until 1908, when he himself gained the great prize.

Constantinople, Europe's easternmost or Asia's westernmost city, is situated on a peninsula studded with seven low hills; the Golden Horn, or Bay of Constantinople, lies to its north, the channel of the Bosporus to its east, and the Sea of Marmara to its south. It is a city of mosques and domes and minarets; of Roman ruins, palaces, fortresses, and columns: beautiful, cultured, cosmopolitan, and lively. The future grand sharif flourished there. The sultan provided him with a furnished home overlooking the Bosporus. Hussein raised four sons (Ali, born in 1879, Abdullah, born in 1882, Feisal, born in 1886, and Zeid, born to a Turkish mother in 1898), for whom he engaged private tutors in every subject except the Quran, which he taught them himself. Already he was known for his piety and knowledge of Islam. His social circle comprised the Turkish and Muslim elites, many of the latter being descended, as was he, from the Prophet. "He enjoyed the high esteem and respect of the Constantinople Statesmen, Ministers and Viziers, and of the Sultan himself," according to the biographer, and as a result he too attained the rank of vizier, and membership of the Council of State, an advisory body to the sultan. Nor would he deviate "by a hair's breadth from the path of honor and virtue thus gaining the deepest love and veneration of the whole nation." But for all its glories, Constantinople was a political hothouse. That Hussein succeeded in becoming grand sharif in 1908, when all his male relatives and their Dwahi Zeid rivals wanted the position too, suggests qualities his biographer failed to mention: tact, for one, which is to say the ability to mask his true thoughts, which is to say political cunning. Also he was lucky.

Cunning and luck were both apparent in 1908, when the CUP decided to replace the acting grand sharif (who happened to be one of Hussein's cousins). Having just taken power and still nourishing progressive and democratic impulses, the CUP had little reason to favor the conservative, deeply religious Hussein, who put himself forward. It chose instead another of his relatives, an uncle. But the latter dropped dead while on his way to Mecca. The Young Turks distrusted Hussein, but some Old Turks held different views. The sultan, for one, appears to have admired and liked Hussein personally. "I pray that God may punish those who have prevented me from benefiting from your talents," Abdul Hamid II told him before dispatching him to Mecca. But the sultan could not have done it alone. Hussein had been courting the English too: He sent a message of thanks to the British ambassador in Constantinople for supporting opponents of the CUP's centralizing policies; and the British dragoman, Gerald Fitzmaurice, may have recommended Hussein to the Anglophile grand vizier. The British influence, coupled with the sultan's, proved too weighty for hardliners in the CUP to overcome. Another possibility is that the CUP hoped to score points with the British by appointing their favorite. In any case, while Hussein's courtship of the sultan was simply elementary politics, that he had bothered to court Fitzmaurice is evidence of political acumen.

Another part of this story needs telling. By now Hussein's second son, Abdullah, aspired to play a political role. Like his father, he had grown up at the feet of elder male relatives spinning political intrigues. When he was alone, he must have ruminated upon what he had heard and nourished the ambition to take part someday in political affairs. In 1908 he was ready. He urged his father to put his claim to the sharifate in writing; he brought the letter himself to the Anglophile grand vizier; he lobbied court officials on his father's behalf. He later claimed these efforts were decisive, which we may doubt. But as markers of his future role they were significant.

Already in 1908 Sharif Hussein despised the Young Turks of the CUP, who heartily returned the sentiment; he supported instead the reactionary sultan, Abdul Hamid II. Upon reaching Mecca, Hussein's first words confirmed his deeply conservative views: He would respect not the CUP constitution but only God's: "This country abides by the constitution of God, the law of God and the teaching of his prophet." He anticipated the counterrevolution of 1909: "When Your Majesty calls, the first country to respond will be the Hejaz," he pledged before his departure. He may have promised the sultan a place of safety from which to plan the countercoup, and it may be that the sultan lived to regret not accepting this invitation. At

any rate, Hussein's general outlook did not augur well for his future relations with the CUP government.

The Hejaz of which Hussein became emir in 1908 was among the most
desolate regions of the Arabian Peninsula, that vast expanse of sparsely settled rock and sand roamed by constantly warring, untamable nomadic
tribes. "The principal superficial characteristic of Hejaz is general barren-
ness," wrote the British archaeologist and agent David Hogarth in a prewar
handbook. Only the occasional oasis and "rare fertility" at the foot of certain upland valleys permitted the practice of agriculture at all. There were
few villages or even hamlets. In Midian, in northern Hejaz, such tiny settlements as did exist consisted solely of mud huts, according to William
Yale, an American engineer who worked as an agent for the State Department in the Middle East during World War I. And Midian as a whole Yale
judged "a miserable country." As for the Bedouins, they were, according to
Hogarth, "of exceptionally predatory character, low morale and disunited
organization."

But Hejaz boasted a significant port, Jeddah, and two relatively prosperous cities, Mecca and Medina. Jeddah, with a population of 30,000, played a
crucial role in the hajj: Muslim pilgrims sailed there from all over the
world, then proceeded on to Mecca. Medina, with a population of 30,000 to
40,000, was a walled town based on a large oasis, well watered by wadis,
and surrounded by palm trees bearing 139 varieties of dates, other fruit
trees, vineyards, wheat, barley, and vegetable gardens. As the terminus of
the railway from Damascus, it supplied the second great stream of Muslim
pilgrims en route to Mecca. In fact, for wealthier pilgrims Medina, final
resting place of the Prophet Muhammad, was a destination city too. Residents of all classes and occupations made large profits from these sojourn-
ers.

Mecca itself was a city of 70,000, surrounded by hills, some fifty miles inland from Jeddah; a nine-hour ride on a fast donkey, a two-day trip by
mule, a three-day journey by camel. It contained a great mosque called the
Beit Allah, with a vast courtyard and colonnades, and major and minor
bazaars in the surrounding neighborhood; three forts stood in districts to
the southeast, west, and north. Chief among the city's houses was the grand
sharif's palace, called the Imaret. Made of five stories, massive "as a mountain," according to one who saw it for the first time, it contained one hundred rooms, some of them exceedingly grand. A second palace, even more
sumptuously furnished, contained the sharif's sleeping quarters and was
the domicile of his wife.

Mecca's other houses were mainly of stone; those near the mosque rose to three or four stories, with large windows facing the outlying hills. Water carriers, with swollen dripping leather skins draped over their shoulders, supplied the houses from pits sunk into an underground conduit that connected with springs outside. There were baths, hospices, hospitals, and a court, where the sharif's *wakil* (or general factotum) dispensed rough justice: "In the event of a quarrel in which knives were used an official measurer of wounds . . . estimates by the depth and length of the wound the amount of the fine payable: the total of the smaller wound having been deducted from that of the larger, the inflictor of the latter has to pay the difference." A single building contained a post office, telegraphs, and telephones. There were three schools and a library, but according to Hussein Ruhi Effendi, a Persian employed by the English in Jeddah and later in Cairo, Mecca possessed "only fifty people who are educated at all and there are not more than three per cent who can read and write." Hogarth thought the place "clean," which is curious since Ruhi deemed it "not clean," and a second Arab agent employed by the English (called only X but who was in fact Ruhi's father-in-law, Ali Effendi), reported, "Everything exceedingly filthy." For what it is worth, Ruhi also claimed that "morality seems to be at a very low ebb, very many of the men having unnatural taste." There were no local industries—the population mainly lived off the annual hajj in one way or another—but a few marts still carried on in several inns, where men might purchase Sudanese and Abyssinian slaves.

Mecca's soil was barren. Fruits and vegetables were brought in from a town called Taif, two days' ride up in the hills, where the emir had another palace as refuge from the summer heat. Rice and foreign products came from the port city, Jeddah; poultry, mutton, milk, and butter arrived from the desert Bedouins. It was almost always hot, the mean annual temperature higher than eighty degrees Fahrenheit. Shielded from most breezes by the surrounding hills, Mecca on a still summer day reminded Hogarth of a furnace: "The heat reflected from the rock-faces [of nearby hills] increases the glare by day and the closeness of the atmosphere at night." And it was dry. Rain rarely fell; when it did, it descended in torrents and routinely flooded the mosque.

Here then was Sharif Hussein's kingdom, intimately known to him since early childhood and now, finally, his inheritance. He took it up like a familiar garment. It fit like a glove. Two of his four sons accompanied him to Mecca; they came to know the tribal sheikhs and local notables almost as well as he did. Together father and sons discussed tactics and strategies. Perhaps they were already dreaming tall dreams: not merely of an autonomous Hejaz, restored to the freedom of action that had preceded 1803, but of a semi-independent principality with a hereditary monarch under the protection of Great Britain, for which Hussein had developed great admiration. Britain would treat the Hejaz as Hussein fondly believed she did Afghanistan, refraining from interference in internal matters.

Did they dream too of uniting the Arab tribes under their own leadership? It is possible. During the spring of 1911 Hussein made common cause with the Turks, to defeat a potential rival and anti-Ottoman rebel whose territory lay immediately to the south of the Hejaz. During the campaign Hussein's sons gained valuable military experience. Meanwhile the grand sharif established friendly relations with the chiefs and notables of most of the other Arabian tribes. Only Imam Yahya of Yemen and Abdul Azziz ibn Saud—the inscrutable, ambitious, indeed ferocious Wahhabi chief in the desert regions called el-Nejd, directly east of the Hejaz—rejected his overtures and denied his religious paramountcy. Nevertheless his position was a platform capable of supporting vast ambitions. Perhaps Hussein already dreamed of wresting the caliphate from Ottoman hands. Or perhaps his son Abdullah cherished it for him, or even for himself.

In the meantime Hussein and his sons played the CUP with consummate skill. No *vali* could outmaneuver them; seven tried during 1908–14; all were defeated and recalled to Constantinople. When CUP directives encroached upon his prerogatives, he evaded, or gave the appearance of acquiescing, while considering future options. Above all he opposed extension of the railway from Medina to Mecca, as it would give the Turks a direct line from Damascus into his stronghold and it would deprive Hejazis of their lucrative trade guiding and supplying the pilgrims traveling on foot or by hired camel. He opposed even the extension of the telegraph to Mecca; and he opposed the abolition of slavery, which the modernizing Young Turks favored. Apparently these reactionary positions were popular among his subjects. "He is very generous, kindhearted and liberal," said one. "He does not refrain from stretching out his hand to salute a rough looking and dirty Arab who puts his sandals round his wrists and holds out his hand to shake the hand of the Sherif."

When war came and the sharif decided to establish contact with the English, he sent his son Abdullah. It was a natural choice, for by now this young man had practical experience as a politician, and some knowledge of the English, perhaps more than his father did.

Abdullah was a short stocky figure, "with merry dark brown eyes, a round smooth face . . . straight nose, brown beard." He was canny and ambitious. When the CUP reinstated the Ottoman parliament, he ran successfully for one of the two seats allocated to the Hejaz, receiving 144 votes. (Very few Hejazis possessed the franchise.) He owed his election to the influence of his father. He does not appear to have been much of a parliamentarian; says one account, "On one occasion he quarreled with the wayward Enver Pasha and cursed him in front of a great multitude and was on the point of striking him." His biographer writes that Abdullah played little part in the Ottoman assembly; the press never mentioned him, and he does not figure in the memoirs of contemporary politicians. Surely aware of the developing nationalist movement, surely sympathetic to the Liberal Union Party's giving voice to opponents of Ottoman centralization, he nonetheless joined no political party and evidently developed little respect for representative government. He believed the Ottoman parliament had been fixed to favor Turkey. "It *purports* [emphasis added] to be a government by the people for the people," he wrote dismissively, many years later, of parliamentary rule.

Abdullah contacted the British not out of respect or admiration but rather because Hussein desired a powerful ally against the CUP. When Abdullah made first contact is uncertain, but the location can be fixed. From 1910 to 1914 he attended Ottoman parliamentary sessions in Constantinople, journeying there every winter and spring via Cairo, where he often stayed with the Egyptian khedive. The latter, although supposedly a vassal of the Ottoman sultan, was in fact little more than a British puppet, because the British had controlled Egyptian finances since 1882. The British felt obliged to control Egypt one way or another since it contained the Suez Canal, in which they owned a majority interest and through which traveled much of their foreign trade. So while Egypt remained ostensibly part of the Ottoman Empire, in reality it was part of the British. And it was in Egypt that Abdullah approached them.

He may have met Sir Ronald Storrs, oriental secretary at the British Agency in Cairo, as early as 1912, for he mentions in his memoirs that by 1914 they had kept up friendly relations for two years. During the same period Abdullah records, he developed great respect for Storrs's chief, the consul general, Lord Kitchener. The British, deeply interested as they were in Arab affairs, likely knew of the sharif's politically active son. But there is no reference to their having made Abdullah's acquaintance during 1912–13, whereas a series of meetings held in February 1914 are well chronicled.

By that month relations between Emir Hussein and Constantinople had sunk to a new low. The CUP dispatched a fresh *vali* to the Hejaz, accompanied by an additional detachment of troops. His orders were to enforce a law passed in 1912 that removed Medina from Hussein's control, and to secure the emir's consent to extension of the railway from Medina to Mecca. Hussein intended to block these moves as he had blocked previous Ottoman encroachments, but he feared the CUP response.

Meanwhile Abdullah was passing through Cairo on his way to Constantinople for the opening of parliament. According to his account, Lord Kitchener called upon him at the khedivial palace. They chatted about unimportant matters. Two days later when Abdullah returned the call, however, "I decided to speak openly to Kitchener." (Records being sparse, we have no indication that his father suggested the meeting.) Abdullah described to Kitchener "the realities of the situation in the Hejaz, the delicacy of the Sharif's position, the causes of the disaffection between Turks and Arabs and the aims of the Arab movement as a whole." He thought Kitchener listened attentively. "When I asked him to tell me whether in the event of a rupture the Sharif could count upon any support from Great Britain, Kitchener replied negatively on the plea that British relations with Turkey were friendly and that in any case the dispute was an internal matter in which it would be improper for a foreign Power to intervene." Abdullah pointed out that Britain had intervened in other countries' internal matters. (He was too tactful to say it, but Kitchener himself had done so, on Britain's behalf.) The consul general only laughed.

Two months later, on his way back from Constantinople, Abdullah appears to have tried again to interest the British in his father's plight. At a second meeting with Kitchener he confined himself to small talk, but a few nights later he requested that Storrs call upon him at the khedive's palace. Storrs obliged. First the two men discussed poetry. "I was astonished and delighted at the range of his literary memory," Storrs recalled. "He intoned for me brilliant episodes of the Seven Suspended odes of Pre-Islamic Poetry, the glories and the lament of Antar ibn Shaddad." Then carefully, obliquely, "by a series of delicately inclined planes," Abdullah broached the true reason for the meeting: "whether Great Britain would present the Grand Sharif with a dozen or even a half dozen machine guns."

Storrs demurred. He thought Abdullah could have expected nothing else, "and we parted on the best of terms." But the son of Sharif Hussein had laid down a marker. When World War I began only six months later, the British would remember it, and they would pick it up.

CHAPTER 3

First Steps Toward the Arab Revolt

ON NOVEMBER 5, 1914, when Turkey entered World War I on the side of Germany, she posed no immediate threat to Great Britain, although that country would have preferred her neutrality or active support. But grave dangers to Britain existed much closer to home. During August and September 1914 the German juggernaut rolled westward, smashing through Belgian and French defenses; it crushed the British Expeditionary Force sent to halt it, the boom of the big guns carrying like the rumble of distant thunder all the way to Dover and Folkestone. The Allies finally did stem the German tide, but they could not throw it back. Soon muddy trenches rimmed by barbed wire extended from the North Sea to the Swiss border, the two sides separated by a thin ribbon of cratered no-man's-land, dotted with mines, unexploded shells, and rotting human and animal corpses, or pieces of them. Now commenced the war of attrition, where advances of even half a mile were rare and not worth the blood spilled and lives lost. The world had never experienced war on so vast a scale, and there would be no let-up for four years. The major powers lost millions of men.

Against this backdrop of carnage on the Western Front, the British strove mightily, sometimes stealthily, sometimes bloodily, for gain in the Middle East; and diplomats maneuvered silkily for their own country's benefit, and contending lobbies and pressure groups vied determinedly for advantage in London, where the decisions were made and directions cabled to British agents around the world.

But if the Middle East was far from the main battlefield, nevertheless war of another kind had begun there. The Ottomans could not immediately bring military force to bear upon British troops, but as the seat of the caliphate, Turkey was revered by Muslims across the world. Already the Ottomans were calling upon believers to wage jihad, holy war, upon the enemies of Turkey. If Britain's Muslim subjects on the Indian subcontinent and in Egypt and Sudan heeded this call, then her position would be more parlous than it was already. The steps taken by British imperialists in India to protect against a Muslim jihad do not concern us. In the Middle East, however, they are of the essence. The Suez Canal was Britain's windpipe. Without that crucial line of trade and communication, she would suffocate.

Having taken charge of Egyptian finances in 1882, Britain now discarded the pretense that the Turks exercised ultimate authority over this Ottoman province and declared her own protectorate. She deposed the Egyptian khedive, Abbas Hilmi, who was inconveniently pro-Ottoman, but conveniently absent in Constantinople, and proclaimed his Anglophile uncle, Hussein Kamel, to be the country's sultan, Hussein I (a new title for the leader of Egypt). Through him Britain decreed martial law. Through him she curtailed civil liberties and imposed censorship.

An imperial power typically fears the people subject to its rule and keeps tabs on individuals and groups who oppose it; an imperial power at war is even more vigilant. The new sultan's puppet government went so far as to outlaw the singing of certain songs, like one that went:

> *The Turkish Army is in the Peninsula of Sinai.*
> *It will come to us during this month . . .*
> *Our khedive will come.*
> *Tomorrow we'll celebrate his return.*
> *And slay Hussein I with a knife, by God we will.*

British intelligence agents identified potential troublemakers in Egypt and collected seditious circulars, pamphlets, and wall posters. "Now the One Powerful God has come forth to take vengeance," threatened a fatwa issued by a cleric in Constantinople and brought to the attention of Sir Ronald Storrs. "Behold the sun of the Glory of Islam and his grandeur rise up over you. Watch it arise out of the horizon which is dyed with crimson gore and lit up with blazing fires." The unflappable oriental secretary placed this document, along with similar messages, in an in-tray on his desk between four telephones presided over by an ivory figure of the Buddha. A warning arrived, issued by the commandant of the Fourth Turkish Army, that the Turkish force would soon be ready to invade Egypt: "The Ottoman Army is coming to embrace you. Shortly by the will of God you will see its sharp swords and glittering bayonets thrust into the hearts of its enemies, tearing their entrails up." Storrs slipped it into the tray.

Storrs was the Englishman to whom Abdullah had appealed for machine guns in April 1914, after the consul general, Lord Kitchener, turned him down. Portraits reveal a squarely built and fine-featured youngish man sporting a dandy's mustache, perhaps to compensate for a receding hairline. He had studied Eastern literature and Arabic at Pembroke College, Cambridge, gaining a first-class degree. But he was not completely at ease with the language, a fact that would have significant repercussions later. Within a year of graduating in 1903, he had gone out to Cairo to work in the Egyptian civil service. He gained the appointment as oriental secretary in 1909. Storrs was urbane, knowledgeable, arrogant, and catty, "too clever by three-quarters," according to one expert, but his boss, Lord Kitchener, regarded him highly.

Even before Turkey entered the war on the German side, Sir Ronald thought it might, and picked up the marker so fortuitously laid down by Abdullah during his visit to Cairo the previous spring. Perhaps Britain could supply machine guns to Abdullah's father after all, and much else besides. Storrs could think of no better figure to undermine a Turkish call for jihad than a descendant of the Prophet himself who was also the grand sharif of Mecca. And no one in Britain could think of a better bridge to the Middle Eastern Muslim world either. The Imam Yahya was pro-Turk or at best neutral in the war and would not oppose the Turkish call for jihad; Ibn Saud had British backers, especially in the British government of India, but the leader of the Wahhabi sect could not speak for a broad Muslim movement. Hussein seemed the obvious choice then, but Storrs, a civilian, lacked authority to send him military aid; nor was he senior enough to set policy. A higher-ranking official, with military connections, must be enlisted.

Storrs consulted Sir Gilbert Clayton. Before the outbreak of war, Clayton had been director of intelligence and Sudan agent in Cairo; with the onset of war, he assumed the additional position of director of military intelligence. (Soon he would become unofficial father figure of a newly established agency, the fabled Arab Bureau, in which swashbucklers like T. E. Lawrence were to cut such a dashing figure.) Clayton sat at the nexus of Egyptian and Sudanese politics and military intelligence. He too had no doubt that Britain should pick up Abdullah's marker. He directed Storrs to put the matter to Lord Kitchener in writing.

Kitchener, however, was no longer in Cairo. When war broke out, he had been in England intending to return to Egypt to resume his duties as consul general. While standing upon the deck of the ferry at Dover, he received the summons from Prime Minister Asquith to become Britain's secretary of state for war.

He was a remarkable character, Kitchener: private, complex, contradictory, powerful. Alone among senior figures in the British establishment, he understood from the outset that victory over Germany would not be quick; it would take at least three years, he thought. Britain's small professional force, he knew, would be insufficient to fight it. Britain would need a vast army. Since she did not (yet) practice conscription, the army must be raised from volunteers. Soon Kitchener's fierce chiseled features, piercing blue eyes, and silvery-gold mustache adorned posters on walls throughout the land, over the following declaration in capital letters: "YOUR COUNTRY NEEDS YOU!" Volunteers practically stampeded to join the colors, testimony to the awe in which so many held the newly appointed secretary of state for war.

A man of few words, he yet had a commanding presence. Many revered him as the victor of Omdurman and thus the avenger of General Gordon, slain by the forces of the Mahdi at Khartoum in 1885. He was known too as the general who had faced down the French at Fashoda thirteen years later, thereby maintaining British supremacy in the Sudan; also as conqueror of the Boer rebels in South Africa two years after that. He had been governor general of eastern Sudan, commander in chief of the armed forces in India, inspector general of the Egyptian police, sirdar (military commander) of Egypt, governor general of Sudan, and finally consul general in Egypt. His great ambition was to become viceroy of India. Had the war not intervened, perhaps he would have realized this dream. He was close to the Cecil family, a fountainhead of Conservative leaders including Prime Ministers Salisbury and Balfour. The former had advanced his career at critical junctures. Among some of his subordinates he inspired great devotion and admiration.

But he had critics too. They drew attention, sotto voce, to defects in the imperial hero's character: an inability to delegate authority or to organize paperwork (they called him "Lord Kitchener of Chaos" behind his back); a predilection for brutality in his dealings with colonized peoples; and very strangely, a kind of kleptomania. When he saw something he wanted (he had a particular fondness for objets d'art, antiques, and silver), he took it—even from the homes of his hosts. One of the doubters, Margot Asquith, the prime minister's wife, said of him: "He may not be a great man—but he *is* a great poster."

Still, Kitchener knew the Middle East very well and grasped Britain's strategic position and needs there. He was a close student of the fledgling Arab nationalist movement, such as it was, and of the intrigues at the Ottoman sultan's court. Despising both Old and Young Turk methods of government, he had long hoped Britain would replace their rule with hers throughout the Middle East, not incidentally guaranteeing the British position at Suez and creating a new swath of imperial territory to complement India. The best way to win the war, he believed, was to concentrate on defeating Germany on the Western Front, but unlike other "westerners" in the British cabinet, he remained attuned to developments in the east. When Storrs's letter reached him, he acted at once. The situation now, he recognized, was potentially more dangerous for the grand sharif than it had been six months earlier. If Hussein displeased the regime in Constantinople, it could call upon Germany to help deal with him. The first step, therefore, must be to ensure that Hussein was still interested in British assistance.

"Tell Storrs," Kitchener directed Sir Milne Cheetham, who was acting in his place in Cairo until a longer-term replacement could be appointed, "to send secret and carefully chosen messenger from me to Sherif Abdullah to ascertain whether 'should present armed German influence at Constantinople coerce Calif against his will and Sublime Porte to acts of aggression and war against Great Britain, he and his father and Arabs of Hejaz would be with us or against us.' "

This directive reached Storrs on September 24, 1914. He acted immediately, choosing as messenger to Abdullah X, "the father-in-law of my little Persian agent Ruhi." Travel to Mecca with all speed, Storrs directed X. But it took X four days to reach his destination, traveling the last fifteen hours by donkey overnight. Then he waited five days more for the grand sharif and his family to return from the summer palace in Taif.

When X finally did enter the palace in Mecca, he dined sumptuously with the grand sharif and his sons. Afterward he gave Abdullah the message Storrs had composed according to Kitchener's instructions. Presumably Abdullah gave it to his father, who quickly read it, for soon a servant appeared: Grand Sharif Hussein would receive X in another room. X climbed stairs to the top of the palace and entered a very fine, large chamber. There the emir, pacing back and forth, informed him that he no longer felt obliged to honor his duties to the Ottomans because they had "made war upon our rights." Throwing back the sleeve of his garment in a dramatic gesture, he declared: "My heart is open to Storrs, even as this. Stretch forth to us a helping hand and we shall never at all help these oppressors. On the contrary we shall help those who do good." As always with Hussein, religious conviction spurred activity: "This is the Commandment of God upon us: Do good to Islam and Moslems—Nor do we fear or respect any save God."

The emir had taken a first step toward rebellion. He thereby risked his life and those of his sons, as Kitchener and the other Britons well knew. But we have no record of the meeting except for Storrs's translation of X's subsequent oral report. When it came to putting his sentiments down on paper, the grand sharif was exceedingly cautious. Since Kitchener had addressed himself to Abdullah, Hussein had his son write and sign the reply and place it in an unaddressed sealed envelope inside a larger one that was addressed to a third party; then he had Feisal convey it to the sharif's agent at Jeddah. The latter finally gave it over to X, but only when he was safely aboard the Japanese freighter that would take him back to Suez.

The written message was carefully conceived, yet is vague in a crucial respect. The first part was plain enough: According to a résumé of the letter that Cheetham sent to Kitchener, Abdullah had replied (for his father of course) that the grand sharif looked forward to "closer union" with England but awaited "written promise that Great Britain will . . . guarantee Emir against Foreign and Ottoman aggression." In short, Hussein would not risk putting his neck into a Turkish noose without receiving written pledges of protection from Britain. But this was not his only caveat: Hussein and his sons also refused to put themselves in jeopardy, only to discover that Britain had replaced Turkey as their foreign overlord. And here in retrospect two ambiguities are apparent.

First, even in this initial letter Hussein appears to have been looking beyond his own kingdom of Hejaz and claiming to speak for Arabs throughout the Middle East. Before he took any sort of action, he warned Kitchener and Storrs, he must receive Britain's promise to "abstain from internal intervention in Arabia." The indeterminate term was crucial: By "Arabia," did he mean not merely the Hejaz but the entire Arabian Peninsula? Did he even perhaps mean Mesopotamia and Syria too, including Palestine? He did not specify.

Let us pursue this ambiguity. On the one hand, Hussein's letter was just what the British had been hoping for. Only a great leader of "Arabia" could

successfully countermand the caliph's appeal for jihad against Turkey's enemies. On the other hand, this first wartime exchange between the two parties sowed the seeds of future conflict and misunderstanding. Cheetham
appears to have discerned the looming difficulty and tried to protect against
it. As he cabled to the Foreign Office, Abdullah's letter was very promising.
"Reply is being prepared subject to your approval disclaiming all intention
of internal intervention and guaranteeing against external aggression *only
independence of Sherifate*" (emphasis added). In other words, the British
wanted the grand sharif to speak for all Arabia, of undefined boundaries,
but they would guarantee to protect his authority only in the territory he
governed already.

"Does Kitchener agree?" Sir Edward Grey, the foreign secretary back in
London, queried in his spiky handwriting at the bottom of Cheetham's
cable. "If so I will approve." But Kitchener did not accept Cheetham's qualification. Instead he directed that the sharif be informed: "If the Arab nation assist England in this war . . . England will guarantee that no internal
intervention takes place in Arabia and will give the Arabs every assistance
against external foreign aggression." He had accepted the emir's original
broad formulation of "Arabia," although whether this meant to him the
Hejaz, or the peninsula, or the peninsula plus Syria and Mesopotamia, remains unclear. And since Grey signed off on it too, he presumably also accepted the broad but vague understanding of "Arabia."

But did they truly accept it? Quite possibly Grey did. A lifelong Liberal,
he soon would argue in a War Council meeting that "Arabia, Syria and
Mesopotamia were the only possible territories for an Arab Empire," and
that in those countries Britain could "set up a new and independent
Moslem State" over which Hussein would be ruler. But Kitchener, hardly a
Liberal, rejected this argument at the War Council, suggesting instead that
Britain should annex Mesopotamia at the least. It is likely, therefore, that he
rejected the idea when Hussein first broached it as well. Probably he was
prepared to fudge the matter of boundaries or was being consciously mis-
leading in order to induce Hussein to take action.

Again, someone recognized the dissonances, and given the imprecision
of future letters from Cairo to Mecca in which his influence was less important, the stickler may have been Cheetham. He, Clayton, and Storrs
would have had input on the letter now to go to Abdullah, and perhaps
under his guidance they took it upon themselves to limit Kitchener's
pledge. They adapted and narrowed the original language so that it now
read: "If the Amir and Arabs in general assist Great Britain . . . Great
Britain will promise not to intervene in any manner whatsoever whether in

things religious or otherwise. Moreover recognizing and respecting the sacred and unique office of the Amir Hosayn Great Britain will guarantee the independence, rights and privileges *of the Sherifate* [emphasis added] against all external foreign aggression, in particular that of the Ottomans."

This early wartime correspondence sowed seeds of future difficulties but also displays the reluctance of at least some British officers *in situ* to engage in ambiguities and sophistries. These were early days; once the French became involved, and the Russians, Italians, and Zionists, the opportunities for obfuscation and double-dealing would multiply. It would lead some British officers nearly to despair.

As for the second ambiguity, Hussein's demand that Britain "abstain from internal intervention": Did he mean that Britain must give him an absolutely free hand in determining the domestic policies of his kingdom? Did he mean that she must give him a free hand in external matters as well? In the letter Abdullah wrote on his behalf, he appears to say so. Abdullah wrote that Britain must promise to protect "clearly and in writing" the emirate's "independence in all respects, without any exceptions or restrictions." But why then, during the previous spring, had he held up to Storrs the relationship between Britain and Afghanistan as his model? There British advisers abstained from interference, even in internal matters, only when it pleased them. In any event, British diplomats had their own interpretation of what an "independent" emirate (whatever its boundaries) would mean: Hussein's kingdom would become independent of Turkey only. On important matters, the grand sharif would refer to them; they would advise; and the grand sharif would consent to their advice. Few in Britain's governing circles doubted the necessity of such an arrangement. They could not conceive of Arabs ruling themselves without Western assistance.

A third aspect of the British reply to Grand Sharif Hussein would prove an additional source of future troubles. Kitchener's letter to Abdullah concluded:

> Till now we have defended and befriended Islam in the person of the Turks; henceforward it shall be in that of the noble Arab. It may be that an Arab of true race will assume the Caliphate at Mecca or Medina, and so good may come by the help of God out of all the evil which is now occurring. It would be well if Your Highness could convey to your followers and devotees, who are found throughout the world in every country, the good tidings of the Freedom of the Arabs and the rising of the sun over Arabia.

This was Kitchener reaching deep into the British arsenal for any deadly weapon to hurl against Turkey. He would nourish, or if need be plant, the seed of religious ambition within the sharif's breast, hoping thereby to cause maximum disruption within the Ottoman realm. But unlike the pope of the Catholics, the caliph of Islam was not solely a spiritual leader. He held both spiritual and temporal authority because he was also sultan of the Ottoman Empire. Indeed, Muslims believed that in the fullness of time the caliph would come to exercise temporal authority over all Muslims, wherever they lived. In dangling the inducement of the caliphate before the grand sharif, therefore, Kitchener was offering far more than Britain ever could deliver or even wish to deliver. Nor would it help the sharif of Mecca to become known as Christian Britain's candidate for caliph. Nor would it help Britain to be seen as meddling this way in Muslim affairs. Even Britons would soon point this out. Kitchener had taken a false step. But then, the letter he had inspired was riddled with false steps.

Once again X made the wearying journey from Suez to Mecca, this time bearing promises and inducements. Once again the emir replied in writing through his son Abdullah: "We are doing that which is more important than the performance of that which is naturally imposed upon us, regardless of whether or not these negotiations take place and whether or not an agreement is arrived at." This characteristically opaque pronouncement seems to mean "We are preparing to rebel against the Turks despite their natural hold over us and we will proceed with or without British support." This was promising news from the British point of view.

X had another audience with the grand sharif in the splendid room at the top of the palace. This time he took shorthand notes. They are more direct than the letter was. "Our relations with the [Ottoman] Empire are waning, dying even as a flickering lamp whose oil had run out," the emir told him. He heaped scorn upon the Young Turks of the CUP. They "declare openly that the cause of the degeneration of the Moslem Nations is Religion and they set themselves to efface it . . . therefore we are no longer bound to obey them." They had betrayed the caliphate: "The Caliphate means this, that the rules of the Book of God should be enforced (and this they do not do)." And they had overthrown Sultan Abdul Hamid, to whom Hussein had sentimental ties: "I cannot forget the favors the Reigning House bestowed upon me. But the reins of power have passed from the hands of this Family."

Nevertheless the grand sharif was not yet prepared to throw down the gauntlet to the Turks. He put it this way in his written response: "Religion which justifies it and which is the sole foundation of action prevents us from working at once." And in that attic chamber he said more plainly to X: "I am of opinion that it will be better now to put off action."

We do not know why "religion" prevented action at this point; perhaps Hussein did not wish to interfere with the annual hajj, which would soon take place. In any event, he was anxious that the British understand that he was merely postponing action, not ruling it out. "When the time shall come, and it is not far distant, we cannot but accomplish it," the letter says, "even though the Ottoman Empire be not occupied and even though it should muster against us all its army." And on the roof he told X, whom he addressed by name: "Ali, do your best to make Mr. Storrs understand that he should not consider my answer as a breaking up of relations. It simply came late, and if she [Britain] had granted our demand when we made it, things would have been better. The day will come when we shall demand more of her than she is now prepared for and perhaps soon."

Certainly this news, faithfully reported by Ali to the authorities in Cairo after the long trek back, lifted their spirits. They would wait until the sharif deemed the moment ripe. In the meantime the focus of anti-Ottoman planning shifted temporarily from Egypt to London.

In the imperial metropolis the mood was robust. The war had stoked a nationalist fever. During its first weeks mobs coursed through the streets of the East End where many immigrants lived, smashing and looting homes and shops owned by people with German-sounding names. Young men crowded the recruiting offices, clamoring to join the armed services. They feared the Allies would win the war before they had a chance to see action and adventure. Soldiers in uniform were everywhere. Soon young women would be handing out white feathers to men still wearing civilian dress, to shame them into joining up too.

The Liberal government that brought Britain into the war was ambivalent about the passions it had unleashed. The prime minister, Herbert Henry Asquith, and the foreign secretary, Sir Edward Grey, knew how to play political hardball, but jingoistic bumptiousness discomfited them and many of their allies and supporters. Moreover the war had unleashed the passions not only of their countrymen but of Britain's foreign allies as well. The Russians, shortly after declaring war upon Turkey, let it be known that one of their war aims would be annexation of Constantinople and control of the Dardanelles. At last they would attain access to the Mediterranean Sea and a warm-water port. At first Britain and France maintained their traditional opposition; such gains by Russia would disrupt the European

balance to their disadvantage. But they desperately needed Russia to keep
German troops busy on the Eastern Front; they even feared Russia might
sign a separate peace with Germany. So eventually they gave way. But if
Russia was to gain from the war at Turkey's expense, then so must they, or
at least some members of the British and French governments thought so.

Here those letters circulating among London, Cairo, and Mecca became
relevant. Grand Sharif Hussein had insisted upon British backing for an independent "Arabia" under his leadership. But to the extent Britain acceded
to this demand, she must deny herself territory in the region. To Liberals
who still believed in the nineteenth-century Gladstonian principles of re-
trenchment and reform, such a renunciation would be no sacrifice. "We
have not the men or the money to make new countries out of barren and
savage deserts," wrote the Liberal secretary of the Committee of Imperial
Defense, "and if we try, and as far as we try, we shall arrest progress at
home and in the other countries for which we are now responsible, and we
shall saddle the British taxpayer with huge liabilities for defense and construction on top of the appalling liabilities of this country." But such sentiments went against the temper of the times.

When the Liberal-dominated War Council met on March 19, 1915, the
traditional Liberals' increasing isolation quickly became apparent. Speaking for the anti-annexationist outlook, Sir Edward Grey asked his colleagues to consider a fundamental question: "If we acquire fresh territory
shall we make ourselves weaker or stronger?" Lord Haldane, the minister
of war, argued that when the German and Ottoman Empires had been defeated, they should not be broken up: "All experience showed that a permanent peace could not be obtained except by general consent." Likewise
the home secretary, Reginald McKenna, urged that "we should put forward a suggestion that none of us take anything."

More characteristic of the country's mood, however, was the position
taken by the sole Conservative Party representative on the War Council,
Arthur Balfour. "In Europe," Balfour explained to Haldane, "he understood there was a general consensus that divisions of territory should be by
nationality. But in Asia we had to deal with countries which had been mis-
governed by the Turks." The often bellicose Winston Churchill, presently
serving as secretary of the navy, seconded: "Surely we did not intend to
leave this inefficient and out-of-date nation which had long misruled one of
the most fertile countries in the world still in possession! Turkey had long
shown herself to be inefficient as a governing Power and it was time for us
to make a clean sweep." At this stage neither Balfour (certainly) nor

Churchill (probably) knew of the correspondence with Grand Sharif Hussein. In arguing for British annexation of portions of Turkey already promised to him, they were not being duplicitous, merely traditionally imperialist. But what of Lord Kitchener, who also weighed in on the side of British territorial aggrandizement? "India [by which he meant British India, which was sending troops to Mesopotamia] would expect some return for her effort and losses." He favored annexation of the land that Indian troops occupied in Mesopotamia, the annexed land to be ruled by the British government in India. And what, finally, of Asquith, who saw which way the wind was blowing and who surely knew of the inducements Kitchener and Grey had held out to the grand sharif? Although "he had great sympathy with Sir Edward Grey's first proposition that we have already as much territory as we are able to hold . . . the fact was we were not free agents . . . If for one reason or another, because we didn't want more territory or because we didn't feel equal to the responsibility, we were to leave the other nations to scramble for Turkey without taking anything ourselves, we should not be doing our duty."

Asquith appointed a committee to study and make recommendations on British desiderata in the Middle East. Its chair was Sir Maurice de Bunsen, an assistant under secretary at the Foreign Office, formerly British ambassador to Vienna and previous to that secretary to the British embassy at Constantinople. The report that his committee wrote did not so much make foreign policy recommendations as explain Britain's foreign policy options. Assuming as it did the breakup of the Ottoman Empire after the war, it was the first British government committee to consider the future of Palestine (it anticipated that an international condominium would govern the place). The individual who dominated its sessions was ultimately as important as Balfour himself among non-Jews, during the events leading up to publication of the Balfour Declaration.

That individual was not the chairman, de Bunsen, but rather Sir Mark Sykes, sixth baronet of Sledmere. Sykes was a Yorkshire squire, the owner of an estate of 34,000 acres. The seat of his estate, Sledmere Hall, "lay like a ducal demesne among the Wolds," writes one of his biographers. It was "approached by long straight roads and sheltered by belts of woodland, surrounded by large prosperous farms." Gates and walls "ornamented with the heraldic triton of the Sykes family . . . [guarded] the mighty four-square residence and the exquisite parish church" adjoining it. The family's famous stud farm lay behind. Sykes could have devoted himself to the pleasures of an extremely privileged life but was destined to cut a larger figure.

We cannot say how much larger because he died in 1919 at age forty, of the influenza epidemic in Paris. He achieved much, but had he lived he probably would have achieved a good deal more.

His father, the ill-tempered Sir Tatton Sykes, took young Mark on frequent and extensive journeys, some through the Middle East and South Asia. Of formal schooling the boy had little, although a succession of tutors ensured an eclectic range of knowledge to complement what he gained by experience and travel. His mother, an unhappy, delicate woman, was chained by marriage to a choleric, intolerant, and uncomprehending husband and found refuge in drink and Catholicism. Over the years she resorted increasingly to both, and the second had lasting influence upon her son. Those who knew Mark Sykes believed that religious devotion constituted the bedrock of his soul.

But he wore his Catholicism lightly. He had an effervescent personality; he could turn a gathering into a party, a party into a festival. He bubbled with ideas, and he swept up his listeners with his enthusiasm. In addition he had a remarkable talent for sketching caricatures and for mimicry. "Mark Sykes had vitality beyond any man I have ever met," wrote a close friend. "When one had been in his company one felt almost as if one had been given a draught from the fountain of life." Despite the miserable marriage of his parents, he radiated happiness. He was, apparently, a sort of human champagne.

A few remained immune to his charm. T. E. Lawrence considered him a lightweight, but Sykes was actually a serious student of politics and war and imperial policy. He went to South Africa for the Boer War, although he did not see combat. For nearly a decade after the war's conclusion, he traveled again. He knew the Ottoman Empire well and regarded it with Disraelian tolerance: In other words, he was prepared to overlook its defects in order to preserve it as a buttress of British interests, especially since it blocked Russian access to the Mediterranean. He shared the prejudices of his era and class: Although he looked down upon Turks by and large, he judged them to be racially superior to the peoples they governed. He was an anti-Semite—during his travels he sketched grotesque cartoons of fat Jews with big noses. But other peoples ranked lower still in his estimation. He wrote in one of his early books, "Even Jews have their good points, but Armenians have none." Given that he would become Chaim Weizmann's staunchest and most effective Gentile ally, and champion of the national aspirations of Armenians as well, we may say at the outset that he was capable of changing his mind and of adapting to circumstances.

During 1907 Sykes served as honorary attaché at the British embassy in

Constantinople. There he met and befriended two other young English-men serving in the same capacity. They were George Lloyd, scion of a wealthy Birmingham industrial family, and Aubrey Herbert, son of the fourth earl of Carnarvon. Like Sykes, both men shared a fascination with the East; both were extremely able. All three returned to Britain, and by 1911 all three had secured seats as Conservatives in the House of Commons, where they formed the nucleus of a group of old-fashioned romantic To-ries. They believed implicitly in the goodness of the British Empire and in its civilizing role. They distrusted Liberal anti-imperialists and reformers, hated trade unions and socialism, and believed in the virtues of a sturdy yeomanry and in the natural bonds connecting peasant with landowner. But they were hardly simple. Sykes, for example, could be both radical and reactionary at the same time: He favored home rule for Ireland (as did Aubrey Herbert), although the vast majority of Conservatives opposed it fanatically; simultaneously he unavailingly supported the hereditary power of the House of Lords to block the Liberal Home Rule Bill in the House of Commons, an anachronistic parliamentary prerogative that more moderate and up-to-date Conservatives eventually abandoned.

With the outbreak of war, Sykes returned to Sledmere Hall to raise a battalion of volunteers from the estate. He hoped to lead them to France. But the government, wishing to make use of his knowledge of the Middle East, attached him to the Intelligence Department. This was a disappoint-ment that he may have inadvertently helped make happen by writing to Sir Edward Grey, urging a more aggressive attitude toward the Turks, even though they were not yet in the war. He expertly summarized recent British policy with regard to the Ottomans and explained what British passivity in the Middle East might lead to among "the Arabs of the Syr-ian desert and those south of the Dead Sea . . . [also those of] S. Meso-potamia . . . [and] the Kurds." Then he laid out the probable repercussions in Afghanistan and India. Shortly thereafter, quite possibly as a response, the summons from Intelligence arrived. In London, Sykes was put to work writing pamphlets urging the people of Syria to rebel against the Ottomans.

He knew already the Foreign Office men with Middle East expertise. One of them introduced him to Lord Kitchener's devoted secretary and as-sistant, Colonel Oswald Fitzgerald. Turkey had not yet entered the war, and in London much wishful thinking had her staying out or even joining the Allies. Sykes told Fitzgerald that Turkey would come in soon, however, and on the side of Germany. He backed up the prediction with an explana-tory letter that Fitzgerald carried to Kitchener. The latter kept it. When the Turks intervened as Sykes had prophesied, Kitchener decided to make use of the prophet. But how? When Prime Minister Asquith formed the de Bunsen Committee to ascertain British desiderata in Asiatic Turkey, Kitchener requested that Sykes be placed upon it. He told Fitzgerald that he wished to be kept informed of its deliberations—this was Sykes's job to begin with. "But," Sykes recalled, "I never saw Lord Kitchener except once and then only for a moment. I used to report to Fitzgerald each night at York House on the various problems that had come up for discussion and received instructions as to the points that Lord Kitchener desired should be considered. This I did as best I could." Sykes was too modest. Historians agree that he crucially influenced the committee's report. Certainly his letters reveal a mind in full flow and a personality more than willing to dispense advice. What preoccupied him? "Turkey must cease to be," he wrote to a friend. But he did not pine for its colonized subjects. "All black people want sound, strict, unbending government," he declared in the same letter.

Once the de Bunsen Committee had concluded its deliberations and written its report, Fitzgerald informed Sykes that Kitchener wanted him to travel "right round the Middle East and report back to him on the various situations." Before he left, Sykes saw Kitchener "for about fifteen minutes and he gave me nothing more than the same instructions Fitzgerald had mentioned to me." It seems a strange way of running the largest empire in the world. "I could never understand what he thought and he could never understand what I thought," Sykes was to remark of Kitchener a year later, but "Fitzgerald was a very good intermediary in that way with a man who was difficult to explain things to or understand what was meant."

To go "right round the Middle East," Kitchener had instructed Sykes, for the war had cast that region into the crucible, and he had to know how Britain might reshape it. The Cairo contingent already had definite plans, as Sykes would learn upon arrival. Clayton, Storrs, and others were pushing for Britain to throw the Turks out of Syria and to attack Alexandretta, a port at the northeast corner of the Mediterranean Sea. This would relieve Turkish pressure, they held, both on Suez and on British soldiers facing difficult conditions in Gallipoli; once taken, Alexandretta might also prove an entryway for British forces into Turkey. Hence its possession might even tilt the balance of the war. At least it afforded Mesopotamia convenient access to the Mediterranean Sea, and they assumed that Britain would take Mesopotamia as a spoil of war. Thus Alexandretta was "the key of the whole place," as T. E. Lawrence, recently arrived in Cairo, wrote to a friend. Even now Lawrence and his superiors in Cairo were thinking of Britain's imperial position after the war and of potential future wars. Alexandretta was "going to be the head of the Baghdad [railway] line and

therefore the natural outlet for Northern Syria and Northern Mesopotamia; it's the only easy road from Cilicia and Asia Minor into Asia, etc.
etc. Also it's a wonderful harbor and . . . can be made impregnable." No
other country but Britain must possess it. "If Russia has Alexandretta it's all
up with us in the near East," Lawrence warned. France must not control it
either since "one cannot go on betting that France will always be our
friend."

Nor had Cairo forgotten the grand sharif of Mecca. Although the British
would not hear from him again until July 14, 1915, they were already spinning elaborate schemes in which he figured prominently. Lawrence, for
one, saw the emir as a crucial player in the British interest, both during the
war and afterward. "I want to pull them all [the smaller Arab principalities
and tribes] together and to roll up Syria by way of the Hejaz in the name
of the Sharif . . . and biff the French out of all hope of Syria. It's a big game
and at last one worth playing." In other words, he wanted Hussein ruling
"Arabia"—still undefined but now including Syria, which would have en-
compassed Lebanon and Palestine—under the influence of Great Britain.
Likewise Storrs looked forward to Hussein's rise—under Britain's indirect control. He would become caliph: "His allegiance to us inspired, as
his revenues derived, from annual subventions and the proceeds of an annual pilgrimage—guaranteed against foreign and especially Turkish aggression . . . it is to this ideal that we should shape our course."

Although the sharif had refrained from contacting the British, he had
hardly been inactive, as Kitchener might have guessed. What he had done,
and what it led to, is the subject of our next chapter. But it is fair to say that
Kitchener expected Sykes, as he traveled the Middle East, to get a grip on
the sharif too.

So the sixth baronet of Sledmere set off from England, on a journey that
would take him, in six months, to Sofia, to British headquarters at the Dardanelles, to Egypt, to Aden, to Simla in India, and back to Egypt. While in
Egypt, he held cheerful reunion with Aubrey Herbert and George Lloyd,
both now Egyptian army intelligence officers; he met often with Clayton
and Storrs and with Cheetham's replacement as high commissioner, Sir
Henry McMahon. From the last we may glean something of the atmosphere of their conferences. "He is a very pleasant change from the ordinary," McMahon wrote to his old chief in India, the Viceroy Lord
Hardinge. "Among other things he is an extraordinarily clever mimic and
you should get him to give some of his impersonations such as the Old
Turk, Young Turk, Syrian, Naval Division, &c."

But Sykes had done much more than indulge his talent for mimicry.

Wherever he went, he reported on the policy options enumerated by the de Bunsen Committee, and he also listened and learned and conferred. The Egyptian high commissioner brought him up-to-date on the promises made and inducements held out to the grand sharif. In mid-July the emir finally ended his seven-month silence and wrote again to Sir Ronald Storrs; Sykes was no longer in Cairo but soon knew of the letter's contents, and of the correspondence that ensued among the parties planning the Arab Revolt. Sykes endorsed that cause immediately. A British-supported Arab uprising to free Arabia (including Syria) from the Turks fit his own outlook and temperament and appealed to his imagination. He returned to England on December 8, 1915, determined to obtain the government's backing for the Arab Revolt and for what the Cairo contingent were calling the "forward policy"—which meant the larger effort to attack Alexandretta and "roll up Syria," refashioning the Middle East to suit Britain's imperial interests. On December 16 he had an audience with the War Council or War Committee, as it now was called. Aside from Sykes, only Asquith, Balfour, David Lloyd George, and Kitchener spoke at this meeting. All the opponents of expanding Britain's reach were absent or silent. Sykes made his report, a masterly performance. "I should just like to conclude," he wound up, "by putting before you the dangers that I think confront us if matters are allowed to slide. If we adopt a perfectly passive attitude . . . the Sharif, I think, will be killed."

"Will be what?" asked Arthur Balfour.

"Will be killed," Sykes repeated, "and a Committee of Union and Progress nominee will be put in his place. That gives the Turks and the Germans Mecca. The Christians in Syria will be exterminated . . . The anti-Committee [of Union and Progress] elements will be destroyed among the Arabs, the intellectual Arabs will be hanged and shot . . . The Arab machine will be captured . . . then we shall be confronted with the danger of a real Jehad."

But Sykes was preaching to the converted.

CHAPTER 4

The Next Steps

WHILE SYKES WAS REPORTING to London, the Ottomans were pressing Grand Sharif Hussein to raise an army: They wished to throw his soldiers against the British at the Suez Canal. More important, they wanted him to endorse their call to jihad: His endorsement would inspire millions of British Muslim subjects in Egypt, Sudan, and India to rise up against their colonial infidel masters, making Britain's worst nightmare come true.

The grand sharif prevaricated. He supported the jihad personally, he told the Turks, but a public declaration was too risky. It would result in an English blockade of his country and perhaps in bombardment of its ports. His people would starve or worse. Moreover the annual hajj would be endangered. He could not in this instance do as they requested. But he would raise troops for the attack on the Canal.

What he did not tell the Turks was that he was secretly dispatching emissaries to the main Arab leaders. Without divulging his own plans, he needed to know their intentions with regard to the war and their likely reaction if he took the English bait and did indeed launch a rebellion. Soon enough his messengers returned with answers. One sheikh hoped to enlist the Turks against the dangerous Ibn Saud: he would declare the jihad as a quid pro quo for Turkish support, but he protested his continuing love for the grand sharif. Another, the Iman Yahya, was noncommittal. The rest, however, including Ibn Saud, supported Britain against Turkey. Saud urged Hussein to ignore the Ottoman call to wage jihad. If the grand sharif decided to move against the Ottomans, then one or two of the great Arab chiefs might disapprove, but none were likely to oppose him actively.

In January 1915 Hussein's oldest son, Ali, led a contingent of Hejazi volunteers into Medina. They were some of the troops his father had raised to take part in the Turkish attack on Suez, which was scheduled to commence on February 2. The Turkish *vali* of the Hejaz accompanied Ali. Somewhere between Mecca and Medina the *vali* misplaced his briefcase. One of Ali's men happened upon it and brought it not to its rightful owner but to his own master. Naturally, given his father's attitude toward the Turkish government, Ali opened the briefcase and read the documents inside. Probably he was not astonished to learn that the *vali* was playing a double game. Although outwardly friendly, this gentleman really intended to depose Hussein and to assert Ottoman control over the Hejaz. Immediately Ali, and the soldiers under his command, turned back to Mecca and brought the briefcase with incriminating documents to his father. The *vali* continued on to Suez where, on February 2, 1915, the British easily repulsed the Turkish attack.

As Ali was arriving back in Mecca, another young man, Fauzi al-Bakri, was setting out from Damascus for the same city. The Turks had conscripted him, but he belonged to a prominent Syrian family that had long been friendly with the family of Grand Sharif Hussein. As a result, the Ottomans awarded him with a decorative posting—they made him a member of the sharif's personal bodyguard. Unknown to them, however, Fauzi had recently joined the Arab secret society al-Fatat. Just before his departure from Damascus, the society commissioned him to sound out the grand sharif. If Arab nationalists rose against the Turks in Syria and Iraq, would he consent to be their leader? And if so, would he send a deputy to concert plans with them beforehand?

Al-Fatat's plans were well advanced already. Since the outbreak of war, its members' views had altered considerably: Arab autonomy within the Ottoman Empire would no longer satisfy them, since the Ottomans likely could no longer protect Arabia from European imperialist designs. Now they believed that Arab interests required complete independence from Turkey. Thus the war hastened the society's transition from Ottomanism to Arabism, as it hastened the development of revolutionary movements in Ireland, Russia, and elsewhere. In Syria, al-Fatat combined forces with the other major secret society, al-Ahd. Together the two groups planned a rising. Arab army officers stationed in Damascus would lead their soldiers into revolt. Syrian desert tribes whose sheikhs already belonged to the societies would join. The leaders hoped the revolt would spread to the Arabian Peninsula as well. Who would lead a rebellion there? They turned first to Ibn Saud, but he politely turned down their emissary—he had to deal with the disaffected sheikh to his north. And then the nationalists recalled the grand sharif of Mecca—and chose Fauzi al-Bakri to approach him.

Fauzi arrived in the holy city late in January 1915 and quickly contrived a meeting alone with the grand sharif. Perhaps it was in the same great room at the top of the palace where Hussein had received X, the emissary from Cairo, for it is recorded that while Fauzi delivered the message from Damascus, the emir stared out the window over the rooftops of his city as he listened without comment, without even acknowledging the young man's presence. The young nationalist, thinking no doubt that other members of the sharif's bodyguard or household might be within earshot and might not be trustworthy, did not raise his voice above a whisper. When he finished, he slipped silently from the room. Hussein, seemingly, took no notice.

In fact, he had listened intently. He was accustomed by now to discuss important political matters with his sons, and a family council ensued. In comparison with Abdullah and Feisal, Hussein's oldest son, Ali, played a minor role in these family conclaves, and the fourth son, Zeid, played little part at all. Feisal distrusted Western imperialist designs in the Middle East and had hitherto favored maintaining relations with the Ottomans. Abdullah, on the other hand, had held anti-Turk and pro-British views since at least early 1914. Abdullah largely accepted the Arab nationalist position, but his father remained, as always, more a pan-Islamist than an Arab nationalist, although increasingly doubtful that he could continue to cooperate with the Ottoman regime. Perhaps the contents of the Ottoman *vali*'s briefcase encouraged him to look favorably upon Fauzi's invitation. At any rate, the result of the meeting was a decision to send Feisal to Constantinople, to convey to the Ottoman authorities his father's outrage at the *vali*'s double-dealing. En route Feisal was to stop at Damascus and stay with the al-Bakri family. He was to meet clandestinely with representatives of the secret societies in order to gauge them and their plans. If appropriate, he was to sound them on their attitude toward the British, with whom the sharif had been in contact. Then he was to report back to his father.

It was an undertaking fraught with peril, but the tall, broad-shouldered, narrow-waisted Feisal had been brought up (like his father and like all his brothers, for that matter) in an atmosphere of political intrigue that could on occasion turn deadly. Hussein was confident that Feisal could cope;

Feisal was too. Not yet thirty years of age, he had gained military experience in his father's prewar campaigns and was, according to David Hogarth, Hussein's "most capable military commander." "Clear-skinned as a pure Circassian," Hogarth described him, "with dark hair, vivid black eyes set a little sloping in his face, strong nose, [and] short chin," he seemed to the Englishman "far more imposing personally than any of his brothers," although he was high-strung: "very quick and restless in movement . . . full of nerves." Yet very much the son of his father, he could keep his face impassive and hold his tongue when necessary, or he could dissemble.

In Damascus the top Ottoman official was Djemal Pasha, minister of marine, commander of the Turkish Fourth Army, and along with Enver Pasha and Talaat Pasha, a member of the Young Turk ruling triumvirate. A formidable not to say intimidating figure, thick-set, black-bearded, with "a pair of cunning cruel eyes," he already knew that Arab nationalists in Syria were planning an uprising. He had learned about it when the French dragoman brought the authorities the incriminating papers that the departing diplomat François Georges-Picot had left in the French consulate safe. Eventually Djemal would take ruthless action against those incriminated, but to begin with he merely directed his agents to keep close watch over them. At this stage he wished to win the goodwill of Syrians, not to provoke them.

Still, when Feisal arrived at the Kadem Station in Damascus on March 26, 1915, he was entering a city on edge, its atmosphere heavy with fear and intrigue. Djemal greeted him warmly, probably with sincerity, having no inkling of the young man's double mission. A few years after the war, he wrote in his memoirs, "Although I had never believed in the honesty of the Sherif of Mecca, I could never have conceived that in a war, upon which the fate of the Khalifate depended, he would ally himself with the States which desired to thrust the Slav yoke upon the whole Mohammedan world." Feisal vindicated his father's wisdom in sending him. He neither said nor did anything to raise Djemal's suspicions—rather the opposite. Already Djemal was planning a second attack upon the Suez Canal. Feisal made a speech to the Ottoman headquarters staff in which "he swore by the glorious soul of the Prophet to return at an early date at the head of his warriors and help them to fight the foes of the Faith to the death."

That, and like declarations, he made during the day. At night, when his ceremonial and official obligations could not be carried out, he was meeting in secret with emissaries from al-Ahd and al-Fatat at the home of the al-Bakri family. There in the eastern suburbs of the city, amid groves of apricot and pomegranate and walnut trees in full spring bloom, these emissaries told him of their aims and something of their plans. They impressed him deeply; in fact, they worked a revolution in his mind. Where previously Feisal had thought his father should stick with the Ottomans and have nothing to do with Arab nationalist schemes, now he thought his father should lead the Arab nationalist attempt to throw off the Ottoman yoke, even if it led to a strengthened role for Britain in the Middle East. Better the British than the Turks. He told the Syrians about his brother's prewar meetings with Storrs and Kitchener and about the correspondence that had ensued. The conspirators talked long and searchingly about what should be their attitude, and the attitude of the grand sharif and his sons, toward England. Then Feisal took the plunge. On one of those scented spring Damascene nights, he swore the blood oaths of both secret societies.

From Damascus he traveled to Constantinople, arriving on April 23. There too he had to maintain a poker face. While meeting with leading Turkish politicians and military figures, he played the loyal subaltern. He complained to them that his father, the faithful grand sharif, had been betrayed by the *vali* with the briefcase. In turn Talaat and Enver, among others, explained that so far as they were concerned, Hussein would have nothing to fear if he publicly endorsed the jihad against Turkey's enemies. Feisal promised to convey this message to his father with all sympathy. He paid his respects to the new sultan. "When he was received in audience by the sultan," recalled Djemal Pasha, "he protested his loyalty and that of his father and family in words of such humble devotion that His Majesty could not have the slightest doubt about his honesty." All the while, however, Feisal was longing to get back to Damascus to continue the discussions with the conspirators in al-Ahd and al-Fatat.

Within a month he had realized this aim and was again lodged at the al-Bakri residence on the outskirts of Damascus. As before, his days were taken up with courtesy calls, public appearances, and the like, but the clandestine meetings recommenced at night; Arab army officers quietly appeared at the back gates and slipped noiselessly inside. The discussions were more urgent than before. The plotters had set the fuse, they told Feisal. It remained only to light it. Feisal promised the support of the Hejazi tribes—without consulting his father. But "we do not need them," answered the Arab chief of staff of the Twelfth Corps of the Ottoman Fourth Army. "We have everything." All they wanted was for the grand sharif of Mecca to lend his prestigious support to their uprising and for Feisal himself, the grand sharif's most effective general, to become their visible leader.

They had settled, too, the question of Great Britain's role in their rebellion and its aftermath:

The recognition by Great Britain of the independence of the
Arab countries lying within the following frontiers:

North: The line Mersin-Adana to parallel 37° N. and thence
along the line Birejik-Urfa-Mardin-Midiat-Jazirat (Ibn Umar)-
Amadia to the Persian frontier;

East: The Persian frontier down to the Persian Gulf;

South: The Indian Ocean (with the exclusion of Aden,
whose status was to be maintained);

West: The Red Sea and the Mediterranean Sea back to
Mersin.

The abolition of all exceptional privileges granted to foreigners . . .

The conclusion of a defensive alliance between Great Britain
and the future independent Arab state.

The grant of economic preference to Great Britain.

This was the Damascus Protocol, at once the foundation document and the
lodestar of the Arab Revolt. It envisioned a federation of Arab countries organized within a single independent Arab state or empire, containing
Palestine, and backed by Britain, which would receive in return economic
preferences. Implicit in the document, Grand Sharif Hussein would pre-
side over the great state. Feisal promised to bring the protocol to his father
and to recommend that he accept it and leadership of the movement that
had produced it. A scribe copied the protocol in tiny letters onto a small
sheet. It was sewn into the lining of a boot worn by one of Feisal's servants.
Should some mishap befall the grand sharif's son on his return journey to
Mecca, the message would nevertheless be delivered. Feisal probably
thought his father's reaction would be positive; but whether Great Britain
would accept the terms of the Damascus Protocol was something none of
the conspirators could predict.

By the beginning of 1915 a new man was running Britain's Cairo operation.
Lieutenant-Colonel Sir Arthur Henry McMahon replaced Sir Milne
Cheetham, who had filled in briefly for the consul general, Lord Kitchener,
detained by war work in London. The Foreign Office viewed McMahon as
a placeholder for Kitchener too, but McMahon himself appears to have regarded the position as permanent. Strangely, although he had extensive experience of the subcontinent, where he had risen to become foreign
secretary of the British government in India, he had no experience of the

The Arab Kingdom envisioned in the Damascus Protocol

Middle East. "I cannot say that I know it more than an ordinary traveler would," he confessed to an Egyptian journalist sent to interview him before his arrival in Cairo. "I don't speak Arabic [but] . . . there are so many Arabic words in Indian languages—Persian, Afghan and Hindustani—which I know well." Even so, near total ignorance of the relevant language seems an unlikely qualification for the top job in the world's cockpit.

A British dispatch boat brought McMahon and his wife to Alexandria, and a special train conveyed them to Cairo, where they were greeted with much pomp and circumstance. The newspapers reported that he had made a good impression. "His eye is kindly," Sir Ronald Storrs remembered an Egyptian of the welcoming party remarking. Storrs himself wrote in his diary that McMahon seemed "quiet, friendly, agreeable, considerate and cautious," estimates he would later considerably revise. Aubrey Herbert, then in Cairo, wrote of McMahon in his own diary: "He seems a stupid little man."

In India, McMahon's last posting, British officials strongly opposed Cairo's plan for an Arab uprising led by Sharif Hussein. They especially opposed Kitchener's suggestion that an Arab might repossess the caliphate from the Turks. That, they argued, would have disastrous repercussions among Muslims everywhere outside Arabia, not least in their own South Asia. Moreover they did not believe for a minute that the Arabs could organize or govern a great kingdom or empire. Specifically, they discounted the sharif's personal influence and abilities. They already had relations with the principalities running along the Arabian coast of the Indian Ocean from Aden to the Gulf of Oman. Insofar as they favored any Arab leader for a larger role, it was Ibn Saud, who as chief of the sectarian Wahhabis could never become caliph. And they nursed annexationist dreams, which the establishment of a great Arabian state headed by Sharif Hussein would render nil. Having sent troops across the Indian Ocean into Mesopotamia, they intended to keep that territory after the war. They assumed that McMahon, so recently one of them, still supported their position. Having departed India, however, the new high commissioner of Egypt was not bound by Indian interests. Once he arrived in Cairo, Storrs, Clayton, Herbert, and other members of the British intelligence community went to work on him. He "understood our design at once and judged it good," T. E. Lawrence recorded with satisfaction.

Despite McMahon's ready acceptance of the plan, for six months it got no further. These were the months when Sharif Hussein was sounding the other Arab leaders and putting off the Ottoman demand that he endorse the jihad, and when Feisal was playing his dangerous double game in

Damascus and Constantinople. Of some of these activities, the British had gleanings: They were aware of Hussein's inquiry to Ibn Saud about the Turkish call for jihad, and of Saud's advice to ignore it. Otherwise they knew little of the sharif's thinking or activities. They were impatient for decisive action on his part, none more so than the governor general and sirdar of Sudan, Sir Francis Reginald Wingate. Although cut off from Cairo by distance (his address was the grandest in the British Empire—"The Palace, Khartoum"), Wingate knew of Kitchener's offer to Hussein from Gilbert Clayton, British director of military intelligence for the Middle East, who was also his protégé, former private secretary, and despite his other duties, still his agent in Egypt.

Once Wingate digested the correspondence between London/Cairo and Hussein, he too understood the design and judged it good. In fact, he had favored something along the same lines since the outbreak of war. Like the Cairo men, India men, and London men, he doubted that Hussein could lead a great independent Arab kingdom: Wingate judged Arabia to be "scarcely an embryo [of a state] and during the process of conception and being actually born and indeed through the boyhood stages some nation will have to mother them." But he believed strongly that an Arab rebellion would aid the British war effort. Moreover he cherished a secret personal ambition: that Cairo would "mother" a great Arab empire, as Delhi had "mothered" Britain's empire in India, and that he would be its viceroy. In one cable after another, therefore, he urged first Clayton, then McMahon, and then, through McMahon, both Grey and Kitchener in London, to make Hussein an offer he could not refuse.

And so the cables poured into London. In those from Khartoum and Cairo, Wingate, Clayton, and McMahon all urged the British government somehow to induce Sharif Hussein to act; in those from Delhi, its viceroy, Lord Hardinge, urged the opposite, that the sharif not be encouraged. Wingate and Hardinge sent each other conflicting cables setting out their positions as well. Debate raged in the Foreign Office, but in the end Cairo and Khartoum prevailed. "You should inform Wingate," Grey instructed McMahon, "that I authorize him to let it be known if he thinks it desirable that His Majesty's Government will make it an essential condition in any terms of peace that the Arabian Peninsula and its Moslem Holy Places should remain in the hands of an independent Sovereign Moslem state." Wingate undertook to spread the news "far and wide, and as it is now authoritative it will be believed and credited."

But still the grand sharif remained silent.

Feisal returned to Mecca on June 20, 1915, and delivered the Damascus

Protocol to his father. The family gathered in council yet again. This time
it deliberated for an entire week, "one of the most difficult weeks of my
life," Feisal would later tell the Anglo-Arab historian George Antonius.
Grand Sharif Hussein balanced on a knife's edge: Depending on which
way he jumped, the British would help or harm him, but so would the
Turks, and it was not clear whose forces could help or harm him more.
Even though Great Britain governed the mightiest empire in the world,
Turkish forces were so far more than holding their own against it. Britain
hardly seemed invincible. Nevertheless Feisal urged his father to jump in
its direction and away from the Turks. The British Empire had great resources; it could sustain terrible losses and still win at the end; and the Syrian conspirators were well organized and powerful. Hussein should accept
leadership of their movement and present the Damascus Protocol to the
British. Abdullah agreed with his younger brother; even before the war
began, he had been urging action against the Ottomans with British aid.
But Hussein knew, perhaps better than his sons, how merciless would be
the Young Turk response, especially during wartime. He hesitated.

In the end his religious beliefs proved decisive, or that is how he presented it afterward, in a typically convoluted justification: "God selected us
to arouse our nation to restrain the unjust and to banish the insolent ones,
the heretics, from the land and from among the true worshipers, requesting
for them what we request for ourselves, namely to make us desire to follow
what He [Muhammad] brought [Sharia, religious law as set forth in the
Quran] and to drive the evil from our tribes and our Arab communities to
whose race, language, customs, comforts and pleasures these heedless ones
showed enmity." Although he denied it, personal ambition cannot have
been absent from his calculations. The British promised to guarantee his independence from foreign interference; their own role in the future Arabian
state remained ambiguous, but surely that was better than the continual Ottoman scheming and plotting against him. Moreover the British seemed to
be waving the caliphate before him as a further inducement to action.
Whether Hussein truly hoped to become caliph at this stage, however, no
one has established. Most historians think not.

Sometime in mid-July Hussein took the plunge, dispatching a trusted
messenger to Cairo carrying two letters. The first was a brief note from Abdullah to Storrs, dated July 14, 1915, requesting that the British allow Egypt
to send to Mecca stores of grain for the annual hajj; they had been held back
for the past two years; their resumption "would be an important factor in
laying the foundations of our mutual advantage. This should suffice for a
person of your grasp." The second letter, undated and unsigned but un-

doubtedly composed by Hussein since it dealt with the crux of the matter, was longer and uncharacteristically clear. Essentially it repeated the Damascus Protocol and asked quite simply whether the British approved it and warned that if they did not, "we will consider ourselves free in word and deed from the bonds of our previous declaration which we made through Ali Effendi [X]." Thus recommenced the fatal McMahon-Hussein correspondence, whose conflicting interpretations have divided Jews, Arabs, and Britons for nearly a hundred years.

Even before the sharif's letter arrived, the British knew of its existence and something of its contents from Wingate, who had established his own line of communication with Mecca. "I think," Wingate crowed to Clayton, "you will find that he will be strongly in favour of obtaining our assistance." True enough. And when the messenger appeared in Cairo on or about August 22, he supplemented the written documents with an oral statement: "On handing [me] the letter at Taif, which was in the presence of his four sons, Ali, Abdullah, Faisal and Zeid, the Sherif told me to tell Mr. Storrs—'We are now ready and well prepared.' His son Abdullah then said: 'Tell Mr. Storrs that our word is a word of honour and we will carry it out even at the cost of our lives; we are not now under the orders of the Turks but the Turks are under our orders.'"

Cairo was delighted—until it read the proposed borders of the new Arab state. Hussein had copied them word for word from the Damascus Protocol, but they were too expansive from the British point of view. "The Sharif had opened his mouth . . . a good deal too wide," Storrs would write afterward. McMahon cabled London: "His pretensions are in every way exaggerated, no doubt considerably beyond his hope of acceptance, but it seems very difficult to treat with them in detail without seriously discouraging him." Eventually, after much consultation with London, he tried to square the circle. "We confirm to you the terms of Lord Kitchener's message . . . in which was stated clearly our desire for the independence of Arabia and its inhabitants, together with our approval of the Arab Caliphate when it should be proclaimed," he wrote to Hussein on August 29. But "with regard to the questions of limits, frontiers and boundaries, it would appear to be premature to consume our time in discussing such details in the heat of war." This was the message carried back to Mecca.

Hussein received it coolly and responded quickly (on September 9), angrily, and at length. Now he spoke as leader of an organized revolutionary movement, he emphasized, not merely for himself; the borders he had indicated were essential to the well-being of any future Arab state. George Antonius, who first translated and published the McMahon-Hussein correspondence in his classic account of the Arab Revolt and who knew and admired the grand sharif, described his writing style: "a tight network of parentheses, incidentals, allusions, saws and apophthegms, woven together by a process of literary orchestration into a sonorous rigmarole." Which is why we quote very selectively here. "The coldness and hesitation which you have displayed in the question of the limits and boundaries . . . might be taken to infer an estrangement," Hussein charged. And a little beneath: "It is not I personally who am demanding of these limits which include only our race, but that they are all proposals of the people who, in short, believe that they are necessary for economic life." And finally, driving home the main point: "I cannot admit that you, as a man of sound opinion will deny to be necessary for our existence [the borders suggested in the Damascus Protocol]; nay, they are the essential essence of our life, material and moral."

The two parties had arrived at a seeming impasse. The matter might have rested there, for if the British declined to accept the borders Hussein wanted, then he might decline to launch the rebellion they favored. Perhaps Hussein could have continued to prevaricate, waiting out the war, albeit on the edge of the knife, without committing to either side. He had waited most of his life for the sharifate, after all. But as is so often the case in wartime, new and unexpected developments altered everything.

"I am a descendant of Omar Ibn El Khattab, the second Khalifa of El Islam who had the title of El Farug, which means separator. He was so called for having separated the right from the wrong. The descendants of Omar El Farug were all living in Damascus, but some centuries ago a part of them emigrated to El Mosul. At present there are thirty families of them living in El Mosul and twenty families in Damascus. I was born in El Mosul in 1891 . . ."

So begins the statement of Sharif Muhammad al-Faruki, an Arab lieutenant in the Turkish army who deserted to the British at Gallipoli in August, to tell them of the Arab plot and to enlist their support. By October the British had brought him to Egypt to be debriefed by their chief intelligence officer in the Middle East, Gilbert Clayton. Faruki told him: "I entered as Member in a secret Society started by the Arab officers in the Turkish Army . . . I have done several services and carried out several missions for the Society in Aleppo and environs." But the reach of the secret society extended beyond Aleppo, Faruki assured the Englishman. It stretched to "Damascus and Beirut provinces . . . a branch being started in every important town or station."

"We know well the real military situation of the two contending forces," Faruki continued, "and we know that our siding with the Allies will diminish greatly the two forces of their enemies and will cause them immense trouble." But he knew much more than that. "Moreover the English have declared publicly that they will help the Arabs against the Turks." In addition: "We also found out that the Sherif of Mecca was in communication with the High Commissioner in Egypt, and the English are willing to give the Sherif the necessary arms and ammunition for the attainment of his object. That the English have given their consent to the Sherif establishing an Arab Empire but the limits of his Empire were not defined." Faruki added that the secret societies had renounced allegiance to the sultan of Turkey and sworn instead to support Hussein. The grand sharif would lead their rebellion.

Faruki knew the terms outlined in the Damascus Protocol and, it would seem, even McMahon's response to it. He had deserted in part in order to argue for the boundaries advocated in the protocol, and although he was not authorized to speak for the secret societies, he acted as though he were, and the British came to treat him as though he were. "A guarantee of the independence of the Arabian Peninsula would not satisfy," Clayton reported glumly after talking with him, "but this together with the institution of an increasing measure of autonomous Government . . . in Palestine and Mesopotamia would probably secure their [secret societies'] friendship. Syria is of course included in their programme." Faruki conceded that France possessed legitimate interests in Syria, but he insisted that French influence there be strictly limited. If it was not, then his societies would resist by force of arms. "Our scheme embraces all the Arab countries including Syria and Mesopotamia, but if we cannot have all [then] we want as much as we can get," he declared imprecisely. More specifically, he said, the plotters insisted on keeping "in Arabia purely Arab districts of Aleppo, Damascus, Hama and Homs." Here is the first mention of a geographical caveat that would prove a stumbling block to all future understanding and goodwill. The formulation appears for the first time in a cable reporting on discussions with Faruki that McMahon sent to London on October 19, 1915.

As for the nature of the Arab state to be established, Faruki explained: "The Arab countries [are] to be governed by the principles of decentralization; each country to have the sort of Government which best suits it, but to be ruled by the Central government, i.e. the seat of the Khalifate. Sherif Hussein of Mecca to be the Khalifa and Sultan of the new empire." Christians, Druze, and Neiria would have the same rights as Muslims in the new state, he promised, "but the Jews will be governed by a special law." This did not augur well, but apparently the British saw no reason to query it.

Essentially Faruki was reiterating the sharif's program as set forth in his most recent letter to Cairo. He added flesh to the bare bones of British knowledge about the secret societies, exaggerating their strength, the extent of their organization, and their influence; also his own importance. Nevertheless the British believed him. They believed too a further embroidery, one of breathtaking audacity—a threat, or rather a bluff, or to put it baldly, a falsehood. Clayton reported that Faruki had "stated that Turkey and Germany are fully alive to the situation and have already approached the leaders of the Young Arab Committee, and indeed have gone so far as to promise them the granting of their demands in full . . . The Committee, however, are strongly inclined towards England."

Historians find no archival evidence that the Turks and Germans were prepared to grant the Arab demands. But really they have no need to search for such documents. Events soon would put the lie to Faruki's assertion. By now, far from wanting to woo Arab nationalists, the Turks wanted only to destroy them, as a series of brutal trials, imprisonments, and hangings in Damascus would disclose within a matter of months.

In October 1915, however, Clayton believed that the Arab plotters were powerful and that Germany and Turkey were near to winning them over. He warned London: "To reject the Arab proposals entirely *or even to seek to evade the issues* [emphasis added] will be to throw the Young Arab party definitely into the arms of the enemy. Their machinery will at once be employed against us throughout the Arab countries . . . the religious element will come into play and the Jihad, so far a failure, may become a very grim reality the effects of which would certainly be far-reaching and at the present crisis might well be disastrous." Note the italicized words: They must refer to McMahon's attempt, in the letter of August 29, to postpone discussion of future boundaries. Now Clayton was repudiating McMahon's strategy. He was pushing for defining the boundaries immediately and in a way that would satisfy Arab aspirations. He thought it was necessary if Britain hoped to outbid the Germans.

Why was Clayton so willing to accept Faruki's embellishments? The young deserter's arrival in Cairo was but one element of a remarkable and, for the British, not particularly happy conjuncture. He appeared before Clayton almost simultaneously with Hussein's chilly letter of September 9. Faruki confirmed the sharif's claims: He *was* speaking not merely for himself but for a larger movement; his ambitions *were* not merely personal; it really *was* the larger movement that had established the boundaries of the future Arabian federation adumbrated in his last letter. This confirmation was worrying enough, but, perhaps more important, Faruki's arrival coincided with a torrent of bad news about the war: Bulgaria had entered it on the side of the Central Powers, affording them not only an increment of strength but a direct overland route from Germany to Constantinople. At Gallipoli, British losses mounted daily; morale there had plummeted; the British beachhead remained insecure, so that withdrawal seemed increasingly likely; but *withdrawal* was another word for *retreat,* and *retreat* was another word for *defeat.* Meanwhile in Mesopotamia, British forces were overextended, and soon would arrive devastating reports of disasters at Ctesiphon and Kut.

For all these reasons the Cairo contingent was disposed not merely to believe Faruki but to act upon the belief. Britain must enlist the sharif and his movement, or else Germany would. In memos and cables they stressed Britain's dire predicament in the Middle East and the grim consequences of inaction. So did Wingate from Khartoum and Sykes at the War Committee meeting. McMahon prepared to write the most important letter of his career, one that would induce Hussein finally to throw down the gauntlet to Turkey. But if he thought he was resolving a difficult situation, he was profoundly mistaken. "Aleppo, Damascus, Hama and Homs": These place-names signified enormous complexities and ramifications; they would haunt his future, and everyone else's.

CHAPTER 5

The Hussein-McMahon Correspondence

THIS BRINGS US to the crux of the matter, the rock on which British-Arab relations subsequently foundered, the misunderstanding, or perhaps the duplicity, that eventually colored everything else.

The most important letter in the Hussein-McMahon correspondence was McMahon's reply to the grand sharif, written while Faruki's farrago of truths, half-truths, exaggerations, and downright lies were fresh and unquestioned in British minds, and while the alarming reports about Bulgaria and Gallipoli and Mesopotamia were likewise fresh. McMahon dated the message October 24, 1915, and immediately took up the question of the boundaries of the future Arab state:

> The districts of Mersina and Alexandretta and portions of Syria lying to the west of the districts of Damascus, Hama, Homs and Aleppo cannot be said to be purely Arab and should be excluded from the proposed limits and boundaries. With the above modification, and without prejudice to our existing treaties with Arab chiefs, we accept those limits and boundaries and, in regard to those portions of the territories therein in which Great Britain is free to act without detriment to the interests of her Ally, France, I am empowered in the name of the Government

of Great Britain to give the following assurances and make the
following reply to your letter.

Subject to the modifications referred to above, McMahon wrote, Britain
would recognize and support the independence of the proposed Arab federation with borders previously defined by Sharif Hussein—that is to say,
with the borders first traced in the Damascus Protocol. She would guarantee the Muslim holy places against external aggression. She would advise
and assist the Arabs in establishing suitable forms of government in the various states that would comprise the federation. In return, the Arabs must
agree to look only to Britain for advice and support and must accept that
Britain could assert special measures of administrative control in the *vilayet*s of Baghdad and Basra.

McMahon wrote in English—he could neither speak nor write in Arabic—so his letter to Hussein had to be translated. Storrs wrote of the translation process in his memoirs: "Our Arabic correspondence with Mecca was
prepared by Ruhi, a fair though not a profound Arabist (and a better agent
than scholar); and checked often under high pressure by myself. I had no
Deputy, Staff or office, so that during my absence on mission the work was
carried on (better perhaps) by others, but the continuity was lost." What
Storrs did not record was that his own knowledge of written Arabic likewise was limited. Conceivably the imbroglio that resulted from this most
infamous letter can be traced to nothing more than an imprecise rendering
of English into Arabic caused perhaps by ignorance or even by haste.

At any rate, once it had been translated, McMahon gave the missive to
Hussein's "trusted and excellent messenger, Sheikh Mohammed Ibn Arif
Arayfan," who set out once again upon the long and difficult journey from
Cairo to Mecca. Hussein would have received and read it with some satis-
faction. But in certain respects he would have found it vague and perhaps
even troubling.

Parts of the crucial paragraph require explanation, but regardless of the
language in which they are read, they are not ambiguous. McMahon's first
qualification to Hussein's suggested boundaries was the districts of Mersina
and Alexandretta: These he wished to exclude from the proposed Arab
kingdom because he suspected that France would claim them after the war,
or even possibly because Britain might wish to claim Alexandretta before
the French did. As for the second qualification regarding "our existing
treaties with Arab chiefs," this referred primarily to the line of principalities along the east coast of Arabia on the Indian Ocean with which the
British government in India had established relations. With regard to the

"portions of territories . . . in which Great Britain is free to act without detriment to the interests of her Ally, France," McMahon simply was recognizing that Britain's most important partner in the war might make additional territorial claims in Syria that Britain would likely be obliged to support, although she did not know precisely what the claims might be and actually rather begrudged them. And finally, as for Baghdad and Basra, McMahon mentioned them to satisfy the territorial ambitions of the British government in India, which still wanted to annex portions of Mesopotamia.

At the time, however, the phrase that may have caused the grand sharif to raise his eyebrows highest, and that created untold trouble afterward, is the one about excluding from the Arab kingdom "the districts of Damascus, Hama, Homs and Aleppo." The key word is "districts," simple enough in the English language but ambiguous when translated, as it was by Ruhi or Storrs or conceivably someone else in Cairo, into the Arabic *wilāyāt*. This is the plural form of the Arabic word *wilāyah,* which means *vilayet,* a political jurisdiction in Turkish, but "vicinity" or "environs," a geographical expression in English. To boil down what became an exceedingly acrimonious, even tortuous argument (one that I have no intention of entering, let alone attempting to settle), Arabs claimed that Hussein understood the word to mean "vicinity" or "environs" and therefore *not* to refer to Palestine, which is south of the line connecting Damascus, Hama, Homs, and Aleppo, not west of it as any glance at a map will quickly show and clearly not within the vicinity or environs of any of those towns. The British and Zionists have argued to the contrary, however, that since *wilāyāt* can mean *vilayet*s and since the *vilayet* or "province" of Damascus extended all the way south to Ma'an and beyond down to Aqaba, therefore McMahon did indeed mean to exclude Palestine from the Arab kingdom because Palestine is indubitably west (not south) of Ma'an.

Perhaps it will be helpful for American readers to think of the problem in the following terms: Presume a line extending from the *districts* of New York, New Haven, New London, and Boston, excluding territory to the west from an imaginary coastal kingdom. If by *districts* one means "vicinity" or "environs," that is one thing with regard to the land excluded, but if one means "*vilayet*s" or "provinces," or in the American instance "states," it is another altogether. There are no states of Boston, New London, or New Haven, just as there were no provinces of Hama and Homs, but there is a state of New York, just as there was a *vilayet* of Damascus, and territory to the west of New York State is different from territory to the west of the district of New York, presumably New York City and environs, just as territory to the west of the *vilayet* of Damascus is different from territory to the west of the district of Damascus, presumably the city of Damascus and its environs.

Which meaning of *district* McMahon really intended, *"vilayet"* or "vicinity," whether he was even aware of the several meanings, and whether the translator was aware of them have been at the crux of the disagreement that ensued.

It is also worth mentioning that in 1915 the French were still claiming that Palestine fell within their Syrian sphere of interest. Therefore McMahon conceivably did not mean to exclude Palestine from King Hussein's proposed Arab kingdom when he referred to the territory lying to the west of the districts of Damascus, Hama, Homs, and Aleppo in the first part of his letter, but that he did mean to exclude it when he referred a little later to the possibility of postwar French claims that Britain would be obliged to support. But we cannot know for certain, since he did not say as much in any part of his correspondence with Sharif Hussein.

The argument over these bare bones would rage first when it came time to recast the Middle East after World War I; then among the champions of the British Mandate in Palestine, their Arab opponents, and their Zionist supporters; and finally, after the establishment of Israel in 1948, among interested parties and academics representing all points of view. Over the years proponents of the Arab side have often made reference to perfidious Albion; they assert that McMahon knowingly misled Sharif Hussein about Palestine. From the other side, Zionist scholars have defended McMahon, arguing that he did not mislead the sharif, who understood and accepted from the start that Britain meant to exclude Palestine from the Arabian kingdom and discovered a longing for that country only after 1917; and that even if McMahon's strictures about territory were vague, as the Arabs charged, Britain's territorial promises depended upon the Arabs carrying out a successful revolt on their own, which they never did, relying instead upon British support to defeat the Turks. In short, the Zionists asserted that even if McMahon's letter did fail to exclude Palestine from the projected Arab kingdom, it made no difference because the letter was not legally binding. Meanwhile assorted historians of the British role in the Middle East have either excoriated the high commissioner for the sloppiness of his language or praised him for being a subtle guardian of his country's imperial interests.

Scholars have assiduously combed the archives in search of a contemporary document that states unambiguously McMahon's intention. Possibly they found it in a self-exculpatory letter he wrote to his former chief in India, the Viceroy Lord Hardinge. Hardinge was furious with McMahon,

Territory south and west of the line Aleppo-Hama-Homs-Damascus ambiguously discussed in the Hussein-McMahon Correspondence

first for giving away the British position in Mesopotamia to the Arabs (he wanted outright annexation and not mere "administrative control") and second, and more generally, for taking Sharif Hussein's ambitions seriously. He did not believe that Hussein or any other Arab could organize and lead a united Arab kingdom. McMahon replied defensively, "What we have to arrive at now is to tempt the Arab people into the right path, detach them from the enemy and bring them on to our side. This on our part is at present largely a matter of words, and to succeed we must use persuasive terms and abstain from academic haggling over conditions."

This remark seems almost an admission of intent to deceive, which is how Hardinge interpreted it. McMahon had "impl[ied] that the negotiations [over Arabian boundaries] are merely a question of words and will neither establish our rights nor bind our hands in that country," he wrote to the secretary of state for India, Austen Chamberlain, in a letter that practically smokes with indignation. "I do not like pledges given when there is no intention of keeping them." But McMahon was not acting very differently from the way his new master in London, Lord Kitchener, had acted one year before, when he trailed the caliphate in front of Sharif Hussein in order to tempt him into an anti-Ottoman rebellion. Kitchener did not consider that Britain's hands were bound by that earlier gesture, and already the Foreign Office was backing away from it. Is it strange, then, that his subordinate, McMahon, who likewise aimed to motivate the grand sharif, made additional "nebulous" (as he termed them) proposals?

At any rate, it was the grand sharif's reaction to McMahon's letter that counted. We may guess that he gathered with his sons again in the palace in Mecca, parsing the Egyptian high commissioner's words very carefully indeed. In his reply of November 5, 1915, he accepted some of them and rejected others. While immediately renouncing claim to the *vilayet*s of Mersina and Adana "in order to facilitate an agreement [with the British] and to render a service to Islam," he held firm with regard to the land west of Damascus, Hama, Homs, and Aleppo. Only now he called this territory "the provinces [*vilayet*s] of Aleppo and Beyrout and their sea coasts." Essentially, and *contra* McMahon, he was reserving for the new Arabian kingdom lands stretching down the Mediterranean shoreline from Alexandretta past Haifa nearly to Jaffa (although not below). Moreover in claiming the *vilayet* of Aleppo, he was not merely refusing McMahon's demand to exclude Alexandretta from his future kingdom; he was reaffirming his claim to it and to adjoining territory reaching to the thirty-seventh parallel. Nor, in Mesopotamia, would he cede unconditionally Britain's right to administrative control of the *vilayet*s of Baghdad and Basra: "We might agree to leave under the British Administration for a short time those districts now occupied by the British troops without the rights of either party being prejudiced thereby . . . and against a suitable sum paid as compensation to the Arab kingdom for the period of occupation." But Hussein extended to the British an inducement of his own: As soon as a "clear and final reply . . . to the questions and problems set forth above" had arrived, he and his followers would take "the necessary action . . . with the least possible delay."

From the sirdar, Reginald Wingate, Hussein's letter wrung a grudging respect: It "proves very conclusively that he is by no means a nonentity, but . . . somewhat of a statesman and diplomat." From the Foreign Office it elicited rather a different response. "For sheer insolence it would be difficult to find any passage to equal Para. 2 of the Sherif's message," fumed one official, and Sir Edward Grey added in red ink in his jagged handwriting, "The proposals are absurd." But if British promises to Hussein were merely a matter of words (as McMahon had asserted to Hardinge), and if they did not commit Britain to any specific future policy, why should Britain even care when Hussein made assertions of his own? Whatever "absurd" objections and stipulations the grand sharif might raise, Britain should simply postpone dealing with them.

Moreover, why should the British not concentrate upon the positive? As if to assuage them, as if to emphasize his offer to take "the necessary action," Hussein had instructed his messenger to deliver oral communications that he knew the British would find to their liking. "Feeling amongst Arabs is very favorable to us," McMahon reported the courier telling him on behalf of Hussein; the "Sherif impressed upon him readiness and intention of Arabs to begin work at once." The grand sharif finally was on the verge of jumping their way. Would McMahon not have thought it best to refrain from raising difficulties that could only delay this long-desired action?

McMahon peppered London with telegrams urging that he be given a green light in his dealings with Sharif Hussein and warning of the repercussions if permission were refused. So did the others in Cairo who favored the forward policy. Clayton urged the War Office to "meet the Arab party generously on the lines of the Sherif's proposals." Mark Sykes brought this same message to London, as did his friend Aubrey Herbert. Herbert left Cairo in October, ahead of Sykes, composing a memorandum for the Foreign Office aboard ship: "If the leaders of the Arabs come in with us . . . the situation will be much eased and our defensive position will be greatly improved." Upon reaching London, he lobbied Grey's private secretary, Sir Eric Drummond; also Lord Robert Cecil, the parliamentary secretary of state for foreign affairs: "If the Germans get to Constantinople while we are negotiating [with the sharif] we have lost the trick." Speed was of the essence, Herbert thought, and yet Britain's messengers to the grand sharif, dispatched by Wingate from Khartoum, "probably eat hashish, ride on donkeys that fall lame or are taken by brigands." He saw Sir Vivien Gabriel at the War Office. "Promise the French big concessions, Nigeria," Herbert advised; "send Curzon or a great man to Paris to say they must make this concession, send Clayton as plenipotentiary across the Red Sea [to Mecca]." "This was . . . a psychological time," Herbert had written in his shipboard memo; "if we don't gain the Arabs now we might well lose them altogether."

Yet Grey and his team of officials hesitated. The exhortations coming in from Cairo and its advocates in London were strong, but a counterblast from India nearly balanced them. "We have been greatly disturbed by the assurances given by McMahon to the Grand Sherif of Mecca," Lord Hardinge wrote to Arthur Nicolson, the under secretary of state for foreign affairs, on November 12, 1915. "I trust that the Foreign Office will be able to get McMahon out of the hole into which he has fallen." And three days later: "I devoutly hope that this proposed independent Arab State will fall to pieces if it is ever created. Nobody could possibly have devised any scheme more detrimental to British interests in the Middle East than this." There was another reason to think twice before plunging, Hardinge added with great percipience: "Two-thirds of the population in Baghdad and Busrah are Shias and the Shia holy places of Kerbela and Nejef are in the province of Baghdad and have no connection whatsoever with Mecca or the Sherif thereof. To place these provinces under the Sunni ruler of Mecca would be the negation of all national and religious claims in those two provinces."

Well founded though his objections to the Cairo plans might be, however, Hardinge had only one strong ally in the cabinet, the secretary of state for India, Austen Chamberlain. Against this single advocate of caution were ranged a variety of bigger guns, of whom (when it came to military and strategic matters) Kitchener was biggest of all. And Kitchener favored the forward policy. In fact, "the Arab movement [is] his and no other man's," Sykes judged. Kitchener, it will be recalled, had been aware of the grand sharif's discontent with the Ottomans even before the war. He was the one who, at Storrs's urging, had directed Cairo to sound out the sharif when the war began. A little later he had sent Mark Sykes as his personal agent to get a grip on the Middle East. While Sykes remained abroad, Kitchener had been encouraging McMahon and the Egyptian military commander, General Sir John Maxwell, to "do your best to prevent any alienation of the Arabs' traditional loyalty to England." He tried hard to persuade Asquith to stake a claim to Ottoman territories before the French could by landing a British force at Alexandretta, but failed, much to his own and Cairo's disappointment. He believed that an Arab revolt would serve Britain's imperial interest. He did not take India's objections to it seriously, although he sympathized with the Indian government's desire to annex portions of Mesopotamia. Moreover he was convinced of the military value to Britain of Arabian help; at the very least it would deny an increment of strength to Germany and Turkey. Kitchener, then, wished McMahon to persuade Grand Sharif Hussein to throw down the gauntlet to Turkey as soon as possible. He was not troubled by Hardinge's scruples about vague language. For his part, Grey thought McMahon should be given flexibility in his dealings with the grand sharif. He opposed Chamberlain too. Against Kitchener and Grey, the officials in the Foreign Office who shared Chamberlain's skepticism were powerless. McMahon received his green light.

Now we may imagine McMahon huddled with his advisers in Cairo drafting the communication they all hoped would conclude the protracted correspondence and bring Grand Sharif Hussein to the sticking point. They worked at a feverish pitch, afraid the Germans and Turks would beat them to the punch. Wingate, who was coaching Clayton from Khartoum on how to approach the man in Mecca, spoke for them all: "I live in almost hourly anticipation of some announcement that the Sultan of Turkey has granted the Arabs of Arabia autonomy." He thought "a reply to the Sherif [should] be dispatched at once containing assurances."

But McMahon, when he wrote the final draft of his letter, cagily reverted to the style of his first letter, which is why to this day we cannot be sure what his intentions were with regard to Palestine. Far from clarifying the crucial points, he chose to leave them in abeyance. Where his second and third messages had been murky about Arabia's future borders, in this one he did not discuss them at all. So he wrote to Grand Sharif Hussein on December 17, 1915: "With regard to the *vilayet*s of Aleppo and Beyrout the Government of Great Britain have taken careful note of your observations, but as the interests of our Ally France are involved the question will require careful consideration and a further communication on the subject will be addressed to you in due course." With regard to Mesopotamia, he wrote that the adequate safeguarding of Britain's interests "calls for a much fuller and more detailed consideration than the present situation and the urgency of these negotiations permits." But as inducement to the sharif to act and as a signal that Britain would be generous with her potential Arabian ally, he added, "I am sending by your trustworthy messenger a sum of £20,000."

Possibly the grand sharif interpreted the money as an earnest of Britain's intention to pay for what he hoped would be the temporary occupation of Baghdad. At any rate, he too was willing to postpone settling the border issue. Why? Because while his relations with the Turks had continued to deteriorate, his relations with the plotters had strengthened; increasingly rebellion seemed to him the most likely and most hopeful course (see Chapter 7). He wanted the British on board as much as they wanted him.

He replied to McMahon in a letter dated January 1, 1916. With regard to "the matter of compensation for the period of occupation [of Mesopotamia:] We . . . leave the determination of the amount to the perception of her [Britain's] wisdom and justice." With regard to "the Northern Parts and their coasts," as he confusingly termed them this time, he was conciliatory too, albeit exceedingly careful. He accepted McMahon's suggestion that their future be decided at a later date in order "to avoid what may possibly injure the alliance of Great Britain and France and the agreement made between them during the present wars and calamities." But he would not yield the point altogether. McMahon "should be sure that at the first opportunity after this war is finished we shall ask (what we avert our eyes from today) for what we now leave to France in Beyrout and its coasts." And as if to underline his determination, he brought the matter up again a few lines below. After the war, he declared, it would be "impossible to allow any derogation that gives France or any other Power a span of land in those regions."

Much as McMahon had ended his letter with a sweetener (of £20,000), so Sharif Hussein ended his with a promise he knew the British would value: "We still remain firm to our resolution which Storrs learnt from us two years ago, for which we await the opportunity suitable to our situation, especially that action the time of which has now come near and which destiny drives towards us with great haste and clearness." Thus the two sides edged closer together, each for its own reason, and each with private reservations.

In his last letter McMahon had assured Hussein that once he launched the rebellion, Britain would prove a staunch and faithful ally; she would not negotiate a peace "of which the freedom of the Arab peoples and their liberation from German and Turkish domination do not form an essential condition." Only one final matter remained. Hussein reminded his potential ally that "we shall have to let you know in due course our requirements in the way of arms, ammunition and so forth." McMahon replied in the fourth and final note of this famous series (they would continue to correspond, but not over essential points, until McMahon returned to London later in 1916): "You will doubtless inform us by the bearer of this letter of any manner in which we can assist you, and your requests will always receive our immediate consideration." This would have to do, and it was good enough. Now the spring was wound up and the plot would move forward. But the deferred question of Syrian, Lebanese, and especially Palestinian borders, and of Britain's role in Mesopotamia, remained a stumbling block to future understanding and good relations.

CHAPTER 6

The Sykes-Picot Agreement

EVEN AS THE HIGH COMMISSIONER of Egypt and the grand sharif of Mecca were conducting their protracted and ultimately unsatisfactory correspondence, British and French representatives closeted in London were also discussing the future of the Middle East. The Foreign Office kept Sir Henry McMahon apprised of these conversations; it told Sharif Hussein nothing about them; nor did McMahon. It was a sin of omission rather than commission, but once again British officials were sowing dragon's teeth. The Anglo-French discussions culminated in the Sykes-Picot Agreement of 1916. This document, although never implemented, created nearly as much ill will and distrust among the principals and their followers, and subsequent disagreement among historians, as the McMahon-Hussein correspondence of 1914–15.

When Aubrey Herbert arrived in Cairo early in 1915, he wrote to Mark Sykes in London, "Our policy has been clear and high in this war. We have not gone out for loot but to protect small people." It was a romantic interpretation and, at this early stage, a common one. Most Britons believed their country was defending little Belgium from mighty Germany; that it would protect tiny Serbia from the bullying military clique in Vienna; that

it would lift the onerous yoke that the Turks had fastened upon various minorities within the Ottoman Empire. Later on a certain amount of disillusionment would set in; even Aubrey Herbert would rethink his early
optimism.

At the outset, however, Foreign Secretary Sir Edward Grey and others
articulated what might be called a liberal imperialist viewpoint. They up-
held the notion of the "white man's burden," doubting the capacity of dark-
skinned peoples, including Arabs, to govern themselves. But they thought
that further extending the empire would be economically expensive and
strategically problematic; in their view, Britain held sufficient territory already. Although he was a Conservative member of Parliament, Aubrey
Herbert shared this liberal imperialist view.

The recipient of his letter, Mark Sykes, who was also a Conservative MP,
took a very different position. He wanted to enlarge the empire for political, economic, and strategic reasons. At this stage he belonged to a group of
aggressively imperialist diplomats, Foreign Office officials, and politicians.
To the dismay of Liberals like Grey, the more sweeping imperialist outlook
increasingly dominated discussion and determined policy in British governing circles.

Early in 1915 Russian diplomats informed their Western allies that they
intended to take and to keep Constantinople, thereby finally satisfying their
country's centuries-old aspiration for a warm-water port and access to the
Mediterranean Sea. They invited Britain and France to claim the parts of
the Ottoman Empire that they would require as compensation. France was
willing. Her cultural influence and financial interest in the Middle East
were strong, especially in Syria, which she defined as extending from Anatolia right down to the Egyptian border, thus including Palestine. Britain
too had important interests in the region, as even the liberal imperialists acknowledged. First and foremost she wished to protect Egypt and the Suez
Canal. Some believed she must guarantee the land route from Egypt to Persia and Mesopotamia and, in the distance, to South Asia by further accre-
tions of territory and influence. The British government in India and its
sympathizers in the Foreign Office coveted parts of Mesopotamia as well.
But Britain also wanted Grand Sharif Hussein of Mecca to rebel against
Turkey and, as we know, had offered him inducements to do so.

Britain may or may not have dealt fairly with Sharif Hussein; in any
case, she must deal also with her ally France. The goal was to persuade her
to support the sharif's rebellion. "Unless this is done," warned Grey, "Egypt
and India may be endangered and the Turk will control the whole of North
Africa." Since France held most of the latter region, this was a warning to

her too. For her own part, Britain was willing to pay a price for the sharif's support. She would "give back Basra &c., if the Arabs came in," Grey promised (although in the event she did not). France must be persuaded to make a sacrifice as well: "The French Government should be asked to resign their immediate hopes of Damascus etc."

It was not that simple. A stated willingness to renounce Basra notwithstanding, if the British kept any part of Mesopotamia after the war, then its northern border might abut the southern boundary of territory in Anatolia occupied by Russia during her march toward Constantinople. Better to create a buffer zone between them, British strategists argued, a shield against possible future Russian aggression. France, with her long-standing interests in the region, immediately came to mind.

As is so often the case with imperial aggrandizement, acquisition of one territory necessitated acquisition of another. In this case, the acquisition of Mesopotamia by Britain would necessitate her acquisition of a port on the Mediterranean Sea, either Haifa or Alexandretta, for strategic and economic reasons. But this meant Britain must persuade France not merely to support the sharif and renounce territorial claims in Syria, as Grey had indicated, but to renounce as well whichever of the two Syrian ports Britain chose to annex, and to take territory between British Mesopotamia and Russian Anatolia as Britain wanted her to do, perhaps instead of taking territory elsewhere.

Grey kept the French informed in a general sense about British contacts with Sharif Hussein in Mecca. By November 1915 it was clear that Britain must bring France more fully into the picture, if only to gain her support for the sharif's planned rebellion. It was time, too, that the two powers hammered out their agreement regarding the future of Ottoman territory in the Middle East, as Russia had suggested. The Foreign Office proposed that Anglo-French discussions take place in London. The French government agreed the time was ripe and it chose François Georges-Picot to represent its interests there.

Picot, at present the first secretary of the French embassy in the British capital, was the consul general who had fled Lebanon at the outbreak of war with Turkey, leaving incriminating documents in the embassy safe. When the French dragoman led the Ottomans to these documents, they used them to identify local nationalists and eventually to arrest, torture, and execute many of them. Picot, however, gave no outward sign that his disastrous oversight troubled him. Tall and elegant, Catholic and conservative, with a long face, thinning gray hair, and a neat mustache, he was a practiced diplomat and tough bargainer with expert knowledge of the Middle

East. He boasted strong imperialist convictions and familial links. (His father was founder of the Comité de l'Afrique Française, and his brother was treasurer of the Comité de l'Asie Française.) Picot was an obvious choice to defend France's Middle East ambitions in discussions with the British.

Meanwhile the war had forced the French to modify their designs on Ottoman territory. Before the war French imperialists had favored maintaining a weak Ottoman presence in the Middle East, which the European powers would divide into spheres of influence. France would have scope to advance her interests in the region without the bother of governing or administering any part of it. With the advent of war, however, French imperialists shifted position. Now they favored terminating Ottoman rule in the Middle East altogether. They wanted direct French control of the eastern Mediterranean coastline, including an enlarged Lebanon. They wanted, too, indirect control through puppet rulers of the Syrian interior, all the way to Mosul in present-day Iraq. These were Picot's goals when he arrived in London in late 1915.

He took part in two extended sessions with representatives of the British Foreign Office, India Office, and War Office in Whitehall, the first of which occurred on November 23. By this date most of the McMahon-Hussein correspondence had been written. The British acquainted him with its particulars and with the sharif's planned rebellion, in effect asking him to accept a fait accompli. Picot refused to be stampeded. He ridiculed the sharif's pretensions and Britain's willingness to accept them. Picot "did not believe in any but a few Arab tribes joining us no matter what we promised," a Foreign Office official reported glumly. Moreover, although (as we now know) he was prepared to concede much Syrian territory to Britain, he absolutely refused to sacrifice any during this first meeting, warning that "No French government would stand for a day which made any surrender of French claims in Syria." Nor would he accept Grey's contention that the Allies must detach the Arabs from Turkey, by supporting the sharif's rebellion, in order to protect their position along the southern and eastern rim of the Mediterranean: "Though an Arab union with Turkey and Germany might be very awkward for us in Egypt and India," the same official recorded Picot as pointing out, "the French were quite happy about Algeria and Tunis."

In short, Picot and the British representatives could not agree on anything. The Frenchman returned to Paris for consultations. When he reappeared in London a few weeks later, he seemed a changed man, willing to make significant concessions. At this point Lord Kitchener directed Mark

Sykes, recently returned from Cairo and fresh from his interview with the War Council, to hammer out an agreement with the Frenchman.

It did not take long. Sykes was a human dynamo, bubbling with enthusiasm, teeming with ideas, easy to like. Picot was urbane and reserved. Perhaps in this case opposites attracted. The two men developed a working relationship that they preserved for the duration of the war. Perhaps their mutual Catholicism provided a basis for trust beneath the feints and gestures of misdirection that each felt obliged to perform. But in fact each man was prepared already to cede most of the territory that the other wished his country to possess. Sykes pretended to be yielding ground when he offered Mosul and land above the Lesser Zab, a tributary of the Tigris River that runs from east to west a little bit north of Kirkuk. He hoped this area would become the French buffer zone, or shield, between British territory in Arabia and Russian Anatolia. But it was the same land that France had wanted all along. Picot pretended to accept it grudgingly. In return he offered British control of land south of the Lesser Zab. This was part of the Mesopotamian territory that the British government in India had its eye on and that France had long been willing to forfeit. Sykes was happy to accept, though we may guess that he too appeared grudging when he did so.

Together Sykes and Picot redrew the Middle Eastern map. We may picture them in a grand conference room at the Foreign Office, crayons in hand. They colored blue the portions on the map that they agreed to allocate to France, and they colored red the portions they would allocate to Britain. Within those areas they proposed that the two countries "should be allowed to establish such direct or indirect administration or control as they desire." Since both parties coveted Palestine, with its sites holy to Christians, Muslims, and Jews alike, they compromised and colored the region brown, agreeing that this portion of the Middle East should be administered by an international condominium. East and south of the blue portion of the map they outlined an Area A also in blue; east and north of the red portion they outlined in that color an Area B. These two contiguous regions, A and B, represented part of the future Arab state or confederation of states. Conceivably its ruler would be Sharif Hussein. But France in Area A and Britain in Area B "should have priority of right of enterprise and local loans [and] . . . should alone supply advisers or foreign functionaries at the request of the Arab confederation." In short, the two areas would become French and British spheres of influence. Finally, within the Brown

Area, Palestine, Britain reserved for herself the ports of Haifa and Acre and the right to construct a railway connecting them with the red-outlined Area B. The two men negotiated less important measures as well. Finally they agreed that if the sharif failed to rebel, or if his rebellion failed, then all the arrangements would be canceled.

This, then, was the famous, or infamous, Sykes-Picot Agreement. Within weeks higher authorities in both London and Paris studied and accepted it. In the British cabinet only Asquith seems to have had doubts. He "thought the Arabs would not be content with the A and B areas," the cabinet meeting minutes record, but "Sir E. Grey pointed out that the four cities Homs, Damascus, Hamma and Aleppo have been assigned to them which would satisfy them." The prime minister's hesitations vanished.

The two governments dispatched Sykes and Picot to Russia to acquaint their partner, the third divider of the anticipated Ottoman carcass, with the agreement's provisions. Sykes, who already had traveled around the Middle East and to India and back again, announced that he would make this further trip under a pseudonym. If he should be captured, the Germans would not know who he was and would not learn of the treaty with France. Unfortunately an English newspaper wrote that he would be journeying to Russia on official business and published his photograph. The disappointed diplomat had to make the passage under his own name. But once he got to Moscow and Picot arrived, the Russians told them they found the agreement good too. After some minor adjustments, the Sykes-Picot Agreement became the Tripartite Agreement, the essentials unaltered.

When Sir Henry McMahon in Cairo learned what Sykes and Picot had wrought, he warned the Foreign Office not to tell the Arabs. "I feel that divulgence of agreement at present time might be detrimental to our good relations with all parties and possibly create a change of attitude in some of them . . . It might also prejudice the hoped for action of the Sherif who views French penetration with suspicion." Here was the crux of the matter. As with the McMahon-Hussein correspondence, so with the Sykes-Picot Agreement: Interested parties at the time and ever since have argued over the aims and motives of the men responsible for it. The issue around which the debate revolves is whether Sykes-Picot contradicted promises that McMahon had conveyed, or was in process of conveying, to Sharif Hussein. In short, did the agreement shortchange the Arabs?

There was first the matter of land west of Damascus, Homs, Hama, and Aleppo. Sykes and Picot allocated it to France. The British could truthfully say that they had reserved that strip of coastline for France in the correspondence with Hussein. But Hussein could reply with equal accuracy that

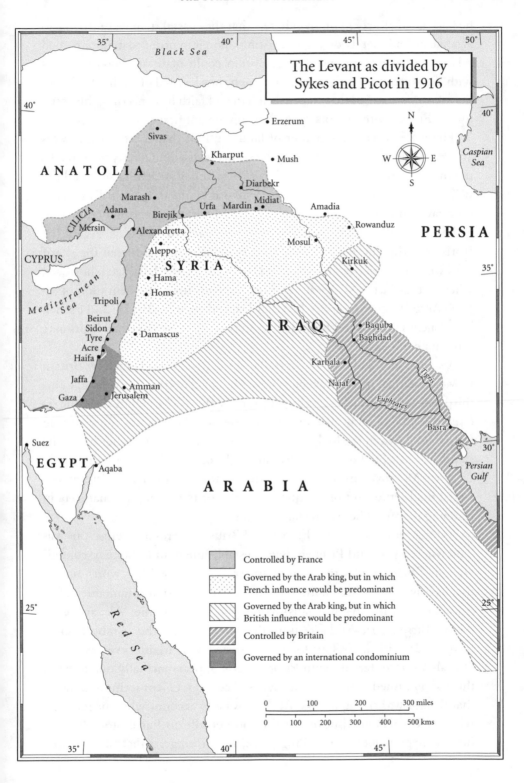

The Levant as divided by
Sykes and Picot in 1916

Controlled by France

Governed by the Arab king, but in which
French influence would be predominant

Governed by the Arab king, but in which
British influence would be predominant

Controlled by Britain

Governed by an international condominium

he had stated clearly in his own letters that the coastal strip was intrinsic to Arabia; he had merely deferred insisting upon it in order to maintain good relations with Britain and so that Britain could maintain good relations with her wartime ally France. Later when they learned of it, the sharif and his followers charged that Britain acted in bad faith by conceding this territory to France without obtaining Arab agreement first.

There was second the matter of land south of that coastal strip. Sykes and Picot had allocated to France the stretch extending nearly to Acre. To the international condominium, they allocated land reaching south all the way to Gaza (except for the British enclave at Haifa and Acre). To Britain, they gave land south of Gaza all the way to the Egyptian border. Taken together, these allocations were essentially the land of Palestine. Again the British could point to McMahon's letters, which withheld from the sharif land west of the *vilayet* or district of Damascus. As we have seen, however, whether that included Palestine or not depends upon the definition of *vilayet*. Accordingly here too, when they learned what the British and French had done, the sharif and his followers may or may not have had legitimate cause for complaint.

A similar cloud of doubt hovers above the Red Area claimed by Britain in Mesopotamia, most of which is now present-day Iraq. McMahon, in his third note to Hussein, had excluded from the sharif's kingdom-to-be the *vilayet* of Baghdad; now Britain could argue that she was not contradicting terms laid down in the high commissioner's letters. On the other hand, the sharif had accepted only that Britain might occupy this land temporarily for a fee. Moreover, in subsequent letters both McMahon and Hussein deferred final settlement of the question. Was Britain acting prematurely in claiming it now? The Arabs charged that she was.

As for Areas A and B, the French and British spheres of interest, this was land where Sykes and Picot envisaged establishment of a "State or confederation of States under the aegis of an Arabian prince." It is worth noting that its original northern border, the upper limit of Area A (amended after consultation with the Russians), corresponded to a line, Alexandretta-Aintab-Birijik-Urfa-Midiat-Zakho-Rowanduz, that the Arab deserter from the Turkish army, Faruki, had suggested to McMahon even as British officials were conferring with Picot. That it appears virtually unaltered in the first published iteration of the Sykes-Picot Agreement seems to indicate that Britain was trying to take Arab views into account while negotiating with her French ally. But the British did not inform Faruki (or Hussein) that the negotiations were taking place, which suggests that they favored

France over Arabia and would sacrifice the interests of the latter to the former if necessary. This is what the Arabs later charged the British had done.

A still more pertinent question about Areas A and B: Would the Arabian prince who governed them be truly independent? Here as elsewhere the evidence is ambiguous, even contradictory. The great Arabist Gertrude Bell prepared a report on the Sykes-Picot Agreement soon after the three powers approved it. "Regarding areas A and B," she wrote, "the elected Council is still the only solution . . . its obvious place of meeting is Damascus. Its president can be no other than an elected native of the country . . . Native representatives of the Red, Blue and Brown areas should also be summoned to it, together with representatives of the Arabian princes, the King of the Hijaz, Ibn Saud etc." She went on to suggest that English and French observers should attend council meetings, although she does not specify what their role should be. Nevertheless her report seems to indicate that at least one important British authority envisioned some form of Arab self-government and determination in that area. T. E. Lawrence appears to have shared her view. "The Sykes-Picot treaty was the Arab sheet-anchor," he argued some years later, after the agreement had been discarded. "It was absurd in its boundaries, but it did recognize the claims of Syrians to self-government." And he added: "It was ten thousand times better than the eventual settlement."

Let us be clear, however. In a different context Lawrence was quite prepared to argue the other way. "Self determination has been a good deal talked about," he said shortly after the war. "I think it is a foolish idea in many ways. We might allow the people who have fought with us to determine themselves [by which he probably meant those Arabs who had supported the grand sharif's rebellion]. People like the Mesopotamian Arabs who have fought against us deserve nothing from us in the way of self-determination." As for Bell, she once wrote to Lord Cromer, the predecessor of Kitchener as high commissioner in Egypt: "They are an easy people to govern, the Arabs . . . to punish is sometimes necessary, to punish thoroughly is frequently salutary, to . . . kill half a dozen men and then go away . . . that's . . . generally harmful," which does not suggest a commitment to Arab self-government on her part after all.

In any event Bell and Lawrence were merely advisers to the men who set British policy, about whom the evidence is also mixed. At meetings of the Eastern Committee, which was a subcommittee of the War Cabinet chaired by Lord Curzon, the subject of Arab independence recurred often. On April 24, 1918, Curzon instructed his committee to assume that Turkey would be defeated. The Ottomans would depart the Middle East alto-gether, leaving British troops in control. Then "we should construct a State with an 'Arab Façade,' ruled and administered under British guidance and controlled by a native Mohammedan and as far as possible an Arab staff." Curzon further pointed out that the titular head of this state need not be Sharif Hussein, despite the "assurances given by Sir H. McMahon . . . [and] never entirely withdrawn."

Seated around the table in Curzon's room at the Privy Council Office were Sir Percy Cox, mastermind of the British army's political relations in Mesopotamia; Lord Hardinge, now removed from India and become per-manent under secretary of the Foreign Office; several of his advisers; Lord Balfour; and Sir Mark Sykes. Not one person demurred from Curzon's statement. Clear-eyed as always, Arthur Balfour observed that the policy of the "Arab Façade" had a "more or less specious inconsistency with the prin-ciple of 'self-determination.'" Since the Arabs were incapable of self-government, a "Façade" was all they could expect. Cox directly contradicted Gertrude Bell, pointing out that "nothing in the nature of a plebiscite could be arranged. It was quite unsuited to Arab thought and habits and could only excite the liveliest misgivings." At another meeting of the Eastern Committee, Lord Robert Cecil, the assistant secretary of state for foreign affairs, offered a classic justification of British imperialism: "From the point of view of the inhabitants we should almost certainly [govern the region] better than anybody else and therefore it would be better for us to do it." No self-determination there; and similar statements may be found scattered throughout the relevant archives.

Even in these unabashedly imperialist circles, however, ambiguity was not absent. On June 18, 1918, Curzon summarized the views of his com-mittee as follows: "1. That His Majesty's Government is still determined to secure Arab independence and to fulfill the promises made at the beginning of the Hejaz revolt; 2. That His Majesty's Government will countenance no permanent foreign or European occupation of Palestine, Iraq (except the province of Basrah) or Syria after the war; 3. That these districts will be in the possession of their natives and that foreign interference with Arab countries will be restricted to assistance and protection." What is a historian to think? We are returned to the original difficulty noted in the early cor-respondence between Lord Kitchener and Sharif Abdullah in 1914. Per-haps the two sides understood the Arab demand for independence differently.

We have no notes or minutes of the meetings between Sykes and Picot, so we cannot know precisely what the two men meant by the word "independence," but this has not kept leading scholars from taking sides. Essentially they fall into three camps. One defends the agreement, arguing that had Hussein known of the negotiations, he would not have been upset, although later he pretended to be; after all, he knew at least in a general sense what French and British claims to Middle Eastern territory were, and still he cast his lot with them. Arab independence, this camp continues, would have developed under the "protective umbrella" offered by the French and British spheres of influence, and Sykes did genuinely attempt to reconcile French and Arab ambitions while the negotiations were taking place, although (as one historian adds) Sykes failed to appreciate how deeply the Arabs longed to be quit of foreign control. Nevertheless, according to this school, Sykes was negotiating in good faith.

A second group of historians who are sympathetic to the Arab position do not mince words: They regard the Sykes-Picot Agreement as "a shocking document . . . the product of greed at its worst . . . a startling piece of double-dealing." But that was written in 1946. More recently a third camp has emerged that accepts that British and French diplomats acted honorably by their own lights, but within a context we no longer find acceptable. This attitude is summarized best, perhaps, by Margaret MacMillan in her *Peacemakers: Six Months That Changed the World* (2001). The Sykes-Picot Agreement, she writes, "was reasonable enough, if you were a western imperialist."

The Sykes-Picot Agreement is important for the light it casts upon British thinking about the Middle East during World War I but not for what it accomplished—for it never was implemented. Shortly after taking power, the Russian Bolsheviks discovered and published what they termed the "secret treaties," revealing that the Entente countries intended to redraw the map of the world in their own interests once they won the war. In keeping with their ideology, however, Russia's new rulers declined to participate in this thieves' banquet. They relinquished previous claims to territory in Asia and the Caucasus, including Constantinople. In powerful and inspiring language, the Bolsheviks called upon colonized peoples not merely to revolt against their foreign overlords but to overthrow their own social elites as well. In words equally stirring, the American president Woodrow Wilson broadcast a competing vision of democratic internationalism: The Western powers must recognize they had no right to dictate to other portions of the globe.

Spurred by Wilson and Lenin and a thousand other causes stemming from the war, the population of each belligerent country became disillusioned with national and military leaders. In the court of public opinion Sykes-Picot, a "secret treaty" if ever there was one, stood branded as an example of all that Leninist and Wilsonian anti-imperialists loathed. To the firestorm of public protest, old-style diplomats bowed with honeyed words; in private they struggled to redefine the new ideology in more traditional and acceptable forms. Surely, said Lord Balfour at the April 24 meeting of the Eastern Committee, President Wilson "did not seriously mean to apply his formula [regarding the self-determination of peoples] outside Europe." But many thought he did. In Britain a revivified liberal and socialist Left clamored for their leaders to define the country's war aims, to include no annexation of additional land, anywhere. Thus, in an unforeseen way, the earlier liberal imperialism of Sir Edward Grey and Aubrey Herbert, who had opposed extending Britain's sway from the outset, was vindicated in the public mind.

The French and British were willing to let Sykes-Picot lapse anyway. Once Russia gave up her claim to Constantinople and territory east of it, the British no longer needed French troops to occupy territory immediately north of her own lands. They had no need for a buffer against the Russians to the north, for there were none. Few French troops remained in the Middle East at the end of the war either. Soldiers fighting for Britain had done all the heavy lifting. Britain could pretty well write her own ticket there, as Curzon and Cox and Balfour recognized. But (and here was the rub) she must do so without incurring the odium that a large fraction of the British public now attached to old-style imperialism.

The British had another factor to consider. When Sykes and Picot were busy with their maps and crayons, they may or may not have been endeavoring to satisfy Arab nationalism in addition to British and French imperialism. Now an additional force, a newly powerful Jewish nationalism, had emerged in the Middle East. The Zionist movement had been gathering strength in fits and starts since the late nineteenth century, when it was founded by the Austrian journalist Theodor Herzl, and ever more quickly since the Ottomans had decided to join World War I. But before we can consider the remarkable story of Zionism's far-from-inevitable rise, and its impact upon British policy and policy makers, we must finish tracing the last steps of Sharif Hussein and his sons, and the movement they led up to June 1916, which culminated in yet another declaration of war.

CHAPTER 7

The Arab Revolt Begins

EARLY IN 1916 Grand Sharif Hussein began laying the groundwork for rebellion in earnest. He knew little if anything of Sir Mark Sykes and François Georges-Picot, and absolutely nothing of the agreement the two men had reached regarding Arabia and that the three Entente powers had subsequently ratified. He had no inkling either that the British government soon would be considering the future role of Jews in Palestine. Had he known of such matters, Middle Eastern history might have unwound very differently. Instead, with the careful but encouraging letters of Sir Henry McMahon fresh in his mind, the emir pushed his chess pieces into position.

To Damascus—headquarters of the dangerous Djemal Pasha and base of the Turkish Fourth Army, of which Djemal was commander in chief— he dispatched his third son, Feisal. Feisal would secretly reestablish links with the nationalist Arab army officers who had framed the Damascus Protocol and with whom he had met the previous spring. Hussein anticipated that they, with the loyal Arabian soldiers under their command and with Feisal at their head, would lead the Syrian wing of his rebellion.

To Medina, which also housed a substantial Ottoman garrison, he sent his eldest son, Ali, and fifteen hundred troops. Ostensibly their mission was to take part in the second invasion of Egypt, planned by the Ottomans; in reality they would undertake the siege of Medina when Feisal threw down the gauntlet in Damascus. In the meantime Ali must win over the regional tribal chiefs, all retainers of the grand sharif.

To the British in Cairo, he sent a series of letters, requesting arms and ammunition for his desert fighters, gold with which to pay them, and British troops to reinforce them.

Finally in Mecca, he kept by his side for the time being his second son, Abdullah, and his youngest son, Zeid. The latter lacked experience and influence, but Hussein depended on the former. He could send Abdullah to parley with local sheikhs. Moreover, aided by Abdullah—and perhaps with young Zeid looking on respectfully and very occasionally making a suggestion—he could ponder the chessboard and discuss future moves. Together father and son would direct their knights in Damascus and Medina to jump at the proper hour onto the proper squares.

For the moment, however, the two knights must rely upon their own good judgment, at a time when any false move might prove literally fatal. We have scant record of Ali's movements and activities in Medina, but he appears to have skirted very near the edge of the precipice. Ali did not much resemble his more active younger brothers, being short while Feisal was tall, slim while Abdullah was stocky, and with a face already weary-looking (although he was only thirty-seven years old); but he had his father's large deep brown eyes and thin nose. A zealous protector of Hussein's prerogatives as the emir of Hejaz, he quickly came into conflict with the Ottoman governor in Medina. Perhaps there was a religious component to his attitude: He was, like the grand sharif, a devout Muslim, "less ready to sink religious prejudices than his brothers." During this period in Medina, Ali was "assuming powers on the pretext that they were part of his authority as Imam," wrote an Ottoman who watched him carefully. This official warned Ali to mend his ways. Ali, perhaps emboldened by the fifteen hundred Hejazi troops at his back, did nothing of the sort. Rather, he became "simply intolerable," the same official remembered. The official was Djemal Pasha, not a man one would wish to antagonize, but the Turks needed Ali because they needed his father. They still wanted the grand sharif to endorse the jihad publicly. They wanted him to raise additional Arab troops for the second invasion of Egypt and to fight the British in Mesopotamia too. So Djemal, whose first instinct when confronted with a troublemaker was to flatten him, stayed his hand. Only in retrospect did he recognize Ali's conduct for what it most probably had been: a harbinger of a total break.

Thus spared, Ali managed a successful passage. His primary mission in Medina was to win over the region's tribal leaders. "The Jehani Kadi has arrived," he wrote to his father, "and I did the necessary with him." In fact he had "compelled" the latter to come to terms with a rival sheikh, then brought them and three more sheikhs into the rebel camp, a considerable achievement. Their tribal armies, when added to the fifteen hundred soldiers already encamped on the outskirts of Medina at Hezret Hamza, constituted a significant if unconventional and undisciplined force. Now they waited on tenterhooks for word from Hussein to advance against the Ottomans.

Feisal's mission in Damascus was more important to Hussein than Ali's in Medina, because that Syrian city had been the main base of the Arab officers in the Ottoman army who drew up the Damascus Protocol and who, he now hoped, would provide the nucleus of a rebel general staff. Damascus was also more dangerous for Feisal than Medina was for Ali, because it was headquarters of the redoubtable Djemal. Feisal would have to plan his part of the rebellion right under the Turkish commander's watchful, unforgiving eye.

Forty picked men accompanied Feisal into this lion's den. They were, Feisal said, soldiers for the invasion of Egypt, but in fact they constituted his bodyguard. With them he approached the familiar city. He may have intended to stay once again with the al-Bakri family and, as before, to meet with the conspirators at the al-Bakri house in the small hours of the morning. As they rode the train into Damascus, Feisal must have thought he would be engaging in work that was perilous but not impossible. After all, he had done it before, unaccompanied.

In fact, by January 1916, when Feisal arrived in Damascus, everything had changed. Almost all the officers with whom he had met the previous year were gone. Djemal had sent the 35th Division, in which most of them were based, to fight the British in Gallipoli. Not only the officers but the Arab soldiers, upon whom the conspirators had counted to act as the revolution's shock troops, were gone as well. This was a major setback for which Hussein and his sons were entirely unprepared.

Moreover, the disruption of trade caused by the war had taken a toll on Damascus. The British had blockaded most of the east coast of the Mediterranean. To cope with scarcities and to feed his armies, Djemal Pasha had levied new taxes and had confiscated much Syrian property. To make fuel for his trains, he had directed the felling of trees, including cherished orchards and olive groves. Hardship for the residents of Damascus led to hunger and eventually to starvation. People weak from lack of food succumb easily to disease, in this case typhus. Historians estimate that during the war between 150,000 and 300,000 Syrians died from famine and sickness. Hussein and Feisal had hoped that when the rebel Arab army challenged the Ottomans, the population of Damascus would rise. But with so much of the city ill and famished, there was little chance of that.

Perhaps worst of all from the Arab nationalist point of view, the political atmosphere in Damascus had grown darker and more ominous than before. Djemal Pasha, who had known from the outset about Arab nationalist activities because Picot had left those incriminating documents in the French embassy safe, had finally turned upon the conspirators. Moreover he had additional evidence of traitorous activities from spies and informers who carried news to him in a constant stream. Some of it was accurate. "I decided to take ruthless action against the traitors," Djemal records.

The results were horrific. The Turks rounded up suspects and brought them for trial and imprisonment to Aleyh, a town southeast of Beirut. There they were beaten bloody; pierced with needles; and pressed by a vise that squeezed their heads until they thought their brains would burst from their eye sockets. They received bread and water only, and that every other day; their jailers kept them awake seventy-two hours at a stretch. How could they defend themselves when finally they were brought into the courtroom? They could not. They would say anything to stop the torture. Eleven men paid with their lives. An English newspaper reported: "The bodies of the hanged remained exposed in Liberty Square [in Beirut] for six hours, after which they were carried to the sands on the western outskirts of the town and there buried ignominiously." That was only the beginning. "Eight more have been hanged and fifteen others [are] expected to meet the same fate," the newspaper reported a little later. Djemal ordered that hundreds of suspected nationalists be deported to the far reaches of Anatolia. Thousands more left of their own accord, fearful that he would turn upon them next.

Feisal and his retinue, forty strong, disembarked from the train at the Damascus railway station to find themselves in a city gripped by hunger, illness, dread, and revulsion. Djemal suspected everyone, possibly even Feisal and his father. He insisted that the grand sharif's son stay with him, at Ottoman army headquarters. Was he trying to keep his enemy close, or was it simple courtesy? Either way Feisal had no option but to accept. Imperturbably he presented his host with gifts from Mecca, including a sword of honor. Djemal claimed to have interpreted this at the time "as the greatest proof of friendship." Did he really? Feisal thought not. He wrote of the Ottoman leadership to his father: "There can be no trust in their sayings or their writings." His letters to Mecca traveled in cakes, in sword handles, in the soles of his servants' sandals. He wrote them in code, in invisible ink.

And meanwhile, in the famished, terrorized city, he attended banquets and receptions arranged by Djemal in his honor.

In Aleyh, to which all eyes had turned, trials of the second batch of suspects proceeded. Among the prisoners now suffering the same vile torments as had been meted out to the first group were Arab deputies to the Ottoman parliament; delegates to the prewar Arab Congress in Paris, including its president; lawyers, journalists, and army officers; indeed, "some of the best known and most influential names in Syria." A few were Christian, but most were Muslim. "In my opinion," wrote Djemal Pasha, "the punishment of a man who betrays his faith and his country should be in proportion to the social position he enjoys." The outcome was a foregone conclusion, although (as we know today) a number of the condemned had in fact held aloof from the nationalist movement. Their innocence did not save them. Now it was Feisal's turn to sail close to the wind. "He came to see me every day," Djemal Pasha continues, "and always brought the conversation round to the question of pardon." From Mecca the grand sharif, too, exhorted the commander of the Fourth Army, and leading Young Turks in Constantinople and even the sultan himself, to show mercy.

There was to be none. On the evening of May 5, 1916, a jailer read out the names of twenty-one prisoners. They were divided into two groups: one entrained for Damascus, while the other boarded horse-drawn carriages bound for Beirut. In the first city soldiers had erected seven gallows in the main square; in the second they had built a scaffold in Liberty Square (known today as Martyrs' Square). "O paradise of my country," cried one prisoner as they placed the rope around his neck, "carry our feelings of brotherly love to every Lebanese, to every Syrian, to every Arab, tell them of our tragic end and tell them: 'For your freedom we have lived and for your independence we are dying!' " Then he kicked away the stool himself, denying that honor to the hangman.

On the very day of the executions, Djemal caused the army to publish a summary of the trials, including some of the evidence used to convict. That morning Feisal was taking his ease with the al-Bakris, at their house five miles outside Damascus. A servant brought them the army summary. One of the Bakri family read aloud the twenty-one names. At last, and only for a moment, the mask slipped from Feisal's face. He leaped to his feet, a cry for vengeance wrenched from deep within him: "Death will now be a pleasure for us!" But two hours later he stood before Djemal protesting his good intentions: "I swear by the memory of my ancestors," he is supposed to have told him, "that had I known how heinous was the offence of those criminals I should not merely have refused to intervene for them. I should have asked for them to be torn limb from limb to prolong their sufferings. God's curse be upon them!"

That was play-acting. The real Feisal met again secretly with the remaining members of al-Fatat at the al-Bakris' house. Their number was much diminished, not only by the dispatch of the 35th Division to Gallipoli but by the transfer of nearly all Arab officers out of Syria and into Turkey, and of course by the executions, deportations, and other removals. Djemal, now also contemplating the chessboard, was taking off as many of his opponents' pieces as possible before the game began. With them gone, and with Damascus effectively traumatized, Feisal and the remaining conspirators came to the only possible conclusion. The revolt could not begin in Syria. Feisal advised his father that the initial blow must be struck elsewhere, in Medina or Mecca or both.

But first he must escape from Damascus and make his way to one or the other of those cities. Once more he appeared before Djemal Pasha, wearing his dissembler's mask. Historians do not agree about precisely what he said, but in some way he gave reason to join his brother Ali in Medina. Djemal believed him (as most would have it) or did not (as Djemal himself later told it, but he was an interested party). Either way, he raised no objection. Feisal left Damascus. Djemal Pasha had had him in his grasp and let him go.

Could the grand sharif launch a successful rebellion without the Syrians playing a leading role? He thought so. He had his two knights now and fifteen hundred warriors in Medina. The tribal desert fighters were champing at the bit in the surrounding wastes. At his signal Ali and Feisal would gather them all and lead them in an attack upon the railway that connected Medina with Damascus. Tear up enough line, and the Ottoman path into Arabia would be blocked. Then they must besiege and capture Medina itself. Simultaneously a portion of the grand sharif's own army would take Mecca, forcing surrender of the Ottoman troops there. Abdullah would lead another force, local tribesmen with whose sheikhs he had been consulting, against Taif, where the Turkish *vali* already was seeking refuge from the early summer heat and where the bulk of Ottoman troops usually posted in the holy city spent the summer months. Still other desert tribes would attack the Turks in the port of Jeddah and other Hejazi towns occupied by Ottoman soldiers.

But first Hussein sought once again to bring even more powerful pieces onto the board. He thought the British should land at Alexandretta. With the eastern Mediterranean's best port as their base, they could fall upon Djemal's Fourth Army and then turn north to join up with the Russians. Together the armies of the two great powers could push west into Anatolia toward the Ottoman capital. Hussein wrote to McMahon: "Since this war started we had thought that this plan will be that of the Allies in the Turkish theatre of war. This is why I could not understand [that] they have preferred to take operations in the Dardanelles." But the British would not land at Alexandretta. They had just accepted the Sykes-Picot Agreement, which among other things allocated that harbor to France. Of course McMahon could not say so; he reiterated instead that given clear evidence of a genuine rebellion, Britain *would* be willing to pay and supply the Arabs and, if necessary, to assist by bombarding the Red Sea ports held by Ottomans. But Britian would provide no significant detachment of troops to aid the rebellion.

Ali wrote to his father from Medina, "The movement should take place in the hot season; i.e., in the middle of the summer, so that the hot climate also might help us against them." This was indeed the schedule, but an unforeseen development precipitated matters earlier. A Turkish force of 3,500 arrived in Medina, aiming to pass through the Hejaz en route to a final destination in Yemen. Stationed there, it would strengthen the Ottoman presence in the Arabian Peninsula as a whole; it would menace British-dominated Aden; it could even prove helpful to German troops across the Red Sea in East Africa.

There was more to this Turkish mission than was apparent. A small party of Germans, led by a major of the general staff, Baron Othmar von Stotzingen, accompanied the Turkish division. Von Stotzingen's servant was a Muslim Indian deserter; his interpreter was "the notorious Jew, ex-storekeeper, ex-prisoner of the caliphate, Heinrich Neufeld." Neufeld had brought with him a Kurdish bride fifty years his junior. The party contained three additional officers, two wireless operators, and a few attendants. As non-Muslims, they were not permitted to travel by train to Medina. Djemal Pasha instructed them to take the coastal road and to rejoin the troops south of the Hejaz. The Ottoman Muslim troops, however, could go right on through.

The arrival of Turkish soldiers in Medina set off alarm bells, and Ali immediately communicated with his father. Suppose the division's real target was not Aden but the Hejaz? Even if it was not, Ali said, the presence of 3,500 Ottoman troops permanently stationed south of the sharif in Yemen would be a direct threat, and the passage through his father's territory an insult. Hussein agreed. He determined that the Ottoman troops would not enter his kingdom at all. It was time to launch the rebellion.

On May 23, 1916, McMahon received a telegram: "Sharif's son Abdallah urgently requires Storrs to come to Arabian coast to meet him. Movement will begin as soon as Faisal arrives at Mecca." The delighted high commissioner informed the Foreign Office back in London: "Will send Storrs as required." He dispatched his oriental secretary almost immediately, and with him Kinahan Cornwallis and David G. Hogarth, both leaders of the newly established Arab Bureau in Cairo, which would oversee British intelligence operations in the Middle East for the rest of the war. The three men carried with them two sacks of a British propaganda newspaper called *al-Haqiqa* (The Truth) for distribution as the sharif saw fit, and £10,000 for his rebellion; also news that Britain would send £50,000 more once it had clear evidence that the revolt was in progress.

From Cairo the trio went to Suez, where they boarded HMS *Dufferin,* which took them down the canal and into the Red Sea all the way to Port Sudan. They sailed under a blistering sun on flat and shining water, with their singular cargo in Storrs's cabin. At Port Sudan the three met with Oreifan, an experienced go-between. Oreifan reported that the grand sharif wished to consult with him one more time before sending Abdullah to meet the British. HMS *Dufferin* ferried Oreifan across the Red Sea, landing him close to Jeddah, the port nearest Mecca. They would rendezvous at the same spot when Oreifan returned from Mecca three days later.

It was a nervous interval. To fill it, HMS *Dufferin* cruised the Arab side of the coast, a forbidding, gorgeous, picturesque shoreline. "We made the near acquaintance of an island as scorched by heaven as any vent of earth's fires, and of long miles of submerged coral, greens and blues dappled with gold," Hogarth would recall. High mountains towered in the near distance. Tiny port villages, still under Turkish control, baked in the sun. Then "a naked fisherman paddled his bark canoe through the shark-infested sea to tell an incredible tale of German officers and a German lady gone southward to Yambo a few days before." It was von Stotzingen's party; the German lady was Neufeld's Kurdish bride.

At one P.M. on Monday, June 5, HMS *Dufferin* anchored off Jeddah. Oreifan was waiting. He had news: Bedouin marauders had murdered seven Germans the previous day—obviously some, or all, of the contingent described to them by the naked fisherman. If the Englishmen wished, Oreifan continued, he would bring them their heads. Storrs declined, telling Oreifan that he would prefer to see the Germans' papers.

Then Oreifan presented a letter, signed by Hussein but written in Abdullah's hand: "I deeply regret my inability to send Abdallah for an urgent reason which bearer will explain: but his brother will represent him with one of his cousins." Oreifan handed over another letter, from Abdullah to Storrs, containing the same message, but ending: "My request of you is to start operations in Syria to the best of your ability." Evidently he and his father still pined for a British landing at Alexandretta. Finally Oreifan proffered a third letter, unsigned, but very much to the point: "Please order by wireless immediately 500 rifles of same pattern as those already sent us . . . also 4 machine guns, both with ammunition."

In addition to conveying the letters, Oreifan delivered a verbal report, which surely came as music to the ears of the waiting Englishmen. The Arab revolt they had so ardently wished for, planned for, and more or less patiently nurtured, finally was about to commence. Oreifan told them that the reason Abdullah could not meet them was that he had left Mecca to begin the siege of Taif. Feisal and Ali were about to attack Medina; the sharif would turn upon the Turks in Mecca; the Harb tribe would fall upon Jeddah. All these actions, so long contemplated by the sharif, were to be launched by the coming Saturday. In the meantime telegraph lines between Mecca and Jeddah already were in the sharif's hands; the line to Medina had been cut; the railway was cut also. Zeid, the sharif's fourth and youngest son, was on his way to Samima, six miles southwest of Jeddah, where he would meet the three British men next day at dawn.

"We had not come so far to see a boy," Hogarth sniffed, "but there was no help for it." HMS *Dufferin* slipped down the six miles of coastline to anchor just outside the reefs at the desolate spot appointed. At five-thirty next morning, Tuesday, June 6, Storrs, Hogarth, and Cornwallis, still carrying their precious cargo of propaganda and £10,000, were taken by a small boat just inside the reef offshore from Samima. There was no sign of Zeid on the beach. But an Arab contact awaited them in a dhow half-full of sacks of maize, with a sail rigged to provide the Englishmen some shade. Even at that early hour the sun was broiling hot. On the shore Oreifan was waiting too, with a tent of honor erected for the conclave soon to occur.

Finally ten camels and riders appeared silhouetted against the shimmering horizon and made their way to the tent by the shore. Moments later Oreifan was paddling a canoe out toward the dhow. He told the Englishmen that Zeid and his cousin wished to meet alone with Storrs. Evidently the Arabs did not wish to be outnumbered in council. The three devised a counterstrategy: Storrs would step ashore alone, as requested, but then so firmly invite the Arabs to return with him to the ship that they could not politely refuse. Even at this initial meeting, maneuvering for precedence was essential; perhaps it is so at every meeting between emissaries of governments. On this occasion it was not a fair fight, however: Zeid, aged twenty, confronted three masters of the game.

"I stepped into Oreifan's canoe, the bottom of which was so full of water that I elected for obvious reasons to stand up in it," Storrs reported. "The last ten yards I was carried to the beach by two slaves." Immediately he commenced to maneuver: "Without looking up I saw Zeid and Shakir [the cousin] slowly advancing upon me. I continued to arrange my clothes so as to bring the two down in front of their guard to welcome on their threshold one who was, after all, representing the High Commissioner."

The three men walked back up the beach to the tent, passing Zeid's protectors. Storrs scrutinized the sharif's youngest son: "He is about 5.5' in height, fair in complexion, with fine eyes and the round face and Greek profile characteristic of Circassians. He is evidently attempting to encourage the growth of a somewhat backward beard." The young man wore a caftan of Egyptian silk. Brilliant gold cords fixed the head shawl. In fact, both Zeid and his relative were so faultlessly attired that Storrs believed they must have stopped and changed costume just before reaching the beach. This was, perhaps, an Arabian attempt at maneuver.

The three waited in the tent for coffee, sitting on divans, the sand beneath their feet covered by two Shirwan rugs (of poor quality, Storrs judged) and two Killim carpets. Zeid confirmed the plan and schedule for the risings. Storrs asked for details. "We will summon the Turks to surrender and shoot them if they refuse," Zeid said. "If they surrender we will imprison them until the end of the war. We intend to destroy the Hijaz railway as far north as Medain Salih, which will be our advance guard." Then Zeid returned to the talking points provided by his father and older brother. The grand sharif wanted guns, ammunition, and money. He asked once more that the British send reinforcements to land on the Syrian coast. "His father felt very strongly on this point," Storrs recorded. Storrs stuck to the British line: Money and weapons would be forthcoming, and perhaps advisers to train Arab soldiers in their use, but not soldiers in any quantity. At this juncture a slave dressed in white and silver served the coffee. "As soon as decently possible after this," Storrs reports, I "took [Zeid's] arm and told him it was time to be getting to the ship."

By now he had taken his measure of the man: "soft in his ways and vague in his ideas . . . and though by no means intelligent quite capable of understanding and conveying to or from his father any instructions or explanation with which he may be entrusted." With this judgment Hogarth concurred: "Zeid struck me as amiable but weak ... not a man of action but a Harem Arab." The business conducted on HMS *Dufferin* therefore, when the men clambered aboard, merely reprised what had taken place earlier on shore. The British promised to send guns and ammunition and, later, more money. Then Storrs arranged a meal, and for the Arabs to be photographed, and a guided tour of the ship: "I had them shewn [sic] and explained the wireless, which appeared to fascinate them, the guns, the Captain's bath-room and other wonders of the deep." Here as elsewhere in Storrs's memoirs and papers, we recognize a tone. That same condescending attitude allowed Sykes so cavalierly to redraw Arabian borders, and the British government in India to look upon Mesopotamia as its own preserve, and McMahon to write to Lord Hardinge that promises made to Arabs need not be binding upon the British government.

Then it was over. The two young men disembarked from the ship into a canoe with the bundles of *al-Haqiqa,* the £10,000, and one thousand cigarettes, which Storrs thoughtfully added as a gift for Feisal and Ali, the only smokers in the sharif's family. Then with the Arabs gone, the three Englishmen shared impressions. That the revolt would now take place none doubted. "The conception, plan and intended execution of the rising have every appearance of genuineness," Storrs concluded. That the revolt was well conceived and would succeed remained an open question in their minds. "Far too much has been left to the last moment and to luck," Hogarth warned.

Still, England had evidently gained a prime objective. Merely by taking place, regardless of its success or failure, the Arab Revolt would divert the Turks; it would blunt their call for jihad; it would convert many Arabs to the Allied cause. And it would have another entirely unforeseen consequence as well. Somehow on their journey across the Hejaz, von Stotzingen's party caught wind of the impending revolt and, frightened by that prospect, decided to turn back. It was then that they met up with the Bedouins, with fatal consequences for some but not all of the party. (Von Stotzingen himself, Neufeld, and Neufeld's bride eventually made it back safely to Germany.) Von Stotzingen's mission had been to recruit soldiers for jihad against the Allies, not only on the Arabian Peninsula but across the Red Sea in the Sudan and Egypt. The repercussions could have reached east too, across the Indian Ocean into South Asia. "Had the sherifian revolt never done anything else than frustrate that combined march of Turks and Germans to southern Arabia in 1916, we should owe it more than we have paid to this day," Hogarth would write in 1920. HMS *Dufferin* steamed slowly northward upon a molten and breathless sea. Upon its deck three Englishmen congratulated themselves on a job well done.

But three thousand miles to the northwest, off the Orkney Islands, Lord Horatio Herbert Kitchener had just perished in icy waters amid gale-force winds. He had been on his way to Russia on a diplomatic mission when his ship, HMS *Hampshire,* struck a German mine. Thus did fate deny the British initiator and prime architect of his country's alliance with Grand Sharif Hussein any chance to see the fruit, whether good or ill, of his labors.

Feisal had gone to Medina, but Djemal Pasha remained uneasy. Anticipating trouble, he decided to send Fakhri Pasha, a seasoned divisional commander, after him. "I explained to him the situation and . . . asked him . . . if occasion required to arrange . . . all necessary measures of defence." Djemal also prepared "two or three battalions and one or two mountain batteries at Damascus . . . they could be entrained within half an hour of receiving the first signal." By this time, late May, Hussein had already dispatched the letter to McMahon asking him to send Storrs to meet Abdullah, and in Medina, Ali and Feisal were busy making preparations for the uprising. Ali secretly contacted the tribal chiefs to warn them that action was pending. Feisal sent word to his bodyguard back in Damascus: They must leave that city immediately. He reviewed the fifteen hundred Mujahid fighters, who everyone supposed would take part in the invasion of Sinai, and discussed its real mission with their officers. When Fakhri arrived in Medina, the two brothers brought him out to Hezret Hamza to review the troops again. "We lunched together," Fakhri reported to Djemal. "The volunteers were indulging in all the sports beloved of the Beduins [sic] and singing songs about the blows they were going to inflict upon the English." On the evening of June 4 he accepted an invitation to dine with Feisal and Ali at their Medina quarters. The brothers assured him that the first contingents of Mujahids would depart for Dara in two days' time. It was an unexceptional occasion.

The next morning, however, Ali sent a note to Fakhri. Perhaps he had written it before dinner the previous evening. Fakhri read it with surprise and growing anger. "In accordance with my father's orders the transport of the volunteers to Palestine will be suspended," Ali wrote. "I have therefore decided to return with the Mujahids to Mecca instead of wasting my time here. I regret that I must go without taking leave of you. Please excuse me!" Ali did not state it plainly, but Fakhri Pasha understood what was about to happen: Ali would not be returning with his troops to Mecca, he would be throwing them against the Turks. Frantically Fakhri sought to contact Djemal Pasha, finally tracking him down by telephone in Beirut. "The railway will be attacked tonight or tomorrow morning at the latest," he warned. "Ali Bey will interrupt our communications between Medina and Syria and attempt a surprise attack on Medina . . . I have assumed command of all the troops." Djemal sent the Damascus battalions and batteries at once. Let the two brothers waste their time in the desert blowing up railway track. That could be repaired. He was determined to hold Medina against all comers.

Ali and Feisal had ridden out to Hezret Hamza at daybreak. There before the fifteen hundred Arab fighters, they fired their rifles into the air and proclaimed the independence of Arabia in the name of their father the Grand Sharif Hussein of Mecca. Then the two brothers led their now-rebel army into the desolate reaches beyond Medina to join the tribes Ali had recruited earlier. They would tear up the railway. They would besiege Fakhri Pasha and his reinforced Ottoman army in Medina. The die was cast. The date was June 5.

Abdullah had arrived in Taif three days earlier. As in Medina, Ottoman soldiers crowded the city, refugees from the blast-furnace heat of Mecca. Likewise seeking relief from the blazing sun, the Turkish *vali* rested there. The grand sharif had either seized or cut the telegraph lines into Mecca, but not yet those extending from it, presumably on the grounds that control of cables in meant control of cables out. Taif, then, remained on line, but its messages could be intercepted in Mecca. During that first week of June no one in Taif knew anything about Ali and Feisal's actions far to the north.

Abdullah consulted with the local sheikhs. All was in readiness; they waited only for the word to strike. Abdullah told them that a date had been set: Saturday, June 10. Then on the morning of June 9 he received a summons to meet with the Turkish *vali* later in the day. A nervous Abdullah accepted quickly enough but took precautions. At the time appointed he rode with four picked men toward the *vali*'s palace. They reined in before it. "I left Faraj with the horses," Abdullah recalled. He entered the building with his three comrades "and posted Hosaan at the top of the stairs;" traversed a long hallway, and stationed the two remaining sheikhs outside the *vali*'s room.

Then Abdullah entered it, with a pistol hidden beneath his cloak. "If there was any trouble I was to shoot the *vali* in the room and they were to dispatch anyone who tried to interfere outside." In fact, the *vali* harbored no designs; he remained ignorant of events in Medina. But the continual jockeying with the emir for control of the Hejaz preyed upon his nerves. When Abdullah appeared before him, the *vali* reiterated these concerns. Then two Ottoman officials entered the room. One of them whispered in the *vali*'s ear. Abdullah tightened his grip upon the pistol. But the *vali* only shook his head and ordered the men to leave. Later Abdullah learned they had been urging the *vali* to arrest him.

It was a narrow escape, and when a shaken Abdullah left the palace, he immediately ordered that the telegraph wires into Taif be severed. Now the city was entirely cut off. The next day, as planned, he launched the siege of Taif.

Back in February the grand sharif already had devised his opening gambit: He would send a letter to Enver Pasha, first among the triumvirate of Young Turks leading the Ottoman Empire. No copy survives, but both Abdullah and Djemal summarize it in their memoirs. Hussein offered, in this communication, to do what the Ottomans wanted: He would send additional troops for the invasion of Egypt and still more to face the British in Iraq; he would endorse the jihad. But he stipulated that the Ottomans must do something for him in return. They must pardon the prisoners in Djemal's jails, grant autonomy to Syria and Iraq within the empire, and recognize him as hereditary emir of the Hejaz. It is impossible that the grand sharif did not understand he was crying for the moon. Therefore he was preparing the way for revolt. When the Ottomans rejected his offer, he would have his casus belli.

Meanwhile he ratcheted up tensions in Mecca. First he asked the British to extend their blockade in the Red Sea to the Arabian coast. He believed, rightly as it turned out, that those affected would blame the Turks for provoking Britain rather than Britain for prosecuting the war. As the blockade tightened, supplies dwindled throughout his kingdom. "Purveyors have begun to refuse to give provisions," reported the acting governor and commandant of Mecca from Hamidiye, the Ottoman headquarters in that city. "Everyone reclaims his money. Even wood ration is now given day by day. . . . provisions sent to Taif have not arrived." A few days earlier he had warned that as a result of the blockade, people in Mecca were showing "an attitude of distrust of the government."

In Constantinople the Ottomans were puzzling over Hussein's letter. Enver Pasha sent it to Damascus, telling Djemal that he could not make heads or tails of it. The latter understood it well enough, according to his account, but he approached the matter obliquely. "Your father," he cautioned Feisal, who was at that point still in Damascus, "has many enemies . . . in Constantinople . . . trying every day to rouse the Government's suspicions against [him]." The grand sharif's son "turned pale," according to Djemal. The commander of the Fourth Army sent a more transparent warning to Hussein: "The men who form the present Government . . . would never forgive anyone who had the audacity to hamper them in the war upon which they have entered for the good of the Mohammedan world."

The time for a parting of the ways was near at hand. We may imagine the grand sharif and his son Abdullah in nearly continual consultation in Mecca; messages in code and invisible ink secreted in sword hilts must have been flying to and fro between Ali and Feisal, both now in Medina, and the sharif and Abdullah in Mecca. When the brothers in Medina finally set the date for their rising and informed their father of it, Hussein wrote to Enver in Constantinople and to Djemal in Damascus: "He [Hussein] considered himself compelled to break off relations with the Government until the request was acceded to which he had made to Enver Pasha two months before." At that point Ali sent his own brief note to Fakhri Pasha. He and Feisal rode off into the desert with their fifteen hundred soldiers.

In Mecca Bimbashi Mehmed Zia Bey, the acting governor and commandant, had no knowledge of these developments. But as tensions grew because of the British blockade and ensuing mutterings, he devised a defense, in case matters should reach the breaking point. He must hold three main Ottoman outposts in the holy city, he concluded: Hamidiye (the headquarters), Fort Jeyad (which was close by), and the Jiyad Barracks (located on the outskirts of town). But he continued to hope that it would not be necessary to implement the plan. The evidence suggests that when the crisis finally arrived, it took him by surprise.

It came not with a rush but by degrees, yet overwhelmed him nonetheless. On the afternoon of June 9, just as Abdullah, pistol hidden beneath his robe, was entering the palace in Taif for his verbal sparring match with the *vali,* "outlaws" blocked the Jeddah-Mecca road and cut the Jeddah-Mecca and Mecca-Taif telegraph lines. In Mecca itself "a number of armed men" could be seen "wandering about in the streets," while others patrolled the surrounding hills. The acting governor sent men to repair the telegraph lines. He telephoned the grand sharif, asking for an explanation of the armed men. "They were simply the young men of the quarter who were strolling about to maintain the peace of the town," the sharif told him. Not entirely clueless, the Turk brought in troops to defend the oven and granary upon which both fort and headquarters depended. And he sent an order to both fortress and barracks: If a battery at the fort fired three blank shots, the barracks should instantly send reinforcements from the Second Battalion, 130th Regiment.

Immediately after prayers at dawn the next morning, gunfire broke out in the streets of Mecca. "I called up the Emir and asked what all this meant," the acting commandant reported. "Do something," he is said to have implored the grand sharif, and Hussein is said to have replied rather ambiguously that he would. But not ambiguously enough; at last the acting commandant, realizing what he confronted, ordered that the three blank shots be fired.

The reinforcements started off from the barracks but immediately ran into a larger detachment of Arab soldiers. The Second Battalion, 130th Regiment, returned to its barracks. "I felt much grieved at this . . . our position in the city was very dangerous," the acting commandant later reported. That was an understatement. Only twenty-two artillerymen occupied the fortress; they had among them only 325 rounds of ammunition. The previous night Hussein's men had cut off their water so that the twenty-two had only a single cistern containing perhaps a day's supply. As a result of the blockade, they had stockpiled very little food.

All that day the Arabs kept up continual firing at Hamidiye. The single detachment of soldiers protecting the bakery and granary returned fire, but the Arabs outnumbered and outgunned them. Increasingly desperate, the acting commandant appealed for help to Taif, not realizing that Ottoman forces there were under attack by Abdullah. He dispatched his personal servant with a plea for help. The Arabs captured this unfortunate man immediately. Eventually the acting commandant tried the barracks once more, this time by telephone, but "the line was cut." Meanwhile the heavy guns at the fort remained strangely mute. "I tried to communicate with the fort but no sooner did the private pass out of the door than he was shot." His own soldiers at the granary and the bakery had only eight to ten rounds of ammunition left.

So passed the first day of the Arab Revolt in Mecca. On the second day, June 11, the fortress at last commenced a bombardment of the ground near and about Hamidiye. But by then the Turkish position was dire. Slowly but inexorably and from all sides, the Arabs advanced upon Ottoman headquarters. They occupied adjoining buildings. Others pumped petroleum onto the great wooden gates. They would burn their way in. Soon flames were licking at the structure. The Turks had no water to put the fire out. They had run out of ammunition. The acting commandant "was overpowered by the smoke . . . in a fainting condition." Then he saw a representative of the grand sharif, striding toward him through the chaos. He "heard him speak to me in reassuring terms . . . A minute later I was being led to the Emaret as a prisoner in the hands of the rebels." The first and most important part of the siege of Mecca was finished, and the Arab rebels were victorious.

It was only a first gust but in mid-June 1916 Britons and Arabs together had loosed a desert wind, a sirocco, upon the Middle East. From Mecca and Medina and Taif it would reach over and down to Basra and up and across to Damascus. Palestine would feel it too, but already a countervailing storm was brewing there. Some of the very same men working the Arab bellows had sufficient strength and purpose to pump a second pair as well. They would stir up a different storm. We turn at last to the subject of London and Zion.

PART II

London and Zion

CHAPTER 8

Prewar British Jews

ON THE THIRD DAY OF MARCH 1913 an elegantly dressed middle-aged man approached the entrance to the British Foreign Office in White-hall. Nahum Sokolow had receding brown hair, blue eyes, a mustache, and a trim goatee. Born fifty-three years earlier in Wyszogrod, Russian Poland, he was descended from a line of distinguished rabbis, and himself a brilliant student, indeed deemed a prodigy by his teachers, he had been destined originally for the rabbinate too. But a religious career did not appeal to him. He left the village shtetl for Warsaw and made his livelihood in the world of letters. He learned to write and speak fluently in more than half a dozen languages. By 1913 he was a newspaper proprietor and editor and one of the best-known and most prolific Jewish journalists and litterateurs in the world.

He also served on the actions committee, or executive board, of the World Zionist Organization, whose headquarters were located in Berlin. Nahum Sokolow's diplomatic and political skills more than equaled his talent for journalism and writing. They were not the result of formal training; he had picked them up, one must assume, in the salons of Warsaw, and in Cologne, where he relocated to serve the Zionists, and later in Berlin; also perhaps from the diplomats and politicians he met as a journalist. In any event he learned them well. As one who knew and worked with him would later write: "His handsome appearance, his air of fine breeding, his distinguished manner, his gentle speech, his calculated expression, his cautious action, his well-cut clothes, his monocle [made him] the diplomatist of the Zionist Movement." Already in 1913 Sokolow had traveled the world for the Zionists, honing his diplomatic expertise on European officials, Turkish bureaucrats, Arab leaders, and fellow Jewish nationalists from many countries. His purpose this day was to meet with Foreign Office representatives and through them to bring the British government up-to-date on Zionist affairs and accomplishments. The long-term goal, of course, was to enlist their support. Nahum Sokolow did not think that would happen anytime soon.

The Foreign Office occupied a grand edifice in 1913, as it does today, within surroundings that could hardly fail to impress. The building's eastern facade stretches the length of Parliament Street in Whitehall; its Italianate western frontage includes a six-story tower overlooking the white-pebbled Horse Guards Parade, where jousting tournaments used to take place during the reign of Henry VIII. In 1913 occasional ceremonies and exhibitions still were held on the parade grounds, but usually red-jacketed, metal-helmeted, mounted sentries from the Queen's Household Cavalry stood permanent guard there. Beyond the parade lies lush St. James's Park and its lake, which together provide an almost pastoral backdrop, suggesting the parkland of a vast royal country estate.

Inside the building marble floors and columns, a grand red-carpeted staircase outlined by polished gleaming banisters, arched windows, glowing chandeliers, and elaborately patterned ceilings and walls could not be more different from the interior of any public building in provincial Poland—or provincial anywhere. The men who worked at the Foreign Office in 1913 knew this. When it came to measuring themselves against visitors, no matter how distinguished and no matter where from, they suffered few insecurities.

The Jew from Wyszogrod had to cool his heels for nearly three months before entering. Soon after his arrival in England he applied for an appointment, and two months later, on February 12, 1913, an official grudgingly got around to acknowledging that "somebody could see him if he calls, but [because Turkey, a friendly power, opposed the Jewish nationalist movement] the less we have to do with the Zionists the better." Three weeks after that Sokolow finally got inside the door. We cannot know what his private feelings and hesitations might have been, but he would have taken in the splendid surroundings without betraying them. When he learned that Foreign Office permanent under secretary Sir Arthur Nicolson had no time to receive him after all, Sokolow would not have allowed even a shadow to cross his face.

Instead he concentrated his well-honed diplomatic skills upon Nicolson's private secretary, the Earl of Onslow. Smoothly, even charmingly no doubt, the Zionist diplomat explained to this gentleman that his movement aspired to till the soil of Palestine; that it had successfully established more than two dozen agricultural colonies there; and that it had its difficulties with Ottoman officials and policies. "It [is] to the advantage of Great Britain," he said, "to have the Jewish element increase in a country next door to Egypt," but the point was not taken. Indeed, little of Sokolow's message seems to have gotten through. "Jews have never made good agriculturalists," Nicolson sniffed after conferring with his aide about the meeting. "In any case we had better not intervene to support the Zionist movement. The implantation of Jews is a question of internal administration on which there is great division of opinion in Turkey. The Arabs and the old Turks detest the movement."

No doubt the Earl of Onslow behaved with impeccable courtesy during his ninety-minute interview with the Zionist diplomat; no doubt, too, so acute an observer as Nahum Sokolow privately registered the earl's unexpressed disdain for Zionism. Still he refused to be discouraged. The World Zionist Federation had had few if any formal contacts with British officials since the death of its founder Theodor Herzl nearly a decade before. The reestablishment of relations, however tenuous, was cause for satisfaction. Moreover, the great powers must consider the question of Palestine *someday,* and then this initial visit would be viewed as "a preparatory step."

In the meantime Nahum Sokolow would work to consolidate the toehold he had gained. A little more than a year later, he wrote to request a second audience. The Zionists had been busy; the Foreign Office should receive an update. It was July 1914, however, and unknown to him, Europe was teetering. Foreign Office mandarins were even less inclined to meet with him than before. "It is not really necessary," one wrote, "that anyone's time should be wasted in this way, but as M. Sokolow has been received before I suppose we might tell him that we shall be happy to see him again. I strongly object, however, to being myself the victim." In the end no one was victimized, except perhaps for Nahum Sokolow, and he had merely wasted his time. "I think," decided the responsible official, "we can safely reply that no useful purpose would be served by a verbal statement but that if he will be good enough to submit a report in writing it will receive careful consideration." Sokolow appears not to have written the report. No doubt its composition was interrupted when, only a few weeks later, the European powers descended into the madness of world war.

Not too many months later, when the Foreign Office discovered an interest in Zionism after all, Sokolow would be back. But prewar indifference to Jewish nationalism was widespread; the British public, including the vast majority of British Jews, shared it. Of 300,000 Jews living in Britain in 1913, only 8,000 belonged to a Zionist organization. Of the 150,000 Jews living in London, fewer than 4,000 called themselves Zionists. The great majority of British Jews were recent immigrants, or were the children of immigrants, refugees from the pogroms of Russia and eastern and southern Europe. They found new homes in the squalid "two-up, two-downs" of East London's narrow streets and alleyways and in the less salubrious quarters of the great industrial cities like Manchester and Leeds and other provincial centers. They labored in sweatshops as tailors and furriers and seamstresses; they served as clerks and shop assistants and bookkeepers; they toiled in northern factories and mills. Some succeeded in opening their own small shops or businesses. Intent upon earning their daily bread, such people had little time for Zionists, who spoke to them of a promised land several thousand miles away in Palestine. Few wished to deny their Jewish heritage, but few wished to assert it by joining a utopian movement, populated, as they thought, by dreamers and visionaries.

Jews whose families had lived in Britain for more than a generation or two were even less likely than the newcomers to identify with the Zionists. Some of them had prospered as businessmen or financiers; others had entered the liberal professions. Among this fortunate minority, an even smaller number had grown extraordinarily rich. In London the families occupying this apex of Jewish society lived in the West End and were referred to as the "Cousinhood." This informally designated body consisted of only a few extended families, often linked by marriage: the Rothschilds, Montefiores, Mocattas, Cohens, Goldsmids, Samuels, and Montagus, to name some of the most prominent. Most of them were active in the worlds of finance and philanthropy; a few had risen in politics to enter Parliament, where they sat on both sides of the House. Two literal cousins belonging to the Cousinhood, Herbert Samuel and Edwin Montagu, served in Asquith's Liberal government.

Such figures lived like other Englishmen of their class, set apart from them, however, by the religion they practiced and the response it evoked

among certain of their fellow citizens. But British anti-Semitism was relatively mild, and as a result most of the Cousinhood viewed with patriotic
affection the country that since 1858 had afforded them and their coreligionists equal civil and political rights. They considered themselves to be
Jewish Britons, not British Jews, and they abhorred Zionists, who insisted
that Jews constituted a separate people or nation, unassimilable by Britain
or by any other country except Palestine.

This did not mean that they ignored the plight of Jews already settled in
Palestine. Some among the Cousinhood were generous in their support.
But they did not wish to live there themselves, and they did not believe that
establishment of a larger Jewish presence there would contribute much to a
solution of the "Jewish problem" in Russia or Romania, or lead to the re-
duction of anti-Semitism more generally. That a latent sympathy for Zionism underlay this prewar indifference became apparent only a few years
later. World War I changed everything, including the attitude of the British
government toward both the so-called Zionist dreamers and the Ottoman
Empire. Once Zionism entered the realm of practical politics, British Jews
flocked to the Zionist banner. Interestingly, however, many among the
Cousinhood continued to hold themselves aloof.

In prewar England three main Zionist associations struggled to gain
purchase. The most important, historically speaking, was the English Zionist Federation (EZF). This body, founded in 1899, was the local branch of
the World Zionist Organization that the Austrian Theodor Herzl had established two years before. On the eve of World War I about fifty EZF
branches dotted the map of Britain in the provincial cities and important
towns, in some of the universities, and in London. Its membership rolls
contained about four thousand dues-payers. But the prewar EZF did not
flourish, lacking impact upon the mass of poor immigrant Jews and upon
the British Jewish establishment, including the Cousinhood. It contained a
number of able men, including a few with outsize personalities; but its impact upon prewar Britain, Jewish and non-Jewish, was negligible.

Aside from its seeming utopianism, the EZF failed to prosper before the
war because its leadership engaged in unedifying quarrels, sniping, and
backstabbing. Plain cussedness and egotism prompted much of it, but a
genuine ideological difference existed as well, mirroring a split in the international movement. Some Zionists held, as Herzl had done, that their
proper role was political and diplomatic: Zionists must focus on persuading
the great powers to support establishment of a Jewish homeland in Palestine. The Turkish sultan and his government must be the first target of
their politicking, since Palestine lay within the Ottoman Empire.

Britain, which was relatively free of anti-Semitism, was both liberal and imperial, held extensive interests in the Middle East, and still possessed some influence over Turkey, should be the second target. Germany represented a third, and Russia a fourth, but especially for British Zionists, the latter two powers were very much an afterthought. They agreed with Herzl that the great fulcrum upon which Zionists could shift world opinion was in England. During his visits to Britain, Herzl met with Liberal and Conservative politicians and other influential people, testified to a parliamentary commission, and addressed public and private meetings. In other words, he did his best to utilize the fulcrum. In 1914 Leopold Greenberg, proprietor and editor of Britain's leading Jewish newspaper, *The Jewish Chronicle,* and Joseph Cowen, a shirt manufacturer and current president of the EZF, still were trying to do that.

Herzl never found the proper lever, however, and because the plight of Jews in Russia especially remained dire, some political Zionists developed an alternative strategy. Herzl himself broached it in 1903 in Basel, Switzerland, at the sixth Zionist Congress, after meeting with British colonial secretary Joseph Chamberlain and British foreign secretary Lord Lansdowne. Lansdowne had offered to allow unrestricted Jewish immigration into Uganda. East Africa was not Palestine, Herzl acknowledged to the Congress, but it could be a safe refuge for any Jew wishing to leave Russia. The recent bloody pogrom in Kishinev, where at least forty-seven Jews had been murdered, many hundreds injured, and their property looted and destroyed, proved the necessity of this new strategy. Moreover Uganda need not be a permanent resting place for the immigrants—they could move on to Palestine if and when it opened to them.

A majority of Zionist delegates supported Herzl's line of reasoning, but the opposition was intense. The very Russian Jews most in danger of pogroms, including the Zionist delegates from Kishinev, led the charge against it. In his willingness to abandon Palestine, even if only temporarily, they charged, Herzl had proved himself a traitor to Zionism. Their feelings ran so high that they marched out of the hall. In the end, without abating their hostility in the slightest degree, they agreed to a temporary compromise: An exploratory group would report back the following year on Uganda's suitability for colonization. But Herzl died that year, of a broken heart according to some, and the East African scheme, although debated again at the next Zionist Congress, in 1905, essentially died with him.

In the years before World War I political Zionists divided between those for whom Palestine was the sine qua non and the territorials, who believed that a way station in Uganda or somewhere else deserved consideration. In the wake of the 1905 congress, when Uganda was taken off the table, some of the territorials, led by a charismatic Englishman, the author Israel Zangwill, broke away from the Zionist Federation altogether to found their own Jewish Territorial Association (ITO). This constituted a second Zionist organization in Britain, apart from the EZF, although since it did not necessarily aim for Palestine, it was Zionist mainly in the sense that it was Jewish nationalist. By 1914 it had a headquarters in London and branches scattered throughout Europe. It had about as many British members as the EZF did. Its strategy was to get the desperate Jews of Russia and Romania somewhere else—in fact, almost anywhere else that was safe. Uganda now was closed to them, but the ITO helped Jews move, or looked into the possibility of helping them move, to Galveston, Texas, Mesopotamia, Western Australia, British Honduras, Brazil, Mexico, and Cyrenaica, among other places. From those locations, if ever it became truly feasible, and if they wished to do so, the Jews could decamp yet again, this time for Palestine.

Meanwhile, within the EZF, a faction of practical Zionists emerged to constitute a powerful opposition to the politicals. Moses Gaster, the *haham* or chief rabbi of the Sephardic Jews in Britain, took the lead among this contingent. An extraordinary figure, Romanian born, bearded and bulky and tall, quarrelsome and egotistical, Gaster was also a profound scholar of Jewish and Middle Eastern history, linguistics (he could speak and write in ten languages), mythology, and even English folklore. Unfortunately Gaster quarreled not only with politicals such as Greenberg and Cowen but with his fellow practicals too. Indeed there appears to have been virtually no one with whom the learned *haham* did not quarrel eventually.

In one respect the practicals resembled Zangwill's territorials: They did not believe that a great power would support establishment of a homeland for the Jews in Palestine anytime soon. Unlike the territorials, however, they failed to find Uganda, or any other temporary substitute for the Promised Land, even slightly beguiling. They fashioned an alternative strategy to both territorial and political Zionism that emphasized building up Jewish society within Palestine as it was, and strengthening Jewish culture throughout the lands of the Diaspora. They worked to settle Jewish immigrants in the agricultural colonies and in Palestinian towns; to improve conditions for them; and to establish schools, hospitals, clinics, and the like. Simultaneously they strove to turn Hebrew into a living language. They founded a Hebrew journal to publish Hebrew literature and poetry. Above all they wished to establish a Hebrew university in Jerusalem. It would be a beacon and a shining example; it would showcase Jewish abilities and accomplishments. They believed that eventually a Jewish homeland would be built upon such practical and cultural accomplishments, that in fact they were its precondition.

Personality clashes and the ideological rift between political and practical Zionists eventually led the latter group, Gaster at their head, to partially secede from the EZF. Without giving up membership in the parent body, the WZF, they managed to take over a third Jewish organization in Britain with Zionist inclinations, a debating society called the Ancient Order of Maccabeans, and to persuade the WZF that Zionist affairs in Britain should be managed by a Joint Zionist Council composed of EZF members and Maccabeans working together. Zangwill's ITO remained an outlier, unrepresented in the WZF. This was the arrangement on the eve of World War I.

Finally, still another tendency arose among these fissiparous English Zionists, although its aim was to bridge the fissures. After all, the practicals had never abandoned politics and diplomacy altogether, only deemphasized them in favor of practical and cultural work. Now a group among the culturals argued for a synthesis of practical, cultural, and political-diplomatic Zionism. At the 1911 WZF congress they carried the day. Just before the outbreak of war, this synthetic approach more or less characterized the international organization, but not the EZF, in which the obstinate politicals Greenberg and Cowen remained influential.

The leader and spokesman of the synthetic Zionists at the 1911 congress was a delegate from Britain belonging to the WZF's actions committee. Chaim Weizmann was also a leader of a so-called Democratic Fraction of Zionists that while not explicitly advocating strategy or tactics, did so implicitly by objecting to Herzl's grand airs and to the grandees surrounding him. This advocate of both synthesis and simplicity was "pre-eminently what the Jewish people call *folks-mensch*," wrote one who came to know Weizmann very well, "a man of the people, of the masses, not of the elite, a leader in whose breast beat the common heart of man." Originally from Russia, the *folks-mensch* was sturdily built, of perhaps a little more than middle height, with a great dome of a forehead and a short dark beard covering his cheeks and jaw. He had attended every Zionist congress except the first. Though well known within the WZF, he was by no means a power in its English branch. In 1911 he successfully ran for election as one of its two vice presidents. That brought him a few steps nearer the top, but he still spent the prewar years in relative obscurity within the world of English Zionism, laboring hard on the practical and cultural fronts, especially on the campaign to build a Hebrew University in Jerusalem. Later all the Zionists

in Britain would recognize that he possessed an unrivaled talent for Her-
zlian political and diplomatic work. Chaim Weizmann, more than any
other individual, would orchestrate the wartime campaign for British support of a Jewish homeland in Palestine.

Born in Motol, near Pinsk, Russia, in 1874, Weizmann was the son of a
relatively prosperous timber transporter. As a child he excelled at his studies, beginning in his village's filthy single-room *cheder* (Jewish elementary
school). At secondary school in Pinsk, which was slightly less insalubrious,
one of his teachers instilled in him an abiding love of science, particularly
chemistry. This subject he chose to pursue at the university level, but in
Germany, not in Russia, where the obstacles placed before Jews who aspired to higher education were humiliating and nearly insuperable. He
then carried out his graduate work in Switzerland and earned his doctorate
summa cum laude in 1899 from the University of Fribourg. In 1904 he took
up a post at the University of Manchester in a chemistry lab. Six years later
he became a naturalized British subject.

Weizmann loved his laboratory and would do important work there,
but he loved Zion more. That was a central theme of the *cheder* he had attended in Motol, where his instructors taught him in Yiddish, not Russian.
It was a central theme of his university days too, when he played a leading
role in the Russian-Jewish Academic Society in Berlin. He had always at
heart been a fervent Zionist, although sometimes, from impatience or disgust or exhaustion, he sought to distance himself from the movement. One
of these episodes occurred in 1904 after Herzl recommended the Uganda
scheme, which Weizmann opposed vehemently. It was then that he
thought to begin a new life in Britain. But such emotions never lasted long.
He stayed in Britain, coming eventually to revere it, but by 1905 he was
back in harness for the Zionists again.

Although Weizmann opposed Herzl's Ugandan gambit, many of the
London politicals, Greenberg and Cowen among them, favored it. In fact
Greenberg, a natural-born wire-puller, had been instrumental in bringing
Herzl and Joseph Chamberlain together. When Weizmann arrived in England, he found himself ostracized by the politicals, who held his opposition to Herzl against him. Greenberg would hardly speak to him. But the
practicals, including the volcanic Gaster, embraced him, indeed sought to
administer a bear hug. But the *haham* was never a reliable or easy ally.
Weizmann would cooperate with him when necessary, but before long he
built up an alternative Zionist base in Manchester, where he continued to
pursue his academic career. This Manchester school of Zionists would later

prove an important source of money and brains for British Zionism; it would come to rival London for influence. Moreover it provided Weizmann with comradeship and spiritual sustenance of incalculable value.

A remarkable trio—Harry Sacher, Israel Sieff, and Simon Marks—constituted the heart of Weizmann's Manchester school. Sacher was born in 1881 in London, the son of naturalized Polish Jews. His father labored as a self-employed tailor. Like Sokolow and Weizmann before him, Sacher excelled as a student. He gained entrance to New College, Oxford, no mean feat for a Jew without important connections, and went on to earn a first in history. He continued his studies at the Universities of Paris and Berlin. But when he failed to win a fellowship at his old college, he took up a position with the great liberal newspaper, *The Manchester Guardian*. For an interlude in London he was called to the bar; and for a time he worked for *The London Daily News;* but soon after 1914 he returned to the *Guardian*. This momentous step would enable him to facilitate a developing friendship between his friend and mentor in Zionism, Chaim Weizmann, and his friend and mentor in British liberalism, the *Guardian*'s editor, C. P. Scott. The latter would prove crucial to Weizmann's political ascent.

Sacher, seven years younger than Weizmann, never escaped the latter's shadow nor even tried to, serving always as a junior collaborator and aide. But he held strong views of his own, indeed appears to have been something of an iconoclast. His opinions did not always coincide with Weizmann's. At times the great man felt that Sacher was a thorn in his side, more trouble than he was worth. They quarreled often; their correspondence is full of accusations and justifications and reconciliations. But neither Sacher nor Weizmann was difficult *au fond,* as Gaster was. No breach between them ever proved so wide that it could not be bridged. The two remained close friends throughout our period.

As for Simon Marks and Israel Sieff, who were, respectively, seven and eight years younger than Sacher and therefore very much junior to Weizmann, they played lesser roles in Zionist deliberations regarding policy and strategy but greater roles as facilitators, fund-raisers, and organizers. Like Sacher, they offered their acknowledged leader valuable spiritual nourishment and friendship. The two had grown up on the same street in Manchester, attended the same primary and secondary schools in the same class, and gone into business together, founding what eventually became the Marks & Spencer chain of department stores. Sieff appears to have been closer to Weizmann, serving as his unpaid personal assistant. He later wrote that when they first met, Weizmann swept him off his feet; Sieff wished to impress him and boasted that he could raise more money for

Weizmann's Zionist efforts than anyone else. Weizmann put him to the test, admitting that he had great need of a good *schnorrer* (Yiddish for an engaging beggar). Sieff passed the test with flying colors.

Sacher, Sieff, and Marks would occupy a secondary tier in the Zionist leadership, subordinate to Weizmann and Sokolow, during the maneuvering that preceded the Balfour Declaration. Their role, especially Sacher's, was more complex than has hitherto been appreciated. It is an odd tangential part of our story that Marks married Sieff's sister and that both Sacher and Sieff married sisters of Simon Marks. The Zionists seemed to have had their own Cousinhood.

The other Zionist to whom Weizmann grew very close before the war was Asher Ginzberg, who he acknowledged was wiser and more experienced in Zionist and Jewish affairs than himself. Ginzberg had moved from Russia to London in 1907 to represent the interests of the Wissotsky Tea Company. At first glance he did not impress, being slight and bald, with a thin, bearded, bespectacled face, but in fact he was formidable, charismatic, and iron-willed. Among all the prominent Zionists of this period, it was Ginzberg who thought most seriously about the Arabs living in Palestine. He criticized Zionist attitudes toward them: "We are used to thinking of the Arabs as primitive men of the desert, as a donkey-like nation that neither sees nor understands what is going on around it. But that is a great error." As early as 1891 he warned against the "repressive cruelty" employed by Zionists in their dealings with Arabs. Instinctively an advocate of underdogs, he belonged to the Democratic Fraction of the WZF, in which Weizmann played an important role.

Ginzberg condemned Herzl's political Zionism, regarding the proposed move to Uganda as a scheme for a quick solution to the "Jewish problem" through emigration. There could be no shortcut to Zion, Ginzberg argued. In fact, negotiating with the sultan, the kaiser, or the British colonial secretary wasted effort and time. Even planting colonies in Palestine missed the point.

Ginzberg was probably the chief and most effective advocate of cultural Zionism. An observant Jew, he was not religious in a conventional sense. While always insisting upon the spiritual value of a Hebrew renaissance, he emphasized Judaism's rational and ethical aspects. Judaism was to him an ethos and approach to life, which he thought must permeate the Jewish people and become inseparable from daily living. Only that way, he wrote, could lovers of Zion attain their great goal. An accomplished journalist, essayist, and when occasion demanded polemicist, he published only in the Hebrew language, in a prose that was remarkably spare and precise. The man who did not waste words adopted the pen name Ahad Ha'am, "one of the people."

So during those years before the war Chaim Weizmann, the *folks-mensch* from Motol, sometimes took the train down to London to visit his fellow Russian, Ahad Ha'am, "one of the people." They would have explored and developed their understanding of spiritual and cultural Zionism; they would have pondered goals and tactics and strategies. They would have deplored the attitudes of the politicals like Greenberg and Cowen and vented, or perhaps chuckled, over the antics of the difficult *haham,* Moses Gaster. When the war broke out, Weizmann naturally turned first of all to his admired friend, Ahad Ha'am, to discuss what Zionists ought to do.

In August 1914 Zionists lacked easy entrée to the Foreign Office, but a Jewish anti-Zionist, Lucien Wolf, did have access to it, if not always easily.

Wolf was director of the Conjoint Foreign Committee of British Jews, the offspring of two parent bodies. One was the Board of Deputies of British Jews, which by 1914 had been offering guidance to the British Jewish community, molding British Jewish opinion, and representing that opinion to the British government for a century and a half. The board consisted of delegates elected by members of British synagogues, but it was not a religious body, let alone a truly representative one. In fact it was dominated by the Cousinhood, and since its foundation in 1760, this elite section of British Jewry had successfully worked the board behind the scenes. True, one of its presidents, Moses Montefiore, became famous for drawing public attention to the persecution of Jews abroad, but he did so in his capacity as a private citizen. The board did not sponsor his ex officio activities. It did not wish to draw attention to itself or to British Jews more generally because it did not wish to give a handle to anti-Semites who might deem the board, or British Jews, too influential. For all that the board spoke for the community to the outside world, it looked inward, conceiving of the community it represented as a distinct and potentially embattled entity, and it strove mightily to protect it.

The other parent of the Conjoint Committee, the Anglo-Jewish Association (AJA), had been founded in 1871 and boasted a membership as socially elite as that of the Board of Deputies. All who belonged to the AJA paid an annual subscription of at least a guinea (a pound and a shilling, which was a substantial sum in those days). The AJA did not even pretend to be a representative body. Nor did it aspire to exercise the kind of communal authority that the board did. It aimed to protect Jews from anti-Semitism both at home and abroad. It took public political positions on their behalf. It held that British Jews differed from Quaker, Congregationalist, and Catholic Britons only in the religious belief system to which they adhered. The Board of Deputies maintained that British Jews constituted a distinct entity; the Zionists contended that they were a distinct nation; but the AJA argued that British Jews were Britons who happened also to be Jewish. One AJA leader went so far as to found a Reform synagogue whose outward forms of worship differed little from Anglican forms.

The Board of Deputies and the AJA, while maintaining their distinct identities, came together in 1878 to found the Conjoint Foreign Committee of British Jews because both groups wished to more effectively sway British foreign policy where Jewish interests were at stake. The AJA welcomed the combination because it thought a conjoint committee could more effectively advocate on behalf of Jews living in countries where assimilation was impossible. The board welcomed it, even though it meant abandoning its traditional low profile, because Moses Montefiore had retired; board members feared that without him they could lose all influence over government foreign policy. The Conjoint Committee numbered fourteen members, six each from the two parent bodies, which maintained their separate existence, plus their presidents, who would serve as president and vice president of the new committee in alternating years.

The two groups established the Conjoint Committee in 1878 specifically to influence the Congress of Berlin, which was about to meet in the wake of the Russo-Turkish War. In its first public intervention the Conjoint Committee lobbied British officials on behalf of Balkan Jews. It wanted them to encourage the congress to establish religious toleration throughout the Near East and especially in Romania. At first the British officials' efforts appeared to bear fruit: The congress mandated religious toleration, just as the Conjoint Committee had hoped it would. But toleration of religious minorities was never put into effective practice in the Balkans before 1914. Romania especially ignored it.

In 1878 the Conjoint Committee's future director, Lucien Wolf, was twenty-one years old. Born in London, he was the son of a Bohemian pipe manufacturer who took part in the revolutions of 1848 and fled to England after their failure. Thus while Lucien Wolf would later work closely with the Cousinhood, he came from a relatively modest background.

He learned from his father to cherish British liberal traditions: political and economic freedom, religious tolerance. He attended schools in Brussels and Paris and learned to write and speak in French and German as fluently

as in English. That he was a patriotic Briton cannot be doubted, but he radiated the cosmopolitanism of a continental sophisticate. A man of medium
height and build, he sported nearly a handlebar mustache; his brown hair
thinned as he aged. His eyes were weak, and he wore thick spectacles. He
smoked cigarettes. Like Nahum Sokolow, Wolf became a brilliant and brilliantly successful journalist, with an interest in Jewish affairs. Simultaneously he honed an untutored genius for diplomacy.

Wolf's attitude toward Jewish matters was complex. He rejected the notion, common in the AJA, that Jewish Britons were indistinguishable from
other Britons except for their faith. Early in the twentieth century Claude
Montefiore, a nephew of Moses Montefiore and a long-serving president of
the AJA, developed Liberal Judaism, which eliminated ritual and national
identification altogether and emphasized moral and ethical values and a
vague monotheism that might appeal to anyone. Wolf publicly rebuked
him. "To denationalize" Judaism, he charged in *The Jewish World* in September 1882, would be "to lose it and with it the work of 50 centuries." In
Judaism, he maintained, the religion and the race were "almost indistinguishable."

At times he seemed almost to embrace cultural Zionism. He actively
nurtured Jewish cultural organizations such as the Jewish Historical Society, the Jewish Literary Society, and the Union of Jewish Literary Societies.
He joined the Ancient Order of Maccabeans, whose aim in part was "the
promotion of the interests of the Jewish race," and which as we have seen
came eventually under the sway of Moses Gaster and other cultural Zionists.

But Wolf was not quite a cultural Zionist: It was the history of the Jewish people (from which their ethnic and religious identities could not be
separated) that moved him most deeply. But ethnic labels meant little to
him, and religion as such even less. He wrote that a friend "once said of me
that my Judaism was not a religion at all but a cult of auld lang syne. I think
he was right." He was too much of a liberal to embrace the Jewish nationalism that was the raison d'être of even the most cultural Zionists. Jews
could assimilate in an adopted homeland without losing their cultural dis-
tinctiveness, he believed, if only their hosts were sufficiently enlightened,
which is to say sufficiently liberal. In fact, he judged Zionism to be a creed
of anti-liberalism and despair, precisely because it rejected assimilation on
the grounds that "anti-Semitism is unconquerable." To his dying day, Wolf
insisted that it could be conquered. In the end he chose to work with
Claude Montefiore, founder of Liberal Judaism, after all, although he con-

tinued to think the creed "chilly" and "high flown." He did not identify with Ahad Ha'am, exponent of cultural Judaism and cultural Zionism.

Wolf abhorred Russia's official anti-Semitism, and his unsparing and trenchant criticisms of it brought him to the attention of the Conjoint Committee. After the pogrom in Kishinev in 1903, the committee approached him for advice on how best to mobilize the Foreign Office to protest to Russia. Ironically, Claude Montefiore, AJA president and therefore one of two protagonists on the Conjoint Committee, must have been instrumental in the decision to contact his former critic. Wolf's connection with the committee would last for twenty years; the relationship with Montefiore lasted even longer. The founder of Liberal Judaism would deliver a moving eulogy at Wolf's funeral in 1930.

Between 1908 and 1914, when Balkan Jews were in continuous danger, Wolf gained control over the Conjoint Committee's relationship with the Foreign Office. Ostensibly subordinate to the committee's two presidents, Montefiore and David Lindo Alexander, in fact Wolf established an ascendancy over them, turning the committee into a sort of shadow Foreign Office. He cemented relationships with various Foreign Office figures. Subtle, dexterous, indefatigable, and knowledgeable, Wolf shuttled between meetings with the Conjoint Committee and meetings at the Foreign Office. His last great prewar effort was to persuade the Foreign Office to reaffirm the commitment to religious liberty that the great powers had stated at the Congress of Berlin in 1878. He got the statement on July 28, 1914. Catastrophe broke upon the world only a week later.

Even better positioned to influence Britain's foreign policy was Herbert Samuel, a member of the Cousinhood who in 1914 belonged to the cabinet of Liberal Prime Minister Herbert Henry Asquith. Son of a prosperous banker, Samuel had graduated from Balliol College, Oxford, with a first-class degree. In 1889 he took part in his older brother Stuart's successful campaign to represent the East End district of Whitechapel on the London County Council. Whitechapel was a filthy, impoverished, and overcrowded neighborhood, the home of many thousands of recent Jewish immigrants. The terrible conditions Samuel saw there moved him deeply. Governments exist to ameliorate poverty, he concluded, a conviction that never left him. His early political connections were with the radical wing of the Liberal Party and the moderate Fabian wing of socialism. In 1902 he published *Liberalism: Its Principles and Proposals,* which would provide a moral and practical foundation for many of the reforms that the Asquith government carried out only a few years later.

Samuel's political ascent also began in 1902, when he gained entrance to Parliament. When the Liberals won the general election of 1905, he gained minor government office, and then in 1909 he gained cabinet rank as chancellor of the Duchy of Lancaster. Five years later he climbed higher still, to become president of the Local Government Board. As he advanced, he learned impassivity. Although he still believed in the meliorating role of government, "he conveys no impression of enthusiasm," wrote a journalist, "and is as free from passion as an oyster." He championed mild, incremental social reform, such as an act ending child imprisonment, restricting corporal punishment, and establishing juvenile courts. His approach was piecemeal and painstaking. The same journalist wrote that he was "a splendidly efficient instrument, but never an inspiration."

Nor was he much liked by his colleagues, who judged him, unfairly, to be both interfering and self-serving. Anti-Semitism may have lain at the root of this dislike. Certainly it was at the root of an ugly episode, the Marconi Scandal, in which he became embroiled in 1912. Journalists discovered that several cabinet ministers, including David Lloyd George and Sir Rufus Isaacs, who was Jewish, had profited from inside knowledge to make gains on the stock market. Samuel attracted criticism too, although he had nothing to do with the business. The critics attacked him because he was Jewish.

Samuel endured this trial with characteristic stoicism, betraying little, which only furthered the false impression that he was a man of stone. But beneath his expressionless exterior, the president of the Local Government Board nursed an unexpected, indeed counterintuitive, emotional bond with the Jewish people and a romantic attachment to the goals of the Zionist movement. "Zionism was the one political passion of a singularly passionless career," writes the best historian of his life and times.

Where it came from, we cannot tell: Samuel himself never said. He seemed the sort of wealthy, assimilated, disconnected Jew whom Zionists despised. Yet he cherished his link with his father's brother and business partner, Samuel Montagu (who had reversed his first and last names). Montagu was in the Cousinhood but not entirely of it. Immensely wealthy and forceful, he took his religion seriously. He visited Palestine more than once and wished to purchase land there. Not a formal Zionist, he had many Zionist connections. When Herbert Samuel's father died unexpectedly, Montagu interested himself in his nephew. Perhaps his preoccupations influenced the younger man.

Samuel had a second, more direct connection with Zionism: none other than the disputatious practical of the EZF, Rabbi Moses Gaster. The link came via Samuel's wife, one of whose childhood friends had gone on to marry the *haham* of England's Sephardic Jews. The wives remained close, and as a result the two couples socialized on occasion. At least once Gaster sought a political favor from Samuel, asking him to help obtain naturalization papers for a Russian émigré, none other than Chaim Weizmann. Samuel obliged. Naturally enough, when sometime later he became acquainted with Zionist ideas, he looked to Gaster for reading material. "I remember Dr. Gaster being associated from time to time with my early inquiries into the Zionist Movement," Samuel later recalled. That happened after 1914, but before the war he held at least "a benevolent goodwill toward the Zionist idea," as he told the West London Zionist Association in 1919. He had no intention in those days of doing anything about it.

The announcement of war on August 4, 1914, fell upon Herbert Samuel like a thunderclap, as it did upon Chaim Weizmann and Nahum Sokolow and Lucien Wolf. For these men, as for so many, it had profound impact upon their lives, which now would intersect in unforeseen ways. At this moment of supreme crisis, prime ministers and monarchs and generals occupied center stage. But the proto-Zionist Herbert Samuel, the *folks-mensch* Chaim Weizmann, the subtle diplomat Nahum Sokolow, and the anti-Zionist Lucien Wolf—the Jewish protagonists in the struggle for and against the Balfour Declaration—were waiting in the wings.

CHAPTER 9

Weizmann's First Steps

THE DECLARATIONS OF WAR in late July and early August 1914 burst upon an unprepared world like a volley of gunshots at a summer garden party. They sliced through illusions, ripping up the pretty picture of great powers at peace and taking their ease. Austria-Hungary declared war on Serbia on July 28; Germany declared war on Russia on August 1 and on France on August 3. Britain declared war upon Germany on August 4. Initial shock quickly gave way to martial ardor, however, and then to apprehension for loved ones serving in rapidly deploying armies all over Europe. British Jews had additional worries. They feared for their coreligionists in Russia, where anti-Semitism was scaling new heights, and in Habsburg Poland, which lay directly in the path of the tsar's advancing forces.

Then Turkey gave British Zionists a reason to hope. When the Ottomans entered the war on the side of the Central Powers in early November, they called into question the future of their own empire, which meant the future of Palestine as well. It took a moment for the implication to sink in. At first even the most sophisticated and best-informed British Zionists foresaw only additional calamities. "The fate of Palestine thus becomes dreadful and, moreover, uncertain," Ahad Ha'am wrote to Weizmann. "Our colonies, our institutions—everything may now be swept away," Weizmann lamented. But then dread gave way to a wild and surging anticipation. Assume that Britain won the war, against Turkey as well as against Germany and Austria-Hungary. The Middle East would drop into the melting pot at last. And then perhaps the ingot of Palestine could be pried loose from the great slab of Turkey's Middle Eastern empire.

But should Zionists hope that Britain won the war? Zionism was a world movement—Jews lived everywhere, fought everywhere, on every front, against each other, for their respective countries of residence. The World Zionist Organization tried to insist that its various branches remain neutral, but this was impossible. Much as socialists from Germany, France, and Britain marched to the trenches (while singing the Internationale), so too Jews, even Zionists, loyally supported the wartime governments of the countries in which they lived. A typical example: Leopold Greenberg wrote on August 14 in *The Jewish Chronicle,* "England has been all she could be to the Jews; the Jews will be all they can to England." Outside his office he put up a giant placard displaying the same words.

For a British government minister such as Herbert Samuel, neutrality was obviously impossible. But the Ottoman attack on Russia in early November, like a flash of lightning, illumined a landscape that had been previously dark to him. "The moment Turkey entered the war the position was entirely changed," he recalled. The prewar proto-Zionist, the self-described "first member of the Jewish community ever to sit in a British Cabinet" (Disraeli, born Jewish, had converted to Christianity at age twelve), emerged as the Zionist movement's most effective and highly placed champion. He could and would combine his duties to Britain with his duties, as he now conceived them, to the Jewish people.

He kept a record of his initial steps as a fully fledged, if as yet publicly undeclared, Zionist and reproduced the relevant passages verbatim in his memoirs. On November 9, 1914, only a week after Turkey entered the war, Samuel met with Foreign Secretary Sir Edward Grey in the grand building with the Italianate facade and six-story tower overlooking Horse Guards Parade and St. James's Park. He was no unfamiliar Jew from Poland seeking audience with a distant and disdainful official. He was a member of the government. For once, a Zionist had entered the inner sanctum on equal terms to discuss the future of Palestine.

He prepared carefully for the interview and came right to the point. "Perhaps," he told Sir Edward, "the opportunity might arise for the fulfillment of the ancient aspiration of the Jewish people and the restoration [in Palestine] of a Jewish state." He ticked off the reasons why Britain should support this "ancient aspiration." Most important, "the geographical situation of Palestine and especially its proximity to Egypt would render its

goodwill to England a matter of importance to the British Empire." But almost equally significant in the present wartime circumstances, if Russia
could be induced to back the Zionist policy, then Russian Jews would have
some reason to support their government. That would benefit Russia's ally
Britain. For that matter, Samuel argued, a pro-Zionist policy would rally
Jewish opinion throughout the world on behalf of the Allies.

Britain should support establishment of a Jewish state in Palestine, he
added, for less self-interested reasons. Such a state would be good not
merely for Britons but for everyone: "It might become the centre of a new
culture. The Jewish brain is rather a remarkable thing, and under national
auspices the state might become a fountain of enlightenment and a source
of a great literature and art and development of science." Obviously it
would be good for the Jews themselves: "If they could see men of their own
kin achieving great things it would have a profound influence on their outlook." And this would benefit their Middle Eastern neighbors as well:
"Raising their [the Jews'] character would add to their usefulness to the
peoples among whom they lived."

How Grey would have responded only weeks before, when Britain was
hoping to keep Turkey's goodwill, can readily be imagined. With Turkey
having chosen the wrong side in the great conflict, however, he could make
only one response. Zionism, which would undermine Turkey in the Middle
East if given free rein, finally had entered the realm of practical politics,
from the British point of view—or at least had got its toe inside the door. So
without actually committing himself to a specific policy, Grey smiled upon
a proposal that his Foreign Office subordinates had rejected, politely but
scornfully, just a few months before when put to them by Nahum Sokolow.
"The idea had always had a strong sentimental attraction for him," Samuel
recalled him saying. "The historical appeal was very strong. He was quite
favourable to the proposal and would be prepared to work for it if the opportunity arose."

Later that day Samuel broached the same subject with another colleague, chancellor of the exchequer David Lloyd George. The previous
April, Lloyd George had described the president of the Local Government
Board as "a greedy, ambitious and grasping Jew with all the worst charac-
teristics of his race"; on November 9, however, when Samuel mentioned the
"ancient aspiration" of Jews to establish a state in Palestine, Lloyd George
replied that he was "very keen to see a Jewish state established there." Thus
encouraged, Samuel prepared a memorandum on the subject for circula-
tion among the other cabinet ministers.

It is worth noting here the parallel evolution of British interest in and sympathy for the rise of both Arab and Jewish nationalism. Before the war, when Sharif Hussein's son Abdullah inquired about British support, he received polite but short shrift from Lord Kitchener and Sir Ronald Storrs in Cairo. At roughly the same time the Zionist Nahum Sokolow was leaving the Foreign Office in London equally empty-handed. But once the war was raging, and the Ottoman Empire was a declared enemy, Lord Kitchener discovered a coincidence of interest among Arabs and Britons after all. Simultaneously Grey and Lloyd George were expressing a newly avowed, but ostensibly long-held, concern for Zionist goals. Did Grey know that Kitchener had approached Abdullah? Perhaps. Did it occur to him that the Arab nationalism that Kitchener now encouraged and the Jewish nationalism that he himself supported were potentially contradictory? Probably not. Sharif Hussein and Herbert Samuel knew nothing of each other, but from now on their two movements would advance in unsuspecting tandem.

Meanwhile in London in the late summer and early fall of 1914, leading Jews were mobilizing for action. Israel Zangwill, head of the ITO, which sought a safe refuge for Jews anywhere that would take them, worried for the Austro-Polish Jews living in the path of the advancing Russian army, and for Russia's own Jews subject to ever harsher repression. Using contacts gained from his ITO work, he lobbied high-placed contacts on their behalf. Leopold Greenberg, of *The Jewish Chronicle,* shared Zangwill's fears, as well as Zangwill's hope that the British government would pressure Russia to treat Jews less vilely. Unlike Zangwill, he also hoped to persuade Britain to help them if they wished to flee to Palestine. The old wire-puller managed a brief audience with several people at the Foreign Office. "Needless to say they have enough on their hands without our 'tsuris,' " Greenberg reported somewhat ruefully. But he discerned in their reaction to him a shift in Britain's Middle Eastern policy: "I think they want to see some settlement of our question." This was before Turkey entered the war.

Despite his earlier relative unimportance, Chaim Weizmann proved during this period to be a more effective champion of Zionism than Greenberg, Zangwill, or anyone else. That he should become the undisputed leader would not have been predicted, and was even counterintuitive. During 1914–18 he mastered the political Zionist approach, which as a practical Zionist he had once condemned. The *folks-mensch* learned to circulate comfortably in august social circles. If the search for British support took him down unanticipated paths, he would follow where they led.

Unlike Greenberg and Zangwill, who looked to the government for immediate intervention on behalf of Austro-Polish and Russian Jews, Weiz-

mann approached the situation from a strategic point of view. He shared
their concern but held that only the Russians could solve the problem of
Russian anti-Semitism. Therefore, as he wrote on September 8 (to a Russian Zionist friend in New York City), he would focus instead upon "the
unification of Jewry, or such part of it as might present definite demands at
a future peace conference." The first demand, of course, would be a homeland for Jews in Palestine. Already he was thinking in terms of political
rather than practical Zionism.

He considered bringing together international Zionist notables to con-
cert their demands for the peace conference but decided instead to focus on
British Zionists. Then he decided that Zionism needed not so much to for-
mulate demands as to produce a memorandum stating the Zionist position.
For this he turned to the Manchester school, notably to Harry Sacher and to
Sacher's friend Leon Simon. Simon was a follower of Ahad Ha'am who
earned his living as a civil servant (he would rise eventually to head the
British Post Office) while serving as president of the University of London
Zionist Organization. Quickly the three set to work. Their correspondence
for the months of November and December 1914 refers often to progress
and lack of progress on the document.

Weizmann also reached out to former opponents, such as the old practicals Cowen and Greenberg. He contemplated approaching Israel Zangwill
too, despite his loathing of the ITO program, but Greenberg warned Weizmann that Zangwill "will be difficult to get into line. He takes such ferocious views and then he sticks to them so ferociously." Weizmann tried
anyway, even offering Zangwill leadership of the movement that he himself was attempting to organize. Zangwill turned him down flat: "It would
be a case of the blind leading the blind." Moreover, "I should find it difficult
to demand that the Jewish minority should rule over the Arab majority [in
Palestine]; a free and equal constitution for both races is all that is in the
British or the modern tradition."

For some months Weizmann unavailingly courted Zangwill, but he had
bigger fish to fry. The most important Jewish family in Britain, indeed in
the world, was the great banking dynasty, the House of Rothschild. Weizmann wanted the family's support for his concert of Jews preparing to submit demands to an eventual peace conference. (When that project lapsed,
he would seek it for Zionism more generally.) His prewar advocacy of a
Hebrew university in Jerusalem had brought him into contact with Baron
Edmond de Rothschild in Paris. In fact, he had visited the baron just as war

was breaking out (and had managed to return to England only with difficulty). Weizmann also knew the baron's son, James, a tall, elegant, monocle-wearing devotee of the racetrack, and owner of prizewinning horses, who in 1913, at age thirty-five, had married Dorothy (Dolly) Pinto, an Englishwoman or girl, really; she was just seventeen. With the outbreak of war, Baron James joined the French army, but Dorothy stayed in London.

On November 7 and 8 Weizmann had two long sessions with Dorothy in lieu of meeting with her husband (who already was serving in the army) or with her father-in-law (who had traveled to Bordeaux). "I tried to learn from Madame James whether Jews like [the English] Lord [Nathan Mayer] Rothschild and his circle would be willing to take any action at present, but Madame James was not well informed on these points." But Weizmann, who could exercise great fascination upon women (and men too), had touched a deep chord. Dorothy wrote to him less than two weeks later: "I have spoken to Mr. Charles Rothschild, not in any sort of way officially, but in the course of conversation he thoroughly approved of the idea [a Jewish Palestine] and in fact thought it would be the only possible future." Charles was the second son of Nathan Rothschild and the younger brother of Walter Lionel Rothschild, who would become the Lord Rothschild to whom the Balfour Declaration would be addressed. Thus were woven the first strands of a great web.

Dorothy, who was now playing the role of a political go-between for Weizmann, reported that she had also spoken with the Earl of Crewe, Asquith's secretary of state for India. Crewe was related to the Rothschilds by marriage. According to Dorothy, he too believed that "our compatriots would not be unwelcome in Palestine . . . if by some chance it became British." Crewe was very much aware of Kitchener's recent approach to Sharif Hussein. On November 12—a few days after speaking with Dorothy Rothschild about the future of Palestine—he wrote to Lord Hardinge, the Indian viceroy: "Supposing that the Arabs took up arms against the Turks I think it would be our policy to recognize a new Khalif at Mecca . . . If this were done there appears to me to be a possibility for allowing Syria to be organized as an Arab state under the Khalif." He then suggested that Europeans might indirectly control the new Arab state. But as we saw in Chapter 3, Kitchener never mentioned any such possibility to Sharif Hussein. In fact, quite the opposite; he had held out to him the prospect of Arab independence. Perfidious Albion aside, did Crewe believe that Palestinian Jews would live contentedly within a new Syrian kingdom under a newly appointed Arab caliph, even if indirectly protected by Euro-

peans? Most probably he did not think about the potential for conflict between Jews and Arabs in Syria at all. This is an early sign of the incomprehension with which some important Britons initially pursued two mutually
exclusive policies.

Weizmann, knowing nothing of Kitchener's plans for Arabia, was delighted with Dorothy Rothschild's letter. "You don't—I am sure—expect
me to acknowledge your very kind letter in ordinary conventional terms of
thanks. The action you undertook and your intention to help on a just cause
is in itself sufficient satisfaction and so much in harmony with the glorious
Jewish traditions of the house to which you belong, that my trivial thanks
would only be superfluous." Then, unexpectedly, he told her that he had
been present "in the cursed town of Kishinev during a Jewish massacre . . .
we defended the Jewish quarter with revolvers in our hands . . . We 'slept'
in the cemetery—the only 'safe' place and we saw 80 Jewish corpses
brought in, mutilated dead." Only he had not been in Kishinev during the
pogrom but in Geneva. He was making it up, trying to impress a twenty-
year-old girl.

He saw Dorothy again three days later, this time with her husband, who
was on leave from the French army. Baron James urged him "to try and influence members of the British government" and, further, to advocate to
them more ambitious goals than practical Zionism had hitherto advanced.
"One should ask for something which . . . tends towards the formation of a
Jewish State." This remark only reinforced Weizmann's developing approach, although he and his allies carefully avoided the word "state," which
they rightly deemed too controversial to introduce at the moment.

Through Baron James and Dorothy Rothschild, Weizmann now came
into contact with other members of the Rothschild family, most important
the Hungarian-born Rozsika, wife of Charles Rothschild, to whom
Dorothy had spoken about Palestine. Through Rozsika he would meet
Charles and Charles's older brother, Walter. Again the *folks-mensch* exer-
cised an irresistible fascination upon the cream of British high society.
Charles, Rozsika, and Walter would become important supporters. Eventually Rozsika outdid Dorothy as a political go-between, introducing
Weizmann to many influential figures, including Robert Cecil, a cousin of
Arthur Balfour and parliamentary under secretary of state for foreign affairs. Cecil reported to his superiors after his first meeting with Weizmann:
"It is impossible to reproduce in writing the subdued enthusiasm with
which Dr. Weizmann spoke, or the extraordinary impressiveness of his attitude, which made one forget his rather repellant and even sordid exterior." This, one suspects, is the authentic voice of the British establishment

and a faithful recapitulation of its reaction to the Zionist leader during the early war years.

Weizmann made one of his most important contacts without Rozsika's help, at a social event in Manchester, to which his wife dragged him early in November 1914. At that tea party someone introduced him to a Mr. Scott. Weizmann did not recognize the editor of Britain's most famous Liberal newspaper, *The Manchester Guardian*. "I saw before me a tall, distinguished-looking gentleman, advanced in years, but very alert and attentive. He was inquisitive about my origin and work." Weizmann told him, "I am a Jew and if you want to talk to me about that, Mr. Scott, I am at your disposal."

It was the beginning of an extraordinary partnership. They did talk, at the party and then more seriously at Scott's *Manchester Guardian* offices, or (accounts vary) possibly at his home, The Firs, a large house surrounded by extensive gardens and noble trees. Weizmann opened his heart to the older man, a complete stranger. Perhaps he sensed political affinities based upon common liberal values; possibly he had a shrewd intimation that more than mere sympathy would be forthcoming. Or conceivably, Weizmann sensed something even deeper in Scott's reaction to him, for the elderly editor would soon take almost a paternal interest in the younger man.

Scott, for his part, found Weizmann "extraordinarily interesting, a rare combination of idealism and the severely practical which are the two essentials of statesmanship." He was struck particularly by Weizmann's "perfectly clear conception of Jewish nationalism, an intense and burning sense of the Jew as Jew, just as strong, perhaps more so, as that of the German as German or the Englishman as Englishman, and secondly arising out of that and necessary for its satisfaction and development, his demand for a country, a home-land which for him and for anyone sharing his view of Jewish nationality can be no other than the ancient home of his race." But for Scott as for Grey and Lloyd George (who spoke with Herbert Samuel at roughly the same time), it was the Ottoman entry into World War I that spelled the difference between mere sympathy and active support. He asked Weizmann for a memorandum encapsulating the Zionist position. This was the document upon which Weizmann and Harry Sacher and Leon Simon worked in November and December and that came to overshadow Weizmann's initial preparations for a future peace conference.

As their second interview came to an end, Scott said to Weizmann: "I would like to do something for you." He knew most of the British government, he said, and would like Weizmann to meet Herbert Samuel, president of the Local Government Board. "For God's sake, Mr. Scott, let's have nothing to do with this man," expostulated Weizmann, assuming that a member of the Cousinhood would oppose Zionism tooth and nail.

So Scott contacted Lloyd George first and asked him to meet the extraordinary Zionist from Manchester. Lloyd George agreed—as he told Scott, he just had been talking about Zionism with Herbert Samuel. Perhaps Dr. Weizmann would meet the two of them together. ("Alas," sighed Weizmann when he heard of it, still unaware of Samuel's Zionist epiphany.) Lloyd George suggested a date; then he had to postpone. He suggested a second date and had to postpone again, but this time he indicated that Weizmann should meet at any rate with his colleague. Meanwhile Weizmann frenziedly exhorted Sacher and Simon to polish the memorandum so that he could present it at the meeting. But it does not appear to have been ready on the afternoon of December 9, when Weizmann took the four-fifteen train from Manchester to London. He spent the night at the home of Ahad Ha'am in Haverstock Hill and met the president of the Local Government Board in his Whitehall office the next morning.

Weizmann expected little from Herbert Samuel. He explained to him the Zionist position—for the first time, as he probably thought. Samuel listened patiently, then floored his visitor. "Since Turkey had entered the war, he [Samuel] had given the problem much . . . consideration . . . Realization of the Zionist dream [now] was possible . . . Big things would have to be done in Palestine . . . The Jews would have to build Railways, harbours, a University, a network of schools, etc." Flabbergasted, Weizmann told Samuel, "If I were a religious Jew I should have thought the Messianic times were near." Shortly after the meeting he repeated this formulation in a letter to his wife: "Messianic times have really come . . . He told me that his programme is more ambitious than mine." In great excitement he returned to Haverstock Hill, where he and Ahad Ha'am went over the details of the meeting again and again. "I have just remembered another of Samuel's remarks which I have not passed on to you," he wrote to his friend three days later. "He said: *We would rebuild the Temple, as a symbol of Jewish unity.*" Weizmann wrote delightedly to Scott, who had made the eye-opening meeting possible, that Samuel "feels the responsibility lying on him, as a British Cabinet Minister and [as] a Jew." Indeed, he reported, Samuel had expressed a desire to meet additional Zionists. Weizmann would be happy to make introductions. An important meeting of minds had taken place, and an important relationship had been established.

Weizmann was on fire. He had lassoed for Zionism important members of the Rothschild family and the influential editor of *The Manchester Guardian;* and he had made contact with the president of the Local Government Board, a political insider. Yet he had his eye on even bigger game, a former prime minister now serving not merely as Conservative member of Parliament for the City of London but also, at Asquith's invitation, as a member of the War Council. He had met Arthur James Balfour eight years ago in Manchester, briefly during the general election of 1905–06, and again shortly thereafter for a more extended discussion of Zionism. Now he asked a mutual friend to request for him a third audience.

It was a shrewd request. So far Weizmann's most important political contacts belonged to the Liberal Party. It seemed only common sense to approach the Conservatives as well, not least since, as Ahad Ha'am warned, "it is very possible that after the war there will be a Conservative Government with Balfour at its head." Moreover, Conservatives did not share the anti-imperialist scruples of certain Liberals, such as Grey. They would not object to Britain expanding her empire by adding Palestine.

A. J. Balfour looms large in the history of Zionism; for the Declaration that bears his name, for his role in events leading up to its release, and for his sympathetic attitude afterward. Yet he seems an odd protagonist, scion as he was of the aristocratic Cecil political dynasty, which began in the sixteenth century with Lord Burghley, the adviser to Queen Elizabeth I, and extended down the years to Balfour's uncle, the third Marquess of Salisbury, who had served as Conservative prime minister after Disraeli. The line had continued to the present generation, with Balfour himself as its most eminent representative among a stable of successful relatives who served in Parliament, the Foreign Office, and the diplomatic corps.

Balfour's manner betrayed his background. He indulged (it was not affectation) a sort of aristocratic indolence and imperturbability. Tall and willowy, he rarely stood straight, but leaned against a wall. In the House of Commons he slouched low in his seat, boots on the railing before him. His spoken interventions in Commons were so graceful that, even when he criticized or directly attacked his opponents, they almost appreciated the attention. In fact there was steel beneath the creamy surface. When he was Irish home secretary under his uncle, Lord Salisbury, his appearance initially earned the ridicule of Home Rulers, who called him "Daddy Long Legs" and "Niminy Piminy." Then when he defended policemen found guilty of willfully murdering three tenants at Mitchelstown during a rent strike, they learned to call him "Bloody Balfour." Eventually "Daddy Long Legs" confounded them even more completely by climbing to the top of the greasy pole, replacing his uncle, who resigned as prime minister in 1902.

Critics accused him of laziness because he could not be bothered to read blue books. They accused him of dilettantism because politics was only one of his myriad interests. He belonged to the Royal Society, to the British Academy, and to the Society for Psychical Research. He wrote thoughtful works of philosophy attempting to reconcile Darwinism and religion. Acute, subtle, detached, and profoundly conservative, he was no democrat; he believed in a representative Parliament for the British and their kin but for few others. "Even in the West," he once pointed out to cabinet ministers, "Parliamentary institutions have rarely been a great success, except amongst the English-speaking peoples." He shared the attitudes of his time and class with regard to the various races of the world. "They have been different and unequal since history began," he once said, and "different and unequal they are destined to remain." He supported British imperialism because it was, he thought, good for Britain and good for the world. In short he was not, on the face of it, a likely ally for the much-despised Jews. Yet he wrote to Weizmann's friend: "I have the liveliest and also the most pleasant recollections of my conversation with Dr. Weizmann in 1906 . . . I shall be happy to see him."

The darkly bearded Zionist, intense and foreign, met the tall, languid aristocrat in the latter's splendid London residence, 12 Carlton Gardens, just across St. James's Park from the Foreign Office, on December 12. Only two days had passed since Weizmann's meeting with Herbert Samuel; he had not returned to Manchester but had spent the time with Ahad Ha'am, likely preparing for the coming audience. Afterward he crowed with delight: "Balfour remembered everything we discussed eight years ago." Weizmann brought him up-to-date on Zionist achievements since 1906 and lamented that the war had interrupted progress. No doubt with the prospective defeat of Turkey in mind, Balfour replied: "You may get your things done much quicker after the war."

But Weizmann was not, at present, asking Balfour to help him get specific things done. His more subtle and difficult task was to explain to a skeptical, patrician philosopher-cum-politician the tragedy of anti-Semitism and how to overcome it. He hoped not to ask for favors, but to educate and to convert. The two men spoke of the Jews in Germany. They had contributed much to German greatness, Weizmann pointed out, "as other Jews have to the greatness of France and England, at the expense of the whole Jewish people whose sufferings increase in proportion to 'the withdrawal' from that people of the creative element which are absorbed into the surrounding communities—those same communities later reproaching us for this *absorption,* and reacting with anti-Semitism." He cannot have expressed himself as drily as in his memoir, however. For Balfour listened intently and was deeply moved—"to *tears,*" Weizmann reported in near disbelief to Ahad Ha'am, "and he took me by the hand and said I had illu-minated for him the road followed by a great suffering nation."

Balfour had immediately grasped the essential difference between Weizmann and other Jews he had met. Claude Montefiore had once asked Balfour to intercede on behalf of Romanian Jews. "What a great difference there is between you and him," he told Weizmann. "For you are not asking for anything . . . you demand, and people have to listen to you because you are a *statesman* of a morally strong state." He added that he "regretted hav-ing known only Jews of one type." As the meeting drew to a close and he led his guest to the door, he said to him: "Mind you come again to see me, I am deeply moved and interested, it is not a dream, it is a great cause and I understand it."

After that almost anything would have seemed anticlimactic, but Weiz-mann continued his political work at the same fever pitch. He met again with Herbert Samuel, this time with their mutual acquaintance, the *haham* Moses Gaster, present as well. They discussed the memorandum that Samuel was preparing for the cabinet. He traveled to Paris and conferred once more with Baron Edmond de Rothschild. On January 15, 1915, he met at last with Lloyd George, Herbert Samuel being present as well. Scott coached him for this meeting:

> You probably will find that he will take the lead in the conver-sation and put questions to you which will give you plenty of openings . . . he will want to discuss with you . . . the present strength of the Jewish element in Palestine and the possibility of its rapid expansion; its relation to the local Arab population which so greatly outnumbers it; the potential value of Palestine as a "buffer" state and the means of evading for ourselves an un-desirable extension of military responsibility; the best way of al-laying Catholic and "Orthodox" jealousy in regard to the custody of the Holy Places.

Weizmann approached the meeting, which took place at 11 Downing Street, with great nervousness. As Scott had predicted, the future prime minister bombarded him with questions: "I answered as best I could." He must have answered very well indeed. With Lloyd George, as with almost everyone else during this extraordinary period, Weizmann worked his magic: The chancellor too would become a firm supporter.

Less than two weeks later Herbert Samuel forwarded his memoran-dum, now amended in light of Weizmann's suggestions, to Grey and

Asquith for approval before submitting it to the cabinet as a whole. He no longer advocated a Jewish state in Palestine but rather the territory's annexation to the British Empire.

> It is hoped that under British rule facilities would be given to Jewish organizations to purchase land, to found colonies, to establish educational and religious institutions, and to cooperate in the economic development of the country, and that Jewish immigration, carefully regulated, would be given preference, so that in course of time the Jewish people, grown into a majority and settled in the land, may be conceded such degree of self-government as the conditions of that day might justify.

And he concluded:

> The Jewish brain is a physiological product not to be despised. For fifteen centuries the race produced in Palestine a constant succession of great men—statesmen and prophets, judges and soldiers. If a body be again given in which its soul can lodge, it may again enrich the world. Till full scope is granted, as Macaulay said in the House of Commons, "let us not presume to say that there is no genius among the countrymen of Isaiah, no heroism among the descendants of the Maccabees."

The prime minister's response was lukewarm. Asquith, either in Liberal anti-imperialist mode or in veiled anti-Semitic mode, confessed to his confidante Venetia Stanley: "I am not attracted by this proposed addition to our responsibilities, but it is a curious illustration of Dizzy's [Disraeli's] favourite maxim that 'race is everything' to find this almost lyrical outburst proceeding from the well-ordered and methodical brain of H.S." But the prime minister did not forbid the preparation of a less lyrical memorandum for the cabinet to consider. Samuel got back to work. Six weeks later the British government duly convened to discuss the future of Palestine as a British Jewish nationalist envisioned it. Thus was a watershed crossed.

During the first months of World War I British Zionism, led primarily by Chaim Weizmann but with Herbert Samuel playing a crucial role and the titular leaders of the EZF very much overshadowed, moved purposefully to establish influence among the men who determined British foreign policy.

It was a brash and successful program that Weizmann conducted, its success all the more extraordinary for largely being planned and executed by a man born not in Britain but in Russia.

Some British Jews, if they had known of Weizmann's activities, would not have approved. Most of the Cousinhood and its auxiliaries, the Board of Jewish Deputies and the Anglo-Jewish Association and their Conjoint Committee, held very different ideas about how to solve the "Jewish problem." When Weizmann first realized the desirability of Jewish unity, he had approached not only Israel Zangwill of the ITO and his former political Zionist opponents Greenberg and Cowen, but the Conjoint Committee as well, in the person of Lucien Wolf. Perhaps this gesture was somewhat pro forma, as it had been with Zangwill. Perhaps, however, Weizmann genuinely expected to work his magic on this representative of assimilated British Jewry. If so, then he was doomed to disappointment. Lucien Wolf and his colleagues regarded Zionism with distaste. They deemed Weizmann an interloper. They had their own wartime program for British Jewry, and it was not his. A significant struggle, a competition for the ear of the British government, was about to commence.

CHAPTER 10

The Assimilationists

AT THE OUTSET OF WORLD WAR I, British Jews who believed in assimilation had very different preoccupations from Zionists. Enjoying full legal and civic equality, they understood themselves to be the beneficiaries of many decades of toil and tears and hard political organizing. Now a mood created by the war seemed to call their hard-earned gains into question. The war stoked nationalist passions, giving scope to xenophobes and anti-Semites who usually inhabited the fringes and dark corners of national life. In 1914, when British Zionists began to anticipate the prospective carve-up of the Ottoman Empire, these other British Jews, the vast majority, were more likely to focus on a prospective carve-up much closer to home—in fact, right at home. British chauvinists and bigots were manifestly gaining an audience, and the Jews had become their target. Rights that had been won over decades, these Jews feared, could be lost in months.

They had grounds for their concern. With the war only three weeks old, two policemen appeared at the door of Lucien Wolf's London home. Despite his prominency someone had denounced him to the authorities, presumably as a pro-German, perhaps as an undocumented alien or likely spy, possibly simply because he was Jewish. Wolf happened to be ill in bed that day. "They threatened to remain outside my door until they saw me," he reported a few days later, "and said to my housekeeper that they would not be 'pleasant for me before my neighbors.' " Wolf rose from his sickbed to invite them inside, but they behaved in a "cruelly aggressive" manner and with "exceptional hostility." They demanded to know his nationality. "They not only catechized me in a very peremptory tone, but insisted on having documentary proof of all my replies." Wolf, born in Britain, thought of himself quite rightly as a patriotic Englishman.

A few weeks later Wolf endured another form of humiliation. Leo Maxse, editor of the anti-Semitic *National Review,* was fulminating in print against German Jews who, he claimed, controlled the British press and favored Britain's enemies. In one article he specifically mentioned Lucien Wolf of *The Daily Graphic.* Explaining the situation to his editor, Wolf hardly thought it necessary to repeat that he was not German, or even to mention that his three sons were serving, or soon would be serving, in the British army. He merely noted that although his column, "Foreign Office Bag," appeared regularly in *The Daily Graphic,* he had no position of authority with that newspaper. Before the war Maxse's campaign might not have mattered much, but now it did. Wolf discovered that many of his colleagues would no longer talk to him. Then his employer suddenly fired him—from a job he had held for a quarter century. No non-Jewish British journalist of this period suffered so harshly, according to Wolf's most recent biographer. Deeply depressed, Wolf wrote at this time: "My misfortunes extend to almost every aspect of my life and I see no prospect of ever being able to overcome them."

He could have been forgiven, then, for concluding that true assimilation for Jews in Britain was unattainable just as the Zionists claimed, and that Jews who thought they had attained it were fooling themselves. But he drew no such conclusion. Rather he judged that the liberal Britain he cherished, in part because it permitted Jewish assimilation, had come under attack by enemies from within as well as from without. Wolf could make only one response, and that was to fight back. He threatened to sue the odious Maxse. As soon as the two policemen had left his house, he telephoned the Special Branch of the CID to complain of his treatment. He followed up with angry letters to the commissioner of police and to the assistant commissioner, protesting the "quite undeserved" indignity that had been placed upon him.

In so energetically defending himself, and defending liberal principles, Wolf provided historians with a lens through which to understand the anti-Zionism of Jews who believed in assimilation. The Zionist, whatever his political inclinations and affiliations, holds that wherever the Jew may reside, he can be truly at home only in one country, Palestine. To him, birth matters more than environment. Wolf rejected this formulation. During this early part of the war, an acquaintance named Spielmann, a third-generation Briton, was nevertheless a target of xenophobes because of his German name. Wolf argued in a letter to a friend that even if Spielmann *had* been born in Germany, it would not matter so long as he had *lived* mainly in England: "All we have to consider are birth, environment and psychology, and psychology owes much more to environment than to the mechanical accident of birth." British jingoes and Jewish nationalists both mistakenly emphasized the accident of birth, according to Wolf; they represented two sides of the same coin, and both sides were inimical to liberalism. Without ever minimizing his own Jewishness, Lucien Wolf insisted, against Maxse and against the Zionists, that Jews could and should assimilate in Great Britain or in any other country where they chose to live. But in defending this bedrock liberal principle, Wolf could only oppose Zionism, which meant eventually opposing its leader, Chaim Weizmann, even though the latter's views on other subjects often were liberal too. On this crucial point the two men differed profoundly; and so in the end, Wolf became Weizmann's chief and most effective British Jewish opponent.

Wolf responded to the outbreak of war as many other British Liberals did, first appalled, then resolute in opposition to Germany. In fact, he saw farther than most. "It is not only the carnage that will be frightful, but the economic exhaustion and the starvation which will be infinitely worse; and then when peace comes . . . desolation and certain revolution everywhere," he wrote to a friend. "There will be no choice between the military dictator and the socialist and in the end socialism must triumph." It was not precisely accurate, but it was a closer forecast of the postwar situation than many made at the time.

Wolf never doubted that Britain had been right to declare war on Germany: "We were bound to fight on the Belgian question." Nor did he query the judgment of Foreign Secretary Edward Grey: "As far as I can see he has acted very well." In fact he articulated the British liberal justification for war with more clarity and force than many professional Liberals. His country was fighting "a war of ethical opinion," he declared. Austria's German-backed invasion of Serbia, Germany's invasion of Belgium, and her threat to Britain's mastery of the seas must all be resisted, but the essence of the problem Germany posed was "the German people—or rather a large section of them—have become saturated with a philosophy which has sought to rationalize and justify their dominating instincts and ambitions, and has actually reached the point of molding and directing the national policy."

That philosophy's progenitor had been Georg Wilhelm Friedrich

Hegel, Wolf explained; its more recent spokesman had been Heinrich von Treitschke, who argued that the individual lived to serve the state, not vice versa; that war was a positive good; that treaties, which limited the state, should be ignored; and that the state should be racially homogenous. This autocratic German creed directly contradicted Britain's liberal one, which was based upon the thought of Jeremy Bentham and John Stuart Mill among others. It contradicted the liberal, tolerant creed of Judaism as well. "With their invincible attachments to things of the spirit and with their strongly marked individualism [Jews] would not easily have embraced the modern German conception of the finality of the military State," Wolf argued. "For them the State was made for the individual, not the individual for the State. Nor could they imagine Jews acquiescing in the doctrine of the necessity and eternity of war as a God-given principle, or in the idea of the citizen as before all and above all a soldier. All this struck at the very root of Jewish teaching."

Here were two sides of another coin, in Wolf's view: liberal Britain and liberal Judaism (not to be confused with Montefiore's religious doctrine of Liberal Judaism). That the German philosophy emphasized anti-Semitism was no mere "political eccentricity." Rather it was "a logical consequence of [Treitschke's] main teaching." This was a crucial linkage: "The makers of Anti-Semitism are the makers of the present war. Both are the logical outcome of the same order of barbarian ideas. They are the hideous twin progeny of a hideous teaching."

Inconveniently for the consistency of Wolf's argument, however, tsarist Russia had allied with liberal England and France against autocratic Germany. So too, within a year, did that other bastion of anti-Semitism and conservatism, Romania. The government of neither country intended to moderate its treatment of Jews. Particularly Jews in Russia, and Jews who lived in the path of the Russian army as it marched west, suffered at its hands from pillage, rapine, false accusations of treason, and summary executions. This Wolf learned from reports that poured into his office from Jewish contacts on the Continent. He knew, however, that to ask the Foreign Office to protest right now would do no good. The Foreign Office had tolerated but hardly welcomed the Conjoint Committee's prewar exhortations to condemn Russian and Romanian anti-Semitism. It would not stand criticism of these allies during wartime. Troubled, Wolf sought to justify his self-imposed silence—to himself perhaps as much as to anyone else: "To me there have always been two Russias. The Russia I am fighting for today is the Russia I have always fought for—the Russia of Liberalism and progress which is now the whole of Russia because it is on the side of my own country—Liberal England—and against the forces of Prussian reaction." The argument was not convincing, but it is illuminating. In 1914 nearly the entire world was convulsed in war, and one side was committed to the defense of liberalism, Lucien Wolf believed. How could he ever bend his knee to those other opponents of liberalism, the Zionists?

He could not. The two branches of political British Jewry—that is to say, the Zionists led by Weizmann and the assimilationists led by Wolf—were fated to engage in a fierce competition for the support of the British government. The competition was as far-reaching, if not as personally dangerous to its protagonists, as anything engaged in by Sharif Hussein and his sons far to the east, and it mainly concerned the fate of the same strip of land. But first the Zionists and the assimilationists explored the possibility of cooperation.

In certain ways the careers of Weizmann and Wolf at this stage run parallel. Weizmann began his ascent to leadership among British Zionists with the onset of the war. Only a month or two later Wolf agreed to become the Conjoint Committee's paid director (having lost his job with *The Daily Graphic*); henceforth he would be the chief public advocate of Jewish assimilation in Britain. Weizmann proposed that influential Jews plan for the peace conference that would end the war. As director of the Conjoint Committee, Wolf had as a primary task planning for that very conference, not least since during wartime the committee could not play its customary role as protector of oppressed Jews in Russia and Romania. It was only natural, then, that Weizmann and Wolf, or their delegates, should come into contact.

And so they did, on November 17, 1914. That day, acting upon Chaim Weizmann's instructions (which may have been concerted with Ahad Ha'am, given the closeness of the two men), Harry Sacher called upon Lucien Wolf at his offices at 2 Verulam Buildings, Grays Inn. Wolf would have received the talented younger Jewish journalist with interest verging on pleasure.

That day Sacher did not represent his position altogether accurately to Wolf. True enough, he reflected Weizmann's views faithfully on the Jewish attitude toward Russia's continuing anti-Semitism. "Silence during the war is our best chance, or rather [our] only chance," he averred, and Wolf agreed, however reluctantly. Sacher was truthful again in stating that he and his friends believed there was at least "a faint chance" of something good for Russian Jews coming out of a peace conference, which was precisely what Wolf also thought. But on the crucial question (for Zionists) of Palestine and his group's plans for it, Sacher misled Wolf, almost certainly wittingly, although his purpose remains obscure. He was a cultural not a political Zionist, he assured his host. The return to Palestine was the prerequisite for developing Jewish culture and nothing more. "Political demands or a Jewish state I should not press for, or raise, if we could get Jewish unanimity on such a basis as this."

That had been true only three weeks earlier, before Turkey entered the war, but since then leading cultural Zionists, as Sacher must have known, had embraced political Zionism and its goal of a Jewish state in Palestine, even if they did not say so publicly. Only seven days after Sacher met with Wolf, James Rothschild would urge Weizmann to "ask for something which . . . tends towards the formation of a Jewish State." But Weizmann's mind had been prepared for this change already, in discussions with Ahad Ha'am and, one must assume, with Harry Sacher.

Wolf did not yet know of these meetings, but well informed as he was, he probably knew that strict cultural Zionism was waning. Nonetheless he took Sacher's statement at face value, discerning in it a possibility for cooperation between Zionists and the Conjoint Committee. A program limited to cultural Zionism "would be welcomed by the 'leaders' " of Britain's Jewish community, Wolf pronounced. "For such work in Palestine there was more sympathy than [Sacher] imagined." Additional discussions between Zionist principals and the heads of the Conjoint Committee might lead to positive results.

In fact, Lucien Wolf was every bit as capable of misdirection as Harry Sacher. In their ensuing correspondence Wolf encouraged the younger man to help arrange the Zionist–Conjoint Committee meeting. Simultaneously, however, he was attempting to undermine the Zionists' credibility with the Foreign Office. He found out that Greenberg and Zangwill already had lobbied there; reports of Weizmann's various triumphs reached him as well. But traditionally the Conjoint Committee represented British Jews' foreign policy interests to the British government, and Wolf meant for that tradition to continue. These other men were interlopers, in his view.

On January 7, 1915, as director of the Conjoint Committee, Wolf cautioned Francis Acland, parliamentary under secretary of state, "against unauthorized persons who approached the Foreign Office on questions concerning the interests of our foreign coreligionists." More specifically, Wolf warned "that Mr. Zangwill had no official connection with our leading organizations," and that Greenberg, while editor of *The Jewish Chronicle,* nevertheless "was very often in conflict with our communal chiefs."

Then he struck a particularly low blow—indeed a stunningly hypocritical one, given that he himself had been the recent target of the xenophobe Leo Maxse. "The Zionist organization," he warned Acland, "was foreign and was almost entirely controlled from alien-enemy countries."

In other words, some of the Jewish protagonists in our tale were as capable of dissimulation as the Emir Hussein and his sons were; as capable, even, as the British politicians who later would simultaneously encourage (or at least not actively discourage) both Arabs and Zionists to think they would someday control the same bit of land, Palestine.

The initial meeting between Wolf and Sacher had established the parameters of the Zionist-assimilationist relationship. The benefits of cooperation were plain to both sides, but disdain, distrust, and dissimulation overshadowed them. Weizmann and Wolf would continue to jockey for influence with the Foreign Office and with high-ranking government officials, even as meetings to define the basis of a joint effort were taking place. Those meetings, however, only served to emphasize the two parties' profound disagreement over the status and role of Jews in Britain and in the world.

On March 13, 1915, Prime Minister H. H. Asquith's Liberal cabinet convened at 10 Downing Street to discuss the revised memorandum prepared by Herbert Samuel on the future of Palestine. Samuel had toned it down since showing the original version to his leader two months earlier. He had eliminated the rhetorical flourishes, to which Asquith referred disdainfully as practically "dithyrambic." And this time he explicitly ruled out any attempt to found a Jewish state there: "Whatever be the merits or the demerits of that proposal, it is certain that the time is not ripe for it." But the justifications for British action in the region remained from the original memorandum, and this time he took great pains to emphasize that non-Jews in the region must receive equal treatment under any future scheme.

Once again Samuel prepared the ground carefully. Prior to submitting the memorandum to the cabinet, he consulted several times with Weizmann, with Moses Gaster, and with various other experts, including a few who had returned recently from the Middle East. Then he sent the modified document to cabinet colleagues whom he judged sympathetic: Viscount Haldane, the lord chancellor; Jackie Fisher, the first sea lord; and Lord Reading, or Rufus Isaacs, the (Jewish) lord chief justice. Reading reported to Samuel that Lloyd George was "inclined to the sympathetic side—your proposal appeals to the poetic and imaginative as well as to the romantic and religious qualities of his mind." Samuel would have known this already from his talks with the man.

But when the cabinet met, according to Asquith, only Lloyd George strongly supported the proposal, and he "does not care a damn for the Jews or their past or their future, but . . . thinks it would be an outrage to let the Christian Holy Places . . . pass into the possession or under the protectorate of 'Agnostic Atheistic France'!" This remark casts rather an unflattering light upon Lloyd George's early wartime sympathy for Zionism. Was he thinking more about keeping France out of Palestine than about letting Jews in? Historians have not made much of Asquith's comment, although they know it well.

The prime minister barely bothered to hide his own distaste for a Palestine into which the scattered Jews of the world "could in time swarm back from all quarters of the globe and in due course obtain Home Rule (What an attractive community!)." But if the letter he wrote to Asquith after the meeting is anything to go by, it was Edwin Montagu, chancellor of the Duchy of Lancaster and Herbert Samuel's own cousin, who objected most strenuously to everything the president of the Local Government Board proposed.

Perhaps no individual better exemplified the success of Jewish assimilation in Britain than Montagu. (Or, perhaps, its failure, depending upon whether you take Wolf's or Weizmann's approach to the question.) Outwardly Montagu had it all: enormous wealth, inherited from his father, the great banker and Liberal politician Samuel Montagu (Lord Swaythling); cabinet rank at an early age; the friendship of important figures such as Prime Minister Asquith, whose parliamentary private secretary he had been; and a country estate called Hickling in Norfolk. Like many country gentlemen who owned estates, he enjoyed the shooting and was himself a fair shot. One morning he "fired about two hundred and thirty shots at pochard and tufted ducks, bagging about forty-five, which was not so bad." He was a big man, with heavy-lidded eyes, large hands, and in 1915 a receding hairline. Despite this rather imposing physiognomy, "children and animals took to him at sight."

Soon too he would have a beautiful and aristocratic wife, Venetia Stanley—the very confidante to whom Asquith had written so disparagingly of Samuel's "dithyrambic" memorandum. Asquith was accustomed to write disparagingly to her about Edwin Montagu too. The prime minister simply could not forget that his close political colleague was a Jew. In his correspondence with her, he referred to Montagu as "the Assyrian" and to his grand London residence as the "silken tent." When she married Montagu, Asquith sent congratulations and presents but felt great dismay, a sentiment compounded of jealousy, loneliness, and, one cannot dismiss it, a genteel but unmistakable anti-Semitism.

Montagu was mordantly witty, politically clever, emotional, malicious, and thin-skinned. He wore his heart upon his sleeve. Surely he was aware that Asquith perceived him not so much as a colleague who happened to be a Jew, but rather as a Jew who happened to be his colleague. And if Asquith thought this way, then what of his other cabinet colleagues, and everybody else? Montagu wished to be recognized as a Briton who practiced the Jewish religion. In this regard his position was that of Lucien Wolf. In fact, he stood in relation to Wolf much as Samuel stood in relation to Weizmann—a Jewish supporter who belonged to the government.

On March 16, 1915, in response to his cousin's memorandum, Montagu wrote a letter to Asquith. It was an attempt at demolition, a complete rejection not merely of the tactical considerations that Samuel had advanced as reasons for a British protectorate in Palestine but also of their underlying premise of eventual Jewish autonomy there.

"Palestine in itself offers little or no attraction to Great Britain from a strategical or material point of view," Montagu charged. Its possession by Britain would facilitate the defense neither of Egypt nor of the Suez Canal. Moreover it was "incomparably a poorer possession than, let us say, Mesopotamia." Nor would Jews find great fulfillment working the land there, whatever Zionists like his cousin might say: "I cannot see any Jews I know tending olive trees or herding sheep."

What Montagu objected to at the most basic level, however, was the Zionist assumption that Palestine was the homeland of a distinct Jewish people: "There is no Jewish race now as a homogenous whole. It is quite obvious that the Jews in Great Britain are as remote from the Jews in Morocco or the black Jews in Cochin as the Christian Englishman is from the moor or the Hindoo." A Jewish homeland in Palestine would be composed of "a polyglot, many-colored, heterogeneous collection of people of different civilizations and different ordinances and different traditions." Unless conditions were completely insupportable where they lived now, the Jews of the world would be better off to stay put and assimilate—as he had done.

If they did not, Montagu argued, and instead moved in great numbers to Palestine and established a homeland there, they would become unwelcome everywhere else. "Their only claim to the hospitality of Russia, Bulgaria, France, Spain, is that they have no alternative home, no State of their own, and they want to be and are patriotic citizens working for the good of the countries in which they live . . . When it is known that Palestine is the Jewish State which is really their home then I can foresee a world movement to get them away at any cost." And he closed with a heartfelt plea: "If only our peoples would . . . take their place as non-conformists [members of a religious sect not belonging to the Church of England], then Zionism would obviously die and Jews might find their way to esteem."

Asquith read this impassioned document and smiled. He thought it "racy," he wrote to Venetia Stanley. He seems not to have shown it to any of his colleagues, but the conflict between Montagu and Samuel served its historical purpose, mirroring the competition between Wolf and Weizmann, and between assimilationists and Zionists more generally. At this stage the assimilationists still had the advantage, but Samuel had performed a great service for Zionism: His memorandum, and its rejection by his own cousin, demonstrated conclusively to cabinet ministers that the British Jewish community had split. The Conjoint Committee no longer voiced the views of a monolithic bloc, if ever it had done. And that Samuel, their most prosaic associate, had been the one to articulate the Zionist position may have gone some way to persuading them that Zionism had entered the realm of practical politics after all.

About a month later, on April 14, 1915, the first formal meeting between the Zionist leadership and the Conjoint Committee convened. Five months had elapsed since Sacher's initial approach to Wolf, testifying to the maneuvering for position in which both sides had since engaged. Ironically, when the two groups finally did get together, neither Sacher nor Weizmann even attended; the latter because he could not take time away from his laboratory, the former perhaps because the Zionist veterans considered him too junior. But during the interval a pair of Zionists from the central office in Berlin had traveled to England: Yehiel Tschlenow, who would soon return to his native Russia, and Nahum Sokolow, whom we have met already. Three additional men represented the Zionists, including the *haham* Moses Gaster. The assimilationist contingent included Claude Montefiore and David Alexander, president and vice president respectively of the Conjoint Committee, and of course Lucien Wolf.

The first thing to become absolutely clear at the meeting was that the cultural Zionist program, to which Sacher had initially referred, no longer applied, if ever it truly had done. Tschlenow, in a long introductory speech, pointed out that at the peace conference following the war, even small nationalities such as Finns, Lithuanians, and Armenians would "put forward their demands, their wishes, their aspirations." He then asked his anti-Zionist friends: "Shall the Jewish 'people,' the Jewish 'nation,' be silent?"

Note here that Wolf, in his written account of the meeting, placed the words "people" and "nation" in quotation marks. Those tiny vertical scratches signaled the profound chasm separating the two camps. Wolf believed that asserting that the Jews constituted a distinct nation would fatally undercut his argument that British Jews really were Jewish Britons. It would deny the possibility of genuine Jewish assimilation in Britain or anywhere else. It contradicted his liberal assumptions. He refused to make the required assertion.

Tschlenow further argued that Turkish entry into the war had upset all previous calculations. For if the Allies defeated the Ottomans, then "there is a good chance that Palestine may fall to England and that England may hand it over and give it to the Jews." It was now or never: "If the Jews do not develop Palestine and make it populous and cultivated and civilized and flourishing, others will do so." He envisioned a "big Jewish Commonwealth . . . 5,000,000 souls . . . or more . . . [as] in days of old." To which Moses Gaster added, "The Zionists intended to go in and work for 'the whole hog,' Nothing less than a Commonwealth would satisfy them."

So much for cultural Zionism! On what basis, then, might political Zionists and the Conjoint Committee find common ground? Tschlenow contended that the Zionist goal of a Jewish commonwealth in Palestine and the Conjoint Committee's desire to ameliorate conditions for Russian Jews were complementary, not antagonistic. Once the Jews possessed Palestine and could immigrate freely to that place, "there would be fewer Jews in Russia," and a smaller Jewish community would be perceived as a lesser threat and therefore attract less persecution. Gaster added that "when the nations knew a Jew could go off to his own country they would persecute him less." And Sokolow chimed in: "If Palestine was a British protectorate, and if England held it as a legally secured home for the Jews, England would be more interested in preventing the persecution of the Jews elsewhere and in obtaining rights for them." But the Zionists insisted on the primacy of their own political program. Efforts to improve the Jewish lot, as noble and useful as they might be, "would and could never be the solution of the Jewish problem. That solution lay only in Zionism."

Wolf and his colleagues seem to have been unsurprised by the jettisoning of the cultural program, which greatly reduced the possibility of meaningful cooperation between the two groups. They asked their guests two pertinent questions: "How would Palestine become a Jewish country?" and of equal importance: Would "special rights . . . be asked for the Jews" once they had entered into it?

The Zionists did not mince words in reply. Special rights would be asked for and would be necessary, Gaster explained, "till the Jews were so numerous, and in so large a minority, that they would predominate by weight of numbers." As to how the Jews should enter Palestine, a Jewish Chartered Company with Britain's backing "would take care that Jews should be the prevailing settlers." Sokolow added that if Britain established some form of control over Palestine, "she would clearly and obviously take such necessary steps as to secure that the Jews should be the predominant people in Palestine [and] that it should be *their* country. The one point followed from the other."

It was an uncompromising performance, albeit politely delivered. The Conjoint Committee promised to consider it and to respond. Within days Wolf wrote a fourteen-page encapsulation of his own optimistic liberal creed:

> The whole tendency of the national life in Eastern Europe is necessarily towards a more enlightened and liberal policy . . . The present war, through the preponderance of Great Britain and France on the side of the Allies, must give a great impulse to liberal reforms in Russia . . . Sooner or later the statesmanship of the countries concerned will, for their own protection, deal with [the Jewish problem] in the way in which it has been successfully dealt with in Western Europe and America . . . There is no solid ground to despair of eventual success.

Therefore, Wolf argued, the Conjoint Committee must reject the Zionist approach. Not even unrestricted Russian Jewish emigration to Palestine, he argued, would improve conditions for the majority who must stay behind; after all, the massive Russian Jewish migration to America had not done so. Moreover, far from improving things, the establishment of a Jewish commonwealth would "at once relieve persecuting countries of much of their present incentive to pursue a policy of emancipation." Like Edwin Montagu, Wolf believed that anti-Semitism would increase, not decrease, upon establishment of a Jewish commonwealth. The Zionist approach ran "counter to all experience and probabilities, and is essentially reactionary."

So much for Zionist tactics; Wolf then dismissed the Zionists' fundamental premise.

> The idea of a Jewish nationality, the talk of a Jew "going home" to Palestine if he is not content with his lot in the land of his birth, strikes at the root of all claim to Jewish citizenship in lands where Jewish disabilities still exist. It is the assertion not merely of a double nationality . . . but of the perpetual alienage of Jews everywhere outside Palestine.

Thus political Zionism threatened to undermine even the most assimilated Jews. It threatened to make strangers of Jews like himself, and his colleagues on the Conjoint Committee, in the land of their birth, England.

Wolf went on to reject the Zionist claim to special privileges for Jews once they had arrived in Palestine. Britain, the likely future suzerain power in Palestine, specifically barred special privileges based upon religion. Moreover "nothing could be more detrimental to the struggle for Jewish liberties all over the world," than for Jews to claim special privileges anywhere. "How could we continue to ask that the Russian Government shall make no distinction between . . . Jews and Christians?" he asked.

In sum, the Zionist scheme if implemented,

> would not only aggravate the difficulties of unemancipated, and imperil the liberties of emancipated Jews all over the world, but in Palestine itself it would make for a Jewish state based on civil and religious disabilities of the most mediaeval kind, a state, consequently which could not endure and which would bring lasting reproach on Jews and Judaism. Indeed it could not be otherwise with a political nationality based on religious and racial tests, and no other Jewish nationality is possible.

The main lines of disagreement could hardly have been more clearly stated. The Zionists replied to Wolf on May 11, 1915; exactly one month later the Conjoint Committee wrote a rejoinder, ending with the pious hope "that the progress of events may lead to such an approximation of the views of the two parties as to render some useful scheme of cooperation yet possible."

It would not happen. On the crucial issue of Jewish nationality, neither side budged. Consultations and discussions would continue, and memo-

randa would be written from both sides, but the gulf remained unbridge-
able. Henceforth their competition for the ear of the government would
grow increasingly fierce. And although Wolf began from the better-
established and therefore more advantageous position, Weizmann was an
absolute master of the political game.

CHAPTER 11

The Road Forks

A YEAR AND A HALF into the war, the British government and the Foreign Office faced a grim situation. On the Western Front, despite appalling sacrifices, the Allies had achieved only a bloody stalemate. In the east a war of comparatively rapid movement had produced equally indecisive results. To the south, Turkey had beaten Britain at Gallipoli; in Mesopotamia it had captured and interned thousands of British troops and officers at Kut. Meanwhile Serbia had fallen to the Austrians, and Italy's belated entry into the conflict on the side of the Entente had done little to help, either in the southern theater or anywhere else.

Thus the view from Whitehall early in 1916: If defeat was not imminent, neither was victory; and the outcome of the war of attrition on the Western Front could not be predicted. The colossal forces in a death-grip across Europe and in Eurasia appeared to have canceled each other out. Only the addition of significant new forces on one side or the other seemed likely to tip the scale. Britain's willingness, beginning early in 1916, to explore seriously some kind of arrangement with "world Jewry" or "Great Jewry" must be understood in this context. The British never believed that the Jews alone could alter the balance of the war, but they did come to believe that the Jews could help fund it; and perhaps more important, they could persuade mightier forces to weigh in or out or to stand firm. Many Britons in 1916,

including policy makers, apparently believed in the existence of a monolithic and powerful Jewish factor in world affairs. But there was no such
thing. The government's wartime decision to appeal to the Jews was based
upon a misconception.

A year and a half into the war, that misconception formed part of the
worldview of Gerald Henry Fitzmaurice, the former British dragoman in
Constantinople whom Grand Sharif Hussein had successfully courted in
1908 when he wanted British support for his candidacy to become emir of
Mecca. Hussein had discerned in the British dragoman a likely ally: When
it came to Ottoman politics, Fitzmaurice was an ultraconservative who
shared the sharif's admiration for Sultan Abdul Hamid II as well as his hatred of the Young Turks. Sharp-featured, with receding ginger hair, piercing eyes, and a full handlebar mustache, the dragoman possessed "an eagle
mind and a personality of iron vigor," according to T. E. Lawrence, who
nevertheless did not like him. He exercised great influence (too much, and
of the wrong kind, as Lawrence saw it) over a series of British ambassadors
to the Ottoman government.

From his appointment to Constantinople as a junior consul in 1905 until
his recall to London in February 1914 (by which time he had been promoted to chief dragoman in Constantinople and first secretary in the diplomatic service), Fitzmaurice did his best to pump life into the moribund
Ottoman court and to sustain its cruel, corrupt, and capricious ruler.
Aubrey Herbert, then an honorary attaché in Constantinople (along with
Mark Sykes and George Lloyd), likened him to the chains of ivy that may
sometimes hold up a great and ancient but rotten oak tree. And like certain
other British diplomats, scholars, and journalists of the era, Fitzmaurice labored under the misperception that the Young Turks who had thrown out
Sultan Abdul Hamid II and taken control of the empire were dominated
by Jews and *dömnes,* or "crypto-Jews." These Jewish puppeteers, according
to this worldview, were part of a wider conspiracy to gain control of the Ottoman Empire in order to acquire Palestine for the world Zionist movement.

Fitzmaurice reenters our tale now because he was probably the first responsible British diplomat to suggest that Jewish power, both in Turkey
and elsewhere, held the key to Entente victory in World War I. He im-
parted this piece of wisdom to Hugh James O'Bierne, CVO (Commander
of the Victorian Order) and CB (Commander of the Order of Bath), an experienced, accomplished, and well-respected British diplomat who apparently saw no reason to doubt it. The two men came into contact in Sofia, to
which Fitzmaurice had been sent in February 1915 to link up with dissi-

dent Turks who opposed their government's alliance with Germany; O'Bierne arrived in July 1915 as part of a British team tasked with bribing Bulgaria to join the Entente. Fitzmaurice took part in this mission as well, but it proved unsuccessful because Britain could not offer Bulgaria what she wanted most—territory in Macedonia that had been occupied by Serbia during the Second Balkan War. Germany, on the other hand, could offer it; unlike Britain, she was Serbia's enemy. After some hesitation the Bulgarian prime minister, Vasil Radoslavov, accepted Germany's inducement to align with her in the war. Mere days later, just before Bulgaria declared war on Britain, O'Bierne and Fitzmaurice beat a hasty retreat. Back in London, the former dragoman took a position with the Intelligence Division at the Admiralty Office, while O'Bierne went to work at the Foreign Office.

Late in 1915 or early in 1916, Fitzmaurice met Moses Gaster; possibly Herbert Samuel provided the introduction. At any rate the former dragoman learned something of the Zionist program from the *haham* of the British Sephardim and applied it to what he thought he knew about who really ruled Turkey. To put it baldly, Fitzmaurice put two and (something less than) two together and came up with five. He reasoned thus: The Allies should offer Palestine to the *dönmes* of Constantinople, in return for which they would withdraw their support from the Ottoman regime. This would result in the latter's collapse. Allied victory would follow. Moreover, as Jews everywhere focused on returning to, and building up, their promised land, the shadowy, malign influence of world Zionism would fade. This was the insight Fitzmaurice shared with Hugh James O'Bierne at about the turn of the year 1915–16.

O'Bierne was primed to entertain the notion and even to appreciate it. Only a month earlier the Foreign Office had received a memorandum that likewise emphasized the power of Jews, in this case American rather than Turkish. Its author, a professor at the University of Wisconsin, was a prominent U.S. Zionist with English connections. Now he wished to warn the Foreign Office about German propaganda among the American Jewish community, which, he stressed, possessed significant political and financial power. Fortunately for the Allies, the professor said, this group held instinctive pro-British and pro-French views, but also, and for obvious reasons, strong anti-Russian ones. To win over American Jews, he recommended, among other measures, "a very veiled suggestion concerning nationalization in Palestine," by which he must have meant some form of French or British control.

Only a few weeks later a second memo reached the Foreign Office, again emphasizing the power of Jews and seconding the American's warning. It came from none other than Sir Henry McMahon in Egypt. In the midst of his ambiguous but far-reaching correspondence with Grand Sharif Hussein, the high commissioner had received a report on the views of "a prominent Italian businessman and head of the Jewish colony at Alexandria." McMahon found the report so suggestive that he summarized it and forwarded it to his masters in London. Apparently his informant feared that the Allies risked losing Jewish support, especially from the all-important American branch, because of Russian anti-Semitism. Also like the American professor, this gentleman thought that Jewish support could be a factor in the war and that it could be obtained easily enough. "What the Jews in America were waiting for," the Italian businessman averred, "was only the knowledge that British policy accorded with their aspirations for Palestine." If Britain did not act quickly to assuage this longing, he warned, then Germany might.

These reports filtered into the Foreign Office entirely unknown to our Jewish protagonists, but they too, each in his own way, continued their attempts to persuade British authorities that the Jewish factor was important. Herbert Samuel gave a copy of his cabinet memorandum to Sir Mark Sykes, who had just finished negotiating his agreement with François Georges-Picot. Sykes and Picot were about to leave for Russia to seek support for their proposed postwar partition of Ottoman territories. Sykes was hardly a Zionist at this point, but on the eve of his departure he reported to Samuel that "I read the memorandum and have committed it to memory and destroyed it—as no print or other papers can pass the R. Frontier except in the F.O. bag." Indeed when Sykes read the report, it lit a lightbulb in his mind. All during the wearying journey to Russia, he would ruminate on the Jewish factor, and his ruminations would soon help to shape British policy. Like O'Bierne, he was primed. It is worth noting that Sykes, O'Bierne, and Fitzmaurice all were devout Catholics who perhaps had learned in their early years that Jews represented a powerful and mysterious world force, one that, they now thought, could be activated on behalf of the Allies if only the proper switch could be found. Alternatively, it is conceivable that the Catholicism of Sykes, O'Bierne, and Fitzmaurice had nothing to do with the fact that they were among the small cadre of British officials who first discerned a potential ally in "world Jewry."

As for Chaim Weizmann, he was hard at work in the laboratory, perfecting a process for fermenting acetone from grain rather than from wood, which was growing scarce. Acetone is an essential ingredient in the manufacture of cordite for explosives. His work was so important and successful that it brought him into further contact with leading government officials, including Lloyd George, whom Asquith just had made minister of munitions. Meanwhile he remained engaged in his great charm offensive, teaching Zionism to Jews and non-Jews alike. By now the Rothschild women had taken him in hand, coaching him on how to speak and act at the nonacademic version of high table. The erstwhile *folks-mensch* proved to be as quick a study in the drawing and dining rooms of the British elite as he was in the chemistry department. A testament to his effectiveness: At one of her dinner parties during this period the Marchioness of Crewe was heard to remark to Robert Cecil, "We all in this house are 'Weizmannites.'" Nancy Astor invited Weizmann to dine one evening with a number of luminaries including Balfour and Philip Henry Kerr, editor of the influential *Round Table* (soon to become a member of Lloyd George's personal secretariat). "You must speak Zionism to Dr. Weizmann," Mrs. Astor instructed as they sat down to dinner. The Zionist leader had developed access to policy makers and managed to keep the issue of Palestine before them.

As for Weizmann's anti-Zionist Doppelgänger, Lucien Wolf was seeking to impress on Britain's governors the importance of the Jewish factor too. He recognized, however, that during a world war Britain and France would never risk the Russian alliance in order to win Jewish sympathy. He knew that the Zionists were suggesting that Britain could win Jewish support by promising to satisfy Jewish aspirations in Palestine. Quite rightly, he feared that this concrete program was more appealing to the Foreign Office than his own more nebulous approach of trying to get Britain and France to pressure Russia without offending her. Then, unexpectedly, an initiative launched from across the English Channel showed him a possible way forward. France also wanted the Allies to woo the Jews, and she asked Lucien Wolf to help.

The French worried that Germany was already outbidding the Entente for Jewish backing and that German success could have serious repercussions, especially in America, where, as they too believed, the Jewish community was financially powerful and politically influential. To counter this possibility, the French government dispatched to New York two professors (both Jewish) as emissaries and appointed a French Committee for Information and Action Among the Jews of Neutral Countries (Comité française d'information et d'action auprés des juifs des pays neutres) to support their efforts. Based on the professors' reports, the French government came to conclusions similar to those reached by the various informants of the British Foreign Office. While French and British pressure on Russia might win friends among American Jews, it would inevitably alienate the Russian government. Dangling the bait of Palestine before American Jews, however, could appeal to them without necessarily estranging the tsar's ministers. The Quai d'Orsay instructed the Jewish professors to tell American Jews that the end of Ottoman rule in the Middle East would lead to an extension of liberty and increased Jewish settlement in Palestine.

Meanwhile the *comité* had concluded that Britain should establish an organization parallel to theirs and asked Lucien Wolf to form it. Wolf recognized a double opportunity. Both as a Jew and as a British patriot, he wanted to win Jewish backing for the Allies; promising Jews an increased role in Palestine after victory, without going so far as to embrace Zionist prescriptions, could win it. Simultaneously such a task would enable him, and the Conjoint Committee, to outflank Dr. Weizmann. Immediately he prepared a memorandum for the Foreign Office. "I am not a Zionist and I deplore the Jewish National Movement," he began, yet now was the moment for the Allies to declare their sympathy with Jewish aspirations in Palestine and to promise to grant them equal rights there after the war; facilitate their immigration to it; guarantee "a liberal scheme of local self-government for the existing colonies"; support construction of a Jewish university in Jerusalem; and recognize Hebrew as one of the languages of the land. If the Allies did these things, Wolf wrote, they "would sweep the whole of American Jewry into enthusiastic allegiance to their cause." The next day Wolf saw Robert Cecil at the Foreign Office and offered to head up a team of propaganda committees in all the Allied capitals, especially in London, to publicize this program. (A supreme British committee was not what the French *comité* had in mind.) He volunteered to carry the message about the future of Palestine to America himself.

The Foreign Office refused to be stampeded. It weighed Wolf's proposal along with Fitzmaurice's recommendation, the American professors' memorandum, and Sir Henry McMahon's report upon the views of the Italian businessman. What Wolf was suggesting, it noted, differed only in degree from what Weizmann wanted. The Foreign Office, which previously had had little time for Zionism, now underwent a crash course. It forwarded Wolf's memo to the British ambassador in Washington, Cecil Spring Rice. Rice had never liked Wolf. His negative response was predictable.

Impatiently awaiting word, Wolf received worrying information from a French contact: "Mr. Lloyd George has formally assured Dr. Weizmann who is his 'right hand man' at the Ministry of Munitions that Great Britain will grant a charter to the Jews in Palestine in the event of that country coming within the sphere of influence of the British Crown." Lloyd George had done no such thing, but Wolf accepted the warning at face value, and it

galvanized him. On March 3, 1916, he sent Robert Cecil a second memorandum, this one containing a "formula" for Palestine that went about as
far as a man who did not believe that Jews constituted a distinct nationality
could go toward Zionism. Wolf proposed:

> In the event of Palestine coming within the spheres of influence
> of Great Britain or France at the close of the war, the Govern-
> ments of those Powers will not fail to take account of the historic
> interest that country possesses for the Jewish community. The
> Jewish population will be secured in the enjoyment of civil and
> religious liberty, equal political rights with the rest of the popu-
> lation, reasonable facilities for immigration and colonization
> and such municipal privileges in the towns and colonies inhab-
> ited by them as may be shown to be necessary.

Then Wolf did his best to precipitate the Foreign Office's decision. In another message sent three days later, he added that if the Foreign Office accepted his "formula," he would announce it at a mass meeting of Jews, to be
held in East London the following Sunday, March 12.

Wolf sensed correctly that his influence among policy makers was
ebbing. "We should inform Mr. Wolf that his suggested 'formula' is receiving our careful and sympathetic consideration, but that we must consult
our allies and that that must take time," Hugh O'Bierne minuted. In other
words, the Foreign Office would not allow Wolf to tell his meeting that the
British government endorsed his "formula" for Palestine. Lord Crewe,
substituting as foreign secretary for Sir Edward Grey, who was ill, added
that "Mr. L. Wolf cannot be taken as the spokesman of the whole [Jewish]
community." Crewe was already a "Weizmannite," according to his wife,
and would have known that the Zionists would not be satisfied with Wolf's
"formula." By now perhaps Robert Cecil had become a "Weizmannite" too:
He repudiated Wolf even more thoroughly than Lord Crewe had done.
"May I add," he appended to O'Bierne's minute, "that if and when we are
allowed by our allies to say anything worth saying to the Jews it should not
be left to Mr. Lucien Wolf to say it?"

Thus the tectonic plates of Britain's Jewish policy began to slide. On February 28, 1916, O'Bierne composed the first Foreign Office minute to link
the fate of Palestine both with Jewish interests and with British chances of
victory. Here the influence of Dragoman Fitzmaurice was dominant, for
O'Bierne aimed at influencing the Jews of Turkey, not of America. "It has
been suggested to me," he told his colleagues, "that if we could offer the

Jews an arrangement as to Palestine which would strongly appeal to them, we might conceivably be able to strike a bargain with them as to withdrawing their support from the Young Turk government which would then automatically collapse." But the influence now of American and Italian and French informants, and of the Quai d'Orsay more generally, as well as of Weizmann and Lucien Wolf, meant that the focus would shift from Turkey's to America's Jews and then to Jews everywhere. "To obtain Jewish support," Lord Reading explained to Edwin Montagu only three weeks after O'Bierne wrote that initial minute, finally had become "the objective of the Foreign Office."

Here two geopolitical matters deserve consideration.

Much as Britain might wish to obtain the support of Jews by dangling the bait of Palestine before them, she could not act as a free agent. She had to consult her partners in the Triple Entente, France and Russia. Russia was likely to approve the idea, so long as the Christian holy places did not fall under non-Christian control, because she would rather offer concessions somewhere far away than relax anti-Semitic policies at home.

French acquiescence, however, could not be taken for granted. France might wish to court the Jews, but France had long-standing claims to Syria, even to "greater Syria" or Syria intégral, which meant Syria defined to include most of Palestine. These claims to territory (except for a northern slice) she had tentatively sacrificed during the Sykes-Picot negotiations in London, which envisioned a condominium of powers governing the region. But the French certainly did not consider that Palestine was Britain's to dangle before the Jews or anyone else. If, after due consideration and consultation, an offer of Palestine to the Jews was to be made, France would want to be among the countries to make it.

But whatever shape such an offer might take, neither Sykes nor Picot had foreseen the need for one while negotiating their agreement in London. The Sykes-Picot Agreement already allocated Palestine, and not to the Jews. Indeed, the Sykes-Picot Agreement did not speak of Jewish interests at all. Herbert Samuel and Edwin Montagu knew this fact, but both men were bound by cabinet etiquette not to speak.

Moreover, an important actor on the Middle Eastern stage might have thought that Britain had already offered Palestine to him. What precisely Grand Sharif Hussein understood to be the likely borders of his projected Arabian kingdom remains obscure; and so do the British negotiators' ideas about them. Some of them were now thinking that it would not contain

Palestine, but precisely to whom Palestine would belong remained unclear. The Sykes-Picot Agreement envisioned a condominium. O'Bierne wrote in his initial minute: "The Jews could be given special colonizing facilities which in time would make them strong enough to cope with the Arab element, when the management of internal affairs might be placed in their hands under America's protection . . . [or] under the administration of some neutral nationality if the United States would not agree." In other memoranda diplomats mentioned Belgium as a neutral power that might serve as trustee. France and Britain nourished their own ambitions as well.

That Jews eventually should form the predominant element, whichever European power or combination of powers oversaw the country, was not in doubt. Already Britain contemplated extending Wolf's "formula" in a direction that would please the Zionists. Crewe informed the British ambassadors to Russia and America that if the Allies did agree to court Jewish opinion, part of the inducement could be that "when in the course of time the Jewish colonists in Palestine grow strong enough to cope with the Arab population they may be allowed to take the management of the internal affairs of Palestine (with the exception of Jerusalem and the Holy Places) into their own hands." Weizmann could have asked for little more.

That the Arabs' reaction would be negative if they learned about such plans, nobody doubted. "It must be admitted," O'Bierne noted, "that if the Arabs knew we were contemplating an extensive Jewish colonization scheme in Palestine (with the possible prospect of eventual Jewish self-government), this might have a very chilling effect on the Arab leaders." So Britain must keep the approach to world Jewry secret. But Lucien Wolf did not realize that his "formula" cut across promises made to Sharif Hussein and continued to push the government to accept it. Eventually Robert Cecil felt obliged to shut him down. "The present time," he warned Wolf, "would, in the interests of the Jews themselves, be badly chosen for the publication of any formula such as that suggested."

In other words, at this very preliminary stage of their courtship of "world Jewry," British officials who had previously been wooing Arabs now understood that they faced a fork in the road. "It is evident," wrote the percipient O'Bierne, "that Jewish colonization of Palestine must conflict to some extent with Arab interests. All we can do, if and when the time comes to discuss details, is to try to devise a settlement which will involve as little hardship as possible to the Arab population. We shall then, of course, have to consult experts." In the initial minute he had indicated which expert he was likely to favor: "I would suggest that we might consult Mr. Fitzmaurice."

The British government could not choose one course without disappointing the advocates of the other. That did not stop them from choosing. They thought that the fate of the British Empire was at stake.

At eight o'clock on the evening of Sunday, June 4, 1916, Hugh James O'Bierne joined Lord Kitchener and his staff at the King's Cross railway station in London. They all boarded the overnight train to Scotland. At Scapa Flow the next day they transferred to the HMS *Hampshire,* a 10,850-ton coal-burning cruiser. Their destination was Russia; O'Bierne had served several terms there as a diplomat, eventually rising to the rank of minister plenipotentiary in Petrograd. He would have proved an invaluable resource for Kitchener there.

But they never arrived in Russia. On the night of Monday, June 5, a German mine sank their ship, killing all but twelve of the *Hampshire*'s 650-man crew and every member of Kitchener's party. Thus the first Briton to conceive the Arab Revolt and the first to write a Foreign Office minute advocating an alliance with the Jews went down together, perishing within minutes of each other in the icy North Sea. Rarely does history afford such a weird and awful symmetry.

But by that date the divergent courses charted by the doomed pair could not be reconciled. Champions of each would compete with ever more fury. Nor were Kitchener's and O'Bierne's the only paths to win advocates. A new phase was opening in the struggle to define a crucial portion of the postwar, post-Ottoman Middle East.

PART III

The Battle for the
Ear of the Foreign Office

CHAPTER 12

Forging the British-Zionist Connection

SIR MARK SYKES and François Georges-Picot both arrived in St. Petersburg at the beginning of March 1916. Their main job was to turn the Anglo-French (Sykes-Picot) agreement into a tripartite Anglo-French-Russian one. That did not prove difficult: Within weeks, Britain and France formally agreed to Russian control of Constantinople, the Turkish straits, and Ottoman Armenia; Russia essentially accepted the remaining division of territory between Britain and France foreseen by Sykes and Picot. Thus did the Triple Entente divide the prospective Ottoman carcass even before they had skinned it, even before it was dead; thus in the spring of 1916 did they fight the war to end all wars, on behalf of small powers, nationality, liberalism, and the like.

Nevertheless, during the long journey to the British embassy in Petrograd, Sir Mark may have been racking his brain to come up with a switch to turn on the Jews. No sooner did he arrive than he read Lord Crewe's remarkable, nearly Zionist, telegram of March 11 to Sir George Buchanan, the British ambassador. Crewe, it will be recalled, had forwarded Wolf's "formula," asking Buchanan to sound the Russians on it. The Foreign Office, Crewe added, believed the scheme "might be made far more attractive to the majority of Jews if it held out to them the prospect that when in course of time the Jewish colonists in Palestine grow strong enough to cope with the Arab population they may be allowed to take the management of the internal affairs of Palestine (with the exception of Jerusalem and the Holy Places) into their own hands." What would the Russians think of this addition to Wolf's "formula"? Crewe wanted to know. Buchanan inquired, and the Russians thought it good, he reported to the Foreign Office. The tsar's ministers would make no difficulties about such promises to Jews, they had informed him, as long as the holy places remained under international control. Eventually this provision would be written into the Tripartite Agreement.

But now the British had to worry about the French, who believed that Palestine belonged to greater Syria and therefore that Palestine's northern parts would belong to them, as Sykes and Picot had arranged when they negotiated their agreement in London only a few short weeks earlier.

After his sessions with Picot, who could better understand French reservations about Palestine than Sir Mark Sykes? Nevertheless he must have read Crewe's wire with mounting enthusiasm. That it reflected policies adumbrated in Herbert Samuel's memorandum (although not Samuel's desire for a British protectorate) provoked from him an effusion of telegrams, on March 14, 16, and 18. He had been thinking about Zionism after all; the cable merely gave him license to express what was in his mind or perhaps helped crystallize what was in it. In any event, those three telegrams inadvertently revealed the hopes, contradictions, tensions, guile, and prejudices now at work in shaping British and Allied wartime policy toward both Jews and Arabs.

Sykes immediately sought out the French diplomat, who had read the relevant portions of the telegram courtesy of the Russian foreign minister, Sergei Dmitrievich Sazonov. The latter had gotten the telegram from Buchanan. Unlike Sykes, Picot did not care for what he read. An international condominium governing Palestine was one thing, he told his friend, but Jewish control of the land was something else entirely. Indeed, he predicted that French patriots would oppose such a policy, with violence if necessary. Sykes insisted upon the necessity of some such move, and enumerated the ostensibly "inestimable advantages to allied cause of active friendship of Jews of the World." Picot "reluctantly admitted" the force of his argument: Conceivably France, as a constituent member of the proposed condominium, could agree to do something in Palestine to satisfy the Jews after all. But that was not what Sykes had in mind. The Jews favored British rule in Palestine, he explained, not French or international rule.

But the two men were accustomed to collaborating. With Sykes leading, one suspects, they concocted a new scheme for Palestine that they hoped would appeal to its three prospective signatories, as well as to the Jews and even to Sharif Hussein. Their plan was that an agent of the sharif (perhaps one of his sons) be made sultan of Palestine under French and British protection and with Russian concurrence; that the three great powers agree upon a method of administering Palestine's holy places; that the new state establish an incorporated chartered company to purchase land for Jewish colonists, who would then become citizens with equal rights to Arabs; that Britain arbitrate any disagreement between the chartered company and the state; and that France arbitrate any disagreement regarding administration of the holy places.

Sir Mark may have thought that he and Picot had squared the circle, but his colleagues in London disagreed. The chartered company would lead to Jewish domination of Palestine, which the Arabs would oppose; and appointment of an Arab sultan would alienate the Jews. They telegraphed Sykes to put the Samuel Memorandum out of his mind. But Sir Mark, original and irrepressible, continued to ruminate. The difficulties of the situation multiplied in his mind. First, Britain needed France in order to win the war against Germany, but Britain's newly revealed interest in Palestine, even if on behalf of the Jews and in order to secure the common cause, might nevertheless estrange her crucial partner. Second, the British and French both needed the Jews (or thought they did), but the Jews' preference for a British protectorate might cause the French to spurn them.

Third, the Allies needed the Arabs to revolt against Turkey. The Arabs might think Britain had promised them Syria including its coastal portions, but France claimed all of Syria, including the coastal portions. Moreover the Arabs had no inkling that Britain and France together were now contemplating making some gesture toward the Jews involving Palestine, which was land the Arabs also wanted and perhaps thought already had been promised to them. Sykes no longer knew what to suggest regarding the conflicting French-Arab claims: "I have repeatedly told Picot that Arabs will not consent to the French holding the whole coast as French territory, but he remains unmovable." As for the proposed gesture toward "Great Jewry," which surely would alienate the Arabs, and as for the general division of Ottoman territory that the three Allies now were planning, Sykes warned: "Keep actual terms of provisional agreement from knowledge of Arab leaders."

Secret diplomacy was the only sort to employ, Sykes argued in his third telegram, when "we bump into a thing like Zionism which is atmospheric, international, cosmopolitan, subconscious, and unwritten, nay often unspoken." He must have spent March 17 pondering the mysteries and powers of international Judaism and discussing them with Buchanan and Picot, and maybe even with the Russians, although their attitudes toward Jews were well known. He concluded, as he now informed the Foreign Office, that the Zionists represented "the key of the situation," by which he meant nothing less than the key to victory in the war. "With 'Great Jewry' against us," he warned, "there is no possible chance of getting the thing thro,' " that is, defeating Germany. Jewish ill will would mean "optimism in Berlin, dumps in London, unease in Paris, resistance to last ditch in C'ople, dissension in Cairo, Arabs all squabbling among themselves." But give the Zionists a reason to support the Allies, and everything would change. "If they want us to win they will do their best which means they will (a) calm their activities in Russia, (b) Pessimism in Germany, (c) stimulate in France, England and Italy, (d) Enthuse in USA." He was heartened because "P[icot] now sees this and understands it and will put it to those who count in France."

In short, Sykes's exposure to Zionism at a crucial moment in the war led him to adapt, but hardly to relinquish, his prewar prejudices and stereotypical thinking about Jews. He continued to believe in their enormous if subterranean power, but where previously he had deemed "Great Jewry" a malign force, now he discerned its positive dimensions and wished to harness them. What seems more remarkable nearly a century later is not that this one individual held such views but rather that they were apparently shared by François Georges-Picot and the men of the Quai d'Orsay in Paris; and by Sir George Buchanan, representing Britain in Russia and the mandarins of the Foreign Office back in London; that is to say, the bulk of the policy-making elite of the two Western liberal great powers. The group in the Foreign Office worried that Sykes had spoken too freely with Picot about Jewish preference for a British rather than a French protectorate in Palestine. They did not want the French to think that they themselves nourished any hopes of gaining that land, although in fact some of them were beginning to. But that Sykes might have gripped the wrong end of the stick altogether; that his notion of Jewish world power was outrageously, egregiously, mistaken; that it was based upon romance and myth and age-old prejudice, not upon fact; and that it was at heart profoundly irrational does not seem to have occurred to any of them. Robert Cecil had expressed the common misconception only a few weeks earlier, upon reading McMahon's report on the views of that Italian businessman in Alexandria: "I do not think it is easy to exaggerate the international power of the Jews."

Although Sykes's and Picot's efforts in Petrograd had direct relevance to Sharif Hussein, who was at that very moment polishing plans for his rebellion against Turkey, the Foreign Office did not even for an instant consider telling him about them.

In Sir Mark Sykes, the Zionists had gained a vigorous, resourceful, and well-placed ally. In early April he returned from Russia to London, where he went to work for the secretariat of the Committee of Imperial Defense. This brought him into close contact with the cabinet's War Committee. As energetic as ever, he authored a series of "Arabian Reports"; launched an investigation into the Zionist movement; and shuttled back and forth as the liaison between government departments concerned with Middle Eastern affairs. The Foreign Office's rejection of his first plan for Palestine does not appear to have daunted him in the least. Nor did the Foreign Office appear to hold that plan against him. Not quite belonging to the tiny number who fashioned government policy, Sykes's views really counted when the policy makers looked for information, context, interpretation, and advice.

Practically his first move upon returning home was to contact Herbert Samuel and explain to him the plan for Palestine that he and Picot had devised. Samuel would have taken it in impassively enough, we may imagine, given what we know of his personality, but it rang a tocsin in his mind. He immediately telephoned Moses Gaster and Chaim Weizmann and proposed a meeting to talk things over. Gaster suggested that Nahum Sokolow be invited as well, and Samuel agreed. The four men gathered at Gaster's home, Mizpah, at 193 Maida Vale, on April 11. Samuel recounted Sykes's plan. Afterward Gaster waxed enthusiastic in his diary: "It practically comes to a complete realization of our Zionist programme. We are offered French-English condominium in Palest. Arab Prince to conciliate Arab sentiment and as part of the Constitution a Charter to Zionists for which England would stand guarantee and which would stand by us in every case of friction." This is the only record of the meeting. We do not know what Weizmann and Sokolow thought, nor even what Samuel thought, but it is doubtful that any of them deemed an Anglo-French condominium to be a realization of *their* Zionist program. It is not clear whether Sykes had mentioned to Samuel, or Samuel to the three Zionists, that in fact the Foreign Office had not approved his and Picot's proposals.

Sykes had also asked Samuel to arrange for him to meet London Zionists. Interestingly, the president of the Local Government Board first put him in touch not with Weizmann (of whose ascent he was well aware), nor with Joseph Cowen (or any other official of the English Zionist Federation), nor even with Nahum Sokolow (who was the highest-ranking official of the World Zionist Organization in Britain), but rather with his old friend Moses Gaster. It was a case of friendship trumping judgment. Samuel wrote to the *haham,* asking him to contact Colonel Mark Sykes: "The suggestion about which I came to see you a few days ago originated with [him] . . . [He] is in very close touch with the Foreign Office and . . . has recently visited Russia in connection with this subject. As the matter should be kept absolutely confidential I think it would be better for him to see you alone, at all events in the first instance." Gaster then wrote to Sykes suggesting alternative times and places for a tête-à-tête. He may not have grasped the golden opportunity this connection represented, saying that if he must go to Sykes, then the meeting should take place the following week, "as I am still suffering from a virulent attack of lumbago." Sykes's reply suggests that making the connection was an urgent matter to him; he did not want to wait until next week. "My Dear Rabbi," he wrote, "If it would be equally convenient for you I should be glad if I might call upon you at 4:30 on Tuesday."

So it began: Mark Sykes made personal contact with English Zionism, a significant moment in the prehistory of the Balfour Declaration. At this preliminary meeting he brought Gaster up-to-date on relevant matters. Then he arranged for Gaster to make contact with the British government (G. H. Fitzmaurice at the War Office, again, and Lancelot Oliphant at the Foreign Office); and with the French government too (François Georges-Picot). Sykes questioned the *haham* closely on Zionist history, present policies, and future goals and requested that he prepare maps locating significant Jewish settlements in Britain, continental Europe, Russia, Ottoman Eurasia, North Africa, and the Middle East including Palestine.

Unfortunately, Sykes had not made contact with the right Zionist. Moses Gaster was jealous, self-important, quick to take offense, and sometimes neither clear-sighted nor clear-minded. He told Sykes that he could speak for and control the Zionist movement in Britain, but that was not true. Although he had enthused about the Franco-British condominium for Palestine in his diary, he strongly opposed it to Sykes in person, indicating that even a German-British condominium would be preferable because at least the Germans were not interested in Egypt. He attributed this idea to Chaim Weizmann, whom Sykes had not yet met, but Weizmann could not conceivably have favored such an idea. In the end Gaster failed to impress: Picot told Sykes that he found the *haham* interesting but lacking a realistic grasp of the situation. He would like to meet someone else. Sykes, who was nothing if not quick, no doubt was thinking along similar lines.

And then Sykes did meet a Zionist with a more realistic grasp, a burly

Jewish Palestinian agronomist (born in Romania) who was on terms with Djemal Pasha in Damascus and who was also a British spy. Aaron Aaronsohn is yet another extraordinary character in a tale replete with them. He flits briefly across the stage now, playing an important role in Mark Sykes's final conversion to Zionism.

Aaronsohn had built a brilliant reputation as Palestine's foremost authority on agriculture and agricultural science. Invited to America by the Department of Agriculture to advise on wheat cultivation in the western states, he made an electric impression. He turned down a professorship at the University of California. After a session with Louis Brandeis, the future Supreme Court Justice wrote: "He is one of the most interesting men I have ever met." American Zionist philanthropists jumped to fund his next project, an agricultural experimental station, to be established in Athlit on the coastal plain at the foot of Mount Carmel. Once war began, it turned out to be the perfect location for making clandestine rendezvous with agents dropped from British naval vessels.

As a prominent Jewish Palestinian, Aaronsohn had served in Jerusalem as an administrator of American relief funds. This brought him into contact with Djemal Pasha. When a plague of locusts descended upon Palestine in the summer of 1915, the Turkish minister of marine appointed Aaronsohn to defeat it. The agronomist had carte blanche to travel the country. He recorded his observations in a diary, and they were not only about locusts. He noted troop movements and gun emplacements too.

Where most Jews in Palestine believed they should do nothing during the war to excite Turkish suspicion, let alone reprisal, Aaronsohn scorned such timidity. Contact with Djemal Pasha convinced him that Zionism had no future under Turkish rule. What precisely he thought should be the relationship between Zionists and the Western powers is obscure, but he had no doubt the Jewish movement needed an Allied victory. His brother Alexander, his two sisters, Rivkah and Sarah, and a colleague at the experimental station in Athlit, Absalom Feinberg, agreed.

In January 1915 Turkish authorities arrested Feinberg, accusing him of contact with British ships anchored in Haifa Bay. The accusation was false, but it gave Feinberg an idea. When he gained his freedom, he went to Aaronsohn with a plan: They would supply the British navy with information they gleaned in their travels as agronomists. Aaronsohn approved. A first attempt to make contact with the British in Cairo failed: Officials there were preoccupied with preparations for the Arab Revolt and thought this unsolicited advance might have been inspired by Germany. A second approach, to British Intelligence in Port Said, proved fruitful—there the responsible official was willing to take a chance. Some two weeks later in the dead of night, a British sailor slipped ashore near Athlit. A packet of papers awaited him. The clandestine organization had made its first delivery. Eventually the Aaronsohns and Feinberg established the NILI spy ring. (NILI was an acronym of a verse from 1 Samuel 15:29, *Netzach Yisrael Lo Yeshaker,* "the eternity of Israel will not lie.") They recruited twenty-one active members; eventually more than a hundred individuals aided the group in one way or another.

The NILI spy ring, whose ultimate goal was the establishment of a Jewish state in Palestine, carried out missions as dangerous to its members as any of Sharif Hussein and his sons' efforts to establish a new Arab kingdom. NILI's informants worked on the land, in the towns and cities, and even in the Ottoman army. But in October 1917 the Turks intercepted one of the carrier pigeons by which the members communicated with one another. Nearly all the NILI activists paid with their lives; some of them, including Aaronsohn's sister Sarah, who took her own life, died after dreadful torture.

The year before this awful dénouement, Aaronsohn had been traveling the country on agricultural business, recording what he saw in his diary. In June 1916 he gained information about a planned Turkish advance upon Suez. He thought a preemptive British counterthrust might enable a Zionist takeover in Palestine. He decided to deliver this message, along with the diary, to the British in person. But he would not go to Cairo, which had rejected his circle's initial approach; and his contact in Port Said had been captured by the Germans while sailing home on leave. So Aaronsohn went to London. His route was perforce circuitous; it required resource and courage. He traveled to Damascus, Constantinople, Vienna, and Berlin (where he connected with American Zionists), then to Stockholm and Copenhagen. In the Danish port he made contact with the British consul. He boarded the Danish liner *Oskar II,* bound for the United States. When she reached the Orkney Islands, not far from where Kitchener and Hugh James O'Bierne perished, a British patrol boat intercepted her. British officials interviewed all passengers in their cabins. Aaronsohn's stateroom, they informed the Danish captain with a wink and a nod (for Aaronsohn had just informed him of the plan), was "full of German stuff." They "arrested" the "German spy" and brought him to London.

It was a funny kind of arrest. The authorities arranged for Aaronsohn to stay at the First Avenue Hotel in High Holborn under an assumed name. They permitted him to attend the theater at night and to sightsee during the day. But Scotland Yard and the War Office thoroughly debriefed the

"Inhabitant of Athlit," as they called him in their reports. Aaronsohn provided them with details on Turkish and German troop movements, the economic and political situation in Syria, and the general mood of people and soldiers. More important perhaps from his own point of view, Aaronsohn marshaled his intimate knowledge of the Palestinian terrain to urge the feasibility of a British invasion. He knew even the most obscure passageways of the Syrian interior, the high and low ground, where water could be found, and so on, arguing for British help in establishing Jewish rule in Palestine. Inevitably the authorities concluded that he should be brought into contact with Sir Mark Sykes.

The two met on October 27 and appear to have talked mainly about Zionism. They met again three days later with the ubiquitous G. H. Fitzmaurice in attendance as well. Aaronsohn reverted to the immediate theme: the need for a British invasion of Palestine. Sykes heard him out. He hoped Britain soon would be in a position to help, he said, but "it requires work." Of course it did. Fitzmaurice, whose idea it first had been for Britain to approach the Jews, must have been pleased. A third meeting took place a week later. By now Aaronsohn realized that his interrogators at the War Office could not commit the Foreign Office to any specific policy; that the Foreign Office sympathized with but would not make a public statement about Zionism; and nor would Mark Sykes. He wrote in his diary, after this third and final meeting, that although his mission had been successful in convincing British authorities that the NILI group could play a useful role, *"Au point de vue diplomatique, fiasco."*

His pessimism was mistaken. Sykes the diplomat gave nothing away, but Aaronsohn had made a strong impression. The Zionist returned to the Middle East, to Cairo, where he went to work for British Intelligence. Thus he avoided the dreadful fate of his sister and other NILI agents. (He would die in an airplane crash in 1919.) In the spring of 1917, when Sykes returned to Egypt on a diplomatic mission, he sought out the charismatic agronomist first of all. He preferred the settler-scientist to the vain and bombastic Moses Gaster. Indeed when he had asked the *haham* about Aaronsohn, the rabbi did little to strengthen his credibility. Aaronsohn was probably a Turkish agent, Gaster warned. "I do not trust [him]. An ambitious man."

If Moses Gaster was not up to the job, and if Aaron Aaronsohn toiled for Great Britain in far-off Cairo, then which Zionist could Mark Sykes productively work with? He did not yet know of Chaim Weizmann, or knew at best only the scantiest details, and Weizmann did not yet suspect the importance of Sir Mark Sykes. But the two could not remain unacquainted for long.

The day after the newspapers broke the story of Lord Kitchener's death in the North Sea, and only shortly after Sykes had returned to England from Russia, a public meeting convened in the vast Egyptian Hall of the Mansion House in the City of London. This imposing building, with its grand marble portico supported by six Corinthian columns, is the official residence of the city's Lord Mayor. Many of the city's formal functions take place there; it is where Britain's chancellors of the exchequer still deliver their annual report on the state of the economy. The purpose of the present meeting was to mark the collection of £50,000 under the auspices of Sir Charles Wakefield, London's lord mayor that year. The fund would provide aid to Armenian Christians living in the war zone with Russia, victims of a brutal Turkish policy of virtual ethnic cleansing. Sir Mark Sykes, among others, addressed this meeting, over which Wakefield presided.

Sykes's interest in the Armenian question had the same root as his interest in the Arab rebellion and his growing interest in Zionism. The three nationalities (he now conceived the Jews to be a nation too) could serve the needs of the British Empire in the former Ottoman dominions, he thought, and the empire could reciprocate by serving the needs of these three long-suffering peoples. Sykes's evolving views on race, nationalism, and imperialism require separate treatment, not least for the light they shed upon Britain's evolving wartime policy on these subjects. Suffice to say here that just as Sykes had sought out Zionists in London with whom to work, so too he had sought out Armenians: hence his presence at the Mansion House on that June afternoon.

A self-conscious Armenian community existed in London. It published a monthly journal called *Ararat;* it sponsored various cultural organizations grouped under an umbrella organization, the Armenian United Association of London; and it supported the British Armenia Committee, which publicized Turkish-inflicted sufferings upon Armenians in their native land and which had a parliamentary branch led by the Liberal MP for North-West Durham, Aneurin Williams. This parliamentary contingent belonged to the radical wing of the Liberal Party and looked to tsarist Russia to liberate Armenia from the yoke of the Young Turks. This was the general attitude of politically conscious Armenians in England, up until about 1919.

One such politically conscious Armenian boasted an Anglicized name. James Aratoon Malcolm was born in Persia, to which his Armenian ancestors had moved in Elizabethan times. There they engaged in shipping and commerce, often with English interests, so that they had come to enjoy a special relationship with the commercial representatives of the United Kingdom. They were well disposed to Jews and accustomed to business dealings with them. In 1881 Malcolm's parents sent their son to study in England (eventually he attended Oxford University), placing him with an old Jewish friend and agent of the family, Sir Albert Sassoon.

After leaving Oxford, Malcolm stayed in London to represent the family firm. Possibly he cut corners in his business dealings. "His previous career as a financier will not bear enquiry," observed an official at the Board of Trade in August 1916. Moreover, if the reaction to him of the famous author John Buchan was typical, he faced obstacles that scarcely could have been anticipated. Buchan had been posted to the News Department of the Board of Trade during the war. The Foreign Office asked for information on Malcolm. "I only once met Malcolm," wrote the author of *The Thirty-nine Steps,* "and he looked an exceedingly unpleasant Jew."

In fact, this Armenian Catholic's true métier appears to have been not commerce and finance (his ostensible British occupations) but rather politics, if not the public kind. He gloried in the role of a fixer, happiest pulling strings or at least thinking he was pulling them, from behind the scenes. During July 1944 he wrote a twelve-page account of his connection with the Zionists during World War I. It is a grandiloquent document and possibly not entirely reliable, but it does suggest the crucial role he played, or liked to think he had played, nearly thirty years earlier.

A few months before Sykes delivered his speech at the Mansion House, the Armenian Catholikos appointed Malcolm to the five-member Armenian National Delegation, whose purpose was to represent Armenian wartime and postwar interests in Europe. Malcolm became its British representative. His work for the delegation brought him into contact with officials at the War Office, Foreign Office, Cabinet Office, and various embassies in London. Possibly it brought him into contact with Sir Mark Sykes.

Malcolm claims in his manuscript to have known Sykes before the war and to have introduced him to Zionists late in the autumn of 1916—an obvious misstatement, for Sykes knew about Zionism as early as March of that year and not as the result of Malcolm's efforts. But the Armenian probably did play a role in introducing Sykes to Chaim Weizmann. By autumn 1916 Sykes was searching for an alternative to Moses Gaster; he had met and been impressed by Aaron Aaronsohn. One day, feeling low about his failure to work Zionism effectively, he bumped into Malcolm in Whitehall Gardens and asked whether he had any Zionist connections. As it happened, the previous year Malcolm had recruited Leopold Greenberg of *The Jewish Chronicle* to the Russia Society, founded to spread knowledge in Britain of the country that Armenians hoped would liberate their homeland from the Turks. On Sykes's suggestion, Malcolm called at Greenberg's offices and explained that his friend wished to meet the true leaders of Zionism in Britain. Greenberg immediately mentioned Weizmann and Sokolow, a self-effacing and generous gesture, given the nature of his relationship with the former at any rate. He promised to introduce Malcolm to them. Shortly afterward the introduction occurred at Weizmann's newly acquired London home in Addison Road. Other Zionist leaders were present as well. "I recounted the gist of my several conversations with Sir Mark," Malcolm recalled. "Dr. Weizmann was most interested and asked his colleagues for their views. All of them, and notably Mr. Sokolow, were skeptical and hesitant. But Dr. Weizmann . . . asked when he could meet Sir Mark Sykes. I said if I could telephone to Sir Mark I might be able to fix it there and then. Accordingly I rang him up, said I was speaking from Dr. Weizmann's house and asked when I could bring him along. Sir Mark fixed the appointment for the very next day, which was a Sunday."

For what it is worth, the Leonard Stein Papers at the New Bodleian Library in Oxford contain a clipping entitled "James Malcolm—the Gentile Zionist," unidentifiable as to author, date, or even publication, that confirms this version of events. But other accounts suggest that Weizmann himself initiated the contact with Sykes, although only after meeting Malcolm, because only then did he understand the crucial role Sykes played in advising the government about Palestine. At any rate we know from Gaster's diary that Weizmann, Greenberg, and Malcolm met with Sykes on Sunday, January 28, 1917. Weizmann called Gaster that evening. "He had met Sir Mark Sykes and found out that he was an old friend of mine," Gaster recorded. "He realized that the whole problem rested now in Sir M's hands and that he was the man on whom our Zionist hopes hang."

The *haham* understood immediately that Weizmann's intrusion threatened his own role. He penned a letter to Sykes the next morning: "Can I see you anywhere just for a few moments? One of my co-workers told me last night of the interview which he had with you . . . it is of some importance that I should put matters and persons in the proper light before you. Caveant Consules." Perhaps in response to this letter, Sykes called him back, but the ensuing conversation only can have confirmed Gaster's fears. Weizmann had made a good impression. "He was earnest in his plea for Zion," Gaster recorded Sykes telling him. Worse still, Sykes had urged Weizmann "to formulate proposals, to prepare for some machinery."

Gaster felt it keenly that Sykes had said this first to Weizmann and not to him—"As I understood him when he now spoke to me!" And unkindest cut of all: "I then learned that W. had another appointment with him that evening."

Sykes clearly recognized in Weizmann the Zionist he had been seeking, while Weizmann immediately recognized in Sykes the highly placed government official with whom Zionists could most effectively work. Gaster had been obstructing the relationship, to the cost of the movement as a whole. Weizmann would deal with the *haham;* meanwhile he and Sykes planned yet another meeting, this time to include a representative group of responsible Zionist leaders. Gaster could take part, but his role would be diminished. This was, in fact, the breakthrough moment for Weizmann and for Zionism. A crucial connection was about to be forged.

CHAPTER 13

Defining the British-Arab Connection

LIKE TWO SHIPS headed for a collision in the dark of night—or rather, given that part of the world, like two desert caravans separated by trackless wastes but following intersecting routes—the Arab and Jewish nationalist movements pushed relentlessly forward, oblivious to each other, fated nonetheless to coincide eventually. During 1916 the Zionists in London gained strength. Early in 1917 Weizmann and his allies made the crucial connection with Sir Mark Sykes, a giant step toward gaining the support of British policy makers for a Jewish homeland in Palestine. During this same period Sharif Hussein and his sons had won British backing for the establishment of an Arab kingdom, part of which, they appear to have expected, would include Palestine. With British encouragement, they launched their rebellion against the Ottoman Empire in early June 1916. Then, during the following months, as the Zionists in London moved toward their ultimate objective, Sharif Hussein and his sons fought their way toward theirs, with this difference: They had to employ the skills not only of diplomacy but of the battlefield as well; and they placed their own lives in the balance.

"What befits a person who has been heaped with the goodwill of the Caliph and who has been elevated to the highest honors, when that person betrays the Caliph by joining the latter's enemy?" asked the leading ulema, or holy men, of Damascus. They had been convened by order of the Ottoman authorities shortly after the sharif proclaimed his revolt. And the ulema answered: "Deposition and death." Hence the fatwa directed against Hussein and his family: It would be, as they always had known it must be, war to the knife.

At the outset of the revolt, Sharif Hussein and his sons had mobilized no more than twenty thousand fighting men, mainly from desert and hill tribes, rarely from towns. The hill tribesmen were "hard and fit, very active, independent, cheerful snipers," but they knew little of military discipline and resisted any attempt to impose it. They consented to serve as soldiers only under their own sheikhs and only for limited periods. If they wished to go home to see their wives and children while on service, no one would stop them so long as they provided someone to take their place. Moreover the various tribes nourished grievances against each other, which could be settled only by blood. As a result, "no man quite trusts his neighbor, though each is usually quite wholehearted in his opposition to the Turks. This would not prevent him working off a family grudge by letting down his private enemy." Weighing them up, T. E. Lawrence concluded that Sharif Hussein's entire army would not be able to defeat a single company of Turks, properly entrenched. Rather, a single company of Turks could defeat the sharif's entire army. Consequently, "the value of the tribes is defensive only, and their real sphere is guerilla warfare."

This realization dawned earlier in some quarters than others. Most British military men, less imaginative than Lawrence, saw the tribesmen merely as picturesque mounted rabble, "a horde of Arabs," as one described them. When confronted by a hostile force, such men on their camels and horses would "spread in a fanlike movement over the whole horizon . . . eternally sweeping about for no apparent reason, unless it be bravado or the instinct of the kite. Drop a shell in front of them and they will swerve like a flight of teal, make a wide detour at full gallop, and appear on the other flank." Orthodox British soldiers did not understand, let alone appreciate, such men and certainly did not know how to make good use of them.

Neither, apparently, did the sharif or his sons, at least to begin with, for all their intimate knowledge of the people of the Hejaz, and for all their prewar military campaigns. Their initial strategy was to mobilize the tribesmen and to hurl them against the cities and towns where Ottoman forces and officials were stationed in numbers—Mecca, Taif, and Medina, most prominently, but also, and crucially in this first stage of rebellion, the Red Sea port of Jeddah. Once those places had been captured, they intended to press the remaining Ottomans gradually from their country. It nearly didn't happen.

In Mecca, as we have seen, the sharif's forces captured the acting Ottoman governor and commandant at his headquarters in the holy city. The fighting had been fierce but relatively brief. An Ottoman detachment held out in a well-defended fortress on the outskirts of the town, however, and the Arabs required big guns transported from Jeddah to bombard and subdue them. Even so they persisted in their defiance for a month—the last Ottoman detachments did not surrender until July 10. The Turkish deserter Muhammad al-Faruki, who had been summoned by Sharif Hussein from Cairo, crowed to Gilbert Clayton, the Cairo intelligence officer who had debriefed him and believed his lies and had thereby helped to set the entire rebellion on its course: "I have drunk the cup of happiness for being able to hit the mean Turks actually. Praise be to GOD . . . Sir, each gun I fired had echoed in my heart with pleasure and gladness . . . No better life than it is now." His celebration was premature.

Consider the circumstances that enabled those guns to be transported from Jeddah to Mecca. They had been removed from Jeddah when its Ottoman defenders surrendered to the emir of the Harb tribe and four thousand of his men, followers of Sharif Hussein. In fact, however, the Harb tribe had not defeated the Ottomans. A Turkish newspaper explained: "Our small force of a few hundred at Jeddah had to cope with brigands by land and the British by sea; [but] they only surrendered when water and ammunition were exhausted." David Hogarth, now chief of the Arab Bureau in Cairo and editor of its *Arab Bulletin,* agreed. At the outset, he wrote, two British patrol boats and a seaplane had softened up the Turkish defenders with bombs and cannonades; when, on Friday, June 16, the town finally gave in, however, it did so "probably more through lack of water and ammunition than Arab attack." A specialist newspaper published in London, *Great Britain and the Near East,* put even a more pacific gloss upon the affair: "At Jeddah, the Shereef's men merely camped outside the walls, until the mayor, delegated by the Commandant and the Mutessarif, came out to parley."

Meanwhile neither the siege of Medina (led by Feisal and Ali) nor the siege of Taif (led by Abdullah) was prospering. At Taif, Abdullah chose to waste time rather than lives, as the British snidely commented, and did not hurry to attack the town, realizing, no doubt, that it was not self-supporting and that therefore time was his ally. Every morning his batteries hammered the town walls; every afternoon his cavalry demonstrated their skills on horseback while harmlessly firing their rifles into the air, within view of the Turks but just out of range of their artillery; and every evening the Turks repaired their walls. So the weeks passed. "The people at Mecca are getting restless at the long resistance at Taif, and the Sherif has asked for an aeroplane to fly over it. He thinks that it would persuade the garrison to surrender at once," reported a British officer in Cairo. The sharif was mistaken, however, for the Turks did not surrender until September 23, three and a half months after the siege had begun. Again, lack of food and ammunition, not Arab military prowess, proved decisive.

Medina turned out to be a much tougher nut to crack than Taif. In fact, it did not crack at all during World War I and only surrendered in January 1919.

Ali and Feisal, it will be recalled, had proclaimed the Arab Revolt outside Medina on June 5, 1916. First they tore up stretches of the railway connecting the city with Damascus; then they stormed in. A fierce and desperate battle ensued. The Turks threw back the Arabs and advanced upon suburban areas in their turn, bringing sword and fire, pillage and rape—indeed, Armenian methods—but no decisive victory. Only then did the siege of Medina commence. The city grew enough food on its own, so it could not be starved as Taif had been, although it could be made to suffer. It boasted walls as sturdy as Taif's, and it contained four forts jammed with well-armed Ottoman soldiers. Worst of all, from the Arab point of view, it still possessed the railway. The Arabs had torn up the track, but Turkish soldiers quickly repaired it. The railway was the Ottoman's lifeline to Damascus; so long as they controlled it, Damascus could send men, guns, ammunition, and other supplies down the line and keep Medina going.

The Ottoman general Fakhri Pasha felt sufficiently confident in Medina's ability to resist the siege that he established a defensive perimeter outside the city walls. Opposing them, Feisal's and Ali's besieging tribesmen formed a loosely maintained circle. They carried a variety of ancient, inaccurate, and oft-mended shooters, as well as British-supplied Japanese rifles that had a disconcerting tendency to explode when fired; the ammunition was of the wrong caliber altogether. To remedy these material deficiencies, the British sent guns and ammunition to Rabegh, a port town on the Red Sea, roughly halfway between Mecca and Medina but to their west. A duplicitous chief in Rabegh, who thought the Turks would win, simply took what the British offloaded and kept it in his own stores. Eventually this man was sent packing and the British equipment was successfully transported inland, but it proved insufficient. As a result, "at Medina the Arab forces appear rather depressed. The Turkish superiority in guns and machine-guns makes them [Arabs] unable to do anything serious." The Arabs and the British worried that when Fakhri Pasha realized the weakness of the forces arrayed against him, he would break through the ring of encircling Arabs and march the hundred miles south to Mecca. If he did so, he could take that city and end the rebellion then and there.

In fact, Fakhri Pasha sent out more than one sortie from Medina but never an army big enough to defeat the besiegers decisively—a lack of initiative the British officers found difficult to explain. During August 3–4 something like a major battle developed about twenty miles south of Medina on the Mecca road, but it had no clear victor. Attention then turned to Rabegh, not merely because it served as a conduit for British equipment but because a strong Arab force there could back up the tribesmen surrounding Medina; and if Fakhri's armies ever did break through the ring and head south, a reserve at Rabegh could cut them off or if necessary take them from the rear. Could the Arabs hold Rabegh themselves, or should the British send troops to help them? They could not send Christian troops, for then the sharif would be seen to depend upon infidels. Eventually Ali and his followers peeled off from the siege to occupy Rabegh themselves. The British sent no troops but promised to help defend the port from the sea if necessary. Feisal, meanwhile, tired of banging his head against the walls of Medina, retired in disgust some miles south to Hamra to recuperate. He left behind soldiers of the Harb tribe to maintain the rather ineffective blockade.

So in the fall of 1916 the Arab Revolt hung fire: Ali occupied Rabegh, indeed was practically pinned there; Feisal sat in Hamra, where at least his forces interposed between Medina and Mecca; and Abdullah finally returned from Taif to Mecca to counsel his father and then after a period of months rode north with troops to station somewhere above Medina, thereby completing the encirclement and threatening the railway line. Nevertheless the trains continued to run, and Medina gave no indication of surrender. "The situation in the Hijaz, though not yet alarming, is decidedly serious," Storrs wrote to George Lloyd. This appraisal appears accurate.

The question occupying minds on both sides was how to break the stalemate. Fakhri Pasha thought to do so by threatening Yanbo, an Arab-controlled port some thirty miles to his west and eighty miles up the coast from Rabegh. Had he taken that town, he might have swept south to take Rabegh as well; in other words, to threaten Yanbo was to threaten Rabegh, which was to threaten Mecca too. Hurriedly the British dispatched a portion of their Red Sea fleet to protect the town. Fakhri's troops backed off, but the threat they posed remained. Meanwhile Feisal thought to take pressure off Yanbo by menacing Wejh, another port, this one some 180 miles farther north. Moreover, if he managed to establish a base at Wejh, then he, like his brother Abdullah, could threaten any number of points along the Damascus-Medina railway line.

Here it is important to point out that the British navy had the power to support any Arab advance upon any Red Sea port by transporting Arab fighting men in ships from port to port, and by shelling the Turkish garrisons from offshore. They controlled the Red Sea.

Feisal decided to capture Wejh with such British assistance. He summoned his youngest brother, Zeid, to take over a portion of his army at Hamra. He intended to lead the remainder along the coastal road to Wejh. What followed illustrates both the strengths and the weaknesses of the Arab military at this point in their national struggle.

At Medina, a Turkish mounted infantry patrol pushed through a weak spot in the line of remaining besiegers; thereupon many Arab soldiers deserted their posts and rushed to save their families in the villages, now threatened, behind them. Zeid himself beat a hasty retreat to Yanbo. When Feisal hurried back to Medina to repair the damage, the left wing of his own army suddenly retreated for no apparent reason. A little later, when Feisal ordered a general retreat, these soldiers stubbornly refused to retire farther but instead chose to engage the Turks on their own in a battle of twenty-four hours' duration. They then broke off to rejoin their commander in chief. Their leaders explained to Feisal that they had retired in the first instance not from cowardice but only because they wished to brew their coffee undisturbed!

Meanwhile Ali's army had marched out of Rabegh to help in the advance to Wejh; then upon hearing a false report of the defection of an allied tribe, it had marched back into Rabegh again.

Feisal finally set out for Wejh with approximately four thousand camel corps and four thousand infantry. It was a much larger native force than had been seen in living memory in Arabia, in fact "the largest Arab force ever assembled," according to one authority. The spectacle amazed and awed all who witnessed it, which was as Feisal intended. The mighty army stirred the Arab imagination; it was a coup de théâtre, a recruiting device. Feisal carried only an eight-day supply of food and thirty-six hours of water, planning to stop along the route where he knew wells to be located. In the end, for the last two and a half days of the advance, his 380 baggage camels went without food, and the army marched the last fifty miles on half a gallon of water per man and no food at all. T. E. Lawrence accompanied them. Even that famous stoic was impressed by the Arab display of endurance. The lack of food and water, he wrote, "did not seem in any way to affect the spirits of the men, who trotted gaily into Wejh singing songs and

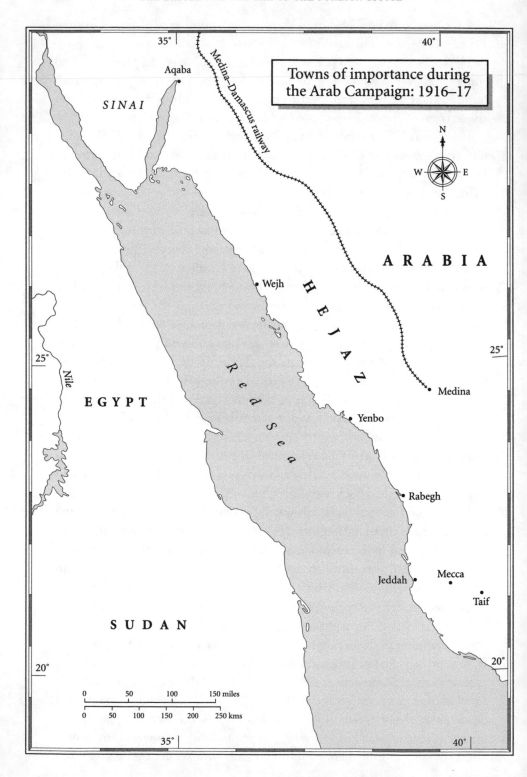

Towns of importance during
the Arab Campaign: 1916–17

executing sham charges; nor did it affect in any way their speed or energy. Feisal said, however, that another thirty-six hours of the same conditions would have begun to tell on them."

Notice, however, that Feisal's army did not capture Wejh; his men entered the town without encountering any resistance. In fact, Feisal had left behind in Yanbo a contingent of 550 Arab troops, deeming them inferior, and arranged for British ships to transport them north; they would attack Wejh from the sea in concert with his own approach by land. But when the 550 arrived, Feisal and his army were nowhere to be seen. While en route to Wejh, Feisal's army had learned that Abdullah's force had fought a successful engagement with the Turks north of Medina, and they immediately halted to celebrate and did not cease celebrating for some time. Up in Wejh, however, the punctual British stuck to the schedule. One warship commenced to fire upon the Turkish positions. Another brought the 550 men to land. They divided into three groups, "about 100 who really meant fighting and advanced directly against the Turkish position," recorded a British captain who observed the battle, "about 300 who moved along the beach and incontinently went off to loot and fight in the town [and] . . . about 100 who sat on the beach and did nothing during the whole operations."

Whatever the British opinion of them, the Arabs who took Wejh had taken a crucial position. Feisal, traveling by land, arrived two days later on January 25, deeply embarrassed to have missed the fight. But local chiefs and tribesmen, impressed by the victory and by the enormous force Feisal had marched up the coast, flocked to join his rebel army anyway. Moreover, now that the port was in Arab hands, General Fakhri Pasha would have to turn his back upon them to attack Yanbo or Rabegh, an impossibly dangerous maneuver. For the same reason, he would hesitate even more to risk a march on Mecca. He was locked in to Medina, the railway his lifeline. At the same time, with Wejh secure, Feisal and his augmented force finally could turn their undivided attention to that railway. It was the Turkish jugular vein. They intended to cut it.

So much for the front lines of the revolt. Simultaneously, in Mecca, the grand sharif was establishing his government. He appointed a cabinet or administrative council of nine members dominated by his sons, even though at the moment they were occupied in the field of battle. Hussein made Ali his grand vizier, Abdullah his foreign minister, and Feisal his minister of the interior. The remainder of cabinet posts—justice, public works, *wakf* and holy places, education, and finance—he filled with notables of Mecca. He appointed a legislative assembly headed by a president and vice president, with twelve members to represent the sharifian clans, the holy places, and the secular population. Also he founded in Mecca a newspaper, *Al Kibla,* for purposes of publicity and propaganda.

At one level the weight of this new regime bore lightly upon the people of the Hejaz. "The return to chthonic conditions has meant the restoration of tribal or family authority and a great decrease in the exercise of the central government," reported Lawrence. The grand sharif understood that his people, whether townsmen or Bedouin, loathed intrusive government officials. He even suspended the collection of taxes (although not the collection of customs in the ports).

At the same time, however, Hussein intended to rule with a heavy hand in that his administration would enforce strict Sharia law, as set out in the Quran. "We fortify ourselves on our noble religion which is our only guide," he declared. That meant undoing reforms carried out by the modernizing Young Turks. The sharif suspended the Turkish civil code, which meant suspending the Young Turk prohibition on slavery. It meant reinstating the archaic Muslim legal approach to women—for did not the good book say, as Hussein fondly pointed out, that "a man shall have twice a woman's share"? In rebelling against the Young Turks, the sharif meant to throw off the onerous Ottoman yoke, but let us be clear: He meant, too, to set back the clock in certain crucial respects. Lawrence wrote in disbelief: "The Sherif intends, when there is time, to extend the principles and scope of the Sharia to cover modern difficulties of trade and exchange!"

He also intended to establish his authority beyond the shadow of a doubt. This, he decided, meant assuming a new and more impressive title than Emir or Grand Sharif. On the morning of October 29, 1916, the notables of Mecca, secular as well as religious, gathered at his palace. Hussein came to greet them. "The deputies of the nation hailed him with hearts full of joy and respect and love," wrote the reporter for *Al Kibla.* Abdullah now "explained" to his father the purpose of this congregation. It wished to present him with a petition which ran in part as follows:

> We have known no Moslem Emir who has feared God and obeyed His word, who has clung to the traditions of His religion—the Koran—in word and deed, more than you have done yourself. We have not known a man more capable to take charge of our affairs than you are . . . We proclaim Your Majesty as King, and we swear to God that we shall always be loyal and obedient to you.

It was a climactic moment, carefully prepared for by the clandestine communiqués with Kitchener and Storrs and McMahon; the establishment of contact with the Syrian conspirators; the risks his sons had run for him in Constantinople, Damascus, and Medina; the risks they all ran still. But Hussein professed before the notables of Mecca to have been taken by surprise: "I have never thought such a thing necessary . . . I swear to you by God Almighty that this thing which you ask me to do now has never occurred to me, nor did I ever think of it when you and I started our blessed movement."

When the coronation was finished, Abdullah, who had helped to stage-manage the event, dispatched a telegram in French to the British high commissioner in Egypt, and to his fellow foreign ministers at The Hague, Christiania, Copenhagen, Petrograd, Bucharest, Berne, Washington, Rome, Paris, Havre, Corfu, and Kabul. The telegram requested that their governments recognize his father's new title, *Malik el Bilad el Arabia.*

What precisely did the title mean? The English translated it as "King of the Arabs" or "King of the Arab Nation." Did that mean king of all Arabs everywhere? The grand sharif seemed to think so. He said in his speech of acceptance to the Meccan notables: "The Arabs of Syria and Iraq . . . are yearning to be united with us and to restore their freedom and glory. I have received messages from their notables to this effect." He intended a loose sort of rule, a kingdom or empire in which important constituents, while recognizing his headship, enjoyed a form of home rule. Abdullah, on the telephone with an English official, did not think other Arab leaders would dare object: "The History of the Emir of Mecca goes back to the Abbasides. It is not important whether those people would agree or not."

But what if the British did not agree? Recall their skepticism of any large, independent Arab kingdom. Recall, too, the ambiguous cribbings and hedgings by which McMahon's letters had attempted to restrict Hussein's territorial ambitions; recall, above all, the Sykes-Picot Agreement, latterly become a Tripartite Agreement, which envisioned a British-dominated Iraq, a French-dominated Syria, and an internationalized Palestine. Finally recall that by this date the mandarins of the Foreign Office were just beginning to consider the possibility of a Jewish-dominated Palestine.

In short the ambitions of the newly declared "King of the Arabs" conflicted with those of Great Britain, which, not surprisingly, determined to rein him in, although without discouraging his revolt. They must design for him a title that both he and they could accept: if not King, then perhaps His Majesty the Sharif, or if that was unacceptable, then perhaps Sultan; or if it must be King, then King over a carefully delimited territory. Finally McMahon suggested King of the Hejaz as a suitable compromise, and the title stuck. It was a comedown, and surely Hussein knew it, but there was nothing he could do. He depended too heavily upon British advice and material support. The episode reveals to us, even if it did not make plain to him, how little he was a free agent, and how wide was the gap between the future he envisioned for himself and his people and the future envisioned for them all by the British government.

Hussein and his soldier sons depended upon British support, but the British argued among themselves about how much to give them. Those who believed the war would be won on the Western Front, the so-called westerners, begrudged sending even a single man to help the Arab Revolt—a sideshow within a sideshow, as they deemed it. Those who believed the Western Front was a killing field from which neither side would emerge victorious sought a way around it. These "easterners," as they were called, favored the landing at Gallipoli, the campaign in Mesopotamia, and support for the sharif's rebellion, among other strategies.

In London the government alternated between the two poles, sometimes favoring one, sometimes the other. In the Middle East, it is safe to say, every Briton who counted advocated the "eastern" position. Of course the British maintained a sizable force in Egypt in order to safeguard the Suez Canal, and no westerner opposed that. But they would not augment it to help the sharif. "With another British Cavalry Division I think I might almost guarantee to clear the Turks out of southern Palestine and relieve the pressure on the Sherif," Sir Archibald James Murray, the normally cautious British commanding officer in Egypt, informed the chief of the Imperial General Staff, Sir William Robertson. Here is Robertson's position: "My sole object is to win the war and we shall not do that in the Hejaz." Murray did not get the extra cavalry division.

The British army in Egypt had beaten off a first Ottoman invasion in February 1915. Under Murray it beat off a second attack in August 1916. Now slowly, warily, systematically, without reinforcements, Murray pushed his line of defense farther north and east into the Sinai. But that was still a long way from Sharif Feisal in Wejh or Grand Sharif Hussein in Mecca or Abdullah and Ali and Zeid in Jeddah and the vicinity of Medina. The British army in Egypt would play no central role in their drama for some time to come.

But a short, blue-eyed, blond-haired, lantern-jawed, hard-as-nails young man whom Hogarth had known at Oxford and now had brought into his intelligence operation in Cairo would do so. T. E. Lawrence, perhaps unfairly, came to overshadow every other British officer and Arab Bureau colleague serving in the Middle East. Some of these men were daredevils themselves, but none of them possessed Lawrence's flair and charisma, or his genius for publicity; and of them all, only he could write like an angel. Even his dispatches back to the Arab Bureau read almost like literature, albeit literature advocating military stratagems and informed by an acute military intelligence. An example:

> The Hejaz war is one of dervishes against regular troops—and we are on the side of the dervishes. Our text-books do not apply to its conditions at all. It is the fight of a rocky, mountainous, illwatered country (assisted by a wild horde of mountaineers) against a force which has been improved—so far as civilized warfare is concerned—so immensely by the Germans as almost to have lost its efficiency for rough-and-tumble work.

His trenchant and beautifully written reports established his reputation, first in the Middle East and then beyond. "Lawrence is quite excellent," Clayton, the director of intelligence in Cairo, informed the director of intelligence in London, "you may take his stuff as being good."

As practically everyone knows, Lawrence emerged from an unconventional background. His father, Thomas Robert Tighe Chapman, heir to an Irish baronetcy, abandoned his wife to live with his daughter's governess. He then changed his surname to Lawrence. They did not marry but had five illegitimate sons, of whom Thomas Edward was the second. The family lived in modest circumstances, eventually moving to Polstead Road, Oxford, where young Ned (as he had been nicknamed) attended high school and then Jesus College, Oxford University. Already he knew that he wanted to become an archaeologist. Before the war he traveled extensively throughout the Ottoman Middle East, learning and mapping the countryside, participating in important digs, studying the people and their language and dialects. When war broke out, he volunteered for service. Inevitably the authorities posted him to Cairo to work for intelligence; but bored with opening mail, answering the telephone, decoding telegrams, and designing postage stamps, Lawrence managed to transfer to his old Oxford mentor, Hogarth, at the Arab Bureau. His duties there bored him too, so in mid-October 1916 he jumped at the chance to accompany Ronald Storrs to Jeddah for consultations with Sharif Abdullah.

The next step in the Lawrence saga is again well known. They journeyed by ship down the Red Sea; Lawrence took potshots at glass bottles lined up on the rail, much to the annoyance of Storrs, who would rather play chess. They arrived in Jeddah to be greeted by the British agent, Lieutenant-Colonel Cyril Wilson, whom they both viewed as dull-witted, even though he served as principal adviser to Grand Sharif (as he still was) Hussein. The French, jealous of Britain's growing influence in the region, had likewise established a consulate in Jeddah under Colonel Edouard Brémond. Their aim was to support the Arab Revolt just enough that it could continue to harass the Turks without actually liberating Syria, for which they had their own postwar plans. Thus the English in Jeddah engaged in an awkward pas de deux with their "froggy Allies," as General Murray once termed them; they were partners in the Great War with common enemies and common purposes, but they had competing interests in the Middle East, which Sykes and Picot had resolved only momentarily. At one dinner, perhaps searching for something to discuss that would not lead to friction, Brémond mentioned that one of his staff had purchased, not for an hour or an evening but body and soul, une *"jeune négresse."* Storrs recalled Brémond going on to explain: "A Negress, [but] she is Circassian; only one calls such women Negresses." This was, Storrs considered, "a curious and pleasing convention."

Lawrence, who as we have seen wanted "to biff the French out of Syria," made the most of the situation. He attended a meeting where Storrs and Wilson informed Abdullah, who had traveled down from Mecca, that the British would not send airplanes or troops for the rebellion, even though these had been promised. In this conference Wilson tried to keep up, but his rudimentary Arabic rendered him the third man out among the Britons. Storrs confided to a friend, "He reminds me of a very low-geared bicycle working at full speed day and night." But "super cerebral Lawrence" impressed Storrs with his knowledge of the language. Moreover he impressed Abdullah "with his extraordinarily detailed knowledge of the Turkish Army." When Abdullah telephoned to his father in Mecca and put Storrs on the line to explain matters, the Englishman suggested, on the spur of the moment, that Lawrence visit Feisal, who was at Hamra, barely maintaining the siege of Medina, to assess the situation. Storrs implied to the grand sharif that Lawrence then might be able to persuade the British government to send troops and airplanes after all. Of course, that was what Lawrence wanted the government to do, if only to keep the French out.

So he leaped at this chance, arranged by Storrs and endorsed by Hussein. Next day he took ship from Jeddah to Rabegh, first stage of the journey to

Hamra. At Rabegh he met Ali and the youngest of the four brothers, Zeid. Ali did not approve of Lawrence's mission. Infidels did not travel in the Hejaz, he reminded him. Moreover hostile tribes stood in the way. He would permit Lawrence to journey inland only in great secrecy, after dark, wearing an Arab cloak and head-cloth and adjured to silence. It was a hard, dangerous passage, difficult for Lawrence, who was as yet unused to traveling by camel, let alone in the desert heat, as he had to do the second day of his journey. But of such experiences would his legend be made, and finally he and his guides arrived in Hamra and the long lean figure of Feisal stood before him: "I felt at first glance that this was the man I had come to Arabia to seek—the leader who would bring the Arab Revolt to full glory."

Lawrence had to report back to his superiors on Feisal's needs and persuade them to make them good—and then the British must actually do so. In this respect it did not hurt that back in London Asquith's government had just fallen, and that a new one led by David Lloyd George, a confirmed easterner, had taken its place. Soon Lawrence and Feisal were planning the assault upon Wejh and then undertaking it. By the time they entered the town and claimed it for the Arab Revolt, the two men were comrades. Feisal gave him his own white silk gold-embroidered wedding garments to wear in the desert heat. The image we all have of Lawrence of Arabia, whitely shimmering in Arab costume, was beginning to take shape. The two men began planning the next stage of the war with Turkey—"to set the desert on fire" as Lawrence put it—by attacking the railway line.

Sykes made his connection with Weizmann, and Lawrence cemented his with Feisal, in January 1917. Thus did the Zionist and the Arab movements hasten at ever increasing speed toward a point of convergence.

CHAPTER 14

Managing the British-Zionist Connection

EUROPE HAD BECOME a charnel house. The number of casualties mounted into the millions, staggering the imagination, beggaring description. No government implicated in such slaughter could survive, not even H. H. Asquith's carefully constructed coalition in England. It fell on December 5, 1916, not long after the Battle of the Somme, in which Britain suffered more than 400,000 dead, wounded, or captured. It was the last British cabinet in which members of the Liberal Party formed a majority.

Asquith's supporters lamented that the war had transformed into liabilities some of Liberalism's proudest prewar features, such as a willingness to compromise and a cautious approach to the expansion of government power. Liberals mourned the inutility of tolerance, judiciousness, and moderation during wartime. On the other side, Asquith's political opponents—and even some of his friends, albeit with more or less reluctance—emphasized the government's indecisiveness, lack of organization, general ineffectiveness, and drift. William Waldegrave Palmer, second Earl of Selborne and a Conservative member of Asquith's coalition in which he served as president of the Board of Agriculture, voiced typical complaints in an aide-mémoire that he wrote upon resigning in June 1916. The prime minister, he thought, would have made a great judge during peacetime. "As a War PM," however, he had been "quite hopeless . . . He had . . . no ounce of drive . . . not a spark of initiative." As for the foreign secretary, Sir Edward Grey, Selborne deemed him equally irresolute: "He never came to the Cabinet and said 'this is the position, this is what I think ought to be done, do you agree?' " Selborne rendered a more positive verdict on David Lloyd George, the man who would replace Asquith as prime minister: "Very clever, with vision, precision, driving power and courage in wonderful combination." But Selborne did not trust Lloyd George: "He would leave anyone in the lurch anywhere if he thought it suited his purpose." (We will have reason to recall this assessment later.) Selborne also made insider observations of Herbert Samuel ("a clever, efficient and straight little Jew") and of Edwin Montagu ("a very clever Jew . . . he will go far").

Six months later, when Lloyd George wrested the premiership from Asquith, he offered cabinet positions to both those clever Jews. Samuel declined without hesitation, remaining characteristically, undemonstratively, and steadfastly loyal to his previous chief. His cousin Montagu, however, agonized. At first he withstood temptation, writing to Asquith, "I do not want you to cease to be Prime Minister because I am certain that any other Prime Minster cannot succeed." He hoped the king would bring Asquith and Lloyd George together and "endeavor to arrange an accommodation between you." It did not happen. The Liberals had split, weakening themselves irreparably. Six months later Montagu accepted a job from Lloyd George after all, as minister without portfolio in charge of reconstruction. He would be the only Jew holding a senior post in Lloyd George's government when it came time to debate the Balfour Declaration. His anti-Zionism remained undiminished.

Meanwhile Lloyd George took measures to streamline his government. Asquith's dozen-strong cabinet had debated and dithered; the new prime minister installed a War Cabinet of only four members in addition to himself. Two were party leaders, Andrew Bonar Law of the Conservatives and Arthur Henderson of Labour. More important, he appointed two conspicuous Conservative imperialists: Lord Nathaniel Curzon, a former viceroy of India, and Sir Alfred Milner, who had been the high commissioner in South Africa during and immediately after the Boer War. Both men had vigorously opposed Lloyd George during the latter's radical anti-imperialist phase, but both possessed administrative genius and a prodigious capacity for work. Wisely, Lloyd George focused on these latter qualities.

But Curzon and Milner had not changed their imperialist spots. When the government discussed the future of the German and the Ottoman Empires, these men staked broad terrorial claims for Britain. Perhaps they influenced their prime minister, for Lloyd George too staked broad claims.

Meanwhile the new, lean cabinet worked efficiently and at full throttle, calling upon other members of government only when necessary. One upon whom it called often was Arthur J. Balfour, the Conservative imperialist whom Lloyd George had made foreign secretary.

The new prime minister, it will be recalled, belonged to the camp of easterners who sought a way around the abattoir on the Western Front. Curzon, the former Indian viceroy, favored the "eastern" strategy too, and so did Milner. All three, Lloyd George in particular, distrusted the commander in chief of Britain's forces on the Continent, Field Marshal Sir Douglas Haig, who could think only to throw more and more men against the Germans. They had no high opinion either of the chief of the Imperial General Staff, Sir William Robertson, who essentially shared Haig's outlook and approach. As civilians, they did not quite dare to overrule these top military experts, but the ascendancy of easterners in the cabinet meant that Lloyd George's government, more than Asquith's, would look with favor upon those who requested support for the Arab Revolt against the Turks, or who asked for reinforcements for the army in Egypt so that it could engage the Turks in Palestine and push them out of Syria altogether. That this approach might help Zionists as much as Arabs, the Zionists in England quickly realized. Given their preference for a British protectorate in Palestine, they realized too that the new government's willingness to expand Britain's imperial reach in the Middle East might redound to their benefit. They had lost their chief advocate in the cabinet, Herbert Samuel, but from the sea change in the British government's general outlook, they gained.

In far-off Egypt, the sea change swept up General Murray. He appears to have been a rather cautious warrior. Slowly, systematically, he pushed his forces beyond the Suez Canal into the Sinai Peninsula, beating off Ottoman attacks, extending supply lines and a water pipe, aiming for the port town of El Arish, only twenty-five miles south of the Palestinian border. "The Turks . . . are fine fighters, especially behind entrenchments," he warned Robertson back in London. "Their handling of machine guns is excellent . . . I am proceeding with all due precautions." A week later El Arish fell to Murray's well-prepared forces. But the easterners who had just taken hold of the government wanted much more than El Arish. Robertson wrote to Murray, "The War Cabinet is very impatient. They want a victory every day and if they do not get it they begin to propose going to some fresh place to find one. They are giving me a good deal of trouble."

Murray attempted to provide his masters in London with a fresh victory. On March 26, 1917, his troops crossed the border into Palestine, aiming for

Alfred James Balfour, Lloyd George's foreign secretary and the author of the Declaration.

Lloyd George, Britain's inspired wartime prime minister; but "he would leave anyone in the lurch anywhere if he thought it suited his purpose," judged one cabinet colleague.

Declaration of jihad on November 14, 1914, in Constantinople. Kitchener feared jihad would take root in South Asia, Egypt, and the Sudan. His counterstroke: the Arab Revolt.

Enver Pasha, the man who brought Turkey into World War I.

Mecca, Islam's holiest city and home to the men who planned the Arab Revolt.

The World Zionist Organization meeting in London in August 1900.

Chaim Weizmann, Zionist leader
and *folks-mensch*.

Walter Rothschild,
titular head of
the British Jewish
community in
1917 and the man
to whom Balfour
addressed the
Declaration.

Nahum Sokolow, "diplomatist of the
Zionist Movement."

Lucien Wolf,
diplomatist of
Britain's Jewish
anti-Zionists.

François Georges-Picot; he sought to advance French imperial interests in the Middle East.

Sir Mark Sykes, British imperialist.

Herbert Samuel, the first British cabinet minister to advocate Zionism.

Edwin Montagu, British cabinet minister and Jewish anti-Zionist.

Jeddah, the port city where Sykes and Picot first told Emir Hussein of their countries' plans for Arabia.

Marmaduke Pickthall, an early British advocate of a separate peace with Turkey.

Aubrey Herbert, another such advocate: "gentle," "gallant," "a sort of survivor from crusading times," and the inspiration for John Buchan's character Greenmantle.

Hejaz Railway was Turkey's lifeline in Arabia, which is why British and Arab guerrillas kept blowing it up.

Emir Hussein, Muhammad's direct descendant, originator of the Arab Revolt; he lived to see all his hopes dashed.

Sharif Abdullah, Emir Hussein's first son and his spur to action.

Sir Henry McMahon, Kitchener's temporary replacement as British consul general in Egypt; his letters helped persuade Hussein to revolt against the Ottomans.

Ronald Storrs, the man who translated McMahon's letters into Arabic, but his knowledge of Arabic was "imperfect."

The attack on Aqaba (1917), a crucial staging post for the Arabs en route to Damascus.

Sharif Feisal, Hussein's second son and best general; he arrived in Damascus too late from the Arab point of view.

T. E. Lawrence, an inspired guerrilla leader, was less effective in advancing the Arab cause after the war.

General Allenby enters Jerusalem: British Zionism's great objective nearly achieved.

Arab protest at the sale of land in Palestine to Jews; British control of Palestine did not please the Arabs.

Gaza, some forty miles farther up the Mediterranean coast. Twice the Turks beat them back, the second time inflicting heavy casualties, although nothing like those on the Western Front. Murray wrote to Robertson, perhaps in propitiation, "I feel that it is a great blessing to have a straight white man at the head of affairs." But Robertson was not all that straight. He never mentioned to Murray what he actually thought: that the War Office had sent Murray to Egypt "in order to get him out of the way . . . and there they have kept him all these months knowing that he was no good." Nor did he inform the man who had taken El Arish of the War Cabinet's growing disillusionment with his stumbling Palestinian campaign. Murray discovered it as a bolt from the blue: "I have just got your telegram notifying that [General Sir Edmund] Allenby takes my place." Lloyd George instructed this new man, whom he had recalled from France, to take Gaza and continue right up through Palestine and into Syria. The ultimate aim was to capture Damascus and to drive the Ottoman Empire from the war, but he wanted Allenby to capture Jerusalem on the way, by Christmas; it would make a fine seasonal gift for the British people. He promised to ensure that Allenby had the means to do it.

The Zionists in London sensed these shifting currents. They caught the tide and rode it, balancing with great skill.

With the help of the Persian Armenian, James Malcolm, Chaim Weizmann made his first contact with Sir Mark Sykes on January 28, 1917. The two protagonists quickly realized each other's importance and the need for fuller discussion and closer cooperation. A second meeting between Sykes, Weizmann, and the latter's Zionist allies must take place soon, but because Herbert Samuel could not attend until the following week, it was put off until February 7. All concerned appear to have realized that Moses Gaster would have to be handled delicately. Malcolm, who happily assumed the role of go-between, wrote to Sykes: "From what I hear it seems that Dr. Gaster wants to take the leading part, whereas the general impression is (including I think both yours and mine) that Dr. Weitzman [sic] . . . should take the leading part in the negotiations."

Malcolm relished his role as intermediary, meeting with Zionists, meeting with Sykes, and interpreting (or occasionally misinterpreting) one to the other. Clearly he aspired to be more than a bit player fostering Sykes's connection with Zionism; he wanted to facilitate an effective Zionist movement. He understood that Sykes increasingly viewed the peoples of the Ottoman Middle East—Armenians, Arabs, and Jews—as links in a future chain of British dependencies. Possibly his own mind had been moving along a similar track, or perhaps he merely wished to curry favor. At any rate he wrote to Sykes, "For some time past I have considered that the greater object of the establishment of the proposed new autonomous States in the Near East should be a defensive federation between them . . . in close sympathy with England and France. This is one of the reasons why I have interested myself in the Palestine question." He wanted each people to be sufficiently organized so as to be able to negotiate with its future protector.

Malcolm took the opportunity to lecture Sykes about Jews: "Most people have misunderstood the Jewish character. The Jew will always stick to his bargain, but he will never consent to readjusting the terms of an agreement." Himself the unwitting target of John Buchan's misdirected anti-Semitism as we have seen, Malcolm was not above indulging in anti-Semitic thinking of his own. Somewhat obscurely, he blamed the Jews for starting World War I: "In the Near East hitherto the Jew has pursued an exclusive policy, which has perhaps contributed more than anything else to bring about the present war." On the other hand, he also believed that the Jews held the key to future peace. "The question of finance will be a great factor in the future," he lectured Sykes. "It would therefore be important to secure the sentimental support, at least, of the Jewish people."

For the Zionists, the week preceding February 7 passed in a blur of small conferences, preparations, and a fair amount of scheming. Weizmann's assiduous cultivation of Rothschilds now began to pay off. James de Rothschild agreed to attend the February 7 meeting; so did Walter Rothschild, who, upon his father's death, had taken up the role of titular head of the British branch of the family and therefore of the British Jewish community. Herbert Samuel agreed to attend as well, as did Nahum Sokolow. Weizmann also mobilized Harry Sacher and tried, unsuccessfully, to bring in Ahad Ha'am. It was to be a gathering of Weizmannites with the man who, they now realized, played the crucial role in advising the British government on its Middle Eastern policy.

Weizmann had determined to end Moses Gaster's role in representing Zionism to such important people. He must have conferred with Sokolow about how to do it; probably the two men together buttonholed James de Rothschild and persuaded him to suggest at the February 7 meeting that Sokolow take up the critical diplomatic role. On Thursday, February 1, Weizmann and Sokolow met with Gaster at his home. They did not mention the plan they had concerted with James Rothschild but managed to antagonize the *haham* nonetheless; this was not hard to do. Gaster "was laying down the law . . . I had to tell him off once or twice," Weizmann noted. On

Monday, February 5, Sokolow and Weizmann met with James Malcolm at the latter's club, the Thatched House. Afterward Malcolm reported to Sykes, reiterating that "it is the opinion of the Jews that Dr. Weitzman [sic] should have the matter in hand here." Finally on the night before the meeting Weizmann met with Gaster yet again. Without mentioning the plan with James de Rothschild, he suggested that the *haham* voluntarily make way for Sokolow. Gaster absolutely refused. When he learned that Weizmann had invited Sacher and Ahad Ha'am to attend the meeting next day, he invited allies of his own, including Joseph Cowen, the outgoing EZF president.

But Gaster's men were already spent forces in the Zionist movement, as he himself soon would be. Weizmann and his allies clearly permitted Gaster to host and to chair the gathering as a matter of form. ("The most important meeting ever held concerning Zionism was held *here* under my chairmanship," Gaster proudly asserted afterward in his diary.) But at this meeting, where a British government official finally met a Zionist delegation and took its claims seriously, Weizmann and Sokolow and their designees dominated; henceforth they, not the *haham,* would negotiate on the movement's behalf. They allowed Gaster to present Sykes with a document encapsulating the Zionist program, but they had drafted and polished it themselves. (Gaster may have had some input.) When Sykes mentioned that on the next day he would be seeing Picot, who was then attached to the French embassy in London, and that it would be useful for a Zionist to accompany him to put the Zionist case, the *haham* assumed he would be the one to do it. But James de Rothschild nominated Sokolow for the job, and the meeting, dominated as it was by Weizmannites, agreed. Weizmann himself did not feel the need to represent Zionism to Picot at this point. As Leonard Stein puts it, "He needed no formal credentials to give him the commanding position he occupied *de facto* in the transactions which followed."

For his part, Sir Mark Sykes went to the meeting on February 7 expecting the eclipse of Gaster and intending to mobilize Zionism's more effective leaders both on behalf of the Allies and on behalf of British suzerainty in Palestine, and to throw this in the face of France. The Weizmannites happily agreed to be thrown. They wanted a British protectorate in Palestine above all. They believed that Britain afforded her (white) colonial subjects more liberty than any other imperial power did. They believed that France insisted upon making her colonial subjects into French citizens, erasing their national identities. As Jewish nationalists, they could never accept that. They believed that a condominium of imperial powers over Palestine, even one consisting of Britain and France, would be nearly as bad as purely French rule; its members would quarrel among themselves, and all Palestinians, including Jews, would suffer. They feared that Britain and France were planning a joint condominium over Palestine, but the only one they would agree to would be international control over Palestine's holy places.

They did not realize that a year previously Sykes and Picot had agreed precisely to international control of Palestine as a whole, the so-called Brown Area, except for the British corridor running west-east and the northern slice that would go to France. Herbert Samuel, who had been a member of the cabinet when the Sykes-Picot Agreement was made, knew of this plan but was bound by cabinet oath not to speak of it. The meeting on February 7, then, was based upon at least three layers of deceit. In the first layer, Sykes was attempting to undermine an agreement with France that he (and Herbert Samuel) knew the British government already had accepted, that he himself actually had helped to negotiate, and that bore his name. In the second layer, Sykes and Samuel both were keeping the Sykes-Picot and Tripartite Agreements secret from everyone else at the meeting. From his French contacts James de Rothschild had gained some inkling of them. Twice he asked Sykes to confirm that Britain had made no promise of Palestinian territory to France. The first time Sykes replied that "no pledges had been given to the French concerning Palestine," an outright lie if Zionist definitions of Palestine's borders are accepted. The second time he referred the question to Samuel: "Mr. Samuel replied that he could not reveal what had been done by the Cabinet."

The third layer, historically speaking, may have been the most important of all. No one at the meeting except for Sykes knew of the McMahon-Hussein correspondence or that Arabs might believe Palestine had been promised to them. On this subject, Sykes merely said: "The Arabs professed that language must be the measure [by which control of Palestine should be determined] and [by that measure] could claim all Syria and Palestine. Still the Arabs could be managed, particularly if they received Jewish support in other matters."

Given this triple burden of ignorance, Sokolow performed amazingly well the very next day when he appeared at 9 Buckingham Gate, Sykes's London residence, to meet Monsieur Picot. He impressed the French diplomat in a way that Moses Gaster never had done. Cagily, Sykes chose to remain in the background. He wanted Sokolow to make the running, and Sokolow obliged. When Picot asked the Zionist for a general explanation of the aims of his movement and Sokolow delivered one, Picot expressed great interest and complimented him on his exposition. But then he wanted to know, how did "the Jews propose to organize themselves as a nation in Palestine?"

> Mr. Sokolow replied that they would establish themselves in the same way as the French and English had established themselves in Canada or the Boers in South Africa, viz. by settling on the land. A nation should be built up like a pyramid on a broad base and strong foundation. This foundation was the land.

Notably, Sokolow did not mention that Arabs already resided on Palestinian land. At this moment they appear to have been as invisible to him as black Africans had been to Boers intending to move to Cape Town, and Native Americans to the French and English colonists on their way to Canada.

> M. Picot expressed his approval of this view and said he had never believed that Jews, who had been out of touch with the land for so many years, would be able to succeed as agriculturists. But having seen with his own eyes the new Jewish Colonies in Palestine he was convinced of the possibility. "What I have seen is marvelous." [*Ce que j'ai vu là-bas est merveilleux.*]

So at this moment the Arabs were invisible to Picot too.

Sokolow then came to the main point, indicating that the Zionists yearned above all for a British protectorate in Palestine. Picot demurred silkenly: "But Sir, you must know as a politician that this is an affair of the Entente." (*Mais Monsieur, vous devez savoir, comme politician, que c'est l'affaire de l'Entente.*) The Jewish diplomat parried with great dexterity: "Mr. Sokolow agreed with this but said that the Entente could not govern Palestine." Picot stuck to his guns: "Ninety-five per cent of the French people were strongly in favor of the annexation of Palestine by France." The crucial disagreement was over which country, England or France, should have the predominant influence in Palestine; and the crucial dynamic for which Sykes had been maneuvering was for Zionism to make Britain's case. But there was no rupture. Sokolow and Picot agreed to discuss matters further the following day. The Frenchman took his leave. Sykes could barely contain his glee. He "expressed to Mr. Sokolow his great pleasure in listening to the discussion. He said that he was very satisfied with the outcome of the meeting."

Sykes would have been equally pleased next day, when Sokolow and

Picot met without him at the French embassy. This time butter would not melt in Sokolow's mouth. "Zionists and Jews generally had the greatest respect for and trust in France," he assured Picot (reads the résumé of the meeting). They believed that France "was destined to play a great part in the East." They "confidently looked forward to her influential moral and material support in their endeavors on behalf of the Jewish people." Moreover, "Zionist aspirations would not prejudice French interests but were on the contrary in perfect harmony with the great traditions of France." Picot, if he did not employ butter, employed honey: "He personally would see that the facts about Zionism were communicated to the proper quarters and he would do his best to win for the movement whatever sympathies were necessary to be won so far as compatible with the French standpoint on this question." It is hard to imagine such an interchange between Picot and the tempestuous Gaster.

Thinking, no doubt, of the rights of Belgians trampled by Germany, and of Serbians trampled by Austria, Picot remarked at one point "In one respect France was specially disposed to take an interest in the Zionist movement. He referred to the cause of the small nationalities which, in France, had been taken up with greatest ardor and was inspiring every citizen to an extraordinary extent." With these words Picot conceded the main Zionist point, that Jews constituted a nation and were not mere adherents of a belief system.

Sokolow pounced at once, justifying Weizmann's faith in his diplomatic skills: "Mr. Sokolow thereon expressed his great satisfaction that the Jews were considered in France as one of the smaller nationalities which were now struggling for liberty. This would be a guarantee that their cause would be treated in the same spirit of justice and equity which France would show the other nationalities."

Picot tried to backpedal. "This point was not yet quite established . . . he was afraid that if the Jewish question was put in this way, viz. as the case of a small nationality, it would meet with considerable opposition, more perhaps from French Jews than from true Jews." Note that he thought French Jews—that is to say, Jews who had assimilated in France—were not "true Jews." He had ceded the Zionist case, possibly without even realizing it.

Smoothly, courteously, Sokolow let him down nicely: "The question whether all the Jews accept the national standpoint was after all a theoretical one . . . when a good practical scheme for the colonization of Palestine by Jews was put forward all opposition would vanish, including the opposition of the French Jews."

Now Picot did introduce the Arab question, "speaking," he assured

Sokolow, "as a friend of the Jews." If the "good practical scheme" to which Sokolow referred meant demanding "special privileges" for Jews in Palestine, then that would encourage the other peoples of the region to demand something similar. "This would almost certainly lead to grave complications which would prejudice the progress of Jewish colonization."

It was like the meeting between Zionists and assimilationists at the rooms of Lucien Wolf all over again. Sokolow in his reply could fall back upon well-honed arguments: "The Zionists had considered every aspect of the problem and knew quite well that every great movement had inevitably to meet with opposition and difficulties of various kinds. The mere granting of equal rights to the [Jewish] inhabitants of Palestine was insufficient to build up a flourishing [Jewish] colony in that country." But he revealed too a blind spot that almost all his fellow Zionists shared. Just as the peoples who lived already in South Africa and Canada had been invisible to the Dutch, British, and French colonists who intended to move to those places, so the Arabs of Palestine remained invisible to Sokolow: "The question of equal rights was rightly raised in a country already populated and settled, which was not the case with Palestine ... Palestine was a country where the chief need was to attract capable and devoted settlers."

As the meeting was drawing to a close, Picot suggested that Jews should do more to show their support for the Allies. Now Sokolow revealed just that bit of steel that distinguished Zionists from other Jews who wished to speak for Jewry. Assimilationists must always ask the great powers for recognition, for favors, for protection from anti-Semites. By contrast, Sokolow spoke as the representative of a power whose support the other powers needed: "To win the sympathies of all the Jews for the Entente the simplest way would be to show them clearly that the cause of Jewish liberty was intimately bound up with the success of the Entente." Anyway, as he also pointed out, "it was not necessary for him to prove the devotion of the Jews to the Entente. The fact that three-quarters of a million Jews were fighting for Russia (in spite of their legal disabilities and sufferings) was the best proof."

Sokolow's had been a formidable performance—that has to have been Sykes's conclusion when he learned of it. As he said next day, when Sokolow and Weizmann arrived at his house to report and to plan the next moves, "the result of the interview [Sokolow's with Picot] would be satisfactory ... it was a valuable thing that Mr. Picot had an opportunity of informing himself of the Zionist demands as approved at the conference held at the residence of Dr. Gaster on the 7th of February." That was as much as Gaster had to do with it now; Sokolow and Weizmann pressed forward without a backward glance. They wanted special facilities to communicate with Zionists in Russia and America. Sykes agreed to expedite the matter. The next day he telephoned to say he had done so. Sokolow and Weizmann must have realized that a corner had been turned: The British government recognized them as leaders of a movement worth facilitating.

A whirlwind of meetings had established the Weizmannite ascendancy in the mind of Sir Mark Sykes. On Sunday, February 11, a meeting of the English Zionist Federation confirmed the ascendancy of Weizmannites among British Zionists as a whole. Joseph Cowen was stepping down as president of the EZF, and there could be only one successor. No one even ran against Chaim Weizmann, who had previously arranged that "those friends of mine with whom I have been in close cooperation all these years" should become members of the EZF council. He meant the Manchester contingent—Sieff, Marks, and Sacher—as well as London allies such as Leon Simon and Samuel Tolkowsky. Chosen by acclamation, his control of the EZF assured, Weizmann offered the delegates as clear a statement of his single-minded vision, and as clear an assessment of the current situation, as they could have wished for:

> From certain information in their [his circle's] possession—information of a very reliable nature—they had every reason to hope that they were standing appreciably nearer the realization of their cherished aims . . . Although Zionism had always been regarded as a dream, it was now easier of achievement and was much simpler than emancipating the Jews [of Russia, Romania, Poland] . . . They were standing at a critical moment and now, more than ever, was it necessary for them to concentrate all their energies for their definite Zionist purpose.

On the very next day, February 12, preliminary reports of a revolution in Russia reached London. The epochal, earth-shattering news was particularly welcome to British Zionists, not merely because it signified the end of the tsar's hated anti-Semitic regime but also because under a new, more liberal Russian government, the job of emancipating Russia's Jews would fall more clearly to Russian Jews than to British Jews or the British government. Moreover, Britain's governors, ascribing enormous power to world Jewry, worried that Jews would determine whether their Russian ally stayed in the war against Germany or succumbed to pacifism and Bolshevism. This consideration made Zionism even more important to Britain's rulers. Thus by mid-February 1917 the road stretching out before the delighted eyes of Chaim Weizmann seemed clearer, and more hopeful, than it had ever been.

It would be a mistake, however, to assume that the followers of Chaim Weizmann constituted a monolithic bloc and that they all agreed about the next steps. In particular, some of the Zionists of Manchester, his closest friends and allies, his most devoted adherents, had ideas of their own.

Early in 1915 Harry Sacher had had "the curious experience of being dismissed from [the *Daily News*] because I was not sufficiently bellicose for a Quaker proprietor." His refusal to join in the general enthusiasm for world war was a tip-off that he made up his own mind and plowed his own furrow. He was something of an iconoclast. So, of course, was his old employer who took him back at *The Manchester Guardian,* C. P. Scott (whose relationship with Chaim Weizmann we noticed earlier). And so was another journalist in Scott's employ, Herbert Sidebotham. Called "Student of War," Sidebotham had written brilliantly on the Boer War and on the Russo-Japanese War; his articles on the current conflict were, according to French general Ferdinand Foch, "the only thing of the kind in the press worth reading."

Sidebotham argued that Britain must protect her position in Egypt, and especially the Suez Canal, by taking not merely the Sinai Peninsula but also Palestine. Once the Turks were thrown out, Britain should permit no other power to occupy that country, not even France, whose long-standing Middle Eastern interests threatened Britain's position there, if not presently, then prospectively. Sidebotham believed, however, that the Jews could control Palestine—not because it was their historical homeland, or because the world owed it to them to make up for past misdeeds (that would be part of his later position), but rather because the Jews, first under British protection but eventually as a Crown colony with dominion status, would constitute an outpost of progressive civilization in the region and a bastion of British support. They would guarantee the canal for Britain. Sidebotham wrote in his autobiography that he came to Zionism "on grounds of British interest and with the single idea of helping the victory of the Allies in the War." But his employer, Scott, sided with the Zionists, and his colleague Sacher played a leading role in the Zionist movement. It would have been strange if the Zionists had not established close relations with so promising a recruit.

Shortly after returning to *The Manchester Guardian,* Harry Sacher married Miriam Marks, sister of Simon Marks. Marks had married the sister of his best friend, Israel Sieff; Sieff had married Marks's other sister. Into this close-knit little society, Sacher introduced Herbert Sidebotham. "He loved music as he loved fine literature . . . He had a taste for good wine and great liking for good company. He could listen as well as talk." Perhaps over good food and drink the four friends discussed ways to turn Sidebotham's expertise to Zionism's advantage.

They consulted with Weizmann and others in London. Sidebotham agreed to write a memo for the Foreign Office outlining the strategic advantages that Britain would gain from supporting the Zionist claim to Palestine. It made no discernible impact. Then the four took the next logical step, forming a British Palestine Committee (BPC), of which they would be the nucleus. (It also contained some of the most important London Zionists in the Weizmann circle, including Weizmann himself, but this contingent rarely if ever attended committee meetings, which took place in Manchester.) The purpose of the committee was "to promote the ideal of an Anglo-Jewish Palestine which it is hoped the War will bring within reach." They sent out a letter to likely supporters, asking them to lend their names as patrons:

> There are many Jewish nationalists in England who look forward to the establishment of a Jewish State in Palestine under the British Crown. There are many Englishmen who hold it to be a very important British interest that Palestine should be part of the British Imperial system in the East. Thus, not for the first time in history, there is a community alike of interest and of sentiment between the British State and Jewish people.

The response was discouraging. Sidebotham writes, "I think we received about ten replies in all, of which half were purely formal acknowledgments. Of the remainder, two were opposed to us." But two positive replies are worth noting: C. P. Scott lent his name immediately. And although Mark Sykes declined to become a patron ("As I am officially employed at the Committee of Imperial Defense, it would be impossible for me to accept the office of Patron of your Committee"), he was not unsympathetic: "I have always considered that Jewish Nationalism is inevitably destined to play a great part in the future." And he added to his letter a postscript: "Could you send me 4 or 5 of your pamphlets?" At this time Sykes was still in closest contact with Moses Gaster, but he may already have been noting Gaster's deficiencies and seeking alternative sources of information on Zionism.

Even without a long list of notable patrons, the BPC pushed forward.

On January 26, 1917, it published the first issue of *Palestine,* a weekly review and journal of opinion. Sacher edited and wrote the occasional piece for it, as did Sieff and Marks, who also provided much of its funding. Sidebotham composed most of its articles, hammering at a few main themes: notably that "unless Palestine comes under the flag of the Power holding Egypt [namely England] it will, in the hands of a hostile Power, be a perpetual menace to its safety"; and "only the Jewish race and our association with the forces of its nationalism can secure [in Palestine] . . . a colony capable of de- velopment into a self-governing dominion of the British Crown." Quickly *Palestine* established itself as an important source of information for anyone interested in Zionism.

Mark Sykes read *Palestine,* which did not always please him. He objected first of all to the BPC publicly advocating a British protectorate for Pales- tine, as it did in the journal's very first issue. Weizmann conveyed Sykes's concern to the committee. Sieff responded, "We . . . must at whatever cost persistently and unequivocally place our views before the F.O. . . . We must close our ears to Sykes' remark re our articles." Sykes reiterated his con- cerns at the meeting with Weizmann and Sokolow on February 10, when the three discussed Sokolow's interviews with Picot: "It was necessary to keep the idea of British suzerainty in the back-ground for the time being, as it was likely to intensify the French opposition." Again he mentioned the journal: It was "much too emphatic in its exposition of the British interests in Palestine." Weizmann and Sokolow agreed, but muzzling their Man- chester colleagues was not so easy.

On February 15 the BPC published an article envisioning a Palestinian state whose western border was the Mediterranean Sea and that stretched north as far as Damascus, southeast to Basra, southwest to the Gulf of Aqaba, and northwest along the existing Turco-Egyptian border. This was too much for Sykes altogether. Again he complained to Weizmann. He must have been quite angry for "it was most unpleasant," Weizmann re- ported afterward to Sokolow. "I wrote to the Manchester people and I hope that they will be careful."

But they would not be. In fact, Sykes's sensitivity to Palestine's borders set them thinking. "There is no doubt in my mind," Sieff wrote again to Weizmann, "that Sir M. has come to an agreement with the Arabs, and his interest in Jewish political aspirations in Palestine is only secondary." In his letter Weizmann must have warned that the BPC risked harming Britain's good relations with France. Sieff shot back, "Yes, our articles do enormous harm, but it is harm in the right direction. It may harm the Arab kingdom, but that is no concern of ours." He then suggested, "You may diplomatically hint that you are not responsible for the 'hot-headed youths' of the British Palestine Committee. If any communication is to be made on our work, let it be made to us."

At this Weizmann threw down the gauntlet in the form of a telegram: "Letter received. Disagree completely, your attitude renders further efforts here useless, we therefore decide to resign everything on Thursday." He meant that he and the other London members would resign from the BPC. Sieff backed down: " 'Palestine' this week will contain a Jewish article which will meet the wishes of Sir M."

But the dispute did not end. On March 1 *Palestine* published Sidebotham's rebuttal of an article in the last week's *Nation* that had argued against a British protectorate. To this Sidebotham riposted, "We must have a projecting bastion in front of a line of communication so vital as that of the [Suez] Canal . . . Let us beware of repeating the mistake of the mid-nineteenth century politicians who regarded every fresh extension of territory as an increase of responsibility that ought to be avoided." Sykes, and Weizmann, must have thrown up their hands.

The refusal of the Manchester contingent to fall into line pointed to a grave danger for Chaim Weizmann. At first glance Manchester and London seemed to be disagreeing merely over whether to advocate a British protectorate in Palestine publicly or to hold back, at Britain's behest, for political reasons; and whether to push a definition of Palestine's borders that was expansive or modest, as Britain preferred, at least for the moment. At a more profound level, however, the dispute called the Zionist alliance with Britain into question. This was to strike at the root of Weizmann's strategy and therefore at Weizmann's role as principal Zionist leader in Britain. It took the boldest and most perspicacious of the Manchester school to see it and to state it, but Harry Sacher did not draw back. When, a few months after the initial disagreement, *Palestine* again published articles that Sykes, and therefore Weizmann, objected to, Sacher wrote to his friend Leon Simon that Weizmann and Sokolow were "tying Zionism up indissolubly with a 'British' policy, even though that should mean partition and condominium." Therefore they were "guilty of sacrificing Zionist interest to British." They risked "preferring British Imperialism . . . to Zionism." "Where we differ from the London folk," Sacher explained to Simon in another letter, "is that they are determined to tie Zionism up with the F.O. [Foreign Office] and to take anything the F.O. is graciously pleased to grant. I don't trust the F.O. and I am convinced that we shall never do anything with them except by convincing them that we are a power. That, Chaim and his tactics will never achieve."

But Sacher underestimated the skill with which Weizmann and Sokolow had been maneuvering. Weizmann, for his part, privately branded Sacher "an extremist and a 'Draufgeher' [fire-eater,] with . . . a very marked lack of the sense of reality." But he did not make the mistake of underestimating him: As Weizmann well knew, Sacher remained among the most talented and formidable of his followers. The relationship between the two men stretched, sometimes to bending, but never to the breaking point. The Zionist leader still had good reason for optimism in the spring of 1917.

CHAPTER 15

Sokolow in France and Italy

MARK SYKES HAD GIVEN Britain's Zionists a key to the Foreign Office door and perhaps much else besides; now they would turn it. Their aim was to familiarize important officials with the Zionist program and to press for the British protectorate in Palestine that they firmly believed would allow that program to flourish. They aimed as well to extract from the British government a statement of support that would constitute a binding form of official recognition. Shrewdly, delicately, implacably, they pressed forward, unaware that Palestine already was spoken for in the Sykes-Picot Agreement and perhaps in the McMahon-Hussein correspondence. As always for the past thirty months, slaughter along the main fronts of war provided a backdrop to all their efforts.

Weizmann saw Lloyd George and Balfour at a dinner hosted by the Astors on March 13. General Murray's forces had recently taken El Arish; they stood poised on the Palestinian border, about to cross over. On the Mesopotamian side, General Sir Frederick Maude's army had taken Baghdad that very day. The news from everywhere else (with the possible exception of America, which seemed to be on the verge of joining the war against Germany) was grim if not appalling, but Lloyd George chose to emphasize the positive. No sooner had he entered the Astors' drawing room than he made for Weizmann, asking how he liked the developing situation

in the Middle East. But serious discussion could not take place during a social occasion, so Weizmann carefully broached the possibility of a more formal meeting. He would have requested one, he said, except that he fully
understood how heavy was the prime minister's schedule. "You must take
me by storm," Lloyd George replied, "and if Davies [one of his private sec-
retaries] says I'm engaged don't be put off but insist on seeing me." They
went on in to dine, but the prime minister had to leave the table early.

Weizmann turned to Balfour. Still, it being a dinner party, they could
discuss Zionism only "academically," in terms of first principles. The foreign secretary must have agreed to a more formal meeting, for nine days
later he received Weizmann at the Foreign Office. Zionism had come a
long way from the days when the private secretary of an under secretary
would only grudgingly deign to grant Nahum Sokolow ninety minutes of
his valuable time.

When they did meet, Weizmann and the foreign secretary got down to
brass tacks. "I have seen Balfour and for the first time I had a real business
talk with him," Weizmann wrote exultantly to Ahad Ha'am afterward. "I
am delighted with the result." As he had been unable to do at the Astor dinner, he hammered at the need for a British protectorate. "I think I succeeded in explaining that to him," Weizmann wrote to C. P. Scott, "and he
agreed with the view, but he suggested that there may be difficulties with
France and Italy." Balfour's hesitation would have been due to the Sykes-
Picot Agreement (now amended into the Tripartite Agreement) and to recent Italian demands to be included in it. Weizmann, ignorant of all this,
thought Balfour essentially accepted his position. Better still, he thought the
prime minister accepted it too: "Mr. Lloyd George took a view which was
identical with" Weizmann's own, Balfour told him, "namely that it is of
great importance to Great Britain to protect Palestine." The foreign secretary thought Weizmann and Lloyd George should discuss matters further.
" 'You may tell the Prime Minister that I wanted you to see him,' " he advised Weizmann. The Zionist did so, indirectly, by quoting this remark in
his letter to Scott, who could repeat it to Lloyd George and make the meeting possible.

To Joseph Cowen, Weizmann wrote, "Things are moving very satisfac-
torily," as indeed they were. Scott prevailed upon the prime minister, and
only a few days later Weizmann had his meeting with Lloyd George. It was
a breakfast at 10 Downing Street. Weizmann was not the only guest, but
the others said little when Lloyd George, perhaps leaning over eggs, bacon,
toast, and coffee, informed his company that the question of Palestine "was
to him the one really interesting part of the war." Music to the Zionist's ears,

the prime minister went on to reject the possibility of Anglo-French control once the war was won. He speculated about alternatives. What was Weizmann's view of international control (the outcome foreseen in Sykes-Picot)? he asked. That "would be a shade worse [than Anglo-French] as it would mean not control but mere confusion and intrigue," the Zionist warned. What about an Anglo-American condominium? asked Lloyd George. That would be acceptable, Weizmann replied, and the prime minister agreed that such an arrangement might work. "We are both thoroughly materialist peoples," he said. Interestingly this idea of a British-American condominium gained some traction in Britain but not much in America; it will not figure prominently in our story again.

Meanwhile Sykes and Sokolow continued to confer. The English Catholic and the Russian Jew got along. Sokolow thought they did so in part because of Sykes's religion: "Often he remarked to me that it was his Catholicism that enabled him to understand the tragedy of the Jewish question, since not so long since Catholics had to suffer much in England." But Sykes must also have realized that in Sokolow he had found the instrument he had been seeking: an effective Zionist diplomat who would help him to revise the Tripartite Agreement and pry Palestine loose from France. This task had been manifestly beyond the powers of Moses Gaster. Sokolow, for his part, clearly understood that Sykes was Zionism's enabler. Having found so valuable an ally, he would not let him go.

At the end of December 1916 the British War Cabinet had agreed to allow a detachment of French Muslim troops to accompany British forces when they finally entered into Palestine. The French government designated François Georges-Picot to serve as French high commissioner for the soon-to-be occupied territories of Syria and Palestine. Inevitably the British chose Mark Sykes to act on their behalf as Picot's counterpart. Now, early in April 1917, with General Murray about to attack Gaza for the second time, the moment for the two diplomats to make the journey eastward approached. But first Picot suggested that Sokolow come to Paris. It would be useful for him, and for the French government he would be representing, to know more about Zionism. Sykes conveyed and endorsed Picot's invitation; he may indeed have suggested it, believing it would be in Britain's interest for France to become better acquainted with Zionist principles. Sokolow accepted Picot's invitation, although Weizmann and others in the Zionist leadership, and even C. P. Scott, thought he would be better employed in England. Perhaps Sokolow understood more clearly than they that the connection with Sykes had paid another dividend, an open sesame to the Quai d'Orsay. Of course Picot would try to convince him that Jewish nationalists should look to France, not to Britain, for protection in Palestine. Sokolow could deal with that.

Sykes arranged for James Malcolm to accompany Sokolow to Paris. Conceivably he wanted a second pair of eyes there; possibly he thought Malcolm had contacts in the French capital that would be of use to the Zionist; quite likely he wanted to foster cooperation between Armenian and Jewish nationalists, two of the three groups he thought would form a friendly association under British direction in the former Ottoman Empire. Sokolow was unenthusiastic, but ever the diplomat, he wrote to Sykes: "I am extremely satisfied to be accompanied by Mr. Malcolm and your idea of an Arab-Armenian-Zionist Entente is excellent indeed." Several weeks later, after he and the Armenian had discussed their prospective alliance at greater length, Sokolow wrote to Weizmann: "You are, of course, acquainted with Mr. M[alcolm]'s idea [derived from Sir Mark] of an entente between Armenians, Arabs and Jews. I regard the idea as quite fantastic. It is difficult to reach an understanding with the Arabs but we will have to try. There are no conflicts between Jews and Armenians because there are no common interests whatever."

Sokolow and Malcolm left for Paris on the last day of March 1917. Weizmann and the others remained unenthusiastic. While Sokolow was gone they would write carping letters about his activities abroad to one another. All of them misjudged entirely. Sokolow's journey would become part of the mythology of Zionist history, an essential step on the path to the Balfour Declaration.

Sykes did his best to prepare French officials for the Zionist's arrival. "If the great force of Judaism feels that its aspirations are not only considered but in a fair way towards realization," he exhorted Picot, not for the first time, "then there is hope of an ordered and developed Arabia and Middle East. On the other hand, if that force feels that its aspirations will be thwarted by circumstance and are doomed to remain only a painful longing, then I see little or no prospect for our own future hopes." Satisfying Zionist aspirations, he said, would also "give a very strong impetus to the Entente cause in the USA," where a decision to enter the war hung in the balance, and where he believed that Jews represented a powerful political and economic force. Thus did he continue to work the notion of an all-powerful, if subterranean, Jewish influence. He wanted Picot to conclude that if the Jews desired a British protectorate in Palestine, then given the war situation, it was in France's interest to let them have one.

Picot did not draw that conclusion quite yet. When Sokolow arrived in Paris, Picot declared to him that neither an Anglo-French nor, certainly, an Anglo-American condominium would be acceptable to his countrymen. Of course he no longer favored international control either. No more than Mark Sykes did he wish to maintain the arrangements they had previously made for Palestine. Each diplomat, representing his respective government, was trying to undercut the Sykes-Picot Agreement at the other's expense. "The French are determined to take the whole of Palestine," Sokolow (who did not know of Sykes-Picot but understood very well what France intended) reported back to Weizmann in London. But clearly Picot did now believe that the Zionists were a force worth courting, for he also promised Sokolow in that first meeting in Paris that "after the invasion of Palestine, a Jewish administration would be set up in all Jewish Colonies and Communities, as a nucleus of a future administration."

Picot spoke for the current French government but only for a slice of French opinion. French politics and attitudes toward Palestine and Zionism were no more monolithic than the British. A powerful group of French businessmen had interests in Syria and hoped for a compromise peace with Turkey that would protect their investments in Palestine; a French imperialist contingent still demanded Syria *intégral,* which meant Palestine too; many French Catholics reflexively opposed Zionist plans for Palestine. Indeed, the Catholic-Protestant split in France meant divided counsels on all its Middle Eastern policy. The Catholics, much more than the Protestants, were determined that their country play a major role in protecting the holy places. After all, in 1856 France had fought a war against Russia to maintain that role. Finally, French Jews themselves split over Zionism; the main French Jewish organization, the Alliance Israélite, was strongly anti-Zionist.

"This work is very difficult," Sokolow wrote to Weizmann, "but [it is] not impossible." As soon as he reached Paris, he met with the Zionists' old ally, Baron Edmond de Rothschild, to whom he often went for advice on the French scene; he met also with the anti-Zionist French Jews of the Alliance Israélite, and with French officials, of whom Picot was only one. By the time Sir Mark arrived in Paris on April 5, on his way to Egypt, Sokolow had convinced the French Foreign Office to accept for study a statement of Zionist aims, their "desiderata in regard to facilities of colonization, communal autonomy, rights of language and establishment of a Jewish chartered company." These rights went far beyond what Picot had just promised Sokolow. Sykes reported to the Foreign Office, however, that the

Zionist thought the French were likely to endorse them. But the proof of the pudding would be in the eating.

On April 9, 1917, the French ate the pudding, and Zionism's diplomat capped his career to date. That morning Sokolow left his room at the Hotel Meurice on the rue de Rivoli and walked around the corner to meet Sykes in his room at the Hotel Lotti on the rue de Castiglione. For several hours the two men prepared for the meeting, to take place later in the day, between Sokolow and the French foreign minister, Jules Cambon, Picot, and other high-ranking French officials. Sokolow intended to press the case laid out in the document he had supplied to the ministry earlier in the week. The Frenchmen would deliver their government's verdict.

At the appointed hour Sokolow would have squared his shoulders, straightened his tie, left the hotel, crossed the Pont de la Concorde, and entered the French Foreign Ministry at the Quai d'Orsay. He intended to report back to Sykes at the hotel as soon as the meeting had finished, but that was to ignore the ebullient nature and personality of Sir Mark. "As I was crossing the Quai d'Orsay on my return from the Foreign Office I came across Sykes," Sokolow later recalled. "He had not had the patience to wait. We walked on together and I gave him an outline of the proceedings. This did not satisfy him; he studied every detail; I had to give him full notes and he drew up a minute report. 'That's a good day's work,' he said with shining eyes."

So it had been. At the meeting Sokolow had glided smoothly over the question of a British protectorate; the French did not raise the subject either; at this stage it would only have muddied the waters. For the rest of it, France would meet the Zionists more than halfway. "I was told," Sokolow jubilantly reported to Weizmann, "they accept in principle the recognition of Jewish nationality in the capacity of National Home, local autonomy, etc. It is beyond my boldest expectations . . . we have achieved here no less—and maybe more—than in your country [England] where we have been working for nearly three years." In his report to the British foreign secretary, Arthur Balfour, Sykes recorded in more restrained language but with almost equal satisfaction: "Zionists' aspirations are recognized as legitimate by the French." Moreover, although "naturally the moment is not ripe for such a proposal . . . the situation should be the more favorable to British Suzerainty [in Palestine] with a recognized Jewish voice in favor of it."

Cold self-interest, if fuzzily conceived, explains the new French concern with Zionism. Sykes and Sokolow, among others, had persuaded the governors of France—or more likely had reinforced existing sloppy thinking among them—of the power of Jews. They had taught that Zionists, not advocates of Jewish assimilation, were the most effective representatives of Jewish power, and the French government now believed them. Cambon and the others would have weighed the strength of the imperialist camp within their country; the power of financiers with interests in Syria; the religious scruples of Catholics concerned about the holy places; and the prospective wrath of the Alliance Israélite. They decided finally that they had more to gain than to lose by supporting Zionist aspirations in Palestine. Of course they intended to be the principal power in the region, and they demanded a quid pro quo for their goodwill—Jewish support of the Allies in the war. At the meeting one French delegate urged Sokolow to rally the Jews of Russia, who were thought to have influence over that country's pacifists and revolutionaries. Possibly someone else mentioned the need for Jewish support in America, which finally, on April 6, had entered the war against Germany. Sokolow did as requested, dispatching a telegram to the American Zionist leader Louis Brandeis, and to the Russian Zionists as well: "After favorable results in London and Paris, was received with goodwill by Ministry here. Have full confidence Allied victory will realize our Palestine Zionist aspirations." Many years later Harry Sacher would observe, about "the belief in the power and the unity of Jewry," that "to exploit it delicately and deftly belongs to the art of the Jewish diplomat." Few were as delicate and deft as Nahum Sokolow.

As the April 9 meeting was winding down, someone among the French group suggested to Sokolow that he could do important work for the Allies in Italy too. Zionism's diplomat readily agreed to travel there; he was hardly in a position to refuse and he was anxious to learn the Italian government's attitude toward his movement. It must have occurred to him that where once he could scarcely get a toe inside the door of a European chancellery, now he was hard-pressed to stay outside.

Sykes preceded him, however, making a special trip before he headed east with Picot. Just as he had done in Paris, he would smooth Sokolow's way. And this time he had more in mind than opening a door into the Foreign Ministry. The Eternal City also contains the Vatican, and Sykes realized that its goodwill, or at least the absence of its bad will, could be as important to Zionism as the goodwill of Italy's temporal government.

Upon arriving in Rome, Sykes sought out the British representative at the Vatican. Through this man he would get to Vatican officials and prime them for meetings with Sokolow. Exuberant, cheerful, and knowledgeable, he simply charmed him. "Sir M. Sykes' visit has been the best thing that has happened to me since I have been here," the representative wrote. Sykes sought out too the British ambassador to Italy, but this gentleman proved somewhat less susceptible to Sykes's charm. Reporting on their discussion, he complained that Sykes had "opened fire on questions which I have been guarding as closely as the riddle of the sphinx." Nevertheless the ambassador, as much as Britain's man in the Vatican, agreed to facilitate matters for Sokolow when the latter arrived in Rome.

But first the British representative to the Vatican brought Sykes to Monsignor Eugenio Pacelli, the pope's assistant under secretary for foreign affairs. (Pacelli would become Pope Pius XII in 1939. His attitude toward Jews remains a matter of contention: He was not very helpful to Italian or foreign Jews during World War II, but his defenders argue that he did what he could.) Sykes tried to start Pacelli on the right path. "I . . . prepared the way for Zionism," he reported back to the Foreign Office, "by explaining what the purpose and ideals of the Zionists were." Sykes suggested that Pacelli meet with Sokolow when the latter arrived. "Of course one could not expect the Vatican to be enthusiastic . . . but he was most interested and expressed a wish to see Sokolow." Sykes being Sykes, he then managed a short interview with Pope Benedict XV as well. Again he was paving the way for Zionism.

The next day he wrote a letter for Sokolow and left it with the ambassador. When speaking with Catholic leaders, "I laid considerable stress on the intensity of Zionist feeling and the objects of Zionism," he reported. He had emphasized Zionism's main object: "to evolve a self-supporting Jewish community which should raise not only the racial self-respect of the Jewish people but should also be a proof to the non-Jewish peoples of the world of the capacity of Jews to produce a virtuous and simple agrarian population." Then he added a stunner:

> I mentioned that you were coming to Rome and I should strongly advise you to visit Monsignor Pacelli and if you see fit have an audience with His Holiness . . . The British representative at the Vatican can arrange this if you will kindly show him this letter.

It is worth pausing here to underline the sheer incongruity of what was about to take place. Picture Sokolow at the grand British embassy in Rome, a building that four years earlier he would probably have had difficulty even entering. Picture him picking up Sykes's letter, reading it, and grasping its import. He had thought he was in Italy to ascertain the government's view of Zionism and its understanding of Palestine's future—project enough for any diplomat. "It never crossed my mind before that I should approach the Vatican," he wrote to Weizmann a few weeks later. It was an amazing ascent. Not without misgivings, he called upon Britain's Vatican representative as directed, and this man, possibly in concert with the British ambassador, arranged for him to meet first with Pacelli and then with Cardinal Gasparri, the papal secretary of state.

So Nahum Sokolow entered the Vatican. In his sessions with the two papal representatives, he outlined the Zionist program. He appears to have spent a good deal of time reassuring them about Jewish intentions regarding the Christian holy places. Both Catholics advised him that the Jews should make no claim upon the area in Palestine in which these were located. Gasparri, however, extended an olive branch: If the Jews did keep out of them, then the Vatican would wish them well in their attempt to build a Jewish state in the rest of the country. Sokolow quickly assured him that the Zionists aspired only to an autonomous home. He made a good impression. Gasparri told the British ambassador afterward that "he had been pleased" to meet Sokolow, and that the Zionist "had given a good account of his aims and objects coupled with assurances that no feelings of hostility were entertained towards the Church."

"Even after approaching the Vatican," Sokolow wrote to Weizmann, "I did not dream of being received by the Pope." Someone, however, suggested that he request an audience, and two days after the meeting with Gasparri, word came that the pope would indeed see him. And so it came to pass that on May 6, 1917, the Jew from Wyszogrod met the pope in Rome. In symbolism it topped even the meeting with the French foreign minister in Paris.

"In spite of my usual calmness, this was rather an exciting, patriotic and emotional piece of ceremony," Sokolow later confessed. He thought the interview had gone very well. "I am not inclined to any credulity or exaggeration," he protested, but still for the pope to have granted so long and so friendly an audience not merely to a Jew but to a Zionist representative suggested to him that "we are not going to have any unsurmountable obstacles on the part of the Vatican." He had been, Sokolow noted also, "the first Jew received during this Pontificate."

Predictably, the pope had wanted from him reassurances about Jewish intentions regarding the holy places. These the Zionist gladly provided. Then he outlined his movement's accomplishments. The pope responded favorably, saying that the return of the Jews to Palestine was a miraculous event. Sokolow outlined Zionist aspirations for the future. "Is there enough room in Palestine to carry out your plans?" asked the pope. "There is the possibility to reach our goal . . . ," Sokolow replied cautiously.

His Holiness: "But what then can we do for you?"
Sokolow: "We desire that Your Holiness accept the assur-
                 ance of our loyalty and accord us your moral
                 support. That is our aspiration."
His Holiness: "Yes, yes—I believe that we shall be good
                 neighbors."

Again we must picture Sokolow, this time exiting the Vatican and making his way through the Roman streets to the British embassy. Was he walking on air? How could he not have been? Upon arriving at his destination, he composed a telegram for Weizmann hinting at the excitement he must have felt.

Have been received by Pope in special audience which lasted three quarters of an hour. Pope attentively listened to my report . . . declared Jewish efforts of establishing national home in Palestine met sympathetically. He sees no obstacle whatever from the point of view of his religious interests concerning only Holy Places which he trusts will be properly safe guarded by special arrangement . . . The whole impression of honouring me with a long audience and tenor of conversation reveal most favourable attitude.

A clerk would have put these words into cipher and sent them to Military Intelligence in London, where another clerk deciphered them. Weizmann read them a day later. So far had the Zionist movement come that now it made routine use of such government facilities. And the hard-headed Weizmann, when he received Sokolow's entirely unexpected message, must have experienced a certain frisson. He had been wrong to doubt Sokolow on the Continent: "Your telegram received heartily congratulate brilliant result."

Six days later the Italian prime minister, Paolo Boselli, granted Sokolow an audience too. Boselli carefully informed him that although Italy could not take the initiative, neither would it oppose another power, more closely concerned with the future of Palestine, if such a power acted in a manner favorable to Zionism. "I am extremely satisfied," Sokolow reported to Weizmann.

Nor was this the end of his remarkable tour. He had thought he would return directly to London from Rome, but the French government called for him to stop in Paris on his way. There the round of discussions resumed: with Cambon, the foreign secretary, and with Prime Minister Alexandre Ribot himself. Satisfied that Italy had no strong objections to the developing understanding with Zionism; intent upon unleashing Jewish power against the pacifists and Bolsheviks of Russia; and hoping still to win Zionism from exclusive reliance upon Great Britain, now the French leaders courted Zionism's diplomat. Shrewdly Sokolow asked for something he had not dared request before: that they put their expressions of support into writing. On June 4, 1917, the French foreign minister, Jules Cambon, obliged:

> You were good enough to present the project to which you are devoting your efforts, which has for its object the development of Jewish colonization in Palestine. You consider that circumstances permitting, and the independence of the Holy Places being safeguarded on the other hand, it would be a deed of justice and of reparation to assist, by the protection of the Allied Powers, in the renaissance of the Jewish nationality in that Land from which the people of Israel were exiled so many centuries ago.
>
> The French Government, which entered this present war to defend a people wrongly attacked, and which continues the struggle to assure the victory of right over might, can but feel sympathy for your cause, the triumph of which is bound up with that of the allies.
>
> I am happy to give you herewith such assurance.

Note that this letter reverses Picot's refusal in London to recognize the Jews as a distinct nationality. The French government had become the first great power to do so. Sokolow had achieved a Zionist benchmark. And more: The very existence of such a declaration by her primary wartime ally would make it easier for Britain to make one too. No wonder, then, that as soon as he returned to London, Sokolow made sure the British Foreign Office received a copy of Cambon's letter.

Sokolow's extraordinary passage in the spring of 1917 marks a watershed. Before it took place, the Zionists in Britain struggled for purchase; afterward they found their footing. They moved forward with a new sense of confidence and self-worth. But the world was still at war. Italy, France, and England would promise much to win it. What weight would the honeyed words of the pope, or the written words of the French foreign minister, or even the assurances of the British prime minister actually bear? Even while Sokolow was still abroad, even as the words were being spoken and written, Chaim Weizmann was discovering that they might not bear all that much.

CHAPTER 16

Revelation of the Sykes-Picot Agreement

ENGLAND AND FRANCE went to war in 1914 in part to defend the rights of small nations like Belgium and Serbia, or so they claimed. Perhaps it was true, but such considerations did not enter into their calculations when they bribed Italy to join the war with promises of Habsburg territory, or when they induced Romania to join with similar promises, or when they helped engineer a government in Greece likewise open to such promises. Nor was it part of the thinking of Sir Mark Sykes and François Georges-Picot when they redrew the map of the Middle East. They did it to benefit their own countries, not the Arabs or the Armenians, let alone the Jews, and at the time they made no bones about it. The Tripartite Agreement, as Sykes-Picot became after Russia slightly amended it in her own interest and then approved it, is a classic example of old-style imperialism and secret diplomacy. Plenty of people in both England and France wanted their governments to live up to the beautiful early rhetoric used to justify war against Germany, but they lacked political power. In 1916 neither Sykes nor Picot felt the need to take them into account. The two diplomats and the men behind them did not foresee that World War I would turn everything topsy-turvy.

But it did. As the war ground on, the number of its critics grew. They believed that secret diplomacy was one of the causes of the war, as well as imperialist rivalries. Germany's annexation of Alsace-Lorraine at the end of the Franco-Prussian War of 1870–71 had poisoned relations between the two countries. The critics demanded "open covenants openly arrived at," "no annexations" of territory, and much else besides. The fall of the tsar and the advent of the liberal internationalist Woodrow Wilson when America joined the war in the spring of 1917 amplified their voices. In May Kerensky's new government proclaimed that "Free Russia does not purpose to dominate other peoples or to take from them their national patrimony, or forcibly to occupy foreign territory." Lloyd George's government replied, "In this sentiment the British Government heartily concur." But of course the Allies had negotiated covenants in secret and had planned imperialist annexations such as the Sykes-Picot Agreement envisioned. Given the growing strength of these critics, there would be hell to pay when Sykes-Picot came to light. And then it did; and then there was.

On the evening of Thursday, April 12, 1917, C. P. Scott met a French journalist, Vicomte Robert de Caix, foreign editor and lead writer of the Parisian *Le Journal des débats*. De Caix, who advised the Quai d'Orsay on Middle Eastern affairs and would go on to help shape postwar French policy there, dropped a bomb; whether he did so intentionally we cannot know. He told Scott that when the war was finished, France would claim Syria down to Acre and Lake Tiberias and across to, and including, the area of the Hauran. That was territory that the Zionists hoped would become theirs under a British protectorate. The rest of Palestine, de Caix asserted, would be put under international control: "It is settled."

It was pretty much what Sykes and Picot had agreed more than a year earlier, unknown to most. Scott thought the French claims grandiose but aspirational and therefore "disquieting" but not calamitous. The British government could nip French pretensions in the bud, he reasoned, by publicly stating its own plans for Palestine. The next day at *The Manchester Guardian* offices, he repeated to Harry Sacher what he had learned and what he hoped Britain would do. He warned Sacher not to trust the Foreign Office to perform as required, however, "because Balfour is weak as water and the officials are tired, indifferent and inefficient." Sacher immediately put it in a letter to Weizmann. Two days later Scott wrote to Weizmann as well, repeating what de Caix had told him.

Thus did the Zionists first glean something of the Sykes-Picot Agree-

ment and experience their first unnerving trickle of doubt about British intentions. Scott went looking for more information in London and got some,
on Friday, April 20, from Sir Alfred Milner of the War Cabinet. Scott reported to Weizmann that Milner "spoke resignedly about the international
solution in Palestine as a whole, and said that 'unfortunate commitments'
had been made a year ago—I gathered to the French." Thus the War Cabinet minister sparked another glimmer of unease, evidence of some sort of
Anglo-French carve-up of the Middle East.

While Scott and Milner were dancing around that very subject, James
Malcolm was arriving in London from Paris. He carried a diary of
Sokolow's activities that the Zionist had entrusted to him, and a glowing report based upon them that he had written. He brought them to Weizmann
next day, but by now the Zionist leader had more than Sokolow's discussions with Jules Cambon on his mind. He questioned Malcolm closely
about French intentions in the Middle East, such as the latter had been able
to glean, and whether Britain accepted them as part of some larger deal.
What Malcolm told him did little to quiet his growing unease.

> Apparently the French are working very hard for a condo-
> minium and . . . the British have secured Haifa and Acre for
> themselves with the right of building a railway from Haifa
> which would join up the Baghdad railway. This information is
> practically official . . . What is not quite clear yet, and I was un-
> able to clear it up, is whether the arrangement is binding or
> whether it is flexible, and whether there is a clear possibility of
> reopening the whole question.

Even without details, the outline of the Anglo-French plan for Palestine
was beginning to take shape in Weizmann's mind, along with a dawning
realization that the British government had been less than frank with him.
Perhaps Sokolow, who must have discerned French intentions while in
Paris, had been less than frank with him too—or perhaps he was planning
to tell all when he returned to London. But Sokolow now was headed for
Rome. Whom could Weizmann better question at this point than Herbert
Samuel, the one (former) cabinet minister who was both Jewish and Zionist? On Tuesday, April 24, Weizmann tried to pin him down, but Samuel
would not be pinned: "His answer was that he could not disclose to me the
nature of the arrangement made because he was a member of the Cabinet
at that time, but he could say this much, that the arrangement was not satisfactory from the British point of view. He sees no objection at all why this

question should not be reopened, especially now when the British army is occupying Palestine."

So "an arrangement" with France did exist! Weizmann hurried from the morning meeting with Samuel to an afternoon meeting at the Foreign Office with Sir Ronald Graham, who, while in Egypt, had hoped to replace McMahon as high commissioner, but who had been posted back to London instead to serve as assistant under secretary of state. Graham confirmed the existence of an Anglo-French deal but little else. "He found this arrangement after he arrived from Egypt," Weizmann reported to Scott. "He does not consider it satisfactory." Graham thought Weizmann should speak to someone higher up the Foreign Office ladder, namely the acting foreign secretary, Lord Robert Cecil. (Balfour was in America.) He arranged for an interview.

At five-thirty the next afternoon Weizmann went "to Bob Cecil in a fine rage," or so William Ormsby-Gore, assistant secretary to the cabinet and Milner's parliamentary private secretary, reported in a letter to Mark Sykes in Egypt. That would have been something to see, but one doubts that Weizmann was actually in a rage. (Perhaps he would have been if he had known that the man who had negotiated the agreement with France was Sykes.) But if Weizmann was too astute to jeopardize his cause with temper tantrums, he was sufficiently self-assured, and sufficiently at home by now in the Foreign Office, not to mince words. Cecil wrote in his report of the meeting: Weizmann "began by saying that he had been told that some kind of arrangement had been made between the British and French Governments, whereby Judea should be internationalized and the northern part of Palestine, Galilea, should be given to the French Government. He objected to both provisions." He objected equally to a purely French administration. That would be tantamount to "a third destruction of the Temple." When at last, without naming its authors, Cecil revealed the parts of the Sykes-Picot Agreement relevant to Palestine, Weizmann objected to them too. Only a British protectorate would suffice, he repeated, and he would rouse "the feelings of Zionist Jews throughout the world in favour of the solution which he desired."

The Zionists spent the next few days in intense debate. A letter from Sacher to Weizmann suggests their likely tenor: "We have been lied to and deceived all along and I shall never forgive the gentry . . . who have done it . . . the permanent officials and Cecil (Sir R[onald]. G[raham]. & M[ark]. S[ykes]. and the like) cannot be trusted." In a second letter, Sacher warned Weizmann that "our affairs are at a crisis." He prepared a document for discussion at the next meeting of the British Palestine Committee that he wanted amended if necessary but then endorsed and sent to the Foreign Office. (Cooler heads prevailed—it never was.) Sacher's memorandum read in part:

> The representatives of the Jewish national movement have no desire to dwell upon the fact that during the whole course of their lengthy negotiations with His Majesty's Government the existence of such an agreement [Sykes-Picot] was not only sedulously concealed from them but was positively denied, but it would be idle not to point out to His Majesty's Government that this mode of dealing with them has made a most painful impression.

But the Zionists were shrewd as well as angry. "Leon [Simon] thinks that the British want to get away from the agreement with the French & to use us as a lever," Sacher observed to Weizmann; this assessment was accurate. One thing was clear to them all. The revelation of British double-dealing reaffirmed the necessity, as Sacher put it, of obtaining from the British government "a written definite promise satisfactory to ourselves with regard to Palestine."

Think back to Weizmann's assiduous and polished networking in the drawing rooms of London's political high society, and to his most recent meetings with Lloyd George and Balfour at addresses even more august. Consider Sokolow's discussions with French and Italian leaders, and with the pope. What were all these, if not instances of secret diplomacy? Certainly there had been no input from the Jewish masses. But the Zionist movement had been touched by the rising radical tide. At his meeting with Cecil, Weizmann promised to rally the Jews of the world on behalf of the British protectorate and warned that "the suggested division of Palestine would raise an outcry which will ring through from one end of the world to the other, as it is contrary to all the principles which have been proclaimed by the Allies since the beginning of the War, and which have lately been so strongly emphasized by America and Russia."

No doubt Zionists and their supporters *would* be outraged to learn of the arrangement's provisions. Perhaps some of Zionism's opponents would be outraged to learn of them too. If the outcry reached all the way to the Hejaz (where the Arab rebel army encamped) and all the way to the holy city of Mecca (seat of the new Arab kingdom), what would Grand Sharif Hussein and his sons make of it? More to the point, what would they make of the arrangements that Sir Mark Sykes and Monsieur Georges-Picot had made regarding the Arabs? In the event, however, they made the discovery on their own before Weizmann had time to raise the outcry.

"Last night [May 24, 1917]," wrote Colonel Cyril Wilson, Britain's "pilgrimage officer" in Jeddah and main liaison with King Hussein, "Feisal said he wanted to talk about his Father . . . The following are some rough notes I took." We may imagine the English colonel in the port town where temperatures had recently scaled a hundred degrees Fahrenheit, sweltering in khaki, sweat dripping from his forehead, pen in hand, conjuring up Feisal's monologue of the previous evening. "The Sharif first got to respect and like Great Britain about 22 years ago when he was at Stambul," Wilson wrote. Hussein's uncle, who happened to be grand sharif at the time, had cheated him of revenue due him from lands in Egypt, but when Hussein complained to Abdul Hamid II, the latter had done nothing. Hussein then "took an action in Cairo" against his uncle, even though this displeased the sultan. His uncle tried to bribe the Egyptian court, "but Justice prevailed and Hussein knew then that British methods were honest."

This initial appreciation grew into something stronger and larger; eventually it helped to shape Arab policies toward Britain and thus, perhaps, the modern world. Hussein had compared British colonial methods with the French and German, Feisal told Wilson. He had arrived at the same conclusion as the Zionists when they performed a similar exercise: British was better. On that steamy night in Jeddah, Feisal put it to Wilson this way: "He saw that India, with millions of people, was administered by comparatively very few British officials and decided that if ever Arabs could do anything, Great Britain, who never interfered with the peoples' religion or freedom, was the best and only power to assist."

Hussein's wartime letters contain one paean after another to Great Britain's history of honorable conduct and integrity. When McMahon's replacement, Sir Reginald Wingate, thought fit to remind the king of the Hejaz that "the British Government is the respecter of treaties, the espouser of Justice, and, in every case, a faithful ally," Hussein replied, "I have to say that it was this world wide and true fame of Great Britain that encouraged me to assume the heavy responsibility of my present task." Many years later, after bitter disappointment and near the end of a long life, Hussein was still repeating the same mantra: "The English, my son, are an honourable kind, in word and in deed, in fortune and in adversity. I say honourable. Only his Excellency, the estimable, energetic Luweed Jurj [Lloyd George] is something of an acrobat and a fox."

As we have seen, even before Lloyd George came to center stage, British officials had kept much from Hussein that honor should have compelled them to reveal. But then someone let something slip. Perhaps the guilty party belonged to the French mission under Colonel Brémond in Jeddah, or to the British contingent there; or perhaps someone in Cairo allowed his tongue to wag. At any rate someone said something, and Hussein learned about it and experienced that first trickle of doubt, just as Chaim Weizmann did in London after learning what Robert de Caix told C. P. Scott.

And like Weizmann, Hussein would not rest until he knew what was up. Sometime in late March 1917 (just as Nahum Sokolow was preparing to set out for Paris) he dispatched a telegram to Wilson requesting a meeting to discuss various points including "another matter of minor importance, that is, the part of the country in the North-West which we were granted in our agreement." Wilson immediately got into touch with Cairo, where with equal swiftness alarm bells began to sound. "The Sharif evidently intends to discuss the question of Syria, probably with special reference to the districts of Damascus, Hama, Homs and Aleppo," Brigadier General Gilbert Clayton warned in a memorandum circulated among high officials both in Cairo and London. Here the reader should recall that McMahon, in his correspondence with Hussein, had intentionally fudged paragraphs dealing with that part of Syria, because he thought France might wish to claim it at the end of the war. Perhaps willfully, Hussein had ignored their vagueness and had simply reasserted his own claim to the territory, including lands stretching south nearly all the way to Jaffa in Palestine. Now, apparently, he wished to revisit the subject.

On the very day that Clayton composed his memorandum of warning, Lloyd George, Lord Curzon, and the cabinet secretary, Maurice Hankey, met at 10 Downing Street with Mark Sykes to go over his instructions for the forthcoming Middle Eastern trip with Picot. Unaware that King Hussein was becoming restless, the four reaffirmed "the signed agreement from which we could not depart," as Curzon described it. In addition, "the Prime Minister suggested that Sir Mark Sykes ought not enter into any political pledges to the Arabs, and particularly none in regard to Palestine," which earlier in the meeting he had said he hoped would become British. (On that part of the signed agreement, then, the British contemplated departing after all, since the Sykes-Picot Agreement had envisioned an international condominium there.) What this all meant was that when Sykes got to the Hejaz, he would have to reassure King Hussein about British and French intentions, without making any promises and knowing all the while that, against Hussein's wishes, Britain had accepted French claims to the territory west of the four crucial towns and aimed at scooping up Palestine for herself.

Meanwhile, and at almost precisely the same moment, the French government was giving its own instructions to François Georges-Picot: "What we want to do is to free a people for long past enslaved by the Turks, granting it such privileges as it is entitled to." What seems a liberal sentiment on first reading appears ambiguous on the second: Precisely what "privileges" would the French be granting? Here is another ambiguity: "It is not a question of imposing foreign rulers upon them, but only of assisting them in the creation of national institutions capable of assuring to them a proper system of government." What did the French deem "a proper system of government" for Arabs?

Sykes and Picot arrived in Cairo toward the end of April. They held preliminary meetings with three Syrian delegates, including a personal representative of Hussein, Fuad al-Khatib, who served as his deputy foreign minister and who had been a founding member of the Ottoman Decentralization Party. Sykes walked his diplomatic tightrope. He and Picot argued that an Anglo-French presence in the Middle East would not threaten, but rather would buttress, Arab independence. They did not mention the disputed territory on the Syrian coast, although by now they both doubtless knew of Hussein's anxiety regarding it. One must assume that they did not specify the "privileges" to which Arabs would be entitled or the "proper system of government" for them.

The Syrians signified their acceptance of some kind of French presence in Syria, but we do not know precisely what kind. With regard to Mesopotamia Sykes bluntly told them, "though I did not know what form of Government H.M.G. would establish there that there could be no doubt that H.M.G. would reserve for itself the right to maintain a permanent military occupation, and that the local government would have to be of kind sufficient to maintain law and order so that British commerce should not suffer." He added in his cable to London: "I hope it won't be concluded that the negotiations were easy or simple. The main difficulty was to maneuver the delegates into asking for what we were prepared to give them, without letting them know what precise geographical agreement had been come to." But the three delegates were not the men who exercised genuine power. The real question was how Feisal, and above all King Hussein, would react when Sykes and Picot told them about the Tripartite Agreement, and more specifically how they would react to French plans for Syria, including the northern coastal portions.

The king let it be known that he wished to speak with Sir Mark Sykes alone. He would come down from Mecca to Jeddah to meet him on May 2. Sykes would have talked matters over with the men of Cairo—Clayton, Storrs, Hogarth, his old friend George Lloyd, and perhaps the new high commissioner, Sir Reginald Wingate—and concluded, reluctantly, as Hogarth of the Arab Bureau, advised London: "The time has now arrived . . . when the general lines of the Anglo-French agreement regarding Syria must be explained to Hussein." Hogarth thought a letter addressed to Hussein by King George, plus an increase in British subventions, would sweeten the pill.

Sykes prepared for his next journey. With some justification, he appears to have thought that he could persuade just about anyone of just about anything. On the way to Jeddah, he stopped at Wejh, where he met with Feisal. "I explained to him the principle of the Anglo-French agreement in regard to an Arab confederation. After much argument he accepted the principle and seemed satisfied." This sounds as though Sykes outlined the Tripartite Agreement, including the envisioned French sphere of interest, but without going into details about French plans for governing the Red Area, including the Syrian coastline. Three days later, in Jeddah, he had a long interview with King Hussein. First he read to him the cable Hogarth had elicited from King George. It expressed "great satisfaction at the progress of the armies of Hejaz." Not to be outdone, Hussein replied, "On the King of England's forehead I plant the kiss of peace; on his Queen I invoke my blessing; and the royal children of England's King I embrace as the children of my children."

Then Sykes got down to business. "In accordance with my instructions I explained the principle of the agreement as regards an Arab confederation or State . . . I impressed upon the King the importance of Franco-Arab friendship and I at last got him to admit that it was essential to Arab development in Syria, but this after a very lengthy argument." Again this is slightly vague: It does not sound as though Sykes explained that France might annex the disputed area, or indeed any area, and that Britain would not oppose if she did so. Sykes, the human whirlwind, albeit a charming one, had convinced Feisal of something, but perhaps not something of the essence. He may simply have overwhelmed the older, much more reserved Hussein. Or he may have mistaken exhaustion (the meeting lasted three and a half hours and the king was not young) for acquiescence. And again, precisely what the king was asked to acquiesce to remains unclear.

We may glean something of the king's point of view from Sykes's letter about the meeting to Wingate in Cairo. "Unless Arab independence were assured," the king had warned, he "feared that posterity would charge him

REVELATION OF THE SYKES-PICOT AGREEMENT   229

with assisting in the overthrow of the last Islamic power [Turkey] without setting another in its place." Moreover, "if France annexed Syria"—perhaps Sykes mentioned this possibility after all—he "would be open to the charge of breaking faith with the Moslems of Syria by having led them into a rebellion against the Turks in order to hand them over to a Christian power." These points were "important and worthy of sympathy," as Sykes himself noted. We may guess then that he had not set the king's mind at rest about them. Perhaps Sykes was not satisfied in his own mind about French, or even British, intentions. Still, he fixed a meeting for Picot and the king two weeks later, on May 19, and headed back to Cairo.

Here then were the main difficulties Sykes faced in mid-May 1917 during his mission to the Middle East. He had to persuade the king and Feisal to accept that France as well as Britain would play a role in Arabia's future and that the two powers had already drawn up its boundaries. He had to let Picot tell them that France might annex a part of Arabia that they believed integral to it. And he had to persuade the French to relinquish claims to northern Palestine in favor of Britain, and to give up the thought of an international condominium in the rest of it. He had to be wondering also when to explain to Hussein that Britain intended to control all Palestine except the holy places, and that Britain probably would favor a significant increase in the Jewish presence there. Finally, he had to square all this with the early wartime statements about fighting on behalf of the rights of small nations, and the more recent ones about "open covenants openly arrived at," and "no annexations." Picot, for his part, would have been struggling to think of a way to convince Hussein that French annexation would strengthen Arab independence.

The meetings immediately preceding, during, and following May 19 are crucial in Middle Eastern history. Some forty-eight hours before the appointed date, Sykes and Picot as well as Colonel Wilson (who must have gone up earlier to Cairo for consultations), George Lloyd, and the French colonel Brémond boarded the *Northbrook*, Britain's flagship in the Red Sea, and headed south for Jeddah. This time when the ship reached Wejh, Feisal came aboard, accompanied by Colonel Stewart Newcombe, a friend of Lawrence's and military adviser to the Arabs. As the *Northbrook* steamed south under a broiling sun, Sykes, Picot, and Feisal held several meetings, the Europeans' aim being to reconcile the Arab to a French presence in Syria. But the results "I understand" were "not entirely satisfactory," Wilson reported. Feisal worried that the Europeans would interpret anything he said as official. Only his father could speak for the projected Arab state.

The *Northbrook* slid down the glassy, tepid Red Sea, putting in at steamy

Jeddah on Friday night, May 18. Next day Sykes and Picot came ashore in the mid-morning heat, accompanied by French, Egyptian, and Arab troops, a colorful, impressive spectacle intended to disabuse any town residents who still thought the Ottomans might win the war. They all made their way to the king's place of residence. As a special mark of consideration, the king advanced to the door to greet the Frenchman. Sykes introduced them. The principals, Sykes, Picot, Hussein, Feisal, Fuad, and interpreters, went upstairs; Wilson and Brémond remained below.

By now the king knew pretty well from his meeting with Sykes, and from reports given him by Fuad and his son Feisal since their arrival, what the French wanted in Syria. He was having none of it.

> He [Hussein] told M. Picot that he feels himself responsible for the Syrian people, [reported Fuad] because he has lately and before the revolution received so many letters from leaders of all classes and seen some of them personally, all of whom promised true allegiance to him as their Leader and protector: and some of them as their Khalifa . . . He said if you want to take the Christians from us and leave the Moslems to us you are creating divisions amongst the people and fostering bigotry. Lebanon need not be ours or yours either. Let it be as its people wish, but I do not want outside people to interfere. You must know that many people died and were hanged, and on the gallows they said "We don't mind. Our King and Khalifa will soon appear and avenge our death." My conscience will torture me if I do not save their families and country; for they died for the Arab Cause only.

Then he quoted an Arab proverb to the Europeans: "If you take one finger from my hand, you will torture me and let me loose, but you gain nothing by taking the finger."

Sykes did what he could for his French ally. "Although it does not concern me," he interjected, "I give my own opinion that if you have European advisers in Syria and give them exclusive power, it will be the best you can do." Fuad reported, "The King was not pleased with the idea and refused it." Sykes recorded Hussein's reaction in almost identical words: "The King disliked the idea naturally." He added, "And Fuad said that this was the end of Arab independence." Picot suggested that the king accept an agreement with France for Syria along the same lines as the one he had accepted with Britain for Baghdad. "The King utterly refused," Fuad wrote. He would allow the French into Syria on his terms or none at all. The meeting lasted nearly three hours. No agreement was reached.

Afterward, on the way to Wilson's Jeddah residence, presumably for a late lunch, Sykes confided to his host that if Picot did not change his attitude, "it appeared hopeless to try and bring France and the Sharif together." No doubt Sykes spent a good part of the afternoon and evening attempting to modify Picot's approach, but at some point he had a brainstorm. He got into touch with Fuad and asked him to come aboard ship. When the latter arrived, he strongly advised him to convince the king to focus on Picot's last point: "that the relations between the Arab Government and France should be the same in Syria as that between the King and the British in Baghdad." Get the king to accept that much, he instructed Fuad, and then leave everything to me. He hammered at this twice more, wiring ashore to Wilson later the same evening and then early the next morning, directing him both times to reiterate the same instructions to Fuad.

Fuad did as the Englishman wanted: "I took three hours to convince the King to accept Sir Mark Sykes' wish." He and the king and Feisal would have huddled all that evening, talking the matter up and down; and here Hussein's romantic, indeed unrealistic understanding of British history and of Britain's future intentions becomes relevant. Hussein finally accepted Fuad's argument, not because he thought France would do good things for Syria, but rather, as Fuad explained, because the king "trusted what the British Commissioner says. He knows that Sir Mark Sykes can fight for the Arabs better than he can himself in political matters, and knows that Sir Mark Sykes speaks with the authority of the British Government and will therefore be able to carry out his promises."

There may have been more to it than that. Hussein must have asked himself why Sykes suddenly insisted that the French have in Syria the same arrangement with him that Britain had in Baghdad. And then he would have remembered what he thought McMahon had promised him at the end of 1915: a temporary occupation of Iraq paid for by a generous monetary compensation. That would be fine for the territory along the Syrian coast too. Triumphantly Hussein turned to Fuad: "I have in my pocket a letter from Sir Henry McMahon which promises all I wish. This I know is all right as the British Government will fulfill her word." Neither Fuad nor Feisal had seen the letter; nor did Hussein show it to them.

Let us recall what McMahon's letters actually said. In his second note to Hussein (October 24, 1915), the high commissioner had written with regard to the *vilayet*s of Baghdad and Basra that his country's "established position and interests there will call for the setting up of special administrative arrangements to protect those regions from foreign aggression, to promote the welfare of their inhabitants, and to safeguard our mutual economic interests." In the third (December 13, 1915), he had written that Britain's interests "in the *vilayet* of Baghdad necessitate a friendly and stable administration such as you have outlined." In his fourth and final note he had added merely that "we shall examine the matter with the utmost care after the defeat of the enemy." It is hard to interpret any of these statements as an unequivocal promise to recognize Arab independence. Either Hussein had received other letters about Baghdad of which historians are unaware, or wearing his rose-tinted glasses, he simply misconstrued British intentions.

For the moment, however, his aperçu was enough. The three Arabs composed a statement for Hussein to read next morning when negotiations resumed, this time aboard the *Northbrook*. The statement does not survive, but records of the next day's meeting agree that it went roughly as follows:

> His Majesty the King of Hejaz learned with great satisfaction of the approval of the French Government of Arab national aspirations and, as he had every confidence in Great Britain, he would be quite content if the French pursued the same policy towards Moslems and Arab aspirations on the Moslem Syrian littoral as the British did in Baghdad.

And so we may guess that King Hussein went to bed that evening with a sense of triumph. He thought he had the French over a barrel.

But had he interpreted Sykes's reasoning correctly? Perhaps he did. Sykes, after all, had read the McMahon-Hussein correspondence; he would have known what Hussein wanted for the Syrian coastal region. Possibly he may have thought he could arrange it for him. At any rate, self-confident and forceful as he was, the Englishman really did believe that he could defend Arab interests better than Hussein could. That has to be why he repeatedly told Fuad to leave everything to him.

Sykes's attitude toward annexation at this date is difficult to pin down. Once, obviously, he had thought it the natural prerogative of a great power. Now he understood that formidable forces in America and Russia, and in England and France for that matter, opposed it. He concluded that "formal annexation is quite contrary to the spirit of the time and would only lay up a store of future trouble." Anyway, as he wrote to Percy Cox, a chief British officer in Mesopotamia, the Anglo-French agreement would enable Britain to get "what we want without infringing the kind of theories [favored by] . . . President Wilson and the new Russian Government." The problem is that he wrote the letter to Cox four days after the meeting on the nineteenth. He wrote against "formal annexation" three months after that. But two days before it, he and Picot prepared a joint statement on "general policy" in which annexation is neither endorsed nor discounted but certainly remains an option. What are we to conclude? Perhaps that Sykes played a completely lone hand during the negotiations of mid-May. Let Hussein leave everything to him; let Picot think the French would annex part of Syria; he would later persuade him, and the great men in London, to forgo annexation. England and France could attain their Middle Eastern objectives without recourse to that counterproductive, anachronistic tactic.

At this stage Sykes likely foresaw an Arab empire or confederation with Hussein as its figurehead in Mecca. It would encompass the territory outlined in the original Sykes-Picot Agreement: Red Area and Area A, Blue Area and Area B, in which France and England would have predominant interest and influence but not absolute control. The two spheres could be ruled by Feisal and one of his brothers. Formal annexation by Britain and France would not be necessary.

King Hussein, Feisal, and Fuad arrived at the jetty next morning at about 9:20, and Wilson, who would attend the negotiations that day, brought them out to the big boat. Sometime during this meeting, Sykes and Picot finally acquainted Hussein with the details of the Tripartite Agreement. They seem not to have spoken precisely of annexation. They did not leave him with a written copy. And they asked him to accept it then and there. "Any criticisms or exclamations were stopped by Sir Mark Sykes asking me [Fuad] to induce the King to agree" to focus on getting the French to act in Syria as Britain would in Iraq. Luckily for Sykes, Fuad shared Hussein's faith in Great Britain: "I am under the belief that Sir Mark Sykes had some very good plan or proposal which will enable the formation of a whole Arab Empire to be realized; and that the plan would only be possible by following his advice and leaving all to him. Hence my course of action."

A little later, perhaps, Hussein read aloud the statement that he, Fuad, and Feisal had prepared the previous night, and he followed up by adding that he had reversed position "because he relied entirely on the British Government keeping their agreement with him . . . he only knew France through Great Britain [but he] . . . had complete confidence in Sykes' word as he came direct from the British government." Sykes expressed great satisfaction. King Hussein wished "to play the game." Picot was "obviously delighted" too: "On such a reply he would have a useful communication to make to his Government and . . . he hoped that after discussing matters with his Government he would have a further communication to make. The interview then concluded with a very good feeling prevailing." But of course it did. Hussein thought he had tricked the French; Picot thought he had tricked Hussein; and Sykes, if our reading is correct, believed he could square this circle at a later date.

If the principals were satisfied, however, some of the lesser figures were not. They shared neither Hussein's faith in Sykes nor Sykes's faith in Sykes. Colonel Cyril Wilson, for one, felt deep unease. When the king read his statement, "it struck me as possible that the sharif [Hussein], one of the most courteous of men, absolutely loyal to us and with complete faith in Great Britain, was verbally agreeing to a thing which he never would agree to if he knew our interpretation of what the IRAQ situation is to be." He took Sykes aside: "Does the Sharif [Hussein] know what the situation at Baghdad really is?"

"They have the proclamation," Sykes replied, referring to the statement, written by himself, and delivered by General Maude upon capturing Baghdad from the Turks. The proclamation is deservedly famous: "Our armies do not come into your cities and lands as conquerors or enemies, but as liberators," it reads. "I [General Maude] am commanded to invite you, through your nobles and elders and representatives, to participate in the management of your civil affairs in collaboration with the political representatives of Great Britain who accompany the British Army."

Sykes asked Fuad if he had read the proclamation, and Fuad replied that he had. The matter dropped.

Wilson "said nothing for a few minutes as I was an onlooker, but later remarked that the Proclamation said nothing more than asking Arabs to co-operate in the Government." In other words, it employed the same ambiguous language that Sykes and Picot were using that day with Hussein. Wilson remained deeply troubled.

Feisal was troubled too. After the meeting he went to his father. "Supposing Great Britain does not carry out the agreement in Iraq or that they have one idea of it and you another?"

Hussein lost his temper. He had the letter from McMahon, he said. "Don't you know the British? I trust them absolutely."

Later that evening Fuad too developed second thoughts. He and Feisal contrived a meeting with George Lloyd and Colonel Newcombe, whom Feisal knew and trusted from the desert campaign against the Turks. The two Arabs aired their worries: that the king relied too heavily upon Mark

Sykes; that he had conceded too much in accepting the Tripartite Agreement and French occupation of Syria; that conceivably he misunderstood what Britain intended for Baghdad and therefore could have no true understanding of what the French would do in Syria. "Certainly," argued Feisal, "the large number of persons hanged in Syria and the Lebanon had not died to liberate their country from the Turks to give it to the French." "Let it be agreed," he said to the two Englishmen, "that France would be offered concessions first, applied to for loans and advisers, but unless the people wished otherwise, let the Government be Arab."

Newcombe and Lloyd appear to have been troubled too by what Feisal and Fuad told them. Lloyd advised Fuad to go to Cairo right away to explain his worries to Clayton and to Wingate. Newcombe composed an extraordinary note for the Cairo contingent to ponder. Basically he condemned the way in which Sykes and Picot had conducted their meetings. Hussein had been told of the Tripartite Agreement "and asked to give a final decision upon [it] at a moment's notice: while French and English governments have had months to consider their point of view." Implicitly he suggested that the two Europeans had acted dishonestly. The king had "agreed to the Syrian coast being governed by the French on the same terms as Baghdad by the British, having no idea what the latter are: It was not pointed out to him either that the two countries and the conditions differ fundamentally." Newcombe hoped that no irreparable damage to British honor had been done. Nothing had yet been signed. "Further and *very much wider* [emphasis in the original] discussion is possible and very desirable."

Newcombe then went directly to Colonel Wilson. Their discussion only heightened Wilson's existing unease. Afterward he put together a twelve-page document, repetitive, poorly organized, but moving—in fact, extraordinary. The essence of his message was:

> As you know I have all along been a strong advocate of being as open as possible with the Sharif [Hussein]. My considered opinion is that we have not been as open and frank as we should been at this last meeting.
>
> Special representatives of Great Britain and France came expressly to fix things up with the Sharif and when the latter agreed to France having the same status in Syria as we are to have in Iraq surely the main points of our agreement re Iraq should have been stated to prevent all chance of a misunderstanding which might have far reaching consequences . . .

Everything may be all right, as Baghdad and Iraq except Basra may be going to be entirely Arab and independent with British advisers, financial control, etc. If so well and good but if the Sharif puts one construction on McMahon's letter and we another, there is likely to be serious trouble.

Several lines later he put the whole thing in a nutshell. He feared that "we have not played a straight forward game with a courteous old man who is, as Sykes agrees, one of Great Britain's most sincere and loyal admirers." And finally he issued a warning: "If we are not going to see the Sharif through, and we let him down badly after all his trust in us, the very 'enviable' post of Pilgrimage Officer at Jeddah will be vacant because I certainly could not remain."

So did the Zionists and the Arabs learn about Anglo-French plans for the Middle East; and so did British officials in Jeddah learn how their superiors treated an Arab potentate. They all could have been forgiven for thinking that Allied statements about the rights of small nations were so much hot air. King Hussein managed to convince himself that all would be well (later he would claim that he learned the details of the Sykes-Picot Agreement only when the Russian Bolsheviks published details of Allied "secret treaties" in December 1917); other leading Jews and Arabs feared that they had been betrayed or tricked. Hussein's credulity and Feisal's disquiet deeply troubled Colonels Wilson and Newcombe, which is much to their credit. As for Mark Sykes, at this crucial moment he appears to have thought he could manage the Zionists, the Arabs, the French, and the British Foreign Office all at once, and perhaps he could, but to what end? Whether in May 1917 he meant for the Anglo-French agreement to be revised, reinterpreted, or implemented without alteration remains an open question. He wrote and said different things about it.

What he most certainly did not yet do was inform the Arabs about his plans for Zionism in Palestine.

PART IV

The Road Not Taken

British Muslims, the Anglo-Ottoman Society, and the Disillusioning of Marmaduke Pickthall

THE OTTOMAN EMPIRE had entered World War I on the side of Germany at the end of October 1914. Three men dominated the empire's CUP government: Enver Pasha, Talaat Pasha, and Djemal Pasha. (The last we have already met, hanging Arab nationalists in Damascus, and bidding Feisal to feast in the intervals.) Of the ruling triumvirate, only Enver Pasha, the minister of war, unambiguously favored the alliance with Germany. Daring, underhanded, and ruthless, convinced that the German war machine would prove invincible, he had secretly maneuvered his country into the conflict on Germany's side. His two partners, and the rest of his government, and indeed his country as a whole, could not but accept the fait accompli.

Nevertheless, doubts about the wisdom of this choice would not disappear. The political strength of those who harbored them, and their willingness to act upon them, waxed and waned depending largely upon Ottoman success in battle. The doubters were strongest and most likely to call for an end to combat when their country seemed liable to defeat; they were weakest when it seemed most likely to win. Still, the possibility that Turkey would negotiate a separate peace with the Entente powers, whether under Djemal, or Talaat, or Enver, or perhaps someone else entirely, hovered always in the air. It was part of the atmosphere.

As we have also seen, Zionists in Britain at first thought Turkish entry into the war presaged disaster for Jews in Palestine. They feared that the Ottoman government would take advantage of the crisis by attacking a traditional scapegoat. They never completely lost this fear, which Djemal Pasha stoked more than once by threatening to employ "Armenian methods" against the Palestinian Jewish population. Nevertheless very quickly a hope surged to overshadow all else among British Zionists. "The Ottoman Government has drawn the sword . . . [It] will perish by the sword," Prime Minister Asquith intoned prophetically on November 9, 1914. "They . . . have rung the death-knell of Ottoman Dominion not only in Europe but in Asia." With the Ottoman Empire gone, so would be gone one of the greatest obstacles to Zionist progress. What would replace it? British Zionists concluded almost immediately that the best solution for Zionism would be a British protectorate in Palestine. Allied victory in the war would make that possible. It followed that they must oppose any compromise peace with Turkey that left her grip on Palestine intact.

As for the British: Asquith might swear that Britain would fight the war against Turkey to the end, but the easterners who sought in Turkey or the Balkans a back door to central Europe might conclude that they could more easily open it by negotiation than by force. When Lloyd George replaced Asquith as prime minister, the easterners took 10 Downing Street. But not only easterners believed that removing the Ottoman Empire from their list of enemies would benefit the Triple Entente. Westerners could think that too. So just as in Turkey where the possibility of a negotiated settlement with the Allies floated always in the minds of some, so in Britain too the possibility of a compromise peace with Turkey never quite disappeared.

Here then are three pieces on a historic chessboard: namely a never-absent, if never-realized, desire on the part of some Turks for a compromise peace with the Allies; an occasional willingness on the part of some among the Allies to consider such an arrangement with Turkey; and an adamant opposition to any such thing on the part of most British Zionists. The maneuvering of these three parties during the lead-up to the Balfour Declaration is a significant aspect of our story.

Turkey and Britain had no sooner declared war upon each other than they opened secret negotiations to try to end it. British agents had been telling the Foreign Office for years that the CUP governments were not popular; now they added that neither had been the CUP decision to enter the war. On January 28, 1915, Sir Mountstuart Elphinstone Grant Duff, British envoy in Berne, was approached by Rechid Bey, a former Liberal Turkish minister of the interior now living in Geneva. An "Old Turk" whom the CUP had chased from his country, Rechid Bey informed the Briton that if certain assurances were forthcoming from the Entente, "the present regime [in Turkey] could be swept away." On that very day, however, the War Council in London was agreeing to a British naval attempt on the Straits of the Dardanelles. Rechid Bey's proposal appears to have been lost in the shuffle.

Nevertheless Foreign Secretary Sir Edward Grey, whom Grant Duff informed about the visit, hoped to achieve by negotiation what would otherwise require the spilling of much blood. He told the cabinet, "What we really relied on to open the Straits was a coup d'état in Constantinople." He had been in touch with director of naval intelligence, Admiral "Blinker" Hall, who just had enlisted into his service the erstwhile chief British dragoman of Constantinople, Gerald Fitzmaurice. Grey, with Hall's knowledge and approval, sent Fitzmaurice on a delicate mission to Sofia, Bulgaria. Grey wrote to the British ambassador there: "When operations against the Dardanelles begin to be successful he may be able . . . to get into touch with the Turkish party at Constantinople who are anti-German and well-known to him."

Fitzmaurice and a couple of subordinates made contact with Turkish dissidents in Greece. Fitzmaurice offered £4 million if they would open the straits to the British navy. The Turks were willing but demanded guarantees, most particularly that no harm should come to Constantinople. They knew well the long-standing Russian desire for this warm-water port, and they would not risk their lives in a dangerous enterprise against Enver and his backers if it meant losing the chief city of the Ottoman Empire. Unfortunately, however, possession of Constantinople was a Russian war aim to which the British government had acceded. Fitzmaurice could not make the guarantee. Instead he warned that every day the Turks delayed, he would reduce the bribe by £100,000. It might have worked if not for Turkish success in battle. The Ottoman forces withstood everything the British and French navies could throw at them and inflicted terrible damage in return. Whatever dismay Turkish negotiators may have experienced as the value of their bribe diminished was balanced, therefore, by increasing confidence in the ability of their countrymen to resist the enemy. Conversely British assurance began to wane. By March 18, with the Turkish forts still holding out and passage along the straits too dangerous to yet attempt, the British cabinet instructed Hall "to spare no expense to win over the Turks." It was too late. Now Britain would commit the army as well as the navy to what soon became another charnel house, the infamous, dreadful battle of Gallipoli. Fitzmaurice, having failed to bribe the Turks to get out of the war, returned to Sofia. There he would soon engage in an equally futile attempt to bribe the Bulgarians to get into it on the Allied side.

Even after these early efforts to end the war with Turkey by negotiation failed, Fitzmaurice kept his ear to the ground. "Those in touch with Young Turk circles state that the latter have been discussing advisability of a separate peace," he cabled to Grey from Sofia on May 7. Sure enough, three weeks later the idea resurfaced in Paris. It proved stillborn because the French could not promise to keep the Russians from Constantinople. It resurfaced in California in August 1915, when an Ottoman commissioner to the San Francisco Exhibition contacted a British official there. He came up against the same stumbling block: Britain could not protect Constantinople either. At the end of the year, Russia tried to bribe Djemal Pasha to end the war—but he would have to give up Constantinople. Arthur Balfour had it right when the Foreign Office informed the War Council of these various maneuvers. "No harm in trying," he scribbled on the F.O. minute, "but it is incredible that the Turks will agree."

In Britain anti-Turkish sentiment ran high during the war. This was nothing new: It had been running high at least since the 1870s, when Britons learned to despise the murderous Sultan Abdul Hamid II along with the corruption of his court, the dead hand of his bureaucracy, and the brutality of his minions, in short everything that the great nineteenth-century Liberal, William Gladstone, summed up in his memorable epithet "the unspeakable Turk." Conservatives did not dispute this judgment, only the foreign policy that flowed from it. From the floor of the House of Commons, Gladstone's great Conservative antagonist, Benjamin Disraeli, said of the Ottomans, they "seldom resort to torture, but generally terminate their connection with culprits in a more expeditious manner." Where opposition to the Ottoman regime constituted a bedrock of Liberal foreign policy, therefore, willingness to overlook Ottoman faults constituted the Conservative. Disraeli held that Britain must practice realpolitik in the real world. She must defend the far-flung interests of the British Empire; she must keep the Russians out of the Mediterranean Sea and far away from the Suez Canal; and if that meant allying with the brutal regime on the Bosporus, so be it.

The advent of the CUP in 1908 changed little. Gladstone was gone, but the Liberal government kept the Young Turk government at arm's length;

it joined the Triple Entente with France and Russia, Turkey's traditional enemy. Disraeli was long gone too, but many Conservatives still preferred a Turkish alliance to one with Russia. Nevertheless they, as much as the Liberals, generally viewed Young Turks as atheists and radicals who aped the West without truly understanding it, and who continued all the while to indulge the inbred Oriental vices: intrigue, treachery, and violence.

British anti-Ottoman sentiment had a religious component. Many Ottoman subjects practiced the Muslim religion, over which the Ottoman sultan presided as caliph. Ironically, Britain too ruled over a Muslim empire whose main outposts were in South Asia, Egypt, and Sudan. The British Muslim empire numbered nearly a hundred million people and was second in size only to the Ottoman Muslim empire. Inevitably British-governed Muslims flocked to the imperial center as students, business and professional men, and tourists. Muslim lascars (seamen) lived in British port cities when their ships docked. By 1914 Britain contained a small but distinct Muslim community.

That community did not receive a warm welcome. When William Quilliam, a prosperous solicitor from the Isle of Man, converted to Islam and established what appears to have been Britain's first mosque, in Liverpool in 1891, the response was harsh. A crowd greeted the muezzin's call to Friday services "with 'discordant yells and loud execrations,' pelted him with mud, stones and filth; and also pelted worshippers leaving the mosque." In 1895 "furious Christians threatened to burn Sheikh Quilliam alive." Ten years later things had not much improved, even in cosmopolitan London. "Opposition was very keen in those days and many obstacles were placed in our path," recalled one who claimed to have been the sole British-born worshipper then taking part in London's Muslim services. During the next decade passions abated, but general ill will did not. When the war was about four months old, that first Anglo-Muslim, who now called himself Sheikh Khalid Sheldrake, wrote to the king: "Your Majesty, May I venture most humbly to bring to your notice the existence of a grave danger at the present crisis? The Press have issued Cartoons and articles in which the Muslim creed, and the Sultan (its Caliph) have been held up to ridicule."

Old habits of thought died hard among the population as a whole, but in December 1914 the last thing the British government wanted was to alienate Muslims. When Turkey entered the war, the sultan/caliph immediately declared jihad against his Christian enemies. Various imams endorsed and repeated his call. The question for Britain was how her hundred million Muslim subjects would react. Starting the Arab hare, setting up the grand sharif as an opposite pole to the Ottoman sultan, suggesting that he might become caliph himself—all this was part of Britain's strategy for vitiating the sultan's holy war and retaining the loyalty of her own Muslim subjects.

The strategy was not completely successful. Muslim agitators, some of them financed by the Ottoman and German governments, made difficulties in South Asia and throughout the Middle East. Their message reached as far as Europe, even Britain. On October 26, 1915, somebody walked into the East Central London post office and dropped a letter into the box. It was a warning to Prime Minister Asquith, the third he had received so far, against making war on "our brothers and the Caliph of Mohammedans . . . The responsibility falls on you alone and the chastisement for deceiving the nation will be your deprivation from life, and in the world to come you will undergo the worst of torture . . . Beware, beware."

During the war British Intelligence kept a weather eye on British Muslims great and small, whether politically moderate, liberal, or radical, and on those who sympathized with them and on the places where they gathered, not merely in South Asia and Egypt but in England too. It kept tabs, for example, on the chief Muslim cleric in Britain, Khwaja Kamal-ud-Din, who appears from his writings to have been a gentle, tolerant soul; also on some of the more radical members of an Islamic Society, including its general secretary, the barrister, poet, author, and pan-Islamist Mushir Hussein Kidwai; and the pan-Africanist, anti-imperialist Dusé Mohamed Ali. It even opened the mail of a troublesome Liberal MP, Joseph King, who although only tangentially concerned with British Muslims publicly attacked the government for permitting the Secret Service to employ agents provocateurs against these and other groups.

Men such as Dusé Mohamed Ali, Mushir Hussein Kidwai, and Khwaja Kamal-ud-Din figure in our story because their aims and aspirations are relevant to the movement for a separate peace with Turkey.

Dusé Mohamed Ali was an Egyptian-born, English-educated son of a Sudanese woman and an Egyptian army officer who had died in the failed nationalist uprising of 1881–82. An erstwhile actor who toured the United States and Canada as well as Britain, Mohamed turned to journalism in 1909 at the age of forty-five. In 1911 he published to critical acclaim *In the Land of the Pharos,* which was said to be the first short history of Egypt written in English by an Egyptian. A year later he founded the *African Times and Orient Review.* This sporadically published journal provided a forum for opponents of British imperialism. It opened its pages not merely to critics who wished to soften what they deemed to be a well-intentioned if occasionally unjust and harsh movement, but also to those like Kidwai who wished to tear up the imperialist movement root and branch. Dusé Mohamed Ali also founded a League of Justice "to defend the rights of native peoples." In a secret summation of his character, an agent of the India Office deemed him to be quite "capable of political mischief."

The barrister Mushir Hussein Kidwai came from a well-connected and politically active South Asian family, against which he rebelled. The India Office thought little of him. "He is so peculiar that occasionally he is spoken of as not quite right in his head. I think he is quite sane, but not sensible," judged one of its agents. When Kidwai arrived in England shortly before the war he joined the League of Justice. He often contributed to the *African Times and Orient Review*: "long letters, almost always taking an extreme view of the matter, whatever it is." The agent deemed Kidwai honest but extreme: "I don't think he would touch swindling in any form. But he is certainly a pro-Turk, and a friend of the advanced political party."

As for Khwaja Kamal-ud-Din, he was a South Asian who had abandoned his legal practice to become a Muslim missionary and to lead the sole mosque in England, at Woking, some thirty miles south of London. By 1914 this institution had become the center of Muslim activity in Britain. With its domes and minarets, set in the grounds of what once had been the Royal Dramatic College, it was (and remains to this day) an impressive albeit incongruous structure. Khwaja Kamal-ud-Din conducted services there; he started a monthly journal, the *Islamic Review;* and he helped to strengthen the London-based Islamic Society that Kidwai served as an officer and that boasted some three hundred members, many of whom made at least a weekly trek to the Woking mosque. Wherever he went and whenever he wrote, Khwaja Kamal-ud-Din emphasized the tolerant, progressive aspects of his religious creed. He and his followers stressed that Islam made no racial distinctions. As one of the followers wrote, when Muslims gathered annually in the early days of the last lunar month to worship in Mecca, "you would see a black presiding over a meeting of white people. Men in Islam were estimated by their moral greatness, and neither color, [nor] rank, nor wealth was any criterion for preference."

When Khwaja Kamal-ud-Din and Mushir Hussein Kidwai spoke at a meeting organized by the Islamic Society in June 1917, the British government took note. The purpose of the meeting was to protest the possibility of Palestine becoming a Jewish state under Britain's protection. Kidwai argued in his opening address that Palestine was "holier to the Muslims than . . . to the Jews or the Christians . . . So if the Zionistic ambitions of our Jewish brothers must be realized; if they have suffered for the last two thousand years . . . suffered, mind, never at the hands of Muslims but always by the hands of Christians . . . then those ambitions can only be realized by the cooperation and under the suzerainty of Muslims." And Khwaja Kamal-ud-Din said in part: "The great Temple of Solomon at present is below the surface of the ground with a large and splendid mosque over it . . . Does not restoration of the Temple of Solomon mean demolishing the mosque and its appurtenances?" Such statements seem mild enough, but on the cover of the Foreign Office file in which the report of this meeting rests, one of the mandarins scrawled, "Christianophobe C.U.P.-ophils."

An ill wind of anti-Ottoman and anti-Muslim sentiment swept through Britain before and during the war, even among members of the government, who worried that British Muslim subjects might join in a holy war against their rulers. But the anxiety did not touch everyone. Those who resisted tended to be people who actually knew something about the Ottoman Empire and its inhabitants: journalists and academics, for example, but also people who had traveled there, or who had worked there either on business or for Britain. Among the latter category, Mark Sykes, Aubrey Herbert, and George Lloyd had overlapped in Constantinople in 1905 as honorary attachés. Of the three, Sykes reacted most publicly to the experience, extolling traditional Ottoman mores and practices, including religious ones, in books, articles, and speeches, presenting them always with flair and élan. He hated the Young Turks, however, whom he accused of diluting the admirable ancient Ottoman conventions with a half-baked and half-understood Western ideology based upon the principles of the French Revolution. Less voluble but equally impressed by what they had seen of the pre-CUP Ottoman Empire, George Lloyd and Aubrey Herbert advocated a renewed Anglo-Ottoman alliance. Unlike Sykes, they continued advocating it even after the Young Turks came to power.

Herbert went further. He took seriously the Young Turk promises of constitutional government, equality before the law of all Ottoman subjects including women, cultural rights of small nationalities within the Ottoman Empire, and so on. He favored an Anglo-Ottoman alliance not merely because he thought it made strategic sense for Britain but also because he thought the Ottoman government worthy of British support, worthier than brutal, reactionary tsarist Russia. Herbert got to know the leading Young Turks, Enver Pasha and, most particularly, Talaat Pasha. What was more, he liked them.

In late December 1913 Herbert, now Conservative MP for South Somerset, received an invitation to join "an Ottoman Association" whose aim would be to foster Anglo-Ottoman understanding. Among the names listed as endorsing this fledgling body was that of his friend George Lloyd, who had also become a Conservative MP, for West Staffordshire. (Sykes too had entered Parliament by this time, as Conservative MP for Kingston-upon-Hull, but as strongly opposed as he was to the CUP, he refused to endorse or join the society.) Unlike Sykes, Herbert did join it. But do not think the Anglo-Ottoman Society was dominated by Conservative politicians. Liberal, Labour, and Irish Nationalist MPs lent their names to it too, as did several members of the House of Lords, one of whom, Lord Lamington, became its president. Then there were the men of business, journalism, and academia. The name of at least one Jew, Jaakoff Prelooker, a Russian refugee and liberal rabbi, figures on the society's early masthead. Startlingly, on the eve of war the names of Moses Gaster and Lucien Wolf are listed as members of the society's executive committee. And at the body's meetings we find Dusé Mohamed Ali, Mushir Hussein Kidwai, and Khwaja Kamal-ud-Din speaking in favor of various motions.

The Anglo-Ottoman Society takes its place in prewar England as a well-intentioned, not particularly effective, but nevertheless active political lobbying group, most notable perhaps for its highly eclectic membership. Unanimity among members was impossible. Conservatives like George Lloyd believed Britain should ally with the Ottomans for strategic reasons; Muslims like Dusé Mohamed Ali and Mushir Hussein Kidwai believed Britain should support a regime that the other powers, great and small, were pecking to death. They saw the Young Turk government both as the victim of imperialism and as the protector of dark-skinned people throughout the world. Some British Muslims, like Khwaja Kamal-ud-Din, wanted an Anglo-Ottoman alliance in part because both empires contained millions of Muslims.

Then came the war. Most British Turcophiles and British Muslims believed that Britain had to enter it. Most members of the Anglo-Ottoman Society agreed. Khwaja Kamal-ud-Din, who thought Germany was the aggressor, endorsed Britain's decision to fight: "Islam teaches that the use of arms in self-defense is perfectly legitimate." Anti-imperialists like Dusé Mohamed Ali held back, although the possibility of German victory appalled even him. "Are the Germans to extend their rule over vast numbers of Black and Brown men?" he asked. "We who know something of what German rule means and of their treatment of Africans in Togoland, Kamerun and their other African Colonies, say fervently, God forbid!" One thing, however, every British Turcophile and every British Muslim agreed upon: War between Britain and Turkey would be disastrous. Britain must do everything in her power to woo the Ottomans, to keep them from the German embrace. Then Enver Pasha engineered his casus belli, and Turkey joined the war. Now British Turcophiles and Muslims reached another shared conclusion: that Britain and the Ottoman Empire must negotiate a separate peace.

It took time for the British Turcophile and Muslim communities to develop spokesmen who could credibly articulate this demand, but once they did so, the British government could not ignore them. In fact, on occasion the easterners made use of them. This uneasy relationship lasted from early 1916 until the end of the war.

One British Turcophile who desperately wanted a separate peace was the deliciously named Marmaduke Pickthall. He was a successful novelist who often wrote about the mysterious, romantic Middle East, with which he had fallen in love as a young man while traveling there, "living native," as he later put it. A second extended visit in 1907 at age thirty-three confirmed his early impressions, and a third trip in 1913 taught him to greatly admire Young Turk politicians as well. He spoke often at prewar and wartime Anglo-Ottoman Society meetings. Dusé Mohamed Ali may have been the instigator of the society, and Lord Lamington may have been its titular president, but Pickthall became its motor. He "did everything for it, except bathe the members," writes his biographer.

Pickthall belonged not only to the British Turcophile community but to the British Muslim community too. Although he was the son of an Anglican minister and the stepbrother of two Anglican nuns, he was drawn to Khwaja Kamal-ud-Din and spent much time at the mosque in Woking. He would convert to Islam in 1917. Many years later he would write the first literal translation of the Quran into English. It is worth pointing out that Pickthall and Aubrey Herbert had formed a friendship. The Conservative MP introduced the novelist to important Young Turks who came to England and wrote introductions for Pickthall when he traveled to Turkey in 1913. Upon his return to England, Pickthall made a point of attending the House of Commons when Herbert spoke on Turkish questions.

With the commencement of the war, Pickthall wrote a steady stream of well-informed articles and letters to the press extolling Young Turk virtues and criticizing Britain's Near Eastern and Middle Eastern policies. He feared, rightly, that Turkey would be drawn into the conflict on the side of Germany. In September 1914, before Enver Pasha maneuvered his country into the war, Pickthall attended an exclusive gathering at the home of Professor R. W. Seton-Watson, an expert on the Habsburg Empire and the Near East. He read a paper to "a group of men who were certainly not ill-informed on the subject of Foreign Affairs." The subsequent discussion left him aghast. No one who spoke thought the Ottoman Empire would be allowed to survive the war. Pickthall wrote incredulously: "The question was how much of Turkey should be left to Turks at the peace settlement!" He determined to find out what the British policy really was (no doubt by questioning his well-connected friends in the Anglo-Ottoman Society) and by February 18, 1915, was in a position practically to predict the Tripartite Agreement. This was about a year before the diplomats inked in its final clauses.

> Our unknown rulers seem so far as I can learn to contemplate a full partition of the Turkish Empire ... Russia will have Eastern Anatolia, Northern Mesopotamia and almost certainly Constantinople ... England will have southern Mesopotamia and probably all the territory southward roughly of a line drawn on the map from a point a little to the north of Samara on the Tigris to a point a little south of Jaffa on the Coast of Palestine. The whole peninsula of Arabia will be included in her "sphere of influence" for gradual absorption. France will have much of Syria.

Long before Mark Sykes began rethinking the arrangements he had arrived at with Picot, Marmaduke Pickthall knew what to make of this plan: "It is essentially a mess and not a settlement, bound to produce another great war."

Some nine months earlier Pickthall had become friendly with another pro-Ottoman, Dr. Felix Valyi, the Hungarian-born editor of a French journal of opinion, *La Revue politique internationale*. When the war began, Valyi moved to Lausanne, continuing to publish his *Revue* and connecting with the Turkish minister there, Fuad Selim al-Hijari. The latter disapproved of Enver Pasha's pro-German policy and maintained contact with like-minded Turks. In the spring of 1916 this group made what appears to have been a concerted effort for a separate peace. Almost simultaneously Prince Sabaheddin, founder of the Turkish Liberal Union Party, sounded the British ambassador in Paris about peace talks; one of his followers approached Sir Henry McMahon in Cairo; and Fuad made discreet inquiries with the Italian ambassador in Switzerland.

By now the British government, which did not believe the Ottoman government was ready to make peace under any circumstances, was telling such men first to depose Turkey's present rulers and then to bring up the matter with Russia, because the issue of Constantinople would have to be dealt with before any separate peace could be arranged, and Russia had specific plans for that city. Even so, the separate peace idea remained alive in the minds of certain liberal Turks and their fellow travelers, including Dr. Valyi.

Valyi once said of himself, "I am more a philosopher than a politician, and my program is to remove politics from the exclusive influence of the personally ambitious and to introduce into its domain those unselfish intellectuals who, up to the present, balk at the idea of associating themselves with politics." "Philosopher" may not have been an accurate self-description, but "unselfish intellectual" was a fair rendering of Marmaduke Pickthall. When Valyi suggested to Fuad Selim al-Hijari that Pickthall was an obvious choice to serve as intermediary between British officials and nonconformist Turks interested in a separate peace, the latter agreed.

Valyi wrote to his English friend from Berne:

> Try to come here as soon as possible. You could be very useful for your country . . . You inspire absolute confidence in the Islamic world and you're the only man able to render services to your country in the question of the East. You may show my letter to whom it is appropriate.

Pickthall, a political innocent, jumped at the opportunity. Unfortunately he could not consult with his more experienced friend Aubrey Herbert, who was now away in the army. He made his initial formal approach to Lord Newton, an assistant under secretary of state for foreign affairs, who warned him that Britain would not undertake anything "directed against the solidarity of the Entente." What was this except a repetition of the recognition that Russia would veto any peace plan threatening its acquisition of Constantinople? It meant, really, that Pickthall's assay in diplomacy was doomed from the start, yet the aspiring peacemaker wrote to Valyi that he was optimistic.

The mail was slow. On pins and needles, Pickthall wrote to Valyi again: "I am awaiting with some anxiety your answer to my letter." He repeated the Foreign Office prescription about the solidarity of the Entente. If the Turks accepted that, then "I have been informed that I would be allowed to go to Switzerland to talk over the matter to which you refer." This was like saying that he would be allowed to go when the Turks proved that the moon was made of cheese.

In Switzerland more experienced heads were mulling the thing over. Valyi might claim to be a better philosopher than he was a politician, but

Fuad Selim al-Hijari knew about politics. He probably understood that the "solidarity of the Entente" could not stand an Anglo-Ottoman peace agreement that left Constantinople in Turkish hands. Could he entice the Foreign Office to let Pickthall come to Switzerland anyway? Who knew what might develop if only discussions could begin? Valyi, undoubtedly coached by Fuad, wrote to his friend: "I cannot say more than this by letter, but there is no risk in granting you a passport. If the results of your voyage are nil you merely return to England. If, however, things are as I think you will find them [then] I am sure that you will be strongly requested to go on with the work."

Before this message arrived, the fretful Pickthall had sought out Mark Sykes, whom perhaps he had met through Aubrey Herbert. Perhaps he thought he was playing a trump card. He did not realize that Sykes's hatred of the Young Turk regime overshadowed his rosy prewar view of the Ottoman Empire—that, in fact, Sykes was one of the men planning its complete dismemberment. Sykes had just returned from Russia, where he had polished details of the Tripartite Agreement with Picot and Russian foreign minister Sergei Sazanov, skinning the Ottoman bear before it was a carcass. The busy, high-powered, roving British agent had little time for novelists and editors spinning dreams of a separate peace. He wrote to Pickthall on May 25, 1916, denying him permission to travel abroad. The invitation from Valyi did not warrant it: "The writer is apparently an Hungarian with no authority to speak on behalf of the Ottoman Government."

Pickthall now appealed to the Reverend H. G. Rosedale, who had introduced him to Dr. Valyi in the first place. Rosedale knew another assistant under secretary at the Foreign Office, Sir Maurice de Bunsen—chairman of the committee that had envisaged carving up and parceling out Ottoman territories the previous year! Rosedale wrote to de Bunsen: "The man whom the Turks like & trust & [who] especially finds an admirer in M. Valyi, is a man I know well, Mr. Pickthall, the writer of many books & an expert on Oriental questions . . . In my opinion there would be no danger in intrusting Mr. Pickthall with a mission to see what really lies behind this 'olive branch.' " But it was not Rosedale's opinion of Pickthall that mattered, it was the Foreign Office's opinion. As to that: "Mr. Pickthall is most undesirable, and should in no way be encouraged. In fact he ought to be interned as an alien enemy!" wrote one mandarin when de Bunsen circulated Rosedale's letter. And another, repeating the now-common British refrain, added: "If Turkey wishes to make peace, then the present Government must be ejected & overtures must be made, not to us, but to Russia." Eventually de Bunsen wrote to Rosedale and in similar vein to Pickthall: "I am directed by Sir Edward Grey to state that, in present circumstances, he regrets his inability to avail himself of Mr. Pickthall's offer."

Still the novelist could not quite let the matter lapse. He wrote again to Valyi, giving vent to his frustration, praising the Ottomans, criticizing the Foreign Office. Unwisely he sent a copy of the letter to Sykes. The latter replied cuttingly, "I do not consider that it is proper that you should assume absolute friendship to an enemy State in writing to the subject of another enemy State, and further speak in a distinctly hostile tone of your own government." This appears finally to have burst Pickthall's bubble. He had written six months before, "I am a nobody and can do nothing to avert the great disaster I have long seen coming." It was true. The Turcophile community would eventually produce an envoy whom the British government took seriously, but Marmaduke Pickthall was not that man.

That the Ottoman Empire would or could have negotiated a separate peace with the Allies during 1915–16 seems unlikely, although serious men wished for it. Meanwhile British Zionists remained ignorant of the Turcophiles' efforts. Had they known of them, they would have been angered and frightened, for a separate peace with Turkey might have left Palestine languishing (as they would have termed it) inside the Ottoman Empire. In those years British Zionists lacked the strength to effectively oppose such an outcome.

A year later they had gained strength—and knowledge. Now they knew what the British Turcophiles and Muslims and a few easterners and dissident Turks wished for. But meanwhile the advocates of a separate peace had grown stronger too. How could it have been otherwise, when the war continued to grind up lives and principles and the will to fight on? The pieces from both sides of the historical chessboard moved purposefully forward; already a pawn, Marmaduke Pickthall, had been sacrificed; now more powerful tokens slid into position. The fate of millions depended on where they would land.

CHAPTER 18

The Curious Venture of J. R. Pilling

ONE SQUARE ON THE CHESSBOARD where advocates of the separate peace landed with growing frequency was located in Switzerland. That country enjoyed "the distinction of being a sort of happy hunting ground for all the political malcontents and intriguers of Europe," wrote Ronald Campbell of the Foreign Office, rather enviously, to his friend Horace Rumbold, who had just replaced Grant Duff as Britain's envoy extraordinary and minister plenipotentiary to the Swiss Republic. Rumbold agreed. "This is the most interesting post in the service at the present moment," he reported gleefully. "I sit in my room like a spider and attract every day news and information which would keep a diplomatist in prewar days going for months." To Ronald Graham at the Foreign Office, he wrote: "This country is crammed full of spies and rascals of every description and it is incredible that such a small country should be able to hold so many of these gentry." Increasingly the gentry with whom he had to deal were dissident Turks and British agents engaging in the pourparlers that could precede the negotiation of a separate peace between their two nations.

The son of a diplomat (also named Sir Horace) and the husband of a diplomat's daughter (Ethelred Constantia Veitch Fane), Rumbold had gone into the family business. When he took the competitive entrance exam for the diplomatic corps in February 1891, he earned the top score. A series of international postings followed. With the commencement of hostilites, he returned to London, where for two years he oversaw affairs having to do with prisoners of war. Then came the assignment in Berne. In old photographs he looks like an English diplomat of the ancien régime, with receding brown-blond hair and mustache, an impeccable three-piece suit and tie, a half-open mouth, and heavy-lidded, sleepy eyes. "He had trained himself," wrote one who served under him in later years, "to appear more English than any Englishman had ever seemed before."

He was a shrewd observer, an able organizer, and a capable representative of his country, but in some respects Rumbold not only looked like a caricature of an old Etonian but thought like one too. He commiserated with his mother about the lower orders back home: "Our . . . servants did not for a moment admit that the War should make any difference to their diet and they always claimed large joints and the best butter." He wrote about foreigners with equal disdain. Of the Italians, he once observed, "What can you expect from a nation the majority of which would be better employed selling ice-cream?" Of Britain's eastern ally: "I always had doubts about the Russians." Of Britain's eastern enemy: "Talk about the clean-fighting Turk is moonshine. He is a brute and that is the end of it." Of the German minister at The Hague, he recalled: "He is as clever as they make them . . . a Jew-dog."

But he ran a network of informants capably enough, including impecunious Turkish refugees and disaffected Ottoman officials whom he had bribed. Such figures supplied him with a steady stream of more or less trustworthy information about conditions and attitudes in Turkey. He relied far more, however, upon a volunteer agent, Dr. Humbert Denis Parodi, a strikingly handsome, dark-skinned Swiss citizen of French and Italian descent, who had worked before the war for the Egyptian government as inspector general of public instruction in Cairo and who now served as overseer of the Egyptian student community in Switzerland. With the outbreak of war, Parodi offered his services to the British envoy at the time, Grant Duff. "My sole aim," he later wrote, "has been to aid as best I can the triumph of right and justice over brutal force." Equally at home in the café society of Egyptian students, some of whom nourished anti-imperialist and even anti-British sentiments, and in the Ottoman expatriate community, he proved an inspired agent and not only about Turkish matters. To give one example, in April 1916 Parodi learned that Swiss socialists were negotiating with German authorities to arrange passage through Germany of Russian revolutionaries who wished to return home. In this manner the British Foreign Office learned that Lenin was headed for the

Finland Station in St. Petersburg possibly even before the tsar's ministers did.

When Rumbold arrived in Berne, he inherited this remarkable agent from Grant Duff. Parodi would prove indispensable to him in bringing together Britons and Turks who wished to discuss the separate peace. His services proved so valuable that Rumbold wished to reward him. Lord Hardinge at the Foreign Office agreed that Parodi deserved generous recompense. The agent seemed "to be really a good man, and much better than one could possibly conceive of a person of Syrian origins." Rumbold responded indignantly at once: "He is not of Syrian origin: In fact he has not a drop of Oriental blood in him . . . I admit that he looks like an Oriental and that if you put a tarboosh on his head you would think that he was an Egyptian or a Turk. But there is nothing Oriental about him save his appearance, although he knows Orientals down to the ground." Parodi got the money.

In the following instance of British and Turkish maneuverings in Switzerland, however, Dr. Parodi appears to have played no role.

One day during the summer of 1916 "a very old friend" of Lloyd George, a Mrs. Evans, asked an English businessman of her acquaintance, one J. R. Pilling, if he "could get Turkey out of the War." Of Mrs. Evans, the historian can learn little except that she was "practically a member of the Lloyd George household." Of Mr. Pilling, we may glean a bit more. At age sixty-seven, he was a Manchester solicitor, banker, and undischarged bankrupt, who during the 1890s had attempted, unsuccessfully, to build railroads in the Middle East, where he had formed the Syria-Ottoman Railway Company. He lived for a time in Constantinople at the Pera Palace Hotel with a German lady, Therese de Koelle, whom the British Foreign Office suspected of being a German agent. His business dealings brought him into contact with important Ottoman officials, including some among the Young Turk leadership. He may have been a member of the Anglo-Ottoman Society. At any rate he knew members; his employee Sir Douglas Pitt Fox, chief engineer of the Syria-Ottoman Railway Company, belonged to it. When the Foreign Office belatedly investigated Mr. Pilling some six months after Mrs. Evans first asked him about making peace with Turkey, it judged him to be "a 'sharper' and of very shady character."

Mrs. Evans believed that all land and water frontiers should be internationalized and guaranteed by the Allies and the United States; that way Russia could gain access to the Mediterranean Sea without having to capture Constantinople. That accomplished, Russia would have no reason to wage war against the Ottomans—and the Ottomans would have no reason to continue fighting Russia and her allies. "This plan appeared to me to constitute the perfect solution of the difficult Turkish question," wrote Pilling. He realized that he could call upon his "long intimate acquaintance with Turkish Ministers and Turkish affairs" in order to propose Mrs. Evans's plan to responsible parties in the Ottoman government. He may have thought that if he did so, and if his overture really did help launch discussions about a separate peace, these figures would help him to recoup some of his losses in the Syria-Ottoman Railway Company.

But first he must put the plan to responsible parties in London. Together he and Mrs. Evans polished the scheme. By October 1916 they felt sufficiently confident to take advantage of Mrs. Evans's connection with the then–minister of war, David Lloyd George. When he met Mr. Pilling, Lloyd George "formed rather a low opinion of him," according to Ronald Campbell of the Foreign Office. But the businessman must have struck a chord. "The day following" the interview, as Pilling remembered, "I was called to the War Office to give a full explanation of the reasons and mode of operation for securing this detachment of Turkey." Here too, according to Campbell, Pilling made no very positive impression. Nevertheless he received the passport to travel abroad that had been denied to Marmaduke Pickthall only a few months earlier. On February 6, 1917, "I left London en route to Constantinople," Pilling recalled, "with instructions to take such measures as I deemed desirable in order to lead the Turkish Government to apply to England for a separate treaty of peace."

One may wonder why the failed businessman gained a passport to travel abroad when the transparently well-intentioned Pickthall did not. The answer must be that the latter never had an audience with Lloyd George. Sir Mark Sykes and others in the Foreign Office cut him off. But Lloyd George, the easterner, could not get the possibility of a separate peace with Turkey out of his head. That such a peace might jeopardize the possibility of a British protectorate in Palestine, which he was simultaneously encouraging Zionists to anticipate, apparently did not matter to him. Certainly it did not matter to him that Pilling might be a seedy character. In pursuit of a separate peace, Lloyd George would employ agents far seedier than Mr. Pilling.

Actually on February 6, Pilling embarked not for Constantinople but for Switzerland. Once arrived, he met Sir Horace Rumbold, who judged him "rather a muddle-headed person and I do not think he should be playing about . . . interviewing Turks." But Pilling could refer, and often did, to the mission entrusted to him by the government. "I . . . told Mr. Pilling," Rumbold complained, "that I knew nothing whatever about him and that I had never received any message from the Foreign Office about his so-called mission." The Foreign Office sympathized: "Altogether it would seem that Mr. Pilling might be summed up as something of a lunatic." Only now was it scrambling to figure out who he was and what he was doing.

As to that, Pilling was holding meetings with the former khedive of Egypt, presently resident in Switzerland; with Rifaat Bey, former president of the Ottoman senate; with the ubiquitous Fuad Selim al-Hijari; and with many others. He wrote two letters to Talaat Pasha, which apparently were conveyed to Constantinople in the Ottoman diplomatic pouch. Later Eric Drummond, private secretary to Prime Minister Asquith and then to Foreign Ministers Grey and Balfour, worried that Pilling had "made proposals to the Turkish Government and . . . took the Prime Minister's name in vain," but that was not how Pilling described his activities. To the contrary, he reported that he made clear to the Turks that he had "no official status but . . . they need have no hesitation in approaching His Majesty's Government with any reasonable proposal for peace"; also that "it is they who must make the first move."

By now Rumbold and the Foreign Office realized that Pilling really did have some connection with Military Intelligence and with Lloyd George; nevertheless they wanted to be rid of him. "These free lances are rather a nuisance," Rumbold fretted. Lord Hardinge instructed him to tell the meddlesome businessman that "after careful reflexion the authorities at home . . . consider it undesirable that he should remain any longer in Switzerland." Rumbold would have looked down his nose at the undischarged bankrupt in his best old Etonian manner. Pilling would have protested, wanting to wait in Berne for a reply from Talaat to his letters. Rumbold would have shown a bit of the iron that underlay his pompous manner. Pilling returned to London. He reported, however, not to Hardinge at the Foreign Office but to the War Office, where the director of Military Intelligence, Sir George MacDonagh, and others "thought him fairly reasonable and were not at all sure there was not something in what he said." Pilling volunteered to go to Turkey to interview Djemal Pasha, if the British could smuggle him into the country. That was a nonstarter, but "I am afraid you have not seen the last of Pilling," Campbell warned Rumbold: The War Office had given permission for him to return to Switzerland to pick up the letter from Talaat that he assured them would be waiting for him there.

By May 11 Pilling was back in Berne, and the next day saw him closeted once again with Fuad Selim al-Hijari at the Turkish legation. Immediately afterward he wrote a letter to the prime minister, put it in an envelope addressed to Mrs. Evans, and put that one in a larger envelope addressed to a common acquaintance, one Mr. Sutherland. By this roundabout route the letter did eventually reach Lloyd George. It can be read today at the House of Lords Record Office, among the Lloyd George papers, and at the National Archive, which has the original.

Pilling reported that no letter from Talaat Pasha had yet arrived for him, but that Fuad Selim al-Hijari "told me he had a message for me from [him]." According to Pilling, Talaat had instructed Fuad to say that Turkey would cede to Britain both Mesopotamia and Egypt, "so securing British interests in the Persian Gulf, Egypt and Cypress." She desired creation of an independent Armenian buffer state between herself and Russia. She would allow free passage through the straits to all nations, including Russia. Significantly, "the Minister in no wise made reference to Syria, Palestine or Arabia, save as to Mesopotamia. Nor did I, as I was a listener only." From this we may deduce that if Fuad and perhaps Talaat Pasha and other Young Turks were really hoping to communicate with England through Fuad and Pilling, they were signaling that they expected to retain some Middle Eastern foothold after the war.

Then Fuad Selim al-Hijari broached subjects far beyond Pilling's remit. "We went to war on account of the Russian danger," he explained. "So did Austria." But, referring to the revolution that had taken place recently in Russia, the ascension of Kerensky, and the new policy of "no annexations": "This danger for both of us is passed. Neither ourselves nor Austria has any reason for going on with the war." Therefore Austria would give up its claim to Serbia in return for an early peace. As Vienna held that the assassination of Archduke Ferdinand by the Serb nationalist Gavrilo Princip had provoked the war in the first place, this was rather a large concession to make. But note that it was a Turk, not an Austrian, who made it.

Apparently, additional concessions were in order on the part of the Central Powers. Fuad claimed that to gain peace with England, Germany would give up the Baghdad Railway and even her fleet. Pilling, according to his report, pointed out that he was "the friend of Turkey, and would not do anything save for Turkey." The minister replied: "If England wishes to be friends with Turkey again she will not object to Turkey being the intermediary for settlement of this terrible war on England's own terms." It having been put this way, Pilling reported breathlessly: "I cannot bear the responsibility of not communicating the whole of this statement to you for the immediate information of the Prime Minister."

What are we to make of this fantastic message—that Talaat Pasha thought he could become the man who ended World War I? More probably, Fuad was interpreting vague intimations reaching him from interested parties in Constantinople to suit his own desire for an all-embracing peace; perhaps he was even inventing them whole cloth, or Pilling was. What is certain is that at this stage of the war Britain had no desire to engage in negotiations with Germany or Austria. When he assumed the premiership, Lloyd George stated categorically that Britain would continue the war until she had delivered a "knock-out blow" to Germany.

Pilling reported to London what, perhaps, Fuad had told him. Then he cooled his heels in Berne, waiting for the letter from Talaat Pasha. Later he would claim to have received it on June 9; he referred in later correspondence to messages to the War Office that he himself wrote that day and the day after, which does suggest that he may have received and been reporting on something. He refers as well to "my other many reports to our Prime Minister." These reports too may have mentioned, or quoted, Talaat's letter, if there was one, but unfortunately no reports have been found. What we do know is that on June 16, when Rumbold called Pilling into his office to tell him he must return permanently to London, Pilling cited no letter from Talaat. Pilling was "very crestfallen," Rumbold reported.

Why would he have been crestfallen if he had received the letter from Talaat a week before? That would have meant that he had successfully completed his mission and that he no longer had any reason to stay in Switzerland. In fact, he should have headed for home already. It seems a fair inference, therefore, that no such letter had arrived.

This inference is strengthened by Pilling's behavior back in London. On June 30, when MacDonagh of the War Office debriefed him, he did not produce the letter or apparently even mention it. On July 10 he wrote ambiguously to Fuad in Berne: "I hope to be in a position very soon to send to your Excellency the desired reply to the request of His Highness, the Grand Vizier [Talaat Pasha] as to the appointment of Peace Delegates." Talaat's request could have been contained in the letter of June 9, if it existed; or it could have been delivered verbally by Fuad at the May 12 meeting. Or Pilling could have made it up.

His failure to hand over the letter lowered his stock. The Foreign Office had already ignored him, but now the War Office turned a cold shoulder too. When Pilling requested that it repay his Swiss expenses, £830, it refused, on the grounds that his mission had emanated not from it but from 10 Downing Street. When he approached the prime minister, Lloyd George likewise declined to help him. Did Pilling fear not merely that he was considerably out-of-pocket but that his chance of recouping his greater financial losses in Turkey might likewise be slipping away? Perhaps so, for apparently he now asked the Americans to sponsor him on another trip to Switzerland. Or was he genuinely determined to help his country? Possibly the greater good and the personal good combined in his mind, for he wrote to Balfour, "The interests of our Empire, equally with the charge against me on the part of Turkey of broken pledges rendering me liable to corresponding consequences, permit of no further delay in the completion of this agreed treaty of peace."

What treaty of peace was that? Pilling maintained that one had been "agreed in June last," presumably in the letter from Talaat. Now (on November 7, 1917), in a rambling message to the foreign secretary, and still without having shown Talaat's letter to anyone, he enumerated the "treaty's" provisions. "1. The cession by Turkey to England of the sovereignty of Egypt, Syria, Mesopotamia, and Yemen." But on May 12, Pilling had written to Mrs. Evans that the Ottomans were willing to cede only Egypt and Mesopotamia. Nothing had happened between May 12 and "June last," when the letter from Talaat allegedly had arrived, to make the Ottomans more generous with their Middle Eastern possessions. Pilling seems to have been listing new Ottoman concessions in order to take into account changed circumstances. "I have arranged for Syria (which includes Palestine) to be entirely ceded to England, leaving England an absolutely free hand as to the establishment of [a] Jewish State," he wrote, two days before publication of the Balfour Declaration! So far as we can tell, he had never mentioned a Jewish state before. Certainly Talaat had not.

Most likely Pilling was simply spinning his own fantasies based on the terms outlined by Fuad Selim al-Hijari on May 12, terms that may or may not have originated with Talaat Pasha. "3," wrote Pilling to Balfour: "Turkish Arabia outside Mesopotamia, Syria and Yemen, to be ceded to the King of the Hejaz by Turkey, or otherwise, as may be directed by England." Nothing suggests that in June 1917 the Turks were willing to surrender the bulk of Arabia to King Hussein. But nearly six months later, with Hussein secure in Mecca and with Allenby's and Feisal's armies preparing to march north toward Damascus, they might have been willing to do so. Again, the only way to know for sure would be to refer to the letter supposedly written by Talaat, but "Pilling . . . has been unable to produce any letter or even a copy of any letter from Talaat," reported the disillusioned MacDonagh. Furthermore, he added, "I have not seen a copy of any 'Treaty' and do not believe in the existence of any such document."

On November 15 Pilling played what he may have considered his trump card; in fact it was a desperate gesture. He wrote to the king of England: "It is impossible for me to remain silent, and to bear alone the grave responsibility which will arise by the neglect or refusal on England's part, to receive and to meet this request of Turkey for peace." Buckingham Palace forwarded his letter to the Foreign Office, which by now had had more than enough of this troublesome figure. "If Mr. Pilling is, as the letter rather foreshadows, about to make 'sensational disclosures' or play at blackmail," warned one official, "the matter should I submit be considered by the Prime Minister."

The mandarins of the Foreign Office were not the only ones needing to rid themselves of this disreputable Quixote. The Armenians and the Zionists, who had probably never heard of Marmaduke Pickthall's attempt to bring Ottomans and Britons together, did hear about Pilling and moved purposefully to defeat him. Conceivably they learned about Pilling from Sir Mark Sykes, who had access to all the relevant Foreign Office files, opposed a separate peace with Turkey, cared not a fig for Foreign Office protocol except when it suited him, and so would not have hesitated to inform them of Pilling's activities.

Early on the evening of November 19, in what was surely a coordinated approach, first James Malcolm and then Chaim Weizmann called upon Ronald Graham at the Foreign Office. They knew about Lloyd George's unlikely emissary to the Turks and did not like what they knew. Graham recorded:

> A Mr. Pilling, known to them as a shady adventurer, was stating broadcast that he had been to Switzerland as agent for the Prime Minister [and] had negotiated a separate peace with Turkey. They knew Mr. Pilling to be a friend of a Mrs. Evans who was a friend of Mr. Lloyd George, and feared that he, Mr. Pilling, might in fact have some mission from the Prime Minister. They drew attention to Mr. Pilling's discreditable antecedents and said that his language and pretensions were causing serious concern not to say alarm in Armenian, Arab and Jewish circles.

This was two weeks after publication of the Balfour Declaration and after various government statements had been made supporting an independent Armenia. Weizmann and Malcolm both realized that a separate peace with the Ottomans might render the government's pledges null and void. So on the historical chessboard they made this move to remove Mr. J. R. Pilling, the pawn advanced by Lloyd George. He was slightly more impor-

tant than Marmaduke Pickthall, the pawn advanced by Fuad Selim al-
Hijari and Dr. Valyi, whom Sir Mark Sykes had removed a year before.
When Lord Hardinge read Graham's report, he suggested immediately
that Lloyd George "should, if possible, take steps to get Mr. Pilling to hold
his tongue." The prime minister evidently did so, for we do not hear from
the Manchester businessman again.

Hammering the last nail in the coffin of Mr. Pilling proved relatively
easy for Chaim Weizmann. But he was, by November 1917, quite accustomed to visiting the Foreign Office to argue against the advocates of a separate peace with Turkey. Only a few months previously in fact, he had
apparently taken the lead in stymieing a much more important initiative in
that direction. That exercise, a better-known episode in the history of Zionism, had required all his diplomatic skill.

CHAPTER 19

Henry Morgenthau and the Deceiving of Chaim Weizmann

AFTER APRIL 6, 1917, a state of war existed between the United States and Germany, but not between the United States and Turkey. Germany wanted her Ottoman ally to join the war against America but could get her only to sever diplomatic relations, and the Turks begrudged having to do even that. President Wilson took this as a good sign. It might mean that the Ottomans were developing second thoughts about their participation in the war altogether. If so, then perhaps his country could serve as a bridge between the Turks and the Entente powers. In other words, President Wilson too hoped to forge a separate peace.

From late 1913 until February 1916, Henry Morgenthau served as Wilson's ambassador to the Ottoman Empire. A member of the New York bar, Morgenthau had made a fortune speculating in real estate, which enabled him to make lavish contributions to the Democratic Party. During the 1912 presidential campaign, he served as chairman of the party's finance committee. The ambassadorship followed. Morgenthau is famous for having tried, while he was ambassador, to persuade his masters in Washington to intervene against the Armenian massacres of 1915, and when that failed, for bravely taking his protests to the Ottomans themselves, notably to Talaat Pasha. Himself a Jew, he played an honorable role during these early war years as a watch guard and protector of Ottoman Jews, especially the

Jews of Palestine, who benefited from a massive relief effort much facilitated by him. But he was impulsive and boastful. In May 1916, for example, in a speech delivered in Cincinnati, he claimed that before he left Constantinople, he had just about arranged for the Ottomans to sell Palestine to the Jews.

As his interest in the future of Palestine demonstrates, Morgenthau sympathized with Zionism. But he was not a Zionist strictly speaking. He said in that same Cincinnati speech: "It is utterly impossible to place several millions of people in Palestine. There would be grave danger from the Arabs . . . If Jews continue there as at present, at the end of the war there will be no friction." This declaration, as much as his grandiloquent statement about purchasing the Jewish Promised Land, caught Mark Sykes's attention. He immediately contacted Moses Gaster, the Zionist he knew best at that early date, and warned him, "Nothing could be more unfortunate or dangerous." Gaster agreed. By the spring of 1917, British Zionists knew something of Henry Morgenthau, and although they respected some of what he had done as ambassador, they did not approve of it all.

The origins of Morgenthau's mission to speak with Turks about a separate peace with the Allies are obscure, although historians of Zionism (including those who know little of Pickthall, Pilling, or other advocates of the policy) have gone over this particular episode with a fine-tooth comb. The idea may have been his, or it may have been the State Department's. At any rate, here is the scheme Morgenthau eventually put to the president: He would persuade Enver and Talaat, with whom he was on "peculiarly cordial and intimate terms," to allow Allied submarines to pass through the Dardanelles straits. The submarines would torpedo the *Goeben* and *Breslau,* the battleship and cruiser that Germany ostensibly had given to Turkey at the outset of the war but that remained under German command, their guns trained upon Constantinople. Once the two ships had been scuppered, the CUP government would be free to do what it really wanted, which was to conclude a separate peace. What Woodrow Wilson thought of this plan is not recorded. In the end, he gave Morgenthau authorization only to listen to and carry back to Washington whatever information or terms the Turks were prepared to offer. Whether Morgenthau understood or intended to abide by this limit is equally uncertain.

It happened that the British foreign secretary, Arthur Balfour, was visiting Washington, D.C., at this time. When Secretary of State Robert Lansing told him about the scheme, Balfour confirmed that the Turks were "nibbling" at the idea of a separate peace. "If matters took a favorable form," he added, "results might be of enormous advantage," which was true so far as the British were concerned, but would have seemed debatable to Zionists who wanted British support for a Jewish homeland in Palestine detached from the Ottoman Empire. Nevertheless, when Balfour wired news of Morgenthau's pending mission to the Foreign Office, no one so much as mentioned the possibility of Zionist objections, although they had been dealing with Zionists for many months. Sir Ronald Graham actually wrote of Morgenthau, "He might in any case work upon the Jewish elements in the C.U.P. and Turkey." Indeed, the Foreign Office suggested only one emendation to Morgenthau's scheme: "Owing to the number of spies in Switzerland it is doubtful if useful work can be done there. Possibly Egypt would be [a] better base of operations." This was the contribution of Robert Cecil.

It seemed a good suggestion to Morgenthau and Lansing, who accepted it. The former American ambassador could claim to be on his way to check the condition of Jews in nearby Palestine. Then Morgenthau had another idea: He would invite additional American Jews to accompany him, thus further camouflaging the expedition. First he invited the distinguished Harvard Law School professor and Zionist (and future Supreme Court justice) Felix Frankfurter, who was working as an assistant to the secretary of war, Newton Baker. Frankfurter accepted the invitation and invited his own assistant, another lawyer, Max Lowenthal. A third figure who joined the team was Eliahu Lewin-Epstein, treasurer of the Zionist Provisional Executive Committee in New York City. By now the mission gave every sign of being a Zionist enterprise, an impression the government fostered with leaks to the press. Zionists began a fund-raising campaign for the mission. About his main goal, however, Morgenthau kept Frankfurter, Lowenthal, and Lewin-Epstein in the dark.

The approach to Turkey could not take place, however, without the knowledge and agreement of America's wartime allies. Morgenthau would stop with his little band at Gibraltar; the State Department requested that both Britain and France send "someone in authority to discuss the question thoroughly" with him there. Then Morgenthau had another brainstorm. If the British sent Chaim Weizmann to meet him, that would lend further credence to his cover story. Apparently it did not occur to him that the British Zionist might oppose his main object. Nor, apparently, did this occur to the State Department. It accepted Morgenthau's suggestion and asked the Foreign Office to send Weizmann to meet their envoy.

Weizmann learned of Morgenthau's mission not from the Foreign Office but from Louis Brandeis, the American Zionist and Supreme Court justice with close ties to President Wilson. Brandeis had learned of it first from Frankfurter—not its true goal, obviously, for Frankfurter himself did not know it—and then from Wilson, who did explain the mission's real purpose. Brandeis immediately cabled to Weizmann that an American commission was headed to the east (he did not say what for), and he suggested that Weizmann intercept it. Given Brandeis's close connection with Wilson, this was as explicit a warning as he could deliver.

Brandeis was not Weizmann's only source of information. The Armenian James Malcolm's sensitive antennae were vibrating to "rumours here [London] in pro-Young-Turk circles about some manoeuvres for a separate peace with Turkey . . . initiated by Mr. Wilson . . . at the instigation of Mr. Morgenthau in tacit cooperation with the British and French Governments." The rumor was as explicit as Brandeis had been vague, and it troubled Mr. Malcolm. A separate peace with Turkey had the potential for undercutting Armenian nationalist aspirations as much as the Zionists'.

On Saturday, June 8, Malcolm attended an Islamic Society meeting at Caxton Hall on "Muslim Interests in Palestine." Its featured speaker was Marmaduke Pickthall; its chairman was Mushir Hussein Kidwai. Malcolm thought the proceedings were "of a definitely treasonable and seditious character." Pickthall "was openly talking about an early Peace with Turkey involving no loss of territory to the Turkish Empire." Others in the audience "were openly bragging that they were about to arrange a separate Peace with Turkey." From what he heard that day, Malcolm concluded not only that Henry Morgenthau was about to approach the Ottomans but also that Pickthall and two British Turcophiles, Aubrey Herbert and Sir Adam Samuel Block, a Jewish anti-Zionist, were engaged in a similar mission.

An agitated James Malcolm was soon knocking at the door of 67 Addison Road, Chaim Weizmann's house. The two men put together what they had gleaned from their various sources. Weizmann knew about the Islamic Society meeting already—he had heard that assimilationist Jews were its instigators. Then the telephone rang. Wickham Steed, an influential foreign correspondent of *The Times,* was on the line. His own antennae had picked up the same signals as Malcolm's, both about Morgenthau and about the Turcophiles. Steed opposed a separate peace with Turkey, albeit for different reasons than Zionists and Armenians. His newspaper argued for total victory over Britain's enemies. To settle for anything less was to play the German game. Historically *The Times* had not been friendly to Jews; nor had been Steed; but both were prepared to play the Zionist card anyway. Better for the British Empire to assume a protectorate over Palestine dominated by Jews, Steed thought, than for Palestine to remain as part of an Ottoman Empire beholden to the Germans.

Recall that in November 1917 Weizmann and Malcolm went to Ronald Graham at the Foreign Office to slam the relative flea, J. R. Pilling. By that time they were accustomed to employing that particular sledgehammer against advocates of separate peace with Turkey. The first time they employed it was five months earlier, right after the telephone call from Wickham Steed. On Sunday, June 9, Graham reported to Robert Cecil: "Dr. Weizmann, whom I happened to see this morning . . . referred in the course of conversation to Mr. Morgenthau whom he described as closely connected with . . . the anti-Zionist Jews in the U.S., and as being pro-German and especially pro-Turkish. He said 'I am expecting to see Mr. Morgenthau employed in some intrigue for a separate peace with Turkey and believe that he is coming to Europe for this purpose. If so the whole thing is a German move.' " Weizmann had taken up the line Steed pursued in his newspaper.

Just as Weizmann was warning Graham against Morgenthau, Malcolm was telephoning another mandarin, William Ormsby-Gore, parliamentary private secretary of Lord Milner and assistant secretary to the cabinet, where he seconded the efforts of Mark Sykes. No doubt Malcolm would have preferred to call Sykes himself, but the latter had not yet returned to London from the discussions with King Hussein in the Middle East. Ormsby-Gore had been converted to Zionism the previous year, during his stint at the Arab Bureau in Cairo, by none other than Aaron Aaronsohn. Weizmann and Malcolm calculated he would give them a sympathetic hearing. Malcolm asked for a meeting "as soon as possible," and Ormsby-Gore "arranged to see him at my office at 12.30."

Ormsby-Gore (later Lord Harlech) was a capable man who would go on to a distinguished career as a Conservative politician, including a stint as colonial secretary during the 1930s. Nevertheless the double team of Malcolm and Weizmann seem to have come close to overwhelming him. "Both Mr. Malcolm and Dr. Weizmann were very much excited and very angry," Ormsby-Gore reported, "and both stated that we were not only playing with fire in approaching the Turks at this juncture but also imperiling the interests of the British Empire and the causes which they have more especially at heart. Dr. Weizmann was open in his denunciation of Mr. Morgenthau." He was open in his denunciation of Aubrey Herbert and Sir Adam Samuel Block too, but he trained his biggest guns on the American, whom he practically accused of being a German agent. Morgenthau "was notoriously pro-German." He acted "on behalf of an international ring of Jewish financiers in Hamburg, Berlin, Vienna, Paris and New York." His aim was "an inconclusive Peace which would give German capital and

German Jews an ascendant importance throughout the Turkish Empire and particularly Palestine." Not knowing that the Americans wanted him present, he ended with a request that would have gladdened them: "If any Jew is to be sent to meet Mr. Morgenthau . . . he, Dr. Weizmann, [should] be sent."

On Tuesday, June 12, Weizmann and Malcolm called, separately this time, on Graham, to continue hammering. They mentioned Herbert and Block but reserved special venom for Morgenthau. Did their efforts have a dampening impact upon British attitudes toward the growing impetus for a separate peace? Without exception, historians agree that they did. Between them, the Zionist and the Armenian reminded British diplomats of their previous promises to free subject peoples from Ottoman tyranny. In fact they affected only the government's attitude toward Mr. Morgenthau's expedition. As will become apparent, Malcolm and Weizmann stymied one peace feeler only.

At the instigation of Weizmann and Malcolm, the British government came to oppose Morgenthau's approach to the Turks, even though it supported the others. Why? Perhaps for two reasons. First of all, despite the assiduously promoted cover story the real reason for Morgenthau's mission had become well known, both in America and in London. Morgenthau himself had been extremely indiscreet (while keeping his traveling companions in the dark). As a result, Sir Ronald Graham warned his colleagues: "As condition of secrecy to which Mr. Morgenthau attaches so much importance no longer exists it is doubtful whether mission could serve useful purpose at present moment, and I would suggest that it should be postponed." The Americans refused to postpone it, but the British ceased to believe in it.

Second, the Foreign Office had concluded that Britain needed the support of "international Jewry" to win the war. In his denunciation of Morgenthau, Weizmann had shrewdly harped upon the power of this cosmopolitan cabal and upon Morgenthau's place within it. Now he wanted to head him off at Gibraltar. Morgenthau no longer enjoyed Foreign Office confidence; Weizmann did; very well, then, the mandarins may have reasoned, keep him happy; let him go.

True, at the meeting of the Islamic Society, James Malcolm caught wind that Aubrey Herbert was planning a mission (see Chapter 20) and he and Weizmann protested about it. Sir Ronald Graham's face betrayed nothing, but he had written the previous day to Horace Rumbold: "Will you be kind to my cousin Aubrey Herbert if he comes to Switzerland which he may do, on a sort of roving mission which he had better explain to you himself?"

Somehow Weizmann and Malcolm came to focus exclusively upon defeating Morgenthau. The Foreign Office did not enlighten them, quite the opposite. Balfour called Weizmann to his office and entrusted him with a secret assignment: "I was to talk to Mr. Morgenthau, and keep on talking till I had talked him out of this mission." He did not know, he never knew, that simultaneously Balfour was giving permission for Aubrey Herbert to go to Switzerland on another peace mission. Thus the British government tricked Chaim Weizmann.

Morgenthau's party, which now included not only the three Zionists but also Ashag K. Schmarvonian, a Turkish Armenian working for the State Department who had served as Morgenthau's interpreter in Constantinople, sailed from New York on June 21. They carried with them eighteen trunks filled with $400,000 in gold for the Jews of Palestine. Their ship zigzagged across the Atlantic, ever watchful for German U-boats. For his part, Weizmann sailed for Le Havre aboard the *Hantonia* on June 29, accompanied only by an intelligence officer, Kennerley Rumford, a well-known baritone who had married the singer Clara Butt. Rumford, Weizmann wrote to his wife Vera, was "either terribly 'profound' or completely innocent: rather the latter, I think." He may have underestimated his minder.

The two stopped first in Paris, where Weizmann met with the British ambassador and with Edmond de Rothschild. Then they entrained for Spain. Weizmann wrote his wife: "From the moment we entered Spanish territory we have been followed by German spies. There were 4 of them and one accompanied us as far as Madrid. It seemed that we had lost him at the railway station but he has just turned up again and will probably follow us still further." Perhaps, however, the "innocent" Rumford now proved his worth. He and Weizmann checked into their Madrid hotel, followed by the German agent. They told the *portier* that they intended to stay the night. The *portier,* an Austrian, repeated this to the spy, a fellow German-speaker. Weizmann went out to pay a call. When he returned to the hotel, "a car drove up with an English guide; we packed hastily, paid the bill, and vanished within 10 minutes. You should have seen the *portier*'s rage."

So the two parties, British and American, converged by land and by sea upon a Gibraltar baking under the summer sun. A third party, a French one, comprising Colonel E. Weyl (a former head of the Turkish tobacco monopoly) and Albert Thomas (the French minister of munitions) arrived on July 4. The next day they all met for discussions, inside the fortress, guarded by British soldiers. They spoke in German, the only language they had in common, and as they kept the windows open because of the heat, Weizmann indulged the fantasy that the Tommies could hear them talk and deemed them to be spies who had been lured into a trap and would be shot next morning.

The discussions, which lasted two days, began with a report from Schmarvonian on conditions in Turkey, which he had left with the rest of the American diplomatic staff only six weeks earlier. The Ottoman army had just about shot its bolt, he thought; bankruptcy loomed over the empire as a whole; most Turks hated and feared the Germans, he continued; and relations between Talaat and Enver had reached the breaking point. "I am not aware whether this information is quite new to the Foreign Office or not, but I am giving this résumé because I consider that these are the only real facts which Mr. Morgenthau was able to communicate to us," Weizmann reported afterward to Ronald Graham.

Where Schmarvonian had been incisive, Morgenthau was vague. Weizmann put it this way in his autobiography: "Mr. Morgenthau had had an idea. He felt that Turkey was on the point of collapse . . . It had occurred to him that perhaps Talaat Pasha might be played off against Enver Bey." But when Weizmann asked him whether the Turks realized they were beaten in the war, and if they did, what their terms for a separate peace would be, neither the American nor anyone in his entourage could answer. Weizmann then told Morgenthau what he understood Britain's terms to be. She must be "satisfied that Armenia, Mesopotamia, Syria and Palestine are to be detached from the present Turkish Empire." Whether this was wishful thinking on Weizmann's part is another matter, but no one at the conference disputed him. Nor did anyone think that "such conditions would be acceptable at present to the Turks." Therefore, and even though it became apparent during the discussions that the French government strongly favored an approach to Turkey (which disquieted Weizmann), "it was no job at all to persuade Mr. Morgenthau to drop the project."

Weizmann also made very clear to the American that it had been a mistake to try to associate his mission with Zionism. "On no account should the Zionist organization be in any way compromised by his negotiations," Weizmann lectured the diplomat. "On no account must the Zionist organization be in any way identified or mixed up even with the faintest attempts to secure a separate peace . . . We Zionists feel about this point most strongly, and we would like assurances from Mr. Morgenthau that he agrees and understands this position." The assurance was offered, with what painful swallowing of pride one may imagine. In fact, the deeply humiliated Morgenthau capitulated on all fronts. He would not continue his journey to Egypt or even to Switzerland but rather would "stay in Biarritz and then try and get into contact with General Pershing." He would take the $400,000 in gold back to America. Morgenthau never forgave the author of his mortification and thenceforth opposed the Zionists.

Weizmann's bravura performance justified Foreign Office confidence in his abilities. He had been "eminently successful," Graham reported to Lord Hardinge; he was "a shrewd observer." Still, he had not quite carried off the diplomatic coup that virtually all historians of the episode celebrate. After all, Weizmann had not killed the separate peace idea, only Morgenthau's version of it, and in that the Foreign Office had ceased to believe anyway.

Weizmann returned to London on July 21 to report to Graham in person. Two days later Graham sent him to Paris to brief Balfour and Lloyd George, who were attending a war conference there. The two were glad to learn that Weizmann had scotched Morgenthau's mission. Nothing they said to him suggested anything except that he had scored a complete triumph.

Back in London again, however, Weizmann soon realized there was a fly in the ointment, or rather two flies, and that they were Harry Sacher and Leon Simon, his close, junior associates. Like every other British Zionist who learned of Weizmann's mission to Gibraltar, they took it at face value, accepting that Weizmann had defeated the advocates of a separate peace with Turkey. But unlike their colleagues, they disapproved of what he had done. They had been arguing for months that their leader was becoming too enamored of Mark Sykes and other Foreign Office mandarins, none of whom were trustworthy. "The Zionists in public must preach pure Zionism and be detached from any Power," Sacher wrote to Simon, who had just expressed similar sentiments in a letter to him. "The Zionist movement as such must of course not stake all on Great Britain. I have never dreamt of such a doctrine." But that meant that they believed Zionists ought not to depend upon complete British victory in the war either. And that meant that they did not necessarily oppose the idea of a compromise peace with Turkey.

Just before Weizmann embarked for Gibraltar, he called Simon to his home for a lengthy discussion. He may have come to regret it. Simon recorded in his diary:

> I said that it was not for us to try to stop peace with Turkey if we could get decent conditions. He said that we could not get de-

cent conditions and that the only terms on which G[reat]
B[ritain] would make peace with Turkey included the detachment from the Turkish Empire of Armenia, Syria, and Palestine, and that of course Turkey would not accept these terms . . .
I expressed the opinion that probably the people of this country,
and certainly the Russians, would not go on fighting Turkey if
they knew that these conditions had been laid down and I further suggested that his going to Gib[raltar] along with representatives of G[reat] B[ritain] whose object was to stop a separate
peace with Turkey would look as though we Zionists were trying to use our influence in the same direction.

But of course Weizmann did go to Gibraltar, not as an observer accompanying British representatives but rather as the sole representative himself.
Simon's doubts multiplied. "Assume [?] the peace proposals break down . . .
and it gets known that a Zionist leader had met the Americans as emissary
of the Government," he worried in his diary. "The movement will incur
well deserved odium . . . For my part I will not tie myself up with the policy, or tendency, this move implies."

Sacher and Simon judged that after three years of bloodshed the peoples
of the belligerent powers had grown weary of war. They thought the forces
of the Left were rising and that "the centre of gravity will shift steadily
towards the 'pacifists.' The future is with them." It made no sense, then,
from a practical point of view, for Zionists to ally with a government that
was publicly wedded to "the knock-out blow." When Sacher saw Weizmann briefly right after the latter returned from Gibraltar, he tried to make
these points but did not have time to develop them. Simon tried on August
1 at the initial meeting of a political committee composed of Weizmann's
closest associates. Sacher could not attend, and so Simon reported to him by
letter the following day:

Chaim gave us an account—a bit discursive—of his mission . . .
What struck me most was that while he was at great pains to
make it clear to Morgenthau that Zionism is not trying to make
a separate peace with Turkey, he had not suggested that Zionism was not trying to stop a separate peace with Turkey—rather
the reverse. I raised a discussion on this question and of course
was in a minority of one . . . If you share my views at all I wish
you would find an opportunity of rubbing them in, if only by
letter.

Sacher did rub them in, the next day, in a long and powerful communication to Weizmann. "I think you were much too emphatic in discouraging and combating the idea itself of a separate peace with Turkey, instead of opposing any form of peace which did not safeguard our interests," he wrote flatly. He reiterated that Zionist and British interests were not identical: "A British protectorate is . . . one form under which our aims in Palestine may be realized . . . There are other forms—an international arrangement; Turkish suzerainty under guarantees." He broadened Simon's earlier critique: "I see the peril that we Zionists in England may be infected with imperialism at the very time when the rest of the world is beginning to cast it off." And he injected a moral note: To oppose the advocates of peace with Turkey meant possibly prolonging the war. "I myself would not buy a British protectorate at the cost of prolonging the war by a single day."

Sacher missed the next meeting of the political committee too. Generously Weizmann had copies of his letter made and "handed around . . . and Simon [Marks] read it out. So you had your innings." Leon Simon thought, "It is a very good letter but it hadn't much effect. These people don't believe that the future is to the pacifists—that is the fundamental difference." Again Simon did his best to argue the position, but as he confessed sadly to his friend, he made little impression. Afterward Sacher fumed: "But think of tying ourselves with [Lloyd] George and his Cabinet swine and getting athwart the world's democracies as our 'leaders' want to do!" Weizmann had become enamored of "the general policy of Imperialism and militarism," and of "Sykes and other 'politicians,' " and of "armies, diplomacy and other muck no good in themselves." Sacher tried to warn his mentor and leader: "In politics one is always dependent on politicians . . . We Jews, like all mankind, are puppets in their hands, and their hands are as clumsy as their morals are base and their intellects feeble."

The warning was prescient but ineffective. Weizmann swatted him down, and Simon too. He maintained and even strengthened his ties with the politicians and the men of the Foreign Office. He continued to insist upon a British protectorate in Palestine and to oppose the separate peace with Turkey. He staked everything on Allied victory, and the gamble paid off. History belongs to the victors. But spare a moment to consider what might have been. Had Weizmann's gamble failed, had Britain lost the war, the history of Zionism (and of the world) would be very different. Or had his two critics on the political committee succeeded in persuading their colleagues to support a separate peace with Turkey (which would have represented a smaller and therefore more plausible wrinkle in the historical record), then too Zionism, and history, would have taken a different path.

Absent Zionist opposition, sentiment in favor of the separate peace might have strengthened, might have proved irresistible. Then perhaps, in return for withdrawing from the war, the Ottomans might have kept part of their Middle Eastern empire, including Palestine, Syria, even Arabia. No one can know where that might have led.

The government and Foreign Office made effective use of Chaim Weizmann to check the Morgenthau mission. They had learned to respect him over the past two years, and he repaid their confidence with a bravura performance at Gibraltar. Nonetheless, the government played him with breathtaking cynicism. Sir Ronald Graham did not tell either him or James Malcolm, when the two called, that J. R. Pilling (not yet discredited) had just returned to London claiming to have a letter from Talaat Pasha spelling out Turkey's peace terms, which, had it ever arrived, the government would have been eager to review. Graham hid from them too that only the day before he had paved the way for his cousin, Aubrey Herbert, to travel to Switzerland to meet dissident Turks to discuss peace. When Weizmann returned triumphant from Gibraltar, Graham sent him to Paris on July 23 to brief Lloyd George and Balfour and to receive their congratulations on scotching the Morgenthau peace mission. Two days later the prime minister and the foreign secretary received Aubrey Herbert, just returned from Berne and carrying an outline of peace terms provided by Turks. They congratulated him too.

CHAPTER 20

"The Man Who Was Greenmantle"

THE FOREIGN OFFICE did not take Marmaduke Pickthall seriously as a British emissary to dissident Turks, and eventually it ceased to take J. R. Pilling seriously either. At first it approved the mission of American ambassador Henry Morgenthau, but when it decided his mission would not bear fruit, it dispatched Chaim Weizmann to cut him off. But the Foreign Office took Aubrey Nigel Henry Molyneux Herbert very seriously indeed. When Herbert made his trip to Switzerland in July 1917 to meet with Turks, he carried with him the good wishes of some of the War Cabinet, of the foreign secretary, Balfour, and of other important Foreign Office figures. Like Pickthall, Pilling, and Morgenthau before him, however, Herbert ran into fierce opposition. In the end it proved too much even for him.

We have previously caught glimpses of Herbert: as a young honorary attaché in Constantinople along with the two men who became his friends, George Lloyd and Mark Sykes; as a Conservative Turcophile MP who joined the Anglo-Ottoman Soceity; as an army intelligence officer in Cairo in 1915; and as a supporter of Marmaduke Pickthall one year later. Now he moves to the center of our narrative.

He came from an august family. His father, the fourth Earl of Carnarvon, served Lord Derby as secretary of state for the colonies, and Disraeli as lord lieutenant of Ireland. His half brother discovered the tomb of Tutankhamen. Tall and slim, with thick, wiry, untamable hair that turned gray during the war, an aquiline nose, and gray, heavy-lidded eyes, he explored the Middle East and the Balkans as a young man, gaining a reputation for bravery, kindness, eccentricity, and dash even among the Albanian bandits who befriended him—and yet he was nearly blind. In 1913 came a startling inquiry from Tirana, the Albanian capital: Would he accept the Albanian throne? He wanted to, but the British government would not let him. He knew and admired Young Turk leaders and remained in touch with them right up until the moment Enver arranged the fateful alliance with Germany. "He loved to dare; he loved adventure; he loved to let people off and to give," Desmond MacCarthy wrote of him, shortly after his friend's untimely death at forty-four in 1924. John Buchan, who modeled his eponymous hero, Sandy Arbuthnot, after Herbert in the thriller *Greenmantle,* adds: "He was the most extraordinary combination of tenderness and gentleness, with the most insane gallantry that I have ever known—a sort of survivor from crusading times."

Herbert joined the House of Commons as Conservative member for South Somerset in 1911, but he was no party man. He sent a telegram of support to the foundation meeting of Dusé Mohamed Ali's League of Justice. During the war he gave money to an impecunious member of the league, one Charles Rosher, who happened to be the subject of British government surveillance (which is how we know of Herbert's generosity). The Conservative Party hierarchy did not know what to make of him; he had no desire to climb or to ingratiate himself; he seemed to them almost indifferent. Desmond MacCarthy judged that he was "the kind of man whom professional politicians do not fear because the hearts of such are clearly not 'in the game'; or rather because they only fight for what they immensely care for and while the impulse is hot within them."

When the war began, Herbert contrived, despite his near blindness, to join the Irish Guards "by the simple method of buying himself a second lieutenant's uniform and falling in as the regiment boarded ship for France." This sounds more like family legend than truth, but however he obtained the uniform, he took part in Britain's first engagement with the Germans, at Mons, and fell wounded. The Germans took him prisoner. In a characteristic passage, Herbert wrote of his experience: "It is only fair to say that both on the battlefield and subsequently we were all shown courtesy and great kindness by the Germans, from all ranks to all ranks; and from Prussians and Bavarians alike." When the French counterattacked, they freed him. Soon he was back in London, in hospital, recuperating. He appears to have been the first British MP to take part in combat during World War I; almost certainly he was the first to take a bullet.

Once he recovered, the government sent him to a part of the world he knew well, Cairo, to work for army intelligence. Serendipitously he traveled out to Egypt with another intelligence officer, his friend George Lloyd, aboard the ship *India*. "Oh Mark," he wrote to Sykes upon arrival, "here is a beginning. I left England in an historic gale. The Ship rolled 37 degrees. She could only roll 44. We went down to the sea that was near as a lion behind his bars." In Cairo he settled in with the others at Shepherd's Hotel. He recorded his impressions of fellow intelligence officers in his diary. Of T. E. Lawrence, who arrived the day after he did, he observed shrewdly: "an odd gnome, half cad, with a touch of genius." The two men became fast friends.

Herbert took part in the Cairo discussions about how to deal with then-sharif Hussein. He read the McMahon-Hussein letters. He wanted Britain to support the Arab Revolt. He knew, too, about the Sykes-Picot Agreement, which he opposed, even though his friend was its joint author. He wrote to Sykes, not specifically about the treaty with France but about British war aims: "We have not gone out for loot but to protect small people." Britain, he was clear, should not annex new territory in Syria, and he regretted that the French intended to annex it for themselves. Already he was thinking that Britain should negotiate a separate peace with the Ottomans and was wondering whether the authorities in Egypt, should they make contact, had authority to carry on discussions with Turkish representatives. On June 22, 1915, he wrote from Cairo to another friend, Robert Cecil, newly installed in the Foreign Office: "Suppose we are able to advance, and by, say, 1st August, find ourselves in the position that the Turkish Government . . . believes to be formidable, and a Turk comes in from my friend Talaat (or it may be from the Liberals), and says 'We will let you through [the Dardanelles] on such-and-such terms,' does G.H.Q. here know what terms we are prepared to accept and has it got the power of negotiating?" At this stage, the answer to his percipient query was negative: "If . . . at any time any proposal for surrender by the Turks were to reach us, we should have to submit it to the Russians before accepting it, and it is therefore impossible to give to anyone out there a free hand, as you desire."

At the end of 1915 Herbert returned to London, in part to push for reorganization of the Cairo intelligence bureau into the Arab Bureau, as Mark Sykes, Gilbert Clayton, and others on the spot wanted. But he did not forget the possibility of a separate peace with Turkey. In February 1916 he lunched with Maurice Hankey, secretary of the War Council, who told him "2 things were in the air: a separate peace with Turkey on the one hand, [and] on the other a speeding up of our attack on Turkey to help the Russians at Erzerum." British pursuit of the second option led to the ill-fated campaign at Gallipoli. Britain declined to pursue the first, Herbert records Hankey as saying, "on the ground that . . . the attempt would only cause friction with Russia." Herbert argued the point, keeping Robert Cecil's strictures in mind. He wanted a British soldier (himself?) to tell the Russians: "We all want to finish the war, and the quickest way is to get rid of unnecessary enemies. Begin with the Turks . . . Make your own terms with the Turks, or let us make terms but only such as are completely satisfactory to you." He would "put the case very friendly but bluffly." Hankey did not bite.

During the next year Herbert served his country in various capacities: on a secret mission to Albania; as a liaison officer at Gallipoli; and in Mesopotamia, where he and Lawrence were sent to bribe the Turkish troops besieging Kut to let the British go (they would not). On one of his trips, passing through Paris, he met with Rechid Bey, the man who approached Grant Duff in Berne in January 1915. At the Hotel du Louvre, after having "passed down corridors that smelt like the parrot house at the Zoo," the two men found a quiet spot to talk. Regretfully Herbert "told him that I thought there was nothing to be done at the present moment. That the sound of battle drowned everything else . . . those who loved his countrymen best were thinking of their own country now, and mourning their own relations, and . . . no one would dream of taking any risk of alienating an ally [Russia] on the chance of getting Turkey out at this moment."

Eighteen months later things had changed. Millions had perished. Russia, now led by Kerensky, no longer claimed Constantinople or any other territory. Britain no longer thought it could force a passage through the Dardanelles. Herbert judged that the time to push for a separate peace with Turkey was finally ripe. And when he broached the possibility this time, the authorities did not turn their backs; quite the opposite.

So far was Aubrey Herbert from being a conventional Tory that by spring 1917 he had begun to think not merely that Britain should sign a separate peace with Turkey but that she should negotiate an end to the war altogether. Otherwise, he predicted to George Lloyd, "we shall simply pass from a European war to European Revolution. You have two civilizations fighting each other, each exhausting their resources . . . I do not know that the last lap of victory will make very much difference." Had he known Harry Sacher and Leon Simon, he would have agreed with them that the future lay with the opponents of war and imperialism. He sympathized to a degree with such figures; at any rate he thought it only realistic to accommodate them, and he did not hesitate to say so. When he bumped into a businessman he knew at the Travelers' Club "going profiteering to Liverpool," he said to him: " 'Time's up for you rich men. If I were you I should be trembling in my shoes, and I should do something very spectacular in the way of charity to save my neck.' " The man turned pale and asked what kind of charity. "I said: 'Something respectable, like orphans.' " A few months later he was equally indiscreet in Paris with the British ambassador, who called him a "dangerous pacifist Turcophile lunatic in khaki."

Herbert thought that whatever its architects had planned, the war spelled the end of traditional imperialism and territorial carve-ups. Britain would now seriously consider a separate peace with Turkey, he judged, not merely because the Russians had repudiated annexations, and because Allied generals had given up hope of forcing the Dardanelles, and because people in general had wearied of the war, but also because British leaders were abandoning their imperialist ambitions, including those enunciated in the Sykes-Picot Agreement. Interestingly, his friend Sykes's mind was traveling down a similar path with regard to imperialism, although not with regard to the separate peace.

Meanwhile the mind of the government likewise was exploring these paths. With regard to the separate peace, neither Pickthall nor Pilling nor Morgenthau had been the person it required. Aubrey Herbert, however, was neither a dreamy novelist, nor a disreputable businessman, nor an indiscreet American former ambassador. He was a Conservative MP, the son of an earl, with extensive experience of the Ottoman Empire. "Yesterday, I had the last of a long series of conversations with R[obert] C[ecil] about getting the Turks out of the war," he recorded in his diary on June 3, 1917. "I sketched a plan, which he agreed." Three days later he wrote: "My departure practically agreed to by the Foreign Office," and two days after that: "I saw Lord Hardinge . . . , and settled the details of my journey to Switzerland." (Again, at almost exactly the same time as it was preparing to dispatch Herbert, the Foreign Office was reassuring Chaim Weizmann and James Malcolm that it would not consider a separate peace with Turkey.)

Herbert would not leave for weeks yet; he still had to convince the biggest guns. On July 4 he met with the foreign secretary himself. At Balfour's request he prepared a memorandum explaining what Britain had to gain from a separate peace with Turkey: "We should free troops in Egypt,

Salonika and Mesopotamia . . . We should avoid a position in Mesopotamia that may become dangerous in the autumn. We should be concentrating instead of dissipating our forces . . . the position of Bulgaria would become precarious and the desire for peace in Vienna would be increased." Oddly, he did not touch upon what the government considered to be "the strongest point of all in favor of a separate peace with Turkey, namely that it means the complete defeat of Germany's Near Eastern and Middle Eastern aspirations, and would undoubtedly cause the gravest unease and possible disturbance in Germany."

For that reason in addition to the others, then, Balfour and most of his colleagues were inclined to smile upon Herbert's offer to meet Turkish emissaries in Switzerland (regardless of what they might say simultaneously to Zionists and Armenians). They had another reason too. During May, June, and July 1917 they kept receiving reports that important Ottoman figures likewise were thinking about peace. These reports culminated in a cable from Rumbold in Switzerland, who had learned from Dr. Parodi that on June 27 prominent Turks in that country had formed an Ottoman League of Peace and Liberation, whose aim was to overthrow the CUP and to negotiate peace with Britain. They had chosen Rechid Bey as their president and Kemal Midhat Bey, a former Albanian minister of public works, to be their secretary. Soon thereafter important Turks began arriving in Zurich. "I am taking steps," Rumbold assured London, "to try and find out if possible [the] results of any meeting these persons hold, as I am informed on good authority that their presence in this country indicates probable peace proposal from Turkey."

"Taking steps" meant asking Dr. Parodi to look further into the matter. The British agent did so, and within the week Rumbold was reporting that the Turks had met in Zurich on July 9 or 10. One of their leaders, Fethy Bey, formerly the Ottoman minister in Sofia, wanted to meet Dr. Parodi in person, and moreover, "a member of the Committee of Union and Progress who is in opposition to . . . Enver Pasha is coming to Switzerland, and the friends of the person in question have sounded Dr. Parodi as to whether this Turkish delegate could meet some prominent Englishman in this country."

The visible outlines of a crucial nexus now grew clear to the men in London. An important Ottoman wished to meet an important Briton in Switzerland to broach the separate peace; an important Briton, Aubrey Herbert, wished to meet an important Ottoman for the very same reason. On July 14 Herbert left for Switzerland. He spent twenty-four hours in the French capital and then entrained to Berne, where he consulted with Rumbold and Parodi among others, finally stopping at Geneva, where, on the evening of July 17, he took a room at the Hôtel de la Cloche.

We turn now to Herbert's diary:

> Next morning [I] was woken up at 6.30 by a man who said: "Mr. Smith is waiting for you." I said: "Tell Mr. Smith to go to the devil," but then remembered and got up and went out and ran into a black man. I found out afterwards that he was the nephew of the ex-khedive [of Egypt], and also of the present Sultan [of Egypt]. He told me that a car should wait for me at three that afternoon . . . At 3, Mr. Smith walked through the room, and I followed him out through a couple of streets to a car, and we went off to his flat. Nobody lived there as far as I could make out, and it was unfurnished except for one oriental picture.

Into this safe house, Herbert records, walked "my friend." He does not identify him in the diary. In the memorandum he prepared afterward he wrote only: "He comes from one of the best and most honourable families of his country; in looks he is like a typical Englishman of the public school class and he talks perfect English."

This gentleman began their conversation: "How are you, Aubrey Herbert? I hope your wound is better. You must have had a filthy time with the Germans." Herbert made his position clear: He was in Switzerland for his health, he had no authorization to discuss anything in particular, and the opinions he expressed would be his alone. His friend made like protestations. They got down to business.

> For the last year [his friend] had devoted himself to organizing an Anglophil party to bring Turkey and England together after the war. This party was now very strong and with help they could effect a change of Government . . . He said that the autonomy of the outlying provinces, Armenia, Arabia, Mesopotamia, Syria and Palestine, was acceptable to his friends and part of their programme . . . I asked him what was meant by autonomy . . . He said that it did mean certainly the Turkish flag and, he thought, garrisons. I answered that, if the occupation was effective, it would mean that there was no real autonomy—for which we were fighting, and that weak garrisons would be an irritation to the native population, and a source of anxiety and possibly of humiliation to the Turkish Government. He said

that he was inclined to agree with [my] reservations, but that he
would find it very difficult to put this to his own people . . . He
suggested that the Egyptian status quo ante might be a satisfactory compromise.

The Egyptian status quo ante meant the fig leaf of Turkish control with
Britain pulling the strings, as it had done in Egypt since Gladstone's day.
This would have satisfied Sacher and Simon, but it would have been anath-
ema to Weizmann and his followers.

When the discussion ended, Herbert found his way back to the hotel by
a circuitous route. He would have been pleased with what had taken place,
but he was not yet finished. Next morning he consulted again with Parodi.
They traveled together by train to Interlaken, "where we separated at the
station. I went to the Kursaal [then a spa, today a casino] and in a short time
P. came along and sat down with a couple of Turks, both Committee men,
at a table near me. He introduced me, and we had an extremely curious
conversation. They had come from a conversation at Zurich [the one reported on by Parodi to Rumbold and by Rumbold to the Foreign Office],
and were anxious to have a revolution in Turkey."

In a second memorandum Herbert gave further details. The Turks were
Hakki Halid Bey, ex-director of the mint at Constantinople, now living in
Geneva, and Dr. Noureddin Bey, an influential member of the CUP and director of a Constantinople hospital, who had arrived in Switzerland only
two weeks before. He was the anti-Enver CUP member who had expressed
the desire to meet an influential Englishman.

"We then went walking in the garden which was completely deserted,"
Herbert continued. "Dr. Parodi at first talked to Noureddin Bey while I
walked with Hakki Halid. The following is a précis of our conversations."

> There are, they said, two parties in the Committee, one com-
> posed of Enver's men, while the others were waiting for Talaat
> to lead them. Talaat was hanging back, waiting for his position
> to become more assured . . . The Anglophil party are afraid of
> two things . . . the guillotine and the partition of Turkey. They
> want moral and financial support from England and guarantees
> that there will be no complete partition amongst the powers of
> Turkey. Hakki Halid and Dr. Noureddin asked me if I had any
> idea as to the terms upon which Great Britain would be pre-
> pared to make a separate peace . . . I answered that I did not
> know what terms the British Government would desire and

that I was not authorized to discuss this question. Hakki Halid
said that they did not wish to negotiate with the Italians or the
Russians and that they preferred to negotiate with us rather
than with the French.

They proposed (and this proposal emanated from the Conference and possibly indirectly from Talaat) that Noureddin Bey
should return to Turkey where he would see Talaat. Talaat
would then appoint an authoritative person with credentials
who would journey to Switzerland on the ground of ill-health
accompanied by Dr. Noureddin as his physician . . . On arriving
in Switzerland this envoy would enter into direct relations with
the British Government.

The stroll in the garden ended. Talking it over a little later, Herbert and
Parodi concluded that the suggestions had been made in good faith and
that Noureddin probably had been sent to Switzerland by Talaat, because
"directly he arrived here in Switzerland Hakki Halid Bey communicated
to Dr. Parodi Noureddin's desire to see him, and if possible, some influential Englishman."

Herbert argued in his memorandum that Britain now had a golden opportunity to take the Ottoman Empire out of the war. "As long as the Turks
believe that the outlying provinces such as Syria . . . are to be annexed by
foreigners who will make these regions the instruments of further en-
croachment, there can be no prospect of peace. If, on the other hand, the
Turks see a chance . . . that their country will be ringed round by a chain of
semi-autonomous friendly Moslem States, half the reason that compelled
them to continue fighting will have gone." He wanted Britain to make its
allies "surrender claims to territories which they cannot take themselves,
and which it is doubtful they could hold even if we could take them for
them." An agreement with the Ottomans would follow.

Herbert thought his mission complete. He packed his bag and prepared
to leave for Paris. Twenty minutes before his train arrived, perhaps even as
he stood on the station platform, someone slipped a memorandum in
French into his hands. It contained the dissident Turks' proposals for a separate peace. "I do not think that it is acceptable," Herbert wrote in his diary,
"but I think that it would form a basis."

He arrived in Paris on the morning of July 25, two days after Weizmann.
Lloyd George and Balfour were in the city, as we know. The latter sent for
him. Herbert records: "I told him what happened. He was interested and
excited . . . In the evening I had an hour with L[loyd] G[eorge] and Hankey.

He sipped his tea and listened while we sat on a balcony and the crowd cheered in the Place de la Concorde . . . I read him my memorandum." What he did not know, but what would have cheered him had he known, was that the day before the prime minister and the foreign secretary had received confirmation of his general message from another Military Intelligence officer stationed in Berne. The latter had held a secret meeting with Dr. Noureddin too. He reported: "Talaat now convinced that Russian revival, failure of submarine warfare, and American intervention have destroyed all hope of satisfactory settlement for Turkey and . . . wishes to . . . make terms with England." Such information would not have cheered Dr. Weizmann, but they withheld it from him too.

In London three days later Herbert had an hour at the Foreign Office with Balfour again, accompanied this time by Lord Hardinge and Robert Cecil. On August 3 MacDonagh told him that the War Cabinet "had seen my memorandum and agreed to it." At this stage Herbert might have been excused for thinking that a compromise peace between Britain and the Ottoman Empire was within reach. But he would have been mistaken. The same forces that had defeated Pickthall and Pilling and Morgenthau had already mobilized against him. Whether Aubrey Herbert's attempt to facilitate a separate peace with Turkey would meet finally with his government's approval remained an open question.

The Foreign Office received conflicting information on the readiness of the Turks to negotiate. While some, as we have seen, thought the Ottomans were prepared to talk, powerful forces in London argued with equal force that they were not. Among the most authoritative was Lord Nathaniel Curzon, the only member of the War Cabinet with personal experience of the Middle East. Early in May, as reports about Turkish readiness to negotiate were turning from a trickle to a stream, and as pressure to explore the option was building in the Foreign Office, he argued that the advocates of peace were pursuing a chimera. Turkey "now knows that she will retain Constantinople . . . Her Government is in the hands of a powerful triumvirate whose hold [on power] . . . has, on the whole, been strengthened by the War. The Entente has at present nothing in the way of inducement to offer." British restoration to the Ottomans of Mesopotamia, including Baghdad, might open the door to negotiations, Curzon conceded, but such concessions "we are not prepared to consider."

Other Middle East experts from within the Foreign Office reached similar conclusions. On the eve of Herbert's journey to Switzerland, Balfour asked two of them to assess his chances of success. The first did not think much of those chances. The German army dominated the Turkish government, he argued, and a coup remained unlikely so long as they did so. Moreover no Turkish government, not even one formed by the conspirators who so unrealistically wished to overthrow the present CUP regime, would accept dismemberment of their empire, which England and France still intended. The second expert, Sir Lewis Mallet, former ambassador in Constantinople, made similar points. The CUP still believed it could win the war. It had lost Baghdad, but it had beaten the British at Kut and Gallipoli and Gaza. That the new Russian government had renounced Constantinople only added to their confidence. "It is not impossible," Mallet darkly hinted, "that there may be some connection between the Jewish wire-pullers at Constantinople and the Jewish element at Petrograd." At any rate, the Turks would not be ready to make peace until their self-belief had been knocked out of them.

Into this debate like an avenging angel swept Sir Mark Sykes, just returned from the Middle East on June 14. He judged the opponents of the separate peace bloodless; he thought the first Foreign Office memo opposing the separate peace tepid and the second based upon "insufficient material." He despised Lord Curzon, whom he had nicknamed "Alabaster." If the faction within the government and Foreign Office who favored the peace were to be defeated, he would have to intervene. He wrote to Gilbert Clayton back in Cairo: "On my arrival I found that the Foreign Office had been carefully destroying everything I had done in the past 2 years." It had been "stimulating anti-Entente feeling and pushing separate negotiations with Turkey ideas. Indeed I just arrived in the nick of time." He consulted with Weizmann, who already had protested the Morgenthau and Herbert missions. "Luckily Zionism held good," Sykes wrote to Clayton. He gathered himself. Weizmann went off to Gibraltar and Herbert to Switzerland. Each returned at the end of July thinking he had succeeded. Sykes knew better: Weizmann's would be a Pyrrhic victory unless Herbert's triumph could be turned into a defeat.

So he let loose, composing two powerful blasts against pursuing negotiations with an emissary from Talaat in Switzerland. His friend Herbert's mission had been misconceived from the start. "The visit of a (to the Turks) notorious Turcophil M.P. to Turkish Agents in Switzerland will certainly be interpreted by the C.U.P. as a proof . . . that . . . the English and their Western Allies believe they cannot win the war." Rather than bring peace closer, Herbert had inadvertently delayed it. In any event, the men with whom Herbert proposed that Britain should parley did not carry sufficient weight. "Hakki Bey, the ex-master of the Turkish mint, is a well intentioned Liberal who had to flee Turkey for participation in an anti-C.U.P. combination. To negotiate with him or such members of the so-called 'opposition' is futile or worse. They are not of the caliber to cope with Talaat Pasha and his Jacobin clique."

Others in the Foreign Office either did not think, or did not care, about how the colonized peoples of the Ottoman Empire would react to Britain making a compromise peace with their colonial masters. The new, anti-imperialist Sykes cared very much. "Before entering on *pourparlers*," he warned in the same scorching memorandum, "it would seem imperative to consult not only France, Italy, America &c, but also the King of Hejaz, representative Armenians and nationalist (i.e.) Zionist Jews, to whom we and the other Entente Powers have obligations and whose fate is bound up with the principle of nationality, the antidote to Prussian military domination." This intriguing man's political evolution was nearly complete. In early 1916 he had put his name to one of the most infamous imperialist deals of the twentieth century; by mid-1917 he had become the advocate of subject peoples whom he wanted his country to champion, albeit with profit for itself.

In a second equally coruscating composition, Sykes shifted ground, arguing that the anti-CUP Liberals with whom Aubrey Herbert had met were actually CUP cats' paws. Perhaps the Ottoman government did desire a separate peace: How else explain why its puppets in Britain, "pacifists . . . financiers . . . Indian and Egyptian Moslem seditionists and their sympathizers such as Pickthall . . . [as well as] Semitic anti-Zionists who are undisguised pro-Turco-Germans," were pushing for one? The government that pulled their strings believed the peoples of Europe were exhausted by the war, that a peace conference would soon end it, and that "it will be useful to get Turkey's situation fixed and settled as advantageously as possible before the conference begins."

How did the CUP want to fix things? It desired "to come out of this war with an assured political and strategic position from which it can henceforth pursue its world policy," the main lines of which were:

1. Pan-Turanianism, reinforced by
2. Political control over the Muslim world.
3. A firm grip on the control levers of international finance.
4. Close cooperation with the various revolutionary movements

in Europe and the United States, such as syndicalism,
Leninism, and cognate forces.

If Britain must negotiate with the Ottomans, she should do so only with the knowledge of her wartime allies and without employing any trickery. More important, she "should stand out for Arab independence [and] . . . a real guarantee of Armenian liberation," his new diplomatic raison d'être. Oddly, he did not refer to Palestine in this paper. Perhaps he assumed that "Arab independence" meant Palestinian independence too, and that the Zionists would benefit from that.

After reading Sykes's second memorandum, two more Foreign Office mandarins weighed in. One wrote: "I find myself in close agreement with what Sir Mark Sykes says." The other, Sir Ronald Graham, Herbert's cousin, backtracked on his support for the separate peace: "If the present Turkish overtures are genuine—as to which I have grave doubts—we must encourage them to the extent (but no further) of hearing what the Turks have to offer . . . It must throughout be borne in mind that any terms under which Turkey would emerge with a semblance of having proved victorious—in Moslem eyes—must lay up endless trouble for us in the future." With Sykes at full throttle, the tide at the Foreign Office seemed to be turning. A few days later, when Herbert had an audience with General Jan Smuts, this most recent addition to the War Cabinet told him that his memoranda "were not sufficient, that an entire re-statement of the case was required." Herbert demurred. He could read the tea leaves.

The British government divided at the highest level over whether to send representatives to Switzerland to meet emissaries from Talaat Pasha to discuss a separate peace. How it might have resolved that internal argument must remain a matter of speculation, however, for developments beyond Britain's control now intruded. In Petrograd Alexander Kerensky still hoped to win the war, but by ordering, contrary to all logic and evidence, that his troops take the offensive once again, he precipitated the final collapse of the Russian army and his own downfall. General Brusilov's weary, famished, disillusioned soldiers gave it up near Lemberg in Galicia, just as Sykes and the other officials were composing their memoranda. This defeat had the effect of instilling new confidence among Turks. While London divided over Aubrey Herbert's proposals, Constantinople began to plot an autumn campaign to recapture Arabia, without worrying that the Russians would attack from behind. Parodi, his ear to the ground as always, reported to Rumbold, who wired to London: "Talaat has no intention of seriously considering separate peace with the Entente . . . he will await result of Mesopotamian campaign in early autumn."

Near the end of August, Herbert called on Lord Hardinge at the Foreign Office, hoping against hope for news from his Turkish contacts. "I told him," Hardinge records, "that as far as I knew nothing had occurred." "The man who was Greenmantle," as his biographer called him, had not been able to jump-start negotiations about a separate peace with Turkey after all.

CHAPTER 21

The Zaharoff Gambit

THE IDEA OF A SEPARATE PEACE with the Ottoman Empire remained very much alive in the mind of the man who mattered most in Great Britain at this time, Prime Minister David Lloyd George. His chosen instrument was not Aubrey Herbert, however, despite the latter's pedigree and connections; indeed, to the eye of a Welsh shoemaker's nephew such as Lloyd George, perhaps those attributes appeared to be drawbacks. He chose instead for this most delicate of diplomatic tasks a self-made man like himself, a subtler, more ruthless figure than Aubrey Herbert, and one who was much more experienced in intrigue: namely, the infamous arms dealer and prototypical "merchant of death," Basil Zaharoff. In a story chock-full of fabulous characters, this gentleman may be the most fabulous of all, although he certainly was not the most admirable.

Zacharias Basileios Zaharoff was born an Ottoman subject in 1849, but he lied about that as about most things. To some he said he was Romanian, to others that he was Greek, or Polish, or Russian. He told Lord Bertie of Thame that he had graduated from Oxford. In fact, as a boy he worked in the streets of Constantinople, touting for brothels and starting fires for a share of the salvage that firemen gained when they extinguished a blaze. A bigamist who changed his name more than once, probably a swindler and embezzler, certainly a risk-taker who had on more than one occasion packed his bags and left town as quickly as possible, he lived his early adult years on the shady side in England, Belgium, the United States, and Cyprus. In Greece in 1877 he discovered his true métier, when he began selling armaments for the Anglo-Swedish firm of Nordenfelt. Immediately his fortunes improved. He sold a submarine to Greece and two more to her traditional enemy, Turkey, and then one to Turkey's other great enemy, Russia. (The craft were unsafe and never used.) He sold weapons to Russia's enemy, Japan, to Germany, to France, and to Spain. Unlike the submarines, these weapons were used, and to deadly effect. The years before 1914 were a golden age for salesmen of weapons and munitions, and Zaharoff proved adept, not least because he well understood how to suborn and corrupt. A brilliant linguist, he could practice his talents in most European languages.

He was more than a successful purveyor of weapons, however. When, as chief salesman for Nordenfelt, he came up against the American Hiram Maxim, inventor of the machine gun, he quickly recognized the superior product. Maxim realized just as quickly who was the superior salesman. The marriage of convenience that resulted strengthened Zaharoff's hand. Already wealthy, he collected enormous commissions after the merger and purchased shares in the business that now had a double-barreled name. By the time British Vickers Steel Company purchased Nordenfelt-Maxim in 1897, Zaharoff was one of its owners. For Vickers he became "general Representative for business abroad." With some of the proceeds of the sale of his old firm, he bought shares in the new one and wound up sitting on its board of directors. Vickers built armaments works across Europe. Zaharoff played a leading role in their development and oversight.

He branched out, founding banks and purchasing newspapers or shares in them. He even lent money to the Monte Carlo casino. He lived opulently in Paris, where he dined off gold plate, which according to some reports was sold later to King Farouk of Egypt. He bought a château in the French countryside. In 1908 he took out French citizenship and sought to establish his bona-fides. He founded a home for retired French seamen. In 1909 he donated £28,000 to the Sorbonne to establish a chair in aviation. Such acts brought him membership in the French Legion of Honor, of which eventually he was made a commander.

The street urchin of Constantinople had climbed to a great height. His profession put him in touch with European leaders, ministers of defense, generals, even royalty, some of whom became his friends. He knew the "tiger" of French politics, the future wartime prime minister, Georges Clemenceau. In Britain he established friendly relations with T. P. O'Connor, the Irish nationalist MP and journalist, and with Baron Murray of Elibank, a member of the prewar and wartime Liberal government. Rumor has it that he became acquainted with Lloyd George during this period. Rumor compounded says the latter once had an affair with Zaharoff's first, abandoned wife. At any rate the arms merchant began to dabble in politics—to facilitate his business dealings, no doubt, but also, it would appear, to satisfy his ego. On one occasion he arranged for the throne of Portugal to be offered to Prince Christopher of Greece.

Eventually the Greek connection provided him with an introduction to the man atop the greasy pole in Britain. When the war commenced, Greek king Constantine resolutely pursued a policy of neutrality. His prime minister, Eleutherios Venizelos, pursued with equal resolution a pro-Entente policy. The French and British supported the latter; the Germans supported the former, hoping he would drop neutrality for an alliance with them. Both sides viewed Greece as a prize to be won. By 1915 it had become a happy hunting ground for men with cloaks and daggers, as well as money and guns. It was more dangerous than Switzerland, whose neutrality never came into question; divisions in Greece nearly precipitated a civil war and French invasion. This situation might have been designed for Basil Zaharoff, "evil and imposing," with his "beaky face . . . hooded eye . . . wrinkled neck . . . [and] the full body" of a vulture. He would fund the Allied propaganda effort in Greece; he would subsidize his "dear friend" Venizelos. "All that is needed is to buy the germanophile papers, also 45 Deputies and one Frontier Commissioner. Last month I bought out and out with my own money the most rabid anti-Venezelist paper." He pressed the British and French governments to provide additional funds for additional suborning. They did so, and Zaharoff knew where to spend it. The results were that Constantine abdicated, and Greece joined the Entente powers. Prime Minister Asquith wrote to Zaharoff: "I beg, on behalf of His Majesty's Government, to tender to you their sincere gratitude for the most valuable service which, at a critical time, you have rendered to the cause of the Allies."

For direct communication with the British government, Zaharoff employed Sir Vincent Caillard, financial director of Vickers. On April 19, 1916, at roughly the same time when Marmaduke Pickthall was responding to the overture from Dr. Felix Valyi in Switzerland, Zaharoff was writing to Caillard: "Mon cher Ami, the following if well managed may become historical."

"The following" was a feeler he had received three weeks previously from Abdul Kerim Bey, formerly cosecretary of Sultan Abdul Hamid II, later Turkish minister to Greece and ambassador to Vienna. "In Norden-felt's time I paid him many a thousand Liras," Zaharoff fondly remembered. Abdul Kerim had "heard that I was playing an important part in Eastern politics." The two met in Marseilles, the Turk traveling there with a false passport, "but said he, anything I may tell you 'comes from me alone, because I have neither an official nor a semi-official mission,' and this he repeated twenty times during our interview." Zaharoff described their ensuing discussion:

> He said that all talk of a separate peace with Turkey was out of the question because the Germans held Constantinople in their iron grip, but, added he, why not open the Dardanelles to you treacherously? What is it worth to the Allies in American dollars payable in American? Would you not be delighted to take Enver & forty or fifty of the Party straight to N.Y.?
>
> I replied that this was very interesting, upon which he said "Keep all this to yourself until I again communicate with you; it may be a month or two or three . . . & then be ready to come & see us at Adrianople and we will make your journey there easy."

The words Zaharoff underlined suggest that he thought that disclaimers notwithstanding, Abdul Kerim Bey was speaking for Enver.

Caillard lost no time in bringing Zaharoff's news to the appropriate people. Eventually Prime Minister Asquith, Chancellor of the Exchequer Reginald McKenna, and Conservative president of the Local Government Board Walter Long discussed the matter with an intelligence officer named Brewis, and with Caillard and Zaharoff, who traveled over from Paris at least once and probably twice. They were reluctant to risk more than £50,000, which Zaharoff thought would be insufficient, even as an earnest of intention. In the end the government ministers would not bite. McKenna thought that if the bribe was successful, it would remove ineffective Ottoman leaders from Constantinople and replace them with effective Germans who would substitute more complete puppets for the men who had fled. Asquith pointed out that if the scheme worked and a new Ottoman government expelled the Germans, the Turks would retain Constantinople, which Russia would not accept. Zaharoff received from Abdul Kerim Bey another communication containing instructions on how he should travel to Adrianople, but he had to reply that at present nothing could be done. In this, if nothing else, he resembled Marmaduke Pickthall, who had come reluctantly to a similar conclusion about Anglo-Turk discussions a little earlier. The time simply was not yet ripe. On the other hand, however, Zaharoff did not sever the link with his Turkish connection. And by now his work as an arms dealer definitely had brought him into touch with the British minister of munitions, Lloyd George.

It is worth pausing for a moment to consider Zaharoff's motivations. Nothing about his professional career suggests that he acted for love or from devotion to abstract principle. To nationalist or patriotic fervor, he remained immune. During 1914–18 he supported the Allies for obvious business reasons: They bought his munitions, at a time when Germany and her partners could not. But he had a personal reason for supporting Allied efforts. This erstwhile tout for Constantinople brothels craved respectability or at least its trappings, and not merely the kind that could be bought in a store and displayed in a house. Of those he had already a plentitude. His correspondence with Caillard reveals that Zaharoff wanted from England the equivalent of the medal of the Legion of Honor that he had received from France, either the Order of Bath or the Order of St. Michael and St. George. He thought his work for the Allies in Greece and later with regard to Turkey should earn him one or the other, but for safekeeping, in the middle of the war, he donated £25,000 to found another chair of aviation, this time at a London university. "This is not the moment to think of self, as we all have but one idea in view and that idea is Victory," he wrote coyly to Caillard. But then he added: "If any of us have contributed towards the victory I have no doubt that their work will be appreciated in due time."

Zaharoff undertook his wartime missions, then, because he had reason to wish for Allied success and also to win "gongs," as the British call them. He himself termed them "pieces of chocolate." At the end of the war he satisfied his craving. King George V conferred upon him a GBE (Knight of the Grand Cross) and a GCB (Knight of the Grand Cross in the Order of Bath). Thenceforth he would be styled "Sir Basil Zaharoff." But one of his biographers adds that the king detested Zaharoff and resented his use of titles, which, since he held French citizenship, were merely honorary anyway.

We come to May 1917. General Maude had taken Baghdad two months earlier, a blow to Ottoman confidence. Russia had renounced the ambition to annex Constantinople, which meant the Ottomans had one less reason to continue to fight. Reports of Turkish interest in a separate peace streamed once again into the Foreign Office. And now the easterner Lloyd George resided at 10 Downing Street. Sir Vincent Caillard, Basil Zaharoff, and Brewis, the intelligence agent, agreed that "the moment might be quite favorable for taking up the Turkish business again." Zaharoff reported from Paris: "I am turning and re-turning that Ottoman matter over in my head . . . I might . . . go as far as Switzerland, where 'by accident,' I am bound to run across some of our Ottoman friends, and that might be a way of re-opening the subject, but . . . if I take this matter up . . . I must be properly backed, and more than ample confidence should be placed in me."

It would be. Brewis spoke with the prime minister, who "was greatly interested and (of course without committing himself) quite sympathetically inclined. He . . . wanted you [Zaharoff] to come over as soon as you could possibly manage it and undertook to see you directly you arrived and to give you as much time as you require for discussion of the project." When we remember how difficult it had been for Chaim Weizmann to see the prime minister, that their meetings were arranged by C. P. Scott for fleeting moments in the interstices of the day, or over breakfast with others present, we may gain insight into the seriousness with which Lloyd George took the prospect of a separate peace with Turkey.

Then fate seemed to intervene. "The enclosed has just reached me in an envelope of the Grand Hotel du Russia, Geneva, addressed by Abdul Kerim," Zaharoff wrote to Caillard on June 5. It was a clipping from a Swiss newspaper, the *Tribune de Genève,* and it said in part:

> We are informed by an authorized source that Turkish civil and military personnel flooding into Switzerland, have been sent by the [Sublime] Porte with a view to arranging a compromise with the Entente Powers. Additional personnel are coming to Switzerland with the goal of finding peace at any price.

The Swiss report exaggerated, but that Abdul Kerim had sent it to Zaharoff at all indicated that the price of peace might be up for negotiation. Lloyd George was ill and recuperating outside London. McKenna no longer belonged to the government. Caillard got in touch with the only government minister in town privy to Abdul Kerim's initial approach. The Turk was "throwing out his hooks again," Caillard reported to Walter Long. "I believe the moment to be a particularly propitious one for the move." But authorization to act could come only from the prime minister. Another sign of Caillard's and Zaharoff's relative importance was that

Lloyd George returned to London on the morning of June 14; Caillard spoke with him that afternoon.

This was precisely when the Foreign Office was authorizing Aubrey Herbert to travel to Switzerland to talk to Turks about a separate peace and authorizing Chaim Weizmann to travel to Gibraltar to oppose talking with Turks about a separate peace. The mandarins cherished hopes for Herbert's mission; they thought Morgenthau's would be fruitless but that it would satisfy Weizmann to defeat it, which probably was why they sent him to Gibraltar. Lloyd George operated at a higher level altogether: He did not entertain much hope for Herbert. "He thought there were only 'second raters' " in Switzerland, Caillard reported, which means the prime minister judged Herbert's contacts there much as Mark Sykes did. Then the man from Vickers told the prime minister of Zaharoff's clipping, and of "the source from whence it came [and] . . . what we knew of that source." He sketched out the scheme of the previous year, which Lloyd George heard now for the first time, and the amount of money involved. "Of the last point he made light in view of the great advantage it would be to break down German influence in Turkey and arrange a separate Peace." This may explain why he had allowed the disreputable J. R. Pilling to travel to Switzerland, and why he did not discourage Aubrey Herbert, despite his misgivings about the men Herbert would contact.

Caillard and Lloyd George got down to brass tacks. The prime minister "said that it was patent that we must guard against a trap,—in other words that our Fleet might get through the Dardanelles, be trapped in the Sea of Marmora, and never get out again." He ticked off British desiderata: "We must retain possession of Mesopotamia, the Russians of the Armenian Provinces of which they are in occupation, a suitable arrangement which would involve at least Internationalization must be made for Palestine." Note that this last would not have satisfied the Zionists, for whom "Internationalization" was the worst possible outcome, as Weizmann had made clear to Lloyd George the previous year. But it appears to have been Lloyd George's fallback position. At this moment he may have hoped for an arrangement that would more completely satisfy the Zionists.

The upshot of the meeting was, as Caillard reported to Zaharoff, that the prime minister "considered it would be very well worth while your undertaking the journey to Switzerland and finding out all you could about the possibilities, as well of course as ascertaining what is the object of Abdul Kerim in opening up again to you now." When Basil Zaharoff received this letter, he embarked for Geneva immediately.

He arrived on June 18 or 19 (just as Horace Rumbold was telling J. R. Pilling that he must return permanently to London, and some two weeks before he would be welcoming Aubrey Herbert). The arms dealer found Abdul Kerim at his hotel. An extraordinary exchange took place. Apparently Zaharoff had only just missed Enver, who had wanted to see him. The Ottoman leader had been waiting at Herculesbad, on the Romanian-Hungarian border. Abdul Kerim too had tired of waiting for Zaharoff to arrive, but Enver had telegraphed: "Stay there and write him to come see you. Enver." Zaharoff asked to view the telegram and copied down the identifying numbers and posting office for British authorities to verify. Presumably they did so. Presumably Enver really had been hoping to meet the British emissary. The archive indicates nothing to the contrary.

"Things had changed" since the previous year, Abdul Kerim then informed Zaharoff. "Turkey was ruined and lost and . . . Enver & Co. were willing to throw up the sponge on 'reasonable conditions' and get out with their lives." Here were their terms:

> They want as a retaining fee $2,000,000 at Morgan's New York, payable now. Of this, he says, he will take, for himself $500,000 and after putting me in communication with Enver and Djavid, who also act for Khalil, the Sheikh-ul-Islam [Constantinople's leading Muslim cleric], Emir Hussein [a high-ranking Ottoman military officer, not to be confused with Sharif Hussein], Ouzoun Ali [another Turkish officer] and Djemal, he will curse Turks and Turkey and go to America and there await the others.
>
> The remaining $1,500,000 would go to the others, above mentioned, who absolutely needed every piaster of it to buy certain people who are indispensable.

Zaharoff asked why Talaat's name had not been mentioned. That member of the ruling triumvirate posed a bit of a problem, Abdul Kerim indicated, but if Talaat refused to listen to reason, "one will give him some coffee," presumably a threat to poison him. ("This tells you what sort of a man I am dealing with," Zaharoff noted piously.) But we know that while Enver was secretly contacting Britain through Abdul Kerim and Zaharoff, Talaat was contacting Britain through Hakki Halid Bey and Aubrey Herbert, and possibly through Fuad Selim and J. R. Pilling. Deceit and intrigue characterized dealings on both sides. On the Ottoman side lives were at stake.

As for the rest of the Turkish terms:

In addition to the $2,000,000, which he distinctly repeated I was to consider as a retainer, $10,000,000 would pay for everything . . .

As soon as the "retainer" was paid to him, Enver and or Djavid (Minister of Finance), he (Abdul Kerim), and I would meet and arrange somewhat on the following lines:

$XXX [meaning a sum in dollars to be determined] to be paid to their nominee when the Turkish troops have been withdrawn from the Mesopotamian Front, to a line indicated by me.

$XXX to be paid to their nominee when the Turkish troops in Palestine have been withdrawn to a line fixed by me . . .

$XXX to be similarly paid when the Turkish troops on both sides of the Dardanelles have allowed the Allies to land and have delivered the forts to them.

$XXX when our Fleet has passed through the Dardanelles and the Turks have asked for an armistice which, in Enver & Co's opinion, will be certain to lead to a general armistice, on account of the terrible state of Germany and Austria (not Hungary).

He said that the above were simply indications but that at the meeting with Enver, Djavid, himself and me, by which time I would know the views of the Money-Bags, we could settle details.

The meeting concluded, and the two men went their separate ways. Zaharoff returned to Paris, where he wrote his report and sent it to Caillard in London. "Your people are to decide," he concluded. "I express no opinion, yet [quoting Dickens] 'Barkis is willin.'" The very next day he sent a second letter to Caillard. "I would like to have the Grand + [Cross]," he reminded his friend.

Caillard saw Lloyd George on June 27. "I had drawn up a Memorandum based on your letter, and handed this to him to start the conversation. After reading it through he said that this was a most important communication—most important—he repeated the words several times." On the other hand, the prime minister doubted that Enver or Djavid could travel to Switzerland without alerting the Germans, and he doubted the wisdom of handing half a million dollars to Abdul Kerim before the meeting with Enver had taken place.

After some further discussion the suggestion we arrived at was this . . . the equivalent of two million dollars should be placed to your credit at some bank that you would indicate, from which bank you could have in your hand a banker's receipt for the amount. This Receipt you could produce to A.K. and state that as soon as he, Enver and Djavid met you in serious discussion you would be ready to transfer the amount to a nominee of theirs. Of course, if it were more easily handled thereby, you could have two banker's receipts, one for the equivalent of $500,000 and the other for $1,500,000, the former for A.K. himself and the latter for the others.

Zaharoff approved this plan, saying it "eases my mind immensely." He sent clippings from the French newspapers *Figaro* and *L'Action française,* both of which had published telegrams announcing that Enver and Djavid were in Switzerland to arrange loans. Caillard brought them to Lloyd George, who doubted their veracity. Nevertheless he agreed that "Zedzed," as Zaharoff signed his letters, should depart for Switzerland again as soon as possible.

Zaharoff left Paris on his second journey to Geneva on July 21, missing Lloyd George, who attended the war conference in the French capital, by a single day. He missed Weizmann, who arrived in Paris to brief the prime minister on events at Gibraltar the day after. He missed Aubrey Herbert, who reported to Lloyd George on his meeting with dissident Turks two days after that, on July 25. He knew nothing of their efforts; they knew nothing of his or of each other's. Lloyd George held all the strings.

In Geneva, Zaharoff found himself jousting with Abdul Kerim. He showed the latter the two receipts from Morgan's Bank in New York City. The Turk

> did not look at them but said once I had the funds I was to deposit $500,000 to his credit at the Credit Swisse, Zurich . . . and that the $1,500,000 were to be deposited to Enver's credit at the Banque Swisse et Francaise. As I did not interrupt him he said in continuation that the moment I had met Enver & Co his part of the bargain ended, and he would leave for the U.S. and prepare the road there for Enver & Co. He further said that Enver had told him last week that he would need some little time to square certain people (mentioned in my last) but that he had fixed our appointment at Lucerne for exactly 35 days after the money was placed to his credit.

Lucerne as a meeting place made sense to Zaharoff. He knew that Enver's wife had been living there since the beginning of 1916.

Then the interview turned sour. Zaharoff repeated his instructions from Lloyd George word for word. He would not pay Abdul Kerim anything until he had actually met with Enver. The Turkish envoy "calmly said 'Take it or leave it!' and notwithstanding all my efforts to reopen the conversation he remained mute, gave me my hat, salaamed me gracefully and dismissed me."

Zaharoff remained for two more days in Geneva, hoping to resume the negotiation. He did not see the Turk. Finally he went to lunch at his hotel. There was Abdul Kerim in the dining room. He "saluted me politely and when I was half through came and smoked at my table, spoke of commonplace things and although I tried to touch upon the question he evaded it, wished me bon voyage and started for the door. He stopped short, came back, whispered in my ear, 'keep your eye on Mesopotamia' and walked out."

Back in Paris, Zaharoff reported immediately to Caillard, who reported in turn to the prime minister. This time it took a couple of weeks before the two could meet face-to-face. Afterward Caillard brought his friend up to date: "The fact is that A.K.'s advice to you to 'keep your eye on Mesopotamia' was genuine, and the Turks are preparing for a big attempt to drive us out of Baghdad." Here is the reason for the failure of Pilling's effort (assuming its reality), and of Herbert's, and of this most recent, but by no means last, of Zaharoff's. Just when the British were most interested in reaching an agreement with the Ottomans, the latter found reason to hope that they could prevail in war after all. But, Caillard continued: "Our military authorities are fully aware of this and are in close communication with Sir Stanley Maude, who expresses the conviction that he can defeat the attack and hold the field." Therefore Lloyd George had not given up on the idea of a separate peace with Turkey after all. "He does not wish you to return the money for the present . . . He has not by any means decided that [it] will not be used for the objects in view when the propitious moment arrives."

So the matter rested for the next three months, until mid-November 1917. By then it had become clear that the threatened Ottoman offensive in Mesopotamia would fail to materialize and that Ottoman forces were falling back on all other fronts. The Young Turks in Constantinople had good reason to revisit the possibility of a separate peace. So did the easterner Lloyd George. Despite the promises of his generals finally to smash a hole in the German line, no breakthrough on the Western Front had occurred, only continual murder on a breathtaking scale. Meanwhile the Bolsheviks had pledged to take Russia out of the war altogether. Britain seemed no closer to winning the war in November 1917 than she had in November 1916, or 1915, or 1914.

Sometime toward the end of the second week in November, Basil Zaharoff learned that Abdul Kerim was on the move again, headed for Switzerland. He wrote to Caillard: "I will be there to meet him." This time Lloyd George empowered him to make the $2 million down payment. At this desperate juncture in the war, the prime minister would go far to bring the Turks to the negotiating table, farther by a great length than the Zionists would have wanted him to. Of course, he did not tell them.

PART V

Climax and Anticlimax

CHAPTER 22

The Ascendancy of Chaim Weizmann

THE BRITISH GOVERNMENT issued the Balfour Declaration in early November 1917. For the twelve months preceding that date, especially for the last six, the Zionists under Weizmann's leadership moved steadily, almost implacably, toward their goal. Obstacles they brushed aside, or overbore, or undermined. Yet Zionist victory never was preordained. To contemporaries, everything seemed to be up in the air almost until the last moment. Furthermore, under certain circumstances even Zionist implacability would have availed them little.

Think back to the fruitless meeting between representatives of the Conjoint Committee and the Zionists at Lucien Wolf's offices in 1915 and the correspondence that preceded and followed it, and to the "formula" Lucien Wolf then devised in hopes of stealing Zionist thunder but which the Foreign Office refused to endorse. Afterward contact between the two Jewish groups lapsed. Wolf's assimilationists on the Conjoint Committee focused on preparing for the postwar settlement, at which they hoped British and French leaders would demand abolition of the cruel disabilities from which Jews in Russia and Romania continued to suffer. They pressed the Foreign Office to promise to make such demands at the appropriate moment. The Zionists, of course, pushed forward with their campaign for a Jewish homeland in Palestine under British auspices. To an outsider, it might have seemed that the two movements would continue along separate and parallel tracks.

In fact the two groups rode upon converging rails. When unavoidable collision came, Zionists would insist that Jews constituted a distinct nationality and must therefore receive distinct privileges while building their homeland in Palestine; against them the assimilationists would insist with equal resolve that Jews cherished a belief system in common and nothing more. As Liberals, the assimilationists held the thought of special privileges for their coreligionists in Palestine, or anywhere else, as anathema.

Another point of convergence made the smashup more complete when it finally occurred: Both groups sought the ear of the Foreign Office with equal determination. Increasingly this aspect of their competition resembled a turf war. But with regard to the future of Palestine, there could be only one victor.

Imagine two railway carriages, one containing British Zionists, the other British advocates of Jewish assimilation, rumbling down the tracks at increasing speed, flashing past signposts warning of an impending collision. One signpost had come into view during the summer of 1916, with publication of *Zionism and the Jewish Future,* edited by Harry Sacher. This book aimed to acquaint non-Zionists with the general history and aims of the movement. Unobjectionable enough, one would have thought, except that two essays in particular deeply offended the advocates of assimilation. The first, by Weizmann, argued bluntly that no matter what success and prominence a Jew who attempts to assimilate achieves, he "is felt by the outside world to be still something different, still an alien." From this it followed that "the position of the emancipated Jew, though he does not realize it himself, is even more tragic than that of his oppressed brother." In other words, unlike the British or French Jew, the Russian or Romanian or Polish Jew, miserable as he might be, at least knew where he stood. Then in a later chapter, Moses Gaster dismissed those who refused to acknowledge that Judaism was the "expression of the religious consciousness of the national life of the Jew." He put his conclusion as bluntly as had Weizmann: "The claim to be Englishmen of the Jewish persuasion—that is, English by nationality and Jewish by faith—is an absolute self-delusion."

Open attacks couched in contemptuous or even pitying terms—the Cousinhood and its "foreign secretary," Lucien Wolf, were unaccustomed to such treatment. Worse than the tone, however, was the accusation of deluded incomprehension. Wolf understood Weizmann and Gaster to be threatening "the position of emancipated Jews as citizens of their native countries." He and Claude Montefiore, president of the Anglo-Jewish Association, published essays of rebuttal in *The Fortnightly Review* for November 1916 and *The Edinburgh Review* for April 1917. "How can a man belong to two nations at once?" Montefiore asked rhetorically in his article, the first of the two to appear. No man *could* belong equally and simultaneously to two nations. One who tried to only opened himself to the charge of divided loyalties. "No wonder that all anti-Semites are enthusiastic Zionists," Montefiore commented bitterly. Wolf dismissed Zionist claims with like decisiveness:

> The Zionist wing of the [Jewish nationalist] movement was never tired of claiming that it expressed an unbroken national yearning of over 2,000 years . . . The Jews were always primarily a religious people and their national life in Palestine was a phase of their greater history as a church. The religion could live without it, and the exiled people soon lost their political yearning and merged their hopes of national restoration with the Messianic teachings of their prophets and sages. The restoration they prayed for was the fulfillment of a Divine Scheme of human redemption.

Wolf's and Montefiore's articles were only the most visible of a number of published replies to Sacher's Zionist book by advocates of assimilation. The Zionists answered back in a further series of articles and pamphlets.

Both parties to the controversy considered themselves aggrieved. "So long as this [Zionist] view was put forward by obscure writers we took no notice," Wolf wrote to a friend in France. When leading Zionists such as Gaster and Weizmann made their charges, however, then the chief advocates of assimilation must reply. Meanwhile Sokolow was charging in a letter to an American Zionist that "the 'campaign' was started by an article in *The Fortnightly Review.*"

For every advance made by the Zionists, Wolf sought a counterstroke. Weizmann had been courting Rothschilds, especially Walter, who in 1915 inherited the baronetcy from Nathan, his father, and with it leadership of the family and of British Jewry, although he was mainly interested in zoology, ornithology, and entomology and seems to have been something of an eccentric. Weizmann made of this unlikely figure a committed Zionist. "As my sister-in-law will have told you I am arranging for an interview with Mr. Balfour," Walter Rothschild wrote to Weizmann in his large, scrawling, almost childish hand. "I fully realize the great importance of doing everything to further the Zionist cause with the Government in view of the persistant [sic] and purile [sic] opposition carried on by Lucien Wolff [sic] and the C[onjoint] C[ommittee]." Meanwhile Wolf was courting Walter's uncle Leopold, who counseled moderation, not attack. Wolf found himself constrained to write placatingly to *his* Rothschild: "I am afraid you imagine that I am eager for the fray but I assure you this is not so . . . but I do feel most strongly and most earnestly that, in the highest interests of the Jewish community, we cannot leave the situation as it is . . . The foolish things published by the Zionists . . . have seriously compromised the situation of the Jews all over the world." But Leopold was ill and would soon pass away. So another signpost flashed by, this one warning that the advocates of assimilation were losing their grip on Britain's most important Jewish family, while the Zionist grip was strengthening.

Weizmann, Wolf knew, had held meetings with mandarins including Balfour at the Foreign Office. Rumors probably reached him of Weizmann's meetings with Prime Minister Lloyd George as well. This was a game two could play, he must have thought, not least since he had been playing it long before Chaim Weizmann arrived upon the British scene. On January 30, 1917, he managed his own interview with Balfour, ostensibly to register Conjoint Committee discontent with the government for refusing to promise to take up the Jewish question at a peace conference after the war. It represented a grave defeat for the Conjoint Committee, and Wolf protested Britain's unwelcome decision to Balfour. But he took at least as much time to educate the foreign secretary on the relative strength of assimilationists and Zionists.

The Conjoint Committee, he explained to Balfour, was

> the only body authorized to speak for the Jewish communities, not only of the United Kingdom, but of the British Empire. It represented 150 congregations, including all the chief synagogues, in addition to the Anglo-Jewish Association and its many branches, and a very considerable section of the foreign Jewish community established in this country who were represented by the delegates of certain of the East End Synagogues, and more especially of the Friendly Societies, which alone have a membership of about 40,000.

By contrast, Zionism "was only a part of the Jewish National Movement, which was largely inspired by the general struggle for Nationalist autonomy and independence in Eastern Europe." Among West European Jews, including British Jews, Wolf insisted, "there was no specifically Jewish National Movement, and relatively very few Zionists."

So far in the interview Wolf had emphasized the turf-war aspect of his struggle against Zionism. But then he stressed that it was a battle over principles as well, and he placed the assimilationists' principles within Britain's liberal tradition. "We should rejoice if the Zionists made Palestine the seat of a flourishing and reputable Jewish community," he informed the foreign secretary. "We should have no objection if that Jewish community developed into a local Jewish nation and a Jewish state." What they did object to was Zionist subversion, as they understood it, of the twin principles of emancipation and assimilation elsewhere, as well as to the "proposal to give to the Jews of Palestine privileges not shared by the rest of the population of that country."

Balfour, as he took it all in, seemed to Wolf to be both patient and sympathetic. But perhaps, inadvertently, the foreign secretary revealed where his true sympathies lay. He strongly objected to anti-Semitism, Balfour told Wolf, but Jews "were exceedingly clever people who in spite of their oppression achieved a certain success which excited the jealousy and envy of the peoples among whom they lived." Conceivably this observation anticipates the view he would publicly express later: that recognition of Jewish nationality and establishment of a Jewish national home would raise the status, and therefore alleviate the treatment, of Jews everywhere. Here then we may notice another signpost warning of the future smashup; if so Wolf did not perceive it.

Additional signposts appeared, and these Lucien Wolf saw well enough. His counterpart in Paris, Jacques Bigart of the Alliance Israélite, reported that Nahum Sokolow (present in that city on the European mission we have treated previously) had said that the British government largely approved the Zionist program already—and so did the French. Alarmed, Wolf immediately contacted the Foreign Office. "The Presidents of the Conjoint Committee are anxious to be informed, if possible, whether this statement is accurate," he wrote. "I am to add that in the opinion of the Presidents . . . a great injustice would be done to the Anglo-Jewish community, and very serious mischief might result, if an agreement on the Palestine Question were concluded without their participation, more especially as the gentlemen with whom His Majesty's Government have so far been in negotiation are all foreign Jews, having no quality to speak for the native Jews of the United Kingdom." (Note that Wolf did not scruple to play the antiforeigner card. By now it had become a staple of the British anti-

Zionist repertoire.) He received in reply a mollifying response from Sir Ronald Graham. Wolf pressed for further assurances, which Robert Cecil provided him at a face-to-face meeting on May 8. But Cecil also warned Wolf against publicly quarreling with the Zionists. It would be inconvenient for the Foreign Office and would do the Anglo-Jewish community no good.

Was Cecil's warning a signpost too? Wolf remained uneasy. With the two presidents of the Conjoint Committee, David Lindo Alexander and Claude Montefiore, he plotted strategy. Montefiore thought he could approach Lord Milner of the War Cabinet, with whom he was personally acquainted. Wolf immediately endorsed this plan. Montefiore saw Milner on May 16. He argued the assimilationists' case and urged the government to stick with the Conjoint Committee because its British-born members better represented Jewish interests than foreign-born Zionists such as Weizmann, Sokolow, and Gaster. Milner tried to reassure him. The Foreign Office would consult the Conjoint Committee before deciding upon its policy for Palestine. On the other hand, he acknowledged that "Mr. Lloyd George was impressed by and sympathetic to many of the ideas of the Zionists," and he downplayed Conjoint Committee fears of the Zionist program: "Anti-Semitism and emancipation depended upon far other considerations than the erection of a small Jewish autonomous community in Palestine." As to whether Britain would grant special privileges to Jews in Palestine if she proclaimed a British protectorate there, he would not be pinned down.

Montefiore left the meeting not reassured. "I would beg of you," he reiterated to Milner the following day in a letter, "to trust your own fellow citizens who, at all events, are Englishmen through and through, and whose sons are serving in England's armies, rather than foreigners who have no love for England, and who, if the fortunes of war went wrong, would throw her over in a trice and hurry over to Berlin to join the majority of their colleagues." It was the chauvinist card yet again, but Milner did not mind. Montefiore "is an able, temperate and most honest man," he wrote to Robert Cecil, "and when he begged me almost passionately to be very careful how we commit ourselves to Sokoloff or Weizmann I am sure that he does so from an honest conviction that they are not reliable guides." But Milner too leaned toward the Zionists. Five months previously he had read Herbert Samuel's Zionist memorandum and wrote to him: "Among the possible alternatives which you review, the one which you yourself favor certainly appears to me the most attractive."

Three days later Wolf received a report of Chaim Weizmann's most recent address to a Zionist conference in London. "I am entitled to state in this assembly," Weizmann had announced, "that His Majesty's Government is ready to support our plans." This repetition of Sokolow's claims in Paris reinforced Wolf's conclusion that Zionism stood upon the verge of a great triumph. Only desperate measures could now rescue the position of the Conjoint Committee; the advocates of Jewish assimilation now must stake all or lose all.

On Tuesday, May 17, Wolf, Alexander, and Montefiore presided over a meeting of the Conjoint Committee to discuss the situation. The group decided "to issue a public statement of their attitude on the Zionist question." They drew it up "there and then . . . and approved [it] with only two dissentients." The statement hammered "the Zionist theory which regards all the Jewish communities of the world as constituting one homeless nationality, incapable of complete social and political identification with the nations among whom they dwell." It condemned the Zionist proposal "to invest the Jewish settlers in Palestine with certain special rights in excess of those enjoyed by the rest of the population, these rights to be embodied in a Charter, and administered by a Jewish Chartered Company." They further resolved to publish the statement not only in the Jewish press but in *The Times*. Those members of the Conjoint Committee, Wolf foremost among them, who claimed that the statement was couched in conciliatory language, were either fooling themselves or attempting to fool others.

Wolf left the meeting accompanied by Joseph H. Hertz, Britain's chief rabbi, who had attended by special invitation and had cast one of the two dissenting votes. The two men stood outside the Regent's Park tube station. As Wolf wrote afterward, Dr. Hertz reiterated "his regret at the action that had been resolved upon. He asked me whether anything could be done to stop it. I said . . . if Dr. Weizmann and Dr. Gaster could be induced to modify or otherwise explain away their published statements obviously there would be no longer any need for the action resolved upon." Hertz reported that Wolf went further: " 'And you would render a great service to the community' he told me, 'if you could induce them to do so.' " Acting upon this advice (although Wolf denied that he ever gave it), the chief rabbi contacted Leopold Greenberg, editor of *The Jewish Chronicle,* "because he was the only man who could bring pressure to bear upon the Zionist leaders." Alarmed, Greenberg got in touch with Wolf.

On Tuesday evening, May 22, the Zionist editor and the Jewish "foreign secretary" met for nearly three hours at Wolf's home. Over the course of a wide-ranging discussion, Greenberg argued that the quarrel between Zionists and anti-Zionists concerned the Anglo-Jewish community primarily and should not be aired outside it. Wolf replied that Zionists had published outside the Jewish press and that the Conjoint Committee, in defending itself, reserved the right to publish where it would. In fact, Wolf and his colleagues had just decided to give their statement to *The Times;* it was published there on Thursday, May 24. But Alexander refused to publish the statement in *The Jewish Chronicle* without Montefiore's explicit assent, and Wolf could not reach Montefiore on Wednesday the twenty-third, so it was too late for the statement to appear there since the *Chronicle* published on Fridays. That *The Jewish Chronicle* did not publish the statement, but *The Times* did, made a bad impression on the Jewish community as a whole and alienated Greenberg further, if that were possible. Nor can it have pleased Sir Robert Cecil, who had warned against a public dispute. That Wolf threw down the gauntlet anyway must be an index of his increasing alarm.

Publication of the Conjoint Committee's statement in *The Times* created a firestorm. Lord Walter Rothschild picked up his copy that morning, read the offending piece, and dashed off a response. He sent it to Weizmann: "If you approve please go and see the Editor personally and hand it to him. I fear it is not in very good style and not as clean as I could wish." Weizmann did better than that. Not only did he polish Rothschild's letter, which *The Times* published on Monday, May 28, but in his own more formidable prose he took on the committee as well: "It may possibly be inconvenient to certain individual Jews that the Jews constitute a nationality. Whether the Jews do constitute a nationality is, however, not a matter to be decided by the convenience of this or that individual. It is strictly a question of fact." The chief rabbi sent in a letter too: "I cannot allow your readers to remain under the misconception that the said statement represents in the least the views held either by Anglo-Jewry as a whole or by the Jewries of the Oversea Dominions."

To Wolf, Alexander, and Montefiore, *The Times* had seemed a natural outlet for expression of the views of the Cousinhood. It was the newspaper of record for England's governing class, of which they formed at least a tangential section. They may even have hoped that *The Times* would endorse their position, but if so they miscalculated. The same Wickham Steed who a few weeks later would warn Weizmann of Henry Morgenthau's pending journey to Gibraltar wrote *The Times* leader for May 29. He endorsed the Zionist movement: "It had fired with a new ideal millions of poverty-stricken Jews . . . It has tended to make Jews proud of their race." And he condemned the Conjoint Committee's statement in Weizmann's own words: "It may possibly be inconvenient to certain individual Jews that the Jews do constitute a nationality. The question is one of fact, not argument."

Other newspapers took a similar line. "Does not the Jew already stamp himself as a stranger and an alien?" asked *The Glasgow Herald.* "Whether it be his religion or his inextinguishable pride of race or his hopes and dreams in the fulfillment of prophecy is he not now 'a stranger and a so-journer' in our midst? The barrier is there and whether he has once more a land of his own . . . or whether he remains as he is . . . it does not seem to us that his status would undergo visible alteration in the near future." Even *The Nation,* an organ of the nonsocialist Left in which Lucien Wolf usually found comfort, failed to comfort him this time. Editors of *The Nation* did not actually endorse the Zionist position but nor did they completely endorse assimilation. Rather they cherished "the hope that for the sake of the very numerous body of Jews who are not and do not want to be assimilated and absorbed, an international regime may be possible in Palestine which would secure a cultural focus for Hebrew Nationalism."

Within the Anglo-Jewish community itself, debate stoked by the Zionists raged fiercely. Samuel Cohen of Manchester, a provincial vice-president of the English Zionist Federation, proudly claimed to be a chief stoker. "It was . . . thanks to the interest I have taken and the energy I have displayed that the Board [of Deputies] . . . were bombarded with letters of protest from the Synagogues and Societies all over England," he boasted to Weizmann. The journal *Palestine,* turning things upside down as only the clever Harry Sacher could, accused Wolf and his partners of being pro-German in thought if not in deed:

> The ordinary non-Jew knows that the Jew whether he admits or denies the existence of a Jewish nation is nevertheless distinguishable and distinct from the non-Jew . . . He does not however deduce from that the conclusion that the Jew is unfitted to be a citizen . . . and when Messrs. Montefiore and Alexander express the fear that he might they are betraying what must be called a Prussian conception of the State. The Prussian idea . . . is that all citizens must be as nearly as possible alike in their outlook upon the world . . . This . . . as we are all beginning to see is the root cause of the war.

Leopold Greenberg, furious that Wolf had ignored his plea to keep the quarrel with Zionism within the family, as it were, wrote more ferociously still. "All that the Committee have achieved is to exhibit the Jewish people in its worst aspect—in a state of strife and disunion—and to injure, *pro tanto,* the Jewish prestige. It is a sorry result but one for which they should be quickly brought to account." Even Israel Zangwill, who was making his way back toward the Zionist position, condemned the committee's "manifesto" in a private letter to Wolf. Its publication had been "a grave error . . . Palestine at your price is not worth having, and is certainly nothing to be thankful for."

On June 2, at a meeting of the council of the Anglo-Jewish Association, one of the two pillars upon which the Conjoint Committee rested, Moses Gaster mounted a Zionist attack: He moved a vote of no confidence in the AJA leaders. Gaster no longer held the chief position among Zionists— Weizmann had that now; but he delivered a stem-winder of a speech, demonstrating the histrionic skills that once had brought him to the fore. The association "had declared the Zionists to be faithless to their past. How dared they take their name and glory away? They were a nation . . . The statement which had been published would be quoted over and over again as if they intended to justify oppression . . . It was an irreparable blunder that such a manifesto should have been given to the world." But, the advocates of assimilation gave as good as they got. Montefiore mocked Gaster: "The most curious thing about the Zionists was that directly the least thing was said in criticism of their acts they set up the most fearful howl and complained bitterly, as though they were a privileged body." Sir Philip Magnus, MP, insisted that advocates of assimilation did not oppose establishment of Jewish colonies in Palestine, only establishment of Jewish rule. Gaster and his friends should accept "the formula put forward by the Conjoint Committee and . . . endeavor to establish in Jerusalem a great center of Jewish learning and culture." The *haham* saw which way the wind was blowing. He withdrew his motion.

Two weeks later, however, on June 15, at the most heavily attended assembly in its history to date, the second pillar of the Conjoint Committee, the Board of Deputies, collapsed entirely. The board had before it the following motion of censure:

> That this Board having considered the views of the Conjoint Committee as promulgated in the communication published in *The Times* of the 24th May, 1917, expresses profound disapproval of such views and dissatisfaction at the publication thereof, and declares that the Conjoint Committee has

lost the confidence of the Board and calls upon its representatives on the Conjoint Committee to resign their appointment forthwith.

One by one the censurers spoke. The statement had been "issued at an inopportune time," said one. "It was disingenuous in origin, defamatory in effect, and altogether unrepresentative." Was there so much trouble "in the community that *The Times* should be the mouthpiece of Anglo-Jewry while the Anglo-Jewish press had been ignored?" wondered another. A third charged that publishing in *The Times* had been "a case of super *chutzpa*." A fourth: "If any man of honor, whether pro-Zionist or anti-Zionist, voted against a resolution of censure he did not deserve to be a member of the Board representing Anglo-Jewry." Although most speakers focused upon the impropriety of the Conjoint Committee airing Jewish linen in public, Lord Rothschild attacked a main plank of the assimilationists' position: "I have always thought that such a Home [a Jewish Palestine under British protection] was only meant for those people who could not or did not desire to consider themselves citizens of the country in which they lived, and I can truly say that the National Zionists have done nothing, and would never do anything, inconsistent with the status of the true British citizen of which I am proud to be one, just as proud as I am of being a Jew."

The supporters of the Conjoint Committee, including Alexander, Magnus, and Wolf himself, ably defended their conduct and outlook, but the vote at the end went against them, 56-51. Wolf would claim that this tally showed how nearly even were the two sides. The scholar who has studied the event most closely points out that the vote reflected provincial jealousy of London leaders and resentment at their high-handed ways more than support of the Zionist position per se. What mattered at the time, however, was perception, and here nuance did not apply. The officers of the board understood themselves to have been defeated and surrendered their posts. Lord Rothschild understood them to have been defeated too. "I write to tell you that we beat them by 56–51 and Mr. Alexander . . . and the rest have all resigned," he reported to Weizmann. "I have written to Mr. Balfour asking for an interview for yourself and me for Tuesday or Wednesday and I shall be able to prove to him that the majority of Jews are in favor of Zionism." Other leading Zionists too perceived the episode as a defeat for the advocates of assimilation. Sacher crowed, "It is a great victory."

With support from the Board of Deputies withdrawn, there could be no Conjoint Committee. This the Foreign Office recognized at once. "This vote signifies the dissolution of the Conjoint Committee," noted Sir Ronald Graham, "and it will no longer be necessary to consult that body."

The smashup had taken place at last. Jewish anti-Zionists had been deprived of their most powerful instrument. Weizmann could have been excused for thinking that the last Jewish obstacle to the great goal finally had been removed.

But he would have been wrong. The Conjoint Committee was dead, but Weizmann's own colleagues remained disputatious as ever. He would have to make them realize, once and for all, that they could not do without him. And even then, before he could finally grasp the nettle and pluck the rose, he would have to overcome, too, his own growing desire to escape from their ceaseless carping by simply throwing up his hands and walking away.

British Zionists argued over at least four major issues. One we have discussed already: the question of a separate peace with Turkey, which pitted Sacher and Simon in particular against Weizmann and most of his colleagues. Another we have also glimpsed: Despite Weizmann's wishes, the British Palestine Committee in Manchester would not wear a bridle fashioned by the Foreign Office. This issue reemerged in early May 1917, just as Lucien Wolf was nerving himself for his ill-fated showdown with Zionism. The BPC organ *Palestine* printed two articles condemning international control of the promised land even though its editors knew that the Foreign Office and, therefore the London Zionists, wished them to keep quiet on the subject. When he saw the articles, Weizmann hit the roof. He threatened to withhold a £500 subsidy for the journal. He accused one BPC member, Israel Sieff, of practicing mere "hobby Zionism."

Sieff, deeply wounded, climbed down immediately: "I intend to send in my resignation to the B.P.C.," he wrote to his leader. "It almost breaks my heart . . . [but] I dare not imperil the cause . . . I am desolated that it should have meant an addition to your burden of anxieties and worries." Harry Sacher would not back down, however. "I don't mind the charge of 'indiscipline.' It's the kind of charge that leaves my withers unwrung." For him the issue encapsulated the essential contradiction between his approach and Weizmann's. The latter was "determined to tie Zionism up with the F.O. and to take anything the F.O. is graciously pleased to grant." Weizmann had become more British than Jewish, Sacher charged. He, however, would remain independent.

The third issue dividing Weizmann's Zionists was the proposal to create a Jewish regiment to fight in Palestine. This scheme found its fiercest proponent in a young Jewish Russian journalist who had made his way to Britain shortly after the outbreak of war, Ze'ev (Vladimir) Jabotinsky. For him, the idea grew naturally from his prewar activities organizing Jewish defense leagues in Russia. At first Weizmann professed neutrality on the subject. But he grew close to Jabotinsky. After a meeting with Lloyd George in April 1917, he realized the government favored creation of a Jewish regiment too. Shortly after the meeting Weizmann came out in support.

Some British Jews saw a myriad of difficulties here. If a distinctly Jewish regiment appeared in Syria to fight the Turks, it might lead to reprisals carried out by Ottoman troops against Jewish civilians. Moreover, who in Britain would join? Most Jewish Britons of military age already served in their country's armed forces. The prospect of combing them out and placing them in separate Jewish battalions offended the advocates of Jewish assimilation—and even many Zionists. Some twenty thousand Russian Jewish immigrants of military age, hitherto exempt from conscription, lived in the East End of London. Perhaps they could be induced to join the regiment. In fact, such men would not join any section of any army that fought on the same side as the tsar. Even after the Russian Revolution overthrew the tsar's anti-Semitic regime, these immigrants remained unenthusiastic about the war. Should they be compelled to enlist in the regiment on pain of deportation? The government thought so, but many Jews, including many Zionists (Weizmann among them), could not stomach forcing such a choice upon them.

Men like Sacher in Manchester and Simon in London opposed the scheme for yet another reason. They thought that in advocating a Jewish regiment, Weizmann once again was sacrificing Jewish needs to British needs. Simon wrote to Nahum Sokolow: "We Zionists are the heirs and the keepers of the great Jewish tradition, and we are false to our trust, and show ourselves incapable of realizing its true worth if we allow ourselves to get into a frame of mind in which the rightness of our cause can be imagined to depend in any way on the success or failure of a petty military scheme—and a scheme which is in no sense our own." Sacher and Simon thought Weizmann had been seduced by the "jingo" Jabotinsky. "Chaim Weizmann has caught from Jabotinsky the disease of Cadetism, that's the long and the short of it," Sacher wrote. When Weizmann would not disavow the regiment, Simon resigned from the Zionist Political Committee in protest.

He rejoined it, however, when Weizmann asked him to. The Zionist leader could turn upon his difficult colleagues the same charm and persuasive powers that he employed when dealing with the great and the grand.

Nevertheless his leadership style often left much to be desired. He could be dictatorial. He could sweetly take the pulse of his associates and then ignore it. Here is the fourth issue bedeviling British Zionists at this critical stage in their history: the personality of Chaim Weizmann himself.

Weizmann was like a great juggler, keeping half a dozen balls in the air at once. During 1917 he courted the Foreign Office and Sykes and Balfour and Lloyd George. He courted Lord Rothschild. He confronted and vanquished Lucien Wolf and the Conjoint Committee. He kept tabs on Sokolow's mission to France and Italy. He traveled to Gibraltar to defeat Henry Morgenthau. He was dealing simultaneously with other matters that we have not even looked at: For example, what should be his group's relations with the representatives of international Zionism, with American and Russian Zionists, with Zionists in Palestine? He was carrying on work of national importance in the laboratory. No man engaged at such a pitch would have responded well to an unending stream of criticism from his closest friends and associates.

On August 16, 1917, the same Samuel Cohen of Manchester who claimed to have stirred up the synagogues against the Conjoint Committee wrote to Weizmann: "You act on your own without acquainting or consulting any of your colleagues . . . it is time that this state of affairs should change and be improved." That day the EZF executive council, of which Weizmann was president, convened its regular monthly meeting. A London delegate made a motion censuring the president for lack of leadership on the question of the Jewish regiment: Most Jews opposed it; Weizmann would not. Something snapped, and he resigned the presidency on the spot. To Israel Sieff that night, he declared that British Zionism was bankrupt. The next day he wrote to Sokolow that he was quitting not only the EZF but also the Zionist Political Committee, which had been formed by his friends largely to ease his burden of work and to provide him with a sounding board.

Faced with the possibility of Zionism sans Chaim Weizmann, his colleagues almost unanimously beseeched him to reconsider. Even Leon Simon, one of the chief critics, did so: "I think it no less my right than my duty to ask you as a friend not to give up the struggle." Thus reassured, Weizmann appeared to relent; he continued to attend meetings. But the air had not yet sufficiently cleared. At a meeting of the Zionist Political Committee held on September 4, the question of the Jewish Regiment was aired yet again. Yet again Weizmann's attitude came in for criticism. Yet again Weizmann declared that he could no longer tolerate such distrust. He wrote that night to Sokolow, "The atmosphere surrounding me is full of suspicion, envy, and [a] certain fanaticism, in the presence of which any fruitful work is impossible to me."

Once more the confidence-restoring letters poured in, begging him to reconsider. Perhaps he would have done so in any event, or perhaps he intended merely to impress upon his colleagues his own indispensability. He wrote afterward to C. P. Scott that his threats to resign "had the effect of sobering them down," as if that had been his intention all along. Or possibly an extraordinary letter from Ahad Ha'am proved decisive. This remarkable figure had remained in the background, but the letter he wrote to Weizmann on September 5, 1917, demonstrates that his voice and influence, whenever he chose to exercise them, must have been powerful, perhaps even decisive.

> For the first time in all the years of our friendship I take the liberty of speaking to you not only as a friend . . . but like an older and more experienced comrade who was in the fight when you were still a schoolboy and who probably directly or indirectly influenced to a certain extent the molding of your opinion in Jewish problems. Now in this capacity I must say that what you intend doing is literally a "stab in the back" to the whole Zionist cause . . . You are too clever to fail to see that the effect of your so-called "resignation" would be the lowering of the prestige of the Zionist representatives in the eyes of those on whom at this critical moment depends the fate of our cause. It is not because you are absolutely indispensable. No man is absolutely indispensable. Had you left the work for some reasons beyond your control, such as serious illness or an accident, that would have been bad and harmful enough. Yet the work could have been carried on by someone else and would not have been shaken in its very foundations. [Or] . . . had you from the start appeared before those in power as the elected representative of the Zionist organization, as its "diplomatic" representative (as it was later the case with Sokolow) your "resignation" would not have caused great surprise either, since they are used to the principle of elected representation and would have found nothing odd in the replacement of one person by another . . .
>
> Your case however is quite exceptional. You did not start as an elected representative of a "collective" unit but as an individual Zionist. Your personal qualities coupled with favorable conditions in a comparatively short period of time have caused a

great number of influential people to regard you as something of a symbol of Zionism. Now suddenly out of the blue you announce that you have resigned. Who did you tender your resignation to? Who were those who elected you to have now the right to accept your resignation? You were elected by the circumstances and the circumstances alone will dismiss you in God's good time, when either complete success or complete failure will render your further work unnecessary. Until then you cannot leave your post without creating a most disastrous impression about the Zionists and Zionism in the minds of those with whom you have been in contact until now . . .

There is of course no need to add that from a personal point of view such an act would be moral suicide. That however is your own affair and you are perfectly aware of it.

Did this letter have a chastening effect? It is hard to imagine otherwise. Did Weizmann's threats to resign chasten the majority of his colleagues? Undoubtedly they had. For whatever combination of reasons, he retracted his threat to resign next day and would not broach the subject again during our period.

CHAPTER 23

Lawrence and the Arabs on the Verge

TODAY WE CAN SEE that the Zionists and the Arabs were entering the home stretch of a historic race for position in Palestine. But during the six months prior to release of the Balfour Declaration on November 2, 1917, neither party really understood that they were in a race at all, and both parties incorrectly identified their adversary. Zionists in Britain fixed their gaze upon Whitehall, hoping that the use of skillful diplomacy would persuade the British government to support them. Of King Hussein and his armies in the Hejaz and Syria, they rarely thought. Meanwhile the Arabs sought to improve their military capacity and effectiveness against the Ottomans, with British aid. If they thought themselves to be in a race, it was not against the Zionists but against the French, who they knew had designs upon Syria. They believed the British would help them to establish control over that country, including most probably a good bit of Palestine. Zionism they rarely considered.

British officers on the spot who knew something about the Sykes-Picot Agreement may also have thought a race was taking place between the Arabs and the French, with the track tilted in favor of the latter and with Syria the prize. They did not consider Palestine, however, because whatever Sykes and Picot had envisioned, they aspired to assert British influence there after the war. Some British officers undoubtedly hoped the Arabs would win their race against France, or would at least gain meaningful authority in the part of Syria that lay east of Palestine and south of Damascus. That would constitute a buffer between a British-dominated Mesopotamia and a French-dominated Syria and Lebanon and it would be more or less under their control. But they were not yet thinking much about Zionism.

At least one British officer, however, may have seen a little further. He even may have hoped the Arabs would establish something more than a mere puppet buffer state.

It seems likely that T. E. Lawrence had developed genuine sympathy for Arab nationalist aspirations by early 1917. He saw too that they would run up against Zionist, French, and British aspirations. He had met Aaron Aaronsohn in Cairo and learned of Zionist plans for Palestine. These troubled him. He knew enough to suspect that McMahon's correspondence with Hussein contradicted aspects of the agreement that Sykes had negotiated with Picot, even though he did not yet know the agreement's details. Like many British officers in the Middle East, Lawrence had concluded, even with only partial knowledge, that Sykes had ceded too much territory to France. In other words, even before he knew its details, he objected to the Sykes-Picot Agreement both for Arab nationalist and for British imperialist reasons.

In July 1917 he interviewed King Hussein and became painfully aware that the latter misunderstood British intentions for Mesopotamia, as well as French plans for the Syrian coastal region. But Lawrence had concluded long since that if Hussein wished to stake any convincing claim to any part of Syria, his troops, led by his son Feisal, must enter Damascus before the troops of any other country did. One night at Wejh he and Feisal and some of the latter's advisers discussed the matter. "We all swore to not go to Mecca till after we had seen Damascus," Lawrence recorded in his diary. But the evidence about his attitude is ambiguous, as is most evidence about this extraordinary figure. Some months after making this pledge, he wrote to Mark Sykes (in a letter never delivered):

> I quite recognize that we may have to sell our small friends [Arabs] to pay our big friends [the international Zionist movement and France] or sell [to France] our future security in the Near East to pay for our present victory in Flanders. If you will tell me once more what we have to give the Jews and what we have to give the French I'll do everything I can to make it easy for us.

He was, he added, "strongly pro-British and also pro-Arab." But he increasingly came to realize that he could not be both, and the realization wore him down.

Lawrence had met Sykes in Cairo in early May 1917, when the latter arrived on the joint mission with Picot, the one that led King Hussein to conclude erroneously that the French would treat Syria's coastal region in the same manner that he thought the British would treat Mesopotamia—that is to say, as temporarily occupied territory, generously paid for. This appears to have been when Lawrence concluded, to the contrary, that the Arabs must stir themselves if they did not wish to lose Syria altogether. Shortly after the meeting with Sykes, he embarked from Wejh on the famous expedition north into Syria dramatized in David Lean's celebrated film. Accompanying him were, among others, seventeen Ageyli soldiers from the towns of central Arabia, and most notably, Auda abu Tayi, sheikh of a section of a northern tribe, the Howeitat, which, with Auda's help, Lawrence intended to mobilize against the Ottomans.

Auda abu Tayi is the fabled figure portrayed by Anthony Quinn in the movie: a warrior who had once reputedly cut the beating heart from a dying enemy and bitten into it, and who had killed seventy-five men in battle—not including Turks, whom he considered not worth counting. He possessed the ravaged face of a tragedian with "large eloquent eyes, like black velvet in richness," Lawrence thought, and a mind "stored with poems of old raids and epic tales of fights." More important, Auda believed in the creation of the greater Arab kingdom envisioned by King Hussein. Lawrence valued him less for his remarkable personal qualities than because he could swing an important tribe, the Howeitat, behind Hussein's revolt.

Their joint expedition has assumed mythic status. It had several purposes: to recruit to Feisal's cause northern Arab tribes in addition to the Howeitat; to make contact with the surviving Syrian revolutionaries in Damascus and perhaps spur them to activity (to facilitate this goal a member of the al-Bakri family accompanied them); to further disrupt Turkish communications with Medina by destroying track along the Hejaz Railway. But by far the most important goal was to capture the tiny but strategically crucial port of Aqaba, at the northernmost point of the Gulf of Aqaba, which extends from the northern end of the Red Sea like a finger pointing farther north into Syria. Famously, the Ottoman defenders of the port kept powerful guns facing the water, protecting against French and British warships. Lawrence and Auda (which man devised the strategy is unclear) intended to surprise them by attacking by land from the east, with Howeitat and other tribal soldiers, although to come out on the right side would require an epic trek through the waterless and broiling desert. Once captured, however, Aqaba could become the jumping-off point for further northern campaigns. The Arab forces engaged in them could constitute the right wing of a largely British army that, as Lawrence correctly anticipated, soon would advance northward into Palestine. As the Arabs moved north from Aqaba in parallel to the British, they could assert control, by virtue of military occupation, of a good part of Jordan and Syria, northern Palestine included. Which aspect of this strategy lay uppermost in Lawrence's mind remains uncertain.

On the afternoon of May 9, 1917, Lawrence and his party left Wejh and headed north into the desert. A report among the papers of General Gilbert Clayton (entitled "Notes on Capt. Lawrence's Journey") provides a bare-bones summary of what followed:

> They marched to Abu Raga where the force was increased to 36 men and thence to the Railway at km. 810.5 which they dyna-mited on 19th May . . . He went west . . . to Ras Baalbek on June 10th and dynamited a small plate girder bridge there . . . From Um Keis they went to Ifdein (Mafrak on map) the first station below Deraa and destroyed a stretch of curved rails . . . thence to Atwi where they failed to take the station but killed 3 out of the 5 of the garrison, captured a large flock of sheep and destroyed a telegraph party of 4 men repairing the wire. They also dyna-mited a stretch of line.

And so they continued, blowing up or digging up railway track, hitting Turkish outposts in deadly lightning attacks and then vanishing back into the desert, recruiting additional members of various tribes until "from Guweira they marched on to El Kethira (wiping out a post of 3 officers and 140 men) and thence to El Khadra in the North of Wadi Ithm, where the Aqaba garrison surrendered at discretion."

This utilitarian account doubtless served its purpose as a military report but perforce left out much interesting material. For example, on May 24, as the scorching sun beat down mercilessly and the heat reflected upward from the desert floor so that the men upon their camels could not tell whether it came from above or below but only how much they suffered from it; as the horizon was dissolved in shimmering mirage so that men could not estimate distance either before or behind; and as each man retreated deep within himself simply in order to endure the brutal day, Lawrence suddenly realized that he could not see his personal servant, Gasim. The man had fallen behind and must be lost—a certain death sentence unless someone quickly rescued him. Lawrence wheeled his camel around and began retracing his steps, alone now in the furnace, with only a compass to guide him. After an hour and a half, he found Gasim "nearly blinded . . . his black mouth gaping open." But he was still alive; Lawrence had saved him.

Another occasion, at night this time: Lawrence and his companions sat by the fire "while the coffee maker boiled up his coffee . . . when there came a volley from the shadowy dunes east of us and one of the Ageyli toppled forward." Death could come unexpectedly and in an instant. And not only from enemy guns—poisonous snakes proved equally dangerous, if slower: "Twice puff-adders came twisting into the alert ring of our debating coffee-circle. Three of our men died of bites; four recovered after great fear and pain and a swelling of the poisoned limb."

Perhaps the most interesting aspect of this fabled adventure took place inside Lawrence's head. "I could see," he wrote in *Seven Pillars of Wisdom,* his famous book about the Arabian campaign, that

> if we won the war the promises to the Arabs [made by McMahon in the correspondence with Hussein] were dead paper. Had I been an honorable adviser I would have sent my men home, and not let them risk their lives for such stuff. Yet the Arab inspiration was our main tool in winning the Eastern war. So I assured them that England kept her word in letter and spirit. In this comfort they performed their fine things: but, of course, instead of being proud of what we did together I was continually and bitterly ashamed.

He finally attempted to resolve this terrible contradiction, at least to his own satisfaction. "I vowed to make the Arab Revolt the engine of its own success, as well as handmaid to our Egyptian campaign," he records in *Seven Pillars.* He "saw the liberation of Syria happening in steps, of which Aqaba was the indispensable first." Successive steps, he now realized, must be taken rapidly thereafter. But first he must ride alone much farther north, indeed all the way to Damascus and beyond, to spy out the land and to plot what those steps should be. "Also," he wrote in his book, "a rash adventure suited my abandoned mood." But at the time, in a message to General Clayton (also never delivered), he wrote: "I've decided to go off alone to Damascus hoping to get killed on the way. For all sakes try and clear this show up before it goes further. We are getting them to fight for us on a lie and I can't stand it."

In this frame of mind, Lawrence embarked upon a journey more extraordinary than the one from which he had just taken temporary leave. His route led from Wadi Sirhan, home base of the Howeitat and their romantic chieftain, Auda, all the way to Ayn al Barida, 130 miles northeast of Damascus, where he made contact with another tribe, the Wuld Ali, whose support would be helpful when it came time to engage the Turks there. From this location he traveled westward into modern Lebanon and then south, to the very gates of Damascus itself. There he met Ali Riza al Rikabi, the Arab nationalist general who had kept his true beliefs secret from the Turks and who had been entrusted by them with defense of this most important Syrian city. The general warned Lawrence that Damascus would not rise up, which would only have confirmed the Englishman in his belief that Feisal's army must make those next steps north if they were to seize control of their homeland. Next he rode south, making contact with the leader of the Druze people and then, more important, with the sheikh of the powerful north Arabian Rwala tribe. He returned to Wadi Sirhan on June 18, having been gone nearly two weeks. He had exorcised the suicidal mood, if ever it had truly existed, with constructive work.

Finally the advance began. It took place in stages: from Wadi Sirhan to Bair; from Bair to El-Jefer; from that town to Ghadir el Haj, where they carried out extensive demolition work on the railway line; and then to "the low rolling grass-covered hills that flank each side of the Aqaba road near Ain Aba el-Lissan." An Ottoman detachment occupied this town and had to be disposed of before the march could continue. Lawrence and his men held the high ground and pinned them there for a day, but "it was terribly hot—hotter than ever before I had felt it in Arabia." Even the hardened Bedouin tribesmen could not take it "and crawled or had to be thrown under rocks to recover in their shade."

At dusk Auda broke the impasse with fifty horsemen in a wild dash down the hill into the teeth of the Ottoman guns. The Turkish defenders broke, just as Lawrence and another detachment rolled in upon them from the flank. A massacre ensued: three hundred Ottoman soldiers dead in just a few minutes. The Arabs lost two men. For once Lawrence wrote of himself not as the hero but as a sort of goat. At the height of the charge, firing wildly, he had shot his own camel in the back of the head. It had fallen as if poleaxed; he had flown from the saddle over its ears and landed hard, and then lay stunned for the remainder of the battle. By contrast, Lawrence records, the Turks had shot Auda's horse out from under him; their bullets had smashed his binoculars, passed through his holster and scabbard, but never touched his body. He had taken part in the bloody work from beginning to end. We do not know how many Auda killed in this battle, perhaps because, as noted, he did not bother to count his victims if they were Turkish.

Lawrence and his army collected capitulations as they marched south toward a still-unsuspecting Aqaba, finally accepting the surrender of the port's only defensive outpost on the landward side. As they approached the town itself, "all the Turks we met were most happy to surrender, holding up their arms and crying 'Muslim, Muslim' as soon as they saw us." So the epic journey ended on July 4, 1917, with Arab troops splashing in the warm salt water of the gulf, and Lawrence already pondering the next move north—but whether primarily in aid of Arab nationalism or British imperialism, we still do not know.

So: As the Zionists in London moved during the spring and early summer of 1917 to assert control over the British Jewish community and to influence the Foreign Office, the Arabs pushed north from Wejh up to Aqaba. They intended to head into Syria proper and claim their homeland—almost certainly they thought that meant claiming Palestine. Had they reached Damascus before November 2, 1917, it is an interesting point whether the British would have felt confident enough about the future of that territory to release the Balfour Declaration at all. The tragedy from the Arab point of view was that the war in the East moved at a significantly slower pace than diplomacy and politicking now moved in the imperial metropolis. It took Feisal much longer to blow up the Hejaz Railway, raise the tribes, help defeat the Ottoman Army, and enter Damascus than it took for Weizmann to arrange meetings with British politicians and vanquish the Conjoint Committee. Feisal did not know that a Balfour Declaration was being contemplated; he moved as fast as he could. The British seemed happy to help, but they had a very different end in view than he did. In any event, Feisal did not move fast enough. And meanwhile poor Lawrence of Arabia, Britain's man on the spot, tore his soul into pieces trying to juggle his country's and Arab interests.

With Aqaba secured, Lawrence drew up a plan for those next quick steps. He envisioned seven roughly simultaneous attacks upon Ottoman positions, to take place in late August. One force would capture the fertile area east and southeast of the Dead Sea. Four separate forces would attack along a 350-mile stretch of the Hejaz Railway between Maan (in modern southern Jordan) and Hama (one hundred miles north of Damascus, in Syria). Then the Druze, with whose leader Lawrence had recently conferred, would descend upon Dara, where the east-west and north-south railways of the region intersected. Yet another force would attack that east-west railway a bit west of Dara in the Yarmuk Valley. The track here represented the Ottoman lifeline into Palestine. Lawrence intended to sever it. He hoped additional Arab tribes would be inspired by such a flurry of offensive activity to rise against Turkish rule and that the culmination would be the occupation of Damascus by Arab troops. If Arab soldiers under Feisal had somehow occupied Damascus before November 2, 1917, and thus perhaps caused the British government to withhold the Balfour Declaration, then Middle Eastern and even world history might have unwound very differently.

The former Oxford student turned desert fighter and military strategist made yet another hard journey by camel, this time from Aqaba to Cairo. There he outlined his plan to General Sir Edmund Allenby, who had recently replaced General Sir Archibald Murray as commander in chief of British forces in Egypt. Allenby, fresh from the front in France, "sat in his chair looking at me—not straight as his custom was, but sideways, puzzled. He did not ask many questions, nor talk much, but studied the map . . . 'Well, I will do for you what I can,' he said finally." What he did not tell Lawrence was that he thought he could use him, and London's growing appreciation of him, to pry men and equipment from the westerner General Robertson, chief of the Imperial General staff (CIGS). "The scheme proposed by Captain Lawrence can only be realized in conjunction with the prosecution of offensive operations by me in this theater," Allenby warned. But he would not be ready to advance into Palestine until mid-September. Thus, the wheels of war were grinding slowly, from the Arab nationalist point of view.

Predictably, Robertson stalled. Convinced that the war could be won only in the West, he begrudged sending Allenby anyone or anything at all. He confided to a friend that he could not stand men who were "dying to go to Jerusalem and Damascus and other places." He thought Allenby should remain on the defensive in Egypt and that British occupation of Palestine would serve no useful purpose. Even the War Cabinet, desperate for a victory in the Middle East since it could not find one in the West, failed to move him. "It is necessary," the War Cabinet instructed, "to strike the Turk as hard as possible during the coming Autumn and Winter." Still he procrastinated. It took Lloyd George himself to get things moving. British heavy guns should be sent from the Western Front to Egypt, he directed the CIGS. "There they could . . . be employed to reinforce General Allenby and enable him to deal the Turks . . . a crushing blow." By now it was September 22, and in the meantime Allenby had postponed his offensive another month.

Lawrence continued with his raiding parties north of Aqaba. He seems to have rethought his schedule of Arab liberation, for we have no evidence that after the initial meeting with Allenby he pressed further for its fulfillment. Perhaps he had concluded that the timetable was unrealistic. The war moved at a pace of its own. He was aware of Zionism but not of its rapid advance in London. Anyway he had developed a malevolent genius for blowing up track and trains, and during the fall of 1917 he gave this talent full scope. Here is an example of his work, in his own words, written at the time for the *Arab Bulletin,* not polished for his book, which came after the war.

In the afternoon of September 18 I laid an electric mine, in about five hours work, over a culvert at kilo. 587, on the outside of a curve towards some low hills, 300 yards away where Stokes and Lewis guns could be placed to rake the lengths of either north- or south-bound trains . . .

At 1 P.M. a train of two engines and two box-wagons came up slowly from the south, shooting hard at us from loopholes and positions on the carriage roofs. As it passed I exploded the mine under the second engine . . . the Lewis guns cleared the roof meanwhile. The mine derailed the front engine, smashing its cab and tender, destroyed the second engine altogether and blew in the culvert. The first wagon upended into the whole and the succeeding ones were shaken up. The shock affected the Turks, and the Arabs promptly charged up to within twenty yards and fired at the wagons which were not armored. The Turks got out on the far side and took refuge in the hollow of the bank (about eleven feet high) and fired between the wheels at us. Two Stokes bombs at once fell among them there and turned them out towards some rough country 200 yards N.E. of the line. On their way there the Lewis gun killed all but about twenty of them, and the survivors threw away their rifles and fled . . . The action took ten minutes.

This was a not-atypical engagement for Lawrence. He returned to Aqaba for a few days, then headed out again on September 27. This time his mines "shattered the firebox of the locomotive (No. 153 Hejaz), burst many of the tubes, threw the l.c. cylinder into the air, cleaned out the cab, warped the frame, bent the two near driving wheels and broke their axles." The mines killed twenty Turks as well.

Slowly—too slowly from the Arab nationalist point of view (but the Arab nationalists did not know it)—Allenby prepared his invasion of Palestine. The Arabs moved slowly as well, at least in comparison with the Zionists in London. Hussein's sons Ali and Abdullah maintained the siege of Medina, which meant they occupied the sidelines. Feisal, who had moved up to Aqaba, built his forces for the northern campaign, but slowly too. He would not rely upon Hejazi tribesmen to take Syria, but rather upon the Syrians themselves—some three thousand Turkish conscripts captured by the British, who had switched sides along with their officers—to form the "Arab Legion." They trained in Egypt, however, and would not arrive in Aqaba until November. Some of their officers had been active in the secret society al-Ahd. They did not get along with the Iraqi officers whom Feisal also employed. Indeed it is a fair point whether they cared about the great Arab empire that Hussein expected to found, or only for an independent Syria. Like the Zionists in London, they sensed the tectonic plates shifting beneath their feet in a direction that might prove favorable to them.

Near the end of October, Allenby launched his offensive. He prepared with care, tricking the Turks into thinking he would repeat General Murray's ill-conceived direct assault upon Gaza of the previous spring. First he sent Colonel Richard Meinertzhagen, a former ornithologist turned daredevil warrior, on reconnaissance. The colonel allowed himself to be seen by the enemy and chased. Purposely he dropped several notebooks as he fled; they contained information suggesting a frontal attack like Murray's. On October 26, Allenby unleashed an extended pounding of Turkish positions in Gaza. The Ottomans, thinking this presaged the main attack, kept most of their troops there. But on October 31 the bulk of Allenby's force attacked Beersheba, thirty-five miles to the southeast, taking the Ottomans completely by surprise. Fearing encirclement, they retreated up the coast, leaving Gaza undefended. Allenby took it and began to chase the Ottomans. Great Britain had entered Palestine at last. But the famous declaration bearing Lord Balfour's name had been written six days before Gaza fell; it would be published the day after. The Arabs had lost the race for Palestine already, although they did not realize it.

Likewise ignorant of developments in London, T. E. Lawrence had ridden north once more. Allenby feared that the Ottomans would reinforce their soldiers in Gaza via the railway that branched west at Dara into the Yarmuk Valley some 420 miles north of Aqaba. That railway represented the main artery connecting Damascus to Palestine. It wound up and down the valley in switchbacks and across gorges along track supported by a series of bridges, eminently suited for destruction by explosive. Lawrence had advocated destroying them back in July; now Allenby wanted him to make the attempt. He should do so as near to the date of the attack upon Gaza as possible. Lawrence accepted his most dangerous assignment. This time he took with him, among others, a British explosives expert, C. E. Wood, as backup in case he himself should be killed; also a number of Indian troops who were adept with the machine gun; and also, for the first part of the expedition, George Lloyd of the Arab Bureau.

George Lloyd is the man who had served as honorary consul with Mark Sykes and Aubrey Herbert at the British embassy in Constantinople twelve years before; who had entered Parliament as a Conservative MP just as his two friends had done; and who had joined the Anglo-Ottoman Society and allowed it to use his name to recruit others, including Herbert. He is important here for the revealing discussion he had with Lawrence as the two rode together on the first leg of the trip.

Lawrence liked and respected Lloyd. He was, Lawrence later wrote, "the rare sort of traveler who could eat anything with anybody, anyhow and at any time." Moreover "he was the only fully taught man with us in Arabia." But these two British experts disagreed fundamentally about Arabia's future. As they rode their camels in the starry night across the desert, Lloyd told Lawrence that he wished to tie "down the Arab movement to its military purpose . . . and to risk no breach of faith with the Arabs by raising hopes beyond it." No doubt he was thinking of King Hussein's various misapprehensions. After all, he had been present at Jeddah when Feisal and Fuad went to Colonel Newcombe with their worries. No doubt, too, his call for plain dealing appealed to Lawrence.

The assumption behind it, however, that the Arabs' role should be merely military and supplemental, cannot have appealed. Lloyd kept a "Diary of a journey with TEL to El Jaffer," in which he scribbled Lawrence's quite different viewpoint. Given that the Balfour Declaration had already been written, it has a rather poignant aspect. Suppose Feisal were triumphantly installed in Damascus as a result of his own efforts, Lawrence posited to Lloyd. Then: "Sharif's flag flies along coast from Acre northwards . . . Feisal's attitude will be non-negotiatory—'What I have, I will keep.'" Note that this meant keeping northern Palestine, which Zionists now believed the British government would assign to them. Note too that Lawrence had no doubt Feisal would be entitled to keep it—or rather that neither Britain nor France would be entitled to, let alone to give it to the Jews. The Sykes-Picot Agreement, Lawrence told Lloyd either that night or sometime during the next day, was "at best one between France and England for partition of a country in armed occupation of forces of Sharif of Mecca."

Lloyd opposed Sykes-Picot for a different reason. Like so many Britons, he thought Sykes had given France too much. Lawrence thought so too, or he may have thought by now that Britain had given both too much to France and not enough to the Arabs. At any rate, both men agreed that the Sykes-Picot Agreement must be revised. Thus Lawrence rejoiced when Lloyd left him three days later, although he would miss his company. Lloyd was headed ultimately for London, where he could work against Sykes-Picot. As Lloyd put it, Lawrence "felt that there was a risk that all his work would be ruined in Whitehall and he thought I could save this." But as far as Palestine was concerned, it had been ruined already.

With Lloyd gone, Lawrence turned his mind exclusively to military matters. Things did not go smoothly. While the Zionists in London were rejoicing at the Balfour Declaration, Lawrence found himself, after yet more hard traveling, in Ain el Beidha, haggling with the sheikh and chief men of the Serahin tribe for recruits. They politely heard him out and then declined to provide any. Lawrence had counted on their help to blow up the Yarmuk Valley bridges. He turned from the sheikh and appealed to the tribesmen themselves, in a "halting, half-coherent speech," which nevertheless struck a chord. They would go after all, they affirmed. Momentarily cheered, he then discovered that one of his men had deserted and would likely warn the Turks of his mission. "We . . . decided to push on none the less, trusting to the usual incompetence of our enemy."

It took another day and night of difficult trekking, part of it in a driving rain, to reach the bridge they intended to take down. When they did reach it, a guard spotted them almost immediately and opened fire. The Serahin tribesmen returned fire. Also they quickly dumped their sacks of gelignite, fearing that incoming fire would detonate them. Lawrence and his men had to retreat, without their explosives. "Our minds were sick with failure," he wrote. It was November 7, two days before the London *Times* reported the Balfour Declaration.

The next morning Lawrence realized he still possessed sufficient gelignite to blow up a train, but the wire connecting the explosive to the trigger would stretch only sixty yards. On another rainy day, down that north-south railway line near Minifer, above Amman, Lawrence laid it all out and waited, in the clammy wood above the track. Twice trains steamed by, and twice the exploder failed to work. The day passed uncomfortably, and another night. Finally, after yet another sunrise, a third train approached, "a splendid two-engined thing of twelve passenger coaches, travelling at top speed." Lawrence was ready, but the sixty yards of wire placed him much too close to the track. "I touched off under the first driving wheel of the first locomotive, and the explosion was terrific. The ground spouted blackly into my face, and I was sent spinning, to sit up with the shirt torn to my shoulder and the blood dripping from long ragged scratches on my left arm. Between my knees lay the exploder, crushed under a twisted sheet of sooty iron. In front of me was the scalded and smoking upper half of a man."

The train had been derailed, both engines irreparably damaged, the carriages zigzagged across the tracks. Lawrence noticed flags flying from one of them. By an extraordinary coincidence, he had blown up the train of Djemal Pasha, who was hurrying to take part in the defense of Jerusalem against Allenby's advancing army. "His motor car was on the end of the train and we shot it up," wrote Lawrence. Djemal himself did not appear, but four hundred Ottoman soldiers had been riding the train with him, and those who had survived the blast now "were under shelter and shooting hard at us." Lawrence's party numbered forty. He had sent back to Aqaba the Indian machine-gunners after the fiasco on November 7. "So we ran in batches up the little stream-bed, turning at each sheltered angle to delay them by pot-shots . . . reached the hill-top [where they had left their camels] . . . and made away at full speed." Lawrence had been grazed by five bullets; his foot had been badly damaged by shrapnel from the explosion.

Blowing up Djemal Pasha's train salvaged pride at least, and the Serahin tribesmen could return to Ain el Beidha with something like honor. But nothing could disguise the fact that they had failed in their primary mission: to destroy at least one of the crucial bridges in the Yarmuk Valley. Lawrence holed up, depressed, in Azraq in the ruins of a fourth-century fortress. He and his remaining group suffered from the weather, which stayed cold and wet. But they were not far from Dara, at the junction of the two railway lines. Lawrence knew that either Feisal's or Allenby's army must take the town eventually. He decided to scout it, to learn its defenses and how it might best be approached. What followed is perhaps the best known although least believable of the great tales Lawrence told of his exploits in Arabia.

On the morning of November 20, Lawrence writes in *Seven Pillars,* he and a companion slipped into Dara. Before long, Turkish soldiers accosted them. They let his companion go but brought Lawrence to the local commandant, who first tried to seduce and then to rape him. When Lawrence resisted, the commandant ordered that he be whipped. It made an unforgettable scene in David Lean's film, but historians doubt that it ever occurred. The commandant died shortly thereafter, but his friends and family convincingly disputed the account. The page of Lawrence's diary that should deal with the episode has been torn out—it is the diary's only missing page. Most probably, then, Lawrence conceived the scene and wrote about it in his book to satisfy a personal compulsion. He writes that after he endured the lashing, "a delicious warmth, probably sexual, was swelling through me." It emerged years later that during the interwar period before his death, he regularly paid various men to beat him.

After the thrashing, according to the account in *Seven Pillars,* he escaped from the room in which the Turks had locked him and returned to the fortress at Azraq. There he remained for nearly two weeks, healing either from the beating or from the wounds suffered in the raid upon the railway. When he reappeared in Aqaba in good health on November 26, he learned that Allenby's army had taken Jaffa on November 14. He left for that town almost immediately to report his failure in the Yarmuk Valley. Then on December 9 word came that Jerusalem too had surrendered. That was exactly a week after the great Zionist celebration at the London Opera House.

The Zionists had closed their deal, or at least had good reason to think they had. Allenby had provided the War Cabinet with the victory it so deeply desired, the Christmas present to the British people that Lloyd George had mentioned when dispatching him to the Middle East. But the Ottomans, although on the run, remained defiant. They retreated to Nablus and Jericho and took up new defensive positions, standing between the Arabs and their great goal, Damascus.

Lawrence would be part of Allenby's retinue when he made his entrance into Jerusalem. Feisal's forces did not attend. They continued training at Aqaba and would not move north against the Turks until the following spring. Then they would remain separated from the British in Palestine by the turpentine waters of the Dead Sea. They took Dara, as Lawrence had foreseen would be necessary, but not until September 18, 1918, and they would not occupy Damascus until September 30. They had helped the British, but too late to help themselves.

CHAPTER 24

The Declaration at Last

IN THE SUMMER OF 1917, months of wrangling and politicking still separated British Zionists from their great goal, but they thought it finally lay within their grasp. Of Lawrence's hair-raising adventures, of his specific attempts at lobbying General Allenby, George Lloyd, and other authorities in support of Arab independence, they knew nothing. Of King Hussein's intentions for Syria and of his British supporters' sympathies, they had some general knowledge. Of the Sykes-Picot Agreement, they had more than an inkling. They realized that with regard to Palestine they must "elicit [from the government] . . . some definite statement beyond the mere verbal assurances with which we have hitherto been contented"—or someone else might. In consultation with sympathetic officials such as Mark Sykes and Ronald Graham, Weizmann and Sokolow worked out a method of approach. They and their colleagues would compose a Zionist statement. When it was ready, Lord Rothschild would send it to the foreign secretary, Arthur Balfour. The latter would present it to the War Cabinet for approval. When this body had sanctioned it, Balfour would inform Rothschild by letter. This would constitute a declaration of British support for Zionism, in fact a Balfour Declaration.

Then, as we know, Weizmann had to travel unexpectedly to Gibraltar to head off Henry Morgenthau, and subsequently to Paris to report to Lloyd George. While he was thus engaged, and while Lawrence and Feisal and Auda were trekking the desert wastes of Arabia blowing up tracks and trestles, the London Zionist Political Committee was meeting at the faux-Gothic, faux-Tudor, and long-since-demolished Imperial Hotel on Russell Square. There, in leafy Bloomsbury in July 1917, Sokolow, Sieff, Marks, Simon, Ahad Ha'am, occasionally Sacher (when on leave from Manchester), and several others discussed and argued and wrote their draft declarations.

Characteristically, Sacher thought Zionists should ask "for as much as possible." "We must control the state machinery in Palestine. If we don't, the Arabs will. Give the Arabs all the guarantees they like for cultural autonomy; but the state must be Jewish." Sokolow overbore him and other maximalists. He remained in constant touch with Sykes; indirectly he had communicated with Balfour himself; and at this stage he knew better than his colleagues what the British government would accept and what it would not. The group must not submit an itemized wish list, he realized; certainly it must not even mention a Jewish state. "Our purpose," Sokolow wrote to Joseph Cowen, who also took part in the deliberations, "is to receive from the Government a general short approval of the same kind as that which I have been successful in getting from the French Government."

On July 12 the group (minus Sacher, who had journalistic duties in the north) boiled down half a dozen more or less militant and detailed drafts into a single, albeit still somewhat prolix, paragraph for the British government to sanction. It argued that Britain should recognize Palestine as the national home of the Jewish people and should establish with the Zionist Organization a "Jewish National Colonizing Corporation," under whose aegis Jews could immigrate to Palestine freely, live autonomously, and develop economically.

Sokolow submitted this statement to Sykes and Graham. They responded within a matter of days, but not positively. Sokolow, reporting their objections, said the paragraph was "too long" and "contained matters of detail which it would be undesirable to raise at the present moment."

Sokolow reconvened the committee on July 17. This time Sacher attended. He had grasped what kind of statement the Foreign Office wanted. While sitting, or pacing, in the hotel room, the Zionists debated what to cut from their earlier paragraph and what to retain. Leon Simon jotted down on a scrap of paper the formulation at which they eventually arrived. Harry Sacher was its principal architect. The scrap survived—someone saved it.

Eighty-eight years later its anonymous owner put it up for auction at Sotheby's in London. An unidentified bidder purchased it for $884,000.

Here is what Simon wrote all those years ago:

1. His Majesty's Government accepts the principle that Palestine should be reconstituted as the National Home of the Jewish people.
2. His Majesty's Government will use its best endeavors to secure the achievement of this object and will discuss the necessary methods and means with the Zionist Organization.

Note that the first sentence implies an unbroken link between Jews and Palestine despite the nearly two-thousand-year separation. Note that the second sentence posits the Zionist Organization as official representative of Jewish interests. Sacher's pithy new statement had taken note of the criticisms offered by Sykes and Graham but ceded little of substance.

Sokolow showed the condensed statement to Sykes and Graham, who approved it. He passed it along to Lord Rothschild, who sent it to Balfour, along with a note: "At last I am able to send you the formula you asked me for. If His Majesty's Government will send me a message on the lines of this formula, if they and you approve of it, I will hand it on to the Zionist Federation and also announce it at a meeting called for that purpose."

Rothschild thought, as did most of the informed Zionists, that the government statement of support would be forthcoming momentarily. Weizmann, who had just returned from Paris, was optimistic too. By this stage the Zionists had defeated the Conjoint Committee; they (himself most of all) had developed extensive and close relations with important officials and had reason to believe the officials supported them; they had nobbled the most important Rothschild, who now served as their emissary to the government; and they had produced the brief, vague, yet apt statement the Foreign Office desired. "The declaration is going to be given us soon I understand," Weizmann informed Sacher on August 1. Even Balfour was sanguine. He drafted a reply to Rothschild: "I am glad to be in a position to inform you that His Majesty's Government accept the principle that Palestine should be reconstituted as the national home of the Jewish people." Zionism stood upon the verge of an epochal step forward. But Balfour did not send the note.

In the same way that much ink has been spilled examining the Hussein-McMahon correspondence, so historians have traced with infinite care

British officials' revisings and rewordings of Sacher's two-sentence message
during the late summer and autumn of 1917, the discussions and meetings
among them to which it gave rise, and the reactions of Jewish Zionists and
anti-Zionists alike. But here historians have no controversy (although inevitably they divide over the motivations of individuals). The War Cabinet
minister Sir Alfred Milner, possibly hoping to assuage the fears of anti-
Zionists such as his friend Claude Montefiore, removed the word "reconstituted" from the statement. Instead of terming Palestine *"the* National
Home *of* the Jewish people" he called it in his new draft *"a* National Home
for the Jewish people." Later, at Milner's request, Leopold Amery, an under
secretary to the War Cabinet, further attenuated Sacher's two sentences, ex-
cising any reference to the Zionist Organization and incorporating language, employed by Zionists in letters to *The Times* during their
controversy with the Conjoint Committee, denying they would damage
Arab interests in Palestine. These changes were important, but they reflected qualified support, not opposition. That came from another quarter
of the cabinet, most irreconcilably from the newly appointed secretary of
state for India and sole remaining Jewish cabinet minister, Edwin Montagu. Ironically, a Jew represented the greatest remaining obstacle to cabinet acceptance of the Balfour Declaration.

   Like his cousin Herbert Samuel, Montagu had resigned his cabinet post
in December 1916, when Asquith relinquished the prime minister's position to Lloyd George. He took this step reluctantly but could do nothing
else. He owed much to the former Liberal leader, whose friendship he still
cherished and whom he greatly admired. He had no inkling of Asquith's
genteel but unmistakably anti-Semitic references to him in his correspondence with Venetia Stanley (although one wonders whether he learned
about them when Venetia Stanley became his wife). He once had written to
Asquith:

> In all the things that matter, in all the issues that frighten, in all
> the apprehensions that disturb, you show yourself clear sighted
> and self possessed, ready to help, to elucidate, to respond, to for-
> mulate, to lead, to inspire. That's why loving you and following
> you is so easy and so profitable . . . Whatever happens, you are
> firm as a rock . . . understanding, shielding.

But Montagu admired Lloyd George too. And he was ambitious and justi-
fiably confident of his own powers, although perhaps socially insecure. He

could not remain content outside government for long. On March 28, 1917, he wrote to Lloyd George:

> *As the desert sand for rain,*
> *As the Londoner for sun,*
> *As the poor for potatoes,*
> *As a landlord for rent,*
> *As drosera rotundifolia for a fly,*
> *As Herbert Samuel for Palestine,*
> *As a woman in Waterloo Road for a soldier*
> I long for talk with you.

Lloyd George must have proved amenable, for shortly thereafter Montagu reentered the cabinet, first as minister without portfolio working on plans for postwar reconstruction, later as replacement for Austen Chamberlain as secretary of state for India. But there was a price to pay. For such disloyalty, as he perceived it, Asquith never forgave him.

Lucien Wolf's Conjoint Committee fell and British Jews who favored assimilation lost their leadership, when the tall, brooding, emotional Montagu, in effect, stepped into the breach. He may not have intended it, but that is what he did. He knew nothing of Zionists drafting paragraphs at the Imperial Hotel or, probably, even of the close connections linking Weizmann and Sokolow to Sykes and various Foreign Office figures. He did not see Sacher's two-sentence statement or Balfour's draft reply until August 22. But when finally he did see it, he was galvanized. He wanted the foreign secretary to redraft his letter and reject the Zionist statement. The scorching memorandum that he composed, five pages of coruscating irony and sarcasm, was titled: "The Anti-Semitism of the Present Government"— not, as he carefully explained, because he thought Lloyd George and his team held anti-Semitic views but rather because he thought their pro-Zionist policy would "prove a rallying ground for anti-Semites in every country in the world."

We have become familiar with the arguments Montagu employed against Zionism. Most cabinet ministers knew them as well, for the arguments had changed little since Montagu's own opposition to Herbert Samuel's 1915 Zionist statement to the cabinet. "I assert that there is not a Jewish nation," Montagu wrote again, two years later. "I deny that Palestine is today associated with the Jews or properly to be regarded as a fit place for them to live in." And further down the page: "When the Jew has a national home surely it follows that the impetus to deprive [him] of the rights of British citizenship must be enormously increased. Palestine will become the world's Ghetto." And finally, and perhaps inevitably: "The Government are asked to be the instrument . . . of a Zionist organization largely run . . . by men of enemy descent or birth." But such quotations do not do justice to the vehemence of Montagu's attack. Cabinet ministers, accustomed to one another's dry formulations and businesslike prose, would have been taken aback when they read their colleague's cri de coeur.

For that was what it was. Montagu took the issue personally. He had once remarked that he had been trying all his life to escape the ghetto. Now he understood the Zionists to be trying to push him, and every other assimilated British Jew, back inside. If the government endorsed the Zionist memorandum, Montagu argued in a desperate letter to Lloyd George, it would mean that "the country for which I have worked ever since I left the University— England—the country for which my family have fought, tells me that my national home . . . is Palestine." He treasured his appointment to the India Office, he reminded the prime minister. He looked forward to championing progressive reforms there, to carrying the ideals of British Liberalism to the subcontinent. But how could a Palestinian—as he must be termed if the government accepted the Zionist statement—represent Britain in India? "Every anti-Semitic organization and newspaper will ask what right a Jewish Englishman, with the status at best of a naturalized foreigner, has to take a foremost part in the Government of the British Empire."

Montagu belonged to the cabinet but had no position in the War Cabinet, that decisive subset of the whole that would render final verdict on the Zionist statement. Nevertheless, his fervent protest ensured him a seat at the table when the body met on September 3. On that day members had before them Sacher's two sentences, Milner's revised version of them, and Montagu's perfervid response. In the discussion that ensued Montagu, according to minutes of the meeting, "urged that the use of the phrase 'the home of the Jewish people' would vitally prejudice the position of every Jew elsewhere and expanded the argument contained in his Memorandum." Bizarrely, neither Lloyd George nor Balfour could attend this particular session; perhaps that fact worked in his favor, although Milner and Robert Cecil (deputizing for Balfour) ably argued the Zionist position. Thus the British War Cabinet divided along lines adumbrated in that first confrontation between Zionists and assimilationists in the offices of Lucien Wolf in early 1915. The result was equally inconclusive. In the end, the War Cabinet agreed only to consult Britain's ally, President Wilson of the United States, before taking action.

News of the cabinet's indecision quickly reached Chaim Weizmann. Balked at this penultimate stage, and furious, he hurled himself into a last great effort to push the declaration through. He mobilized American Zionists to extract a pledge of support from Wilson, and urged British Zionists to press forward one more time. At his indirect instigation, hundreds of telegrams, from Jewish congregations across the length and breadth of the British Isles, all urging government support of the declaration, flooded into the Foreign Office. By the fall of 1917 Weizmann could turn the key to most doors in Whitehall. He met with Foreign Office officials, cabinet ministers, the prime minister's closest advisers, finally even with the prime minister himself (although for only three minutes). With Lord Rothschild he drew up a toughly worded restatement of the Zionist position that could also be read as a barely concealed reproach to the government for stalling: "We have submitted the text of the declaration on behalf of an organization which claims to represent the will of a great and ancient, though scattered, people. We have submitted it after three years of negotiations and conversations with prominent representatives of the British nation." Montagu took steps too. He prepared a second anti-Zionist memorandum for the War Cabinet to consider. But he stood at a disadvantage. He had no organization behind him and scarcely an ally in the government.

The War Cabinet convened again, on October 4, this time with Lloyd George in the chair and Balfour at his right hand. The foreign secretary explained briefly and lucidly what Zionism meant and why he supported it. Unexpectedly a powerful voice intervened—in opposition to him. Here was Montagu's only cabinet-level ally, the Marquess Curzon of Keddleston, lord president of the council. But he was an ally only up to a point. He intended to offer the War Cabinet a cold douche of realism. He opposed Zionism for practical reasons, he explained. He would not concern himself with philosophical speculation about the possibility of Jewish assimilation in the countries of the Diaspora. Alone among the men sitting at 10 Downing Street, he had been to Palestine: "barren and desolate . . . a less propitious seat for the future Jewish race could not be imagined." Anyway, how would Jews get there in significant numbers? What would they do when they arrived? And what would happen to the present Muslim population? Zionism he regarded "as sentimental idealism, which would never be realized and [with which] His Majesty's Government should have nothing to do."

Montagu would have been glad of Curzon's unforeseen, if frigidly offered, support, but he may have understood that it came too late. This meeting would be his swan song. His duties as Indian secretary called him to the subcontinent, and he would be leaving England in a matter of weeks.

Still he continued to hammer, arguing not on practical grounds, as Curzon had, but rather on intensely personal ones. "How would he negotiate with the peoples of India on behalf of His Majesty's Government if the world had just been told that [Britain] regarded his national home as being in Turkish territory?" He pointed out too that "the only trial of strength between Zionists and anti-Zionists in England had resulted in a very narrow majority for the Zionists, namely 56 to 51 of the representatives of Anglo-Jewry on the Conjoint Committee." Surely the government could not choose one side over the other on this slight basis? And he could not refrain from underlining once again the foreign origins of leading Zionists in Britain.

For a second time the War Cabinet deferred a decision, this time so that members could read a paper Curzon wished to prepare and ascertain more precisely the views of President Wilson. The latter's aide, Colonel Edward House, had sent on the president's behalf a noncommittal response to the original cabinet inquiry, but then Wilson had permitted the American Zionist Louis Brandeis to send a more positive one. They decided as well to canvass representative Zionist and anti-Zionist Jews in Britain to ascertain their views of the draft declaration. Montagu composed a third anti-Zionist memorandum, his most outspoken and personal yet, criticizing Weizmann specifically: "On this matter he is near to being a religious fanatic." The secretary of state for India appears to have understood, however, that he was rowing against the current and that the tide was too strong. Except for Curzon, the cabinet's big guns opposed him: Lloyd George, Balfour, Milner. He told C. P. Scott the day after submitting this last memorandum that the big three could not be moved. Therefore "the thing will go through."

Poor Edwin Montagu! For all his worldly success, he embodied the dilemmas and tragedies of early-twentieth-century assimilated British Jewry. He believed passionately in assimilation. At War Cabinet meetings and in his written memoranda, he fought for this ideal with all the tools of an upper-class Englishman: the irony and wit and logic he had imbibed in the debating clubs at Cambridge, the Liberalism he had learned from Asquith, the rhetorical skills he had acquired over years of political campaigning in the flatlands of Norfolk. He even allowed to appear, as an upper-class Englishman might have done when pressed, a glimpse of the antiforeigner sentiment so pervasive in wartime Britain. We cannot know whether his colleagues perceived him to be an Englishman who happened to be Jewish (as he so desperately wished) or rather as a Jew who happened to have been born and raised in England (as Asquith did). We cannot know whether true assimilation was possible for Jews in Britain in 1917.

But surely the response Montagu elicited only a few weeks after the cabinet meeting from none other than Aubrey Herbert, recently returned from his secret mission to Switzerland, is suggestive. Let us give to Herbert, a brave and interesting man, every benefit of the doubt. Let us posit that he sympathized with Jews as he did with other oppressed and persecuted peoples. Now he was on his way, on secret government duty, to Albania to assist in the nationalist struggle against the Ottomans. Montagu had started out for India. Their paths intersected in Turin, Italy, where they dined together. Herbert described the event in his diary. He simply could not regard "Edwin of the Saxon Sword," as he snidely called him (but not to his face), as anything other than a Jew who happened to have been born in Britain. "It's ridiculous to pretend he is an Englishman," Herbert wrote. "He is every inch an Oriental." Then the son of the Earl of Carnarvon, and the son of Lord Swaythling, both on British government service, continued along their separate ways.

Meanwhile the cabinet had received replies to their circular from four Zionists, including Weizmann, Sokolow, and Rothschild, and from four anti-Zionists, including Claude Montefiore and Sir Philip Magnus, MP, with responses to the proposed declaration. President Wilson, decisively influenced by Justice Brandeis via Colonel House, had telegraphed finally an unambiguous message of support for Zionism. Lord Curzon had completed his anti-Zionist memorandum. Cabinet ministers read and digested all this. A third meeting of the War Cabinet was scheduled. It would convene on Wednesday, October 31, 1917.

We know the outcome. On that day the War Cabinet agreed to what has become known as the Balfour Declaration. The document authorized the foreign secretary to reply to Lord Rothschild in the following terms:

> His Majesty's Government view with favor the establishment in Palestine of a national home for the Jewish people, and will use their best endeavors to facilitate the achievement of this object, it being clearly understood that nothing shall be done which may prejudice the civil and religious rights of existing non-Jewish communities in Palestine, or the rights and political status enjoyed by Jews in any other country.

On November 2 Balfour sent this message to Rothschild. The press would publish it exactly one week later. Thus did Weizmann's long, unlikely campaign finally gain its object. Thus too did the campaign of T. E. Lawrence, King Hussein, and Sharif Feisal for some form of Arab confederation or empire (albeit one whose borders remained a matter of contention and misunderstanding) receive a grave setback. Their projected greater Arabia, if ever it came into existence, would not include Palestine.

In the last part of the last sentence of the Balfour Declaration, the War Cabinet attempted to take Edwin Montagu's primary fear into account. They failed to satisfy him. Montagu reached India, where he learned what the War Cabinet had done. Irreconcilable to the last, he wrote in his diary: "The Government has dealt an irreparable blow to Jewish Britons, and they have endeavored to set up a people which does not exist." From the vantage point of nearly a hundred years on, however, we may say that what Montagu dreaded has not come to pass. Indeed, that last reassuring phrase of the Declaration seems almost superfluous. Anti-Semitism has scaled heights beyond Montagu's imagining since 1917, in fact has risen and fallen more than once in different countries, but without regard to Britain's recognition of Palestine as "a national home for the Jewish people." As for the Indian secretary's anguished prediction that the Balfour Declaration would make assimilation in Britain less attainable for Jews: perhaps it did, or perhaps it did not. One cannot prove or disprove a negative.

The War Cabinet attempted also to meet the objections raised by Lord Curzon. Members had read his memorandum before the meeting on October 31. In it Curzon referred to the Syrian Arabs, mainly Muslims, who had "occupied [Palestine] for the best part of 1,500 years," and asked what would become of them. "They will not be content either to be expropriated for Jewish immigrants or to act merely as hewers of wood and drawers of water to the latter." It was a good prophecy, but he did not press it. Perhaps the Declaration's promise to uphold "the civil and religious rights of existing non-Jewish communities in Palestine" persuaded him. It is proper to note, however, that these words have persuaded few Arabs.

In his memorandum Curzon advanced a second reason for opposing the Declaration. The Jewish world population amounted to twelve million. He did not believe that tiny, arid Palestine could become the national home of even a small fraction of this number. Here he ran into a buzz saw wielded by Sir Mark Sykes. Alerted to Curzon's opposition, Sykes prepared and caused to be circulated a powerful paper of his own. He knew Palestine better than "Alabaster," as he called the Marquess of Keddleston, whom he happened to detest. He had seen with his own eyes Jewish colonies that made the desert bloom with flowers. With proper management Palestine eventually could accept a population five times its present size. No one need be dispossessed. During the War Cabinet discussion Balfour, relying on Sykes, dismissed Curzon's warning with relative ease: "There were considerable differences of opinion among experts regarding the possibility of the settlement of any large population in Palestine, but he was informed that if Palestine were scientifically developed a very much larger population could be sustained than had existed during the period of Turkish rule."

Curzon, then, did not maintain his opposition to the Declaration, as Montagu, had he been present, undoubtedly would have done. For Montagu, the issues raised by Zionism were too profound for compromise. For Curzon, they could be subsumed by what he perceived to be larger issues. He and other cabinet ministers were increasingly worried that Germany intended to play the Zionist card herself. She would force Turkey to promise autonomy to the Jews of Palestine. That would rally world Jewish opinion to the Central Powers and alienate them from the Entente. Jewish American support for war bonds would dry up; Jewish Russian support for the moderate Kerensky government would be withdrawn; the Bolsheviks would seize power and make a separate peace. Such considerations overwhelmed Curzon's hesitations regarding the dispossession of Arabs and the inability of Palestine to support a larger population.

He also would have believed, as did everyone else in the room, that if Britain preempted Germany with her own Zionist declaration, then she rather than Germany would reap the benefits. Balfour put it to the War Cabinet this way: "The vast majority of Jews in Russia and America, as indeed all over the world, now appeared to be favorable to Zionism. If we could make a declaration favorable to such an ideal we should be able to carry on extremely useful propaganda both in Russia and America." Curzon "admitted the force of the diplomatic arguments in favor of expressing sympathy." Some such expression, he thought, "would be a valuable adjunct to our propaganda," not least since "the bulk of the Jews held Zionist rather than anti-Zionist opinions."

Implicit here is the wildly unrealistic estimate of the power and unity of "world Jewry" that we have seen such British officials as Hugh O'Bierne and Sir Mark Sykes to have displayed. Let an infamous notation, jotted down by Robert Cecil relatively early in the war on a Foreign Office document, stand for all such miscalculations: "I do not think it is possible to exaggerate the international power of the Jews." In his memorandum, and despite its title, Montagu had discounted "the anti-Semitism of the present government." But stereotypical thinking about Jews did play a role in the War Cabinet's decision to issue the Balfour Declaration.

It is a further irony that British Zionists had done what they could to foster such thinking. The inimitable Harry Sacher wrote long afterward: "Many . . . have a residual belief in the power and the unity of Jewry. We suffer for it, but it is not wholly without its compensations. It is one of the imponderabilia of politics, and it plays, consciously or unconsciously, its part in the calculations and the decisions of statesmen. To exploit it delicately and deftly belongs to the art of the Jewish diplomat." During 1917 the Zionists did just that. Starting in June 1917, they began warning that Germany was courting Jews. Usually they did not say, indeed it was better left unsaid, that if Germany won Jewish support, then the Entente would lose it—and possibly the war. British officials were capable of reaching this conclusion themselves. On one occasion, however, Weizmann went even that far. The Germans had "recently approached the Zionists with a view to coming to terms with them," he warned William Ormsby-Gore on June 10. "It was really a question whether the Zionists were to realize their aims through Germany and Turkey or through Great Britain. He [Weizmann], of course, was absolutely loyal to Great Britain." Meanwhile the British Jewish press had taken up the issue. Lord Rothschild repeated it to Balfour: "During the last few weeks the official and semi-official German newspapers have been making many statements, all to the effect that in the Peace Negotiations the Central Powers must make a condition for Palestine to be a Jewish settlement under German protection. I therefore think it important that the British declaration should forestall any such move." Thus did the Zionists indirectly play "delicately and deftly" upon the ignorance and prejudice of British officials; thus did they employ a mirror image of the same card that Sharif Muhammad al-Faruki had played two years earlier, when he claimed that the Germans would help the Arabs if the British did not.

It helped that the British government was receiving independent confirmation of the Zionist warnings. A Bavarian major, Franz Carl Endress, had authored a series of potent articles on the subject for the *Frankfurter Zeitung*. "This man displays a matchless eloquence in order to persuade the Jews that Germany and Turkey are disposed to support Zionism," reported a War Office informant. Nor was Endress the only German to write such articles. The same War Office official listed more than half a dozen others. On October 8, Balfour received a warning from a British agent in Berne: "A meeting is said to have taken place lately at Berlin at which Herr von

Kuhlmann [former German ambassador to Constantinople, now the German foreign minister], Jemal Pasha and a leading Zionist were present in order to discuss the Palestine question. Certain promises were made to the Jews in order to obtain their cooperation in the new war loan." The same cable went on to advise that the current German ambassador to Turkey, Count von Bernstorff, had been courting Jews in Constantinople and that the German minister at Berne was in touch with prominent Jews in that city as well.

British officials, then, could reasonably conclude that they must take preventive measures because something was definitely going on between German leaders and Jewish representatives. But they erred. Historians, recognizing the real basis of their suspicions, unanimously discount their conclusions. The Ottomans never would have allowed unrestricted Jewish immigration into Palestine, let alone autonomy for Jews once they had arrived there. Nor could the Germans ever have forced them to do so. British leaders overestimated German influence upon Constantinople, and Jewish influence everywhere. In this sense, the Balfour Declaration sprang from fundamental miscalculations about the power of Germany and about the power and unity of Jews.

"It's a boy," Sykes reported gleefully to Weizmann, minutes after the War Cabinet sanctioned the Declaration. The ebullient British diplomat, who back in April could not sit still in the Paris hotel waiting for Nahum Sokolow to report on his meeting with the French foreign minister but had to dash into the streets to intercept him, could be excused this time for rushing from the War Cabinet meeting (he had been present) to the anxiously waiting Weizmann. And the Zionist leader, although disappointed that the Declaration did not go further, nevertheless greeted the news Sykes brought with elation. If the government of Lloyd George had not promised specific action, it had promised general support. Weizmann could reasonably assume this meant removal of Ottoman rule in Palestine, the main obstacle as Zionists perceived it.

What would follow could not be certain, but given all the previous discussions, Weizmann was confident it would be some form of British oversight. We may be sure he felt a great weight lift from his shoulders and ecstatic happiness enter into his heart. Moments later he was speeding in a taxi to share the glad tidings with Ahad Ha'am. Another member of the Political Committee, Shmuel Tolkowsky, accompanied him. Weizmann was so filled with pleasure, Tolkowsky recorded, that he "behaved like a child: He embraced me for a long time, placed his head on my shoulder and pressed my hand, repeating over and over *mazel tov.*" That night, at his home, at an impromptu celebration, Weizmann and his wife and friends literally danced for joy.

But here let us step back for just a moment. Finally Zionism had the backing of the British government. It had pledged its word. Chaim Weizmann never doubted that its word was good. Now think back to King Hussein the previous May. "The British Government will fulfill her word," he had rebuked his doubting son Feisal and his aide Fuad al-Khatib on that steamy night in Jeddah, just before agreeing that France should treat the coastal portion of Syria exactly as Britain would treat Mesopotamia. In their admiration for Britain, at any rate, Weizmann and Hussein were more alike than they ever knew—and strange to say of such experienced and sophisticated men, in this one respect perhaps they were equally naïve. The remaining chapter in our history of the Balfour Declaration treats a subject of which Chaim Weizmann and Grand Sharif Hussein remained always, and blissfully, unaware.

CHAPTER 25

The Declaration Endangered

AT THE END OF OCTOBER 1917 the door to a third option for the Middle East remained ajar, even as Chaim Weizmann strained every nerve to close it by dragging the War Cabinet toward Zionism, even as T. E. Lawrence and George Lloyd rode their camels north from Aqaba and the great desert raider confided his dream of an independent Arab kingdom. The war ground on, mercilessly, bloodily, with no end in sight, nor even, despite growing war-weariness in every belligerent power, the likelihood of compromise between the main antagonists.

But many Turks continued to ponder the possibility of breaking free from Germany and negotiating a separate peace with Britain and her allies. The Ottoman leaders themselves were full of distrust for one another, Enver on one side, Talaat and Djemal on the other, intriguing constantly, and they played for high stakes, perhaps even for life itself. In autumn 1917 both Turkish camps made a move; or rather between them they made several moves, which cracked open the door a little wider to that alternative future in which the Ottomans would continue to perform a Middle Eastern role. British officials made sure that neither Weizmann nor Hussein heard anything about them.

At this point both the partisans of Enver and the partisans of Talaat had high hopes of mounting an Ottoman counteroffensive in Mesopotamia.

Nevertheless, they simultaneously had a desperate foreboding that whichever side won the war, Turkey already had lost it. So independently of each other, both camps wanted to talk to Britain. They realized that the Allies intended to carve up the empire after the war, although they did not yet know the details. They certainly knew that Britain had held out promises to Jews and Arabs. They thought, however, that perhaps they could forestall some of them. What they did not realize was that important people in Britain also wanted to deal. At a time when Germany seemed as powerful and impregnable as ever, "we are watching all the time for an opportunity to detach Turkey," wrote Lord Hardinge a few days after the War Cabinet approved the Balfour Declaration. Had they known it, Zionists might have hesitated before celebrating "the most momentous occasion in the history of Judaism for the last 1,800 years," as Lord Rothschild would put it on December 9.

In late 1917 Talaat's proxies approached their British enemy on a variety of fronts. At the end of October, Charlton Giraud, a French national with extensive business interests in Smyrna, where he made his home, appeared at the British consulate in Athens. He had been dispatched by Rahmi Bey, the liberal Ottoman *vali* of Smyrna, ostensibly to discuss an exchange of interned Allied and Turkish civilians. Soon, however, it became apparent that he had a more important mission. Giraud reported to A. T. Waugh, British attaché at the Athens legation, that Rahmi Bey "would welcome an understanding with us . . . The main obstacle . . . is Enver, who is committed to the Germans. But for him Rahmi might be able to win over Talaat and Djemal, the only other men who count." Rahmi Bey would not have acted without Talaat's implicit consent. The latter was fishing: The *vali* of Smyrna was his rod, Giraud was his lure.

Waugh approached the bait warily. He and a subordinate who also interviewed the Frenchman deemed Rahmi's indirect advances "only of a kind which might be expected in similar circumstances from any oriental of his class, and one of the objects of which may be to gauge the Allies' general condition from their readiness to negotiate." Yet ultimately, despite such suspicions, they concluded, as the British ambassador to Greece, Lord Granville, put it, "this is an opportunity which might be seized."

Meanwhile Talaat was fishing in Switzerland. Here he dangled bait before two old hands, Dr. Parodi and Sir Horace Rumbold. This pair knew something about pourparlers with dissident Turks. In early November they happened to be helping arrange a meeting in Zurich regarding treatment and exchange of Allied and Turkish prisoners of war. Now they passed along the news that the Turks wished to take advantage of this conference on neutral ground to meet secretly with British delegates to discuss broader issues—that is, a separate peace. Rumbold also reported that the same Dr. Noureddin who had met with Aubrey Herbert in Interlaken the previous July had broken silence, was optimistic about "the project," and intended to return to Switzerland soon.

During the second and third weeks of November 1917, Lloyd George's War Cabinet engaged in serious deliberations about these signals emanating from Turkey. Balfour argued that Rahmi Bey's twitch upon the line merely indicated how Turkey would approach Britain when circumstances finally compelled her to do so. He advised that Britain not bite. Alfred Milner disagreed: "The time has come when we must rely upon diplomacy as well as upon arms in order to detach Turkey . . . There is a growing party in Turkey which is very anxious for peace . . . notably Talaat and Djemal." Then came word via Switzerland of the additional approaches; this tipped the balance. The War Cabinet began discussing specifically what terms to offer the Ottomans. Recall Dr. Weizmann's reaction when he learned of J. R. Pilling's trip to Switzerland to speak with Turks about a compromise peace. Recall his fury when he heard of Aubrey Herbert's similar mission and how decisively he responded to Henry Morgenthau's intended journey. It is safe to bet that five months later, had he known the War Cabinet was debating Talaat's overtures, he would have reacted with comparable outrage. Such knowledge probably would have stopped Zionists celebrating the Balfour Declaration in their tracks.

The War Cabinet attempted to define its negotiating position. Ministers agreed that Britain and her allies must have permanent free passage through the Dardanelles Strait into the Sea of Marmara and thence into the Black Sea. In return Turkey should receive financial aid and protection from Germany if necessary; also that the state of Turkey itself should not be dismembered and should be allowed to keep Constantinople as its capital. (Russia had renounced her claim to that city after the February Revolution.) What to do about the rest of the Ottoman Empire proved a much more difficult subject.

Milner had supported Zionism in the War Cabinet and was an architect of the Balfour Declaration. Nevertheless, two weeks later, when he learned of Rahmi Bey's approach, he argued that Britain should persuade the Ottomans they "could now get out of the war . . . without the loss of what still remains to them of Europe and of Asia Minor." What did this mean for Palestine? Milner explained further during ensuing War Cabinet discussions. France and Italy would have to relinquish their territorial ambitions in the Middle East, at least partially. Britain could concede titular power over some of the lands occupied by her troops. The Turkish flag could be allowed to fly over Mesopotamia, over Syria—over Palestine!

Lord Curzon responded furiously: "I ask how far our own pledges and commitments will enable us to make any concession, even that of a purely ostensible or nominal sovereignty, to the Turks in respect of the Asiatic possessions which we have in part or in whole lopped off from her. Almost in the same week that we have pledged ourselves, if successful, to secure Palestine as a national home for the Jewish people, are we to contemplate leaving the Turkish flag flying over Jerusalem?"

Mark Sykes, likewise outraged, weighed in with yet another powerfully argued paper prepared at the request of War Cabinet secretary, Sir Maurice Hankey. "We are pledged to Zionism, Armenian liberation, and Arabian independence," he wrote. These should be Britain's "only desiderata." As for the question of the flag, "it is impossible to ask Armenians and the King of Hejaz to accept Turkish suzerainty, symbolized by a flag which connotes the old doctrine of the integrity of the Ottoman Empire." He did not mention the Zionists, but surely the Ottoman flag offended them too. Sykes concluded: "This is not palatable reading for those who desire easy and swift things."

Perhaps it was not, yet Milner digested it and prevailed. The War Cabinet arranged for A. T. Waugh and another intelligence officer, C. E. Heathcote-Smith, who had known Rahmi Bey before the war, to sound out the *vali* of Smyrna. They could meet with him ostensibly to discuss an exchange of interned civilians. The War Cabinet also empowered a British delegate to the Zurich conference on prisoners of war to speak about a separate peace with Turkish representatives there. Ironically they chose the man whom Marmaduke Pickthall had first approached at the Foreign Office back in 1916, Thomas Legh (the second Baron Newton), a Conservative MP and an assistant under secretary of state for foreign affairs. Unlike Waugh and Heathcote-Smith, who were instructed merely to get Rahmi Bey talking, Lord Newton was told that while he must not initiate discussions about peace, he could outline what he understood the British position would be if formal talks took place. This included the Ottoman flag over Palestine.

Then everything changed. At a meeting on December 2, the date on which Zionists celebrated the Balfour Declaration in London at the Opera House, Rahmi Bey explained that earth-shaking news had just arrived from the Eastern Front, news that significantly reduced his country's interest in a separate peace. "This is the most favorable moment of the war for Turkey," Heathcote-Smith reported Rahmi Bey as saying, although "I got the impression that it was Talaat rather than Rahmi who was talking." The *vali* continued: "We had only one real enemy and this was Russia. Russia today is offering an armistice and peace on the basis of the freedom of nationalities." German military might had prevailed in the East after all. It could save the Ottoman Empire yet. Why then discuss a separate peace with Great Britain? Turkish interest in that subject would revive only if she again feared imminent defeat. In the meantime Rahmi Bey was happy to leave open the channel of communication.

Discussions in Switzerland developed along different lines from those in Greece because they began later in December and took place over a more protracted period of time. By then Britain had recouped the loss of Russia, to a certain extent, with victories in Palestine, culminating for the moment in Allenby's entrance into Jerusalem on December 11. Zionists cheered these victories, not realizing that they revived to a degree Turkish interest in reaching a settlement.

In Switzerland, Newton made contact, through Sir Horace Rumbold, with two Turks already stationed there. Rumbold thought little of them. The first belonged to the Ottoman legation but "the fact that he is known to be Anglophil would probably cause any communications made by him through his Minister to the Turkish Government to be discounted." The second, whose brother was the *wakil,* or general factotum, of a former grand vizier, suffered from the same lack of credibility. He received his Egyptian pension from British officials in Berne. Nevertheless one or the other or possibly a third Turk altogether (for no name is mentioned) had expressed a "strong desire" to meet the British emissary when he should arrive. Lord Newton agreed to a conference. There he followed instructions, stating only what he thought British policy toward Turkey would be. In reply the "Agent, who is believed to be in the confidence of Talaat, stated that large section of Turks would recommend anything which would free them from Enver and German domination . . . He is considering advisability of proceeding to Turkey and personally communicating our views to Talaat."

Newton also made contact with a Turkish delegate to the conference on prisoners of war, Mouktar Bey, former Ottoman ambassador to Berlin, who was, according to Rumbold, "the only important Turk from our point of view." What then transpired cannot quite be pieced together. Mouktar Bey had reason to be cautious. Of the five Ottoman delegates to the conference, three had been chosen by Talaat, two by Enver: "Needless to say, they watched each other very carefully." Mouktar quickly realized that a German and a Turkish spy were tracking him. The German had booked a room next to his at the hotel in Zurich. Nevertheless he managed to get a telegram to Talaat. He reported that "Lord Newton had given [me] to understand that England would be quite ready to come to an arrangement with Turkey if the latter would embark on *pourparlers* for a separate peace." How do we know this? "We get all the details about Mouktar's proceedings from his friend Hakki Halid Bey," Rumbold reported smugly to Lord Balfour.

Lord Newton, however, denied he had made any such declaration to the Turk. Perhaps then Mouktar was making it up in order to impress his master. Or conceivably he was reporting his interpretation of something said to him by Dr. Parodi, for we know that they talked too. At any rate, and despite the waxing and waning and perhaps waxing again of Turkey's interest in a separate peace, British interest remained strong. Not surprisingly, the next move appears to have come from her.

For some months the War Cabinet had been contemplating trying to detach Austria too from the Central Powers. Just as it had been receiving feelers from Talaat, it had been receiving them from Count Albert von Mensdorff, Austria's prewar ambassador in London. Amazingly, Horace Rumbold relayed these overtures too; really, he did occupy the center of the spider's web. And just as the War Cabinet debated how to respond to the Turks, so it considered what to do about Austria. In mid-December, at the same time as Lord Newton was conducting his negotiations with Mouktar Bey, the South African Jan Smuts, who was the War Cabinet's newest addition, made a secret journey to Geneva to talk matters over with the count, who likewise traveled there incognito. Their discussions proved unproductive. Mensdorff aimed at a general peace; Smuts aimed at separating Austria from Germany. But while in Switzerland Smuts and a second Briton, Phillip Kerr, private secretary to Lloyd George and a future British ambassador to Washington, spoke with Turks too.

Again we cannot be precise about what was said or even to whom, but we do know that afterward Kerr and Rumbold arranged for Dr. Parodi to "cause a communication in the following sense to be made unofficially and verbally to Mouktar Bey." Then they laid out the terms we have seen Milner outline in mid-November at the War Cabinet, except apparently in one respect. Kerr first submitted the instructions for Parodi to his superior, Smuts. The latter made a single alteration: "to include Palestine in the area over which the Allies might be willing to allow the Turkish flag to fly." So he was a Milnerite too. Like Milner, he had supported authorization of the

Balfour Declaration the previous month. The Zionists thought him a strong supporter.

Two days before Smuts amended Kerr's instructions for Parodi, Foreign Office mandarins debated how far British agents might go to reassure Turks, and specifically what should be said regarding the Turkish flag in Palestine. They must have had before them the memorandum in which Milner first argued for the separate peace. "I trust that the language regarding Palestine may be modified," Sir Ronald Graham urged. "To agree to any form of Turkish suzerainty over Palestine would be regarded by the Zionist Jews as a complete betrayal and alienate all their sympathies from us. Dr. Weizmann, for instance, would drop the whole scheme at once." Lord Hardinge, who was prepared to revise Sykes-Picot, as we have seen, nevertheless found Graham's warning persuasive. "I doubt the wisdom of saying so much to Mouktar Bey," he cautioned Balfour. The foreign secretary concurred too as he made clear in a cable to Rumbold.

In other words, the War Cabinet and the Foreign Office came to contradictory conclusions on this crucial matter. Moreover apparently they gave out contradictory instructions. On March 21, 1918, while Parodi remained engaged in talks with Mouktar Bey, Rumbold received a wire from Balfour drawing attention to a telegram he had "sent at the end of December"— obviously the one referred to above—"in which the Foreign Office state that His Majesty's Government could not grant the Turkish flag in Palestine." Likely Balfour sent this reminder because he wanted to change the instructions Smuts and Kerr had issued a few months earlier. Possibly confirming this, in August 1918, in a letter to the newspaper magnate Lord Beaverbrook, who was serving as the government's minister of information, Balfour explained the instructions "we" had given to Lord Newton and to Rumbold and Dr. Parodi the previous winter. "We thought it of great importance that the Turkish flag should not be flown in either Palestine or Syria." Who "we" refers to must remain ambiguous, but clearly it did not mean Milner or Smuts or perhaps even the War Cabinet. It may have meant the Foreign Office. What view Prime Minister Lloyd George took of this apparent disagreement, we will discover in our next section.

But first: Mouktar and Parodi continued their clandestine meetings. Britain continued to take them seriously. On February 6, 1918, before Balfour reminded Rumbold of the Foreign Office position with regard to Palestine and the Turkish flag, he telegrammed Parodi to inform Mouktar that if Talaat sent a Turkish representative to discuss peace terms, "my Government will be ready to send negotiators of equal authority to meet him." Whether in these prospective negotiations Britain would have promised to let Turkey fly her flag over Palestine remains a moot point. Mouktar Bey returned to Constantinople at the end of March. Neither Rumbold nor Parodi heard from him again. Perhaps Talaat Pasha had concluded that a separate peace with Britain was not in Turkey's interest after all.

But Turkey's most serious effort to reach an understanding with Great Britain at this point in the war had not come from Talaat Pasha anyway. It had come from Enver.

"Abdul Kerim will arrive [in Geneva] next week and I will be there to meet him," Basil Zaharoff wrote to Sir Vincent Caillard on November 18, 1917. This latest approach from the emissary of Enver Pasha did not take the arms dealer by surprise. Only two days previously he had returned to Paris from London, where he had spent more than a month at the request of Lloyd George. The two men met for breakfast shortly after November 6. (The precise date cannot be ascertained.) Still, some time before Rahmi Bey sent Charlton Giraud to Athens and Mouktar Bey to Switzerland, the prime minister predicted to Zaharoff that a new overture from Enver would also be forthcoming.

Zaharoff had kept two million American dollars of Britain's money in one of his bank accounts. Lloyd George instructed him to pay it next time he saw Abdul Kerim. Risking this relatively small amount as an earnest of Britain's good intentions would be worth it, said the prime minister. He also outlined what Britain's attitude should be toward the Ottoman Empire's Middle Eastern possessions. Anticipating Milner's position at the War Cabinet, he envisioned "Egyptian conditions" for most of them. It will be recalled that until 1914 Egypt remained nominally under Turkish rule, although in fact Britain exercised there what historians have called a "veiled protectorate." Up until the war, then, the Turkish flag continued to fly in Egypt. Lloyd George saw "no difficulty" in allowing it to go on flying if that would ease Turkey toward a separate peace. This would have been about a week after publication of the Balfour Declaration.

Andrew Bonar Law, the Conservative Party leader and chancellor of the exchequer, knew what Lloyd George contemplated. As chancellor he would be responsible for arranging the much larger payment to Enver, $10 million, that Abdul Kerim had mentioned to Zaharoff the previous July. There is no evidence that anyone else in the War Cabinet discussed or even knew about it. On the British side the only men involved, so far as the evidence shows, were the prime minister and chancellor, the prime minister's principal private secretary J. T. Davies, the intelligence officer Brewis, and Caillard and Zaharoff.

Zaharoff set out to meet Abdul Kerim. The two men arrived in Geneva almost simultaneously on about November 20. It quickly became apparent that the Turk was fishing, not prepared to negotiate serious matters, for with much regret and "using a very coarse expression," he turned down the bribe that Zaharoff immediately offered. He could not accept it, he explained, because Enver had told him not to without consulting him first. So now he did. "The moment he gets a reply he will communicate with me," reported the arms merchant in a letter to Caillard, "and I will pay into the Banque Suisse et Française and then your people will have to consult the experts as to the Turkish lines to be withdrawn so that I can meet Enver with a program." Zaharoff returned to Paris and discovered the prime minister was in the city attending an Allied council. "I have just sat with your Chairman at breakfast for half an hour. Lloyd George 'took written notes of my statement on which he paid me a great compliment . . . He is a lovely chappie.' "

The expected summons from Abdul Kerim to another meeting arrived less than a week later. Zaharoff needed to know what would be Britain's negotiating position with regard to Constantinople, Armenia, and the Middle East, including Palestine, now that Russia was out of the war. "No time should be lost in seeing the Chairman" to ascertain the position, he exhorted Caillard. But he was not in too much of a hurry to remind his friend that he still wanted "chocolate," as he called it—that is to say, an English title. "If the previous Chairman's letter to me about 'critical time' and my present work merit recognition, I shall be proud, very proud."

Lloyd George lay sick in bed with influenza. He could not see Caillard but wrote out for him directions for Zaharoff. They contained no reference to "chocolate," and they represented the prime minister's " 'personal opinion' " only, Caillard warned, "the special board [War Cabinet] not having been consulted . . . (but *you* know the weight the Chairman carries with his Board)." *Pace* Curzon, Sykes, Balfour, and the Foreign Office, the instructions regarding Palestine remained unchanged: "Mesopotamia and Palestine must be run on Egyptian lines; the flag, you observe, remains untouched." This does seem to indicate again that 10 Downing Street and the Foreign Office took opposite positions on the issue that Zionists would have found critical.

Zaharoff embarked upon his journeys once more. When he met Abdul Kerim in Switzerland for the fourth time on Wednesday, December 12, "I did not go one iota from your letter. He took notes as I repeated item per item." The Turk reported what was obvious already, that Enver was willing to talk and would accept the bribe. So this time Zaharoff really did pay into the Crédit Suisse et Française $500,000 for the envoy and $1,500,000 for his chief. The two men went to dinner. Imagine a first-class hotel dining room in neutral Switzerland at the height of World War I: bone china, silver cutlery, crystal goblets and snifters, dinner jackets, the hum of conversation in a variety of languages. Zaharoff made sure that the champagne and brandy flowed copiously. In this incongruous setting Abdul Kerim described conditions in Turkey and relations among the leaders of the Central Powers. He let his tongue wag. Enver and Talaat were at daggers drawn, he said, siding with his own boss and again introducing the possibility of poison: "I myself will give Talaat his coffee." He was drunk and under tremendous pressure. He let his ugly side show. "He [Abdul Kerim] only had to lift a finger and I [Zaharoff] would be arrested as a spy conspiring in a neutral country against friendly belligerents at the instigation of the Allies," Zaharoff reports him saying. "I laughed it out [but] it makes me think."

Enver had instructed Zaharoff to meet him at Lucerne during January 25–31. "Send me full instructions," Zaharoff told Caillard, "about the Turks withdrawing to a certain line and our paying a certain sum, and then withdrawing to another fixed line and our again paying and finally opening the Straits." He then headed off to Monte Carlo to recover his health, for he suffered from a debilitating skin condition.

At 10 Downing Street on January 9 at three-thirty in the afternoon, Lloyd George's secretary, Davies, handed to Caillard for transmission to Zaharoff the precise negotiating instructions that the arms merchant had requested. They read as follows:

> We should be prepared to pay the sum of ten million dollars to secure a permanent safe passage through the Dardanelles and Sea of Marmora. This would entail the evacuation of the forts and defenses in the Dardanelles and on the islands of the Sea of Marmora and their occupation by British forces. When the above is secured we will endeavor to obtain the revictualling of Constantinople from Southern Russia through the Bosphorus, which would have to be opened.

The second paragraph remained as before.

> It is agreed that in the event of all Turkish troops in PALESTINE and on the HEJAZ Railway being withdrawn North of the rail-

way line from HAIFA to DERAA a sum of $2,000,000 will be paid and the following guarantees will be given:

1. The Turkish forces will not be molested while carrying out the withdrawal.
2. PALESTINE will not be annexed or incorporated in the British Empire.

A few days earlier Lloyd George had delivered a famous speech to a conference of the Labour Party in which he defined Britain's war aims. With regard to Ottoman possessions in the Middle East, he said: "Arabia, Armenia, Mesopotamia, Syria and Palestine are in our judgment entitled to a recognition of their separate national conditions. What the exact form of that recognition . . . should be need not here be discussed." Caillard flagged this immediately: "You did not mention that Mesopotamia, Palestine &c. would remain under the Turkish flag, although not under Turkish Administration. It would, I think, be effective if I instructed Zaharoff from you to confirm this." Lloyd George provided the reassurances, and Caillard sent them on to Zaharoff: "Please explain to them [the Turks] that your previous communication concerning the retainment of their flag in those districts to be placed under the system of 'conseils judiciaires' (Egyptian model as a general illustration) has been confirmed . . . It is considered desirable you should do this, as the Chairman (consulted) agrees because that particular point about the flag was not mentioned in the Chairman's speech."

This exchange is important because it shows Lloyd George yet again contradicting the Foreign Office position that Balfour had cabled to Rumbold a few weeks earlier.

To make things as clear as possible in an extraordinarily murky situation: In late December 1917 Smuts instructed Dr. Parodi to tell Mouktar Bey, Talaat's emissary, that part of a larger arrangement for peace between Britain and the Ottomans would include provision for Turkey to continue to fly her flag over Palestine. The Foreign Office warned against this course. Balfour sent a countermanding telegram to Rumbold also in December 1917 and reiterated its message in March 1918, and referred to it yet again in the letter to Beaverbrook in August 1918. In mid-January 1918, however, Lloyd George repeated the Smuts position to Zaharoff. He should tell Abdul Kerim and Enver Pasha that the Turkish flag *could* continue to fly over Palestine. As far as can be told, Balfour did not know about this. He sent no countermanding telegrams. Anyway, one doubts that a

British foreign secretary can ever countermand a prime minister. Really, we have come upon a mystifying thicket of contradictory orders and instructions. One thing, however, is clear: In July 1917 Weizmann and his colleagues had judged *any* discussion of peace with Turkey out of bounds. Had they known that Lloyd George proposed to accept any form of Ottoman suzerainty in Palestine, they would have deemed it a gross betrayal. So would have the Arabs.

Zaharoff embarked upon an extraordinary journey from Monte Carlo to Geneva on January 23, 1918. His skin remained bad, and a personal physician accompanied him. He rented an entire saloon car of the train for the price of twenty-four first-class tickets. Upon crossing into Italy, however, soldiers invaded the carriage, driving him and his doctor into the corridor. They stole his food and cutlery and then his money. "We were four days and four nights getting to the Swiss frontier, hardly any food except sometimes soldiers' rations, no bed, no wash, etc. etc., and useless complaining to officers." When they reached the border, Swiss authorities searched him: "(I had not a single paper with me, and had learnt my instructions from your Chairman by heart)." They forced him and the doctor to strip naked and took their clothing into another room to examine. Then they noticed Zaharoff's skin condition. A quarantine doctor sent him to bed in a local hospital: "God, what a bed, what a place!"

Zaharoff deduced that the Swiss border authorities had recognized his name and were stalling while awaiting instructions from their superiors. When eventually they allowed him to continue his journey, he noticed that Swiss detectives were following him.

More extraordinary than the journey were the meetings that followed. Zaharoff arrived in Geneva on January 27, two days late. Abdul Kerim greeted him with the news that Enver was on his way from Lucerne. The three would meet next day. When Enver arrived, however, he refused to meet Zaharoff face-to-face, "claiming that all his movements were being always watched by the inquisitive Swiss; that A.K. was badly suspected of intriguing with me [Zaharoff], that the Swiss were more Niémtze (German) than the Germans." As a result, "I did not see E. but A.K. kept going backwards and forwards as a sort of telephone." Is it possible that either Zaharoff or Abdul Kerim lied about Enver's presence? Probably not: Zaharoff was too experienced to be fooled by Abdul Kerim; Lloyd George was too experienced to be fooled by Zaharoff. The prime minister never renounced the arms merchant; in fact, he saw to it that he received his "chocolate" after the war. It seems that Enver had come to Geneva to speak, however indirectly, with the representative of Lloyd George.

So: Abdul Kerim shuttled back and forth, whether between hotels or even possibly between rooms in the same hotel, we do not know. It quickly became apparent that the news he carried was disappointing for Britain. At the last moment Enver had developed cold feet. He would pay back most of his share of the bribe, five million French francs, into Zaharoff's Paris account. When the arms dealer arrived home, he found that the payment had been made. Abdul Kerim, however, did not return his share. He feared to contradict his chief, but to Zaharoff he said "he would not part with one piaster; he had honestly done his share, and if E. was now backing out, through fear, it was not his fault."

Through Abdul Kerim, Enver told Zaharoff that six months earlier he and Talaat had wanted to make a separate peace with Britain, "but when Russia and Rumania began crumbling Talaat sold him—'but that is my affair.' " Zaharoff had heard Abdul Kerim twice allude to poison in Talaat's coffee. Here was another veiled threat. He did not believe everything the Turks told him, but "E. certainly means to do away with Talaat in some way or other."

All that afternoon Abdul Kerim padded back and forth between the two men. At one point he reported to Zaharoff that Enver said the war would be decided "by the Americans putting or not their whole heart in it, and quickly." At another, through his intermediary, he lamented to Zaharoff that "if the Germans won this War Turkey would become Germany's vassal." At still another he promised to help the Allies by arranging "for the Turkish Armies in Palestine and on the Hejaz Railway to be withdrawn north of the Railway line from Haifa to Deraa." This suggests that Zaharoff at least broached the terms Britain was willing to offer for a separate peace, in which case the British government really did propose a continuing Ottoman presence, with flag flying, in Palestine, nearly three months after the Balfour Declaration was made public.

So Enver Pasha, architect of the Young Turk regime and of the disastrous Ottoman-German wartime alliance, parleyed with Basil Zaharoff, the infamous "merchant of death." Between them shuttled Abdul Kerim, Enver's not-so-faithful aide—he twice that day warned Zaharoff to beware: "He [Enver] is a traitor. Do not believe him. He will sell you. For him there is nothing in this great world but himself." The day finally ended, perhaps on this note. Zaharoff may have hoped for more clarity during a second round of discussion. But "next morning I found that E. and A.K. had taken French leave." He caught the next train for France. "I have given my heart and soul to this scheme and its failure has quite broken me up," he informed Caillard.

Britain and Turkey would make no separate peace during World War I. The two countries never were in sync. When one seemed willing to make a deal, the other found reason to pull back. Abdul Kerim contacted Zaharoff again in August 1918. The arms dealer entrained for Geneva yet again. When he got there, "the time to deal had arrived," Abdul Kerim reported Enver saying. He added: "When you meet E----you should have $25,000,000." Zaharoff backed off. "I replied that I would do nothing of the sort, but that if a definite proposal was made, I would see what it was worth to me in dollars . . . A.K. said I was a fool." Then the erstwhile intermediary went freelance. He asked what Zaharoff would pay for verbatim reports of all the Central Powers' war councils at which Turkish delegates were present. "On my replying that such reports might be interesting, he said, 'Man, they are worth millions, very many millions.' "

Once perhaps they would have been, but Zaharoff's record of this meeting reveals why that was no longer the case. "I purposely stayed with him 5 days and 4 nights so as to induce him to talk over his brandy, without my appearing to be questioning him." Abdul Kerim described breakdown among the Central Powers. At the last war council, Austrian, Turkish, and Bulgarian delegates had criticized the Germans. Hindenburg and Ludendorff threw the blame on each other. The Kaiser "abused his Austrian Ally with strong language." At this same meeting "the Turkish General Izzet Pasha Schishman had spat at King Ferdinand [of Bulgaria], and if anything the Pasha was applauded." No wonder England turned a deaf ear to Enver this time. The quarreling among her opponents reflected the fact that the tide of the war had turned finally in her favor.

When it had flowed the other way, British attitudes had been very different. Then Lloyd George was prepared to risk much for a separate peace with Turkey, not merely many millions of dollars but Arab and Zionist goodwill as well. Jewish and Arab nationalists would have recoiled in horror at the sight of a Turkish flag flying over Syria, Mesopotamia, or Palestine, no matter that Ottomans had no administrative control. Lloyd George must have calculated that they would accept the situation in the end. He rode the Arab horse and the Zionist horse and the separate-peace-with-Turkey horse too, and those were only the horses in the southeastern stable. That the horses pulled in different directions demonstrates the extraordinary skill of the rider.

Had Enver Pasha kept the bribe given him in December 1917 and taken Turkey out of the war, however, could Lloyd George have continued to ride the Zionists? Would we today term the Balfour Declaration a great Zionist triumph and a foundation stone of modern Israel? Or rather would we lump it among other beautiful phrases and promises made by wartime leaders intent upon persuading men to fight: "covenants openly arrived at," "war to end war," "no annexations or indemnities"? Not to discount the genius of Weizmann or the greatness of Balfour, but the famous declaration bearing the foreign secretary's name seems to have just missed the side track. And the genius of Lloyd George notwithstanding, what might have happened then is anybody's guess.

Conclusion

CHAPTER 26

A Drawing Together of Threads

"NEXT YEAR IN JERUSALEM," Jews avow at the conclusion of their annual Passover celebration. For nearly two thousand years the phrase could operate only as a metaphor, expressing an aspiration about Jewish collective destiny in the distant future. But after November 2, 1917, "Next year in Jerusalem" might be a practical plan of action for an individual Jew in the here and now, a genuinely possible sequence of events culminating soon in relocation to the Promised Land. On that second day in November during the third year of the most awful war in history up until then, Zionism formally gained a powerful ally. As a result, the greatest obstacles to realization of the metaphor had been, or were about to be, removed. Or at least so it seemed.

The Balfour Declaration was the result of a process that some consider practically inevitable. Certainly it is true that conditions created by the war enabled Chaim Weizmann and his colleagues to work wonders. During 1914–17 they gained access to the elite among British Jews and converted many of them to Zionism. They defeated advocates of Jewish assimilation, such as Lucien Wolf of the Conjoint Committee, whose raison d'être, lobbying the Foreign Office on behalf of foreign Jews, especially Russian and Romanian, had been swept away by the war. They gained entrance to

British governing circles and converted some of its most important members too.

During this period Weizmann and those who worked with him acted as inspired opportunists. Finally they could argue convincingly that a community of interest linked Zionist aspirations with those of the Entente. Zionists wanted the Ottomans out of Palestine; Britain and France wanted them out of the Middle East altogether. Zionists wanted a British protectorate in Palestine; Britain did too (although initially Sir Mark Sykes had bargained it away in negotiations with Georges-Picot of France).

More generally, Weizmann and his colleagues persuaded powerful men in Britain, France, and Italy that support of Zionism would benefit their wartime cause and the peace to follow. "International Jewry" was a powerful if subterranean force, they claimed, although this was a notable exaggeration if not an outright fantasy, whose goodwill would reap dividends for the Allies. Specifically, they suggested that Jewish finance in America, and Jewish influence upon antiwar forces in Russia, could help determine the conflict's outcome. Weizmann warned the Foreign Office that Germany recognized the potential of Jewish power and had begun to court it already. He advised the Allies to trump their enemy by declaring outright support for Zionism. His arguments worked upon the minds of anti- and philo-Semites alike among the British governing elite, who were desperate for any advantage in the wartime struggle. Eventually, to gain Jewish backing in the war, they promised to support establishment of a homeland for Jews in Palestine. It did them little good. Historians have discovered that in America Jewish financiers overwhelmingly favored the Allies already. In Russia the Bolsheviks seized power five days after the War Cabinet agreed to the Balfour Declaration. Lenin and Trotsky would take their country out of the war no matter what Russian Jews said.

Meanwhile Grand Sharif Hussein of Mecca and his sons were playing as expertly upon British hopes and fears as the Zionists were. Cautiously, shrewdly, bravely, they forged their own contacts: with the underground societies of Damascus already plotting to cast off the Ottoman yoke; and with representatives of the British government stationed in Cairo, whom they recognized as potential allies in their conflict with the CUP. The Damascene plotters offered Sharif Hussein leadership of their movement. The British, represented by Sir Henry McMahon, the high commissioner in Egypt, offered Hussein pledges of support if he would rebel against the Turks, and recognition of the geographical boundaries and political independence of the kingdom he would then establish. Or, at least Hussein interpreted McMahon's famous letters this way.

So he marshaled his forces, deployed them, and struck when he judged the moment ripe. In his own milieu Sharif Hussein was as cunning and subtle as Chaim Weizmann was in his. He had to be, for he occupied a personally dangerous position. To break with Constantinople was to risk his life and the lives of his sons and his followers. He did it anyway. His armies took Mecca, Taif, Jeddah, Wejh, and Aqaba. They besieged Medina. They arrived in Damascus almost simulataneously with the British. When they acted as guerrilla forces, they harried the Turks mercilessly, blowing up track and trestles and trains, cutting telegraph lines, slaughtering the unwary. They could not defeat their enemy alone, but they contributed to Britain's successful Middle Eastern military campaign. Hussein thought the British owed him. Men like T. E. Lawrence, who was in a position to know, thought the British owed him too.

That was not how the British government saw it. Consider the entire business from its point of view. As soon as the Ottomans entered the war, Lord Kitchener approached Sharif Hussein because he thought Hussein had authority to counter the Ottoman caliph's call for Muslims to wage jihad against Great Britain and her allies. Also he remembered Hussein's prewar opposition to the CUP. Now he hoped to aim and launch him against their common foe. He offered the grand sharif inducements to act: the caliphate once the Ottomans had been defeated, pledges of material support for his rebellion, recognition of an Arab kingdom under his leadership after the war. Did British officials intentionally encourage Hussein to believe that Palestine would form part of that kingdom? The McMahon letters are too ambiguous for us to tell. Did McMahon mean for them to be ambiguous? He did. The point was to galvanize a potential ally, he explained to Lord Hardinge. Details could be worked out later.

Simultaneously other Foreign Office mandarins engaged in like behavior with the Zionists. Accustomed to dealing with the Conjoint Committee and Lucien Wolf when Jewish interests impinged upon British foreign policy, they proved reluctant at first even to meet with Weizmann or his colleagues. Then the Zionist leader worked his magic. The Foreign Office learned from him to believe in Jewish influence upon the world (not hard, many of them believed in it already) and, more to the point, in Zionist influence upon the Jews. Weizmann told them that Jews wanted a homeland in Palestine above all else. The Foreign Office believed this too. So it encouraged Zionists to think it supported their chief aspiration, even though it might conflict with what McMahon had allowed Sharif Hussein to think. Once again the point was to galvanize a potential ally.

And all the while they had been busy galvanizing, or keeping galvanized, a third and much more important ally, one that had its eye upon the same fatal strip of land, among other strips. British imperialists did not want France in the Middle East at all, but if a postwar French presence in Syria was the price of her continued and wholehearted participation in the war against Germany, then that was a price Britain would pay, even if it meant deceiving Arabs and Zionists in the meantime.

But France thought that Syria included Palestine, and this Britain could not accept. It was one thing for Zionists to claim that land as home under a British protectorate, or for Arabs to govern it under some form of British tutelage; it was quite another for a great power like France to have power over territory bordering Egypt and overlooking, albeit from a distance, the Suez Canal. Sykes persuaded Picot that neither Britain nor France should govern Palestine, but rather an international condominium. Palestine was not "a twice promised land," as some have written then, but rather a thrice-promised one: to the Arabs (or at least the Arabs thought so), to the Zionists, and to a prospective international consortium whose members had yet to be determined.

Nor is this the end of the very tangled web Great Britain wove for that eastern shore of the Mediterranean Sea. To detach the Ottomans from the Central Powers would do more to win the war for Britain than anything connected to Arabs or Jews. From October 1914 onward certain Britons bent their minds precisely to that task. At first they could not gain much purchase on events. But when the easterner David Lloyd George became prime minister, the project gained a supremely influential advocate, and various pourparlers went forward. Eventually through his emissaries Lloyd George offered to the Turks, among other inducements, that their flag continue to fly over Palestine if they would make a separate peace, even as other British officials were promising to Zionists and Arabs that the Ottomans and their flag would be expelled from the Middle East altogether. In the end Enver Pasha spurned Lloyd George's offer. Nevertheless, it seems right to suggest that Palestine was not thrice-promised really. It was promised, or at any rate dangled as bait, four times: before the Zionists and the Arabs, before Picot by Sykes in the shape of an as-yet-unformed international consortium, and before the Turks, who would otherwise lose it as a result of the war.

Of course during most of our period, for imperial-economic-strategic reasons, Britain meant to keep the primary governing role in Palestine for herself.

———————

The Balfour Declaration was the highly contingent product of a tortuous process characterized as much by deceit and chance as by vision and diplomacy. Weizmann was a genius, but his triumph, even among his British coreligionists, was hardly preordained. The victory over Lucien Wolf was near-run and not entirely edifying. His paramount position among British Zionists was secure, but that did not stop members of his inner circle from severely criticizing his judgment. Nor did it inhibit others among the larger Zionist community from condemning his authoritarian manner, so that more than once Weizmann felt obliged to offer them his resignation. Had Harry Sacher and Leon Simon prevailed in the argument over his attitude toward the separate peace with Turkey, or had Weizmann carried through on any of his several threats to resign, the history of Palestine, and of the world, might be very different.

So might it be if King Hussein's forces had been able to occupy parts of Syria a little bit earlier than they did. That was what T. E. Lawrence thought would happen. On the night he rode out of Aqaba with George Lloyd, he predicted that Hussein's writ would run "along the coast from Acre northwards." He did not realize it was already too late, that the War Cabinet had just endorsed Balfour's letter to Lord Rothschild.

Or imagine that Hussein had possessed in London an advocate for Arab nationalism who was as skillful and eloquent as Chaim Weizmann. He himself could not travel there to play that role, so he relied instead upon British proxies such as Lawrence and Mark Sykes. Both these men possessed genius, but Sykes—juggling Jews, Arabs, Armenians, French, and various Britons, among others—could never advocate solely for the Arabs even if he wished to, which he never did. As for Lawrence, his views must be termed ambiguous. He was pro-Arab, he wrote to Sykes, and pro-British too. Anyway, during the war he was not often in London, and afterward it was too late. Perhaps one of Hussein's sons, Abdullah or Feisal, could have lobbied for Arab nationalism as Weizmann did for Zionism, although one doubts they would have exhibited his extraordinary combination of skills. In any event Hussein needed them both in Arabia. Nevertheless, just because that was how it was does not mean that was how it had to be.

Moreover, the movement for a separate peace with Turkey had the potential for spoiling Zionist and Arab plans altogether. In June and July 1917, with three British agents (Pilling, Herbert, and Zaharoff) and one American (Morgenthau) engaged in talks with Turks or preparing to talk with them, the Ottomans still held Syria, including Palestine. A separate peace with the Allies at that juncture might well have left them with more

than symbolic control over those lands. That was why Weizmann opposed
the idea so fiercely. He managed to stymie Morgenthau. He could not
stymie Herbert, but the Turks did, in the sense that they did not follow up
on their initial contact with him. Weizmann learned about J. R. Pilling in
late November, after publication of the Balfour Declaration. We have evidence that he realized that everything gained by that document still could
be lost. He and the Armenian, James Malcolm, called immediately upon
Ronald Graham at the Foreign Office to express their "serious concern not
to say alarm." Graham reassured them: Pilling had no authority. He did not
mention the role of Basil Zaharoff, because neither he nor anyone else in the
Foreign Office knew about it.

Zaharoff's several journeys to speak with Turks would have caused
Weizmann much greater alarm, for they had a greater chance of success.
His penultimate trip was most dangerous from the Zionist point of view.
Even after publication of the Balfour Declaration, Lloyd George offered to
allow the Turkish flag to continue flying over Jerusalem. Imagine that
Enver Pasha, through his intermediary, Abdul Kerim, had sealed the deal
with the arms merchant in that Swiss hotel room and arranged the separate
peace early in 1918. In that case one may doubt that Jews celebrating
Passover in subsequent years would have charged their annual vow with
the new practical meaning they thought the Declaration made possible.

Because it was unpredictable and characterized by contradictions, decep-
tions, misinterpretations, and wishful thinking, the lead-up to the Balfour
Declaration sowed dragon's teeth. It produced a murderous harvest, and
we go on harvesting even today.

When the Zionists learned of the Sykes-Picot Agreement, which envisioned an international condominium administering Palestine, they were
enraged. It contradicted everything British officials had led them to believe
they could hope for in the Middle East. They concluded they must obtain
from the British government a written guarantee of support. They took the
Balfour Declaration to be that guarantee. In fact, Britain's deceptive practices never ceased. During the summer of 1917, after Zionists learned of the
Sykes-Picot Agreement but before they obtained the Declaration, the Foreign Office satisfied Weizmann by allowing him to checkmate Morgenthau
on his way to speak with Turks about a separate peace. Simultaneously it
encouraged Aubrey Herbert to travel to Switzerland to speak with Turks
about that very subject. Needless to say, it did not tell Weizmann. After the
Declaration it remained true that what Lloyd George gave with one hand

he might negotiate away with the other—if only Enver Pasha would let him. Of the discussions between Zaharoff and Abdul Kerim, the Zionists never learned. Still, the prime minister's conduct did not augur well for future transparency or good relations between Jewish nationalists and the British government.

King Hussein and the Arab nationalists felt British duplicity more keenly than Weizmann and the Zionists did. The Sykes-Picot Agreement contradicted their aspirations too. But when Sykes told Hussein in Jeddah that France would treat the Syrian littoral including northern Palestine just as Britain would treat Mesopotamia, Hussein made a fatal mistake. He remembered his correspondence with Sir Henry McMahon and references in it to a temporary British occupation of Baghdad and Basra. We know that McMahon was purposely vague in his letters, but Hussein did not. He thought he had ironclad guarantees for Mesopotamia and now for Syria too. He trusted Sykes implicitly. Hussein's son Feisal and his adviser Fuad Selim, not to mention even a few British imperial officials, feared he misjudged. We shall never know—perhaps Sykes could somehow have squared even this circle. Unfortunately he died in Paris on February 16, 1919, of Spanish influenza. And then at Versailles Lloyd George allowed France to take Syria so long as Britain could take Iraq and Palestine "from Dan to Beersheba." So with Clemenceau he bargained away part of the Arab nationalist dream, just as months earlier he had been prepared to bargain away part of the Zionist dream with Enver.

Historians who have written about the Hussein-McMahon correspondence and the Sykes-Picot Agreement have spilled oceans of ink tracing the initial reaction of Hussein and his sons to the Balfour Declaration. Did they promise to welcome and work with Jewish colonists and only develop reservations later, or did they express disquiet at the outset? We can no more settle this debate than the others; the evidence, as always for this subject and period, is mixed and ambiguous. When Hogarth of the Arab Bureau traveled to Jeddah to explain the Declaration to Hussein, the "King seemed quite prepared for [the] formula and agreed enthusiastically, saying he welcomed Jews to all Arab lands." But note that Hussein considered Palestine to be Arab land. Then Sykes coached Feisal on the subject in an extraordinary letter that reveals his own fantastic understanding of Jews:

> I know that the Arabs despise, condemn and hate the Jews, but passion is the ruin of princes and peoples . . . Those who have persecuted or condemned the Jews could tell you the tale. The Empire of Spain in the old days and the Empire of Russia in our

time show the road of ruin that Jewish persecution leads to. You
say to yourself what is this race despised, rejected, abhorred, that
cannot fight, that has no home and is no nation? O Feisal, I can
read your heart and your thought, and there are counselors
about you who will whisper similar things in your ear. Believe I
speak the truth when I say that this race, despised and weak, is
universal, is all powerful and cannot be put down.

Feisal replied: "I do not, and never did, despise anyone on account of his
religion . . . Therefore on general grounds I would welcome any good understanding with the Jews." Was the Balfour Declaration a "good understanding"? Feisal was not sure. He continued in this letter to Sykes: "But I
do not know what is going on, nor what is the basis of the arrangement intended to be concluded about Palestine for Jews and Arabs." To Hakki Bey,
a prominent Muslim from Damascus, he expressed doubts in December
1917. He did not look favorably upon the Balfour Declaration, he told him,
but he was not yet prepared to protest it.

Whatever Hussein and his immediate family thought of the Declaration, it produced grave reservations among Arabs and Muslims more generally. Hakki Bey found that when Arab leaders with Feisal in Aqaba
learned of it, they did not hesitate to denounce "the ambitions and designs
of Great Britain and France." Elsewhere, two days after publication,
William Yale of the U.S. State Department was reporting that "the Syrians
have held meetings to protest against Zionism to all the Allies, and the
younger and more hot-headed among the Moslems are laying plans for the
future that bode no good for the peace of Palestine." The Syrian leaders dispatched a telegram to Balfour:

> With reference to the recent publication of your Excellency's
> declaration to Lord Rothschild regarding the Jews in Palestine,
> we respectfully take the liberty to invite your Excellency's atten-
> tion to the fact that Palestine forms a vital part of Syria—as the
> heart is to the body—admitting of no separation politically or
> sociologically, more especially as Palestine is looked upon both
> by Islam and Christendom as the polar star and birthplace of
> their religious ideals as much as by Jewry.

In London the Islamic Society convened on November 5 at 46 Great Russell Street in Bloomsbury, not far from the Imperial Hotel on Russell
Square where the Zionists had gathered the previous summer to draft the

claim to their Promised Land. The Muslims, however, wished "to remind the British government of its pledge to keep inviolate the places of Moslem worship including Masjid-i-Aksa which is synonymous with the Latin name of Palestine." They passed a second even more pointed resolution:

> That we members of the Islamic Society regard with great concern the mischievous movement started by some people calling themselves Zionists, and we hope that the British government will once more make a declaration of its policy at an early date in order to remove any misapprehension which may exist in the minds of the Moslems.

Five days after that an eminent member of the Anglo-Muslim London community, the barrister Amir Ali, founder of the Red Crescent Society, reiterated these concerns: "Palestine is unquestionably regarded by Moslems as a Holy Land, and Jerusalem as next in sanctity to Mecca and Medina," he wrote to Lord Hardinge. "The soul of their Prophet rested in Jerusalem on its ascent to communication with the Divinity. Jerusalem and its environs are covered with Moslem shrines, mosques and mausoleums. Your Lordship will readily realize how offensive the idea must be to them that their holiest places in Palestine should be placed under Jewish control."

To such objections, the British always replied that the Balfour Declaration specifically protected the rights of non-Jews in Palestine. But in 1917 Arabs outnumbered Jews there by six or seven to one. A promise to protect the vast majority from a tiny minority seemed upside down to them. And British officials sometimes grew impatient with expressions of Arab unease. When he learned of the Syrian telegram to Balfour, General Clayton called its authors to a meeting. He told them "the Zionists were very powerful . . . Throughout the world the Jews controlled the capital . . . In their determination to obtain Palestine as a Home for the Jews they would undoubtedly succeed." So, he advised, the Arabs had better cooperate when the Zionists arrived in Palestine. When Sykes read the resolutions submitted by the Islamic Society to the Foreign Office, he scrawled upon the file in his round, boyish hand: "I strongly urge no notice be taken of this . . . crew of seditionists and C.U.P. agents . . . Most of the members ought to be behind the barbed wire. In any other country they would be." This almost makes one wonder whether he intended to square Arab-Zionist conflict after all.

Whether he could have done so remains moot, for in 1919 Sykes passed unwilling from the scene. The Britons who followed him, to whom the

League of Nations gave a mandate for governing Palestine in 1920, certainly could not keep the peace there, but then wartime British officials who had done so much to facilitate the Zionist and Arab movements had never aimed primarily to keep the peace in Palestine, they aimed to win the First World War and to maintain their country's place in the world. Here are the primary motivations (although not the only ones) for all their dealings with Grand Sharif Hussein and Chaim Weizmann. Of course neither man, nor any of their followers, acted as mere pawns in British hands. Zionists and Arabs fought fiercely and tenaciously for their goals during the war and after. But we cannot be surprised at the results of so complex and fraught a process as the lead-up to the Balfour Declaration.

The most famous result was the Declaration itself. Zionists and many others have viewed it ever since as a terrific achievement, a foundation stone along the way to the establishment of modern Israel. Many Arabs, on the other hand, have seen it as a terrible setback, the real starting point of their dispossession and misery.

An equally consequential result of the process was the development of profound mistrust, of all parties by all parties; and growing from that mistrust a bitterness that would lead to the spilling of much blood.

At the end of the war Britain ruled Palestine by virtue of military occupation. The Paris Peace Conference in 1919 and the San Remo Conference in 1920 ratified her rule and extended it indefinitely within the mandate system established by the League of Nations. Zionism had achieved its objective, yet Zionist doubts about Britain were reviving. Many Zionists thought Ronald Storrs, Britain's first military governor of Jerusalem, favored the Arabs over them; and that the new colonial secretary, Winston Churchill, hitherto a staunch ally, favored Arabs too, at least at a conference in Cairo in 1922, when he carved Transjordan out of Palestine and established Hussein's son, Abdullah, as its ruler. Even Herbert Samuel, British Palestine's first high commissioner, shocked and displeased Zionists by temporarily suspending Jewish immigration after anti-Zionist riots in May 1921 and by pardoning jailed rioters. That certain British officials continued to express anti-Semitic views did not improve matters.

Tension between Zionists and British officials eased after 1922, but in 1930 a Labour Government, wishing to assuage Arab resentment of the Jewish presence, accepted a white paper issued by Colonial Secretary Lord Passfield, the Fabian socialist formerly known as Sidney Webb. Webb questioned the very bases of the Zionist program: Jewish immigration into Palestine (again); exclusive labor practices; the wholesale purchase of Arab land. Against this paper Zionists protested so vehemently that the govern-

ment backed down, but in 1937 a Conservative government, hoping to settle the problem once and for all, accepted the recommendations of another
investigative commission, this one led by Lord Peel: Palestine should be divided into a Jewish state, an Arab state, and a territory still under British
mandate. Among Zionists this plan aroused grave suspicion and a storm of
protest, although Weizmann ultimately urged acceptance. Then in 1939
Neville Chamberlain's government repudiated the Peel Report: Palestine
should not be partitioned; it should become an independent binational
Arab-Jewish state. Over the next five years seventy-five thousand more
Jews would be allowed to enter; then Jewish immigration should cease altogether. At this point Arabs outnumbered Jews in Palestine by about three
to one, and Zionist mistrust of British intentions scaled new heights. It
hardly diminished even during World War II, despite the fact that Chamberlain's plan remained on the drawing boards only.

Arab mistrust and resentment also grew after 1918. Hussein did not get
his Arab kingdom but merely the kingdom of Hejaz (and that only until
1924, when Ibn Saud and his Wahhabi fundamentalists overthrew him and
established Saudi Arabia). Feisal never became king of an independent
Syria: The French expelled him from Damascus in 1920; a year later the
British established him as their puppet ruler of Iraq and his brother Abdullah as an equally dependent ruler of Transjordan. Were they better off with
British or Ottoman overlords? It seems fair to conclude at least that their attitudes toward Britain, and the attitudes of their followers, were not simple.

As for the majority of Palestinian Arabs, they directed their resentment
against Jews (whom they thought were stealing their land) and against
British officials (whom they thought were protecting the Jews). In 1920 and
1921 Arab rioters killed more than half a dozen. In 1929 pogroms in
Jerusalem, Hebron, Safed, and elsewhere resulted in the deaths of 133, the
injury of hundreds more, and the destruction of much property. In 1936 a
full-blown Arab Palestinian revolt developed. The recommendations of
the Peel Commission, which were meant to tamp it down, only added fuel
to the fire. Arab leaders denounced Peel even more vociferously than Zionists did and rejected his proposals unanimously. A general strike of Arab
Palestinians demanded immediate cessation of Jewish immigration, prohibition of the sale of Arab land to Jews, and establishment of a national government. Something like civil war ensued. Volunteers from throughout the
Arab world poured into Palestine to fight Zionists and Britons alike.

Britain had a mandate to govern Palestine but lacked the means. Her
empire reached the zenith of its extent just after World War I weakened it
irreparably. In the Middle East during the spring of 1919, General Allenby

was demobilizing soldiers at the rate of twenty thousand a month. A year later the chief of the general staff complained, "In no single theatre are we strong enough. Not in Ireland, nor England, not on the Rhine, not in Constantinople, nor Batoum, nor Egypt, nor Palestine, nor Mesopotamia, nor Persia, nor India." Britain would experience during the coming half century something like what the Ottomans endured half a century before: gradual diminution of an empire whose subject peoples demanded control of their own destinies and would take up arms to gain them. In Palestine, Jews and Arabs took up arms; Britain had not the strength to keep the peace.

The Jews established a paramilitary organization, Haganah, in 1920 because Britain failed to defend them effectively during the pogroms of that year. Two additional armed groups appeared in the 1930s: Etzel (which the British called Irgun), and Lechi (which they called the Stern Gang), a breakaway from Etzel. Both groups moved from defensive to offensive operations and eventually to terrorist campaigns against Arabs and Britons too. They reached a bloody climax in the years immediately after the Second World War, when Etzel and Lechi carried out assassinations, beatings, and bombings, most notoriously against the King David Hotel in Jerusalem, where they killed 91 and injured 46.

To such a low ebb had sunk British-Zionist relations, but British-Arab relations sank lower still. The most important Palestinian leader of the Mandate period, Haj Amin al-Husseini, gained the lifetime post of grand mufti, the highest Muslim religious office in Jerusalem, with the support of none other than Herbert Samuel, who thought he would help maintain order among Arabs. In fact, al-Husseini was an uncompromising Palestinian nationalist, thus an implacable enemy of British occupation and Zionism both. He led the Arab Revolt in 1936. Hunted by the British, he fled, landing finally in Nazi Germany during World War II, where he sought Hitler's support for Arab independence. Al-Husseini would be sidelined during the 1948 war between Arabs and the nascent state of Israel when hatred and violence overboiled yet again, this time with decisive results. But al-Husseini's viewpoint was not sidelined. It remains potent as ever.

During World War I, then, Britain and her allies slew the Ottoman dragon in the Middle East. By their policies they sowed dragon's teeth. Armed men rose up from the ground. They are rising still.

Acknowledgments

I had a lot of help on this project.

First I want to thank the archivists with whom I worked in the United States, Britain, and Israel. All of them went out of their way to help me, none more than Debbie Usher at the Middle East Centre Archive, St. Antony's College, Oxford University, and Merav Segal, director of the Weizmann Archives, Weizmann Institute, Rehovot.

I am grateful to Bruce Henson, a librarian at Georgia Tech, who managed after much effort to track down the weather report with which this book begins.

Then I wish to thank Natalya Staros for helping with translations from Russian, Uri Rosenheck for helping with translations from Hebrew, and Shari Youngblood for helping with translations from French. I am grateful, too, to Luke Dickens, and to an old friend, Jim Obelkevich, both of whom tracked down, photographed, and sent as email attachments documents I realized I wanted from England months after I had left the country. Alexandra Ramirez helped me find images for reproduction in the book.

I am grateful to Leonard Smith for inviting me to lecture on the Balfour Declaration at Oberlin College, and to Oded Irshai, who arranged for me to give a seminar on the same subject at the Hebrew University in

Jerusalem. In both places students and faculty in the audience asked questions that helped me to clarify my thinking.

Peter Oppenheimer, former director of the Oxford Centre for Hebrew and Jewish Studies at Yarnton Manor, oversaw my stay there, enabling me to visit British archives; Tony Judt arranged my stint as a visitor at the Erich Remarque Center, New York University, which enabled me to work at the Yivo Institute for Jewish Research and at the New York Public Library. Thanks to both of you.

Tony Judt, Lisa Anderson, Stephen P. Cohen, David Taal, Dorothy Gilbert Goldstone, John Drucker, and John Krige all read the manuscript, or sections of it, and gave good advice for which I am grateful. But I alone am responsible for errors of fact and interpretation and for such infelicities of style as remain.

During the years this book has been in preparation, I have discussed it, always to my advantage, with many friends, including Bernard Wasserstein, David Gilbert, Chris Clark, Peter Weiler, David Large, Ross McKibbin, Peter Schizgal, Peter Mandler, Peter Dimock, Gary Kornblith, Carol Lasser, Kurt Tauber, and most of my colleagues in the School of History, Technology and Society at Georgia Tech. Thank you all.

My editors, Amy Black in Toronto, Bill Swainson in London, and Will Murphy in New York City, have encouraged me when necessary and offered helpful suggestions when a draft of the manuscript finally became available. To them too I offer thanks.

I acknowledge with thanks the Georgia Tech Foundation, which twice granted subventions for travel to archives abroad.

My agents Peter Robinson and Christie Fletcher have been terrific.

So have been my wife and two sons. By now they realize I am happiest when working on a big project.

Jonathan Schneer
Atlanta, Georgia
August 10, 2009

Notes

POSTLUDE AS PRELUDE

xxvii London on December 2, 1917 . . . "Cold Northerly wind all day gradually increasing in force. Rain gradually dropping off from 12 hrs. Clear intervals in evening." *Symon's Meteorological Magazine.*

CHAPTER 1: PALESTINE BEFORE WORLD WAR I

3 And it was small . . . But the entry for "Palestine" in the *Encyclopaedia Britannica* states that Palestine is 140 miles long and between 23 and 80 miles wide depending on the latitude.

4 "cool, shady, hung . . ." Twain, *Innocents Abroad,* 334–35, 351.

4 A horseman riding . . . *Great Britain and the Near East,* March 23, 1917. The rider on horseback was Dr. E.W.G. Masterman of the Royal Geographical Society.

4 "of a Scotch glen . . ." *Palestine,* February 8, 1917.

5 "many more whose names . . ." Estelle Blythe, daughter of Jerusalem's last Anglican bishop, writing in *Great Britain and the Near East,* December 15, 1916.

5 other European visitors . . . See, for example, ibid., August 14, 1914.

6 "such as his poverty . . ." Entry for "Fellah," *Encyclopaedia Britannica.*

6 When on the move . . . Entry for "Bedouin," ibid.

6 "striking want of beauty . . ." Entry for "Jerusalem," ibid. For an evocative portrait of the city, see Marcus, *Jerusalem 1913.*

7 Meanwhile Jerusalem had . . . The walls were 38½ feet high according to Baedeker, *Palestine and Syria,* 23.

7 "The streets are ill-paved . . ." Ibid.

7 "fanatical and quarrelsome" . . . Ibid., 220.

7 "They usually crowd . . ." Ibid., 128.

8 The so-called Young Turks . . . Although not sufficiently, according to Arab critics: "Eighty per cent of the public funds were spent exclusively in Turkish areas." See Graves, *Memoirs of*

King Abdullah, 98. Still, as a result of Tanzimat, at the outset of Abdul Hamid II's rule it took three days to journey by horse from Jaffa to Jerusalem; in 1912 it took eight hours, along newly built or improved roads, by horse, and four hours by rail. This speed of travel expedited internal trade. Moreover, what had been grown in the interior could be conveyed by rail to the ports and exported, while goods shipped to the ports from abroad could be transported inland. Palestine's foreign trade increased annually by 1 percent from 1875 to 1895 and by 5 percent from 1895 to 1913.

9 They were not themselves . . . Land prices rose from 300 to 500 francs per hectare to 3,000 to 5,000 francs per hectare.

9 Now a new source . . . On Palestine before World War I, see especially Divine, *Politics and Society,* from which much of the material and all the statistics above are drawn; see also McDowall, *Palestinians,* 3–7. For conditions in south Palestine, see *Arab Bulletin,* no. 38.

10 "aboriginal Palestinian Jews," T. E. Lawrence, "Syria, the Raw Material," Oxford University, St. Antony's College, Middle East Centre, William Yale Papers, box 2, file 1. For more on pre-1914 Jews in Palestine, see Roth, *History of Jews,* 366–74; Eban, *My People,* 312–25; *Great Britain and the Near East,* February 9, 1917.

11 Together Russians and Romanians . . . See Shaw, *Jews of Ottoman Empire,* 215–16; and Blumberg, *Zion Before Zionism,* 158–60.

12 self-consciously Jewish nationalists . . . Mandel, *Arabs and Zionism,* xxi.

12 "There was scarcely . . ." Ibid., 37. See too Porath, *Emergence,* 25.

12 "Had we permitted . . ." *Arab Bulletin,* no. 64, p. 389. The author is described merely as "one of the leaders of the Jewish movement."

13 "Ignorant and stupid . . ." Conder, *Eastern Palestine,* 17.

13 "The Jewish planters obtain . . ." *Palestine,* October 17, 1917.

13 In 1891 authorities . . . Mandel, *Arabs and Zionism,* 39.

13 The quarter century before . . . Porath, *Emergence,* 29.

13 "Their labor competes . . ." Quoted in Mandel, *Arabs and Zionism,* 81.

14 "[The Jews'] right . . ." The young Arab nationalist was Khalil al-Sakakini. See his diary entries for February 23, 1914, "and a few days later," quoted ibid., 211–12.

14 But it was Palestine . . . For Ottoman policy toward the Jews during this period, see Shaw, *Jews of Ottoman Empire,* 206–33.

CHAPTER 2: OTTOMANISM, ARABISM, AND SHARIF HUSSEIN

17 full-fledged Arab nationalism . . . See first of all C. Ernest Dawn, "The Origins of Arab Nationalism," in Khalidi et al., *Origins of Arab Nationalism,* 3–30, and Rashid Khalidi, "Ottomanism and Arabism in Syria Before 1914: A Reassessment," ibid., 50–69. Among the most important of the early nationalists were Jamal al-Din al-Asadabadi (1838–97), commonly known as al-Afghani, an early pan-Islamist; Abdullah al-Nadim (1843–96), an advocate of Muslim unity but also of imitating Western political practices; Abd al-Rahman al-Kawakibi (1849–1902), who believed that Islam and tyranny were incompatible; and Muhammad Abduh, an Egyptian advocate of an Arab-led Muslim revival. See Haim, *Arab Nationalism,* 6–29, and Dawn, *From Ottomanism,* 122–35.

18 Nothing could disguise . . . For Abdul Hamid II, see Haslip, *Sultan;* see too Antonius, *Arab Awakening,* 60–75.

19 On July 3, 1908 . . . The CUP major was Ahmed Niyazi.

19 The CUP deposed him . . . It replaced Abdul Hamid II with Prince Reshad, now styled Mehmed V, and when he died, it installed his brother as Mehmed VI.

20 One of them shot . . . The minister of war was Nezim Pasha.

21 "to awaken the Arab . . ." Quoted in Duri, *Historical Formation,* 226.

21 Secret societies emerged . . . For al-Ahd, see NA, FO371/2486/157740, October 25, 1915, see too Antonius, *Arab Awakening,* 118–19, and Duri, *Historical Formation,* 225.

22 Telegrams of support . . . Dawn, *From Ottomanism,* 154.

22 On June 21 the congress . . . NA, FO371/1827/29037. "Il import d'établir dans chacun des vi-

layets syriens et arabes un régime décentralisateur approprié à ses besoins et à ses aptitudes";
"La langue arab doit être reconnue au Parlement Ottoman et considérée comme officielle dans
les pays syriens et arabes."

22 Turkish spies kept . . . "At the moment the Syrians in Cairo are very active . . . spurring each
other on," one spy reported on March 28, 1913. Cairo was headquarters of the Decentralization Committee. Early in 1914 the CUP established an intelligence bureau there to keep more
systematic tabs on the various societies and activists. During the bureau's first year of existence,
it spent 182,500 gold Turkish liras ("an immense sum"). During its second year it employed
513 agents, received 4,131 reports, and maintained files on 8,938 suspects, but such extraordinary assiduity may be explained in part by the fact that Turkey had just entered World War I.
See Tauber, *Arab Movements,* 37.

22 "The heart's desire . . ." Quoted in Djemal Pasha, *Memories,* 229. The French dragoman was
Philippe Zalzal.

23 "It is to be hoped . . ." Mallet to Grey, October 29, 1913, NA, FO371/1848/50838.

23 "There is every sign . . ." NA, FO371/1822/23816.

23 a new Islamic university . . . NA, FO371/1848/5519298. The Egyptian pan-Islamist was
Sheikh Abdul Aziz Shawish.

23 "With one or two exceptions" . . . NA, FO371/1822/24353.

23 "large and expressive brown . . ." Hogarth, *Hejaz,* 54.

23 "He is such an old dear" . . . Lawrence to General Clayton, October 18, 1916, OUNBL, T. E.
Lawrence Papers, MS Eng. C. 6737/f.12.

24 "outwardly so gentle . . ." Hogarth, *Hejaz,* 54.

25 "integrity, energy . . ." *El Qibla,* no. 87, June 15, 1917.

26 It chose instead another . . . It chose his uncle, Abd al-Ilah.

26 "I pray that God . . ." Quoted in Graves, *Memoirs of King Abdullah,* 45.

26 Hussein had been courting . . . Report #2, "The Arabia and Hejaz Situation," November 5,
1917, p. 6, Oxford University, St. Antony's College, Middle East Centre, William Yale Papers.
See also Wilson, *King Abdullah,* 15. The Anglophile grand vizier was Kamil Pasha.

26 But as markers . . . Ibid.

26 "This country abides . . ." Quoted in Graves, *Memoirs of King Abdullah,* 62.

26 He may have promised . . . "If your Majesty were to come to the Hejaz with our household,
money would be brought to you and you would be beyond the reach of any insurgents." Ibid.

27 "a miserable country" . . . Report #2, p. 2, Oxford University, St. Antony's College, Middle East
Centre, Yale Papers.

27 "of exceptionally predatory . . ." Hogarth, *Hejaz,* 16.

27 Residents of all classes . . . Ibid., 27–28.

27 "as a mountain" . . . Sharif of Mecca, Verbal Report of "X," October 29, 1914, Sir Ronald Storrs
Papers, Adam Matthew Publications Microfilm, reel 4, box 2, folder 3.

28 "In the event of a quarrel . . ." Ibid.

28 "clean" . . . "not clean" . . . Storrs, *Memoirs,* 164. Storrs wrote: "I . . . chose for secret messenger
X the father-in-law of my little Persian agent Ruhi."

28 "morality seems to be . . ." "A report written by Hussein Ruhi Effendi, a member of Colonel
Wilson's staff at Jeddah," NA, FO371/3047/13365.

29 Britain would treat . . . "I had it last Spring from the lips of his favorite son Abdullah that the
State of Afghanistan is always before their eyes as an attainable summum bonum." Storrs to illegible, February 22, 1915, Storrs Papers, reel 4, box 2, folder 3.

29 his position was a platform . . . An untitled, unnumbered paper by Mark Sykes on the Arab
situation, September 11, 1916, Hull University, Mark Sykes Papers. Hussein had helped the
Turks defeat the Idrisi of Asir; he had established good relations with tribes led by Ibn el
Rashid and Ibn Sha'alan.

29 He opposed even . . . Dawn, *From Ottomanism,* 6.

29 "He is very generous . . ." NA, FO371/2486/112369. But note that the sentiments, according to
Captain G. S. Symes, are those of "a soi-disant Turcophobe and an associate of Sherif Abdalla,

the son of Sherif Hussein." For a helpful analysis of Sharif Hussein's relations with the Ottoman government and the *valis* it sent to the Hejaz, see Kayali, *Arabs,* 181–84.

29 "with merry dark brown eyes . . ." Hogarth, *Hejaz,* 55.

30 "On one occasion . . ." NA, FO371/2486/112369.

30 His biographer writes . . . Wilson, *King Abdullah,* 14. But George Antonius, the great historian of the Arab Revolt, writes that Abdullah was "foremost among the Arab deputies in the Ottoman Parliament." Antonius, *Arab Awakening,* 126.

30 "It *purports* . . ." Graves, *Memoirs of King Abdullah,* 97.

30 Ottoman parliamentary sessions . . . The Egyptian khedive was Abbas Hilmi.

30 He may have met . . . Ibid., 112.

30 Lord Kitchener . . . Ibid., 112–14.

31 "and we parted on the best . . ." Storrs, *Memoirs,* 135.

CHAPTER 3: FIRST STEPS TOWARD THE ARAB REVOLT

33 *"The Turkish Army is in . . ."* "By order of H.E. the Minister, the Cairo Police have been directed to punish anyone who might be caught singing this song." Sir Ronald Storrs Papers, Adam Matthew Publications Microfilm, reel 4, box 2, folder 3, Egypt 1914–15.

33 British intelligence agents . . . For example, "Mousam El Din . . . a most dangerous suspicious character"; "Calal Bey, Sami Bey, El Hag Abdel Maim: All live in No 5 Sharia Shura, opposite Tewfikieh School . . . Their movements are quite suspicious. They should be supervised." "Notes on Turks suspected of spying for Turkey," ibid.

34 "The Ottoman Army is . . ." "Translation of a Proclamation Issued by the Commandant of the Fourth Turkish Army and Minister of Marine," ibid.

34 "too clever by . . ." Introduction to the Microfilm by Bernard Wasserstein, Storrs Papers. For more on Storrs, see his entry in the *New Dictionary of National Biography* and Storrs, *Memoirs.*

36 "He may not be . . ." There are many biographies of Kitchener, such as Royle, *Kitchener Enigma.*

36 "Tell Storrs . . ." Kitchener to Cheetham, September 24, 1914, NA, FO371/2770/69301. This file contains correspondence between the British and Hussein and family down to March 10, 1916. I will not cite the file again in this chapter unless referring to correspondence after that date.

37 "This is the Commandment . . ." Quoted in Storrs, *Memoirs,* 165.

37 "closer union" . . . I have quoted here Cheetham's recapitulation to the Foreign Office of Abdullah's letter, NA, FO371/2770/69301. But see also Oxford University, St. Antony's College, Middle East Centre, Felix Frankfurter Papers, GB165-0111; this is a microfilm of extracts of the William Yale Papers. It contains the text of part of Abdullah's letter promising that the sharif will support England against the Turks, "so long as she [Britain] protects the rights of our country and the rights of the person of His Highness our present Emir and Lord, and the rights of his Emirate and its independence in all respects, without any exceptions or restrictions, and so long as she supports us against any foreign aggression and in particular against the Ottomans, especially if they wish to set up anyone else as Emir with the intention of causing internal dissension—their principle of government—and provided that the Government of Great Britain would guarantee these fundamental principles clearly and in writing. This guarantee we expect to receive at the first opportunity." Here there is no reference to "Arabia." But then why did Cheetham mention it?

38 "Does Kitchener agree?" See the copy in NA, FO800/48.

38 "Arabia, Syria . . ." "Secretary's Notes of a War Council held at 10 Downing Street, March 19, 1915," NA, Cab42/2/132.

40 "Our relations with the . . ." For X's shorthand notes, see Durham University, Sir Ronald Wingate Papers, 134/8/52.

42 "We have not the men . . ." M.P.A. Hankey to Lord Fisher, April 22, 1915, OUNBL, H. H. Asquith Papers.

43 "he had great sympathy . . ." "Secretary's Notes of a War Council held at 10 Downing Street, March 19, 1915," NA, Cab42/2/132.

43 "lay like a ducal demesne . . ." Leslie, *Mark Sykes,* 6.

44 "Mark Sykes had vitality . . ." Aubrey Herbert, tribute to Sykes at his memorial service, Somerset Record Office, Herbert Papers, DD/HER/53.

44 "Even Jews have their . . ." Quoted in Leslie, *Mark Sykes,* 62.

45 "the Arabs of the Syrian desert . . ." Sykes to Grey, September 14, 1914, NA, FO800/104-112/485.

45 One of them . . . Lancelot Oliphant introduced Sykes to Fitzgerald.

46 "I never saw Lord Kitchener . . ." Sykes to George Arthur, September 12, 1916, OUNBL, Leonard Stein Papers, box 2, PRO30/57/91.

46 "Turkey must cease . . ." For example, the Arab desert tribes "should be done up to the nines and given money and food . . . Then premiums might be offered for camels . . . then a price for telegraphic insulators . . . then a price for interruption of Hejaz railway line and a good price for Turkish Mausers and a good price for deserters from the Turkish Army . . . if possible keep the whole of the Hejaz Railway in a ferment and destroy bridges." This was not a bad description of what T. E. Lawrence would accomplish in his famous guerrilla desert campaign a year and a half later. Sykes to Herbert, n.d. (but from internal evidence spring 1915), Somerset Record Office, Herbert Papers, DD/HER/34.

46 "All black people . . ." Sykes to Herbert, April 1, 1915, Somerset Record Office, Herbert Papers, DD/HER/53.

46 "I could never understand . . ." "War Committee. Evidence of Lieut.-Col. Sir Mark Sykes, Bart., M.P., at a Meeting held at 10 Downing Street on Thursday, July 6, 1916, at 11:30," Hull University, Sykes Papers.

46 "the key of the whole . . ." Lawrence to Hogarth, March 18, 1915, OUNBL, Lawrence Papers, MS Eng. D. 3335/f.146.

47 "I want to pull them . . ." Lawrence to Hogarth, March 22, 1915, OUNBL, Lawrence Papers, MS Eng. D. 3335/f.148.

47 "His allegiance to us . . ." Storrs to illegible, February 22, 1915, Storrs Papers, reel 4, box 2, folder 3.

47 "He is a very pleasant . . ." McMahon to Hardinge, August 4, 1915, CUL, Lord Hardinge of Penshurst Papers, vol. 94, no. 74.

48 "I should just like to conclude" . . . "War Committee. Meeting held at 10 Downing Street on Thursday, December 16, 1915, at 11:30 a.m.," and "Evidence of Lieutenant-Colonel Sir Mark Sykes, Bart., MP on the Arab Question," Hull University, Sykes Papers.

CHAPTER 4: THE NEXT STEPS

49 Soon enough his messengers . . . Ibn Rashid declared the jihad in order to keep Turkish support against Ibn Saud.

50 Saud urged Hussein to ignore . . . Clayton to Wingate, October 2, 1915, Durham University, Wingate Papers, 134/2/29.

50 The Turkish *vali* of the Hejaz . . . The *vali* was Wahib Pasha. But Hasan Kayali doubts this version of events since Constantinople had been urging the *vali* to conciliate Sharif Hussein and this is what the discovered documents would probably have revealed. See Kayali, *Arabs,* 190.

51 Feisal distrusted Western . . . I largely rely on Antonius, *Arab Awakening,* 149–50, for this episode. But see also Tauber, *Arab Movements,* 60–66.

52 "most capable military . . ." Hogarth, *Hejaz,* 55–56.

52 "a pair of cunning cruel . . ." Stuermer, *Two War Years,* 117.

52 "Although I had never . . ." Djemal Pasha, *Memories,* 211.

52 "he swore by the glorious . . ." Ibid., 213. Note that according to Djemal, Feisal delivered this speech in September 1915. Antonius, however, does not even mention a trip to Damascus by Feisal in September.

53 "When he was received . . ." Ibid.

53 But "we do not need them . . ." The speaker was Yasin al-Hashimi, a future prime minister of Iraq.

56 "quiet, friendly, agreeable ..." Storrs, *Memoirs,* 205–06; Herbert, diary entry, January 30, 1915, Somerset Record Office, Herbert Papers, reel 1.

56 He "understood our design ..." Lawrence, *Seven Pillars,* 41.

57 "scarcely an embryo ..." Wingate to Clayton, February 24, 1915, Durham University, Clayton Papers, 469/8/46.

57 "You should inform ..." Grey to McMahon, April 14, 1915, NA, FO371/2486/44598.

57 "far and wide ..." Wingate to Clayton, April 20, 1915, Durham University, Clayton Papers, 469/9/8.

58 "one of the most difficult ..." Antonius, *Arab Awakening,* 159.

58 "God selected us ..." Quoted in Dawn, *From Ottomanism,* 78.

58 dispatching a trusted messenger ... The messenger was Mohammed Ibn Arif Ibn Oreifan.

58 "would be an important ..." "Correspondence with the Grand Sherif of Mecca, 7, Communication from Sherif of Mecca to Mr. Storrs, Oriental Secretary to British Representative, Cairo," NA, FO371/12770/69301.

59 "we will consider ourselves ..." Ibid.

59 "I think, you will find ..." Wingate to Clayton, August 14, 1915, Durham University, Clayton Papers, 469/10/24.

59 "On handing [me] the letter . . ." Statement of Mohammed Arif Ibn Oreifan, NA, FO371/2486/125293.

59 "The Sharif had opened ..." Storrs, *Memoirs,* 167.

59 "His pretensions ..." McMahon to Grey, August 22, 1915, NA, FO371/2486/117236.

59 "We confirm to you ..." McMahon to Hussein, August 29, 1915, NA, FO371/2770/69301.

60 "a tight network of parentheses ..." Antonius, *Arab Awakening,* 167.

60 "I cannot admit that you ..." NA, FO371/2770/69301.

60 "I am a descendant of Omar ..." "Memo on Mulazim Awal (lieutenant) Mohammed Sherif El Farugi, Staff Officer (Infantry) Mosul Corps, Turkish Army," NA, FO371/2486/157740.

61 The formulation appears . . . McMahon to Grey, October 19, 1915, NA, FO371/2468/153/045.

CHAPTER 5: THE HUSSEIN-MCMAHON CORRESPONDENCE

64 "The districts of Mersina ..." McMahon to Hussein, October 24, 1915, NA, FO371/2770.

65 "Our Arabic correspondence ..." Storrs, *Memoirs,* 168.

65 What Storrs did not record ... Ritchie Ovendale, entry on Storrs, *Oxford Dictionary of National Biography.*

66 The British and Zionists have argued ... Note a further complication. While some historians (such as C. Ernest Dawn) refer to the *vilayet* of Damascus, others (notably Antonius and Sanders) point out that there was no *vilayet* of Damascus but rather a *vilayet* of Syria in which Damascus was located!

67 Meanwhile assorted historians . . . It would be tedious to recapitulate the protracted, wide-ranging dispute in detail. For the Zionist point of view the interested reader may refer to Friedman, "McMahon-Hussein Correspondence," published in 1970 in *Journal of Contemporary History;* he reprinted it without emendation but strengthened it in subsequent chapters of his *Palestine, Twice-Promised,* vol. 1. For a lengthy, tempered rebuttal of Friedman's original article, see Dawn, *From Ottomanism,* chap. 4. Friedman's and Dawn's essays are the most comprehensive and persuasive statements of the opposing positions. In late 2009, however, one with no stake in the quarrel might discern, at least among scholars, the emergence of a rough consensus, although Friedman remains conspicuously outside it. Most researchers now believe that McMahon was intentionally vague, not sloppy, in order to give his superiors in London all possible scope for maneuver when the war was finished. See, for instance, Sanders, *High Walls,* 253, and Fromkin, *Peace,* 184. The most recent verdict on the debate, and probably a typical one, is that of Tom Segev: "at most the Arabs won [the historical debate] on a technicality; [for] the letters did not decisively confirm that Palestine would be included in the independent state the British had promised the Arabs." But neither did they explicitly deny it. *One Palestine,* 438.

69 "What we have to arrive at . . ." McMahon to Hardinge, December 4, 1915, CUL, Lord Hardinge Papers, vol. 94, no. 180.

69 "I do not like pledges . . ." Hardinge to Chamberlain, December 24, 1915, CUL, Lord Hardinge Papers, vol. 121, no. 76.

69 "We might agree to leave . . ." Hussein to McMahon, November 5, 1915, NA, FO371/2770/69301.

70 "proves very conclusively . . ." Wingate to Clayton, November 15, 1915, Durham University, Clayton Papers, 469/11/16.

70 "For sheer insolence . . ." Grey's note on the file, NA, FO371/2486/172416.

70 "Feeling amongst Arabs is very . . ." McMahon to Grey, November 8, 1915, NA, FO371/2486/170981.

70 "meet the Arab party . . ." Clayton to Lieutenant-Colonel A. C. Parker, December 10, 1915, Oxford University, St. Antony's College, Middle East Centre, Mark Sykes Papers, GB 165-0275.

70 "If the leaders of the Arabs . . ." Aubrey Herbert, memo to Foreign Office, November 5, 1915, NA, FO371/2486/164659.

71 "Promise the French big . . ." Herbert, diary entries, November 2 and 4, 1915, Somerset Record Office, Herbert Papers.

71 "This was . . . a psychological . . ." Herbert to Clayton, November 7, 1915, NA, FO882/2.

71 "We have been greatly . . ." Hardinge to Nicolson, November 12, 1915, CUL, Lord Hardinge Papers, vol. 94, no. 134.

71 "I devoutly hope . . ." Hardinge to Nicolson, November 15, 1915, CUL, Lord Hardinge Papers, vol. 94, no. 136.

71 "Two-thirds of the population . . ." Hardinge to Wingate, November 28, 1915, CUL, Lord Hardinge Papers, vol. 94, no. 142.

71 "the Arab movement [is] his . . ." Sykes to George Arthur, September 12, 1916, OUNBL, Stein Papers, box 2, PRO30/57/91.

71 "do your best . . ." Sykes to Arthur, September 12, 1916, OUNBL, Stein Papers, ibid.

72 "I live in almost hourly . . ." Wingate to Clayton, December 14, 1915, Durham University, Clayton Papers, 469/11/39.

72 "a reply to the Sherif . . ." Wingate to Clayton, December 14, 1915, NA, FO882/2, fol. 167.

72 "With regard to the *vilayet*s . . ." McMahon to Hussein, December 17, 1915, NA, FO371/2770/69301.

73 "We still remain firm . . ." Hussein to McMahon, January 1, 1916, NA, FO371/2770/69301.

73 "we shall have to let you . . ." Rather than the Foreign Office translation, I use here the more grammatical translation by Antonius, *Arab Awakening,* 426.

CHAPTER 6: THE SYKES-PICOT AGREEMENT

75 "Our policy has been . . ." Herbert to Sykes, February 9, 1915, Somerset Record Office, Aubrey Herbert Papers, DD/DRU/33.

76 "Unless this is done . . ." Grey's note on report of "Interdepartmental Conference on the Arab Question," NA, FO371/2486/34982.

78 These were Picot's goals . . . Fromkin, *Peace,* 190–91.

78 He took part in two . . . Picot's second meeting with the British delegates in London took place on December 21, after he had had a chance to confer again with his political masters in Paris.

78 "did not believe in any but . . ." Grey's note on report of "Interdepartmental Conference on the Arab Question," NA, FO371/2486/34982.

79 Sykes pretended to be yielding . . . Sykes to Clayton, December 28, 1915, NA, FO882/2/7.

79 "should be allowed to establish . . ." "Arab Question: Suggested method of settling various difficulties arranged with M. Picot. Map annexed," January 5, 1916, NA, FO371/2767/2522.

80 "thought the Arabs would not be . . ." Extracts from War Cabinet meeting, March 23, 1916, NA, Cab42/11.

80 The disappointed diplomat . . . Herbert diary entry, February 26, 1916, Somerset Record Of-

fice, Herbert Papers. He had chosen "Elihu P. Bergman" as a pseudonym; the newspaper that broke the story was the *Sketch.*

80 "I feel that divulgence . . ." McMahon to Grey, May 3, 1916, NA, FO882/2/63.

82 As for Areas A and B . . . "Arab Question," McMahon to Grey, November 20, 1915, NA, FO371/2767/23579.

83 "Regarding areas A and B . . ." Gertrude Lowthian Bell, June 23, 1917, NA, FO882/3, pp. 49–57.

83 "The Sykes-Picot treaty . . ." Lawrence to William Yale, October 22, 1929, OUNBL, Lawrence Papers, MS. Eng. C. 6737.

83 "They are an easy people . . ." "Minutes of a Meeting of the Eastern Committee held in Lord Curzon's room at the Privy Council Office," December 5, 1918, OUNBL, Alfred Milner Papers, MSS, Milner dep (microfilm reel 20) #137, War Cabinet, Eastern Committee. See also Bell to Lord Cromer, June 12, 1916, CUL, Lord Hardinge Papers, vol. 23.

84 "we should construct a State . . ." "Minutes of a Meeting of the Eastern Committee held in Lord Curzon's room at the Privy Council Office," April 24, 1918, OUNBL, Alfred Milner Papers, MSS, Milner dep (microfilm reel 20) #137, War Cabinet, Eastern Committee. It was not only the McMahon-Hussein correspondence that Curzon proposed to ignore. He would ignore the Sykes-Picot Agreement too, although France might demand compensation for Britain's territorial gains in the Middle East: "The problem had been considered by the Imperial War Cabinet last year and the Cameroons had been mentioned in this connection."

84 "From the point of view of . . ." "Minutes of a Meeting of the Eastern Committee held in Lord Curzon's room at the Privy Council Office," December 5, 1918, OUNBL, Alfred Milner Papers, MSS, Milner dep (microfilm reel 20) #137, War Cabinet, Eastern Committee.

84 "1. That His Majesty's . . ." "Minutes of a Meeting of the Eastern Committee held in Lord Curzon's room at the Privy Council Office," June 18, 1918, ibid.

85 One defends the agreement . . . Friedman, *Question of Palestine,* 109; Fromkin, *Peace,* 193–94. Other works that generally accept the positive interpretation of the agreement include, among many, Glubb, *Britain and Arabs;* Ovendale, *Origins;* Rose, *Palmerston to Balfour;* Nevakivi, *Britain, France;* Sanders, *High Walls;* Stein, *Balfour Declaration;* Tauber, *Arab Movements;* and Monroe, *Britain's Moment.*

85 A second group of historians . . . Antonius, *Arab Awakening,* 248; Erskine, *Palestine of Arabs;* Wingate, *Wingate of Sudan;* and Avi Shlaim, "The Balfour Declaration," in Lewis, *Yet More Adventures.* Another who was deeply critical of the Sykes-Picot Agreement was Arnold Toynbee, quoted in Friedman, *Palestine, Twice-Promised.*

85 "was reasonable enough . . ." MacMillan, *Peacemakers,* 394. Though very briefly treated, this is pretty much the verdict also in Segev, *One Palestine;* in Barr, *Setting the Desert;* and in Darwin, *Britain, Egypt.*

CHAPTER 7: THE ARAB REVOLT BEGINS

88 the Ottoman governor in Medina. The Ottoman governor in Medina was Basri Pasha. *Arab Bulletin,* no. 27, p. 387.

88 "less ready to sink . . ." Hogarth, *Hejaz,* 54.

88 "assuming powers on the . . ." Djemal Pasha, *Memories,* 215, 220.

88 "The Jehani Kadi has . . ." Ali to Hussein, n.d., NA, FO371/2767/88001.

89 a rival sheikh . . . He was the Awagir El Ghazu; the three other sheikhs were Al Awali, Ibn El Sifr, and Al Sawaid.

89 Djemal had sent . . . In some accounts it is Gallipoli; in others, Mesopotamia.

89 Historians estimate . . . Tauber, *Arab Movements,* 37.

90 "I decided to take . . ." Djemal Pasha, *Memories,* 207.

90 They received bread . . . Tauber, *Arab Movements,* 37–38.

90 "The bodies of the hanged . . ." *Great Britain and the Near East,* September 24, 1915.

90 "Eight more . . ." Ibid., December 31, 1915.

90 "as the greatest proof . . ." Djemal Pasha, *Memories,* 214.

90 "There can be no trust . . ." Feisal to Hussein, n.d., NA, FO371/2767/88001.

91 "some of the best known . . ." Antonius, *Arab Awakening,* 188.

91 "In my opinion . . ." Djemal Pasha, *Memories,* 214.

91 "He came to see . . ." Ibid., 217.

91 "O paradise of my . . ." Robert Fisk, *Independent,* May 21, 2005.

91 "Death will now . . ." Antonius writes of Feisal's cry, "Literally it is equivalent to: 'Death has become sweet, O Arabs!' But the Arabic is much richer in meaning and amounts to an appeal to all Arabs to take up arms, at the risk of their lives, to avenge the executions in blood" (191).

91 "I swear by the . . ." Djemal Pasha, *Memories,* 220.

93 "Since this war . . ." Hussein to McMahon, April 18, 1916, NA, FO370/2767/95498.

93 "The movement should . . ." Ali to Hussein, n.d., NA, FO371/2767/88001.

93 A Turkish force . . . It was led by the Ottoman general Khairy Bey.

93 Neufeld had brought . . . Hogarth, "Mecca's Revolt," 410.

94 "Sharif's son Abdallah . . ." Report written June 14, 1916, Storrs Papers, reel 5, box 2, folder 4, Egypt 1916–17. See also Storrs, *Memoirs,* 169.

94 "Will send Storrs . . ." Quoted in David Gill, "David George Hogarth," *Oxford Dictionary of National Biography,* 6.

94 "We made the near acquaintance . . ." Hogarth, "Mecca's Revolt," 169.

95 "I deeply regret my inability . . ." Abdullah's cousin was Sharif Shakir, emir of the Ataibah. Ibid.

95 "Please order by . . ." Storrs's report to McMahon, June 14, 1916, Storrs Papers, reel 5, box 2, folder 4, Egypt 1916–17; Storrs, *Memoirs,* 174.

95 All these actions . . . But in the letter that Oreifan delivered to Storrs, the grand sharif wrote that Ali and Feisal would launch the attack against Medina on the coming Monday.

95 "We had not come so far . . ." Hogarth, "Mecca's Revolt," 411.

96 "I stepped into Oreifan's . . ." Storrs Papers, reel 5, box 2, folder 4, Egypt 1916–17; Storrs, *Memoirs,* 172.

96 "He is about 5.5' . . ." Storrs Papers, ibid.; Storrs, *Memoirs,* 174.

96 The grand sharif wanted guns . . . Hogarth, "Mecca's Revolt," 411.

97 "Zeid struck me . . ." Hogarth Report, June 10, 1916, Storrs Papers, reel 5, box 2, folder 4, Egypt 1916–17.

97 "The conception . . ." Storrs's report written June 14, 1916, Storrs Papers, ibid.

97 "Far too much . . ." Hogarth Report, June 10, 1916, Storrs Papers, ibid.

97 "Had the sherifian revolt . . ." Hogarth, "Mecca's Revolt," 411.

98 "two or three battalions . . ." Djemal Pasha, *Memories,* 222–23.

98 "The volunteers were . . ." Quoted ibid., 224.

98 On the evening of June 4 . . . Djemal writes (ibid.) that this event took place on June 2, but that makes no sense, because it was the evening before Ali and Feisal declared the revolt, which occurred on Monday morning, June 5.

99 Then on the morning of June 9 . . . The Turkish *vali* was Ghalib Pasha.

99 "If there was any trouble . . ." For this episode see Graves, *Memoirs of King Abdullah,* 144–46.

100 No copy survives . . . Ibid., 136; Djemal Pasha, *Memories,* 215.

100 "Everyone reclaims . . ." "Translation of an Account of the Events leading to the Revolution in Arabia as given by Bimbashi Mehmed Zia Bey, Acting Governor and Commandant at Mecca," *Arab Bulletin,* no. 21, pp. 256–60, September 15, 1916.

101 "The men who form . . ." Djemal Pasha, *Memories,* 215–16.

101 "He [Hussein] considered himself . . ." Ibid., 225.

101 "They were simply . . ." "Translation of an Account," *Arab Bulletin,* no. 21, p. 257.

CHAPTER 8: PREWAR BRITISH JEWS

107 Nahum Sokolow . . . Sokolow owned and edited a Warsaw newspaper, *Ha Tzefira;* he served as editor of two Zionist journals, the movement's official organ, *Die Welt,* and the Hebrew weekly *Ha-Olam;* he regularly contributed articles on Russian and Jewish subjects to a range

of European newspapers, including *The Times* of London. In addition he wrote histories, biographies, geographical studies, and language primers, even a historical novel.

108 "His handsome appearance . . ." Sacher, *Zionist Portraits,* 36.

109 "It [is] to the advantage . . ." For Sokolow's first visit to the Foreign Office, see NA, FO371/1794. See too Rawidowicz, "Nahum Sokolow."

109 "a preparatory step" . . . Sokolow to executive committee of the Zionist Organization, quoted in Rawidowicz, "Nahum Sokolow."

109 "I think . . . we can safely . . ." NA, FO511/2136.

111 the English Zionist Federation . . . For membership figures, see Cohen, *English Zionists,* 106–07.

112 But Herzl died . . . In fact he died of pneumonia.

114 "pre-eminently what the . . ." Sieff, *Memoirs,* 67.

117 Weizmann put him . . . Ibid., 68.

117 "repressive cruelty" . . . Quoted in Segev, *One Palestine,* 104.

118 two parent bodies . . . For this treatment of the Board of Deputies and the Anglo-Jewish Association, I rely primarily upon Levene, *War, Jews,* 1–19.

119 Lucien Wolf . . . Wolf wrote for and edited *The Jewish World,* an English newspaper. He edited the centenary edition of Disraeli's novels. He wrote a biography of Moses Montefiore. His journalism brought him into touch with European politicians, diplomats, and officials. He courted their English counterparts. By the 1890s he was contributing a remarkably well-informed regular column called "The Foreign Office Bag" to *The Daily Graphic.* He wrote frequently for *The Fortnightly Review* as "Diplomaticus." In addition he served as London correspondent of the French *Le Journal.* He claimed to have influence over events, notably in 1898, when possibly at Arthur Balfour's prompting he suggested to the Russian ambassador in London a solution to Anglo-Russian difficulties over Manchuria, which Russia adopted.

120 "almost indistinguishable." Quoted in Finestein, *Scenes and Personalities,* 209.

120 "once said of me . . ." Wolf to Sam G. Asher, September 28, 1915, Yivo Institute, Wolf Papers, microfilm reel 2.

120 "anti-Semitism is . . ." Finestein, *Scenes and Personalities,* 214.

121 He did not identify . . . Wolf to Asher, September 28, 1915.

121 He cemented relationships . . . Levene, *War, Jews,* 16.

121 His last great prewar . . . Ibid., 19.

122 "he conveys no impression . . ." Quoted in Wasserstein, *Herbert Samuel,* 129.

122 "Zionism was the one . . ." Ibid., 204.

123 The link came . . . Samuel's wife was Beatrice Miriam Franklin. The childhood friend who went on to marry Gaster was Lucy Friedlander.

123 "I remember Dr. Gaster . . ." Samuel to Stein, December 6, 1951, OUNBL, Stein Papers, box 7.

123 "a benevolent goodwill . . ." Quoted in Stein, *Balfour Declaration,* 109; see also Samuel, *Memoirs,* 139.

CHAPTER 9: WEIZMANN'S FIRST STEPS

124 "The fate of Palestine . . ." Ahad Ha'am to Weizmann, November 1, 1914, WI.

124 "Our colonies . . ." Weizmann to Jacobus Kann, November 2, 1914, Stein, *Letters,* letter no. 27, 7:33.

125 "The moment Turkey . . ." Samuel, *Memoirs,* 139.

125 He kept a record . . . Numerous historians have quoted these pages, for example, Stein, *Balfour Declaration,* Sanders, *High Walls,* and Friedman, *Question of Palestine,* to name a few.

125 "Perhaps . . . the opportunity . . ." Samuel, notes to himself, November 9, 1914, House of Lords Record Office, Herbert Samuel Papers, Correspondence, vol. 1, 1915–17.

126 "a greedy, ambitious . . ." Quoted in Wasserstein, *Herbert Samuel,* 144. Samuel, notes to himself, November 9, 1914, House of Lords Record Office, Samuel Papers, Correspondence, vol. 1, 1915–17.

127 "Needless to say they ..." Greenberg to Weizmann, October 10, 1914, WI, Letters to Weizmann.

128 "the unification of Jewry ..." Weizmann to Levin, September 8, 1914, in Stein, *Letters,* letter no. 4.

128 "will be difficult to ..." Greenberg to Weizmann, October 10, 1914, WI, Letters to Weizmann.

128 "I should find it ..." Zangwill to Weizmann, October 28, 1914, WI, Letters to Weizmann.

129 "I tried to learn ..." "Report submitted to the members of the Executive of the International Zionist Organization, January 7, 1915," in Stein, *Letters,* letter no. 95, 7:113.

129 Crewe was related ... Crewe had wed the granddaughter of a Rothschild, Lady Margaret Primrose, youngest daughter of the Earl of Rosebery, himself a former Liberal prime minister.

129 "our compatriots ..." Dorothy Rothschild to Chaim Weizmann, November 19, 1914, CZA.

129 "Supposing that the Arabs ..." Crewe to Hardinge, November 12, 1914, OUNBL, Stein Papers, box 3; Extracts from Crewe Papers; CUL, Crewe Mss I 19/2.

130 "You don't—I am sure ..." Weizmann to D. Rothschild, November 22, 1914, Stein, *Letters,* letter no. 43, 7:51.

130 "to try and influence ..." "Summary of a conversation with Baron James de Rothschild, Wednesday, November 25, 1914," WI.

130 Eventually Rozsika outdid ... She introduced Weizmann to, among others, Lady Crewe, Theo Russell (private secretary of Sir Edward Grey), and Lord Haldane (Asquith's lord chancellor).

130 "It is impossible ..." August 18, 1915, NA, FO800/104 R.C.

131 "I saw before me ..." Weizmann, *Trial and Error,* 1:149.

131 "I would like to do ..." Ibid.

132 "Since Turkey had entered ..." "Report submitted to the members of the Executive of the International Zionist Organization, January 7, 1915," Stein, *Letters,* letter no. 95, 7:111–12.

132 "Messianic times . . ." Weizmann to Vera Weizmann, December 10, 1914, ibid., letter no. 65, 7:77–78.

132 "I have just remembered ..." Weizmann to Ahad Ha'am, December 13, 1914, ibid., letter no. 68, 7:82. The letter was written in Russian, but the words in italics were written in English.

132 "feels the responsibility ..." Weizmann to Scott, December 13, 1914, in Stein, *Letters,* letter no. 67, 7:79–80.

133 "it is very possible ..." Ahad Ha'am to Weizmann, December 16, 1914, OUNBL, Stein Papers, box 7.

134 "Even in the West ..." Appendix 1, Note A 189 (14–15), August 14, 1917, NA, Cab23/3.

134 "They have been different ..." Quoted in Tomes, *Balfour and Foreign Policy,* 29.

134 "I have the liveliest ..." Quoted in Stein, *Balfour Declaration,* 153.

134 "Balfour remembered ..." Weizmann to Ahad Ha'am, December 14–15, 1914, in Stein, *Letters*, letter no. 68, 7:81–83.

135 "What a great difference ..." "Report submitted to the members of the Executive of the International Zionist Organization," January 7, 1915, ibid., letter no. 95, 7:115. Letters no. 68 and 95 both reprise the meeting in essentially the same terms.

135 "You probably will find ..." C. P. Scott to Weizmann, January 14, 1915, WI.

135 "I answered ..." Weizmann, *Trial and Error,* 150.

136 "It is hoped . . ." "The Future of Palestine," January 1915, House of Lords Record Office, Samuel Papers, Break up of Ottoman Empire (Palestine) file, DR. 588.25.

136 "I am not attracted ..." Quoted in Samuel, *Memoirs,* 142.

CHAPTER 10: THE ASSIMILATIONISTS

138 "They threatened to remain ..." Wolf to Chief Commissioner of Police, August 31, 1914; Wolf to Assistant Commissioner of Police, September 7, 1914; Yivo Institute, Lucien Wolf Papers, microfilm reel 5.

139 Leo Maxse, editor ... *National Review,* September 1914.

139 No non-Jewish ... Levene, *War, Jews,* 34.

139 "My misfortunes extend . . ." Wolf to Coumbe, January 5, 1915, Yivo Institute, Wolf Papers, microfilm reel 2.

139 He threatened to sue . . . Wolf to Hutchinson, October 16, 1914, ibid., microfilm reel 5.

140 "All we have to consider . . ." Wolf to Bulloch, November 30, 1914, ibid., Wolf Papers.

140 "It is not only the carnage . . ." Wolf to Neil Primrose, August 7, 1914, ibid., microfilm reel 4. Neil Primrose was a Liberal MP for the Wisbech division of Cambridgeshire and second son of Hannah Rothschild and former Liberal Prime Minister Lord Rosebery; ironically, he was later a Weizmann ally.

140 "We were bound . . ." Wolf to Lady Primrose, August 11, 1914, ibid., microfilm reel 7.

140 "the German people . . ." Wolf, *Jewish Ideals and the War,* 3.

141 "With their invincible . . ." *Jewish Chronicle,* December 11, 1914.

141 "To me there have always . . ." Wolf to G. De Wesseslitsky, May 25, 1915, Yivo Institute, Wolf Papers, microfilm reel 5.

142 Harry Sacher called upon Lucien Wolf . . . Sacher to Weizmann, November 17, 1914, WI.

143 In their ensuing correspondence . . . Wolf to Sacher, November 26, November 30, December 3, December 11, December 18, and December 24, 1914, WI. For example, Wolf had wanted to know more precisely whom Sacher represented; he wanted a written record of Sacher's position; he wanted assurances that the meeting, when it finally did take place, would be with formal representatives of the Zionist organizations; he wanted to be sure that Sacher or other Zionists were not approaching other members of the Conjoint Committee.

143 "against unauthorized persons . . ." Wolf to Alexander and Montefiore, January 7, 1915, CZA, A7732.

144 "Whatever be the merits . . ." Palestine Memorandum, March 1915, House of Lords Record Office, Samuel Papers.

144 "inclined to the sympathetic . . ." Haldane to Samuel, February 12, 1915; Fisher to Samuel, illegible date but probably February 21, 1915, Reading to Samuel, February 5, 1915, ibid., Correspondence, vol. 1, 1915–17.

145 "does not care a damn . . ." Quoted in Reinharz, *Weizmann,* 26.

145 "fired about two hundred . . ." Jim Vincent, "Memoir" [of Edwin Montagu], *Norfolk Post,* November 22, 1924.

145 "children and animals . . ." *Times,* November 19, 1924.

147 the first formal meeting . . . "The Palestinian Question. Negotiations between the Conjoint Committee & the Zionists. London, July 20, 1915," Yivo Institute, Wolf Papers, microfilm reel 6. All quotations are taken from this source. A fourth assimilationist at the meeting was H. S. Henriques, a lawyer.

147 Five months had elapsed . . . When Wolf realized that the Zionists were less interested in the cultural aspect than Sacher had claimed, he sought to pin them down, to nail them to it. Who better to provide the hammer than Herbert Samuel, with whom Weizmann had recently conferred? Wolf met with Samuel on February 28, 1915, in Samuel's offices. As their discussion drew to a close, Wolf asked Mr. Samuel whether I might take it that we were agreed on the two following points:

1. Palestine does not and cannot offer an effective solution for the Jewish question as we know it in Russia, Poland, Rumania, etc.
2. The "Cultural" plan, including perhaps a Hebrew University, free immigration and facilities for colonization, together with, of course, equal political rights with the rest of the population, should be the limit of our aim at the present time.

He answered unhesitatingly "Yes." (Interview with Herbert Samuel, Yivo Institute, Wolf Papers, microfilm reel 6.)

Pleased with this outcome, Wolf sought to balance Weizmann's meeting with Lloyd George too, for the chancellor was an even bigger hammer than the president of the Board of Trade.

But Lloyd George must have been too busy to see him at this point, for the meeting does not appear to have taken place. (Wolf to Sir Charles Henry, March 30, 1915, CZA, A7731.)

147 Three additional men . . . The other two were Joseph Cowen, president of the EZF, and Herbert Bentwich, a veteran of the English Zionist movement, who in fact had been a founding member of the EZF and who currently served as president of the Ancient Order of the Maccabeans.

CHAPTER 11: THE ROAD FORKS

153 *dönmes,* or "crypto-Jews." *Dönmes* were a community descended from the disciples and adherents of Sabbatai Tsvi, who abandoned Judaism and adopted Islam in the late seventeenth century. See Moorehead, *Gallipoli,* 19.

153 These Jewish puppeteers . . . Berridge, *Fitzmaurice,* 145–48.

153 Hugh James O'Bierne . . . O'Bierne served in St. Petersburg, Washington, D.C., and Constantinople, steadily rising in rank until being appointed minister plenipotentiary in the Russian capital in 1913. See his obituary in *Great Britain and the Near East,* June 9, 1916.

153 The two men came into contact . . . Miller, *Straits.*

154 After some hesitation . . . But this is a simplification. For a blow-by-blow account, see Hall, *Bulgaria's Road,* 285–323.

154 possibly Herbert Samuel . . . This is the speculation of Sanders, *High Walls,* 334.

154 the shadowy, malign . . . Berridge, *Fitzmaurice,* 233–34.

154 "a very veiled suggestion . . ." Quoted in Sanders, *High Walls,* 325. The American professor was Horace Kallen.

155 "What the Jews . . ." "Palestine," January 27, 1916, February 28, 1916, NA, FO371/2671/138708. The Italian businessman was Edgar Suarez.

155 If Britain did not act . . . For the German dimension, see Friedman, *Question of Palestine,* 53.

155 "I read the memorandum . . ." Sykes to Samuel, February 26, 1916, House of Lords Record Office, Samuel Papers, Correspondence, vol. 1, 1915–17.

156 "You must speak Zionism . . ." Reinharz, *Weizmann,* 79–80.

156 The French worried . . . The two French Jewish professors were Dr. Nahum Slousch, a Zionist, and Victor Basch, an anti-Zionist. It is a historic irony, given Germany's later role with regard to Jews, that during World War I she could appear to them, at least on some occasions, as a savior. In the Russian and Polish territories that came under her control, Germany abolished anti-Semitic regulations, encouraged various social, cultural, and educational initiatives that would benefit Jews, favored appointing Jews to municipal councils, and appointed a Jew to head the Jewish department of her civil administration in Poland. Whatever the underlying motives, Germany announced that the Jews of Warsaw would be emancipated as soon as German soldiers had liberated the city. See Levene, *War, Jews,* 85.

157 "I am not a Zionist . . ." "Suggestions for a Pro-Allies Propaganda among the Jews of the United States," December 15, 1916, Yivo Institute, Wolf Papers, microfilm reel 7.

157 "Mr. Lloyd George has . . ." Wolf to Lord Reading, February 24, 1916. Ibid. The French contact was Professor Basch.

158 "In the event of Palestine . . ." Wolf to Cecil, March 3, 1916, NA, FO371/ 2817.

158 "We should inform . . ." Ibid.

158 "It has been suggested . . ." O'Bierne, minute, February 28, 1916, NA, FO371/2671.

159 "To obtain Jewish . . ." Reading to Montagu, March 19, 1916, Lord Reading Papers, Mss. Eur. F118/95. For two blow-by-blow accounts, see Friedman, *Question of Palestine,* 48–64, focusing upon the Zionist perspective, and Levene, *War, Jews,* 77–107, focusing on Wolf's perspective.

160 "when in the course of time . . ." Crewe to Sir George Buchanan, March 11, 1916, NA, FO371/2817.

160 "It must be admitted" . . . O'Bierne, minute, March 22, 1916, NA, FO371/2671.

160 "The present time" . . . Cecil, minute, June 29, 1916, NA, FO371/2817.

160 "It is evident" . . . O'Bierne, minute, March 15, 1916, NA, FO371/2767.

CHAPTER 12: FORGING THE BRITISH-ZIONIST CONNECTION

165 "might be made . . ." Crewe to Sir George Buchanan, March 11, 1916, NA, FO371/2817.

166 "inestimable advantages . . ." Sykes, telegram, March 14, 1916, NA, FO371/2767.

167 "I have repeatedly told Picot . . ." Sykes, telegram, March 16, 1916, NA, FO371/2767.

167 "we bump into a thing . . ." Sykes, telegram, March 18, 1916, NA, FO800/381.

168 "I do not think it easy . . ." Cecil, March 3, 1916, NA, FO371/2817.

169 "It practically comes to . . ." Quoted in Stein, *Balfour Declaration,* 278–79, n27.

170 "The suggestion about which . . ." Samuel to Gaster, April 20, 1916, CZA, A203227.

170 "My Dear Rabbi" . . . Sykes to Gaster, April 28, 1916, CZA, A203227.

170 Sykes questioned . . . Gaster to Sykes, November 3, 1916, Hull University, Sykes Collection, Zionism file, 4/203. He delivered at least the maps of Britain and Palestine.

170 Picot told Sykes . . . Stein, *Balfour Declaration,* 361, n3.

171 Aaron Aaronsohn . . . Historians have been aware of Aaronsohn's role ever since the 1963 publication of Stein, *Balfour Declaration.*

171 "He is one of the . . ." Quoted in Sanders, *High Walls,* 408.

172 The NILI spy ring . . . Ibid., 413.

172 So Aaronsohn went to London . . . All information on Aaronsohn, including diary quotations, is taken from Sanders, *High Walls,* 405–416; Stein, *Balfour Declaration,* 285–95; and www.hagshama.org.il/en/resources/view.asp?id=1854.

174 a public meeting convened . . . *Ararat,* June 1916.

175 "His previous career . . ." Board of Trade official, August 1916, NA, FO668/1601.

175 "I only once met Malcolm . . ." John Buchan, minute, August 14, 1916, NA, FO668/1601.

176 "I recounted the gist . . ." James Malcolm, "Origins of the Balfour Declaration: Dr. Weizmann's Contribution," Oxford University, St. Antony's College, Middle East Centre, J&ME, LSOC/2.

176 "James Malcolm—the Gentile Zionist" . . . Unidentifiable clipping, OUNBL, Stein Papers, box 8. It may simply be based upon the Malcolm manuscript.

176 But other accounts suggest . . . Stein, *Balfour Declaration,* 361–68; and Sanders, *High Walls,* 451–54.

176 "He had met Sir Mark . . ." Quoted in Stein, *Balfour Declaration,* 367.

176 "Can I see you anywhere . . ." Gaster to Sykes, January 29, 1917, Hull University, Sykes Papers, Zionism file 4/203.

177 "I then learned that W. . . ." Quoted in Stein, *Balfour Declaration,* 367.

CHAPTER 13: DEFINING THE BRITISH-ARAB CONNECTION

179 "Deposition and death" . . . Quoted in Kayali, *Arabs,* 197.

179 At the outset of the revolt . . . The Harb, the Ateibah, and the Juheinah most prominently, although they drew from tribes farther north and south of central Hejaz as well. *Arab Bulletin,* February 6, 1917, no. 41, p. 55. During the later stages of the revolt, as many as seventy thousand Arabs belonged to the Sharifian forces.

179 "the value of the tribes . . ." "Military Notes," *Arab Bulletin,* October 26, 1916, no. 32, p. 478.

179 "spread in a fanlike movement . . ." *Great Britain and the Near East,* March 31, 1916.

180 "I have drunk the cup . . ." "Faruki's Report to His Excellency General Clayton, C.M.G.," n.d., NA, FO882/4, Arab Bureau, 4.

180 "Our small force . . ." *Tanin,* July 26, 1916, quoted in *Arab Bulletin,* August 30, 1916, no. 17, p. 192.

180 "probably more through . . ." "Arab Revolt in the Hejaz," *Arab Bulletin,* June 18, 1916, no. 5, p. 44.

180 "At Jeddah, the Shereef's . . ." *Great Britain and the Near East,* August 4, 1916.

180 "The people at Mecca . . ." *Arab Bulletin,* August 30, 1916, no. 17, p. 195.

181 Opposing them . . . Lawrence, *Seven Pillars,* 78–80; Barr, *Setting the Desert,* 27.

181 "at Medina the Arab . . ." *Arab Bulletin,* August 30, 1916, no. 17, p. 195.

182 "The situation in the Hijaz . . ." Storrs to Lloyd, September 5, 1916, Cambridge University, Churchill College, George Lloyd Papers, 8/6.

183 When Feisal hurried back . . . Greaves, *Lawrence of Arabia,* 81.

183 "did not seem in any . . ." *Arab Bulletin,* February 6, 1917, no. 41, p. 68.

185 They divided into three . . . The British observer was Captain N.N.E. Bray of the 18th Bengal Lancers. Here is his description of the battle. Of the first group, who "really meant fighting," he recorded that about twenty "advanced at a very sharp pace straight toward the Turks, who were in position about two thousand yards away. At one thousand yards they came under fire but took no notice and showed no excitement. Indeed, they appeared, but for the pace they were walking, to be out for an ordinary constitutional. When within five hundred yards, they halted a moment or two to see exactly where the fire came from and, without taking advantage of any cover or extending to any unusual extent, wandered on till they eventually halted in some dead ground within fifty yards of the Turks. Here they remained, firing snap-shots and crouching down again, suffering no casualties whatever, but inflicting a fair number on their opponents. There was no noise or confusion."

The remaining eighty Arabs from this first group engaged the Turks a little to the south of the village proper. "These men behaved in a similar manner and remained cool in action till ordered to retire so that the naval guns might shell the Turkish trenches. They retired quietly and extended, walking slowly away and taking no notice of the stray Turkish bullets amongst them."

Bray had nothing but scorn for the remainder of Arab troops, however. According to him, the second group, numbering three hundred men and representing the bulk of Arab soldiers present, "rushed for the town and at once began looting and fighting in a completely disorganized manner. The Turks fought very hard in the town, from house to house, and the Arabs suffered a fair number of casualties." Nevertheless by the next morning they had driven the Turks out. "The town was in an utter state of confusion and had been ransacked from roof to floor."

Of the third group, the hundred soldiers who sat on the beach until the fighting was over, Bray did not deign to write anything further.

185 Simultaneously, in Mecca . . . *Arab Bulletin,* October 26, 1916, no. 27, pp. 386–90.

186 "The return to chthonic . . ." *Arab Bulletin,* November 26, 1916, no. 32, p. 476.

186 "We fortify ourselves . . ." Quoted in *Great Britain and the Near East,* September 1, 1916.

186 "The Sherif intends . . ." *Arab Bulletin,* November 26, 1916, no. 32, p. 476.

187 The telegram requested . . . For this episode, see NA, FO882/5, from which all quotations are taken.

187 The English translated it as . . . Antonius translates it as "King of the Arab Countries," *Arab Awakening,* 213.

188 King of the Hejaz . . . Tauber, *Arab Movements,* 160.

188 These "easterners" . . . Two quotations from the opposing schools will suffice to summarize their argument. Sir William Robertson, CIGS, a committed "westerner," explained to the cabinet why he opposed sending troops to the Hejaz: "The only way to win this war is to beat the German Armies, and as I have consistently held ever since I became Chief of the Imperial General Staff, we must accordingly concentrate every available man against those Armies." W. R. Robertson, "Assistance to the Shereef," September 20, 1916, NA, WO 106/1510. In opposition to this point of view, General Gilbert Clayton, in a memorandum, also addressed to the cabinet, explained why Britain should support the Arab Revolt: It had "shattered the solidarity of Islam in that Moslem is against Moslem. It has emphasized the failure of the Jehad and endangered the Khalifate of the Sultan . . . One way and another the best part of 3 Divisions is being held up in Arabia without costing us a man." Moreover, if the sharif failed, that "would give the eastern coast of the Red Sea to the Turks, thus increasing for the Navy the strain of guarding the sea route to India. It would furnish the Turks with a base in Arabia for

military and political activity which might well extend to the Euphrates, Aden, Abyssinia and the Southern Sudan and Somaliland." Finally, since the revolt was widely perceived to have been British-inspired, its failure would lead to a diminution of British prestige throughout the East. Clayton, memorandum to the Foreign Office, September 28, 1916, Durham University, Clayton Papers, 693/10/65. See too Clayton to Hall, September 10, 1916, ibid., 693/10/57.

188 "With another British Cavalry . . ." Murray to Robertson, January 10, 1917, British Library, Murray-Robertson Papers, Add. 52462/f.35.

188 "My sole object is . . ." Robertson to Murray, October 16, 1916, ibid., Add. 52462/f.13.

189 "The Hejaz war is . . ." *Arab Bulletin,* November 26, 1916, no. 32, p. 480.

189 "Lawrence is quite . . ." Quoted in Barr, *Setting the Desert,* 56.

190 They arrived in Jeddah . . . "Extract from a letter dated January 31, 1917, from the C.G.S., Egyptian Expeditionary Force, to the D.M.O., War Office," NA, FO800, Balfour Miscellaneous.

190 "A Negress, [but] she . . ." Storrs, diary entry, October 17, 1916, Storrs Papers, reel 6, box 2, folder 5.

190 "He reminds me of . . ." Storrs to "My Dear Colum," December 21, 1916, ibid., reel 5, box 2, folder 4, Egypt 1916–17.

190 "with his extraordinarily . . ." Storrs, diary entry, October 16, 1916, ibid.

191 "I felt at first glance . . ." Lawrence, *Seven Pillars,* 76.

CHAPTER 14: MANAGING THE BRITISH-ZIONIST CONNECTION

193 "a clever, efficient . . ." OUNBL, Selborne Papers, 80/285. This is part of Selborne's recollection of the entire cabinet.

193 "I do not want you . . ." Montagu to Asquith, December 5, 1916, OUNBL, Asquith Papers, 17.

194 "The Turks . . . are fine fighters . . ." Murray to Robertson, December 13, 1916, British Library, Murray-Robertson Papers, Add. 52462/f.27.

194 "The War Cabinet is very . . ." Robertson to Murray, January 31, 1917, ibid., Add. 52462/f.43.

195 "in order to get him . . ." Hardinge to Sir Valentine Chirol, April 26, 1917, CUL, Lord Hardinge Papers.

195 "I have just got . . ." Murray to Robertson, May 20, 1917, June 12, 1917, British Library, Murray-Robertson Papers, Add. 52462/ff. 96, 103.

195 "From what I hear . . ." Malcolm to Sykes, February 3, 1917, Hull University, Sykes Papers, DDSY/2.

196 "was laying down the . . ." Weizmann to Sieff, February 3, 1917, in Stein, *Letters,* letter no. 303, 7:326.

197 "it is the opinion . . ." Malcolm to Sykes, February 5, 1917, Hull University, Sykes Papers, DDSY/2.

197 When he learned . . . Gaster also invited Herbert Bentwich of the Maccabeans.

197 "The most important . . ." Quoted in Reinharz, *Weizmann,* 112. See also Gaster to James de Rothschild, February 9, 1917, WI, Moses Gaster Papers.

197 a document encapsulating . . . The statement ended with a by-now-familiar assertion of the main Zionist claims: that Palestine be recognized as the Jewish national home; that Jews be free to immigrate there from all countries; that their colonies be self-governing; and that Hebrew be recognized as their official language.

197 "He needed no formal . . ." Stein, *Balfour Declaration,* 374.

198 "Mr. Samuel replied . . ." Quoted in Stein, *Balfour Declaration,* 372. Copies of Sokolow's résumé of the meeting may be found at the Weizmann Archive, the CZA, and the Moses Gaster Papers.

198 "The Arabs professed . . ." Ibid., 373.

199 "Mr. Sokolow replied . . ." Sokolow's résumé of the meeting may be found in various archives. I quote from copies in the OUNBL, Stein Papers, box 6.

200 "Zionists and Jews generally . . ." "Notes of a meeting held on Saturday, February 10, 1917, at 9 Buckingham Gate, London SW," CZA Z440/661.

202 "those friends of mine . . ." Weizmann to Harris J. Morgenstern, February 1, 1917, in Stein, *Letters,* letter no. 302, 7:324.

202 "From certain information . . ." Quoted in Sanders, *High Walls,* 472.

203 "the curious experience . . ." Sacher, *Zionist Portraits,* 104.

203 "the only thing of the . . ." Ibid., 107

203 "on grounds of British . . ." Sidebotham, *Great Britain,* 32–33.

204 "He loved music . . ." Sacher, *Zionist Portraits,* 109.

204 "I think we received . . ." Sidebotham, *Great Britain,* 41–42.

204 "As I am officially . . ." Sacher, Sieff, Simon to C. P. Scott, October 16, 1916, online at http://www.mucjs.org/EXHIBITION/12bpctoscott.html.

204 "I have always considered . . ." Sykes to "Dear Sir," October 14, 1916, WI.

205 "unless Palestine comes . . ." *Palestine,* February 1, 1917; "The Policy of the Palestine Committee," n.d., OUNBL, Stein Papers, box 1.

205 Quickly *Palestine* established . . . For example, Sir Reginald Wingate, who had replaced McMahon as Egypt's high commissioner, requested that copies be sent to him in faraway Cairo.

205 "We . . . must at whatever . . ." Sieff to Weizmann, February 2, 1917, WI.

205 "it was most unpleasant . . ." Weizmann to Sokolow, February 18, 1917, in Stein, *Letters,* letter no. 309, 7:330.

205 "There is no doubt . . ." Sieff to Weizmann, February 19, 1917, WI.

206 "Letter received . . ." Weizmann to Sieff, February 20, 1917, quoted in Stein, *Letters,* letter no. 311, 7:332.

206 " 'Palestine' this week . . ." Sieff to Weizmann, February 20, 1917, WI.

206 "tying Zionism up . . ." Sacher to Simon, May 13, 1917, WI.

206 "Where we differ from . . ." Sacher to Simon, May 9, 1917, CZA, Leon Simon Collection, CZA/A298114.

207 "an extremist and . . ." Weizmann to Tolkowsky, February 28, 1917, WI (filed under Miscellaneous). Interestingly, the printed version of this letter in Stein, *Letters,* letter no. 313, 7:335, does not contain this sentence.

CHAPTER 15: SOKOLOW IN FRANCE AND ITALY

209 "You must take me . . ." C. P. Scott, diary (photocopy), March 15, 1917, WI. C. P. Scott's diaries are available at a number of archives.

209 "I have seen Balfour . . ." Weizmann to Ahad Ha'am, March 24, 1917, in Stein, *Letters,* letter no. 324.

209 " 'You may tell the Prime . . .' " Weizmann to Scott, March 23, 1917, ibid., letter no. 323.

209 a breakfast at 10 Downing Street . . . C. P. Scott, diary entry, April 3, 1917, British Library.

210 "Often he remarked . . ." Sokolow, *History of Zionism,* 2:xviii–xix.

211 "I am extremely satisfied . . ." Sokolow to Sykes, March 28, 1917, CZA, Sokolow Papers.

211 "You are, of course, acquainted . . ." Sokolow to Weizmann, April 20, 1917, quoted in Stein, *Balfour Declaration,* 394, n3.

211 "If the great force . . ." Sykes to Picot, February 28, 1917, Oxford University, St. Antony's College, Middle East Centre, Sykes Papers, GB 165-0275/32B.

212 "The French are determined . . ." Sokolow to Weizmann, April 4, 1917, CZA, Sokolow Papers.

213 For several hours . . . The other officials included Jules Cambon's brother Paul, who was the French ambassador to Britain, and Prime Minister Alexandre Ribot's chef de cabinet, Pierre de Margerie.

213 "As I was crossing the Quai . . ." Sokolow, *History of Zionism,* 2:xxx.

213 "I was told . . ." Sokolow to Weizmann, April 19, 1917, CZA, Sokolow Papers.

213 "Zionists' aspirations . . ." NA, FO371/3045. Weizmann, upon receiving a copy of this wire, worried that it gave the impression that Zionists would look to France as well as to England, or rather instead of to England, for protection in Palestine. He thought Sokolow had let down

the movement and said so in a rather undiplomatic telegram. Sokolow replied: "Astonished fallacious commentaries . . . My programme were our demands for which enlisted official sympathy without slightest allusion to French alternative or any engagement . . . My ideal solution is naturally British Palestine." See Sokolow to Weizmann, May 4, 1917, CZA, Sokolow Papers.

213 "naturally the moment . . ." Sykes to Balfour, April 9, 1917, Hull University, Sykes Papers, DDSY/2/13.

214 "the belief in the power . . ." Sacher, *Zionist Portraits,* 37.

214 Upon arriving in Rome . . . The British representative was Count T. de Salis.

215 "Sir M. Sykes' visit . . ." De Salis to Drummond, April 17, 1917, House of Lords Record Office, Lloyd George Papers, box 95, folder 2, no. 16.

215 Sykes sought out too . . . The British ambassador was Sir Rennel Rodd.

215 "opened fire on questions . . ." Rodd to Hardinge, April 12, 1917, CUL, Lord Hardinge Papers, vol. 31.

215 "I . . . prepared the way . . ." Sykes to Graham, April 15, 1917, NA, FO371/3052.

215 "I laid considerable stress . . ." Sykes to Sokolow, April 14, 1917, Oxford University, St. Antony's College, Middle East Centre, Sykes Papers, 42B.

216 Sokolow quickly assured . . . I never found Sokolow's account of this meeting and rely upon Stein's account in *Balfour Declaration,* 407.

216 "he had been pleased" . . . Rodd to Drummond, May 11, 1917, Hull University, Sykes Papers.

216 Someone, however . . . "It was then suggested that I should ask for an audience with the Pope." Sokolow to Weizmann, May 12, 1917, CZA, Sokolow Papers.

216 "In spite of my usual . . ." Sokolow to Weizmann, May 7, 1917, CZA, Sokolow Papers.

217 "There is the possibility . . ." Florian Sokolow, *Nahum Sokolow,* 151.

217 "But what then . . ." Stein, *Balfour Declaration,* 408.

217 "Your telegram received . . ." Weizmann to Sokolow, May 9, 1917, Stein, *Letters,* letter no. 380, 7:405.

218 "I am extremely satisfied" . . . Sokolow to Weizmann, May 25, 1917, CZA, Sokolow Papers.

218 "You were good enough . . ." Quoted in Stein, *Balfour Declaration,* 416–17.

CHAPTER 16: REVELATION OF THE SYKES-PICOT AGREEMENT

221 "In this sentiment the British . . ." British reply to Russian note regarding the Allied war-aims, December 7, 1917, NA, FO371/3062/232332.

221 "It is settled" . . . Scott to Weizmann, April 16, 1917, WI, Weizmann Papers.

221 Sacher immediately put . . . Sacher to Weizmann, April 14, 1917, ibid.

222 "spoke resignedly . . ." Scott to Weizmann, April 24, 1916, ibid.

222 "Apparently the French . . ." Weizmann to Scott, April 26, 1917, Stein, *Letters,* letter no. 357, 7:379.

222 "His answer was that . . ." Ibid.

223 "He found this arrangement . . ." Ibid.

223 "to Bob Cecil in . . ." Ormsby-Gore to Sykes, May 8, 1917, WI, Weizmann Papers.

223 "began by saying that . . ." Cecil, memorandum, April 25, 1917, ibid.

223 "We have been lied to . . ." Sacher to Weizmann, April 28, 1917, ibid.

223 "our affairs are at a . . ." Sacher to Weizmann, May 1, 1917, ibid.

224 "The representatives . . ." Sacher, memo, May 1, 1917, OUNBL, Stein Papers, box 8.

224 "the suggested division . . ." "Notes on an interview which took place at the Foreign Office on Wednesday the 25th of April at 5.30 P.M. with Lord Robert Cecil," WI, Weizmann Papers.

225 "Last night . . . Feisal said . . ." Wilson to Cairo (Wingate?), May 25, 1917, Cambridge University, Churchill College, George Lloyd Papers, Arabian file, January–June 1917, 9/9.

225 "I have to say . . ." Hussein to Wingate, April 28, 1917, NA, FO371/3059.

225 "The English, my son, are . . ." Antonius, *Arab Awakening,* 183.

226 "The Sharif evidently . . ." Clayton, memorandum, April 3, 1917, WI, Gilbert Clayton file.

226 "the signed agreement . . ." "Notes of a Conference held at 10 Downing Street, at 3:30 PM on April 3, 1917," WI, Arabs file.

227 "What we want to do . . ." Leonard Stein, "Some Footnotes to the History of the War in Asia," *Near East and India,* July 9, 1925, OUNBL, Stein Papers, box 130.

227 "though I did not know . . ." Sykes, telegram to London, April 29, 1917, WI, material from Mark Sykes.

228 "The time has now arrived . . ." Hogarth to Balfour, April 27, 1917, Oxford University, St. Antony's College, Middle East Centre, Sykes Papers, 41D.

228 "Unless Arab independence . . ." Sykes to Wingate, May 5, 1917, ibid.

229 As the *Northbrook* steamed . . . Sykes to high commissioner, May 23, 1917, Oxford University, St. Antony's College, Middle East Centre, Sykes Papers, 41B.

229 "I understand . . . not entirely . . ." Colonel Cyril Wilson to Cairo (Wingate?), May 24, 1917, Cambridge University, Churchill College, Lloyd Papers, Arabian file, January–June 1917, 9/9.

230 "He [Hussein] told M. Picot . . ." Fuad al-Khatib, note taken down by Lt. Colonel Newcombe, May 19, 1917, Cambridge University, Churchill College, Lloyd Papers, Arabian file, January–June 1917, 9/9.

230 "The King disliked the idea . . ." Sykes to Wingate, May 23, 1917, Oxford University, St. Antony's College, Middle East Centre, Sykes Papers, 41B.

231 "that the relations between . . ." Note by Lt. Colonel Newcombe, D.S.O., March 20, 1917 [NB: the date is obviously May 20, 1917], Cambridge University, Churchill College, Lloyd Papers, Arabian file, January–June 1917, 9/9.

232 "we shall examine the matter . . ." Letters quoted from Antonius, *Arab Awakening,* 414–27.

232 His Majesty the King of Hejaz . . . Sykes to Wingate, May 23, 1917, Oxford University, St. Antony's College, Middle East Centre, Sykes Papers, 41B.

232 "formal annexation is quite . . ." "Memorandum by Sir Mark Sykes on Mr. Nicholson's Note Regarding our Commitments," August 14, 1917, Hull University, Sykes Papers, DDSY/2/4/151.

233 "what we want without . . ." Sykes to Cox, May 23, 1917, Oxford University, St. Antony's College, Middle East Centre, Sykes Papers, 42C.

233 a joint statement on "general policy" . . . "General Policy," May 17, 1917, Hull University, Sykes Papers, DDSY/2/4.

233 "Any criticisms or exclamations . . ." "Note by Fuad al-Khatib taken down by Lt. Colonel Newcombe." Cambridge University, Churchill College, Lloyd Papers, Arabian file, January–June 1917, 9/9.

233 "obviously delighted" . . . Colonel Cyril Wilson to Cairo (Wingate?), May 24, 1917, Cambridge University, Churchill College, Lloyd Papers, Arabian file, January–June 1917, 9/9.

234 "On such a reply . . ." Sykes to high commissioner, May 23, 1917, Oxford University, St. Antony's College, Middle East Centre, Sykes Papers, 41B.

234 "it struck me as possible . . ." Colonel Cyril Wilson to Cairo (Wingate?), May 24, 1917, Cambridge University, Churchill College, Lloyd Papers, Arabian file, January–June 1917, 9/9.

234 "They have the proclamation" . . . Ibid.

235 "Certainly . . . the large number of . . ." Ibid.

CHAPTER 17: BRITISH MUSLIMS, THE ANGLO-OTTOMAN SOCIETY, AND THE DISILLUSIONING OF MARMADUKE PICKTHALL

240 "The Ottoman Government has drawn . . ." Quoted in Sanders, *High Walls,* 58.

241 "the present regime . . ." Duff to Grey, January 29, 1915, NA, FO371/2489.

241 "What we really relied on . . ." Quoted in Berridge, *Fitzmaurice,* 216. I rely on Berridge's account of these first negotiations.

242 the idea resurfaced in Paris . . . T. P. to Bertie, July 12, 1915, NA, FO800/181. "An important

personage," a French businessman with interests in Turkey, approached the French foreign
minister Théophile Delcassé. He wanted to know "whether he would send someone to talk
with Djavid Bey [the Ottoman finance minister currently traveling] in Switzerland as to terms
of peace with Turkey." Interested but wary, Delcassé's first move was to contact Russia, asking
whether the position with regard to Constantinople had changed. Russia's foreign minister,
Sergei Sazanov, promptly informed him that it had not. The report by "T. P." to the British
ambassador in Paris, Lord Bertie, is dated July 12, 1915.

242 It resurfaced in California . . . September 21, 1915, NA, FO371/2489. Vahan Cardashian, Ottoman high commissioner to the San Francisco Exposition, sounded a member of the British
consular staff, Sir Arthur Herbert, on the separate peace, possibly with the knowledge of Talaat Pasha.

242 Russia tried to bribe . . . The Russians suggested to their allies that Armenian intermediaries
contact Djemal Pasha. If Djemal overthrew Enver and took Turkey out of the war, the Allies
would recognize him as sultan of Turkey with a hereditary title and supply him with weapons.
The Allies also would accept Ottoman claims in Asia and Arabia. But Djemal must pledge to
take steps for the salvation of the Armenians and cede Constantinople and the Dardanelles to
Russia. Interestingly, Britain did not reject this plan out of hand, although it would have
meant abandoning Sharif Hussein, with whom McMahon was just concluding his notorious
correspondence. But the French objected strongly. They would have to give up their annexationist schemes in Syria and elsewhere, which they were not willing to do. The Russian design,
like those before it, led nowhere. Leonard Stein, article in *Near East and India,* July 2, 1925,
clipped and kept in Stein Papers, box 130.

242 "No harm in trying" . . . minute, telegram from Lord Bertie, June 1, 1915, NA, FO371/2777.

243 "with 'discordant yells . . .' " Ansari, *Infidel Within,* 82, quoting *Liverpool Review,* November
28, 1891.

243 "Opposition was . . ." Khalid Sheldrake, *Islamic Review,* February 1914.

243 "Your Majesty, May I venture . . ." Sheldrake to His Majesty the King, December 19, 1914,
NA, FO371/2480.

244 "our brothers and the Caliph . . ." "Translation of an anonymous letter addressed to H.E. the
Prime Minister," Ronald Storrs Papers, reel 4, box II, folder 3, Egypt 1914–15.

244 British Intelligence kept . . . Of Rosher, the War Office spy, noted: "He and his wife are in very
straitened circumstances and have pawned nearly everything." War Office 106/1420.

244 Joseph King . . . "Mr. Joseph King MP, Police Report on," NA, FO371/3121.

245 "capable of political mischief" . . . "Mr. Duse Mohammed and the Islamic Society," British Library, India Office L/P&J/12/752, file 416/916.

245 "He is so peculiar . . ." "Note by Mr. Rose, CSI," ibid. See also Ansari, *Infidel Within,* 128.

245 "I don't think he would . . ." "Mushir Hussein Kidwai," British Library, India Office
L/P&J/12/752, file 416/916.

245 Khwaja Kamal-ud-Din . . . He wrote a pamphlet called *Jesus—An Ideal of Godhead and Hu-
manity* to demonstrate that Islam did not condemn other religions. He wrote a pamphlet called
The Problem of Human Evolution to reconcile religion and science. His two pamphlets *The Status of Women in World Religions and Civilisations,* and *Woman from Judaism to Islam,* argue that
Muslims recognized women's rights.

245 "you would see a black . . ." Ismail Bey, *How Muhammad (peace be upon him!) found the world
and how he left it,* 293.

246 "The great Temple of Solomon . . ." "Muslim Interests in Palestine," Report of a lecture given
by Mr. M. Pickthall, June 9, 1917, NA, FO371/3053. So thoroughly did the British government
infiltrate Muslim activist groups during the war, and so much did it fear their possible disloyalty, that by November 1918 it could receive a nearly verbatim account of a meeting held at 71
Talbot Road, London, of four prominent British Muslims who were merely discussing how to
bring Muslim issues before the pending peace conference. One of the four must have been the
informer. See "Muslims in England, Confidential, November 25, 1918," NA, FO371/3419.

246 "an Ottoman Association" . . . For the founding meeting of the Ottoman Society, see clipping

NOTES

of the *African Times,* "Xmas 1913," Somerset Record Office, Aubrey Herbert Papers, DD/DRU/43.

246 Among the names listed . . . E. N. Bennett, William H. Leed, Joint Hon. Secretaries, to Herbert, December 13, 1913, Somerset Record Office, Herbert Papers, DD/DRU/33.

247 the names of Moses Gaster and Lucien Wolf . . . *African Times,* June 9, 1914.

247 at the body's meetings . . . *Islamic Review,* February 1914.

247 Khwaja Kamal-ud-Din, who . . . Ibid., September 1914.

247 "We who know something . . ." *African Times,* August 4, 1914.

248 "did everything for it . . ." Fremantle, *Loyal Enemy,* 230.

249 "Our unknown rulers . . ." Marmaduke Pickthall, *New Age,* February 18, 1915.

249 Some nine months . . . He met Valyi at a meeting at the Cannon Street Hotel organized by yet another well-connected Turcophile, the Reverend H. G. Rosedale. In this company Pickthall had called for a revival of Disraeli's old pro-Ottoman policy. Afterward Valyi introduced himself and asked for permission to publish the paper. Pickthall agreed.

249 Fuad Selim al-Hijari . . . Granville to Grey, April 18, 1916, NA, FO371/2777.

250 "I am more a philosopher . . ." *Dial,* June 8, 1916.

250 "Philosopher" may not have been . . . Rev. H. G. Rosedale to Sir Maurice de Bunsen, June 16, 1916, NA, FO371/2777. Rosedale thought Valyi "may be said in some way to represent the [Ottoman] Government & at least has great influence in that direction."

252 "I am directed by Sir Edward . . ." De Bunsen to Rosedale, June 23, 1916, NA, FO371/2777.

252 "I am a nobody . . ." *New Age,* December 30, 1915. For the correspondence between Pickthall and Sykes, see Fremantle, *Loyal Enemy,* 270–79.

CHAPTER 18: THE CURIOUS VENTURE OF J. R. PILLING

253 "the distinction of being . . ." April 26, 1917, OUNBL, Papers of Sir Horace Rumbold, box 21.

253 "This is the most . . ." Rumbold to Lady Fane, February 12, 1917, ibid.

253 "This country is crammed . . ." Rumbold to Graham, June 22, 1917, ibid., box 22.

254 "He had trained . . ." Harold Nicolson, quoted in T. G. Otte, "Horace Rumbold," in *New Dictionary of National Biography.*

254 "Our . . . servants did not . . ." Rumbold to "Mama," February 18, 1918, OUNBL, Rumbold Papers, box 24.

254 "What can you expect . . ." Rumbold to Lord Newton, November 10, 1917, ibid., box 23.

254 "I always had doubts . . ." Rumbold to Lord Newton, November 10, 1917, re Russians and February 16, 1918, re Turks, ibid., box 24.

254 "He is as clever . . ." Rumbold to Lord Newton, May 19, 1917, ibid., box 21.

254 "My sole aim . . ." Parodi to Rumbold, April 27, 1918, ibid., box 24.

254 Swiss socialists were negotiating . . . C. French to Sykes, n.d., Hull University, Sykes Papers, DDSY/2/11/59.

255 "to be really a good . . ." Hardinge to Rumbold, April 2, 1918, OUNBL, Rumbold Papers, box 24.

255 "He is not of Syrian . . ." Rumbold to Ronald Campbell, April 5, 1918, ibid.

255 "practically a member . . ." For Mrs. Evans, see Rumbold to Campbell, February 27, 1917, ibid., box 21.

255 Anglo-Ottoman Society . . . *New York Times,* May 6, 1899.

255 "a 'sharper' and of very shady . . ." For biographical material regarding Pilling, see Gilbert, *Sir Horace Rumbold,* 149, n1; October 17, 1917, NA, FO371/3057; and Hardinge to Lord Lansdowne, November 24, 1917, CUL, Lord Hardinge Papers, vol. 35.

256 "long intimate acquaintance . . ." Pilling to Balfour, November 8, 1917, NA, FO371/3057.

256 "formed rather a low . . ." Campbell to Rumbold, March 3, 1917, OUNBL, Rumbold Papers.

256 "The day following . . ." Pilling to Balfour, November 9, 1917, NA, FO371/3057.

256 "rather a muddle-headed . . ." Rumbold to Campbell, February 27, 1917, OUNBL, Rumbold Papers, box 21.

257 "Altogether it would seem . . ." Campbell to Rumbold, March 3, 1917, ibid.

257 "made proposals to the . . ." Drummond to Balfour, October 19, 1917, NA, FO371/3057.

257 "no official status but . . ." DMI interview with Pilling, April 30, 1917, OUNBL, Rumbold Papers, box 21.

257 "These free lances are . . ." Rumbold to Campbell, February 27, 1917, ibid.

257 "I am afraid you have . . ." Campbell to Rumbold, March 22, 1917, ibid.

258 "so securing British interests . . ." Pilling to Mrs. Evans, May 12, 1917, NA, FO371/3057.

259 "my other many reports . . ." Pilling to Balfour, November 9, 1917, ibid.

259 When he approached . . . Hardinge, minute, November 9, 1917, ibid.

260 another trip to Switzerland . . . MacDonagh to Campbell, November 15, 1917, ibid. "I hear that Pilling has been worrying the American Embassy for the last four months, and is now trying to secure an interview with the Ambassador."

260 "agreed in June last" . . . Pilling to Balfour, November 7, 1917, ibid.

260 "Pilling . . . has been unable . . ." MacDonagh to Campbell, November 15, 1917, ibid.

CHAPTER 19: HENRY MORGENTHAU AND THE DECEIVING OF CHAIM WEIZMANN

263 Germany wanted her Ottoman . . . Rumbold to Cecil, May 23, 1917, NA, FO371/3050.

264 speech delivered in Cincinnati . . . *New York Times,* May 22, 1916.

264 "Nothing could be . . ." Sykes to Gaster, May 22, 1916, CZA, Gaster Papers, A203/227/35.

264 Morgenthau's mission . . . See, for example, Stein, *Balfour Declaration,* 353–60; Friedman, *Question of Palestine,* 211–18; Sanders, *High Walls,* 551–56; Reinharz, *Weizmann,* 154–66; and Reinharz, "His Majesty's Zionist Emissary," 259–77. My account is based on these secondary sources, supplemented by primary sources as noted.

264 The idea may have . . . Morgenthau and Secretary of State Robert Lansing discussed the matter on May 16. Twenty-four hours later Lansing reported on that discussion to the president. Nine days after that Morgenthau and Wilson reviewed the idea again, and the president agreed to it in principle. The two men met once more on June 7.

264 "peculiarly cordial and . . ." Quoted in Reinharz, "His Majesty's Zionist Emissary," 261.

264 Turks were "nibbling" . . . Quoted in Yale, "Morgenthau's Special Mission," 311.

264 "If matters took . . ." Quoted in Friedman, *Question of Palestine,* 211.

265 This was . . . Notes on the cover of the file by various Foreign Office figures, May 24, 1917, NA, FO371/3057.

265 About his main goal . . . "Lewin-Epstein went without knowing the political background of the business . . . Frankfurter . . . had no idea why they came." Weizmann to Vera Weizmann, July 8, 1917, in Stein, *Letters,* letter no. 456, 7:469.

265 "someone in authority . . ." Mr. Barclay to Cecil, May 31, 1917, NA, FO371/3057.

266 "rumours here . . ." Malcolm to Nubar Pasha, June 22, 1917, ibid.

266 "Muslim Interests in Palestine" . . . Ormsby-Gore, report to Cecil on meeting with Malcolm and Weizmann, June 10, 1917, Hull University, Sykes Papers, DDSY/2/12/8.

266 Weizmann knew about . . . Weizmann to Lord Walter Rothschild, June 2, 1917, WI, "Arabs."

267 "Dr. Weizmann, whom I . . ." Graham, minute, June 9, 1917, NA, FO371/3057.

267 "Both Mr. Malcolm . . ." Ormsby-Gore, report, "Secret and Confidential," June 10, 1917, Hull University, Sykes Papers, DDSY/2/12/8.

268 On Tuesday, June 12 . . . Graham, first minute, June 13, 1917, NA, FO371/3057.

268 extremely indiscreet . . . Yale, "Morgenthau's Special Mission," 313.

268 "As condition of . . ." Graham, second minute, June 13, 1917, NA, FO371/3057.

268 "Will you be kind . . ." Graham to Rumbold, June 8, 1917, OUNBL, Rumbold Papers, box 22.

269 "I was to talk . . ." Weizmann, *Trial and Error,* 196.

269 eighteen trunks . . . Ibid., 197.

269 Rumford . . . Weizmann to Vera Weizmann, June 29, 1917, in Stein, *Letters,* letter no. 446, 7:455.

269 "either terribly 'profound' . . ." Weizmann to Vera Weizmann, July 2, 1917, ibid., letter no. 448, 7:457.

269 "From the moment . . ." Weizmann to Vera Weizmann, July 3, 1917, in Stein, *Letters,* letter no. 449, 7:458.
269 Weizmann went out . . . He paid a call on Max Nordau, a venerable Zionist and native Austrian who had left Paris when the war began. He bumped into another Zionist in the street, Abraham S. Yahuda.
270 "I am not aware . . ." Weizmann to Sir Ronald Graham, July 6, 1917, in Stein, *Letters,* letter no. 453, 7:461. To Schmarvonian, Weizmann "took an instantaneous, cordial and enduring dislike."
270 "Mr. Morgenthau had . . ." Weizmann, *Trial and Error,* 1:198.
270 "such conditions . . ." Weizmann to Sir Ronald Graham, July 6, 1917, in Stein, *Letters,* letter no. 453, 7:463.
270 "On no account . . ." Ibid.
271 "eminently successful" . . . Graham to Hardinge, July 13 and July 21, 1917, NA, FO371/3057.
271 "The Zionists in public . . ." Sacher to Simon, May 9, 1917, CZA, Sacher Papers, CZA/A289/114.
271 "The Zionist movement as such . . ." Sacher to Simon, n.d. (but May 1917 from internal evidence), ibid.
271 "I said that it was not . . ." Simon, diary entry, June 24, 1917, CZA, Simon Papers, CZA/AK2001.
272 "Assume [?] the peace . . ." Simon to Sacher, July 1, 1917, ibid.
272 "the centre of gravity . . ." Sacher to Weizmann, August 3, 1917, WI, Sacher letters.
272 "Chaim gave us an account . . ." Simon to Sacher, August 2, 1917, CZA, Simon Papers, CZA/AK2001.
273 "I think you were much . . ." Sacher to Weizmann, August 3, 1917, WI, Sacher letters.
273 "But think of tying . . ." Sacher to Simon, August 11, 1917, ibid.
273 "the general policy . . ." Sacher to Simon, August 17 and August 21, 1917, ibid.
273 "In politics one is . . ." Sacher to Weizmann, September 16, 1917, ibid.

CHAPTER 20: "THE MAN WHO WAS GREENMANTLE"

276 "He loved to dare . . ." Herbert, *Mons, Anzac & Kut,* 12. He died of blood poisoning after having all his teeth removed, which he had been told would cure his blindness.
276 "He was the most . . ." Quoted in Fitzherbert, *Man Who Was Greenmantle,* 1.
276 "the kind of man . . ." Herbert, *Mons, Anzac & Kut,* 14.
276 "by the simple . . ." Auberon Waugh (Herbert's grandson), "Aubrey Herbert," in *New Dictionary of National Biography.*
276 "It is only fair . . ." *Western Morning News,* October 16, 1914.
277 "Oh Mark . . ." Herbert to Sykes, February 9, 1915, Somerset Record Office, Herbert Papers, DD/DRU/33.
277 "an odd gnome . . ." Herbert, diary entry, January 11, 1915, ibid.
277 "We have not gone . . ." Herbert to Sykes, February 9, 1915, ibid., DD/DRU/33.
277 "If . . . at any time . . ." Cecil to Herbert, July 17, 1915, ibid.
278 "2 things were in . . ." Herbert, diary entry, February 27, 1916, ibid.
278 "passed down corridors . . ." December 8, 1915, ibid.
278 "we shall simply . . ." Herbert to Lloyd, May 14, 1917, Cambridge University, Churchill College, Lloyd Papers, GLLD9/1, 1917–18.
279 " 'Time's up for you . . .' " Herbert, diary entry, June 4, 1917, Somerset Record Office, Herbert Papers.
279 "dangerous pacifist . . ." Quoted in Fisher, *Gentleman Spies,* 18.
279 On July 4 . . . Before meeting Balfour, Herbert met with Milner. Herbert, diary entry, July 6, 1917, Somerset Record Office, Herbert Papers.
279 "We should free troops . . ." Herbert, memo, July 4, 1917, NA, FO800/18/226.
280 "the strongest point . . ." Eric Drummond to Balfour, July 7, 1917, NA, FO800/18/223.
280 During May, June . . . To give only a few examples: From the British ambassador in Petrograd,

Sir George Buchanan: "Minister for Foreign Affairs told me today that he had heard from Berne that Turkish Minister had stated that time had come for organizing a movement against young Turks and in favor of peace." Buchanan to Balfour, May 23, 1917, NA, FO371/3050. From Rumbold in Berne on June 4: "Suraya Bey Vlera, a former Albanian official who has been at Vienna with Prince of Wied has just returned to Switzerland. He states Talaat Pasha recently told Germans at Berlin that having regard to present economic and military conditions in Turkey latter could no longer continue to fight and would be obliged to make a separate peace with Allies." On June 17 Rumbold enclosed a long report from Parodi on the views of Turkish Liberals: They wished to overthrow the CUP and make peace, the peace to be based upon the retention of Constantinople, the opening of the straits under an international guarantee, autonomy for Armenia, Syria, Palestine, and Mesopotamia, independence for the various Arab emirs, including Sharif Hussein, and financial assistance from the Allies. Rumbold to Balfour, June 17, 1917, NA, FO371/2770. At the War Office, on June 19, MacDonagh interviewed Elkus, the former American envoy in Constantinople: "He believes that both Talaat and Djavid earnestly desire peace . . . Mr. Elkus suggests a M. Orosti Blocket Cie of Paris as a possibly suitable intermediary."

280 Rechid Bey as . . . Rumbold to Balfour, July 1, 1917, NA, FO371/3057.

280 "I am taking steps . . ." Rumbold to Balfour, July 7, 1917, ibid. The important Turks included Fethy Bey, Ottoman minister at Sofia; Rifaat and Mutak Effendi, respectively president and secretary of the Ottoman senate; Hadji Adil Bey, president of the Ottoman Chamber of Deputies; and various Turkish army officers convalescing at Davos.

280 "a member of the Committee . . ." Rumbold to Grey, July 12, 1917, NA, FO371/3050.

281 "Next morning [I] was . . ." Herbert, diary entry, July 21, 1917, Somerset Record Office, Herbert Papers.

281 "He comes from one . . ." Herbert, memorandum, July 28, 1917, NA, FO371/3057.

282 "We then went . . ." Herbert, memorandum, July 22, 1917, NA, FO371/3057.

283 "I do not think . . ." Herbert, diary entry, July 24, 1917, Somerset Record Office, Herbert Papers.

284 "Talaat now convinced . . ." Binns to London, July 22, 1917, NA, FO371/3057.

284 "now knows that she . . ." Lord Curzon, memorandum, May 12, 1917, NA, CAB24/10/13.

285 The first did not . . . Arthur Ryan, memorandum, July 13, 1917, NA, FO800/18/237-241.

285 "It is not impossible . . ." Lewis Mallet, memorandum, July 14, 1917, NA, FO800/18/243-248.

285 "On my arrival I found . . ." Sykes to Clayton, July 22, 1917, Hull University, Sykes Papers, DDSY/2/4/69.

285 "The visit of a . . ." Sykes, note, n.d., ibid., DDSY/2/11/62.

287 "I find myself in . . ." "Minutes by Sir G. Clerk and Sir R. Graham," July 31 and August 1, 1917, NA, FO371/3057.

287 "were not sufficient . . ." Herbert, diary entry, August 6, 1917, Somerset Record Office, Herbert Papers.

288 "Talaat has no intention . . ." Rumbold to Balfour, July 27, 1917, NA, FO371/3058.

288 "I told him that . . ." Hardinge note, August 28, 1917, NA, FO371/3057.

CHAPTER 21: THE ZAHAROFF GAMBIT

291 "evil and imposing" . . . Quoted in Richard Davenport Hines, "Basil Zaharoff," in *New Dictionary of National Biography.* See also Allfrey, *Man of Arms;* McCormick, *Pedlar of Death;* and Engelbrecht and Hanighen, *Merchants of Death,* 95–107.

291 "All that is needed . . ." Zaharoff to Caillard, undated fragment, probably November 1915, NA, Caillard Papers, file 1.

291 "I beg . . ." Asquith to Caillard, March 6, 1916, Zaharoff copy, ibid., file 4.

291 "Mon cher Ami . . ." Zaharoff to Caillard, April 19, 1916, ibid., file 3.

293 "This is not the moment . . ." Zaharoff to Caillard, June 29, 1916, ibid.

293 But one of his biographers . . . Hynes, in *New Dictionary of National Biography.*

294 "the moment might . . ." Zaharoff to Caillard, June 29, 1916, and Caillard to Zaharoff, May 21, 1917, NA, Caillard Papers.

294 "I am turning . . ." Zaharoff to Caillard, May 23, 1917, ibid.

294 "was greatly interested . . ." Caillard to Zaharoff, May 31, 1917, ibid., file 7.

294 "The enclosed . . ." Zaharoff to Caillard, June 5, 1917, ibid.

294 "throwing out . . ." Caillard to Walter Long, June 11, 1917, ibid.

295 "considered it would be . . ." Caillard to Zaharoff, June 14, 1917, ibid.

296 He arrived on June 18 . . . "What a nest of spies Switzerland must be at this moment," Sir Ronald Graham had just written to Britain's man in Berne—neither of them knowing about Zaharoff's mission. Graham to Rumbold, June 8, 1917, OUNBL, Rumbold Papers, box 22.

296 "Things had changed . . ." Zaharoff to Caillard, June 23, 1917, NA, Caillard Papers.

297 "Your people are to . . ." Zaharoff to Caillard, June 24, [1917], ibid.

297 "After some further . . ." Caillard to Zaharoff, June 27, 1917, ibid.

298 "eases my mind . . ." Zaharoff to Caillard, July 2, 1917, ibid.

299 "saluted me politely . . ." Zaharoff to Caillard, July 28, 1917, ibid.

299 "The fact is that . . ." Caillard to Zaharoff, August 17, 1917, ibid.

300 "I will be there . . ." Quoted in Caillard to Lloyd George, November 23, 1917, ibid.

CHAPTER 22: THE ASCENDANCY OF CHAIM WEIZMANN

304 "is felt by the outside . . ." Weizmann, "Introduction," in Sacher, *Zionism and Jewish Future,* 6–7; Gaster, "Judaism a National Religion," ibid., 93.

304 "the position of emancipated . . ." Wolf to Bigart, June 5, 1917, Conjoint Committee, Report no. 11, May 17, 1917–July 15, 1917, Yivo Institute, Lucien Wolf Papers.

305 "How can a man . . ." Montefiore, "Englishman of Jewish Faith," 823.

305 "The Zionist wing . . ." Wolf, "Jewish National Movement."

305 "So long as this . . ." Wolf to Bigart, June 5, 1917, Conjoint Committee, Report no. 11, May 17, 1917–July 15, 1917, Yivo Institute, Wolf Papers.

305 "the 'campaign' was . . ." Sokolow to Brandeis, April 7, 1917, OUNBL, Stein Papers, box 6.

305 "As my sister-in-law will . . ." Walter Rothschild to Weizmann, April 10, 1917, WI.

306 "I am afraid you . . ." Wolf to de Rothschild, January 3, 1917, CZA, A7732.

307 "were exceedingly . . ." Wolf, memorandum, January 31, 1917, FO800/129, Balfour Miscellaneous.

307 "The Presidents of the . . ." Wolf to Oliphant, April 21, 1917, Conjoint Committee, Report no. 10, February 6, 1917–May 17, 1917, Yivo Institute, Wolf Papers.

308 a mollifying response . . . "I am authorized to inform you that no new agreement on the Palestine question has been concluded. His Majesty's Government are sincerely anxious to act in all matters affecting the Jewish community not only in its best interests but with a due regard to the wishes and opinions of all its sections." Graham to Wolf, April 27, 1917, ibid.

308 Wolf immediately endorsed . . . Wolf to Montefiore, May 11, 1917, ibid., microfilm reel 3.

308 As to whether Britain . . . Claude Montefiore, interview with Lord Milner, May 16, 1917, ibid., microfilm reel 7.

308 "I would beg of you . . ." Montefiore to Milner, May 17, 1917, CZA, A/7731.

308 "is an able, temperate . . ." Milner to Cecil, May 17, 1917, NA, FO800/198.

308 "Among the possible . . ." Milner to Samuel, January 17, 1917, Oxford University, St. Antony's College, Middle East Centre, Samuel Papers, GB165-0252.

309 "I am entitled . . ." "English Zionist Federation. Meeting at Armfield's Hotel . . . May 20, 1917," NA, FO371/3053.

309 "to issue a public . . ." Conjoint Committee, Report no. 11, May 17, 1917–July 15, 1917, Yivo Institute, Wolf Papers.

309 "the Zionist theory . . ." Wolf, "Conjoint Foreign Committee . . . Statement on the Palestine Question," CZA, A/7731.

309 "his regret at . . ." Wolf to Montefiore, June 1, 1917, Yivo Institute, Wolf Papers.

309 " 'And you would render . . .' " Hertz to Montefiore, May 30, 1917, ibid.

310 Over the course . . . Wolf, enclosure with letter to Montefiore, May 23, 1917, CZA, A/7732.

310 But Alexander refused . . . Wolf to Montefiore, May 23, 1917, Yivo Institute, Wolf Papers, microfilm reel 3.

310 "If you approve . . ." Walter Rothschild to Weizmann, May 24, 1917, WI.

311 "the hope that for . . ." Both quoted in *Jewish Chronicle,* June 1, 1917.

311 "It was . . . thanks . . ." Samuel Cohen to Weizmann, August 16, 1917, WI.

311 "The ordinary non-Jew . . ." *Palestine,* June 9, 1917.

312 "All that the Committee . . ." *Jewish Chronicle,* June 1, 1917.

312 "a grave error . . ." Zangwill to Wolf, May 26, 1917, WI.

312 "had declared the Zionists . . ." *Jewish Chronicle,* June 8, 1917.

313 "issued at an inopportune . . ." Ibid., June 22, 1917.

313 The scholar who . . . Cohen, *English Zionists,* 261–75.

313 "I write to tell you . . ." Walter Rothschild to Weizmann, June 17, 1917, WI.

313 "It is a great victory" . . . Sacher to Simon, June 20, 1917, and Sacher to Weizmann, June 22, 1917, ibid.

313 "This vote . . ." Graham, minute, June 20, 1917, NA, FO371/3053.

314 "I intend to send . . ." Sieff to Weizmann, May 7, 1917, WI.

314 "I don't mind . . ." Sacher to Simon, May 9, 1917, CZA, A/289114.

315 "We Zionists . . ." Simon to Sokolow, August 3, 1917, WI.

315 "Chaim Weizmann has caught . . ." Sacher to Simon, September 2, 1917, CZA, A/289114.

316 "You act on your . . ." Cohen to Weizmann, August 16, 1917, WI.

316 A London delegate . . . The London delegate was Benjamin Grad.

316 "I think it no less . . ." Simon to Weizmann, August 17, 1917, ibid. Of the principals, only the iconoclast, Harry Sacher, remained mute.

316 "The atmosphere . . ." Weizmann to Sokolow, September 5, 1917, in Stein, *Letters,* letter no. 490, 7:499.

317 "had the effect . . ." Weizmann to Scott, September 13, 1917, in Stein, *Letters,* letter no. 501, 7:510.

317 "For the first time . . ." Ginzberg to Weizmann, September 5, 1917, OUNBL, Stein Papers, box 6.

CHAPTER 23: LAWRENCE AND THE ARABS ON THE VERGE

320 "We all swore . . ." Quoted in Barr, *Setting the Desert,* 103.

320 "I quite recognize . . ." Lawrence to Sykes, September 9, 1917, Durham University, Clayton Papers, 693/11/4.

322 "They marched to Abu . . ." "Notes on Capt. Lawrence's Journey," Durham University, Clayton Papers, 694/5/26.

323 "nearly blinded . . ." Lawrence, *Seven Pillars,* 246.

323 "while the coffee . . ." Ibid., 251.

323 "Twice puff-adders . . ." Ibid., 261.

323 "I could see . . ." Ibid., 267.

323 "Also . . . a rash . . ." Ibid., 266–67.

323 "I've decided . . ." Quoted in Barr, *Setting the Desert,* 137.

324 "the low rolling . . ." *Arab Bulletin,* no. 59, August 12, 1917, p. 337.

324 "it was terribly hot . . ." Lawrence, *Seven Pillars,* 292–95.

325 "all the Turks . . ." *Arab Bulletin,* no. 59, August 12, 1917, p. 339.

325 With Aqaba secured . . . Barr, *Setting the Desert,* 154.

326 "sat in his chair . . ." Lawrence, *Seven Pillars,* 312–13.

326 "The scheme . . ." Quoted in Barr, *Setting the Desert,* 156.

326 "dying to go . . ." Quoted ibid., 160.

326 "It is necessary . . ." War Cabinet, August 10, 1917, NA, Cab23/13.

327 "There they could . . ." Secretary (for Lloyd George) to Robertson, September 22, 1917, House of Lords Record Office, David Lloyd George Papers, box 71.

327 "In the afternoon . . ." *Arab Bulletin,* no. 65, October 8, 1917, p. 402.

328 "shattered the firebox . . ." Ibid., no. 66, October 21, 1917, p. 414.

328 Slowly—too slowly . . . Report No. 2, p. 13, Oxford University, St. Antony's College, Middle East Centre, William Yale Papers, DS 244.4.

328 They did not . . . See Tauber, *Arab Movements,* 127.

329 "the rare sort . . ." Lawrence, *Seven Pillars,* 386.

329 "he was the only . . ." Ibid., 393.

330 "felt that there was . . ." Quoted in Barr, *Setting the Desert,* 187.

330 "Our minds were . . ." Lawrence, *Seven Pillars,* 405–16.

331 "a splendid two-engined . . ." Ibid., 422.

331 "His motor car . . ." Ibid., 423–25.

332 When Lawrence resisted . . . Barr, *Setting the Desert,* 195–200.

332 "a delicious warmth . . ." Lawrence, *Seven Pillars,* 436.

CHAPTER 24: THE DECLARATION AT LAST

333 "elicit [from the . . .]" Gaster to Weizmann, May 7, 1917, WI.

334 "for as much as . . ." Sacher to Sokolow, July 10, 1917, OUNBL, Stein Papers, box 5.

334 "We must control . . ." Sacher to Sokolow, July 11, 1917, ibid.

334 "Our purpose . . ." Sokolow to Cowen, July 9, 1917, ibid.

334 "Jewish National . . ." Sokolow to Sacher, July 13, 1917, ibid.

334 "too long . . ." Sokolow to Sacher, July 18, 1917, ibid.

335 "1. His Majesty's . . ." *New York Times,* June 19, 2005.

335 "At last I am able . . ." Rothschild to Balfour, July 18, 1917, WI.

335 "The declaration is . . ." Weizmann to ——, August 1, 1917, in Stein, *Letters,* letter no. 468, 7:481.

335 "I am glad to be . . ." Reinharz, *Weizmann,* 180.

336 Later, at Milner's request . . . Stein, *Balfour Declaration,* 520–21.

336 "In all the things . . ." Montagu to Asquith, June 15, 1915, OUNBL, Asquith Papers.

337 *"As the desert sand . . ."* Quoted in Sanders, *High Walls,* 563.

337 "I assert that . . ." Edwin Montagu, "The Anti-Semitism of the Present Government," August 23, 1917, NA, Cab24/24.

338 "the country for which . . ." Montagu to Lloyd George, October 4, 1917, WI.

338 "urged that the use . . ." September 3, 1917, 26(2), NA, Cab23/4.

339 "We have submitted . . ." Quoted in Stein, *Balfour Declaration,* 514.

339 "barren and desolate . . ." October 4, 1917, 80(5–7), NA, Cab23/4.

340 "On this matter . . ." Edwin Montagu, "Zionism," October 9, 1917, NA, Cab24/28.

340 "the thing will go . . ." Scott, diary entry, October 14, 1917, WI.

341 "It's ridiculous . . ." Herbert, diary entry, October 21, 1917, Somerset Record Office, Herbert Papers.

342 "The Government has . . ." Quoted in Vital, *Zionism,* 291, n50.

342 "occupied [Palestine] . . ." Lord Curzon, "The Future of Palestine," October 26, 1917, NA, Cab21/58.

343 No one need be . . . Sykes, memorandum, October 30, 1917, NA, FO371/3083.

343 "There were considerable . . ." October 31, 1917, 137(5–6), NA, Cab21/58.

343 "The vast majority . . ." Ibid.

343 "admitted the force . . ." Ibid.

343 "I do not think . . ." Cecil, minute, March 3, 1916, NA, FO371/2671.

344 "Many . . . have a residual . . ." Sacher, *Zionist Portraits,* 37.

344 "recently approached . . ." Ormsby-Gore to Cecil, June 10, 1917, Hull University, Sykes Papers, DDSY/(2)/12/8.

344 Meanwhile the British . . . See, for example, *Jewish Chronicle,* September 21, 1917, and *Palestine,* September 22, 1917.

344 "During the last few . . ." Rothschild to Balfour, September 22, 1917, WI.

344 "This man displays . . ." Abraham Braunstein, "The Influence of British Successes in Palestine and the British Declaration Concerning a Jewish State on the Zionists in the Central Empires," June 12, 1917, NA, WO106/1419.

344 "A meeting is said . . ." The message from "Mr. Goodhart in Berne to Mr. Balfour" may be found in a file along with Cab21/58 "Attitude of enemy governments towards Zionism," February 15, 1918, which lists additional pro-Zionist press articles and expressions of sympathy from German officials. OUNBL, Stein Papers, box 12.

345 "behaved like a . . ." Quoted in Reinharz, *Weizmann,* 205.

CHAPTER 25: THE DECLARATION ENDANGERED

348 "we are watching . . ." Hardinge to General [MacDonagh?], November 8, 1917, NA, WO106/1516.

348 He had been dispatched . . . Arthur Balfour, "Circulated to the War Cabinet," November 1917, NA, FO371/3057.

348 "would welcome . . ." "Notes of conversation held by Mr. Waugh with Mr. Charlton Giraud: October 29, 1917," ibid.

348 "only of a kind . . ." Colonel Gabriel, memorandum on discussion with Giraud; Granville to Hardinge, November 1, 1917, ibid.

349 Rumbold also reported . . . For example, Rumbold to Foreign Office, September 1, 1917 and November 29, 1917, ibid.

349 Rahmi Bey's twitch . . . Arthur Balfour, "Circulated to the War Cabinet," November 1917, ibid.

349 "The time has come . . ." Lord Milner, memorandum, November 12, 1917, ibid.

350 "I ask how far . . ." Curzon of Keddleston, "Peace Negotiations with Turkey," November 16, 1917, NA, WO800/214.

350 "We are pledged . . ." Sykes to Hankey, November 14, 1917, Hull University, Sykes Papers, DDSY/2/4/161.

350 Unlike Waugh . . . Balfour to Lord Beaverbrook, August 9, 1918, NA, WO800/206.

351 "This is the most favorable . . ." Granville to Balfour, December 15, 1918, NA, FO371/3057; Waugh to Granville, December 4, 1918; Heathcote-Smith, memorandum on two conversations with Rahmi Bey, December 3, 1918, ibid.

351 "the fact that he is . . ." The two Turks were Chevky Bey and Begjet Wahby. Rumbold to Balfour, January 7, 1918, NA, WO800/206.

351 "Agent, who is believed . . ." Rumbold to Foreign Office, December 28, 1917, OUNBL, Rumbold Papers, box 23.

352 Lord Newton, however . . . Newton to Rumbold, January 5, 1918, ibid.

352 Amazingly, Horace . . . Palmer, *Victory in 1918,* 148–49.

352 "to include Palestine . . ." Smuts to Rumbold, December 19, 1917, OUNBL, Rumbold Papers, box 23.

353 "I trust that . . ." Minutes by various officials, December 15, 1917, NA, FO371/3057.

353 a wire from Balfour . . . I have found no copy of this cable, but Balfour refers to it twice in correspondence (see below).

353 "sent at the end . . ." Rumbold to Parodi, March 21, 1918, OUNBL, Rumbold Papers, box 23.

353 "We thought . . ." Balfour to Beaverbrook, August 9, 1918, NA, WO800/206.

353 "my Government will . . ." Rumbold to Parodi, February 6, 1918, OUNBL, Rumbold Papers, box 23.

354 "Abdul Kerim will . . ." Zaharoff to Caillard, November 18, 1917, NA, Caillard Papers, file 8.

354 Only two days . . . Zaharoff to Caillard, October 15, 1917, ibid.

354 The two men met . . . W. H. Fisher to Caillard, November 6, 1917, ibid.

354 "Egyptian conditions" . . . Owen, "Influence of Cromer's Indian Experience," 109–39; Al-Sayyd-Marsotm, "The British Occupation of Egypt from 1882," in Porter, ed., *Oxford History of the British Empire,* 3:651–64.

355 "using a very coarse . . ." Zaharoff to Caillard, November 27, 1917, NA, Caillard Papers, file 7.

355 "If the previous . . ." Zaharoff to Caillard, December 4, 1917, ibid.

355 " 'personal opinion' " . . . Zaharoff to Caillard, December 7, 1917, ibid.

355 "I did not go one . . ." Zaharoff to Caillard, December 15, 1917, House of Lords Record Office, Lloyd George Papers, Zaharoff file.

356 "Send me . . ." Ibid.

356 "We should be . . ." Davies to Caillard, January 21, 1918, ibid.

356 "It is agreed . . ." "Instructions of January 9, 1918," ibid.

357 "You did not mention . . ." Caillard to Lloyd George, January 12, 1918, ibid.

357 "Please explain . . ." Caillard to Zaharoff, January 16, 1918, ibid.

358 "We were four days . . ." Zaharoff to Caillard, January 29, 1918, ibid.

358 "claiming that all . . ." Zaharoff to Caillard, August 21, 1918, ibid.

CHAPTER 26: A DRAWING TOGETHER OF THREADS

370 "serious concern not . . ." Ronald Graham, minute, November 22, 1917, NA, FO371/3057.

371 "King seemed quite . . ." Quoted in Stein, *Balfour Declaration,* 633.

371 "I know that the Arabs . . ." Sykes to Feisal, March 3, 1918, NA, FO882/3, Arab Bureau.

372 "I do not, and never did . . ." Feisal to Sykes, July 18, 1917, NA, FO800/221.

372 He did not look . . . Yale Report no. 10, December 31, 1917, Oxford University, St. Antony's College, Middle East Centre, Yale Papers.

372 "the ambitions and . . ." Yale Report no. 3, November 12, 1917, ibid.

373 "The soul of their Prophet . . ." Amir Ali to Lord Hardinge, November 10, 1917, NA, FO371/3053.

373 "the Zionists were very . . ." Yale Report no. 9, December 26, 1917, Oxford University, St. Antony's College, Middle East Centre, Yale Papers.

373 "I strongly urge . . ." Islamic Society Resolutions, November 5, 1917, NA, FO371/3053.

375 Britain had a mandate . . . Macmillan, *Peacemakers,* 411.

376 "In no single theatre . . ." Quoted in Porter, *Lion's Share,* 252.

Bibliography

UNPUBLISHED SOURCES

GREAT BRITAIN

BRITISH LIBRARY
Arthur Balfour Papers
Robert Cecil Papers
Lord Curzon Papers
Edwin Montagu Papers
Murray-Robertson Papers
Lord Reading Papers
C. P. Scott Diary
India Office: "Notes on Mushir Husain Kidwai and Duse Mohamed," 1916, file number
   L/P&J/12/752; File 416/916.

CAMBRIDGE UNIVERSITY LIBRARY
Hardinge Papers

CHURCHILL COLLEGE, CAMBRIDGE UNIVERSITY
George Lloyd Papers

DURHAM UNIVERSITY
Sir Gilbert Clayton Papers
Sir Reginald Wingate Papers

HOUSE OF LORDS RECORD OFFICE
David Lloyd George Papers
Herbert Samuel Papers

HULL UNIVERSITY
Mark Sykes Papers

MIDDLE EAST CENTRE, ST. ANTONY'S COLLEGE, OXFORD UNIVERSITY
Edmund Allenby Papers
Balfour Declaration Papers
Sir Wyndham Deedes Papers
Felix Frankfurter Papers
David Hogarth Papers
Sir Henry McMahon Papers
Herbert Samuel Papers
Sir Mark Sykes Papers
William Yale Papers

NATIONAL ARCHIVE AT KEW
War Cabinet Papers: Cab23, Cab24, 1914–18
Foreign Office Papers: FO371 1914–18: America, Egypt, Russia, Turkey files
Foreign Office Papers: FO800 Balfour files, Grey files, miscellaneous files
Foreign Office Papers: FO882, Arab Bureau Papers
War Office Papers: WO106, papers pertaining to the Middle East
Sir Vincent Caillard Papers

NEW BODLEIAN LIBRARY, OXFORD UNIVERSITY
H. H. Asquith Papers
Geoffrey Dawson Papers
T. E. Lawrence Papers
Alfred Milner Papers
Sir Rennell Rodd Papers
Sir Horace Rumbold Papers
Earl of Selborne Papers
Leonard Stein Papers
Sir Ronald Storrs Papers (microfilm)
Sir Alfred Zimmern Papers

SOMERSET RECORD OFFICE, TAUNTON
Aubrey Herbert Papers

UNIVERSITY COLLEGE, LONDON
Moses Gaster Papers

UNITED STATES

YIVO INSTITUTE, NEW YORK CITY
Lucien Wolf Papers

ISRAEL

CENTRAL ZIONIST ARCHIVE
H. Bentwich Papers
N. Bentwich Papers
Akiva Ettinger Papers
Moses Gaster Papers
Simon Marks Papers
Claude Montefiore Papers
Harry Sacher Papers
Israel Sieff Papers
Leon Simon Papers
Nahum Sokolow Papers
Zionist Papers
Lucien Wolf Papers
Israel Zangwill Papers

WEIZMANN INSTITUTE
Letters Received 1914–1918

PUBLISHED SOURCES

NEWSPAPERS AND PERIODICALS 1914–18

Arab Bulletin
Arab Bulletin Supplementary Papers
Ararat, a Searchlight on Armenia
African Times and Orient Review
Dial
Great Britain and the Near East
Islamic Review
Jewish Chronicle
New Age
New Europe
Palestine
Zionist Review

PAMPHLETS

Anon. *Central Islamic Society*. London, 1916.
Berlin, Isaiah. *Chaim Weizmann*. Second Herbert Samuel Lecture. London, 1958.
Conder, Claude Reignier. *Eastern Palestine*. London, 1892.
Dugdale, Mrs. Edgar. *The Balfour Declaration, Origins and Background*. London, 1940.
"Falastin." *The Balfour Declaration, an Analysis*. Jaffa, n.d.
Ismail Bey, Mohammad A. *How Muhammad (peace be upon him!) found the world and how he left it*. London, 1918.
Landman, Samuel. *Origins of the Balfour Declaration: Dr. Hertz's Contribution*. London, n.d.
Lowry, Heath W. *The Story behind "Ambassador" Morgenthau's Story*. Istanbul, 1990.

Pickthall, Marmaduke. *War and Religion*. Woking, 1919.

Sacher, Harry. *Jewish Emancipation: The Contract Myth*. London, 1917.

Schor, Samuel. *Palestine for the Jew*. London, 1907.

Simon, Leon. *Zionism and the Jewish Problem*. London, 1915.

———. *The Case of the Anti-Zionists: A Reply*. London, 1917.

Stein, Leonard. *Weizmann and England*. Presidential Address to the Jewish Historical Society, delivered in London, November 11, 1964. London, 1964.

Tibawi, Abdul-Latif. *The Husain-McMahon Correspondence, or Palestine is covered by the British Pledge of 1915 Regarding the Arab Independence*. Jaffa, 1939.

Tolkowsky, S. *Achievements and Prospects in Palestine*. 1917.

Waley, S. D. *Edwin Montagu, A Memoir and an Account of His Visits to India*. London, 1924.

Weizmann, Chaim. *What Is Zionism*. London, 1918.

Wolf, Lucien. *Jewish Ideals and the War, an Address to the Historical Society of England*. London, December 7, 1914.

JOURNAL ARTICLES

Friedman, Isaiah. "The McMahon-Hussein Correspondence and the Question of Palestine." *Journal of Contemporary History* 5 (1970), 83–122.

Hogarth, D. G. "Mecca's Revolt against the Turk." *Century,* July 1920.

Johnson, Maxwell Orme. "The Arab Bureau and the Arab Revolt: Yanbu' to Aqaba." *Military Affairs* 46, no. 4 (December 1982), 194–201.

Lebow, Ned. "Woodrow Wilson and the Balfour Declaration." *Journal of Modern History* 40, no. 4 (December 1968), 501–23.

Levene, Mark. "The Balfour Declaration: A Case of Mistaken Identity." *English Historical Review* (January 1992), 54–77.

Montefiore, Claude. "An Englishman of the Jewish Faith." *Fortnightly Review,* November 1916.

Mousa, Suleiman. "A Matter of Principle: King Hussein of the Hijaz and the Arabs of Palestine." *International Journal of Middle East Studies* 9 (1978), 183–94.

Oke, Mim Kemal. "The Ottoman Empire, Zionism and the Question of Palestine 1880-1908," *International Journal of Middle East Studies* 14 (1982), 329–41.

Owen, E.R.J. "The Influence of Lord Cromer's Indian Experience on British Policy in Egypt, 1883–1907." *St. Antony's Papers* 17 (1965), 109–39.

Rawidowicz, S. "Nahum Sokolow in Great Britain." *New Judea,* May 1941.

Reinharz, Jehuda. "His Majesty's Zionist Emissary: Chaim Weizmann's Mission to Gibraltar in 1917." *Journal of Contemporary History* 27 (1992), 259–77.

———. "The Balfour Declaration and Its Maker: A Reassessment." *Journal of Modern History* 64 (September 1992), 455–92.

Renton, James. "The Historiography of the Balfour Declaration: Toward a Multi-causal Framework." *Journal of Israeli History* 19 (Summer 1998), 109–28.

Smith, Charles. "The Invention of a Tradition: The Question of Arab Acceptance of the Zionist Right to Palestine during World War I." *Journal of Palestine Studies* 22, no. 2 (Winter 1993), 48–61.

Wolf, Lucien. "The Jewish National Movement." *Edinburgh Review,* April 1917.

Yale, William. "Ambassador Heny Morgenthau's Special Mission of 1917." *World Politics* 1, no. 3 (April 1949).

DICTIONARIES AND ENCYCLOPEDIAS

Encyclopaedia Britannica. London, 1911.

Encyclopedia of Islam. Leiden, 1995.

New Dictionary of National Biography. Oxford, ongoing project.
Oxford Dictionary of National Biography.

BOOKS

Abu-Lughod, Ibrahim, ed. *The Transformation of Palestine.* Evanston, Ill., 1987.

Adelson, Roger. *London and the Invention of the Middle East: Money, Power and War, 1902–1922.* New Haven, Conn., 1995.

Allfrey, Anthony. *Man of Arms: The Life and Legend of Sir Basil Zaharoff.* London, 1989.

Amery, Leo. *My Political Life, vol. 2, War and Peace 1914–1929.* London, 1953.

Ansari, Humayun. *The Infidel Within: Muslims in Britain Since 1800.* London, 2004.

Antonius, George. *The Arab Awakening.* London, 2000.

Baedeker, Karl. *Palestine and Syria.* London, 1912.

Barr, James. *Setting the Desert on Fire: T. E. Lawrence and Britain's Secret War in Arabia, 1916–1918.* London, 2006.

Berridge, G. R. *Gerald Fitzmaurice, 1865–1939, Chief Dragoman of the British Embassy in Turkey.* Leicester and Boston, 2007.

Blumberg, Arnold. *Zion Before Zionism, 1838–1880.* Syracuse, N.Y., 1985.

Brook, Stephen. *The Club: The Jews of Modern Britain.* London, 1989.

Butt, Gerald. *The Arabs: Myth and Reality.* London, 1997.

Cesarani, David, ed. *The Making of Modern Anglo-Jewry.* Oxford, 1990.

Charmley, John. *Lord Lloyd and the Decline of the British Empire.* London, 1987.

Chelwood, Viscount Cecil. *All the Way.* London, 1949.

Cohen, Stuart A. *English Zionists and British Jews.* Princeton, N.J., 1982.

Daly, M.W. *The Sirdar: Sir Reginald Wingate and the British Empire in the Middle East.* Philadelphia, 1997.

Darwin, John. *Britain, Egypt and the Middle East: Imperial Policy in the Aftermath of War, 1918–22.* New York, 1981.

Dawn, C. Ernest. *From Ottomanism to Arabism: Essays on the Origins of Arab Nationalism.* Urbana, Ill., 1973.

Divine, Donna Robinson. *Politics and Society in Ottoman Palestine.* London, 1994.

Djemal Pasha. *Memories of a Turkish Statesman, 1913–1919.* London, n.d.

Dugdale, Blanche E. C. *Arthur James Balfour.* New York, 1937.

Duri, A. A. *The Historical Formation of the Arab Nation.* Translated by Lawrence I. Conrad. London, 1987.

Eban, Abba. *My People.* New York, 1968.

Emin, Ahmed. *Turkey in the World War.* New Haven, Conn., 1930.

Engelbrecht, H. C., and F. C. Hanighen. *Merchants of Death.* New York, 1934.

Erskine, Mrs. Steuart. *Palestine of the Arabs.* London, 1935.

Finestein, Israel. *Scenes and Personalities in Anglo-Jewry, 1800–2000.* London, 2002.

Fisher, John. *Gentleman Spies: Intelligence Agents in the British Empire and Beyond.* Stroud, 2002.

Fitzherbert, Margaret. *The Man Who Was Greenmantle: A Biography of Aubrey Herbert.* Oxford, 1985.

Fremantle, Anne. *Loyal Enemy.* London, 1938.

Friedman, Isaiah. *The Question of Palestine, 1914–18.* New York, 1973.

———. *Germany, Turkey and Zionism, 1897–1918.* Oxford, 1977.

———. *Palestine, A Twice-Promised Land? The British, the Arabs and Zionism, 1915–1920.* New Brunswick, N.J., 2000.

Fromkin, David. *A Peace to End All Peace, Creating the Modern Middle East, 1914–1922.* New York, 1989.

Gaillard, Gaston. *The Turks and Europe*. London, 1921.

Gilbert, Martin. *Sir Horace Rumbold, Portrait of a Diplomat, 1869–1941*. London, 1973.

Gilmour, David. *Curzon*. London, 1994.

Glubb, Sir John Bagot. *Britain and the Arabs*. London, 1959.

Goldberg, Rabbi P. Selvin. *The Manchester Congregation of British Jews 1857–1957*. Manchester, 1957.

Graves, Philip. *The Life of Sir Percy Cox*. London, 1941.

Graves, Philip, ed. *Memoirs of King Abdullah of Transjordan*. London, 1950.

Greaves, Adrian. *Lawrence of Arabia*. London, 2007.

Grigg, John. *Lloyd George, From Peace to War, 1912–16*. London, 1985.

———. *Lloyd George, War Leader, 1916–1918*. London, 2002.

Haim, Sylvia G., ed. *Arab Nationalism: An Anthology*. Berkeley, Calif., 1974.

Hall, Catherine, ed. *Cultures of Empire*. Manchester, 2000.

Hall, Richard C. *Bulgaria's Road to the First World War*. New York, 1996.

Hammond, J. L. *C. P. Scott of the Manchester Guardian*. London, 1934.

Hancock, W. K. *Smuts: The Sanguine Years, 1870–1919*. Cambridge, 1962.

Hardinge, Lord of Penshurst. *Old Diplomacy*. London, 1947.

Haslip, Joan. *The Sultan: The Life of Abdul Hamid II*. New York, 1958.

Herbert, Aubrey. *Mons, Anzac & Kut*. London, 1930.

Hogarth, David George. *Hejaz before World War I: A Handbook*, 2nd ed., 1917. New York, 1978.

Hovannisian, Richard. *Armenia: On the Road to Independence, 1918*. Berkeley, Calif., 1967.

Huneidi, Sahar. *A Broken Trust: Herbert Samuel, Zionism and the Palestinians, 1920–25*. London, 2001.

Kayali, Hasan. *Arabs and Young Turks, Ottomanism, Arabism and Islamism in the Ottoman Empire, 1908–1918*. Berkeley, Calif., 1997.

Kedourie, Elie. *England and the Middle East: The Destruction of the Ottoman Empire 1914–21*. London, 1987.

Keynes, John Maynard. *Essays in Biography*. London, 1951.

Khalidi, Rashid Ismail. *British Policy Towards Syria and Palestine, 1906–1914*. London, 1980.

Khalidi, Rashid, et al., eds. *The Origins of Arab Nationalism*. New York, 1991.

Kimche, Jon. *The Unromantics: The Great Powers and the Balfour Declaration*. London, 1968.

Lawrence, T. E. *Seven Pillars of Wisdom*. 1922; Ware, Hertfordshire, 1997.

Lennox, Lady Algernon Gordon, ed. *The Diary of Lord Bertie of Thame 1914–18*. London, 1924.

Leslie, Shane. *Mark Sykes: His Life and Letters*. New York, 1923.

Levene, Mark. *War, Jews and the New Europe: The Diplomacy of Lucien Wolf, 1914–1919*. Oxford, 1992.

Levy, Avigdor, ed. *The Jews of the Ottoman Empire*. Princeton, N.J., 1994.

Louis, Roger, ed. *Yet More Adventures with Britannia; Personalities, Politics and Culture in Britain*. Texas, 2005.

MacMillan, Margaret. *Peacemakers: Six Months That Changed the World*. London, 2001.

Mandel, Neville. *The Arabs and Zionism before World War I*. Berkeley, Calif., 1976.

Marcus, Amy Dockser. *Jerusalem 1913: The Origins of the Arab-Israeli Conflict*. New York, 2007.

McCormick, Donald. *Pedlar of Death: The Life of Sir Basil Zaharoff*. London, 1965.

McDowall, David. *The Palestinians: The Road to Nationhood*. London, 1994.

Miller, Geoffrey. *Straits: British Policy Towards the Ottoman Empire and the Origins of the Dardanelles Campaign*. Hull, 1997.

Monroe, Elizabeth. *Britain's Moment in the Middle East, 1914–56*. London, 1964.

Moorehead, Alan. *Gallipoli*. London, 1959.

Morgenthau, Henry. *All in a Life-Time*. London, 1923.

———. *Ambassador Morgenthau's Story*. Reading, 2003.

Nevakivi, Jukka. *Britain, France and the Arab Middle East, 1914–1920*. London, 1969.

Ovendale, Ritchie. *The Origins of the Arab-Israeli Wars*. London, 1992.

Palmer, Alan. *Victory in 1918.* New York, 2000.

Porath, Y. *The Emergence of the Palestinian-Arab National Movement, 1918–1929.* London, 1974.

Porter, Andrew, ed. *Oxford History of the British Empire.* Vol. 3, *The Nineteenth Century.* Oxford, 1999.

Porter, Bernard. *The Lion's Share.* London, 1975.

Ranowicz, Oskar K. *Fifty Years of Zionism, A Historical Analysis of Dr. Weizmann's "Trial and Error."* London, 1952.

Reinharz, Yehuda. *Chaim Weizmann: The Making of a Statesman.* Oxford, 1993.

Renton, James. *The Zionist Masquerade, The Birth of the Anglo-Jewish Alliance, 1914–1918.* London, 2007.

Rose, Norman. *Chaim Weizmann.* New York, 1986.

Rose, Norman, ed. *From Palmerston to Balfour: Collected Essays of Mayir Vereté.* London, 1992.

Roth, Cecil. *History of the Jews.* New York, 1966.

Royle, Trevor. *The Kitchener Enigma.* London, 1985.

Sacher, Harry. *Zionism and the Jewish Future.* London, 1916.

———. *Zionist Portraits and Other Essays.* London, 1959.

Said, Edward. *The Question of Palestine.* New York, 1979.

———. *Orientalism.* New York, 1979.

Samuel, Herbert. *Memoirs.* London, 1945.

Sanders, Ronald. *The High Walls of Jerusalem: A History of the Balfour Declaration and the Birth of the British Mandate for Palestine.* New York, 1983.

Segev, Tom. *One Palestine, Complete: Jews and Arabs under the British Mandate.* New York, 1999.

Shaw, Stanford. *The Jews of the Ottoman Empire and the Turkish Republic.* New York, 1991.

Sidebotham, Herbert. *Great Britain and Palestine.* London, 1937.

Sieff, Israel. *Memoirs.* London, 1970.

Sokolow, Florian. *Nahum Sokolow.* London, 1975.

Sokolow, Nahum. *History of Zionism 1600–1918.* London, 1919.

Stein, Leonard. *The Balfour Declaration.* London, 1961.

Stein, Leonard, ed. *The Letters and Papers of Chaim Weizmann, Series A, Letters Volume 7, August 1914–November 1917.* Oxford, 1975.

Storrs, Sir Ronald. *The Memoirs of Sir Ronald Storrs.* New York, 1937.

Strum, Philippa. *Louis D. Brandeis, Justice for the People.* Cambridge, Mass., 1984.

Stuermer, Harry. *Two War Years in Constantinople: Sketches of German and Young Turkish Ethics and Politics.* London, 2004.

Sugarman, Sidney. *The Unrelenting Conflict: Britain, Balfour, and Betrayal.* Sussex, 2000.

Susser, Asher, and Aryeh Shmuelevitz, eds. *The Hashemites in the Modern Arab World: Essays in Honor of the Late Professor Uriel Dann.* London, 1995.

Sykes, Sir Mark. *The Caliphs' Last Heritage.* London, 1915.

Tauber, Eliezer. *The Arab Movements in World War I.* London, 1993.

Tibawi, A. L. *Anglo-Arab Relations and the Question of Palestine, 1914–1921.* London, 1977.

Tomes, Jason. *Balfour and Foreign Policy.* Cambridge, 1997.

Toynbee, Arnold. *Acquaintances.* London, 1938.

Twain, Mark. *The Innocents Abroad.* Pleasantville, N.Y., 1990.

Urofsky, Melvin. *A Mind of One Piece: Brandeis and American Reform.* New York, 1971.

Vital, David. *Zionism: The Crucial Phase.* Oxford, 1987.

Wasserstein, Bernard. *The British in Palestine: The Mandatory Government and the Arab-Jewish Conflict 1917–29.* London, 1978.

———. *Herbert Samuel: A Political Life.* Oxford, 1992.

Westrate, Bruce. *The Arab Bureau: British Policy in the Middle East, 1916–1920.* University Park, Penn., 1992.

Weizmann, Chaim. *Trial and Error,* vol. 1. Philadelphia, 1949.

Williams, Bill. *The Making of Manchester Jewry, 1740–1875.* Manchester, 1985.

Wilson, Mary. *King Abdullah, Britain, and the Making of Jordan.* Cambridge, 1987.

Wingate, Sir Ronald. *Wingate of the Sudan.* London, 1955.

Wolf, Lucien. *Essays in Jewish History,* edited by Cecil Roth. London, 1934.

Yardley, Michael. *Backing into the Limelight: A Biography of T. E. Lawrence.* London, 1985.

Zürcher, Eric Jan. *The Unionist Factor: The Role of the Committee of Union and Progress in the Turkish National Movement, 1905–26.* Leiden, 1984.

Index

Page numbers in *italics* refer to illustrations.

About the Author

JONATHAN SCHNEER, a specialist in modern British history, is a professor at Georgia Tech's School of History, Technology, and Society. He is the author of five additional books as well as numerous articles and reviews. A fellow of the American Council of Learned Societies in 1985–86, he has also held research fellowships at Oxford and Cambridge universities in the UK and at the Erich Remarque Center of New York University. He was a founding editor of *Radical History Review* and is a member of the editorial board of *20th Century British History* and *The London Journal.*